MASTERWORKS
OF
CHILDREN'S
LITERATURE

MASTERWORKS
OF
CHILDREN'S
LITERATURE

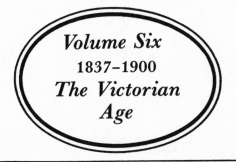

Volume Six
1837–1900
The Victorian
Age

EDITED BY **Robert Lee Wolff**

GENERAL EDITOR: *Jonathan Cott*

THE STONEHILL PUBLISHING COMPANY
IN ASSOCIATION WITH
CHELSEA HOUSE PUBLISHERS
NEW YORK

GENERAL EDITOR: Jonathan Cott
ADVISORY EDITOR: Robert G. Miner, Jr.
VOLUME EDITOR: Robert Lee Wolff
PROJECT DIRECTOR: Esther Mitgang
DESIGNER: Paul Bacon
EDITORIAL STAFF: Joy Johannessen, Philip Minges III, Claire Bottler
PRODUCTION: Coco Dupuy, Heather White, Sandra Su, Susan Lusk,
  Christopher Newton, Carol McDougall

First Printing
Printed and Bound in the United States of America
ISBN: 0-87754-449-2
LC: 79-89986

Chelsea House Publishers
  Harold Steinberg, Chairman and Publisher
  Andrew E. Norman, President
  Susan Lusk, Vice President
A Division of Chelsea House Educational Communications, Inc.
133 Christopher Street, New York, NY 10014

Contents

The King of the Golden River; or, The Black Brothers

A Legend of Stiria

By JOHN RUSKIN

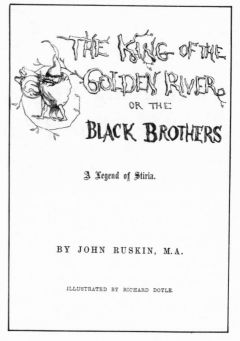

THE KING OF THE GOLDEN RIVER,

OR THE

BLACK BROTHERS

A Legend of Stiria.

BY JOHN RUSKIN, M.A.

ILLUSTRATED BY RICHARD DOYLE.

J OHN RUSKIN (1819–1900), art critic, critic of society, and a great Victorian sage, wrote many books, among which is a single short fairy tale, *The King of the Golden River*. Written in 1841 at the request of a young girl named Euphemia Grey, whom Ruskin married seven years later, it was first published in 1851, anonymously. Its fine illustrations by "Dicky" Doyle (one of the leading draughtsmen of the period and a frequent contributor to *Punch*) helped ensure its popularity then and ever since, but quite apart from these it richly deserves revival.

The King of the Golden River followed by only two years Uncle David's story, in *Holiday House* (see Volume 5, Part I), of the lazy No-book and his transformation into an active studious boy, the earliest original Victorian fairy tale, and far transcends it artistically. Deeply influenced by the brothers Grimm, whom he had read in his youth, Ruskin set his story in Stiria, an Austrian province, and gave his characters German names. He followed the well-known pattern of many *Volksmärchen*, in which there are three brothers, the elder two powerful and wicked, the youngest weak and good. One after the other the elder brothers fail to meet a series of ordeals, often because they disregard instructions or lack the virtue to surmount their difficulties, while the youngest wins through triumphantly. This pattern enables the narrator to recount the essential stages of the adventure three times, with only slight variations, and gives comforting reassurance to the listener.

But if the framework is that of folk literature, *The King of the Golden River* is nonetheless a *Kunstmärchen*, a work of art by an individual author. The splendor of the mountain scenery, beautifully depicted, Ruskin derived from the Wordsworthian passion for the Alps, shared by the Romantics and by many Victorians, and serving as a positive source of spiritual inspiration of a kind wholly alien to folk fairy tales. And, although later in life Ruskin maintained that fairy tales did not need morals (see his "Fairy Stories," reprinted in this volume), he certainly put a moral in *The King of the Golden River*. It is not only that overbearing cruelty and unkindness must be punished, while meekness and generosity will be rewarded—a lesson familiar enough even in fairy tales. It is that true riches are not to be found in the gold that the wicked elder brothers so covet and believe they will obtain when the Golden River is transformed into gold for them. True riches consist instead of the rich harvests and nourishing food that grow again upon the lands once made desolate by the vengeance of the Southwest Wind, when they are transformed back into fertile farms by the Golden River itself, after little Gluck (and the name itself of course means "luck") has won the promised reward. In this way, although it is a very early effort by a young man of twenty-two, *The King of the Golden River* may be seen to foreshadow Ruskin's later social criticism, in which he condemned the Victorian plutocracy and its worship of gold, and called for a reorganization of society along vaguely socialistic and Utopian lines.

Ruskin's marriage to Euphemia Grey was a failure and was eventually annulled. It brought them both much anguish, and scandal. She married the celebrated artist John Millais, with whom she was happy, and by whom she had eight children. Ruskin's life was stormy and tormented. Of the tragic association between the brilliant young student of the arts and the beautiful girl, who mistakenly thought that they loved one another, the only literary relic remains this fairy story he wrote for her when she was twelve.

The text of The King of the Golden River, *with illustrations by Richard Doyle, is reprinted from the seventh English edition (Kent: George Allen, 1882).*

3

ADVERTISEMENT

The Publishers think it due to the Author of this Fairy Tale, to state the circumstances under which it appears.

THE KING OF THE GOLDEN RIVER was written in 1841, at the request of a very young lady, and solely for her amusement, without any idea of publication. It has since remained in the possession of a friend, to whose suggestion, and the passive assent of the Author, the Publishers are indebted for the opportunity of printing it.

The Illustrations, by Mr. Richard Doyle, will, it is hoped, be found to embody the Author's ideas with characteristic spirit.

CHAPTER I

*How the Agricultural System of the Black Brothers
was interfered with by South-West Wind, Esquire.*

IN A SECLUDED and mountainous part of Stiria there was, in old time, a valley of the most surprising and luxuriant fertility. It was surrounded, on all sides, by steep and rocky mountains, rising into peaks, which were always covered with snow, and from which a number of torrents descended in constant cataracts. One of these fell westward, over the face of a crag so high, that, when the sun had set to everything else, and all below was darkness, his beams still shone full upon this waterfall, so that it looked like a shower of gold. It was, therefore, called by the people of the neighbourhood, the Golden River. It was strange that none of these streams fell into the valley itself. They all descended on the other side of the mountains, and wound away through broad plains and by populous cities. But the clouds were drawn so constantly to the snowy hills, and rested so softly in the circular hollow, that in time of drought and heat, when all the country round was burnt up, there was still rain in the little valley; and its crops were so heavy, and its hay so high, and its apples so red, and its grapes so blue, and its wine so rich, and its honey so sweet, that it was a marvel to every one who beheld it, and was commonly called the Treasure Valley.

The whole of this little valley belonged to three brothers, called Schwartz, Hans, and Gluck. Schwartz and Hans, the two elder brothers, were very ugly men, with overhanging eyebrows and small dull eyes, which were always half shut, so that you couldn't see into *them*, and always fancied they saw very far into *you*. They lived by farming the Treasure Valley, and very good farmers they were. They killed everything that did not pay for its eating. They shot the blackbirds, because they pecked the fruit; and killed the hedgehogs, lest they should suck the cows; they poisoned the crickets for eating the crumbs in the kitchen; and smothered the cicadas, which used to sing all summer in the lime trees. They worked their servants without any wages, till they would not work any more, and then quarrelled with them, and turned them out of doors without paying them. It would have been very odd, if with such a farm, and such a system of farming, they hadn't got very rich; and very rich they *did* get. They generally contrived to keep their corn by them till it was very dear, and then sell it for twice its value; they had heaps of gold lying about on their floors, yet it was never known that they had given so much as a penny or a crust in charity; they never went to mass; grumbled perpetually at paying tithes; and were, in a word, of so cruel and grinding a temper, as to receive from all those with whom they had any dealings, the nick-name of the "Black Brothers."

The youngest brother, Gluck, was as completely opposed, in both appearance and character, to his seniors as could possibly be imagined or desired. He was not above twelve years old, fair, blue-eyed, and kind in temper to every living thing. He did not, of course, agree particularly well with his brothers, or rather, they did not agree with *him*. He was usually appointed to the honourable office of turnspit, when there was anything to roast, which was not often; for, to do the brothers justice, they were hardly less sparing upon themselves than upon other people. At other times he used to clean the shoes, floors, and sometimes the plates, occasionally getting what was left on them, by way of encouragement, and a wholesome quantity of dry blows, by way of education.

Things went on in this manner for a long time. At last came a very wet summer, and everything went wrong in the country around. The hay had hardly been got in, when the haystacks were floated bodily down to the sea by an inundation; the vines were cut to pieces with the hail; the corn was all killed by a black blight; only in the Treasure Valley, as usual, all was safe. As it had rain when there was rain no where else, so it had sun when there was sun no where else. Every body came to buy corn at the farm, and went away pouring maledictions on the Black Brothers. They asked what they liked, and got it, except from the poor people, who could only beg, and several of whom were starved at their very door, without the slightest regard or notice.

It was drawing towards winter, and very cold weather, when one day the two elder brothers had gone out, with their usual warning to little Gluck, who was left to mind the roast, that he was to let nobody in, and give nothing out. Gluck sat down quite close to the fire, for it was raining very hard, and the kitchen walls were by no means dry or comfortable looking. He turned and turned, and the roast got nice and brown. "What a pity," thought Gluck, "my brothers never ask any body to dinner. I'm sure, when they've got such a nice piece of mutton as this, and nobody else has got so much as a piece of dry bread, it would do their hearts good to have somebody to eat it with them."

Just as he spoke, there came a double knock at the house door, yet heavy and dull, as though the knocker had been tied up—more like a puff than a knock.

"It must be the wind," said Gluck; "nobody else would venture to knock double knocks at our door."

No; it wasn't the wind: there it came again very hard, and what was particularly astounding, the knocker seemed to be in a hurry, and not to be in the least afraid of the consequences. Gluck went to the window, opened it, and put his head out to see who it was.

It was the most extraordinary looking little gentleman he had ever seen in his life. He had a very large nose, slightly brass-coloured; his cheeks were very round, and very red, and might have warranted a supposition that he had been blowing a refractory fire for the last eight-and-forty hours; his eyes twinkled merrily through long silky eyelashes, his

moustaches curled twice round like a corkscrew on each side of his mouth, and his hair, of a curious mixed pepper-and-salt colour, descended far over his shoulders. He was about four feet six in height, and wore a conical pointed cap of nearly the same altitude, decorated with a black feather some three feet long. His doublet was prolonged behind into something resembling a violent exaggeration of what is now termed a "swallow tail," but was much obscured by the swelling folds of an enormous black, glossy-looking cloak, which must have been very much too long in calm weather, as the wind, whistling round the old house, carried it clear out from the wearer's shoulders to about four times his own length.

Gluck was so perfectly paralyzed by the singular appearance of his visitor, that he remained fixed without uttering a word, until the old gentleman, having performed another, and a more energetic concerto on the knocker, turned round to look after his fly-away cloak. In so doing he caught sight of Gluck's little yellow head jammed in the window, with its mouth and eyes very wide open indeed.

"Hollo!" said the little gentleman, "that's not the way to answer the door: I'm wet, let me in."

To do the little gentleman justice, he *was* wet. His feather hung down between his legs like a beaten puppy's tail, dripping like an umbrella; and from the ends of his moustaches the water was running into his waistcoat pockets, and out again like a mill stream.

"I beg pardon, sir," said Gluck, "I'm very sorry, but I really can't."

"Can't what!" said the old gentleman.

"I can't let you in, sir,—I can't, indeed; my brothers would beat me to death, sir, if I thought of such a thing. What do you want, sir?"

"Want?" said the old gentleman, petulantly. "I want fire, and shelter; and there's your

great fire there blazing, crackling, and dancing on the walls, with nobody to feel it. Let me in, I say; I only want to warm myself."

Gluck had had his head, by this time, so long out of the window, that he began to feel it was really unpleasantly cold, and when he turned, and saw the beautiful fire rustling and roaring, and throwing long bright tongues up the chimney, as if it were licking its chops at the savoury smell of the leg of mutton, his heart melted within him that it should be burning away for nothing. "He does look *very* wet," said little Gluck; "I'll just let him in for a quarter of an hour." Round he went to the door, and opened it; and as the little gentleman walked in, there came a gust of wind through the house, that made the old chimneys totter.

"That's a good boy," said the little gentleman. "Never mind your brothers. I'll talk to them."

"Pray, sir, don't do any such thing," said Gluck. "I can't let you stay till they come; they'd be the death of me."

"Dear me," said the old gentleman, "I'm very sorry to hear that. How long may I stay?"

"Only till the mutton's done, sir," replied Gluck, "and it's very brown."

Then the old gentleman walked into the kitchen, and sat himself down on the hob, with the top of his cap accommodated up the chimney, for it was a great deal too high for the roof.

"You'll soon dry there, sir," said Gluck, and sat down again to turn the mutton. But the old gentleman did *not* dry there, but went on drip, drip, dripping among the cinders, and the fire fizzed, and sputtered, and began to look very black, and uncomfortable: never was such a cloak; every fold in it ran like a gutter.

"I beg pardon, sir," said Gluck at length, after watching the water spreading in long, quicksilver-like streams over the floor for a quarter of an hour; "mayn't I take your cloak?"

"No, thank you," said the old gentleman.

"Your cap, sir?"

"I am all right, thank you," said the old gentleman rather gruffly.

"But,—sir,—I'm very sorry," said Gluck, hesitatingly; "but—really, sir,—you're—putting the fire out."

"It'll take longer to do the mutton, then," replied his visitor drily.

Gluck was very much puzzled by the behaviour of his guest; it was such a strange mixture of coolness and humility. He turned away at the string meditatively for another five minutes.

"That mutton looks very nice," said the old gentleman at length. "Can't you give me a little bit?"

"Impossible, sir," said Gluck.

"I'm very hungry," continued the old gentleman: "I've had nothing to eat yesterday, nor to-day. They surely couldn't miss a bit from the knuckle!"

He spoke in so very melancholy a tone, that it quite melted Gluck's heart. "They promised me one slice to-day, sir," said he; "I can give you that, but not a bit more."

"That's a good boy," said the old gentleman again.

Then Gluck warmed a plate, and sharpened a knife. "I don't care if I do get beaten for it," thought he. Just as he had cut a large slice out of the mutton, there came a tremendous rap at the door. The old gentleman jumped off the hob, as if it had suddenly become inconveniently warm. Gluck fitted the slice into the mutton again, with desperate efforts at exactitude, and ran to open the door.

"What did you keep us waiting in the rain for?" said Schwartz, as he walked in, throwing his umbrella in Gluck's face. "Ay! what for, indeed, you little vagabond?" said Hans, administering an educational box on the ear, as he followed his brother into the kitchen.

"Bless my soul!" said Schwartz when he opened the door.

"Amen," said the little gentleman, who had taken his cap off, and was standing in the middle of the kitchen, bowing with the utmost possible velocity.

"Who's that?" said Schwartz, catching up a rolling-pin, and turning to Gluck with a fierce frown.

"I don't know, indeed, brother," said Gluck in great terror.

"How did he get in?" roared Schwartz.

"My dear brother," said Gluck, deprecatingly, "he was so *very* wet!"

The rolling-pin was descending on Gluck's head; but, at the instant, the old gentleman interposed his conical cap, on which it crashed with a shock that shook the water out of it all over the room. What was very odd, the rolling-pin no sooner touched the cap, than it flew out of Schwartz's hand, spinning like a straw in a high wind, and fell into the corner at the further end of the room.

"Who are you, sir?" demanded Schwartz, turning upon him.

"What's your business?" snarled Hans.

"I'm a poor old man, sir," the little gentleman began very modestly, "and I saw your fire through the window, and begged shelter for a quarter of an hour."

"Have the goodness to walk out again, then," said Schwartz. "We've quite enough water in our kitchen, without making it a drying house."

"It is a cold day to turn an old man out in, sir; look at my grey hairs." They hung down to his shoulders, as I told you before.

"Ay!" said Hans, "there are enough of them to keep you warm. Walk!"

"I'm very, very hungry, sir; couldn't you spare me a bit of bread before I go?"

"Bread, indeed!" said Schwartz; "do you suppose we've nothing to do with our bread, but to give it to such red-nosed fellows as you?"

"Why don't you sell your feather?" said Hans, sneeringly. "Out with you."

"A little bit," said the old gentleman.

"Be off!" said Schwartz.

"Pray, gentlemen."

"Off, and be hanged!" cried Hans, seizing him by the collar. But he had no sooner touched the old gentleman's collar, than away he went after the rolling-pin, spinning round and round, till he fell into the corner on the top of it. Then Schwartz was very angry, and ran at the old gentleman to turn him out; but he also had hardly touched him, when away he went after Hans and the rolling-pin, and hit his head against the wall as he tumbled into the corner. And so there they lay, all three.

Then the old gentleman spun himself round with velocity in the opposite direction; continued to spin until his long cloak was all wound neatly about him; clapped his cap on his head, very much on one side (for it could not stand upright without going through the ceiling), gave an additional twist to his corkscrew moustaches, and replied with perfect coolness: "Gentlemen, I wish you a very good morning. At twelve o'clock to-night I'll call again; after such a refusal of hospitality as I have just experienced, you will not be surprised if that visit is the last I ever pay you."

"If ever I catch you here again," muttered Schwartz, coming, half frightened, out of the corner—but, before he could finish his sentence, the old gentleman had shut the house door behind him with a great bang: and there drove past the window, at the same instant, a wreath of ragged cloud, that whirled and rolled away down the valley in all manner of shapes; turning over and over in the air; and melting away at last in a gush of rain.

"A very pretty business, indeed, Mr. Gluck!" said Schwartz. "Dish the mutton, sir. If ever I catch you at such a trick again—bless me, why the mutton's been cut!"

"You promised me one slice, brother, you know," said Gluck.

"Oh! and you were cutting it hot, I suppose, and going to catch all the gravy. It'll be long before I promise you such a thing again. Leave the room, sir; and have the kindness to wait in the coal-cellar till I call you."

Gluck left the room melancholy enough. The brothers ate as much mutton as they could, locked the rest in the cupboard, and proceeded to get very drunk after dinner.

Such a night as it was! Howling wind, and rushing rain, without intermission. The brothers had just sense enough left to put up all the shutters, and double bar the door, before they went to bed. They usually slept in the same room. As the clock struck

twelve, they were both awakened by a tremendous crash. Their door burst open with a violence that shook the house from top to bottom.

"What's that?" cried Schwartz, starting up in his bed.

"Only I," said the little gentleman.

The two brothers sat up on their bolster, and stared into the darkness . The room was full of water, and by a misty moon-beam, which found its way through a hole in the shutter, they could see in the midst of it, an enormous foam globe, spinning round, and bobbing up and down like a cork, on which, as on a most luxurious cushion, reclined the little old gentleman, cap and all. There was plenty of room for it now, for the roof was off.

"Sorry to incommode you," said their visitor, ironically. "I'm afraid your beds are dampish; perhaps you had better go to your brother's room: I've left the ceiling on, there."

They required no second admonition, but rushed into Gluck's room, wet through, and in an agony of terror.

"You'll find my card on the kitchen table," the old gentleman called after them. "Remember, the *last* visit."

"Pray Heaven it may!" said Schwartz, shuddering. And the foam globe disappeared.

Dawn came at last, and the two brothers looked out of Gluck's little window in the morning. The Treasure Valley was one mass of ruin and desolation. The inundation had swept away trees, crops, and cattle, and left in their stead, a waste of red sand, and grey mud. The two brothers crept shivering and horror-struck into the kitchen. The water had gutted the whole first floor; corn, money, almost every moveable thing had been swept away, and there was left only a small white card on the kitchen table. On it, in large, breezy, long-legged letters, were engraved the words:—

CHAPTER II

*Of the Proceedings of the Three Brothers after the Visit
of South-West Wind, Esquire; and how little Gluck had an Interview
with the King of the Golden River.*

SOUTH-WEST WIND, ESQUIRE, was as good as his word. After the momentous visit above related, he entered the Treasure Valley no more; and, what was worse, he had so much influence with his relations, the West Winds in general, and used it so effectually, that they all adopted a similar line of conduct. So no rain fell in the valley from one year's end to another. Though everything remained green and flourishing in the plains below, the inheritance of the Three Brothers was a desert. What had once been the richest soil in the kingdom, became a shifting heap of red sand; and the brothers, unable longer to contend with the adverse skies, abandoned their valueless patrimony in despair, to seek some means of gaining a livelihood among the cities and people of the plains. All their money was gone, and they had nothing left but some curious old-fashioned pieces of gold plate, the last remnants of their ill-gotten wealth.

"Suppose we turn goldsmiths?" said Schwartz to Hans, as they entered the large city. "It is a good knave's trade; we can put a great deal of copper into the gold, without any one's finding it out."

The thought was agreed to be a very good one; they hired a furnace, and turned goldsmiths. But two slight circumstances affected their trade: the first, that people did not approve of the coppered gold; the second, that the two elder brothers, whenever

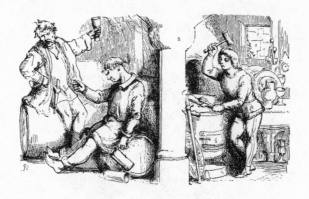

they had sold anything, used to leave little Gluck to mind the furnace, and go and drink out the money in the ale-house next door. So they melted all their gold, without making money enough to buy more, and were at last reduced to one large drinking mug, which an uncle of his had given to little Gluck, and which he was very fond of, and would not have parted with for the world; though he never drank anything out of it but milk and water. The mug was a very odd mug to look at. The handle was formed of two wreaths of flowing golden hair, so finely spun that it looked more like silk than metal, and these wreaths descended into, and mixed with, a beard of whiskers of the same exquisite workmanship, which surrounded and decorated a very fierce little face, of the reddest gold imaginable, right in the front of the mug, with a pair of eyes in it which seemed to command its whole circumference. It was impossible to drink out of the mug without being subjected to an intense gaze out of the side of these eyes; and Schwartz positively averred, that once, after emptying it, full of Rhenish, seventeen times, he had seen them wink! When it came to the mug's turn to be made into spoons, it half broke poor little Gluck's heart; but the brothers only laughed at him, tossed the mug into the melting-pot, and staggered out to the ale-house: leaving him, as usual, to pour the gold into bars, when it was all ready.

When they were gone, Gluck took a farewell look at his old friend in the melting-pot. The flowing hair was all gone; nothing remained but the red nose, and the sparkling eyes, which looked more malicious than ever. "And no wonder," thought Gluck, "after being treated in that way." He sauntered disconsolately to the window, and sat himself down to catch the fresh evening air, and escape the hot breath of the furnace. Now this window commanded a direct view of the range of mountains, which, as I told you before, overhung the Treasure Valley, and more especially of the peak from which fell the Golden River. It was just at the close of the day, and, when Gluck sat down at the window, he saw the rocks of the mountain tops, all crimson, and purple with the sunset; and there were bright tongues of fiery cloud burning and quivering about them; and the river, brighter than all, fell, in a waving column of pure gold, from precipice to precipice, with the double arch of a broad purple rainbow stretched across it, flushing and fading alternately in the wreaths of spray.

"Ah!" said Gluck aloud, after he had looked at it for a while, "if that river were really all gold, what a nice thing it would be."

"No, it wouldn't, Gluck," said a clear metallic voice, close at his ear.

"Bless me, what's that?" exclaimed Gluck, jumping up. There was nobody there. He looked round the room, and under the table, and a great many times behind him, but there was certainly nobody there, and he sat down again at the window. This time he didn't speak, but he couldn't help thinking again that it would be very convenient if the river were really all gold.

"Not at all, my boy," said the same voice, louder than before.

"Bless me!" said Gluck again, "what *is* that?" He looked again into all the corners, and cupboards, and then began turning round, and round, as fast as he could in the middle of the room, thinking there was somebody behind him, when the same voice struck again on his ear. It was singing now very merrily, "Lala-lira-la;" no words, only a soft running effervescent melody, something like that of a kettle on the boil. Gluck looked out of the window. No, it was certainly in the house. Up stairs, and down stairs. No, it was certainly in that very room, coming in quicker time, and clearer notes, every moment. "Lala-lira-la." All at once it struck Gluck, that it sounded louder near the furnace. He ran to the opening, and looked in: yes, he saw right, it seemed to be coming, not only out of the furnace, but out of the pot. He uncovered it, and ran back in a great fright, for the pot was certainly singing! He stood in the farthest corner of the room, with his hands up, and his mouth open, for a minute or two, when the singing stopped, and the voice became clear, and pronunciative.

"Hollo!" said the voice.

Gluck made no answer.

"Hollo! Gluck, my boy," said the pot again.

Gluck summoned all his energies, walked straight up to the crucible, drew it out of the furnace, and looked in. The gold was all melted, and its surface as smooth and polished as a river; but instead of reflecting little Gluck's head, as he looked in, he saw meeting his glance from beneath the gold, the red nose, and sharp eyes of his old friend of the mug, a thousand times redder, and sharper than ever he had seen them in his life.

"Come, Gluck, my boy," said the voice out of the pot again, "I'm all right; pour me out."

But Gluck was too much astonished to do anything of the kind.

"Pour me out, I say," said the voice rather gruffly.

Still Gluck couldn't move.

"*Will* you pour me out?" said the voice passionately, "I'm too hot."

By a violent effort, Gluck recovered the use of his limbs, took hold of the crucible, and sloped it, so as to pour out the gold. But instead of a liquid stream, there came out, first, a pair of pretty little yellow legs, then some coat tails, then a pair of arms stuck a-kimbo, and, finally, the well-known head of his friend the mug; all which articles, uniting as they rolled out, stood up energetically on the floor, in the shape of a little golden dwarf, about a foot and a half high.

"That's right!" said the dwarf, stretching out first his legs, and then his arms, and then shaking his head up and down, and as far round as it would go, for five minutes, without stopping; apparently with the view of ascertaining if he were quite correctly put together, while Gluck stood contemplating him in speechless amazement. He was dressed in a slashed doublet of spun gold, so fine in its texture, that the prismatic colours gleamed over it, as if on a surface of mother of pearl; and, over this brilliant doublet, his hair and beard fell full half way to the ground, in waving curls, so exquisitely delicate, that Gluck could hardly tell where they ended; they seemed to melt into air. The features of the face, however, were by no means finished with the same delicacy; they were rather coarse, slightly inclining to coppery in complexion, and indicative, in expression, of a very pertinacious and intractable disposition in their small proprietor. When the dwarf had finished his self-examination, he turned his small sharp eyes full on Gluck, and stared at him deliberately for a minute or two. "No, it wouldn't, Gluck, my boy," said the little man.

This was certainly rather an abrupt, and unconnected mode of commencing conversation. It might indeed be supposed to refer to the course of Gluck's thoughts, which had first produced the dwarf's observations out of the pot; but whatever it referred to, Gluck had no inclination to dispute the dictum.

"Wouldn't it, sir?" said Gluck, very mildly, and submissively indeed.

"No," said the dwarf, conclusively, "No, it wouldn't." And with that, the dwarf pulled his cap hard over his brows, and took two turns, of three feet long, up and down the room, lifting his legs up very high, and setting them down very hard. This pause gave time for Gluck to collect his thoughts a little, and, seeing no great reason to view his diminutive visitor with dread, and feeling his curiosity overcome his amazement, he ventured on a question of peculiar delicacy.

"Pray, sir," said Gluck, rather hesitatingly, "were you my mug?"

On which the little man turned sharp round, walked straight up to Gluck, and drew himself up to his full height. "I," said the little man, "am the King of the Golden River." Whereupon he turned about again, and took two more turns, some six feet long, in order to allow time for the consternation which this announcement produced in his auditor to evaporate. After which, he again walked up to Gluck and stood still, as if expecting some comment on his communication.

Gluck determined to say something at all events. "I hope your Majesty is very well," said Gluck.

"Listen!" said the little man, deigning no reply to this polite inquiry. "I am the King of what you mortals call the Golden River. The shape you saw me in, was owing to the malice of a stronger king, from whose enchantments you have this instant freed me. What I have seen of you, and your conduct to your wicked brothers, renders me willing to serve you; therefore, attend to what I tell you. Whoever shall climb to the top of that mountain from which you see the Golden River issue, and shall cast into the stream at its source, three drops of holy water, for him, and for him only, the river shall turn to gold. But no one failing in his first, can succeed in a second attempt; and if any one shall cast unholy water into the river, it will overwhelm him, and he will become a black stone." So saying, the King of the Golden River turned away and deliberately walked into the centre of the hottest flame of the furnace. His figure became red, white, transparent, dazzling—a blaze of intense light—rose, trembled, and disappeared. The King of the Golden River had evaporated.

"Oh!" cried poor Gluck, running to look up the chimney after him; "Oh, dear, dear, dear me! My mug! my mug! my mug!"

CHAPTER III

How Mr. Hans set off on an Expedition to the Golden River,
and how he prospered therein.

THE KING OF THE GOLDEN RIVER had hardly made the extraordinary exit related in the last chapter, before Hans and Schwartz came roaring into the house, very savagely drunk. The discovery of the total loss of their last piece of plate had the effect of sobering them just enough to enable them to stand over Gluck, beating him very steadily for a quarter of an hour; at the expiration of which period they dropped into a couple of chairs, and requested to know what he had got to say for himself. Gluck told them his story, of which, of course, they did not believe a word. They beat him again, till their arms were tired, and staggered to bed. In the morning, however, the steadiness with which he adhered to his story obtained him some degree of credence; the immediate consequence of which was, that the two brothers, after wrangling a long time on the knotty question, which of them should try his fortune first, drew their swords and began fighting. The noise of the fray alarmed the neighbours, who, finding they could not pacify the combatants, sent for the constable.

Hans, on hearing this, contrived to escape, and hid himself; but Schwartz was taken before the magistrate, fined for breaking the peace, and, having drunk out his last penny the evening before, was thrown into prison till he should pay.

When Hans heard this, he was much delighted, and determined to set out immediately for the Golden River. How to get the holy water, was the question. He went to the priest, but the priest could not give any holy water to so abandoned a character. So Hans went to vespers in the evening for the first time in his life, and, under pretence of crossing himself, stole a cupful, and returned home in triumph.

Next morning he got up before the sun rose, put the holy water into a strong flask, and two bottles of wine and some meat in a basket, slung them over his back, took his alpine staff in his hand, and set off for the mountains.

On his way out of the town he had to pass the prison, and as he looked in at the windows, whom should he see but Schwartz himself peeping out of the bars, and looking very disconsolate.

"Good morning, brother," said Hans; "have you any message for the King of the Golden River?"

Schwartz gnashed his teeth with rage, and shook the bars with all his strength; but Hans only laughed at him, and advising him to make himself comfortable till he came back again, shouldered his basket, shook the bottle of holy water in Schwartz's face till it frothed again, and marched off in the highest spirits in the world.

It was, indeed, a morning that might have made any one happy, even with no Golden River to seek for. Level lines of dewy mist lay stretched along the valley, out of which rose the massy mountains—their lower cliffs in pale grey shadow, hardly distinguishable from the floating vapour, but gradually ascending till they caught the sunlight, which ran in sharp touches of ruddy colour, along the angular crags, and pierced, in long level rays, through their fringes of spear-like pine. Far above, shot up red splintered masses of castellated rock, jagged and shivered into myriads of fantastic forms, with here and there a streak of sunlit snow, traced down their chasms like a line of forked lightning; and, far beyond, and far above all these, fainter than the morning cloud, but purer and changeless, slept, in the blue sky, the utmost peaks of the eternal snow.

The Golden River, which sprang from one of the lower and snowless elevations, was now nearly in shadow; all but the uppermost jets of spray, which rose like slow smoke above the undulating line of the cataract, and floated away in feeble wreaths upon the morning wind.

On this object, and on this alone, Hans' eyes and thoughts were fixed; forgetting the distance he had to traverse, he set off at an imprudent rate of walking, which greatly exhausted him before he had scaled the first range of the green and low hills. He was, moreover, surprised, on surmounting them, to find that a large glacier, of whose existence, notwithstanding his previous knowledge of the mountains, he had been absolutely ignorant, lay between him and the source of the Golden River. He entered on it with the boldness of a practised mountaineer; yet he thought he had never traversed so strange or so dangerous a glacier in his life. The ice was excessively slippery, and out

of all its chasms came wild sounds of gushing water; not monotonous or low, but changeful and loud, rising occasionally into drifting passages of wild melody, then breaking off into short melancholy tones, or sudden shrieks, resembling those of human voices in distress or pain. The ice was broken into thousands of confused shapes, but none, Hans thought, like the ordinary forms of splintered ice. There seemed a curious *expression* about all their outlines—a perpetual resemblance to living features, distorted and scornful. Myriads of deceitful shadows, and lurid lights, played and floated about and through the pale blue pinnacles, dazzling and confusing the sight of the traveller; while his ears grew dull and his head giddy with the constant gush and roar of the concealed waters. These painful circumstances increased upon him as he advanced; the ice crashed and yawned into fresh chasms at his feet, tottering spires nodded around him, and fell thundering across his path; and though he had repeatedly faced these dangers on the most terrific glaciers, and in the wildest weather, it was with a new and oppressive feeling of panic terror that he leaped the last chasm, and flung himself, exhausted and shuddering, on the firm turf of the mountain.

He had been compelled to abandon his basket of food, which became a perilous incumbrance on the glacier, and had now no means of refreshing himself but by breaking off and eating some of the pieces of ice. This, however, relieved his thirst; an hour's repose recruited his hardy frame, and with the indomitable spirit of avarice, he resumed his laborious journey.

His way now lay straight up a ridge of bare red rocks, without a blade of grass to ease the foot, or a projecting angle to afford an inch of shade from the south sun. It was past noon, and the rays beat intensely upon the steep path, while the whole atmosphere was motionless, and penetrated with heat. Intense thirst was soon added to the bodily fatigue with which Hans was now afflicted; glance after glance he cast on the flask of water which hung at his belt. "Three drops are enough," at last thought he; "I may, at least, cool my lips with it."

He opened the flask, and was raising it to his lips, when his eye fell on an object lying on the rock beside him; he thought it moved. It was a small dog, apparently in the last agony of death from thirst. Its tongue was out, its jaws dry, its limbs extended lifelessly, and a swarm of black ants were crawling about its lips and throat. Its eye moved to the bottle which Hans held in his hand. He raised it, drank, spurned the animal with his foot, and passed on. And he did not know how it was, but he thought that a strange shadow had suddenly come across the blue sky.

The path became steeper and more rugged every moment; and the high hill air, instead of refreshing him, seemed to throw his blood into a fever. The noise of the hill cataracts sounded like mockery in his ears; they were all distant, and his thirst increased every moment. Another hour passed, and he again looked down to the flask at his side; it was half empty; but there was much more than three drops in it. He stopped to open it, and again, as he did so, something moved in the path above him. It was a fair child, stretched nearly lifeless on the rock, its breast heaving with thirst, its eyes closed, and its lips parched and burning. Hans eyed it deliberately, drank, and passed on. And a dark grey cloud came over the sun, and long, snake-like shadows crept up along the mountain sides. Hans struggled on. The sun was sinking, but its descent seemed to bring no coolness; the leaden weight of the dead air pressed upon his brow and heart, but the goal was near. He saw the cataract of the Golden River springing from the hill-side, scarcely five hundred feet above him. He paused for a moment to breathe, and sprang on to complete his task.

At this instant a faint cry fell on his ear. He turned, and saw a grey-haired old man extended on the rocks. His eyes were sunk, his features deadly pale, and gathered into an expression of despair. "Water!" he stretched his arms to Hans, and cried feebly, "Water! I am dying."

"I have none," replied Hans; "thou hast had thy share of life." He strode over the prostrate body, and darted on. And a flash of blue lightning rose out of the East, shaped like a sword; it shook thrice over the whole heaven, and left it dark with one heavy, impenetrable shade. The sun was setting; it plunged toward the horizon like a red-hot ball.

The roar of the Golden River rose on Hans' ear. He stood at the brink of the chasm through which it ran. Its waves were filled with the red glory of the sunset; they shook their crests like tongues of fire, and flashes of bloody light gleamed along their foam. Their sound came mightier and mightier on his senses; his brain grew giddy with the prolonged thunder. Shuddering he drew the flask from his girdle, and hurled it into the centre of the torrent. As he did so, an icy chill shot through his limbs: he staggered, shrieked, and fell. The waters closed over his cry. And the moaning of the river rose wildly into the night, as it gushed over

THE BLACK STONE.

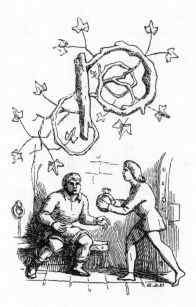

CHAPTER IV

*How Mr. Schwartz set off on an Expedition to the Golden River,
and how he prospered therein.*

POOR LITTLE GLUCK waited very anxiously alone in the house, for Hans' return. Finding
he did not come back, he was terribly frightened, and went and told Schwartz in the
prison, all that had happened. Then Schwartz was very much pleased, and said that
Hans must certainly have been turned into a black stone, and he should have all the
gold to himself. But Gluck was very sorry, and cried all night. When he got up in the
morning, there was no bread in the house, nor any money; so Gluck went, and hired
himself to another goldsmith, and he worked so hard, and so neatly, and so long every
day, that he soon got money enough together, to pay his brother's fine, and he went,
and gave it all to Schwartz, and Schwartz got out of prison. Then Schwartz was quite
pleased, and said he should have some of the gold of the river. But Gluck only begged
he would go and see what had become of Hans.

Now when Schwartz had heard that Hans had stolen the holy water, he thought to
himself that such a proceeding might not be considered altogether correct by the King
of the Golden River, and determined to manage matters better. So he took some more
of Gluck's money, and went to a bad priest, who gave him some holy water very readily
for it. Then Schwartz was sure it was all quite right. So Schwartz got up early in the
morning before the sun rose, and took some bread and wine, in a basket, and put his
holy water in a flask, and set off for the mountains. Like his brother he was much

surprised at the sight of the glacier, and had great difficulty in crossing it, even after leaving his basket behind him. The day was cloudless, but not bright: there was a heavy purple haze hanging over the sky, and the hills looked lowering and gloomy. And as Schwartz climbed the steep rock path, the thirst came upon him, as it had upon his brother, until he lifted his flask to his lips to drink. Then he saw the fair child lying near him on the rocks, and it cried to him, and moaned for water.

"Water indeed," said Schwartz; "I haven't half enough for myself," and passed on. And as he went he thought the sunbeams grew more dim, and he saw a low bank of black cloud rising out of the West; and, when he had climbed for another hour the thirst overcame him again, and he would have drunk. Then he saw the old man lying before him on the path, and heard him cry out for water. "Water, indeed," said Schwartz, "I haven't half enough for myself," and on he went.

Then again the light seemed to fade from before his eyes, and he looked up, and, behold, a mist, of the colour of blood, had come over the sun; and the bank of black cloud had risen very high, and its edges were tossing and tumbling like the waves of the angry sea. And they cast long shadows, which flickered over Schwartz's path.

Then Schwartz climbed for another hour, and again his thirst returned; and as he lifted his flask to his lips, he thought he saw his brother Hans lying exhausted on the path before him, and, as he gazed, the figure stretched its arms to him, and cried for water. "Ha, ha," laughed Schwartz, "are you there? remember the prison bars, my boy. Water, indeed! do you suppose I carried it all the way up here for *you?*" And he strode over the figure; yet, as he passed, he thought he saw a strange expression of mockery about its lips. And, when he had gone a few yards farther, he looked back; but the figure was not there.

And a sudden horror came over Schwartz, he knew not why; but the thirst for gold prevailed over his fear, and he rushed on. And the bank of black cloud rose to the zenith, and out of it came bursts of spiry lightning, and waves of darkness seemed to heave and float between their flashes, over the whole heavens. And the sky where the sun was setting was all level, and like a lake of blood; and a strong wind came out of that sky, tearing its crimson clouds into fragments, and scattering them far into the darkness. And when Schwartz stood by the brink of the Golden River, its waves were black, like thunder clouds, but their foam was like fire; and the roar of the waters below, and the thunder above met, as he cast the flask into the stream. And, as he did so, the lightning glared in his eyes, and the earth gave way beneath him, and the waters closed over his cry. And the moaning of the river rose wildly into the night, as it gushed over the

Two Black Stones.

CHAPTER V

How little Gluck set off on an Expedition to the Golden River,
and how he prospered therein; with other matters of interest.

WHEN GLUCK FOUND that Schwartz did not come back, he was very sorry, and did not know what to do. He had no money, and was obliged to go and hire himself again to the goldsmith, who worked him very hard, and gave him very little money. So, after a month, or two, Gluck grew tired, and made up his mind to go and try his fortune with the Golden River. "The little king looked very kind," thought he. "I don't think he will turn me into a black stone." So he went to the priest, and the priest gave him some holy water as soon as he asked for it. Then Gluck took some bread in his basket, and the bottle of water, and set off very early for the mountains.

If the glacier had occasioned a great deal of fatigue to his brothers, it was twenty times worse for him, who was neither so strong nor so practised on the mountains. He had several very bad falls, lost his basket and bread, and was very much frightened at the strange noises under the ice. He lay a long time to rest on the grass, after he had got over, and began to climb the hill just in the hottest part of the day. When he had climbed for an hour, he got dreadfully thirsty, and was going to drink like his brothers, when he saw an old man coming down the path above him, looking very feeble, and leaning on a staff. "My son," said the old man, "I am faint with thirst, give me some of that water." Then Gluck looked at him, and when he saw that he was pale and weary, he gave him the water; "Only pray don't drink it all," said Gluck. But the old man drank a great deal, and gave him back the bottle two-thirds empty. Then he bade him good speed, and Gluck went on again merrily. And the path became easier to his feet, and two or three blades of grass appeared upon it, and some grasshoppers began singing on the bank beside it; and Gluck thought he had never heard such merry singing.

Then he went on for another hour, and thirst increased on him so that he thought he should be forced to drink. But, as he raised the flask, he saw a little child lying panting by the road-side, and it cried out piteously for water. Then Gluck struggled with himself, and determined to bear the thirst a little longer; and he put the bottle to the child's lips, and it drank it all but a few drops. Then it smiled on him, and got up, and ran down the hill; and Gluck looked after it, till it became as small as a little star, and then turned and began climbing again. And then there were all kinds of sweet flowers growing on the rocks, bright green moss, with pale pink starry flowers, and soft belled gentians, more blue than the sky at its deepest, and pure white transparent lilies. And crimson and purple butterflies darted hither and thither, and the sky sent down such pure light, that Gluck had never felt so happy in his life.

Yet, when he had climbed for another hour, his thirst became intolerable again; and, when he looked at his bottle, he saw that there were only five or six drops left in it, and he could not venture to drink. And, as he was hanging the flask to his belt again, he saw a little dog lying on the rocks, gasping for breath—just as Hans had seen it on the day of his ascent. And Gluck stopped and looked at it, and then at the Golden River, not five hundred yards above him; and he thought of the dwarf's words, "that no one could succeed, except in his first attempt;" and he tried to pass the dog, but it whined piteously, and Gluck stopped again. "Poor beastie," said Gluck, "it'll be dead when I

come down again, if I don't help it." Then he looked closer and closer at it, and its eye turned on him so mournfully, that he could not stand it. "Confound the King and his gold too," said Gluck; and he opened the flask, and poured all the water into the dog's mouth.

The dog sprang up and stood on its hind legs. Its tail disappeared, its ears became long, longer, silky, golden; its nose became very red, its eyes became very twinkling; in three seconds the dog was gone, and before Gluck stood his old acquaintance, the King of the Golden River.

"Thank you," said the monarch; "but don't be frightened, it's all right;" for Gluck showed manifest symptoms of consternation at this unlooked-for reply to his last observation. "Why didn't you come before," continued the dwarf, "instead of sending me those rascally brothers of yours, for me to have the trouble of turning into stones? Very hard stones they make too."

"Oh dear me!" said Gluck, "have you really been so cruel?"

"Cruel!" said the dwarf, "they poured unholy water into my stream: do you suppose I'm going to allow that?"

"Why," said Gluck, "I am sure, sir—your majesty, I mean—they got the water out of the church font."

"Very probably," replied the dwarf; "but," and his countenance grew stern as he spoke, "the water which has been refused to the cry of the weary and dying, is unholy, though it had been blessed by every saint in heaven; and the water which is found in the vessel of mercy is holy, though it had been defiled with corpses."

So saying, the dwarf stooped and plucked a lily that grew at his feet. On its white leaves there hung three drops of clear dew. And the dwarf shook them into the flask which Gluck held in his hand. "Cast these into the river," he said, "and descend on the other side of the mountains into the Treasurey Valley. And so good speed."

As he spoke, the figure of the dwarf became indistinct. The playing colours of his robe formed themselves into a prismatic mist of dewy light: he stood for an instant veiled with them as with the belt of a broad rainbow. The colors grew faint, the mist rose into the air; the monarch had evaporated.

And Gluck climbed to the brink of the Golden River, and its waves were as clear as crystal, and as brilliant as the sun. And, when he cast the three drops of dew into the stream, there opened where they fell, a small circular whirlpool, into which the waters descended with a musical noise.

Gluck stood watching it for some time, very much disappointed, because not only the river was not turned into gold, but its waters seemed much diminished in quantity. Yet he obeyed his friend the dwarf, and descended the other side of the mountains, towards the Treasure Valley; and, as he went, he thought he heard the noise of water working its way under the ground. And, when he came in sight of the Treasure Valley, behold, a river, like the Golden River, was springing from a new cleft of the rocks above it, and was flowing in innumerable streams among the dry heaps of red sand.

And as Gluck gazed, fresh grass sprang beside the new streams, and creeping plants grew, and climbed among the moistening soil. Young flowers opened suddenly along the river sides, as stars leap out when twilight is deepening, and thickets of myrtle, and tendrils of vine, cast lengthening shadows over the valley as they grew. And thus the Treasure Valley became a garden again, and the inheritance, which had been lost by cruelty, was regained by love.

And Gluck went, and dwelt in the valley, and the poor were never driven from his door: so that his barns became full of corn, and his house of treasure. And, for him, the river had, according to the dwarf's promise, become a River of Gold.

And, to this day, the inhabitants of the valley point out the place where the three drops of holy dew were cast into the stream, and trace the course of the Golden River under the ground, until it emerges in the Treasure Valley. And at the top of the cataract of the Golden River, are still to be seen two BLACK STONES, round which the waters howl mournfully every day at sunset; and these stones are still called by the people of the valley

THE BLACK BROTHERS.

THE END

The Enchanted Doll

A Fairy Tale for Little People

By MARK LEMON

THE ENCHANTED DOLL.

A Fairy Tale for Little People.

・・・・・・

BY MARK LEMON.

THE ILLUSTRATIONS BY RICHARD DOYLE.

EIGHT YEARS AFTER Ruskin wrote *The King of the Golden River* but two years before it was first published, Mark Lemon (1809–1870), one of the founders of *Punch*, published *The Enchanted Doll*. He could not have known Ruskin's tale; so his must rank as an equally early and original effort in what was still almost an untrodden field. Like Ruskin, Lemon was fortunate in having Richard Doyle as his illustrator. Journalist, humorist, eventually editor-in-chief of *Punch*, Mark Lemon wrote several novels for adults, and many shorter tales and sketches; and several times later in life he returned to the fairy tale. Some of his later stories are probably more skillful than *The Enchanted Doll*, yet its experimental nature and its freshness lend it special interest. Lemon dedicated it to the two young daughters of his good friend Charles Dickens, Mary and Kate, who probably each got a dedication copy as a Christmas present in 1848: for, ever since Dickens had published *A Christmas Carol* in 1843, short Christmas tales had become the rage and often bore the next year as a publication date on the title page but were already widely available for sale in the weeks just before Christmas. A warm-hearted, benevolent, genial man, Lemon had many friends among Victorian men of letters, and his personal qualities can be inferred from *The Enchanted Doll*.

Like Ruskin, Lemon was influenced by Grimm, and the repeated appearances to Jacob Pout, the doll-maker, of the Black Fairy, Malice, as well as her dubious present, derive from the tradition of the folk fairy tale. But the story is firmly set in sixteenth-century England; many of its episodes, including Jacob's experiences at the bear-baiting, and many details of the setting, notably the suggestion that it was Jacob who carved the famous Guildhall statues, Gog and Magog, were calculated to teach and to delight the London child. *The Enchanted Doll* of course has a moral: indeed it is all moral: envy is a bad thing, a lesson Jacob Pout might—the reader thinks—have learned earlier, except that then there would have been less of a story to tell.

In fact, Jacob's churlishness ("I have often heard you grumbling in a manner which has done my heart good," the Black Fairy says to him) is reminiscent of Scrooge's: and although envy was not Scrooge's besetting sin, Jacob is avaricious enough as well as essentially jealous. So the Dickens-format Christmas book, the Dickens-like character, and the association of *The Enchanted Doll* with Dickens's children render it a sufficiently interesting example of an early Victorian *Kunstmärchen* to warrant its reissue here.

The text of The Enchanted Doll, *with illustrations by Richard Doyle, is reprinted from the first edition (London: Bradbury and Evans, 1849).*

CHAPTER I

Jacob Pout's First Interview with the Black Fairy.

THE STORY I am about to tell you happened many years ago, long before the railroads had cut up the dancing-grounds of the Fairies, or the shrill whistle of the locomotive had frightened the "good people" from the green dells and quiet nooks wherein they are said to have held their merry-makings by the clear moonlight. We never see a fairy now-a-days: nevertheless we are glad to talk about them and their doings in the old time! What a pretty sight it must have been to have seen King Oberon's state balls! Let us imagine one of those elfin revels.

There Oberon sits upon his pretty little mushroom throne, under a canopy of feathery fern, while tiny gnats hum merry tunes within the bells of the fox-glove and wild convolvulus. See! how his minikin courtiers dance round and round until the grass shows a circle of the deepest green! How gracefully their robes of film float in the air or twine about their fragile limbs! And now, tired with their sport, they throw themselves at the root of some huge field-flower, and drink bright dew from cups gathered from the yellow cowslip, and tell of the mad pranks they have played poor mortals, like Shakspere's *Puck.*—

> "That shrewd and knavish sprite
> Call'd Robin Goodfellow; . . .
> That fright the maidens of the villagery,
> Skim milk; and sometimes labour in the quern,*
> And bootless make the breathless housewife churn,
> And sometimes make the drink to bear no barm,
> Mislead night wand'rers, laughing at their harm.

---

*Handmill.

I think Shakspere must have been at King Oberon's court some time or the other, and that his *Midsummer's Night's Dream* was no dream after all, but what he saw and felt in Elf-land, so if you want to know about the "good people," read what he has written of them.

As I have said, the story I am about to tell you happened years ago, long before the fairies had left us, and begins at that pleasant time of the year when the trees (like good little folk at school) are putting forth the blossoms which give promise of fruit hereafter. The doors and shutters of Jacob Pout's booth (as a shop was called in those days) were thrown open to let in the little breeze that was playing among the lavender and marjoram in the garden at the back of his dwelling, and to let out the whizzing noise of the lathe at which Jacob was at work.

Jacob Pout was a doll-maker, and generally admitted to be the cleverest craftsman in his trade. He made wooden dolls only, (for no one had as yet thought of making dolls out of wax,) but they were considered marvels of beauty by all the young ladies who were fortunate enough to possess one. They had such red cheeks, such curly hempen wigs, and legs and arms as good as any wooden doll could wish for. And then they were such dolls to last! You might leave them on the window-sill, in the broad glaring sunshine, without their noses melting away; or you might drop them out of the nursery window without damaging more than a leg or an arm, or perhaps only chipping off a little of the paint. I know there was one that descended to six little girls in succession, and at last had lost nothing but its wig and the tip of its nose.

Ah! Jacob Pout ought to have been a happy man, for his customers were always satisfied with their purchases, and his lathe might have been going every working-day of the week if its owner had not been rather lazy and very envious.

Opposite the doll-maker lived Anthony Stubbs, a clever worker in gold and silver, and moreover an industrious, good-tempered fellow. The shutter of his booth was always the first to be taken down, and there he might be heard whistling and hammering all day, as cheerful as a lark, and as busy as a bee. True, he had not many customers, but then his wares were costly in their material, and took a long time to work into cups, and salvers, and spoons.

Jacob Pout never thought of this as he stood idling his time away at the door of his booth, murmuring within himself that he should have been brought up to doll-making, whilst Tony Stubbs never worked upon anything baser than silver. And then, when he saw the alderman of the ward tell down upon Tony's counter twenty pounds for a silver tankard, he nearly choked with envy at his neighbour's good fortune, never thinking how many long days it had cost the honest silversmith to hammer into form the dogs and horsemen which made the cup so valuable. Neither did he think how much time and travail had been spent by Tony Stubbs before he acquired the art of chasing gold and silver; for he had gone over the sea as far as Florence, to study in the workshop of the great Benvenuto Cellini, the most renowned craftsman of his time, and whose productions are esteemed to this day the masterpieces of their kind. Jacob Pout never thought of all this, and felt no gratitude for the good with which God had blessed him, but envied Tony his hard-earned gains.

Jacob had passed the greater part of a fine summer's afternoon in this discontented spirit, and, having closed his booth, had taken a long walk into the country. London was not the large city that it is now, and its suburbs were not all brick and mortar as they are at present, but shady woods and open meadows were to be found everywhere around it, and thither would the good citizens resort on high days and holidays. Jacob Pout, idler that he was, made twice as many holidays as any of his neighbours, and there was not a pleasant place in wood or field but Jacob knew of it.

There was no pleasanter spot round London than Maude's Dingle, in the middle of the small wood which skirted the boundary wall of the Priory Garden, at Kilbourne. When the wind set in that direction you could hear Bow Bells plain enough; but, at other times, not a sound of the neighbouring city could be heard. Here. on the summer's evening to which our tale refers, at the foot of an old gnarled oak, was seated Jacob Pout. A solitary thrush was singing its hymn to the evening; no other sound was heard, except the soft murmurs of the little Bourne, which gave a name to the locality.

The song, both of bird and brook, was lost upon Jacob Pout; for his mind was full of envious and discontented thoughts, which destroyed the charm of all things round about him. His eye looked not upon the velvet sward upon which he was lying; no, he saw only visions of the glittering wares of Tony Stubbs. He heard not the mellow notes of the thrush, nor the tinkling melody of the brook; no, his ear was filled by ideal sounds, like the noise of beaten metals. The twilight came and went, yet there he lay sulky and miserable; he had no wish to return to the city so long as there was a risk of encountering any one that he knew, for he felt that to "love his neighbour" not "as himself," but even to love him at all, was that night impossible.

The thrush had long since finished its hymn and was at rest; but the little brook could not be silent until it reached the distant river. Jacob heard it at last, and as he listened, the sounds seemed to become more and more distinct, until he thought he could define a tune. Yes, it was a march, and played, so it seemed at least, by drums, trumpets, and cymbals. Every moment it became more audible, and evidently proceeded from a hollow beech-tree not twenty yards from him.

As he looked in the direction of the sound, he saw—bless me! how he rubbed his eyes!—he saw coming from a little hole at the foot of the hollow beech, a procession of pigmy people, all gaily dressed, and marching with measured tread to the music of a full band of elfin players. In the midst, seated in a car not bigger than a walnut shell, was a lady, black as an Ethiopian. As the procession came nearer, Jacob saw that she wore armlets and bracelets of gold, and bands of the same precious metal were round her ankles; her dress was of the costliest materials, and made in the picturesque fashion of the East. Jacob felt rather frightened when the procession halted opposite to him, and his teeth fairly chattered when he saw the Black Fairy descend from her car and advance, with her maids of honour, directly towards the knoll upon which he was lying.

The Black Fairy evidently noticed his trepidation, for she smiled, not very prettily it must be confessed, but she did smile, as though to give Jacob courage; but as her condescension appeared to have a contrary effect to that which it was intended to produce—she spoke. Oh! what a voice she had! It was sharp and small, and sounded like the noise produced by blowing in the barrel of a watch-key; Jacob could hardly hear her words at first, but he became so interested in what she said to him, that, before she had spoken a minute, he could understand every syllable.

"I have often wished to speak to you," said the Black Fairy, "but it would not be considered etiquette in one of my degree to venture abroad, except by moonlight. I

have taken a great fancy to you; I have often heard you grumbling in a manner which has done my heart good, I assure you. I hate people to be contented and grateful; it shows a mean spirit. For my own part, I have never felt satisfied since I was born, and I am now nearly five thousand years old."

"You look remarkably well for your age," remarked Jacob.

"Not I," said the black lady; "I've seen fairies looking much better, who are my seniors by a day or two. But to your own affairs. I have come to take you under my especial protection. You are delightfully envious of that miserable milksop, Tony Stubbs. Ha! Ha! Depend upon it, Jacob, it's not all gold that glitters in that quarter; half his wares are sham, rely upon it. However, you are a good subject of mine, and deserve to be encouraged."

"Who are you?" *thought* Jacob.

"I am the Fairy Malice," said the black lady; "and I am only sorry that, as you are a mortal, I cannot make you my prime minister; you are admirably qualified for the post. But, never mind; if you can't serve me in Elf-land, you can do so in your own sphere. Tony Stubbs can't be worth, stock and all, more than three hundred pounds."

"Not that," shouted Jacob; "not that. If he were sold up to-morrow two hundred pounds would buy him."

"So much the worse for you then," said the Black Fairy; "you are one hundred pounds the poorer; for I intend to make you just as rich as Tony Stubbs."

"What a fool I've been," thought Jacob. "This black hag shouldn't have got off so easily had I known that."

"That's right, abuse me; grumble away," said the fairy. "I can hear your thoughts, and like you the better for having them. Oh, how I love ingratitude! Now, see what I am going to do for you; look at this." And Jacob saw, in the Fairy's hand, an ebony doll not bigger than his little finger; it was exquisitely carved, and had bracelets and armlets and ankle bands of silver. Jacob had never seen anything so well done since he had been a doll-maker.

"What do you think that is?" said the Fairy Malice: "that is an ENCHANTED DOLL. Take it home with you, it will sell for just one hundred pounds, and that sum, with what you are worth already, will place you on an equal footing with Tony Stubbs."

Jacob's eyes glistened with delight.

"So long as you are contented—it breaks my heart to think you may cease to be envious and covetous;—but so long as you are contented, the ENCHANTED DOLL will be of no service to you, but should you again deserve my assistance it will return to you, though her then possessor be living at the Antipodes. Good night, darling!" And then the procession departed in the same order in which it had arrived.

Jacob went home to bed, and slept soundly until daybreak. When he awoke he thought he must have been dreaming. No, there was the ENCHANTED DOLL upon the table.

He soon dressed himself and opened the shutter of his booth; it was a golden morning! He placed the fairy gift upon his board, and sat down to breakfast; but before he had swallowed a mouthful a strange looking person entered the shop, and inquired the price of the little black doll.

"One hundred and fifty pounds," answered Jacob.

"Too much," said the stranger, "I am ordered not to exceed one hundred."

There was something in his customer's manner that made Jacob anxious to get rid of him, and, therefore, he did not chaffer about the matter, but took the stranger's money and gave him the ENCHANTED DOLL.

"What a lucky fellow I am," said Jacob, as the stranger turned to depart.

"Very," said the doll-buyer, "at present."

CHAPTER II

The Enchanted Doll Returns to Jacob Pout.

WHEN THE STRANGER was out of sight, Jacob Pout recounted the money he had received for the ENCHANTED DOLL, ringing each coin on his board as loud as he could ring it, in order to attract the attention of the silversmith over the way. But Tony was too busy with his own work to notice what his neighbour was doing, and kept hammering away, to the great annoyance of the ill-natured doll-maker. Jacob put his money into his pouch, and placing his flat cap jauntily upon one side of his head, took two or three turns in front of the silversmith's booth, rattling the money in his pouch every time that he passed; but his trick was lost upon Tony Stubbs, who never once looked up from his work, but still kept fashioning the lump of silver on his small anvil. Jacob grew desperate, and entered the silversmith's booth.

"Good morrow, neighbour Stubbs," said the doll-maker.

"Ah!" replied Tony, "is it you, neighbour Pout? I am very glad to see you; for though we live opposite to each other, we seldom exchange more than a nod from week's end to week's end. But that is my fault. I believe I am always so hard at work that I have no time for a little friendly gossip."

"Just my case too," said Jacob; "I am always at work;" (what a fib that was!) "I cannot make dolls fast enough to supply the customers" (that was really true, but he might have done so had he been less idle). "But I have no right to grumble; I make money faster than I can spend it;" and Jacob again rattled the coins in his pouch.

"I am rejoiced to hear of your well-doing, neighbour," said Tony, but showing neither by look nor word that he envied Jacob his good fortune. "We have both great reason to be grateful to God, neighbour."

Jacob gave a short cough, and answered, "Yes!" but gratitude had no place in his heart. He was vexed that the silversmith appeared deaf to the jingling of the money in his pouch, and he resolved to try what the sight of the bright coins would produce.

"I have received a large sum—a *very* large sum—this morning," said Jacob, "and I have some doubt as to the goodness of the coin, which has been paid to me. Will you assay a few pieces for me, neighbour, and set my mind at rest."

"With great pleasure indeed," replied Tony; "let me see them."

"There is a small portion of them," said Jacob, throwing down upon the counter a handful of coins, all seemingly new and bright from the mint.

Tony examined them carefully, and tested them by means known in his art. When he had done so, he pronounced them to be of the finest silver, and worth even more than their rateable value: "Unless," said Tony, laughing, "they are made of fairy silver, and if so, neighbour, you have made a bad bargain."

"How?" inquired Jacob.

"Some morning you will find them turned into dirt and stones: at least so it runs in the legend," answered Tony.

"I have no fear of that," said Jacob, gathering up his money and pouring it into his pouch with as much display as possible. He then wished the silversmith a good morning, and crossed over to his own booth.

"Fairy silver—ha, ha! dirt and stones," thought Jacob. "I have made him envious at last." And with this bad thought the wicked doll-maker was contented.

At twelve o'clock the next day Tony Stubbs was seen to close the shutter of his booth, and then hurriedly walk eastward.

"Just like me," thought Jacob; "when I have a fit of the spleen I can never rest at home; I will be bound he is off to the woods for the rest of the day. Just like me."

Jacob was mistaken; in an hour or two the silversmith returned, and his hammer was heard ringing long after the usual hour of work. Again, in the morning, his neighbours were awakened, before cock-crow, by the sounds which proceeded from Tony's anvil. And so it was, day after day, the noise only ceasing at very long intervals, except about mid-day, when Tony closed the shutter of his booth and took his hurried walk eastward. All the neighbours remarked that he looked fatigued and unhappy, and the stock of his booth became less and less in spite of his incessant labour. Something was wrong with the silversmith, and every one pitied him, except the doll-maker.

I dare say you would like to know what took him away from home every day, and made him work early and late, and yet grow poorer and poorer? Well, I will tell you, because I know you are not like Jacob Pout, and I think you will be pleased with what the silversmith has done.

In the easternmost part of the city was a booth, above which was the sign of the Golden Shears, (I shall have to tell you more about signs presently), a sure indication that the owner pursued the ancient and honourable trade of tailor. The place was very clean, but scantily furnished with broadcloth, serge, and taffety, and for some days no one had been seen at work on the tailor's board but little Tom Tit, the apprentice. A good little fellow he was, for though he had no one to keep an eye upon him, he never idled away his time, but honestly stuck to the task his master had set him. It was to this shop that the silversmith paid his daily visit, for the tailor was Tony's father.

"Master is better to-day," said Tom Tit about a week after Tony's first journey; "and the alderman's been here who wanted to put master in the Fleet, and said that as you had paid some of the money, he need not be frightened any longer about going to prison."

"The alderman has been very kind, Tom," remarked Tony; "he has given me time to pay his debt, and in a month or so I hope to see my father a free man again. You are a good boy, Tom, and I shall not forget your kindness and service."

Tom tried to say "Thank you, Master Tony," but something in his throat would not let him; he only wiped his eyes with the back of his hand, and then stitched away ten times harder than ever.

While Tom was doing this, Tony had entered a room upstairs, and kneeling down by the bedside had asked his father's blessing.

The sick man laid his thin hand upon the head of his son, and prayed in silence for a few moments. When he had finished, the old man's eyes filled with tears, whilst a faint smile lighted up his pallid face. "Anthony," said he, "but for your filial love I should now be in a gaol."

"I hardly think that, father," replied Tony, gaily, "for I had no sooner told the alderman how cruelly you had been cheated of your goods, than he offered to forego part of the debt; but this I declined, as the money was justly due."

"You did rightly, my dear son, but it grieves me to think that my misfortunes should have made you almost a beggar," replied the old man; "but I know that the good God will bless you, perhaps not with wealth, for that is not always a blessing, but with a happy and contented mind, the sure reward of virtuous actions."

You know now why Tony worked early and late, and why he became poorer and poorer every day, until he had made his father a free man; but he had kept his secret quite snug, and, unless I had told you, I am certain you would never have heard a word about it. Well, it was on May-day that Tony went to the alderman to make the last payment of his father's debt: May-day was a great holiday in the old time, and the young Londoners used to go to the neighbouring woods to bring home the May-pole, which was a straight tree shorn of its branches and dressed out with gay streamers of ribbons and garlands of flowers. They used to dance round the May-pole to the music of a pipe and tabor, and sing merry songs in praise of Maid Marian and Robin Hood;

but I question whether the lady or gentleman deserved such honour. Sometimes there were grand pageants of knights in armour, and morris-dancers covered over with bells and ribbons. May-day is but a shabby affair now-a-days, with its tawdry "My Lord" and "My Lady," and would be worth nothing without Jack-in-the-Green.

There had never been a grander pageant than the one in Fenchurch Street on the morning when Tony Stubbs paid Alderman Kersey the balance of his father's debt; "all the world and his wife" had come out to see it, and where there was a sight to be seen there Jacob Pout was sure to be. Yes; he was the foremost in the crowd, shouting more loudly and pushing more rudely than any one else. He had received one or two blows on his crown from the staves of the javelin-men who were keeping clear the passage to the stand set apart for the Lord Mayor and Aldermen, and some of their friends, the richest merchants in the City. As the different aldermen passed along they were cheered and saluted by the bye-standers, for in those days it was considered a great honour to be a member of the corporation of London. Even Jacob Pout took off his cap as Alderman Kersey passed by, and it was not until the worthy magistrate stopped to speak to some one he recognised in the crowd, that Jacob perceived he was hanging on the arm of—Tony Stubbs. On they went, until they came to the Lord Mayor's stand, the steps of which they ascended together. There they stood, in the midst of the grandees of the great city of London; many of whom came to Tony and took him kindly by the hand. Jacob Pout could hardly believe his eyes; but what he saw was the truth, nevertheless. The alderman had told a great number of his friends the story of Tony's conduct, and so pleased were they with his filial love and honesty, that all resolved to befriend him as much as they could.

Jacob did not remain to see any more of the show, but walked home as fast as he could and shut himself up in his workshop. The sun shone brightly into the room, but Jacob drew the curtain to prevent the cheerful light from gaining admission; for his heart was full of envy and all uncharitableness, and the pleasant sunlight annoyed him. At last twilight came, and then night; the moon shone clear and bright, and sent a light into the room in spite of the curtain.

As Jacob sat brooding over what he had seen, the wheel of his lathe turned round, slowly at first, and then revolved with the greatest rapidity. Jacob started up in surprise, and saw a swarm of little fairies busily engaged in shaping a large block of ebony into the rude form of a doll. The chips of hard wood flew about in all directions; and the wheel whizzed round like a mad thing. At length the lathe ceased, and Jacob saw the pigmies, with chisels and mallets, fashion the head and limbs into the exact resemblance, only a hundred times larger, of the ENCHANTED DOLL he had brought away from Maude's Dingle.

When the fairies had finished their work they expressed their delight by playing about in the most fantastic manner; now swinging by cobwebs from the ceiling, then climbing up the legs of the table and turning head over heels from that frightful precipice on to the ground. At length Jacob heard the same music he had heard in the woods, and saw the Fairy Malice and her elfin train come forth from a mouse-hole in the corner of the room.

"Well, Jacob, my dear child," said the black lady, "I am glad you have come to your senses again; I was afraid you would never more be envious enough to release the ENCHANTED DOLL from the power of her last possessor. You see, it gives my people some

trouble to restore her form, but never mind about that; you are such a dear envious creature that I could do anything for you."

"But what can this lump of wood do for me? Can it introduce me to the Lord Mayor and Aldermen, and make me as great a man as Tony Stubbs seems likely to be?" said Jacob, with a sneer.

"That's right, dear; abuse my gift, sneer at me; I like to see you ungrateful," exclaimed the fairy.

"Besides, who will buy such a lumbering thing as this? The ENCHANTED DOLL was a wonder in doll-making, but this is a clumsy—ugly——"

"Stop, dear, stop," said the fairy; "the increased size of the doll is all owing to the increase of your desires, and so it will be, my pretty one, until—but you must excuse me for the present: I have to attend a family party in the Dog-star." And without further ceremony, she and her elfin troop disappeared down the mouse-hole.

In the morning Jacob placed the ENCHANTED DOLL on his board; but though a number of persons stopped to look at it, no one seemed disposed to become a purchaser.

Meanwhile, the shop of the silversmith began to assume a very improved appearance, for the alderman and his friends had given Tony as much work as he could do; and such was Jacob Pout's envy, that I think he would never have sold his ENCHANTED DOLL (for it was only when he was contented that he could part with it), had not Tony fallen dangerously sick, and Jacob envied him no longer.

When reading was a much rarer accomplishment than it is now, and but few of the porters and servants of the citizens knew even the letters of the alphabet, the shopkeepers of London used to hang, in the front of their houses, pictures and models, which were called signs, to enable persons to distinguish one trader from another. Some of the devices used were very curious, and among those which have come down to us,

none seems less suited to the trade which it designates than the Black Doll, which we have all seen hanging over the door of the marine-store dealer.

I have no doubt that our ENCHANTED DOLL was the original of the sign, for it was Tristram Tattersall, dealer in ship's stores, who became the new possessor of Jacob's fairy gift. He had it a great bargain, for it only cost him a few pounds and (at Jacob's earnest solicitation) a seat at the Lord Mayor's dinner; for even in the old time good eating was a favourite pastime with the citizens of London.

Jacob enjoyed himself greatly during the early part of the banquet; he ate of everything that looked luscious and tempting, chuckling all the time at the thought that poor Tony was lying in a sick chamber taking nothing by physic, which was then quite as unpleasant in flavour as it is at present. As the feast proceeded, Jacob drunk so much wine that he became very noisy and troublesome, and before the dinner was over the attendants of the Lord Mayor were compelled to carry the doll-maker out of the Guildhall. It was even said that, for more than an hour, he sat in the stocks, to the great delight of a number of little boys in Cheap.

Before we finish this chapter, you will be glad to know that Tony became a great deal better, and that Alderman Kersey called upon him daily; and at length, when Tony was able to sit up, the good alderman took his only daughter, Dorothy, to see him, and there is great reason to believe that the silversmith improved rapidly after the visit.

And Jacob Pout was more envious of his neighbour than ever.

CHAPTER III

Jacob Goes to a Bear Garden, and afterwards to a Christmas Party.

T HE MONEY which Jacob had received from Tristram Tattersall was soon expended, for the doll-maker had resolved to make what he called "a figure in the world;" and he did so, to the great amusement of his neighbours, among whom he was no favourite, as his envy and selfishness were well known. He dressed himself in the extreme of the fashion, which was most fantastic and ridiculous. He had a monstrous ruff round his neck, which made his closely-cropped head look like a small dumpling in a large platter. He wore stockings of two colours, and bows in his shoes. His breeches were so puffed out about the hips with buckram and wadding that his body seemed to rest upon two drumsticks. How the plain, sober citizens laughed at him as he strutted up and down the street with the intention of exciting the envy and admiration of his neighbours! When he thought he had accomplished his object he resolved to favour the court end of the town with a visit. As he could not walk with any comfort he made his way to London Bridge stairs, and hailing a waterman, got into a boat, and desired to be taken to the palace at Westminster. There were no hackney coaches in those days, and persons of all ranks used "the silent highway" (as the river Thames has been called) when they wished to avoid the bustle and noise of the streets. The watermen were generally quick-witted fellows, from being brought in contact with the many people who rode in their boats, and, being bold and impudent, they did not hesitate to pass some very free remarks upon the patrons of each other. You can imagine how Jacob must have fared in his progress up the river, seated, as he was, in the stern of the boat, in his large breeches and ruff, and a little peaked hat with a cock-tail feather in it. Some said he looked like a peg-top turned upside down, whilst others compared him to

a Dutch dram-bottle. Jacob was very angry at first, but became reconciled to his situation when his cunning sculler told him (seeing what a vain fellow he was) that "it was the custom of the river for the low watermen to jibe at all the noblemen and gentry about the court."

When they arrived at Westminster, Jacob was astonished at the large sum demanded by the waterman for rowing him so short a distance, but when he was assured that the scullers "never carried *noblemen* for less," Jacob pulled out his purse with an air and paid the money. Poor dolt! if he had only known how he was jeered and laughed at the moment his back was turned; for persons who pretend to be other than they really are will at all times be exposed to ridicule and imposition.

"Are you for the bear-baiting to-day," said a gaily dressed young man to Jacob, shortly after he had landed; "rare sport is expected, I am told, and the best of the nobility and gentry are to be present."

"Why, sir," replied Jacob, "I have never seen a bear baited. Is the Bear Garden easy of access?"

"It is if you have friends," returned the young man; "I shall be happy to introduce you; I am of the Duke of Northumberland's household, and shall be glad to be of service to so brave a gentleman."

Jacob thanked him for his politeness, and wished heartily that his city neighbours could see him in such good company. Good company, indeed! The young fellow was a London foist, or thief, who instantly saw that Jacob was a very likely person to be imposed upon; so whilst the inflated doll-maker thought he was in the society of a duke's gentleman, he was but the companion of a rogue and a vagabond.

When they came to the Bear Garden, Jacob's friend suddenly discovered that he had no money; of course the doll-maker was too glad to lend a piece of gold to such a desirable acquaintance. None but the best seats would serve the turn of Jacob and his friend, and they were therefore conducted by one of the bear-wards to the gallery set aside for the most distinguished ladies and gentlemen.

"Ladies in a bear garden?" Yes, in the "good old times," of which we hear so much, the most cruel sports were witnessed by gentlewomen, who from their earliest childhood were accustomed to hear deeds of violence and bloodshed spoken of as praiseworthy actions, and thus became inured to think lightly of physical suffering, and to applaud the endurance and the infliction of pain. Books were rare things in those days, and few had the means of knowing what vast stores of elevating enjoyment were to be found among the stars, among the flowers, and in the earth, and under the waters.

It was the ignorance of the past which made cruelty endurable, and it will be the increase of knowledge in the time to come, teaching us that God is everywhere, which will make the meanest creature of value in the eyes of men, and thus preserve from wanton outrage, or wicked neglect, all things endowed with the consciousness of suffering. Be diligent, therefore, my little friends, to gain and to diffuse knowledge, that you may help onward that good time, when kindliness and good will shall inhabit the bosoms of all the human race.

I will not describe the sufferings of the bear or the dogs, for the victim and its tormentors were alike subject to pain and injury, but proceed with our story. The sport was at an end, and the visitors were leaving their seats, when a loud outcry was raised in that part of the garden where Jacob and his friend had taken their position. "Here's a thief, bear-ward," cried one, seizing the duke's gentleman.

"Here's his comrade," shouted another, taking a firm hold of Jacob's ponderous ruff.

The bear-wards were not slow in securing the denounced persons, as their show was likely to suffer in the estimation of the public from the presence of thieves, and without much parley they hurled Jacob and his distinguished acquaintance into the arena, where the bear was still chained to the post. The poor brute, smarting from his previous ill-treatment, and fearing, no doubt, that the new comers were also his enemies, made two or three blows at the doll-maker, who chanced to roll near to him, and rent Jacob's fine clothes into shreds, and with his sharp claws scratched the face of the duke's gentleman. The ridiculous appearance of the suspected thieves roused the mirth of the assemblage, and even the angry bear-wards could not help laughing heartily.

"Let them go now, Robert," said a young nobleman and a great patron of the bear-garden; "they are well served for their knavish practices."

The bear-ward, obedient to his patron's command, conducted the two suspected rogues to the door, and giving each a sound rap with his quarter-staff, bid them not venture within his walls again, at the peril of their ears.

The duke's gentleman instantly took to his heels, and Jacob, ragged, bruised, and disgraced, walked hurriedly to the river-side, intending to take water to the City, but he found that his ill reputation had preceded him, and he was only jeered and ill-used by the watermen. In this tattered condition, therefore, he was obliged to take his way homeward, accompanied by a troop of the rabble, who are always inclined to enjoy the misfortunes of any one.

More than a week had passed since this unlucky occurrence, and Jacob Pout had never crossed the threshold of his booth, for he thought that the story was known among his neighbours, and he feared to encounter their jokes and laughter. The good-natured silversmith became at length greatly concerned for his neighbour, and resolved to pay him a visit. When Tony got to the doll-maker's door he was surprised to see Jacob with a large axe endeavouring to cut in pieces a beautiful black doll, dressed like an Eastern princess, but the hard ebony resisted every effort made to destroy it. Jacob's old friend had come back to him, but larger than before, for his envy and hatred of his neighbours had increased greatly since his own misfortune. During the week that Jacob had shut himself up he had had no other companion but the ENCHANTED DOLL, and that at last be-

came so intolerable to him that he resolved to cut it in pieces and burn it; but his fairy gift was not to be so easily disposed of.

"Good morrow, neighbour Pout," said Tony, holding out his hand, which the other took with evident confusion, but the silversmith attributed Jacob's coolness to his recent misfortune, and not to the real cause, which was the presence of the ENCHANTED DOLL.

"What a capital piece of workmanship," said Tony; "I think I never saw anything so exquisitely made. Surely you were not cutting this up for firewood."

Jacob stammered out something about nobody buying black dolls, as silly little girls were frightened at black people.

"What is the price of it?" inquired Tony. "I have been thinking for a long time of a sign for my booth, and the Indian Princess would be a very good one for my craft. What is the price, neighbour?"

Jacob was delighted at the thought of getting rid of what had become to him a horrible thing, and he therefore named a very small sum.

"Agreed!" said Tony, "I will buy it of you, provided you go with me to-night and spend Christmas Eve at the house of a kind friend of mine. I will promise you a hearty welcome."

Jacob was willing to consent to any terms—even had they been less agreeable than those proposed by the silversmith.

"Then bring the sign over to my booth as soon as you like, and I will pay you the money," said Tony, "and I hope that when you see your handicraft over my door you will think oftener of its owner, and call upon me as a neighbour should do."

Tony shook Jacob heartily by the hand, and then took his leave.

"You shall not wait long for your bargain," said the doll-maker, as soon as Tony's back was turned. "An Indian Princess, forsooth! Will nothing suit you for a sign but an Indian Princess? Well, I'll gratify your proud stomach, and rid me of this odious piece of fairy work."

Jacob Pout took the ENCHANTED DOLL in his arms with the intention of carrying it to the silversmith, but at every step he made towards his own door the doll became heavier and heavier, until at last he was obliged to place it on the floor, quite unable to carry it any further. The ENCHANTED DOLL could only be parted with when Jacob ceased to be envious and discontented, and at that moment he envied everybody.

The ENCHANTED DOLL did not remain long quiet, but hopped back in the oddest way imaginable to the little room at the back of the shop.

"I'll not endure this!" cried Jacob, in a great fury, "I will take it to Tony Stubbs, and he shall keep it;" but he was reckoning without the ENCHANTED DOLL, which then began to hop about the room, over the chairs, and on to the bed, and the great walnut-tree chest in which Jacob kept his Sunday clothes. The doll-maker pursued it as fast as he was able, but the ENCHANTED DOLL always continued to elude his grasp, until, heated and exhausted, Jacob threw himself on a chair and fairly cried with vexation.

We will leave him to himself if you please, and take an imaginary stroll to Holbourne, as it was in the time of the ENCHANTED DOLL.

There are very few houses to be seen, but all are of a substantial character, and evidently belonging to persons of large means. The gardens in front are kept with great care, and though it is winter-time the broad gravel paths have not a withered leaf upon them. In the parlour windows of one or two of the houses a scarlet geranium is to be seen: in others are ostrich's eggs suspended by silk cords from the ceiling, and here and there are beautiful yellow canary birds, and in one that rare creature, a cockatoo, all presents, no doubt, from sea captains who make the long voyage to the warm countries of the East. That clear, swift stream is the Fleet River (the time will come when it will be a foul ditch), and that large brick house with the bow-windows, lighted from within by a blazing fire, is the dwelling of Alderman Kersey. As we are friends of Tony Stubbs, I am sure he will be glad to welcome us. Here we are in the hall. As it is Christmas time there is a table loaded with good cheer, to which all comers are welcome; and those happy-looking folk crowding round the large sea-coal fire are drinking to the good alderman's health in double ale. This way leads to the principal sitting-room. The floor is strewn with dried rushes and lavender, for the rich Turkey carpet is thought too beautiful to tread upon, and it is therefore thrown over the carved table which stands in the centre of the room. The embroidery on the high backs of the chairs is all the work of Miss Dorothy's fingers, who stands arranging her pretty curls by that mirror of polished steel in a velvet-covered framework, whilst her mother and the maids decorate the buffet with the "white plate," which is only displayed on high-days and holidays. From the bosses and pendants of the ceiling hang bunches of red-berried holly and beaded mistletoe intermingled with bows of gay coloured ribbons. The door opposite leads to the kitchen, which looks like a green bower, so thickly is it covered with ivy and holly. The pewter platters on the shelves shine as brightly as the silver ware in the parlour, and as dinner has been long past (for it is nearly four o'clock) the servants are preparing for the dance which is to take place in the evening. Before the huge fire sits the turnspit, dozing and enjoying the warmth after the labours of the morning. Poor dog! he has to work hard at feast-times. He sits up (as our little dog Timber does when he begs) and with his short fore legs turns the great spit, which bends with the weight of the mighty baron of beef. But his work is over for the day. Here are the fiddlers, who prepare themselves for their forthcoming exertions by a hearty assault on the beef and ale. And here come the guests. Those are the alderman's clerks and warehousemen, with their wives and sweethearts. Those two lads shaking hands with Mrs. Kersey and Dorothy are the alderman's apprentices, and the persons just entering the hall are neighbours and old customers of the house, with their wives, sons, and daughters. There are old Mr. Stubbs, and good little Tom Tit! Those two who have just entered I

hope you know by this time. Tony Stubbs is heartily welcomed by the alderman and
Mrs. Kersey, whilst both Dorothy and the silversmith meet each other kindly, but rather
sheepishly. What *can* be the reason? for he has asked her to dance the first dance with
him, and Dorothy has answered "Yes, thank you," although her face is red with blushes.
Jacob Pout has been introduced to the alderman and his family by Tony, but the
doll-maker seems to be ill at ease with his new friends.

There go the fiddles! The alderman and a buxom dame of forty lead off, whilst old
Mr. Stubbs has the honour of following with Mrs. Kersey; Tony and Dorothy are in the
middle of the set and dancing merrily, to the great admiration of the servants, who one
and all take part in the dance. What peals of laughter are heard every now and then as
some blunder is made in the figure, when Charles, who should have turned to the right,
wheels round to the left, and bumps against Mary, who nearly tumbles over Kate, who
falls into the arms of Walter, whilst Frank, and Alfred, and Sidney clap their hands and
declare that Kate did it on purpose. What a shout of laughter! Huzza! Alderman Kersey
has kissed his partner under the mistletoe. There's romping! All the women are
pretending to run away from the kissing-bough, and all the men are dragging them
back again; all but Jacob Pout.

Another dance, and another, and blind man's buff and hot cockles have brought us
to supper time. All the young men assist in laying out the tables and placing the benches
round them. What a huge Christmas pie is drawn from the oven where it has been
quietly baking unknown to every one but the good-tempered cook and her mistress.
There's the baron of beef which the poor little turnspit roasted yesterday, and yonder
comes John, the alderman's apprentice, bearing the pride of the Christmas feast, the
boar's head, decked out with twigs of rosemary. Can you not smell the spiced wine that
is steaming in the silver flagon which the alderman bought of Tony? who thought not
when he sold it that he should ever drink from it as a guest, and perhaps something
more, for pretty Dorothy has nodded to him before she tastes the reaming liquor.

Supper is over, and the kitchen again cleared for dancing; certainly the fiddlers play
better than they did before, and everybody dances with twice as much spirit. Everybody
seems merrier and happier, except Jacob Pout, who is stealing away from the house and
taking the road to the Fields at Finsbury.

You had better remain with the pleasant people at Alderman Kersey's, and join in the

carol which will be sung at midnight to usher in the coming Christmas-day. Besides, there will be other games of blind man's buff, hot cockles, and forfeits, and, I have no doubt, snap-dragon and hunt the slipper. I will follow Jacob Pout and tell you all that happened in the next chapter.

CHAPTER IV

Jacob Parts from the Enchanted Doll at Last.

W HEN JACOB went forth from the house of Alderman Kersey, the noiseless snow was falling fast; but nevertheless the doll-maker pursued his way to the fields, quite regardless of the weather. "It is as plain as the nose on my face," thought Jacob, "the alderman's daughter is to be the wife of Tony Stubbs, and then, of course, the alderman's wealth will all come to Tony, and who knows but some day or other he may become Lord Mayor of London. Just like his luck. A mean, sneaking fellow as he is: always pretending to be at work; never taking a day's holiday except upon the regular feasts and festivals. I hate him! I don't know why, but I can't help it."

I could have told him the reason. Jacob was like many other people in the world who envy and hate every one more successful than themselves.

The moon was shining brightly in the heavens, and the beautiful snow (which seems to have been made for moonlight) sparkled like powdered diamonds. The trees which had lately stretched forth their bare limbs, as though in supplication to the distant spring-time to come and clothe them, were now bending beneath the pearly garlands. Here and there were dark masses of buildings, from whose chimneys the graceful smoke was winding upwards: the windows were glowing with the lights within, and the pleasant sounds of music and merry voices seemed to come forth to greet each other in the silent fields. Jacob was sick with envy.

The path (which Jacob had tracked with some difficulty) was crossed by a stile, and as he felt wearied by his walk, he resolved to rest there for a time, and then return home. As he drew near to the stile, he saw on the topmost rail some living thing, which moved rapidly from one end to the other. He continued to approach, until he was close enough to discover that it was no other than his dingy patroness, the Fairy Malice. She was evidently in a very ill humour, in fact she seemed to be in a positive rage, for she walked with her arms folded together, and her little black lips compressed as closely as though they had been glued to each other. Now and then she would stop, stamp her tiny foot, and shake her clenched pigmy hand in the air. Jacob felt desirous to avoid her, and was about to make a hasty retreat, but the fairy was too quick for him.

"Stay where you are," she screamed as loudly as she could. "Stay where you are, or I will rack every nerve in your body."

Jacob felt quite powerless.

"So, you graceless fellow," continued the Fairy. "You thought to go unpunished for your cruel treatment of that priceless treasure, The ENCHANTED DOLL. You thought you could hack its beauteous limbs and batter its delicate body with impunity, did you? You thought that precious creature was only hewn out of an insensible log, like your own abominable toys, and could be made into fire-wood at your will and pleasure? Look here, every blow that you inflicted on that incomparable being was by elfish sympathy endured by me," and the fairy pointed to her bandaged arms and legs, which had hitherto escaped the notice of Jacob.

"But I will be revenged. I am here to-night to punish your brutality and ingratitude. It is not often that you find fairies out on a snowy night like this, but my people shall have plenty of work to keep them warm, I warrant you. Advance, archers! and give this ungrateful mortal a proof of your ability."

Jacob heard the old march played, and the surface of the snow swarmed with black fairies. Their bright helmets and breastplates glittered in the moonlight as they deployed before their potent ruler, until at last they formed themselves into columns and marched past the terror-stricken Jacob, who, in a few minutes, found himself completely surrounded by the pigmy army. The officers of the different companies then advanced towards each other, and having conferred for a few seconds returned to their respective places, and, at a signal from the commander-in-chief, led their men still closer

to Jacob. They then halted, and instantly a myriad of arrows, as fine as hairs, flew from their bows into the body of the unhappy doll-maker. Jacob roared with pain, but found himself deprived of motion.

The Fairy Malice rubbed her hands with delight, and laughed long and loud at the torture of the unhappy doll-maker.

"Well done, my gallant archers! well done!" cried the Black Lady. "Let our cavalry acquit themselves as well and they shall be rewarded. Charge!"

As she screamed out her command a humming noise was heard in the air, and a legion of fairies, mounted upon horned beetles, flew at the head and hands of the doll-maker; who, powerless to defend himself, endured intolerable pain from the lances of his foes. Malice was more delighted than before, and laughed so immoderately that she was obliged to lean, from exhaustion, upon her attendants. When she had recovered her breath sufficiently to speak, she addressed Jacob as follows:—

"Master Doll-maker, you now know what it is to injure a fairy, and especially the Fairy Malice. As I think I have punished you sufficiently this time, you may go home, Jacob. We are friends again."

"Never!" cried Jacob. "Never! I will throw your horrible gift into the river."

"Don't," said Malice; "if you do it will swim, and come back to you again."

"I will burn it then!" exclaimed Jacob almost beside himself with rage. "I'll consume it to ashes and cast them to the winds."

"Try such a thing at your peril," screamed the fairy; "torture that charming creature with fire, and you shall rue the day. You shall."

"I defy you! You and your enchantments," roared Jacob.

"Ha! ha!"—and all the fairies laughed in concert.

"Your own bad heart gives me the power over you, and until *that* changes you are the slave of my servant." So saying the fairy waved her wand, and the bright moonlight was instantly changed into darkness. At first Jacob thought a black cloud had passed between him and the moon, but he discovered to his great dismay that he was surrounded by myriads of bats. He found, however, that the power of motion was restored to him, and began to run homewards as he thought, but the bats flew with him, and, unable to see his path, he was presently crashing through the thin ice of a pond, from which he emerged dripping with water and shivering with cold. Fear still impelled him onward, but with no better success, and it was not until the church bells of London rung out in concert the advent of the day of promise of "Peace and good will to men," and from mansion and cottage a thousand voices were heard carolling a welcome to the

blessed Christmas-tide, that his tormentors quitted him. Jacob found he was some distance from home, and it was not without great difficulty, bruised and tired as he was, that he reached the door of his own booth as the sun rose on the Christmas morning.

All the way home Jacob has been contrasting his miserable condition with the happy position of Tony Stubbs, never considering that the silversmith owed his prosperity to his own industry and honourable conduct. "Had it not been for him," thought Jacob, as he unlocked the door of his shop, "I should never have gone to the woods and found this accursed fairy gift, which I can never part with so long as I am envious, and envious I shall be until Tony Stubbs is a beggar!"

Thus musing, the doll-maker entered his bed-chamber, and there was the ENCHANTED DOLL larger and more hideous than ever.

The morning wore on, and Jacob very miserable still sat at the window, gazing intently at his neighbour's house. By and bye the door opened, and Bridget, Tony's old housekeeper, came out dressed in her best bib and tucker, a sure sign that she was going to make holiday. In a few minutes more the silversmith made his appearance, and locking the door, strangely enough walked away leaving the key in the lock. Perhaps he was thinking of pretty Dorothy Kersey—no matter.

Jacob saw all this, but instead of doing the part of a good neighbour by calling Tony back, the wicked doll-maker hoped that the key would attract the attention of some thief who would not hesitate to plunder the silversmith. With this bad feeling Jacob Pout watched all day at the window, but no one passed and saw the key. As the evening set in, Jacob's thoughts grew worse and worse, until at last it occurred to him to carry the DOLL over to his neighbour's house and there, by kindling a fire, destroy at once the wealth which he envied and the creature which he dreaded. To his surprise he found the ENCHANTED DOLL as light as a feather, and taking it in his arms he carried it over to his neighbour's house. In a few minutes he returned, and taking his seat again at the window prepared to watch the result of the wickedness he had done. Presently a stream of dark coloured smoke issued from the crevices in the shutters of Tony's booth, and then a bright red flame crept out and showed that the fire was raging fiercely within. Unfortunately for the silversmith, as this was Christmas time the streets were quite empty, and the city watch had taken so much good cheer during the day that they were sleeping at their posts, or the fire might possibly have been discovered and extinguished, but as it was, the wicked doll-maker was the only person who knew of it.

Jacob Pout was rejoicing in the success of his malice and wickedness, when to his great horror he saw Tony's door fly open and from it come the ENCHANTED DOLL, a glowing mass of fire, and make directly for his own booth.—In a minute the room in which he was sitting became filled with smoke, and he heard the wood in his work-shop crackling with the flames.—At the same moment, a great noise at a distance in the street told him that the conflagrations were observed, and Jacob rushed out just as the city watch came up with their ladders and fire-buckets. By great exertion the fire in Tony's house was put out, but nothing seemed to have power over that which was consuming the booth of the doll-maker.

Jacob stood stupified for some time; at last it occurred to him that the first money which he had received for the ENCHANTED DOLL was locked up in his old walnut-tree chest, and without a moment's pause he dashed through the flames to secure his treasure, although the room was full of fire and smoke; Jacob contrived to open the chest, but lo! there was nothing but dirt and stones, for the coins he had received were all of Fairy silver! His disappointment was so great that he remained kneeling by the side of the chest until the flames gathered all around him, and he would no doubt have perished, had not a young man forced his way through the fire and dragged the bewildered doll-maker into the street.

The rescuer and the rescued were both nearly suffocated by the heat and smoke, and it was not until some minutes had elapsed that Jacob could find sense or words to thank his preserver. What must have been his feelings when he found that to Tony Stubbs he was indebted for his preservation!

"This is a sad night for us both, neighbour Pout," said the silversmith, "but worse for you than for me. You have lost all, but my shop only has suffered by the flames, some of my wares are damaged, but a little later to bed and a little earlier to rise will put all that right. But neighbour" and Tony paused, greatly moved by the expression of Jacob's face, "you are in great pain! and no wonder, for your arm is flayed bare. Here! some one run for a surgeon whilst I help him to bed."

The doll-maker from shame and suffering could make no answer, but allowed the much injured Tony to lead him to a bed.

The surgeon came, and pronounced Jacob's state to be very desperate, and desired that he should be kept perfectly quiet, or he would not answer for his life a day. And so for many days Tony Stubbs could not take any steps to repair the damage done by the fire, in case he should disturb his suffering neighbour, but devoted all his time to watching by his bed-side, and, with the aid of old Bridget, preparing and applying the cooling cataplasms ordered for his relief.

Some three weeks had passed since the night of the fire, and Jacob was able to sit up in a chair, and now and then, by the aid of his kind nurse, to walk a few times up and down his room. Still he was very weak, and continued to suffer great pain from the burns which he had received.

One night Tony had retired to rest after talking very cheerfully, and telling how little damage the fire had done his wares, and promising Jacob, that as soon as he was well enough to pursue his calling, a new lathe should be bought, and a booth furnished for him.

One would have thought that so much kindness from a person he had wronged so deeply would have awakened nothing but feelings of gratitude in Jacob Pout, but envy, hatred, and malice, had been too long the cherished passions of his breast, to be dismissed without a struggle.

"So!" thought Jacob; "it seems I am to be indebted for my daily bread to the man I have most hated and envied! Just like my luck! Whilst not one stick of my booth or stock is left unconsumed, this fellow can laugh at his loss and afford to lend me money to boot. He will be richer shortly, for everybody says he is to marry pretty Dorothy Kersey. What has he done to deserve this?"

"What, indeed!" said a shrill voice close to his ear

Jacob shook from head to foot, for he knew it was the Black Fairy who had spoken.

"What, indeed!" repeated the Fairy. "He envies nobody! He sets fire to no man's dwelling! He thinks not only of his own dear self! Fool that he is! But you, my darling, deserve all you get, and a great deal more into the bargain."

"Leave me!" cried Jacob, "leave me! I wish to have done with you for ever."

"How very cruel of you," sobbed the Fairy, "after all I have suffered for you. Why, I have not yet recovered from the effects of the fire; neither has your pretty pet, the ENCHANTED DOLL!"

"Recovered!" gasped Jacob. "Surely it was consumed in the flames!"

"Not so, dear," replied the Fairy, with the most horrible grin. "I was afraid at one time that this silversmith might have been the death of her, but your love and constancy have quite worked a cure. She is beside you!"

And there it was, sure enough, charred and almost shapeless, but still with enough of form left to distinguish the ENCHANTED DOLL.

The next morning Jacob was much worse. He was in a high state of fever, and wandering and raving in his sleep like one mad. The doctor could not account for the change, and appeared greatly perplexed what to do. However, he prescribed certain remedies, which had the effect of composing the patient but not of restoring him to consciousness. Jacob continued in this state for more than three days. When at last his reason returned to him, he heard the sweet voice of a woman earnestly engaged in prayer for his recovery. The suppliant entreated God to restore the sufferer to reason,

that he might not die in his sin; but to grant him life, that he might repent of the evil of his ways, and obtain pardon and salvation.

Jacob's heart was softened, and the tears rolled down his cheeks as fast as they did down those of Dorothy (for it was she who prayed for him); and when the prayer was finished, Jacob breathed a fervent "Amen!"

As country air was considered to be necessary for Jacob's recovery, Alderman Kersey had him taken in a litter to his house at Holbourne, where—thanks to the careful nursing of Mrs. Kersey and the gentle Dorothy—he was gradually restored to health.

And what became of the ENCHANTED DOLL?

You shall hear.

From the hour that Jacob said "Amen!" to Dorothy's prayer, his cruel tormentor began to diminish in size, until, the day before his removal to the house of Alderman Kersey, it had dwindled down to the length of a little finger. It would have gone away altogether, but Jacob could not help (from long habit) altogether at times contrasting his condition with that of Tony Stubbs, and wishing—for a very little while—that he and the silversmith could change places.

One morning towards the end of May, the bells of Holbourne church were ringing merrily. All the people at Alderman Kersey's were dressed in their holiday clothes, decked out with large bows of white ribbon, and went smiling about the house, as though some happy event had occurred in the family. And so there had! Dorothy Kersey had become the wife of Tony Stubbs. There never was a happier bridal party. Never was? There never could be! And Jacob Pout had been to church to see the marriage ceremony performed; and as he knelt beside them at the altar, he had prayed that God would bless them and reward them for all the good they had done to him, and pardon him all the evil he had done them.

From some strange impulse Jacob (who was now quite strong again) resolved in the afternoon to go to Maude's Dingle. When he arrived there he soon found the knoll on which he had sat when he received his fatal fairy gift, and down he threw himself, rather wearied by his walk. The thrush was singing, and Jacob thought the bird's song seemed full of thankfulness, and that the little brook ran babbling on of a thousand happy things!

He wondered he had never thought so before, until he remembered the evil passions which had hitherto been his companions when he visited the pleasant dingle.

Jacob went back with a light heart to the alderman, and joined heartily in the merry-making. He bade the musicians play their merriest tunes, and was, in fact, the last person left dancing at the end of a jovial reel.

When the guests had left, Jacob went up to his bed-chamber and opened a little box, in which he kept his ENCHANTED DOLL, but to his great joy he discovered that it had vanished!—for Jacob had ceased to envy—even a little.

The doll-maker was set up in business by his kind friends, Alderman Kersey and Tony Stubbs; and, through the influence of the former, Jacob received a commission from the Lord Mayor to execute two of the largest dolls in the kingdom. I will not vouch for the fact, but it is more than suspected that Gog and Magog, which occupy so prominent a position in the Guildhall of London, are the identical dolls made by Jacob Pout.

"Frauds on the Fairies"

By CHARLES DICKENS

GEORGE CRUIKSHANK (1792–1878), the artist and caricaturist, in his early days in the 1820s and 1830s illustrated the first English translation of Grimm's *Fairy Tales* and the popular historical romances of W. Harrison Ainsworth, as well as Dickens's *Sketches by Boz* (1836) and *Oliver Twist* (1838). But as time went on, Cruikshank became more and more eccentric, believing that he himself had provided the literary ideas for both Ainsworth's *Tower of London* and *Oliver Twist*. Moreover, he became a passionate advocate of Temperance, which in Victorian England meant total abstinence, and put his brilliantly talented pencil at the disposal of his cause.

In 1853, he began to issue his *Fairy Library*, a series of old familiar fairy stories he had been invited to illustrate. But, he said, upon rereading them he found much in them that was "unfit" for children, and so "much against my will," as he put it, he had done some rewriting. And, in rewriting, he introduced "a few *Temperance Truths*, with a fervent hope that some good may result therefrom." Thus, for example, in *Cinderella*, the king is forestalled from making the fountains run with wine at the prince's wedding by a temperance sermon from the fairy godmother, and is moved to collect all alcoholic beverages and burn them in a great bonfire. Of course, such tampering with the great old fairy tale was sacrilege. And Cruikshank's former friend, Charles Dickens, writing in the magazine *Household Words*, seized the occasion to protest.

The brilliance and wit with which Dickens imagines the ridiculous profanations of the sacred texts to which Cruikshank's example could lead reach a hilarious climax in a new version of *Cinderella* as rewritten by a "commercial traveller," a Victorian traveling salesman of religious and other nostrums. Although he refers to Cruikshank as his old friend, Dickens may have welcomed the opportunity to poke fun at him in public (*Household Words*—which Dickens himself edited—had an enormous circulation). But whatever the personal motivations may have been, the essay itself is a little gem. Because it is now little known, and because it struck a blow against the practice of using fairy tales as a vehicle for propaganda, it is reproduced here.

The text of "Frauds on the Fairies" is reprinted from Household Words, *Vol VIII, No. 184, October 5, 1853, pp. 97–100.*

Wᴇ ᴍᴀʏ ᴀssᴜᴍᴇ that we are not singular in entertaining a very great tenderness for the fairy literature of our childhood. What enchanted us then, and is captivating a million of young fancies now, has, at the same blessed time of life, enchanted vast hosts of men and women who have done their long day's work, and laid their grey heads down to rest. It would be hard to estimate the amount of gentleness and mercy that has made its way among us through these slight channels. Forbearance, courtesy, consideration for the poor and aged, kind treatment of animals, the love of nature, abhorrence of tyranny and brute force—many such good things have been first nourished in the child's heart by this powerful aid. It has greatly helped to keep us, in some sense, ever young, by preserving through our worldly ways one slender track not overgrown with weeds, where we may walk with children, sharing their delights.

In an utilitarian age, of all other times, it is a matter of grave importance that Fairy tales should be respected. Our English red tape is too magnificently red ever to be employed in the tying up of such trifles, but every one who has considered the subject knows full well that a nation without fancy, without some romance, never did, never can, never will, hold a great place under the sun. The theatre, having done its worst to destroy these admirable fictions—and having in a most exemplary manner destroyed itself, its artists, and its audiences, in that perversion of its duty—it becomes doubly important that the little books themselves, nurseries of fancy as they are, should be preserved. To preserve them in their usefulness, they must be as much preserved in their simplicity, and purity, and innocent extravagance, as if they were actual fact. Whosoever alters them to suit his own opinions, whatever they are, is guilty, to our thinking, of an act of presumption, and appropriates to himself what does not belong to him.

We have lately observed, with pain, the intrusion of a Whole Hog of unwieldy dimensions into the fairy flower garden. The rooting of the animal among the roses would in itself have awakened in us nothing but indignation; our pain arises from his being violently driven in by a man of genius, our own beloved friend, Mʀ. Gᴇᴏʀɢᴇ Cʀᴜɪᴋsʜᴀɴᴋ. That incomparable artist is, of all men, the last who should lay his exquisite hand on fairy text. In his own art he understands it so perfectly, and illustrates it so beautifully, so humorously, so wisely, that he should never lay down his etching needle to "edit" the Ogre, to whom with that little instrument he can render such extraordinary justice. But, to "editing" Ogres, and Hop-o'-my-thumbs, and their families, our dear moralist has in a rash moment taken, as a means of propagating the doctrines of Total Abstinence, Prohibition of the sale of spirituous liquors, Free Trade, and Popular Education. For the introduction of these topics, he has altered the text of a fairy story; and against his right to do any such thing we protest with all our might and main. Of his likewise altering it to advertise that excellent series of plates, "The Bottle," we say nothing more than that we foresee a new and improved edition of Goody Two Shoes, edited by E. Moses and Son; of the Dervish with the box of ointment, edited by Professor Holloway; and of Jack and the Beanstalk, edited by Mary Wedlake, the popular authoress of Do you bruise your oats yet.

Now, it makes not the least difference to our objection whether we agree or disagree with our worthy friend, Mr. Cruikshank, in the opinions he interpolates upon an old fairy story. Whether good or bad in themselves, they are, in that relation, like the famous definition of a weed; a thing growing up in a wrong place. He has no greater moral justification in altering the harmless little books than we should have in altering his best etchings. If such a precedent were followed we must soon become disgusted with the old stories into which modern personages so obtruded themselves, and the stories themselves must soon be lost. With seven Blue Beards in the field, each coming at a gallop from his own platform mounted on a foaming hobby, a generation or two hence would not know which was which, and the great original Blue Beard would be confounded with the counterfeits. Imagine a Total abstinence edition of Robinson Crusoe, with the rum left out. Imagine a Peace edition, with the gunpowder left out, and the rum left in. Imagine a Vegetarian edition, with the goat's flesh left out. Imagine a Kentucky edition, to introduce a flogging of that 'tarnal old nigger Friday, twice a week. Imagine an Aborigines Protection Society edition, to deny the cannibalism and make Robinson embrace the amiable savages whenever they landed. Robinson Crusoe would be "edited" out of his island in a hundred years, and the island would be swallowed up in the editorial ocean.

Among the other learned professions we have now the Platform profession, chiefly exercised by a new and meritorious class of commercial travellers who go about to take the sense of meetings on various articles: some, of a very superior description: some, not quite so good. Let us write the story of Cinderella, "edited" by one of these gentlemen, doing a good stroke of business, and having a rather extensive mission.

ONCE UPON A TIME, a rich man and his wife were the parents of a lovely daughter. She was a beautiful child, and became, at her own desire, a member of the Juvenile Bands of Hope when she was only four years of age. When this child was only nine years of age her mother died, and all the Juvenile Bands of Hope in her district—the Central district, number five hundred and twenty-seven—formed in a procession of two and two, amounting to fifteen hundred, and followed her to the grave, singing chorus Number forty-two, "O come," &c. This grave was outside the town, and under the direction of the Local Board of Health, which reported at certain stated intervals to the General Board of Health, Whitehall.

The motherless little girl was very sorrowful for the loss of her mother, and so was her father too, at first; but, after a year was over, he married again—a very cross widow lady, with two proud tyrannical daughters as cross as herself. He was aware that he could have made his marriage with this lady a civil process by simply making a declaration before a Registrar; but he was averse to this course on religious grounds, and, being a member of the Montgolfian persuasion, was married according to the ceremonies of that respectable church by the Reverend Jared Jocks, who improved the occasion.

He did not live long with his disagreeable wife. Having been shamefully accustomed to shave with warm water instead of cold, which he ought to have used (see Medical Appendix B. and C.), his undermined constitution could not bear up against her temper, and he soon died. Then, this orphan was cruelly treated by her stepmother and the two daughters, and was forced to do the dirtiest of the kitchen work; to scour the saucepans, wash the dishes, and light the fires—which did not consume their own smoke, but emitted a dark vapour prejudicial to the bronchial tubes. The only warm place in the house where she was free from ill-treatment was the kitchen chimney-corner; and as she used to sit down there, among the cinders, when her work was done, the proud fine sisters gave her the name of Cinderella.

About this time, the King of the land, who never made war against anybody, and allowed everybody to make war against him—which was the reason why his subjects were the greatest manufacturers on earth, and always lived in security and peace—gave a great feast, which was to last two days. This splendid banquet was to consist entirely of artichokes and gruel; and from among those who were invited to it, and to hear the delightful speeches after dinner, the King's son was to choose a bride for himself. The proud fine sisters were invited, but nobody knew anything about poor Cinderella, and she was to stay at home.

She was so sweet-tempered, however, that she assisted the haughty creatures to dress, and bestowed her admirable taste upon them as freely as if they had been kind to her. Neither did she laugh when they broke seventeen stay-laces in dressing; for, although she wore no stays herself, being sufficiently acquainted with the anatomy of the human figure to be aware of the destructive effects of tight-lacing, she always reserved her opinions on that subject for the Regenerative Record (price three halfpence in a neat wrapper), which all good people take in, and to which she was a Contributor.

At length the wished for moment arrived, and the proud fine sisters swept away to the feast and speeches, leaving Cinderella in the chimney-corner. But, she could always occupy her mind with the general question of the Ocean Penny Postage, and she had in her pocket an unread Oration on that subject, made by the well known Orator, Nehemiah Nicks. She was lost in the fervid eloquence of that talented Apostle when she became aware of the presence of one of those female relatives which (it may not be generally known) it is not lawful for a man to marry. I allude to her grandmother.

"Why so solitary, my child?" said the old lady to Cinderella.

"Alas, grandmother," returned the poor girl, "my sisters have gone to the feast and speeches, and here sit I in the ashes, Cinderella!"

"Never," cried the old lady with animation, "shall one of the Band of Hope despair! Run into the garden, my dear, and fetch me an American Pumpkin! American, because in some parts of that independent country, there are prohibitory laws against the sale of alcoholic drinks in any form. Also; because America produced (among many great pumpkins) the glory of her sex, Mrs. Colonel Bloomer. None but an American Pumpkin will do, my child!"

Cinderella ran into the garden, and brought the largest American Pumpkin she could find. This virtuously democratic vegetable her grandmother immediately changed into a splendid coach. Then, she sent her for six mice from the mouse-trap, which she changed into prancing horses, free from the obnoxious and oppressive post-horse duty. Then, to the rat-trap in the stable for a rat, which she changed to a state-coachman, not amenable to the iniquitous assessed taxes. Then, to look behind a watering-pot for six lizards, which she changed into six footmen, each with a petition in his hand ready to present to the Prince, signed by fifty thousand persons, in favour of the early closing movement.

"But grandmother," said Cinderella, stopping in the midst of her delight, and looking at her clothes, "how can I go to the palace in these miserable rags?"

"Be not uneasy about that, my dear," returned her grandmother.

Upon which the old lady touched her with her wand, her rags disappeared, and she was beautifully dressed. Not in the present costume of the female sex, which has been proved to be at once grossly immodest and absurdly inconvenient, but in rich sky-blue satin pantaloons gathered at the ankle, a puce-colored satin pelisse sprinkled with silver flowers, and a very broad Leghorn hat. The hat was chastely ornamented with a rainbow-coloured ribbon hanging in two bell-pulls down the back; the pantaloons were ornamented with a golden stripe; and the effect of the whole was unspeakably sensible, feminine, and retiring. Lastly, the old lady put on Cinderella's feet a pair of shoes made of glass: observing that but for the abolition of the duty on that article, it never could have been devoted to such a purpose; the effect of all such taxes being to cramp invention, and embarrass the producer, to the manifest injury of the consumer. When the old lady had made these wise remarks, she dismissed Cinderella to the feast and speeches, charging her by no means to remain after twelve o'clock at night.

The arrival of Cinderella at the Monster Gathering produced a great excitement. As a delegate from the United States had just moved that the King do take the chair, and as the motion had been seconded and carried unanimously, the King himself could not go forth to receive her. But His Royal Highness the Prince (who was to move the second resolution), went to the door to hand her from her carriage. This virtuous Prince, being completely covered from head to foot with Total Abstinence Medals, shone as if he were attired in complete armour; while the inspiring strains of the Peace Brass Band in the gallery (composed of the Lambkin Family, eighteen in number, who cannot be too much encouraged) awakened additional enthusiasm.

The King's son handed Cinderella to one of the reserved seats for pink tickets, on the platform, and fell in love with her immediately. His appetite deserted him; he scarcely tasted his artichokes, and merely trifled with his gruel. When the speeches began, and Cinderella, wrapped in the eloquence of the two inspired delegates who occupied the entire evening in speaking to the first Resolution, occasionally cried, "Hear, hear!" the sweetness of her voice completed her conquest of the Prince's heart. But, indeed the whole male portion of the assembly loved her—and doubtless would have done so, even if she had been less beautiful, in consequence of the contrast which her dress presented to the bold and ridiculous garments of the other ladies.

At a quarter before twelve, the second inspired delegate having drunk all the water in the decanter, and fainted away, the King put the question, "That this Meeting do now adjourn until to-morrow." Those who were of that opinion holding up their hands, and then those who were of the contrary, theirs, there appeared an immense majority in favour of the resolution, which was consequently carried. Cinderella got home in safety, and heard nothing all that night, or all next day, but the praises of the unknown lady with the sky-blue satin pantaloons.

When the time for the feast and speeches came round again, the cross stepmother and the proud fine daughters went out in good time to secure their places. As soon as they were gone, Cinderella's grandmother returned and changed her as before. Amid a blast of welcome from the Lambkin family, she was again handed to the pink seat on the platform by His Royal Highness.

This gifted Prince was a powerful speaker, and had the evening before him. He rose at precisely ten minutes before eight, and was greeted with tumultuous cheers and waving of handkerchiefs. When the excitement had in some degree subsided, he proceeded to address the meeting: who were never tired of listening to speeches, as no good people ever are. He held them enthralled for four hours and a quarter. Cinderella forgot the time, and hurried away so when she heard the first stroke of twelve, that her beautiful dress changed back to her old rags at the door, and she left one of her glass shoes behind. The Prince took it up, and vowed—that is, made a declaration before a magistrate; for he objected on principle to the multiplying of oaths—that he would only marry the charming creature to whom that shoe belonged.

He accordingly caused an advertisement to that effect to be inserted in all the newspapers; for, the advertisement duty, an impost most unjust in principle and most unfair in operation, did not exist in that country; neither was the stamp on newspapers known in that land—which had as many newspapers as the United States, and got as much good out of them. Innumerable ladies answered the advertisement and pretended that the shoe was theirs; but, every one of them was unable to get her foot into it. The proud fine sisters answered it, and tried their feet with no greater success. Then, Cinderella, who had answered it too, came forward amidst their scornful jeers, and the shoe slipped on in a moment. It is a remarkable tribute to the improved and sensible fashion of the dress her grandmother had given her, that if she had not worn it the Prince would probably never have seen her feet.

The marriage was solemnized with great rejoicing. When the honeymoon was over, the King retired from public life, and was succeeded by the Prince. Cinderella, being now a queen, applied herself to the government of the country on enlightened, liberal, and free principles. All the people who ate anything she did not eat, or who drank anything she did not drink, were imprisoned for life. All the newspaper offices from which any doctrine proceeded that was not her doctrine, were burnt down. All the public speakers proved to demonstration that if there were any individual on the face of the earth who differed from them in anything, that individual was a designing ruffian and an abandoned monster. She also threw open the right of voting, and of being elected to public offices, and of making the laws, to the whole of her sex; who thus came to be always gloriously occupied with public life and whom nobody dared to love. And they all lived happily ever afterwards.

Frauds on the Fairies once permitted, we see little reason why they may not come to this, and great reason why they may. The Vicar of Wakefield was wisest when he was tired of being always wise. The world is too much with us, early and late. Leave this precious old escape from it, alone.

The Rose and The Ring; or, The History of Prince Giglio and Prince Bulbo

A Fire-side Pantomime
for Great and Small Children

By WILLIAM MAKEPEACE THACKERAY

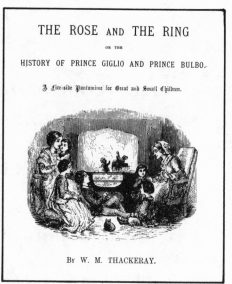

THE ROSE AND THE RING

OR THE

HISTORY OF PRINCE GIGLIO AND PRINCE BULBO.

A Fire-side Pantomime for Great and Small Children.

BY W. M. THACKERAY.

Hᴏᴡ ᴘᴇᴅᴀɴᴛɪᴄ ᴄᴀɴ a pedant bear to be? All the following statements are absolutely true.

Writing under the pseudonym "M. A. Titmarsh," Thackeray published *The Rose and the Ring* in December 1854, in time for Christmas, with the date 1855 on the title page. In that winter of 1854–1855, all eyes in England were turned to the struggle in the Crimea, and for the first time "Crimea," "Crim Tartary," and other place names, historic and contemporary, of the regions about the Black Sea, were in everybody's minds, even the minds of young children. So to invent the kingdoms of Crim Tartary and Paflagonia (a high-sounding word, and once a Byzantine province in northern Asia Minor across the Black Sea from the Crimea) would not mystify children but would hold their attention. Bosforo (Bosphorus) as the name of a town needed no explanation.

At the same time, an author of many dozens of historical romances for adults, George Payne Rainsford James (1799–1860), though still popular, was beginning to appear stilted and ridiculous in the public eye, and was a legitimate target for good-natured satire. "Had I the pen of G. P. R. James," Thackeray lamented during the course of *The Rose and the Ring*, he would rise to the occasion and show how three cavaliers set forth, &c. &c. &c.: but alas, he moaned, he did not have James's pen, and so . . . well, so he proceeded to parody typical passages of James's prose with devastating effect, as he had done several times before.

The word Cavolfiore (the name of the late King of Crim Tartary) means "cauliflower" in Italian; and the nobility of his kingdom—the Spinachi and the rest—are mostly vegetables. Padella, the usurper, on the other hand, has a name that means "warming-pan." If you pronounce the name of the capital city of Paflagonia—Blombodinga—you will discover that it is an Italianate way of saying the English words "plum pudding." All of this was entirely suitable if one remembers that the story was written for two little girls spending Christmas in Rome, and picking up Italian: in an unheated Roman palazzo in December of 1853, no Italian word would have been more useful than *padella*. And of course one would learn the Italian names for vegetables. But there *was* no Italian name for plum pudding, which would be indispensable at Christmas: so you simply pronounced the English words as if they were Italian, and there you were. When a court painter is named Tomaso Lorenzo, translate, and he turns into Thomas Lawrence (1769–1830), a celebrated English painter.

Moreover, there had been a famous Russian general called Kutuzov: why not add the name Hedzoff, when inventing the name for the Paflagonian captain of the guard: Kutasoff Hedzoff? Read it aloud and it will become clearer still. In fact, better read *The Rose and the Ring* aloud anyhow. It was originally read aloud, and there is no other way to savor the marvelously bombastic blank verse, with occasional end rhymes, pseudo-Shakespearean, with which Thackeray embellished it. King Valoroso of Paflagonia almost always speaks in blank verse; and, after his deposed nephew, Giglio, the rightful monarch, claims the throne and leads his rebellion, Giglio (naturally) talks nothing else either.

It would be possible to go on in this vein some time longer (but not indefinitely), yet why break a butterfly upon the wheel? *The Rose and the Ring* is a delightful piece of Victorian fooling, and can stand without footnotes. But, the editor would beg, kindly notice how Thackeray makes fun of the standard machinery of fairy tales. Although she appears only rarely, the Fairy Blackstick is absolutely fundamental to the story, enchanting and disenchanting Gruffanuff the footman-knocker, giving her dubious christening gifts, supplying the extraordinary rose and the extraordinary ring; and yet she is wholly scornful of her profession. After two or three thousand years of turning "numberless wicked people into beasts, birds, millstones, clocks, pumps, bootjacks, umbrellas, or other absurd shapes" as "one of the most active and officious of the whole College of fairies," she herself is disillusioned, and goes out of business. All this would have delighted a child well-read, as they all were, in ordinary fairy tales. And, of course, Blackstick returns to her trade whenever necessary to solve important problems. There had been no fairy like Blackstick before. Neither Ruskin nor Mark Lemon could have invented her. They took themselves too seriously. But Thackeray—and here is another key—was writing a "Fireside Pantomime," a Christmas entertainment for children, of a kind peculiar to the English stage, designed to be absurd: only it had to be read aloud, not acted, since the children were in Rome. Its moral: "let us laugh and be as pleasant as we can . . . a little joking, and dancing, and fooling will do . . . you no harm."

The text of The Rose and the Ring, *with illustrations by the author, is reprinted from an English edition (London: Smith, Elder, and Co., 1909).*

PRELUDE

IT HAPPENED THAT the undersigned spent the last Christmas season in a foreign city where there were many English children.

In that city, if you wanted to give a child's party, you could not even get a magic lantern or buy Twelfth-Night characters—those funny painted pictures of the King, the Queen, the Lover, the Lady, the Dandy, the Captain, and so on—with which our young ones are wont to recreate themselves at this festive time.

My friend, Miss Bunch, who was governess of a large family, that lived in the *Piano Nobile* of the house inhabited by myself and my young charges (it was the Palazzo Poniatowski at Rome, and Messrs. Spillmann, two of the best pastry-cooks in Christendom, have their shop on the ground-floor); Miss Bunch, I say, begged me to draw a set of Twelfth-Night characters for the amusement of our young people.

She is a lady of great fancy and droll imagination, and having looked at the characters, she and I composed a history about them, which was recited to the little folks at night, and served as our FIRE-SIDE PANTOMIME.

Our juvenile audience was amused by the adventures of Giglio and Bulbo, Rosalba and Angelica. I am bound to say the fate of the Hall Porter created a considerable sensation; and the wrath of Countess Gruffanuff was received with extreme pleasure.

If these children are pleased, thought I, why should not others be amused also? In a few days Dr. Birch's young friends will be expected to re-assemble at Rodwell Regis, where they will learn everything that is useful, and under the eyes of careful ushers continue the business of their little lives.

But, in the meanwhile, and for a brief holiday, let us laugh and be as pleasant as we can. And you elder folks—a little joking, and dancing, and fooling will do even you no harm. The author wishes you a merry Christmas, and welcomes you to the Fire-side Pantomime.

M. A. TITMARSH
DECEMBER, 1854

I

Shows How the Royal Family Sate Down to Breakfast.

T HIS IS VALOROSO XXIV., King of Paflagonia, seated with his Queen and only child at their royal breakfast-table, and receiving the letter which announces to his Majesty a proposed visit from Prince Bulbo, heir of Padella, reigning King of Crim Tartary. Remark the delight upon the monarch's royal features. He is so absorbed in the perusal of the King of Crim Tartary's letter, that he allows his eggs to get cold, and leaves his august muffins untasted.

"What! that wicked, brave, delightful Prince Bulbo!" cries Princess Angelica; "so handsome, so accomplished, so witty—the conqueror of Rimbombamento, where he slew ten thousand giants!"

"Who told you of him, my dear?" asks his Majesty.

"A little bird," says Angelica.

"Poor Giglio!" says mamma, pouring out the tea.

"Bother Giglio!" cries Angelica, tossing up her head, which rustled with a thousand curl-papers.

"I wish," growls the King—"I wish Giglio was . . . . ."

"Was better? Yes, dear, he is better," says the Queen. "Angelica's little maid, Betsinda, told me so when she came to my room this morning with my early tea."

"You are always drinking tea," said the Monarch, with a scowl.

"It is better than drinking port or brandy-and-water," replies her Majesty.

"Well, well, my dear, I only said you were fond of drinking tea," said the King of Paflagonia, with an effort as if to command his temper. "Angelica! I hope you have plenty of new dresses; your milliners' bills are long enough. My dear Queen, you must see and have some parties. I prefer dinners, but of course you will be for balls. Your everlasting blue velvet quite tires me: and, my love, I should like you to have a new necklace. Order one. Not more than a hundred or a hundred and fifty thousand pounds."

"And Giglio, dear," says the Queen.

"GIGLIO MAY GO TO THE—"

"Oh, sir," screams her Majesty. "Your own nephew! our late King's only son."

"Giglio may go to the tailor's, and order the bills to be sent in to Glumboso to pay. Confound him! I mean bless his dear heart. He need want for nothing; give him a couple of guineas for pocket-money, my dear; and you may as well order yourself bracelets, while you are about the necklace, Mrs. V."

Her Majesty, or *Mrs. V.*, as the monarch facetiously called her (for even royalty will have its sport, and this august family were very much attached), embraced her husband, and, twining her arm round her daughter's waist, they quitted the breakfast-room in order to make all things ready for the princely stranger.

When they were gone, the smile that had lighted up the eyes of the *husband* and *father* fled—the pride of the *King* fled—the MAN was alone. Had I the pen of a G. P. R. James, I would describe Valoroso's torments in the choicest language; in which I would also depict his flashing eye, his distended nostril—his dressing-gown, pocket-handkerchief, and boots. But I need not say I have *not* the pen of that novelist; suffice it to say, Valoroso was alone.

He rushed to the cupboard, seizing from the table one of the many egg-cups with which his princely board was served for the matin meal, drew out a bottle of right Nantz or Cognac, filled and emptied the cup several times, and laid it down with a hoarse "Ha, ha, ha! now Valoroso is a man again.

"But oh!" he went on, (still sipping, I am sorry to say,) "ere I was a king, I needed not this intoxicating draught; once I detested the hot brandy wine, and quaffed no other fount but nature's rill. It dashes not more quickly o'er the rocks, than I did, as, with blunder-buss in hand, I brushed away the early morning dew, and shot the partridge, snipe, or antlered deer! Ah! well may England's dramatist remark, 'Uneasy lies the head that wears a crown!' Why did I steal my nephew's, my young Giglio's—? Steal! said I? no, no, no, not steal, not steal. Let me withdraw that odious expression. I took, and on my manly head I set, the royal crown of Paflagonia; I took, and with my royal arm I wield, the sceptral rod of Paflagonia; I took, and in my outstretched hand I hold, the royal orb of Paflagonia! Could a poor boy, a snivelling, drivelling boy—was in his nurse's arms but yesterday, and cried for sugar-plums and puled for pap—bear up the awful weight of crown, orb, sceptre? gird on the sword my royal fathers wore, and meet in fight the tough Crimean foe?"

And then the monarch went on to argue in his own mind (though we need not say that blank verse is not argument) that what he had got it was his duty to keep, and that, if at one time he had entertained ideas of a certain restitution, which shall be nameless, the prospect by a *certain marriage* of uniting two crowns and two nations which had been engaged in bloody and expensive wars, as the Paflagonians and the Crimeans had been, put the idea of Giglio's restoration to the throne out of the question: nay, were his own brother, King Savio, alive, he would certainly will away the crown from his own son in order to bring about such a desirable union.

Thus easily do we deceive ourselves! Thus do we fancy what we wish is right! The King took courage, read the papers, finished his muffins and eggs, and rang the bell for his Prime Minister. The Queen, after thinking whether she should go up and see Giglio, who had been sick, thought "Not now. Business first; pleasure afterwards. I will go and see dear Giglio this afternoon; and now I will drive to the jeweller's, to look for the necklace and bracelets." The Princess went up into her own room, and made Betsinda, her maid, bring out all her dresses; and as for Giglio, they forgot him as much as I forget what I had for dinner last Tuesday twelvemonth.

I I

How King Valoroso Got the Crown, and Prince Giglio Went Without.

P AFLAGONIA, ten or twenty thousand years ago, appears to have been one of those kingdoms where the laws of succession were not settled; for when King Savio died, leaving his brother Regent of the kingdom, and guardian of Savio's orphan infant, this unfaithful regent took no sort of regard of the late monarch's will; had himself proclaimed sovereign of Paflagonia under the title of King Valoroso XXIV., had a most splendid coronation, and ordered all the nobles of the kingdom to pay him homage. So long as Valoroso gave them plenty of balls at Court, plenty of money and lucrative places, the Paflagonian nobility did not care who was king; and, as for the people, in those early times they were equally indifferent. The Prince Giglio, by reason of his tender age at his royal father's death, did not feel the loss of his crown and empire. As long as he had plenty of toys and sweetmeats, a holiday five times a week, and a horse and gun to go out shooting when he grew a little older, and, above all, the company of his darling cousin, the King's only child, poor Giglio was perfectly contented; nor did he envy his uncle the royal robes and sceptre, the great hot uncomfortable throne of state, and the enormous cumbersome crown in which that monarch appeared from morning till night. King Valoroso's portrait has been left to us; and I think you will agree with me that he must have been sometimes *rather tired* of his velvet, and his diamonds, and his ermine, and his grandeur. I shouldn't like to sit in that stifling robe, with such a thing as that on my head.

No doubt, the Queen must have been lovely in her youth; for though she grew rather stout in after life, yet her features, as shown in her portrait, are certainly *pleasing*. If she was fond of flattery, scandal, cards, and fine clothes, let us deal gently with her infirmities, which, after all, may be no greater than our own. She was kind to her nephew; and if she had any scruples of conscience about her husband's taking the young Prince's crown, consoled herself by thinking that the King, though a usurper, was a most respectable man, and that at his death Prince Giglio would be restored to his throne, and share it with his cousin, whom he loved so fondly.

The Prime Minister was Glumboso, an old statesman, who most cheerfully swore fidelity to King Valoroso, and in whose hands the monarch left all the affairs of his kingdom. All Valoroso wanted was plenty of money, plenty of hunting, plenty of flattery, and as little trouble as possible. As long as he had his sport, this monarch cared little how his people paid for it: he engaged in some wars, and of course the Paflagonian newspapers anounced that he gained prodigious victories: he had statues erected to himself in every city of the empire; and of course his pictures placed everywhere, and in all the print-shops: he was Valoroso the Magnanimous, Valoroso the Victorious, Valoroso the Great, and so forth;—for even in these early times courtiers and people knew how to flatter.

This royal pair had one only child, the Princess Angelica, who, you may be sure, was a paragon in the courtiers' eyes, in her parents', and in her own. It was said she had the longest hair, the largest eyes, the slimmest waist, the smallest foot, and the most lovely complexion of any young lady in the Paflagonian dominions. Her accomplishments

were announced to be even superior to her beauty; and governesses used to shame their idle pupils by telling them what Princess Angelica could do. She could play the most difficult pieces of music at sight. She could answer any one of "Mangnal's Questions." She knew every date in the history of Paflagonia, and every other country. She knew French, English, Italian, German, Spanish, Hebrew, Greek, Latin, Cappadocian, Samothracian, Aegean, and Crim Tartar. In a word, she was a most accomplished young creature; and her governess and lady-in-waiting was the severe Countess Gruffanuff.

Would you not fancy, from this picture, that Gruffanuff must have been a person of the highest birth? She looks so haughty that I should have thought her a Princess at the very least, with a pedigree reaching as far back as the Deluge. But this lady was no better born than many other ladies who give themselves airs; and all sensible people laughed at her absurd pretensions. The fact is, she had been maid-servant to the Queen when her Majesty was only Princess, and her husband had been head footman; but after his death or *disappearance*, of which you shall hear presently, this Mrs. Gruffanuff, by flattering, toadying, and wheedling her royal mistress, became a favourite with the Queen (who was rather a weak woman), and her Majesty gave her a title, and made her nursery governess to the Princess.

And now I must tell you about the Princess's learning and accomplishments, for which she had such a wonderful character. Clever Angelica certainly was, but as *idle as possible*. Play at sight, indeed! she could play one or two pieces, and pretend that she had never seen them before; she could answer half-a-dozen "Mangnal's Questions;" but then you must take care to ask the *right* ones. As for her languages, she had masters in plenty, but I doubt whether she knew more than a few phrases in each, for all her pretence; and as for her embroidery and her drawing, she showed beautiful specimens, it is true, but *who did them?*

This obliges me to tell the truth, and to do so I must go back ever so far, and tell you about the FAIRY BLACKSTICK.

I I I

Tells Who the Fairy Blackstick Was,
and Who Were Ever So Many Grand Personages Besides.

BETWEEN THE KINGDOMS of Paflagonia and Crim Tartary, there lived a mysterious personage, who was known in those countries as the Fairy Blackstick, from the ebony wand or crutch which she carried; on which she rode to the moon sometimes, or upon other excursions of business or pleasure, and with which she performed her wonders.

When she was young, and had been first taught the art of conjuring, by the necromancer, her father, she was always practising her skill, whizzing about from one kingdom to another upon her black stick, and conferring her fairy favours upon this Prince or that. She had scores of royal godchildren; turned numberless wicked people into beasts, birds, millstones, clocks, pumps, bootjacks, umbrellas, or other absurd shapes; and in a word was one of the most active and officious of the whole College of fairies.

But after two or three thousand years of this sport, I suppose Blackstick grew tired of it. Or perhaps she thought, "What good am I doing by sending this Princess to sleep for a hundred years? by fixing a black pudding on to that booby's nose? by causing diamonds and pearls to drop from one little girl's mouth, and vipers and toads from another's? I begin to think I do as much harm as good by my performances. I might as well shut my incantations up, and allow things to take their natural course.

"There were my two young goddaughters, King Savio's wife, and Duke Padella's wife: I gave them each a present, which was to render them charming in the eyes of their husbands, and secure the affection of those gentlemen as long as they lived. What good did my Rose and my Ring do these two women? None on earth. From having all their whims indulged by their husbands, they became capricious, lazy, ill-humoured, absurdly vain, and leered and languished, and fancied themselves irresistibly beautiful, when they were really quite old and hideous, the ridiculous creatures! They used actually to patronise me when I went to pay them a visit;—*me*, the Fairy Blackstick, who knows all the wisdom of the necromancers, and who could have turned them into baboons, and all their diamonds into strings of onions, by a single wave of my rod!" So she locked up her books in her cupboard, declined further magical performances, and scarcely used her wand at all except as a cane to walk about with.

So when Duke Padella's lady had a little son (the Duke was at that time only one of the principal noblemen in Crim Tartary), Blackstick, although invited to the christening, would not so much as attend; but merely sent her compliments and a silver papboat for the baby, which was really not worth a couple of guineas. About the same time the Queen of Paflagonia presented his Majesty with a son and heir; and guns were fired, the capital illuminated, and no end of feasts ordained to celebrate the young Prince's birth. It was thought the Fairy, who was asked to be his godmother, would at least have presented him with an invisible jacket, a flying horse, a Fortunatus's purse, or some other valuable token of her favour; but instead, Blackstick went up to the cradle of the child Giglio, when everybody was admiring him, and complimenting his royal papa and mamma, and said, "My poor child, the best thing I can send you is a little *misfortune*;" and this was all she would utter, to the disgust of Giglio's parents, who died very soon after, when Giglio's uncle took the throne, as we read in Chapter I.

In like manner, when CAVOLFIORE, Ki•g of Crim Tartary, had a christening of his only child, ROSALBA, the Fairy Blackstick, who had been invited, was not more gracious than in Prince Giglio's case. Whilst everybody was expatiating over the beauty of the darling child, and congratulating its parents, the Fairy Blackstick looked very sadly at the baby and its mother, and said, "My good woman—(for the Fairy was very familiar, and no more minded a Queen than a washerwoman)—my good woman, these people who are following you will be the first to turn against you; and, as for this little lady, the best thing I can wish her is a *little misfortune*." So she touched Rosalba with her black wand, looked severely at the courtiers, motioned the Queen an adieu with her hand, and sailed slowly up into the air out of window.

When she was gone, the Court people, who had been awed and silent in her presence, began to speak. "What an odious Fairy she is (they said)—a pretty Fairy, indeed! Why, she went to the King of Paflagonia's christening, and pretended to do all sorts of things for that family; and what has happened—the Prince, her godson, has been turned off his throne by his uncle. Would we allow our sweet Princess to be deprived of her rights by any enemy? Never, never, never, never!"

And they all shouted in a chorus, "Never, never, never, never!"

Now, I should like to know, how did these fine courtiers show their fidelity? One of King Cavolfiore's vassals, the Duke Padella just mentioned, rebelled against the King, who went out to chastise his rebellious subject. "Any one rebel against our beloved and august Monarch!" cried the courtiers; "any one resist *him*? Pooh! He is invincible, irresistible. He will bring home Padella a prisoner, and tie him to a donkey's tail, and drive him round the town, saying, 'This is the way the great Cavolfiore treats rebels.'"

The King went forth to vanquish Padella; and the poor Queen, who was a very timid, anxious creature, grew so frightened and ill, that I am sorry to say she died; leaving injunctions with her ladies to take care of the dear little Rosalba.—Of course they said they would. Of course they vowed they would die rather than any harm should happen to the Princess. At first the "Crim Tartar Court Journal" stated that the King was obtaining great victories over the audacious rebel: then it was announced that the troops of the infamous Padella were in flight: then it was said that the royal army would soon come up with the enemy, and then—then the news came that King Cavolfiore was vanquished and slain by his Majesty, King Padella the First!

At this news, half the courtiers ran off to pay their duty to the conquering chief, and the other half ran away, laying hands on all the best articles in the palace; and poor little Rosalba was left there quite alone—quite alone; and she toddled from one room to another, crying, "Countess! Duchess! (only she said 'Tountess, Duttess,' not being able to speak plain) bring me my mutton sop; my Royal Highness hungy! Tountess! Duttess!" And she went from the private apartments into the throne-room and nobody was there;—and thence into the ball-room and nobody was there;—and thence into the pages' room and nobody was there;—and she toddled down the great staircase into the hall and nobody was there;—and the door was open, and she went into the court, and into the garden, and thence into the wilderness, and thence into the forest where the wild beasts live, and was never heard of any more!

A piece of her torn mantle and one of her shoes were found in the wood in the mouths of two lioness's cubs, whom King Padella and a royal hunting party shot—for he was King now, and reigned over Crim Tartary. "So the poor little Princess is done for," said he; "well, what's done can't be helped. Gentlemen, let us go to luncheon!" And one of the courtiers took up the shoe and put it in his pocket. And there was an end of Rosalba!

IV

How Blackstick Was Not Asked
to the Princess Angelica's Christening.

WHEN THE PRINCESS ANGELICA was born, her parents not only did not ask the Fairy Blackstick to the christening party, but gave orders to their porter, absolutely to refuse her if she called. This porter's name was Gruffanuff, and he had been selected for the post by their Royal Highnesses because he was a very tall fierce man, who could say "Not at home" to a tradesman or an unwelcome visitor with a rudeness which frightened most such persons away. He was the husband of that Countess whose picture we have just seen, and as long as they were together they quarrelled from morning till night. Now this fellow tried his rudeness once too often, as you shall hear. For the Fairy Blackstick coming to call upon the Prince and Princess, who were actually sitting at the open drawing-room window, Gruffanuff not only denied them, but made the most *odious vulgar sign* as he was going to slam the door in the Fairy's face! "Git away, hold Blackstick!" said he. "I tell you, Master and Missis ain't at home to you:" and he was, as we have said, *going* to slam the door.

But the Fairy, with her wand, prevented the door being shut; and Gruffanuff came out again in a fury, swearing in the most abominable way, and asking the Fairy "whether she thought he was a going to stay at that there door hall day?"

"You *are* going to stay at that door all day and all night, and for many a long year," the Fairy said, very majestically; and Gruffanuff, coming out of the door, straddling before it with his great calves, burst out laughing, and cried, "Ha, ha, ha! this *is* a good un! Ha—ah—what's this? Let me down—O—o—H'm!" and then he was dumb!

For, as the Fairy waved her wand over him, he felt himself rising off the ground, and fluttering up against the door, and then, as if a screw ran into his stomach, he felt a dreadful pain there, and was pinned to the door; and then his arms flew up over his head; and his legs, after writhing about wildly, twisted under his body; and he felt cold, cold, growing over him, as if he was turning into metal; and he said, "O—o—H'm!" and could say no more, because he was dumb.

He *was* turned into metal! He was from being *brazen, brass!* He was neither more nor less than a knocker! And there he was, nailed to the door in the blazing summer day, till he burned almost red hot; and there he was, nailed to the door all the bitter winter nights, till his brass nose was dropping with icicles. And the postman came and rapped at him, and the vulgarest boy with a letter came and hit him up against the door. And the King and Queen (Princess and Prince they were then), coming home from a walk that evening, the King said, "Hullo, my dear! you have had a new knocker put on the door. Why, it's rather like our Porter in the face! What has become of that boozy vagabond?" And the housemaid came and scrubbed his nose with sandpaper; and once, when the Princess Angelica's little sister was born, he was tied up in an old kid glove; and another night, some *larking* young men tried to wrench him off, and put him to the most excruciating agony with a turnscrew. And then the Queen had a fancy to have the colour of the door altered, and the painters dabbed him over the mouth and eyes, and nearly choked him, as they painted him pea-green. I warrant he had leisure to repent of having been rude to the Fairy Blackstick!

As for his wife, she did not miss him; and as he was always guzzling beer at the public-house, and notoriously quarrelling with his wife, and in debt to the tradesmen, it was supposed he had run away from all these evils, and emigrated to Australia or

America. And when the Prince and Princess chose to become King and Queen, they left their old house, and nobody thought of the Porter any more.

V

How Princess Angelica Took a Little Maid.

ONE DAY, when the Princess Angelica was quite a little girl, she was walking in the garden of the palace, with Mrs. Gruffanuff, the governess, holding a parasol over her head, to keep her sweet complexion from the freckles, and Angelica was carrying a bun, to feed the swans and ducks in the royal pond.

They had not reached the duck-pond, when there came toddling up to them such a funny little girl! She had a great quantity of hair blowing about her chubby little cheeks, and looked as if she had not been washed or combed for ever so long. She wore a ragged bit of a cloak, and had only one shoe on.

"You little wretch, who let you in here?" asked Gruffanuff.

"Dive me dat bun," said the little girl, "me vely hungry."

"Hungry! what is that?" asked Princess Angelica, and gave the child the bun.

"Oh, Princess!" says Gruffanuff, "how good, how kind, how truly angelical you are! See, your Majesties," she said to the King and Queen, who now came up, along with their nephew, Prince Giglio, "how kind the Princess is! She met this little dirty wretch in the garden—I can't tell how she came in here, or why the guards did not shoot her dead at the gate!—and the dear darling of a Princess has given her the whole of her bun!"

"I didn't want it," said Angelica.

"But you are a darling little angel all the same," says the governess.

"Yes; I know I am," said Angelica. "Dirty little girl, don't you think I am very pretty?" Indeed, she had on the finest of little dresses and hats; and, as her hair was carefully curled, she really looked very well.

"Oh, pooty, pooty!" says the little girl, capering about, laughing and dancing, and munching her bun; and as she ate it she began to sing, "Oh what fun to have a plum bun! how I wis it never was done!" At which, and her funny accent, Angelica, Giglio, and the King and Queen began to laugh very merrily.

"I can dance as well as sing," says the little girl. "I can dance, and I can sing, and I can do all sorts of ting." And she ran to a flower-bed, and, pulling a few polyanthuses, rhododendrons, and other flowers, made herself a little wreath, and danced before the King and Queen so drolly and prettily, that everybody was delighted.

"Who was your mother—who were your relations, little girl?" said the Queen.

The little girl said, "Little lion was my brudder; great big lioness my mudder; neber heard of any udder." And she capered away on her one shoe, and everybody was exceedingly diverted.

So Angelica said to the Queen, "Mamma, my parrot flew away yesterday out of its

cage, and I don't care any more for any of my toys; and I think this funny little dirty child will amuse me. I will take her home, and give her some of my old frocks."

"Oh, the generous darling!" says Gruffanuff.

"Which I have worn ever so many times, and am quite tired of," Angelica went on; "and she shall be my little maid. Will you come home with me, little dirty girl?"

The child clapped her hands, and said, "Go home with you—yes! You pooty Princess! —Have a nice dinner, and wear a new dress!"

And they all laughed again, and took home the child to the palace, where, when she was washed and combed, and had one of the Princess's frocks given to her, she looked as handsome as Angelica, almost. Not that Angelica ever thought so; for this little lady never imagined that anybody in the world could be as pretty, as good, or as clever as herself. In order that the little girl should not become too proud and conceited, Mrs. Graffanuff took her old ragged mantle and one shoe, and put them into a glass box, with a card laid upon them, upon which was written, "These were the old clothes in which little BETSINDA was found when the great goodness and admirable kindness of her Royal Highness the Princess Angelica received this little outcast." And the date was added, and the box locked up.

For a while little Betsinda was a great favourite with the Princess, and she danced, and sang, and made her little rhymes, to amuse her mistress. But then the Princess got a monkey, and afterwards a little dog, and afterwards a doll, and did not care for Betsinda any more, who became very melancholy and quiet, and sang no more funny songs, because nobody cared to hear her. And then, as she grew older, she was made a little lady's-maid to the Princess; and though she had no wages, she worked and mended, and put Angelica's hair in papers, and was never cross when scolded, and was always eager to please her mistress, and was always up early and to bed late, and at hand when wanted, and in fact became a perfect little maid. So the two girls grew up, and, when the Princess came out, Betsinda was never tired of waiting on her; and made her dresses better than the best milliner, and was useful in a hundred ways. Whilst the Princess was having her masters, Betsinda would sit and watch them; and in this way she picked up a great deal of learning; for she was always awake, though her mistress was not, and listened to the wise professors when Angelica was yawning or thinking of the next ball. And when the dancing-master came, Betsinda learned along with Angelica;

and when the music-master came, she watched him, and practised the Princess's pieces when Angelica was away at balls and parties; and when the drawing-master came, she took note of all he said and did; and the same with French, Italian, and all other languages—she learned them from the teacher who came to Angelica. When the Princess was going out of an evening she would say, "My good Betsinda, you may as well finish what I have begun." "Yes, Miss," Betsinda would say, and sit down very cheerful, not to *finish* what Angelica began, but to *do* it.

For instance, the Princess would begin a head of a warrior, let us say, and when it was begun it was something like this.

But when it was done, the warrior was like this (only handsomer still if possible),

and the Princess put her name to the drawing; and the Court and King and Queen, and above all poor Giglio, admired the picture of all things, and said, "Was there ever a genius like Angelica?" So, I am sorry to say, was it with the Princess's embroidery and other accomplishments; and Angelica actually believed that she did these things herself, and received all the flattery of the Court as if every word of it was true. Thus she began to think that there was no young woman in all the world equal to herself, and that no young man was good enough for her. As for Betsinda, as she heard none of these praises, she was not puffed up by them, and being a most grateful, good-natured girl, she was only too anxious to do everything which might give her mistress pleasure. Now you begin to perceive that Angelica had faults of her own, and was by no means such a wonder of wonders as people represented her Royal Highness to be.

V I

How Prince Giglio Behaved Himself.

AND NOW LET US SPEAK about Prince Giglio, the nephew of the reigning monarch of Paflagonia. It has already been stated, in page [70], that as long as he had a smart coat to wear, a good horse to ride, and money in his pocket, or rather to take out of his pocket, for he was very good-natured, my young Prince did not care for the loss of his crown and sceptre, being a thoughtless youth, not much inclined to politics or any kind of learning. So his tutor had a sinecure. Giglio would not learn classics or mathematics, and the Lord Chancellor of Paflagonia, SQUARETOSO, pulled a very long face because the prince could not be got to study the Paflagonian laws and constitution; but, on the other hand, the King's gamekeepers and huntsmen found the Prince an apt pupil; the dancing-master pronounced that he was a most elegant and assiduous scholar; the First Lord of the Billiard Table gave the most flattering reports of the Prince's skill; so did

the Groom of the Tennis Court; and as for the Captain of the Guard and Fencing Master, the *valiant* and *veteran* Count KUTASOFF HEDZOFF, he avowed that since he ran the General of Crim Tartary, the dreadful Grumbuskin, through the body, he never had encountered so expert a swordsman as Prince Giglio.

I hope you do not imagine that there was any impropriety in the Prince and Princess walking together in the palace garden, and because Giglio kissed Angelica's hand in a polite manner. In the first place they are cousins; next, the Queen is walking in the garden too (you cannot see her, for she happens to be behind that tree), and her Majesty always wished that Angelica and Giglio should marry: so did Giglio: so did Angelica sometimes, for she thought her cousin very handsome, brave, and good-natured: but then you know she was so clever and knew so many things, and poor Giglio knew nothing, and had no conversation. When they looked at the stars, what did Giglio know of the heavenly bodies? Once, when on a sweet night in a balcony where they were standing, Angelica said, "There is the Bear." "Where?" says Giglio. "Don't be afraid, Angelica! if a dozen bears come, I will kill them rather than they shall hurt you." "Oh, you silly creature!" says she: "you are very good, but you are not very wise." When they looked at the flowers, Giglio was utterly unacquainted with botany, and had never heard of Linnæus. When the butterflies passed, Giglio knew nothing about them, being as ignorant of entomology as I am of algebra. So you see, Angelica, though she liked Giglio pretty well, despised him on account of his ignorance. I think she probably valued *her own learning* rather too much; but to think too well of one's self is the fault of people of all ages and both sexes. Finally, when nobody else was there, Angelica liked her cousin well enough.

King Valoroso was very delicate in health, and withal so fond of good dinners (which were prepared for him by his French cook, Marmitonio), that it was supposed he could not live long. Now the idea of anything happening to the King struck the artful Prime

Minister and the designing old lady-in-waiting with terror. For, thought Glumboso and the Countess, "when Prince Giglio marries his cousin and comes to the throne, what a pretty position we shall be in, whom he dislikes, and who have always been unkind to him. We shall lose our places in a trice; Gruffanuff will have to give up all the jewels, laces, snuff-boxes, rings, and watches which belonged to the Queen, Giglio's mother; and Glumboso will be forced to refund two hundred and seventeen thousand millions, nine hundred and eighty-seven thousand, four hundred and thirty-nine pounds, thirteen shillings, and sixpence halfpenny, money left to Prince Giglio by his poor dear father." So the Lady of Honour and the Prime Minister hated Giglio because they had done him a wrong; and these unprincipled people invented a hundred cruel stories about poor Giglio, in order to influence the King, Queen, and Princess against him; how he was so ignorant that he could not spell the commonest words, and actually wrote Valoroso Valloroso, and spelt Angelica with two l's; how he drank a great deal too much wine at dinner, and was always idling in the stables with the grooms; how he owed ever so much money at the pastrycook's and the haberdasher's; how he used to go to sleep at church; how he was fond of playing cards with the pages. So did the Queen like playing cards; so did the King go to sleep at church, and eat and drink too much; and, if Giglio owed a trifle for tarts, who owed him two hundred and seventeen thousand millions, nine hundred and eighty-seven thousand, four hundred and thirty-nine pounds, thirteen shillings, and sixpence halfpenny, I should like to know? Detractors and tale-bearers (in my humble opinion) had much better look at *home*. All this back-biting and slandering had effect upon Princess Angelica, who began to look coldly on her cousin, then to laugh at him and scorn him for being so stupid, then to sneer at him for having vulgar associates; and at Court balls, dinners, and so forth, to treat him so unkindly that poor Giglio became quite ill, took to his bed, and sent for the doctor.

His Majesty King Valoroso, as we have seen, had his own reasons for disliking his nephew; and as for those innocent readers who ask why?—I beg (with the permission of their dear parents) to refer them to Shakspeare's pages, where they will read why King John disliked Prince Arthur. With the Queen, his royal but weak-minded aunt, when Giglio was out of sight he was out of mind. While she had her whist and her evening parties, she cared for little else.

I dare say *two villains*, who shall be nameless, wished Doctor Pildrafto, the Court

Physician, had killed Giglio right out, but he only bled and physicked him so severely, that the Prince was kept to his room for several months, and grew as thin as a post.

Whilst he was lying sick in this way, there came to the Court of Paflagonia a famous painter, whose name was Tomaso Lorenzo, and who was Painter in Ordinary to the King of Crim Tartary, Paflagonia's neighbour. Tomaso Lorenzo painted all the Court, who were delighted with his works; for even Countess Gruffanuff looked young and Glumboso good-humoured in his pictures. "He flatters very much," some people said. "Nay!" says Princess Angelica, "I am above flattery, and I think he did not make my picture handsome enough. I can't bear to hear a man of genius unjustly cried down, and I hope my dear papa will make Lorenzo a knight of his Order of the Cucumber."

The Princess Angelica, although the courtiers vowed her Royal Highness could draw so *beautifully* that the idea of her taking lessons was absurd, yet chose to have Lorenzo for a teacher, and it was wonderful, *as long as she painted in his studio*, what beautiful pictures she made! Some of the performances were engraved for the Book of Beauty: others were sold for enormous sums at Charity Bazaars. She wrote the *signatures* under the drawings, no doubt, but I think I know who did the pictures—this artful painter, who had come with other designs on Angelica than merely to teach her to draw.

One day, Lorenzo showed the Princess a portrait of a young man in armour, with fair hair and the loveliest blue eyes, and an expression at once melancholy and interesting.

"Dear Signor Lorenzo, who is this?" asked the Princess. "I never saw any one so handsome," says Countess Gruffanuff (the old humbug).

"That," said the painter, "that, madam, is the portrait of my august young master, his Royal Highness Bulbo, Crown Prince of Crim Tartary, Duke of Acroceraunia, Marquis of Poluphloisboio, and Knight Grand Cross of the Order of the Pumpkin. That is the Order of the Pumpkin glittering on his manly breast, and received by his Royal Highness from his august father, his Majesty King PADELLA I., for his gallantry at the

battle of Rimbombamento, when he slew with his own princely hand the King of Ograria and two hundred and eleven giants of the two hundred and eighteen who formed the King's body-guard. The remainder were destroyed by the brave Crim Tartar army after an obstinate combat, in which the Crim Tartars suffered severely."

What a Prince! thought Angelica: so brave—so calm-looking—so young—what a hero!

"He is as accomplished as he is brave," continued the Court Painter. "He knows all languages perfectly: sings deliciously: plays every instrument: composes operas which have been acted a thousand nights running at the Imperial Theatre of Crim Tartary, and danced in a ballet there before the King and Queen; in which he looked so beautiful, that his cousin, the lovely daughter of the King of Circassia, died for love of him."

"Why did he not marry the poor Princess?" asked Angelica, with a sigh.

"Because they were *first cousins*, Madam, and the clergy forbid these unions," said the Painter. "And, besides, the young Prince had given his royal heart *elsewhere*."

"And to whom?" asked her Royal Highness.

"I am not at liberty to mention the Princess's name," answered the Painter.

"But you may tell me the first letter of it," gasped out the Princess.

"That your Royal Highness is at liberty to guess," says Lorenzo.

"Does it begin with a Z?" asked Angelica.

The Painter said it wasn't a Z; then she tried a Y; then an X; then a W, and went so backwards through almost the whole alphabet.

When she came to D, and it wasn't D, she grew very much excited; when she came to C, and it wasn't C, she was still more nervous; when she came to B, *and it wasn't B*, "O, dearest Gruffanuff," she said, "lend me your smelling bottle!" and, hiding her head in the Countess's shoulder, she faintly whispered, "Ah, Signor, can it be A?"

"It was A; and though I may not, by my Royal Master's orders, tell your Royal Highness the Princess's name, whom he fondly, madly, devotedly, rapturously loves, I may show you her portrait," says the slyboots: and leading the Princess up to a gilt frame, he drew a curtain which was before it.

O goodness, the frame contained A LOOKING GLASS! and Angelica saw her own face!

VII

How Giglio and Angelica Had a Quarrel.

THE COURT PAINTER of his Majesty the King of Crim Tartary returned to that monarch's dominions, carrying away a number of sketches which he had made in the Paflagonian capital (you know, of course, my dears, that the name of that capital is Blombodinga); but the most charming of all his pieces was a portrait of the Princess Angelica, which all the Crim Tartar nobles came to see. With this work the King was so delighted, that he decorated the Painter with his Order of the Pumpkin (sixth class), and the artist became Sir Tomaso Lorenzo, K.P., thenceforth.

King Valoroso also sent Sir Tomaso his Order of the Cucumber, besides a handsome order for money, for he painted the King, Queen, and principal nobility while at Blombodinga, and became all the fashion, to the perfect rage of all the artists in Paflagonia, where the King used to point to the portrait of Prince Bulbo, which Sir Tomaso had left behind him, and say, "Which among you can paint a picture like that?"

It hung in the royal parlour over the royal sideboard, and Princess Angelica could always look at it as she sat making the tea. Each day it seemed to grow handsomer and handsomer, and the Princess grew so fond of looking at it, that she would often spill the tea over the cloth, at which her father and mother would wink and wag their heads, and say to each other, "Aha! we see how things are going."

In the meanwhile poor Giglio lay up stairs very sick in his chamber, though he took all the doctor's horrible medicines like a good young lad; as I hope *you* do, my dears, when you are ill and mamma sends for the medical man. And the only person who visited Giglio (besides his friend the captain of the guard, who was almost always busy or on parade), was little Betsinda the housemaid, who used to do his bed-room and sitting-room out, bring him his gruel, and warm his bed.

When the little housemaid came to him in the morning and evening, Prince Giglio used to say, "Betsinda, Betsinda, how is the Princess Angelica?"

And Betsinda used to answer, "The Princess is very well, thank you, my Lord." And Giglio would heave a sigh, and think, if Angelica were sick I am sure *I* should not be very well.

Then Giglio would say, "Betsinda, has the Princess Angelica asked for me to-day?" And Betsinda would answer, "No, my Lord, not to-day;" or, "she was very busy practising the piano when I saw her;" or, "she was writing invitations for an evening party, and did not speak to me:" or make some excuse or other, not strictly consonant with truth: for Betsinda was such a good-natured creature, that she strove to do everything to prevent annoyance to Prince Giglio, and even brought him up roast chicken and jellies from the kitchen (when the Doctor allowed them, and Giglio was getting better) saying, "that the Princess had made the jelly or the bread sauce, with her own hands, on purpose for Giglio."

When Giglio heard this he took heart, and began to mend immediately; and gobbled up all the jelly, and picked the last bone of the chicken—drumsticks, merry-thought, sides'-bones, back, pope's-nose, and all—thanking his dear Angelica: and he felt so much better the next day, that he dressed and went down stairs, where, whom should he meet but Angelica going into the drawing-room. All the covers were off the chairs, the chandeliers taken out of the bags, the damask curtains uncovered, the work and things carried away, and the handsomest albums on the tables. Angelica had her hair in papers: in a word, it was evident there was going to be a party.

"Heavens, Giglio!" cries Angelica: "*you* here in such a dress! What a figure you are!"

"Yes, dear Angelica, I am come down stairs, and feel so well to-day, thanks to the *fowl* and the *jelly*."

"What do I know about fowls and jellies, that you allude to them in that rude way?" says Angelica.

"Why, didn't—didn't you send them, Angelica dear?" says Giglio.

"I send them indeed! Angelica dear! No, Giglio dear," says she, mocking him, "*I* was engaged in getting the rooms ready for his Royal Highness the Prince of Crim Tartary, who is coming to pay my papa's Court a visit."

"The—Prince—of—Crim—Tartary!" Giglio said, aghast.

"Yes, the Prince of Crim Tartary," says Angelica, mocking him. "I dare say you never heard of such a country. What *did* you ever hear of? You don't know whether Crim Tartary is on the Red Sea or on the Black Sea, I dare say."

"Yes, I do, it's on the Red Sea," says Giglio, at which the Princess burst out laughing at him, and said, "O you ninny! You are so ignorant, you are really not fit for society! You know nothing but about horses and dogs, and are only fit to dine in a mess-room with my Royal Father's heaviest dragoons. Don't look so surprised at me, sir: go and put your best clothes on to receive the Prince, and let me get the drawing-room ready."

Giglio said, "O, Angelica, Angelica, I didn't think this of you. *This* wasn't your language to me when you gave me this ring, and I gave you mine in the garden, and you gave me that k—"

But what k was we never shall know, for Angelica, in a rage, cried, "Get out, you saucy, rude creature! How dare you to remind me of your rudeness? As for your little trumpery twopenny ring, there, sir, there!" And she flung it out of the window.

"It was my mother's marriage ring," cried Giglio.

"*I* don't care whose marriage ring it was," cries Angelica. "Marry the person who picks it up if she's a woman, you shan't marry *me*. And give me back *my* ring. I've no patience with people who boast about the things they give away! *I* know who'll give me much finer things than you ever gave me. A beggarly ring indeed, not worth five shillings!"

Now Angelica little knew that the ring which Giglio had given her was a fairy ring: if a man wore it, it made all the women in love with him; if a woman, all the gentlemen. The Queen, Giglio's mother, quite an ordinary looking person, was admired immensely

whilst she wore this ring, and her husband was frantic when she was ill. But when she called her little Giglio to her, and put the ring on his finger, King Savio did not seem to care for his wife so much any more, but transferred all his love to little Giglio. So did everybody love him as long as he had the ring; but when, as quite a child, he gave it to Angelica, people began to love and admire *her*; and Giglio, as the saying is, played only second fiddle.

"Yes," says Angelica, going on in her foolish ungrateful way, "*I* know who'll give me much finer things than your beggarly little pearl nonsense."

"Very good, Miss! You may take back your ring, too!" says Giglio, his eyes flashing fire at her, and then, as if his eyes had been suddenly opened, he cried out, "Ha! what does this mean? Is *this* the woman I have been in love with all my life? Have I been such a ninny as to throw away my regard upon *you*? Why—actually—yes—you are a little crooked!"

"O, you wretch!" cries Angelica.

"And, upon my conscience, you—you squint a little."

"Eh!" cries Angelica.

"And your hair is red—and you are marked with the small-pox—and what? you have three false teeth—and one leg shorter than the other!"

"You brute, you brute, you!" Angelica screamed out: and as she seized the ring with one hand, she dealt Giglio one, two, three smacks to the face, and would have pulled the hair off his head had he not started laughing, and crying,

"O dear me, Angelica, don't pull out *my* hair, it hurts! You might remove a great deal of *your own*, as I perceive, without scissors or pulling at all. Oh, ho, ho! ha, ha, ha! he, he he!"

And he nearly choked himself with laughing, and she with rage, when, with a low bow, and dressed in his Court habit, Count Gambabella, the first lord-in-waiting, entered and said, "Royal Highnesses! Their Majesties expect you in the Pink Throne-room, where they await the arrival of the Prince of CRIM TARTARY."

VIII

How Gruffanuff Picked the Fairy Ring Up,
and Prince Bulbo Came to Court.

P RINCE BULBO'S ARRIVAL had set all the Court in a flutter: everybody was ordered to put his or her best clothes on: the footmen had their gala liveries; the Lord Chancellor his new wig; the Guards their last new tunics; and Countess Gruffanuff you may be sure was glad of an opportunity of decorating *her* old person with her finest things. She was walking through the court of the Palace on her way to wait upon their Majesties, when she spied something glittering on the pavement, and bade the boy in buttons who was holding up her train, to go and pick up the article shining yonder. He was an ugly little wretch, in some of the late groom-porter's old clothes cut down, and much too tight for him; and yet, when he had taken up the ring (as it turned out to be), and was carrying it to his mistress, she thought he looked like a little Cupid. He gave the ring to her; it was a trumpery little thing enough, but too small for any of her old knuckles, so she put it into her pocket.

"O, mum!" says the boy, looking at her, "how, how beyoutiful you do look, mum, to-day, mum!"

"And you, too, Jacky," she was going to say; but, looking down at him—no, he was no longer good-looking at all—but only the carroty-haired little Jacky of the morning. However, praise is welcome from the ugliest of men or boys. and Gruffanuff, bidding the boy hold up her train, walked on in high good-humour. The guards saluted her with peculiar respect. Captain Hedzoff, in the ante-room, said, " My dear madam, you look like an angel to-day." And so, bowing and smirking, Gruffanuff went in and took her place behind her Royal Master and Mistress, who were in the throne-room, awaiting the Prince of Crim Tartary. Princess Angelica sat at their feet, and behind the King's chair stood Prince Giglio, looking very savage.

The Prince of Crim Tartary made his appearance, attended by Baron Sleibootz, his chamberlain, and followed by a black page, carrying the most beautiful crown you ever saw! He was dressed in his travelling costume, and his hair, as you see, was a little in disorder. "I have ridden three hundred miles since breakfast," said he, "so eager was I to behold the Prin—the Court and august family of Paflagonia, and I could not wait one minute before appearing in your Majesties' presences."

Giglio, from behind the throne, burst out into a roar of contemptuous laughter; but all the Royal party, in fact, were so flurried, that they did not hear this little outbreak.

"Your R. H. is welcome in any dress," says the King. "Glumboso, a chair for his Royal Highness."

"Any dress his Royal Highness wears *is* a Court dress," says Princess Angelica, smiling graciously.

"Ah! but you should see my other clothes," said the Prince. "I should have had them on, but that stupid carrier has not brought them. Who's that laughing?"

It was Giglio laughing. "I was laughing," he said, "because you said just now that you were in such a hurry to see the Princess, that you could not wait to change your dress; and now you say you come in these clothes because you have no others."

"And who are you?" says Prince Bulbo, very fiercely.

"My father was King of this country, and I am his only son, Prince!" replies Giglio, with equal haughtiness.

"Ha!" said the King and Glumboso, looking very flurried; but the former, collecting himself, said, "Dear Prince Bulbo, I forgot to introduce to your Royal Highness my dear nephew, his Royal Highness Prince Giglio! Know each other! Embrace each other! Giglio, give His Royal Highness your hand!" and Giglio, giving his hand, squeezed poor Bulbo's until the tears ran out of his eyes. Glumboso now brought a chair for the Royal visitor, and placed it on the platform on which the King, Queen, and Prince were seated; but the chair was on the edge of the platform, and as Bulbo sat down, it toppled over, and he with it, rolling over and over, and bellowing like a bull. Giglio roared still louder at this disaster, but it was with laughter; so did all the Court when Prince Bulbo got up; for though when he entered the room he appeared not very ridiculous, as he stood up from his fall for a moment, he looked so exceedingly plain and foolish, that nobody could help laughing at him. When he had entered the room, he was observed to carry a rose in his hand, which fell out of it as he tumbled.

"My rose! my rose!" cried Bulbo; and his chamberlain dashed forwards and picked it

up, and gave it to the Prince, who put it in his waistcoat. Then people wondered why they had laughed; there was nothing particularly ridiculous in him. He was rather short, rather stout, rather red-haired, but, in fine, for a Prince not so bad.

So they sat and talked, the royal personages together, the Crim Tartar officers with those of Paflagonia—Giglio very comfortable with Gruffanuff behind the throne. He looked at her with such tender eyes, that her heart was all in a flutter. "Oh, dear Prince," she said, "how could you speak so haughtily in presence of their Majesties? I protest I thought I should have fainted."

"I should have caught you in my arms," said Giglio, looking raptures.

"Why were you so cruel to Prince Bulbo, dear Prince?" says Gruff.

"Because I hate him," says Gil.

"You are jealous of him, and still love poor Angelica," cries Gruffanuff, putting her handkerchief to her eyes.

"I did, but I love her no more!" Giglio cried. "I despise her! Were she heiress to twenty thousand thrones, I would despise her and scorn her. But why speak of thrones? I have lost mine. I am too weak to recover it—I am alone, and have no friend."

"Oh, say not so, dear Prince!" says Gruffanuff.

"Besides," says he, "I am so happy here *behind the throne,* that I would not change my place, no, not for the throne of the world!"

"What are you two people chattering about there?" says the Queen, who was rather good-natured, though not over-burthened with wisdom. "It is time to dress for dinner. Giglio, show Prince Bulbo to his room. Prince, if your clothes have not come, we shall be very happy to see you as you are." But when Prince Bulbo got to his bed-room, his luggage was there and unpacked; and the hairdresser coming in, cut and curled him entirely to his own satisfaction; and when the dinner-bell rang, the royal company had not to wait above five-and-twenty minutes until Bulbo appeared, during which time the King, who could not bear to wait, grew as sulky as possible. As for Giglio, he never left Madam Gruffanuff all this time, but stood with her in the embrasure of a window, paying her compliments. At length the Groom of the Chambers announced his Royal Highness the Prince of Crim Tartary! and the noble company went into the royal dining-room. It was quite a small party; only the King and Queen, the Princess, whom Bulbo took out, the two Princes, Countess Gruffanuff, Glumboso the Prime Minister,

and Prince Bulbo's chamberlain. You may be sure they had a very good dinner—let every boy or girl think of what he or she likes best, and fancy it on the table.*

The Princess talked incessantly all dinner time to the Prince of Crimea, who ate an immense deal too much, and never took his eyes off his plate, except when Giglio, who was carving a goose, sent a quantity of stuffing and onion sauce into one of them. Giglio only burst out a laughing as the Crimean Prince wiped his shirt-front and face with his scented pocket-handkerchief. He did not make Prince Bulbo any apology. When the Prince looked at him, Giglio would not look that way. When Prince Bulbo said, "Prince Giglio, may I have the honour of taking a glass of wine with you?" Giglio *wouldn't* answer. All his talk and his eyes were for Countess Gruffanuff, who you may be sure was pleased with Giglio's attentions—the vain old creature! When he was not complimenting her, he was making fun of Prince Bulbo, so loud that Gruffanuff was always tapping him with her fan, and saying, "O you satirical Prince! O fie, the Prince will hear!" "Well, I don't mind," says Giglio, louder still. The King and Queen luckily did not hear; for her Majesty was a little deaf, and the King thought so much about his own dinner, and, besides, made such a dreadful noise, hob-gobbling in eating it, that he heard nothing else. After dinner, his Majesty and the Queen went to sleep in their arm-chairs.

This was the time when Giglio began his tricks with Prince Bulbo, plying that young gentleman with port, sherry, madeira, champagne, marsala, cherry brandy, and pale ale, of all of which Master Bulbo drank without stint. But in plying his guest, Giglio was obliged to drink himself, and, I am sorry to say, took more than was good for him, so that the young men were very noisy, rude, and foolish when they joined the ladies after

_____

*Here a very pretty game may be played by all the children saying what they like best for dinner.

dinner; and dearly did they pay for that imprudence, as now, my darlings, you shall hear!

Bulbo went and sat by the piano, where Angelica was playing and singing, and he sang out of tune, and he upset the coffee when the footman brought it, and he laughed out of place, and talked absurdly, and fell asleep and snored horridly. Booh, the nasty pig! But as he lay there stretched on the pink satin sofa, Angelica still persisted in thinking him the most beautiful of human beings. No doubt the magic rose which Bulbo wore, caused this infatuation on Angelica's part; but is she the first young woman who has thought a silly fellow charming?

Giglio must go and sit by Gruffanuff, whose old face he too every moment began to find more lovely. He paid the most outrageous compliments to her: There never was such a darling—Older than he was?—Fiddle-de-dee! He would marry her—he would having nothing but her!

To marry the heir to the throne! Here was a chance! The artful hussey actually got a sheet of paper, and wrote upon it, "This is to give notice that I, Giglio, only son of Savio, King of Paflagonia, hereby promise to marry the charming and virtuous Barbara Griselda Countess Gruffanuff, and widow of the late Jenkins Gruffanuff, Esq."

"What is it you are writing? you charming Gruffy!" says Giglio, who was lolling on the sofa, by the writing-table.

"Only an order for you to sign, dear Prince, for giving coals and blankets to the poor, this cold weather. Look! the King and Queen are both asleep, and your Royal Highness's order will do."

So Giglio, who was very good-natured, as Gruffy well knew, signed the order immediately; and, when she had it in her pocket, you may fancy what airs she gave herself. She was ready to flounce out of the room before the Queen herself, as now she was the wife of the *rightful* King of Paflagonia! She would not speak to Glumboso, whom she thought a brute, for depriving her *dear husband* of the crown! And when candles came, and she had helped to undress the Queen and Princess, she went into her own room, and actually practised, on a sheet of paper, "Griselda Paflagonia," "Barbara Regina," "Griselda Barbara, Paf. Reg.," and I don't know what signatures besides, against the day when she should be Queen, forsooth!

IX

How Betsinda Got the Warming-Pan.

LITTLE BETSINDA came in to put Gruffanuff's hair in papers; and the Countess was so pleased, that, for a wonder, she complimented Betsinda. "Betsinda!" she said, "you dressed my hair very nicely to-day; I promised you a little present. Here are five sh—no, here is a pretty little ring, that I picked—that I have had some time." And she gave Betsinda the ring she had picked up in the court. It fitted Betsinda exactly.

"It's like the ring the Princess used to wear," says the maid.

"No such thing," says Gruffanuff, "I have had it this ever so long. There—tuck me up quite comfortable; and now, as it's a very cold night (the snow was beating in at the window), you may go and warm dear Prince Giglio's bed, like a good girl, and then you may unrip my green silk, and then you can just do me up a little cap for the morning, and then you can mend that hole in my silk stocking, and then you can go to bed, Betsinda. Mind, I shall want my cup of tea at five o'clock in the morning."

"I suppose I had best warm both the young gentlemen's beds, ma'am," says Betsinda.

Gruffanuff, for reply, said, "Hau-au-ho!—Grau-haw-hoo!—Hong-hrho!" In fact, she was snoring sound asleep.

Her room, you know, is next to the King and Queen, and the Princess is next to them. So pretty Betsinda went away for the coals to the kitchen, and filled the royal warming-pan.

Now, she was a very kind, merry, civil, pretty girl; but there must have been something very captivating about her this evening, for all the women in the servant's hall began to scold and abuse her. The housekeeper said she was a pert, stuck-up thing: the upper-housemaid asked, how dare she wear such ringlets and ribbons, it was quite improper! The cook (for there was a woman-cook as well as a man-cook) said to the kitchen-maid that *she* never could see anything in that creetur: but as for the men, every one of them, Coachman, John, Buttons the page, and Monsieur, the Prince of Crim Tartary's valet, started up, and said—

"My eyes!"
"O mussey!"
"O jemmany!"
"O ciel!"
} "What a pretty girl Betsinda is!"

"Hands off; none of your impertinence, you vulgar, low people!" says Betsinda, walking off with her pan of coals. She heard the young gentlemen playing at billiards as she went upstairs: first to Prince Giglio's bed, which she warmed, and then to Prince Bulbo's room.

He came in just as she had done; and as soon as he saw her, "O! O! O! O! O! O! what a beyou—oo—ootiful creature you are! You angel—you peri—you rose-bud, let me be thy bulbul—thy Bulbo, too! Fly to the desert, fly with me! I never saw a young gazelle to glad me with its dark blue eye that had eyes like thine. Thou nymph of beauty, take, take this young heart. A truer never did itself sustain within a soldier's waistcoat. Be mine! Be mine! Be Princess of Crim Tartary! My Royal father will approve our union: and, as for that little carrotty-haired Angelica, I do not care a fig for her any more."

"Go away, your Royal Highness, and go to bed, please," said Betsinda, with the warming-pan.

But Bulbo said, "No, never, till thou swearest to be mine, thou lovely, blushing, chamber-maid divine! Here, at thy feet, the Royal Bulbo lies, the trembling captive of Betsinda's eyes."

And he went on, making himself so *absurd and ridiculous*, that Betsinda, who was full of fun, gave him a touch with the warming-pan, which, I promise you, made him cry "O-o-o-o!" in a very different manner.

Prince Bulbo made such a noise that Prince Giglio, who heard him from the next room, came in to see what was the matter. As soon as he saw what was taking place, Giglio, in a fury, rushed on Bulbo, kicked him in the rudest manner up to the ceiling, and went on kicking him till his hair was quite out of curl.

Poor Betsinda did not know whether to laugh or to cry; the kicking certainly must hurt the Prince, but then he looked so droll! When Giglio had done knocking him up and down to the ground, and whilst he went into a corner rubbing himself, what do you think Giglio does? He goes down on his knees to Betsinda, takes her hand, begs her to accept his heart, and offers to marry her that moment. Fancy Betsinda's condition, who had been in love with the Prince ever since she first saw him in the palace garden, when she was quite a little child.

"Oh, divine Betsinda!" says the Prince, "how have I lived fifteen years in thy company without seeing thy perfections? What woman in all Europe, Asia, Africa, and America, nay, in Australia, only it is not yet discovered, can presume to be thy equal? Angelica? Pish! Gruffanuff? Phoo! The Queen? Ha, ha! Thou art my Queen. Thou art the real Angelica, because thou art really angelic."

"Oh, Prince! I am but a poor chambermaid," says Betsinda, looking, however, very much pleased.

"Didst thou not tend me in my sickness, when all forsook me?" continues Giglio. "Did not thy gentle hand smooth my pillow, and bring me jelly and roast chicken?"

"Yes, dear Prince, I did," says Betsinda, "and I sewed your Royal Highness's shirt-buttons on too, if you please, your Royal Highness," cries this artless maiden.

When poor Prince Bulbo, who was now madly in love with Betsinda, heard this declaration, when he saw the unmistakeable glances which she flung upon Giglio, Bulbo

began to cry bitterly, and tore quantities of hair out of his head, till it all covered the room like so much tow.

Betsinda had left the warming-pan on the floor while the princes were going on with their conversation, and as they began now to quarrel and be very fierce with one another, she thought proper to run away.

"You great big blubbering booby, tearing your hair in the corner there; of course you will give me satisfaction for insulting Betsinda. *You* dare to kneel down at Princess Giglio's knees and kiss her hand!"

"She's not Princess Giglio!" roars out Bulbo. "She shall be Princess Bulbo, no other shall be Princess Bulbo."

"You are engaged to my cousin!" bellows out Giglio.

"I hate your cousin," says Bulbo.

"You shall give me satisfaction for insulting her!" cries Giglio in a fury.

"I'll have your life."

"I'll run you through."

"I'll cut your throat."

"I'll blow your brains out."

"I'll knock your head off."

"I'll send a friend to you in the morning."

"I'll send a bullet into you in the afternoon."

"We'll meet again," says Giglio, shaking his fist in Bulbo's face; and seizing up the warming-pan, he kissed it, because, forsooth, Betsinda had carried it, and rushed down stairs. What should he see on the landing but his Majesty talking to Betsinda, whom he called by all sorts of fond names. His Majesty had heard a row in the building, so he stated, and smelling something burning, had come out to see what the matter was.

"It's the young gentlemen smoking, perhaps, sir," says Betsinda.

"Charming chambermaid," says the King (like all the rest of them), "never mind the young men! Turn thy eyes on a middle-aged autocrat, who has been considered not ill-looking in his time."

"Oh, sir! what will her Majesty say?" cries Betsinda.

"Her Majesty!" laughs the monarch. "Her Majesty be hanged. Am I not Autocrat of Paflagonia? Have I not blocks, ropes, axes, hangmen—ha? Runs not a river by my palace wall? Have I not sacks to sew up wives withal? Say but the word, that thou wilt be mine own,—your mistress straightway in a sack is sewn, and thou the sharer of my heart and throne."

When Giglio heard these atrocious sentiments, he forgot the respect usually paid to Royalty, lifted up the warming-pan, and knocked down the King as flat as a pancake; after which, Master Giglio took to his heels and ran way, and Betsinda went off screaming, and the Queen, Gruffanuff, and the Princess, all came out of their rooms. Fancy their feelings on beholding their husband, father, sovereign, in this posture!

X

How King Valoroso Was in a Dreadful Passion.

As SOON AS the coals began to burn him, the King came to himself and stood up. "Ho! my captain of the guards!" his Majesty exclaimed, stamping his royal feet with rage. O piteous spectacle! the King's nose was bent quite crooked by the blow of Prince Giglio! His Majesty ground his teeth with rage. "Hedzoff," he said, taking a death warrant out of his dressing-gown pocket, "Hedzoff, good Hedzoff, seize upon the Prince. Thou'lt find him in his chamber two pair up. But now he dared, with sacrilegious hand, to strike the sacred night-cap of a king—Hedzoff, and floor me with a warming-pan! Away, no more demur, the villain dies! See it be done, or else,—h'm!—ha!—h'm! mind thine own eyes!" and followed by the ladies, and lifting up the tails of his dressing-gown, the King entered his own apartment.

Captain Hedzoff was very much affected, having a sincere love for Giglio. "Poor, poor Giglio!" he said, the tears rolling over his manly face, and dripping down his moustachios; "My noble young Prince, is it my hand must lead thee to death?"

"Lead him to fiddlestick, Hedzoff," said a female voice. It was Gruffanuff, who had come out in her dressing-gown when she heard the noise—"The King said you were to hang the Prince. Well, hang the Prince."

"I don't understand you," says Hedzoff, who was not a very clever man.

"You Gaby! he didn't say *which* Prince," says Gruffanuff.

"No; he didn't say which, certainly," said Hedzoff.

"Well then, take Bulbo, and hang *him!*"

When Captain Hedzoff heard this, he began to dance about for joy. "Obedience is a soldier's honour," says he. "Prince Bulbo's head will do capitally," and he went to arrest the Prince the very first thing next morning.

He knocked at the door. "Who's there?" says Bulbo. "Captain Hedzoff?" Step in, pray, my good Captain; I'm delighted to see you; I have been expecting you."

"Have you?" says Hedzoff.

"Sleibootz, my Chamberlain, will act for me," says the Prince.

"I beg your Royal Highness's pardon, but you will have to act for yourself, and it's a pity to wake Baron Sleibootz."

The Prince Bulbo still seemed to take the matter very coolly. "Of course, Captain," says he, "you are come about that affair with Prince Giglio?"

"Precisely," says Hedzoff, "that affair of Prince Giglio."

"Is it to be pistols, or swords, Captain?" asks Bulbo. "I'm a pretty good hand with both, and I'll do for Prince Giglio as sure as my name is my Royal Highness Prince Bulbo."

"There's some mistake, my Lord," says the Captain. "The business is done with *axes* among us."

"Axes? That's sharp work," says Bulbo. "Call my Chamberlain, he'll be my second, and in ten minutes, I flatter myself you'll see Master Giglio's head off his impertinent shoulders. I'm hungry for his blood. Hoo-oo, aw!" and he looked as savage as an ogre.

"I beg your pardon, sir, but by this warrant, I am to take you prisoner, and hand you over to—to the executioner."

"Pooh, pooh, my good man!—Stop, I say,—ho!—hulloa!" was all that this luckless Prince was enabled to say, for Hedzoff's guards seizing him, tied a handkerchief over his mouth and face, and carried him to the place of execution.

The King, who happened to be talking to Glumboso, saw him pass, and took a pinch of snuff, and said, "So much for Giglio. Now let's go to breakfast."

The Captain of the Guard handed over his prisoner to the Sheriff, with the fatal order,

"AT SIGHT CUT OFF THE BEARER'S HEAD.

"VALOROSO XXIV."

"It's a mistake," says Bulbo, who did not seem to understand the business in the least.

"Poo—poo—pooh," says the Sheriff. "Fetch Jack Ketch instantly. Jack Ketch!"

And poor Bulbo was led to the scaffold, where an executioner with a block and a tremendous axe was always ready in case he should be wanted.

But we must now revert to Giglio and Betsinda.

X I

What Gruffanuff Did to Giglio and Betsinda.

GRUFFANUFF, who had seen what had happened with the King, and knew that Giglio must come to grief, got up very early the next morning, and went to devise some plans for rescuing her darling husband, as the silly old thing insisted on calling him. She found him walking up and down the garden, thinking of a rhyme for Betsinda (*tinder* and *winda* were all he could find), and indeed having forgotten all about the past evening, except that Betsinda was the most lovely of beings.

"Well, dear Giglio," says Gruff.

"Well, dear Gruffy," says Giglio, only *he* was quite satirical.

"I have been thinking, darling, what you must do in this scrape. You must fly the country for a while."

"What scrape?—fly the country? Never without her I love, Countess," says Giglio.

"No, she will accompany you, dear Prince," she says, in her most coaxing accents. "First, we must get the jewels belonging to our royal parents, and those of her and his present Majesty. Here is the key, duck; they are all yours, you know, by right, for you are the rightful King of Paflagonia, and your wife will be the rightful Queen."

"Will she?" says Giglio.

"Yes; and having got the jewels, go to Glumboso's apartment, where, under his bed, you will find sacks containing money to the amount of £217,000,987,439 13s. 6½d., all belonging to you, for he took it out of your royal father's room on the day of his death. With this we will fly."

"*We* will fly?" says Giglio.

"Yes, you and your bride—your affianced love—your Gruffy!" says the Countess, with a languishing leer.

"*You* my bride!" says Giglio. "You, you hideous old woman!"

"Oh, you, you wretch! didn't you give me this paper promising marriage?" cries Gruff.

"Get away, you old goose! I love Betsinda, and Betsinda only!" And in a fit of terror he ran from her as quickly as he could.

"He! he! he!" shrieks out Gruff; "a promise is a promise, if there are laws in Paflagonia! And as for that monster, that wretch, that fiend, that ugly little vixen—as for that upstart, that ingrate, that beast Betsinda, Master Giglio will have no little difficulty in discovering her whereabouts. He may look very long before finding *her*, I warrant. He little knows that Miss Betsinda is——"

Is—what? Now, you shall hear. Poor Betsinda got up at five in winter's morning to bring her cruel mistress her tea; and instead of finding her in a good humour, found Gruffy as cross as two sticks. The Countess boxed Betsinda's ears half-a-dozen times whilst she was dressing; but as poor little Betsinda was used to this kind of treatment, she did not feel any special alarm. "And now," says she, "when her Majesty rings her bell twice, I'll trouble you, miss, to attend."

So when the Queen's bell rang twice, Betsinda came to her Majesty and made a pretty little curtsey. The Queen, the Princess, and Gruffanuff were all three in the room. As soon as they saw her they began.

"You wretch!" says the Queen.

"You little vulgar thing!" said the Princess.

"You beast!" says Gruffanuff.

"Get out of my sight!" says the Queen.

"Go away with you, do!" says the Princess.

"Quit the premises!" says Gruffanuff.

Alas! and wo is me! very lamentable events had occurred to Betsinda that morning, and all in consequence of that fatal warming-pan business of the previous night. The King had offered to marry her; of course her Majesty the Queen was jealous: Bulbo had fallen in love with her; of course Angelica was furious: Giglio was in love with her, and O what a fury Gruffy was in!

"Take off that $\begin{Bmatrix} \text{cap} \\ \text{petticoat} \\ \text{gown} \end{Bmatrix}$ I gave you," they said, all at once,

and began tearing the clothes off poor Betsinda.

"How dare you flirt with $\begin{Bmatrix} \text{the King?"} \\ \text{Prince Bulbo?"} \\ \text{Prince Giglio?"} \end{Bmatrix}$ cried the Queen, the Princess, and Countess.

"Give her the rags she wore when she came into the house, and turn her out of it!" cries the Queen.

"Mind she does not go with *my* shoes on, which I lent her so kindly," says the Princess; and indeed the Princess's shoes were a great deal too big for Betsinda.

"Come with me, you filthy hussey!" and taking up the Queen's poker, the cruel Gruffanuff drove Betsinda into her room.

The Countess went to the glass box in which she had kept Betsinda's old cloak and shoe this ever so long, and said, "Take those rags, you little beggar creature, and strip off everything, belonging to honest people, and go about your business;" and she actually tore off the poor little delicate thing's back almost all her things, and told her to be off out of the house.

Poor Betsinda huddled the cloak round her back, on which were embroidered the letters PRIN . . . ROSAL . . . and then came a great rent.

As for the shoe, what was she to do with one poor little tootsey sandal? the string was still to it, so she hung it round her neck.

"Won't you give me a pair of shoes to go out in the snow, mum, if you please, mum?" cried the poor child.

"No, you wicked beast!" says Gruffanuff, driving her along with the poker—driving her down the cold stairs—driving her through the cold hall—flinging her out into the cold street, so that the knocker itself shed tears to see her!

But a kind Fairy made the soft snow warm for her little feet, and she wrapped herself up in the ermine of her mantle, and was gone!

"And now let us think about breakfast," says the greedy Queen.

"What dress shall I put on, mamma? the pink or the pea-green?" says Angelica. "Which do you think the dear Prince will like best?"

"Mrs. V.!" sings out the King from his dressing-room, "let us have sausages for breakfast! Remember we have Prince Bulbo staying with us!"

And they all went to get ready.

Nine o'clock came, and they were all in the breakfast-room, and no Prince Bulbo as yet. The urn was hissing and humming: the muffins were smoking—such a heap of muffins! the eggs were done, there was a pot of raspberry jam, and coffee, and a beautiful chicken and tongue on the side-table. Marmitonio the cook brought in the sausages. O, how nice they smelt!

"Where is Bulbo?" said the King. "John, where is his Royal Highness?"

John said he had a took up his Roilighnessesses shaving-water, and his clothes and things, and he wasn't in his room, which he sposed his Royliness was just stepped hout.

"Stepped out before breakfast in the snow! Impossible!" says the King, sticking his fork into a sausage. "My dear, take one. Angelica, won't you have a saveloy?" The Princess took one, being very fond of them; and at this moment Glumboso entered with Captain Hedzoff, both looking very much disturbed. "I am afraid your Majesty—" cries Glumboso. "No business before breakfast, Glum!" says the King. "Breakfast first, business next. Mrs. V., some more sugar!"

"Sire, I am afraid if we wait till after breakfast it will be too late," says Glumboso. "He—he—he'll be hanged at half-past nine."

"Don't talk about hanging and spoil my breakfast, you unkind vulgar man you," cries the Princess. "John, some mustard. Pray who is to be hanged?"

"Sire, it is the Prince," whispers Glumboso to the King.

"Talk about business after breakfast, I tell you!" says his Majesty, quite sulky.

"We shall have a war, Sire, depend on it," says the Minister. "His father, King Padella . . ."

"His father, King *who?*" says the King. "King Padella is not Giglio's father. My brother, King Savio, was Giglio's father."

"It's Prince Bulbo they are hanging, Sire, not Prince Giglio," says the Prime Minister.

"You told me to hang the Prince, and I took the ugly one," says Hedzoff. "I didn't, of course, think your Majesty intended to murder your own flesh and blood!"

The King for all reply flung the plate of sausages at Hedzoff's head. The Princess cried out Hee-karee-karee! and fell down in a fainting fit.

"Turn the cock of the urn upon her Royal Highness," said the King, and the boiling water gradually revived her. His Majesty looked at his watch, compared it by the clock in the parlour, and by that of the church in the square opposite; then he wound it up; then he looked at it again. "The great question is," says he, "am I fast or am I slow? If I'm slow, we may as well go on with breakfast. If I'm fast, why, there is just the possibility of saving Prince Bulbo. It's a doosid awkward mistake, and upon my word, Hedzoff, I have the greatest mind to have you hanged too."

"Sire, I did but my duty; a soldier has but his orders. I didn't expect after forty-seven years of faithful service that my sovereign would think of putting me to a felon's death!"

"A hundred thousand plagues upon you! Can't you see that while you are talking my Bulbo is being hung?" screamed the Princess.

"By Jove! she's always right, that girl, and I'm so absent," says the King, looking at his watch again. "Ha! Hark, there go the drums! What a doosid awkward thing though!"

"O Papa, you goose! Write the reprieve, and let me run with it," cries the Princess— and she got a sheet of paper, and pen and ink, and laid them before the King.

"Confound it! Where are my spectacles?" the Monarch exclaimed. "Angelica! Go up into my bed-room, look under my pillow, not your mamma's; there you'll see my keys. Bring them down to me, and—Well, well! what impetuous things these girls are!" Angelica was gone, and had run up panting to the bed-room, and found the keys, and was back again before the King had finished a muffin, "Now love," says he, "you must go all the way back for my desk, in which my spectacles are. If you *would* but have heard me out . . . . Be hanged to her. There she is off again. Angelica! ANGELICA!" When his Majesty called in his *loud* voice, she knew she must obey, and came back.

"My dear, when you go out of a room, how often have I told you, *shut the door.* That's a darling. That's all." At last the keys and the desk and the spectacles were got, and the King mended his pen, and signed his name to a reprieve, and Angelica ran with it as

swift as the wind. "You'd better stay, my love, and finish the muffins. There's no use going. Be sure it's too late. Hand me over that raspberry jam, please," said the Monarch. "Bong! Bawong! There goes the half hour. I knew it was."

Angelica ran, and ran, and ran, and ran. She ran up Fore Street, and down High Street, and through the Market-place, and down to the left, and over the bridge, and up the blind alley, and back again, and round by the Castle, and so along by the Haberdasher's on the right, opposite the lamp-post, and round the square, and she came—she came to the *Execution place*, where she saw Bulbo laying his head on the block!!! The executioner raised his axe, but at that moment the Princess came panting up and cried Reprieve. "Reprieve!" screamed the Princess. "Reprieve!" shouted all the people. Up the scaffold stairs she sprang, with the agility of a lighter of lamps; and flinging herself in Bulbo's arms, regardless of all ceremony, she cried out, "O my Prince! my lord! my love! my Bulbo! Thine Angelica has been in time to save thy precious existence, sweet rosebud; to prevent thy being nipped in thy young bloom! Had aught befallen thee, Angelica too had died, and welcomed death that joined her to her Bulbo."

"H'm! there's no accounting for tastes," said Bulbo, looking so very much puzzled and uncomfortable, that the Princess, in tones of tenderest strain, asked the cause of his disquiet.

"I tell you what it is, Angelica," said he, "since I came here, yesterday, there has been such a row, and disturbance, and quarrelling, and fighting, and chopping of heads off, and the deuce to pay, that I am inclined to go back to Crim Tartary."

"But with me as thy bride, my Bulbo! Though wherever thou art is Crim Tartary to me, my bold, my beautiful, my Bulbo!"

"Well, well, I suppose we must be married," says Bulbo. "Doctor, you came to read the Funeral Service—read the Marriage Service, will you? What must be, must. That will satisfy Angelica, and then, in the name of peace and quietness, do let us go back to breakfast."

Bulbo had carried a rose in his mouth all the time of the dismal ceremony. It was a fairy rose, and he was told by his mother that he ought never to part with it. So he had kept it between his teeth, even when he laid his poor head upon the block, hoping vaguely that some chance would turn up in his favour. As he began to speak to Angelica, he forgot about the rose, and of course it dropped out of his mouth. The romantic Princess instantly stooped and seized it. "Sweet rose!" she exclaimed, "that bloomed upon my Bulbo's lip, never, never will I part from thee!" and she placed it in her bosom. And you know Bulbo *couldn't* ask her to give the rose back again. And they went to breakfast; and as they walked, it appeared to Bulbo that Angelica became more exquisitely lovely every moment.

He was frantic until they were married; and now, strange to say, it was Angelica who didn't care about him! He knelt down, he kissed her hand, he prayed and begged; he cried with admiration; while she for her part said she really thought they might wait; it seemed to her he was not handsome any more—no, not at all, quite the reverse; and not clever, no, very stupid; and not well bred, like Giglio; no, on the contrary, dreadfully vul—

What, I cannot say, for King Valoroso roared out *"Pooh,* stuff!" in a terrible voice. "We will have no more of this shilly-shallying! Call the Archbishop, and let the Prince and Princess be married off-hand!"

So, married they were, and I am sure for my part I trust they will be happy.

X I I

How Betsinda Fled, and What Became of Her.

Betsinda wandered on and on, till she passed through the town gates, and so on the great Crim Tartary road, the very way on which Giglio too was going. "Ah!" thought she, as the diligence passed her, of which the conductor was blowing a delightful tune on his horn, "how I should like to be on that coach!" But the coach and the jingling horses were very soon gone. She little knew who was in it, though very likely she was thinking of him all the time.

Then came an empty cart, returning from market; and the driver being a kind man, and seeing such a very pretty girl trudging along the road with bare feet, most good-naturedly gave her a seat. He said he lived on the confines of the forest, where his old father was a woodman, and, if she liked, he would take her so far on her road. All roads were the same to little Betsinda, so she very thankfully took this one.

And the carter put a cloth round her bare feet, and gave her some bread and cold bacon, and was very kind to her. For all that she was very cold and melancholy. When after travelling on and on, evening came, and all the black pines were bending with

snow, and there, at last, was the comfortable light beaming in the woodman's windows; and so they arrived, and went into his cottage. He was an old man, and had a number of children, who were just at supper, with nice hot bread-and-milk, when their elder brother arrived with the cart. And they jumped and clapped their hands; for they were good children; and he had brought them toys from the town. And when they saw the pretty stranger, they ran to her, and brought her to the fire, and rubbed her poor little feet, and brought her bread-and-milk.

"Look, Father!" they said to the old woodman, "look at this poor girl, and see what pretty cold feet she has. They are as white as our milk! And look and see what an odd cloak she has, just like the bit of velvet that hangs up in our cupboard, and which you found that day the little cubs were killed by King Padella, in the forest! And look, why, bless us all! she has got round her neck just such another little shoe as that you brought home, and have shown us so often—a little blue velvet shoe!"

"What," said the old woodman, "What is all this about a shoe and a cloak?"

And Betsinda explained that she had been left, when quite a little child, at the town with this cloak and this shoe. And the persons who had taken care of her had—had been angry with her, for no fault, she hoped, of her own. And they had sent her away with her old clothes—and here, in fact, she was. She remembered having been in a forest—and perhaps it was a dream—it was so very odd and strange—having lived in a cave with lions there; and, before that, having lived in a very, very fine house, as fine as the King's, in the town.

When the woodman heard this, he was so astonished, it was quite curious to see how astonished he was. He went to his cupboard, and took out of a stocking a five-shilling piece of King Cavolfiore, and vowed it was exactly like the young woman. And then he produced the shoe and the piece of velvet which he had kept so long, and compared them with the things which Betsinda wore. In Betsinda's little shoe was written, "Hopkins, maker to the Royal Family," so in the other shoe was written, "Hopkins, maker to the Royal Family." In the inside of Betsinda's piece of cloak was embroidered, "PRIN ROSAL;" in the other piece of cloak was embroidered, "CESS BA. No. 246." So that when put together you read, "PRINCESS ROSALBA. No. 246."

On seeing this, the dear old woodman fell down on his knee, saying: "O my princess, O my gracious royal lady, O my rightful Queen of Crim Tartary,—I hail thee—I

acknowledge thee—I do thee homage!" And in token of his fealty, he rubbed his venerable nose three times on the ground, and put the Princess's foot on his head.

"Why," said she, "my good woodman, you must be a nobleman of my royal father's Court!" For in her lowly retreat, and under the name of Betsinda, HER MAJESTY, ROSALBA, Queen of Crim Tartary, had read of the customs of all foreign Courts and nations.

"Marry, indeed am I, my gracious liege—the poor Lord Spinachi, once—the humble woodman these fifteen years syne. Ever since the tyrant Padella (may ruin overtake the treacherous knave!) dismissed me from my post of First Lord."

"First Lord of the Toothpick and Joint Keeper of the Snuff-box? I mind me! Thou heldest these posts under our royal Sire. They are restored to thee, Lord Spinachi! I make thee knight of the second class of our Order of the Pumpkin (the first class being reserved for crowned heads alone). Rise, Marquis of Spinachi!" And with indescribable majesty, the Queen, who had no sword handy, waved the pewter spoon with which she had been taking her bread-and-milk, over the bald head of the old nobleman, whose tears absolutely made a puddle on the ground, and whose dear children went to bed that night Lords and Ladies Bartolomeo, Ubaldo, Catarina, and Ottavia degli Spinachi!

The acquaintance HER MAJESTY showed with the history, and *noble families* of her empire, was wonderful. "The House of Broccoli should remain faithful to us," she said; "they were ever welcome at our Court. Have the Articiocchi, as was their wont, turned to the Rising Sun? The family of Sauerkraut must sure be with us—they were ever welcome in the halls of King Cavolfiore." And so she went on enumerating quite a list of the nobility and gentry of Crim Tartary, so admirably had her Majesty profited by her studies while in exile.

The old Marquis of Spinachi said he could answer for them all; that the whole country groaned under Padella's tyranny, and longed to return to its rightful sovereign; and late as it was, he sent his children, who knew the forest well, to summon this nobleman and that; and when his eldest son, who had been rubbing the horse down and giving him his supper, came into the house for his own, the Marquis told him to put his boots on, and a saddle on the mare, and ride hither and thither to such and such people.

When the young man heard who his companion in the cart had been, he too knelt down and put her royal foot on his head; he too bedewed the ground with his tears; he was frantically in love with her, as everybody now was who saw her: so were the young Lords Bartolomeo and Ubaldo, who punched each other's little heads out of jealousy: and so, when they came from east and west at the summons of the Marquis degli Spinachi, were the Crim Tartar Lords who still remained faithful to the House of Cavolfiore. They were such very old gentlemen for the most part, that her Majesty never suspected their absurd passion, and went among them quite unaware of the havoc her beauty was causing, until an old blind Lord who had joined her party, told her what the truth was; after which, for fear of making the people too much in love with her, she always wore a veil. She went about privately, from one nobleman's castle to another: and they visited amongst themselves again, and had meetings, and composed proclamations and counter-proclamations, and distributed all the best places of the kingdom amongst one another, and selected who of the opposition party should be executed when the Queen came to her own. And so in about a year they were ready to move.

The party of Fidelity was in truth composed of very feeble old fogies for the most part; they went about the country waving their old swords and flags, and calling "God save the Queen!" and King Padella happening to be absent upon an invasion, they had their own way for a little, and to be sure the people were very enthusiastic whenever they saw the Queen; otherwise the vulgar took matters very quietly, for they said, as far as they could recollect, they were pretty well as much taxed in Cavolfiore's time, as now in Padella's.

XIII

How Queen Rosalba Came to the Castle of the Bold Count Hogginarmo.

Her Majesty, having indeed nothing else to give, made all her followers Knights of the Pumpkin, and Marquises, Earls, and Baronets; and they had a little court for her, and made her a little crown of gilt paper, and a robe of cotton velvet; and they quarrelled about the places to be given away in her court, and about rank and precedence and dignities;—you can't think how they quarrelled! The poor Queen was very tired of her honours before she had had them a month, and I dare say sighed sometimes even to be a lady's-maid again. But we must all do our duty in our respective stations, so the Queen resigned herself to perform hers.

We have said how it happened that none of the Usurper's troops came out to oppose this Army of Fidelity: it pottered along as nimbly as the gout of the principal commanders allowed: it consisted of twice as many officers as soldiers: and at length passed near the estates of one of the most powerful noblemen of the country, who had not declared for the Queen, but of whom her party had hopes, as he was always quarrelling with King Padella.

When they came close to his park gates, this nobleman sent to say he would wait upon her Majesty: he was a most powerful warrior, and his name was Count Hogginarmo, whose helmet it took two strong negroes to carry. He knelt down before her and said, "Madam and liege lady! it becomes the great nobles of the Crimean realm to show every outward sign of respect to the wearer of the Crown, whoever that may be. We testify to our own nobility in acknowledging yours. The bold Hogginarmo bends the knee to the first of the aristocracy of his country."

Rosalba said, "The bold Count of Hogginarmo was uncommonly kind." But she felt afraid of him, even while he was kneeling, and his eyes scowled at her from between his whiskers, which grew up to them.

"The first Count of the Empire, madam," he went on, "salutes the Sovereign. The Prince addresses himself to the not more noble lady! Madam, my hand is free, and I offer it, and my heart and my sword to your service! My three wives lie buried in my ancestral vaults. The third perished but a year since; and this heart pines for a consort! Deign to be mine, and I swear to bring to your bridal table the head of King Padella, the eyes and nose of his son Prince Bulbo, the right hand and ears of the usurping Sovereign of Paflagonia, which country shall thenceforth be an appanage to your—to *our* Crown! Say yes; Hogginarmo is not accustomed to be denied. Indeed I cannot contemplate the possibility of a refusal; for frightful will be the result; dreadful the murders; furious the devastations; horrible the tyranny; tremendous the tortures, misery, taxation, which the people of this realm will endure, if Hogginarmo's wrath be aroused! I see consent in your Majesty's lovely eyes—their glances fill my soul with rapture!"

"O, Sir!" Rosalba said, withdrawing her hand in great fright. "Your Lordship is exceedingly kind; but I am sorry to tell you that I have a prior attachment to a young gentleman by the name of—Prince—Giglio—and never—never can marry any one but him."

Who can describe Hogginarmo's wrath at this remark? Rising up from the ground, he ground his teeth so that fire flashed out of his mouth, from which at the same time issued remarks and language, so *loud, violent, and improper*, that this pen shall never repeat them! "R-r-r-r-r—Rejected! Fiends and perdition! The bold Hogginarmo rejected! All the world shall hear of my rage; and you, Madam, you above all shall rue it!" And kicking the two negroes before him, he rushed away, his whiskers streaming in the wind.

Her Majesty's Privy Council was in a dreadful panic when they saw Hogginarmo issue from the royal presence in such a towering rage, making footballs of the poor negroes—a panic which the events justified. They marched off from Hogginarmo's park very crestfallen; and in another half-hour they were met by that rapacious chieftain with a few of his followers, who cut, slashed, charged, whacked, banged and pommelled amongst them, took the Queen prisoner, and drove the Army of Fidelity to I don't know where.

Poor Queen! Hogginarmo, her conqueror, would not condescend to see her. "Get a horse-van!" he said to his grooms, "clap the hussey into it, and send her, with my compliments, to his Majesty King Padella."

Along with his lovely prisoner, Hogginarmo sent a letter full of servile compliments and loathsome flatteries to King Padella, for whose life, and that of his royal family, the *hypocritical humbug* pretended to offer the most fulsome prayers. And Hogginarmo promised speedily to pay his humble homage at his august master's throne, of which he begged leave to be counted the most loyal and constant defender. Such a *wary* old *bird* as King Padella was not to be caught by Master Hogginarmo's *chaff*, and we shall hear presently how the tyrant treated his upstart vassal. No, no; depend on't, two such rogues do not trust one another.

So this poor Queen was laid in the straw like Margery Daw, and driven along in the dark ever so many miles to the Court, where King Padella had now arrived, having

vanquished all his enemies, murdered most of them, and brought some of the richest into captivity with him for the purpose of torturing them and finding out where they had hidden their money.

Rosalba heard their shrieks and groans in the dungeon in which she was thrust; a most awful black hole, full of bats, rats, mice, toads, frogs, mosquitoes, bugs, fleas, serpents, and every kind of horror. No light was let into it, otherwise the gaolers might have seen her and fallen in love with her, as an owl that lived up in the roof of the tower did, and a cat, you know, who can see in the dark, and having set its green eyes on Rosalba, never would be got to go back to the turnkey's wife to whom it belonged. And the toads in the dungeon came and kissed her feet, and the vipers wound round her neck and arms, and never hurt her, so charming was this poor Princess in the midst of her misfortunes.

At last, after she had been kept in this place *ever so long,* the door of the dungeon opened, and the terrible KING PADELLA came in.

But what he said and did must be reserved for another Chapter, as we must now back to Prince Giglio.

XIV

What Became of Giglio.

T HE IDEA OF MARRYING such an old creature as Gruffanuff, frightened Prince Giglio so, that he ran up to his room, packed his trunks, fetched in a couple of porters, and was off to the diligence office in a twinkling.

It was well that he was so quick in his operations, did not dawdle over his luggage, and took the early coach, for as soon as the mistake about Prince Bulbo was found out, that cruel Glumboso sent up a couple of policemen to Prince Giglio's room, with orders that he should be carried to Newgate, and his head taken off before twelve o'clock. But the coach was out of the Paflagonian dominions before two o'clock; and I daresay the express that was sent after Prince Giglio did not ride very quick, for many people in Paflagonia had a regard for Giglio, as the son of their old sovereign; a Prince who, with all his weaknesses, was very much better than his brother the reigning, usurping, lazy, careless, passionate, tyrannical, reigning monarch. That Prince busied himself with the balls, fêtes, masquerades, hunting parties, and so forth, which he thought proper to give on occasion of his daughter's marriage to Prince Bulbo; and let us trust was not sorry in his own heart that his brother's son had escaped the scaffold.

It was very cold weather, and the snow was on the ground, and Giglio, who gave his name as simple Mr. Giles, was very glad to get a comfortable place on the coupé of the diligence, where he sat with the conductor and another gentleman. At the first stage from Blombodinga, as they stopped to change horses, there came up to the diligence a very ordinary, vulgar-looking woman, with a bag under her arm, who asked for a place. All the inside places were taken, and the young woman was informed that if she wished to travel, she must go upon the roof; and the passenger inside with Giglio (a rude person, I should think), put his head out of the window, and said, "Nice weather for travelling outside! I wish you a pleasant journey, my dear." The poor woman coughed very much, and Giglio pitied her. "I will give up my place to her," says he, "rather than she should travel in the cold air with that horrid cough." On which the vulgar traveller said, "*You'd* keep her warm, I am sure, if it's a *muff* she wants." On which Giglio pulled his nose, boxed his ears, hit him in the eye, and gave this vulgar person a warning never to call him *muff* again.

Then he sprang up gaily on to the roof of the diligence, and made himself very comfortable in the straw. The vulgar traveller got down only at the next station, and Giglio took his place again, and talked to the person next to him. She appeared to be a most agreeable, well-informed, and entertaining female. They travelled together till night, and she gave Giglio all sorts of things out of the bag which she carried, and which indeed seemed to contain the most wonderful collection of articles. He was thirsty—out there came a pint bottle of Bass's pale ale, and a silver mug! Hungry—she took out a cold fowl, some slices of ham, bread, salt, and a most delicious piece of cold plumpudding, and a little glass of brandy afterwards.

As they travelled, this plain looking, queer woman talked to Giglio on a variety of subjects, in which the poor Prince showed his ignorance as much as she did her capacity. He owned, with many blushes, how ignorant he was; on which the lady said, "My dear

Gigl—my good Mr. Giles, you are a young man, and have plenty of time before you.
You have nothing to do but to improve yourself. Who knows but that you may find use
for your knowledge some day? When—when you may be wanted at home, as some
people may be."

"Good Heavens, madam!" says he, "do you know me?"

"I know a number of funny things," says the lady. "I have been at some people's
christenings, and turned away from other folks' doors. I have seen some people spoilt
by good fortune, and others, as I hope, improved by hardship. I advise you to stay at
the town where the coach stops for the night. Stay there and study, and remember your
old friend to whom you were kind."

"And who is my old friend?" asked Giglio.

"When you want anything," says the lady, "look in this bag, which I leave to you as a
present, and be grateful to—"

"To whom, madam?" says he.

"To the Fairy Blackstick," says the lady, flying out of the window. And when Giglio
asked the conductor if he knew where the lady was?

"What lady?" says the man; "there has been no lady in this coach, except the old
woman, who got out at the last stage." And Giglio thought he had been dreaming. But
there was the bag which Blackstick had given him lying on his lap; and when he came to
the town he took it in his hand and went into the inn.

They gave him a very bad bed-room, and Giglio, when he woke in the morning,
fancying himself in the Royal Palace at home, called, "John, Charles, Thomas! My
chocolate—my dressing-gown—my slippers;" but nobody came. There was no bell, so he
went and bawled out for waiter on the top of the stairs.

The landlady came up, looking—looking like this—

"What are you a hollaring and a bellaring for here, young man?" says she.

"There's no warm water—no servants; my boots are not even cleaned."

"He, he! Clean 'em yourself," says the landlady. "You young students give yourselves pretty airs. I never heard such impudence."

"I'll quit the house this instant," says Giglio.

"The sooner the better, young man. Pay your bill and be off. All my rooms is wanted for gentlefolks, and not for such as you."

"You may well keep the Bear Inn," said Giglio. "You should have yourself painted as the sign."

The landlady of the Bear went away *growling*. And Giglio returned to his room, where the first thing he saw was the fairy bag lying on the table, which seemed to give a little hop as he came in. "I hope it has some breakfast in it," says Giglio, "for I have only a very little money left." But on opening the bag, what do you think was there? A blacking-brush and a pot of Warren's jet, and on the pot was written,

> "Poor young men their boots must black:
> Use me and cork me and put me back."

So Giglio laughed and blacked his boots, and put back the brush and the bottle into the bag.

When he had done dressing himself, the bag gave another little hop, and he went to it and took out—

1. A tablecloth and a napkin.
2. A sugar-basin full of the best loaf sugar.
4, 6, 8, 10. Two forks, two teaspoons, two knives, and a pair of sugar-tongs, and a butter-knife, all marked G.
11, 12, 13. A teacup, saucer, and slop-basin.
14. A jug full of delicious cream.
15. A canister with black tea and green.
16. A large tea-urn and boiling water.
17. A saucepan, containing three eggs nicely done.
18. A quarter of a pound of best Epping butter.
19. A brown loaf.

And if he hadn't enough now for a good breakfast, I should like to know who ever had one?

Giglio, having had his breakfast, popped all the things back into the bag, and went out looking for lodgings. I forgot to say that this celebrated university town was called Bosforo.

He took a modest lodging opposite the Schools, paid his bill at the inn, and went to his apartment with his trunk, carpet-bag, and not forgetting, we may be sure, his *other* bag.

When he opened his trunk, which the day before he had filled with his best clothes, he found it contained only books. And in the first of them which he opened there was written—

> "Clothes for the back, books for the head;
> Read, and remember them when they are read."

And in his bag, when Giglio looked in it, he found a student's cap and gown, a writing-book full of paper, an inkstand, pens, and a Johnson's dictionary, which was very useful to him, as his spelling had been sadly neglected.

So he sat down and worked away, very, very hard for a whole year, during which "Mr. Giles" was quite an example to all the students in the University of Bosforo. He never got into any riots or disturbances. The Professors all spoke well of him, and the students liked him, too; so that, when at examination, he took all the prizes, viz:—

The Spelling Prize	The French Prize
The Writing Prize	The Arithmetic Prize
The History Prize	The Latin Prize
The Catechism Prize	The Good Conduct Prize,

all his fellow students said, "Hurray! Hurray for Giles! Giles is the boy—the student's joy! Hurray for Giles!" And he brought quite a quantity of medals, crowns, books, and tokens of distinction home to his lodgings.

One day after the Examinations, as he was diverting himself at a coffee house, with two friends—(Did I tell you that in his bag, every Saturday night, he found just enough to pay his bills, with a guinea over, for pocket-money! Didn't I tell you? Well, he did, as sure as twice twenty makes forty-five)—he chanced to look in the "Bosforo Chronicle," and read off quite easily (for he could spell, read, and write the longest words now) the following—

"ROMANTIC CIRCUMSTANCE.—One of the most extraordinary adventures that we have ever heard has set the neighbouring country of Crim Tartary in a state of great excitement.

"It will be remembered that when the present revered sovereign of Crim Tartary, his Majesty King *Padella*, took possession of the throne, after having vanquished, in the terrific battle of Blunderbusco, the late King *Cavolfiore*, that Prince's only child, the Princess Rosalba, was not found in the royal palace, of which King Padella took possession, and, it was said, had strayed into the forest (being abandoned by all her attendants), where she had been eaten up by those ferocious lions, the last pair of which were captured some time since, and brought to the Tower, after killing several hundred persons.

"His Majesty King Padella, who has the kindest heart in the world, was grieved at the accident which had occurred to the harmless little Princess, for whom his Majesty's known benevolence would certainly have provided a fitting establishment. But her death seemed to be certain. The mangled remains of a cloak, and a little shoe, were found in the forest, during a hunting party, in which the intrepid sovereign of Crim Tartary slew two of the lions' cubs with his own spear. And these interesting relics of an innocent little creature were carried home and kept by their finder, the Baron Spinachi, formerly an officer in Cavolfiore's household. The Baron was disgraced in consequence of his known legitimist opinions, and has lived for some time in the humble capacity of a wood-cutter, in a forest on the outskirts of the Kingdom of Crim Tartary.

"Last Tuesday week Baron Spinachi and a number of gentlemen attached to the former dynasty, appeared in arms, crying, 'God save Rosalba, the First Queen of Crim Tartary!' and surrounding a lady whom report describes as '*beautiful exceedingly*.' Her history *may* be authentic, *is* certainly most romantic.

"The personage calling herself Rosalba states that she was brought out of the forest, fifteen years since, by a lady in a car drawn by dragons (this account is certainly *improbable*), that she was left in the Palace Garden of Blombodinga, where her Royal Highness the Princess Angelica, now married to his Royal Highness Bulbo, Crown Prince of Crim Tartary, found the child, and, with *that elegant benevolence* which has always distinguished the heiress of the throne of Paflagonia, gave the little outcast a *shelter and a home!* Her parentage not being known, and her garb very humble, the foundling was educated in the Palace in a menial capacity, under the name of *Betsinda*.

"She did not give satisfaction, and was dismissed, carrying with her, certainly, part of a mantle and a shoe, which she had on when first found. According to her statement she quitted Blombodinga about a year ago, since which time she has been with the Spinachi family. On the very same morning the Prince Giglio, nephew to the King of

Paflagonia, a young Prince whose character for *talent* and *order* were, to say truth, *none of the highest*, also quitted Blombodinga, and has not been since heard of!"

"What an extraordinary story!" said Smith and Jones, two young students, Giglio's especial friends.

"Ha! what is this?" Giglio went on, reading—

"Second Edition, Express.—We hear that the troop under Baron Spinachi has been surrounded, and utterly routed, by General Count Hogginarmo, and the *soi-disant* Princess is sent a prisoner to the capital."

"University News.—Yesterday, at the Schools, the distinguished young student, Mr. Giles, read a Latin oration, and was complimented by the Chancellor of Bosforo, Dr. Prugnaro, with the highest University honour—the wooden spoon."

"Never mind that stuff," says *Giles*, greatly disturbed. "Come home with me, my friends. Gallant Smith! intrepid Jones! friends of my studies—partakers of my academic toils—I have that to tell shall astonish your honest minds."

"Go it, old boy!" cried the impetuous Smith.

"Talk away, my buck!" says Jones, a lively fellow.

With an air of indescribable dignity, Giglio checked their natural, but no more seemly, familiarity. "Jones, Smith, my good friends," said the Prince, "disguise is henceforth useless; I am no more the humble student Giles, I am the descendant of a royal line."

"*Atavis edite regibus*, I know, old co—," cried Jones, he was going to say old cock, but a flash from the royal eye again awed him.

"Friends," continued the Prince, "I am that Giglio, I am in fact, Paflagonia. Rise, Smith, and kneel not in the public street. Jones, thou true heart! My faithless uncle, when I was a baby, filched from me that brave crown my father left me, bred me, all young and careless of my rights, like unto hapless Hamlet, Prince of Denmark; and had I any thoughts about my wrongs, soothed me with promises of near redress. I should espouse his daughter young Angelica; we two indeed should reign in Paflagonia. His words were false—false as Angelica's heart!—false as Angelica's hair, colour, front teeth! She looked with her skew eyes upon young Bulbo, Crim Tartary's stupid heir, and she preferred him. 'Twas then I turned my eyes upon Betsinda—Rosalba, as she now is. And I saw in her the blushing sum of all perfection; the pink of maiden modesty; the nymph that my fond heart had ever woo'd in dreams," &c., &c.

(I don't give this speech, which was very fine, but very long; and though Smith and Jones knew nothing about the circumstances, my dear reader does, so I go on.)

The Prince and his young friends hastened home to his apartment, highly excited by the intelligence, as no doubt by the *royal narrator's* admirable manner of recounting it, and they ran up to his room where he had worked so hard at his books.

On his writing-table was his bag, grown so long, that the Prince could not help remarking it. He went to it, opened it, and what do you think he found in it?

A splendid long, gold-handled, red-velvet-scabbarded, cut-and-thrust sword, and on the sheath was embroidered "ROSALBA FOR EVER!"

He drew out the sword, which flashed and illuminated the whole room, and called out, "Rosalba for ever!" Smith and Jones following him, but quite respectfully this time, and taking the time from his Royal Highness.

And now his trunk opened with a sudden pong, and out there came three ostrich feathers in a gold crown, surrounding a beautiful shining steel helmet, a cuirass, a pair of spurs, finally a complete suit of armour.

The books on Giglio's shelves were all gone. Where there had been some great dictionaries, Giglio's friend found two pairs of Jack boots labelled "Lieutenant Smith," "—Jones Esq.," which fitted them to a nicety. Besides, there were helmets, back and breast plates, swords, &c., just like in Mr. G. P. R. James's novels; and that evening three cavaliers might have been seen issuing from the gates of Bosforo, in whom the porters, proctors, &c., never thought of recognising the young Prince and his friends.

They got horses at a livery stable-keeper's, and never drew bridle until they reached the last town on the frontier before you come to Crim Tartary. Here, as their animals were tired, and the cavaliers hungry, they stopped and refreshed at an hostel. I could make a chapter of this if I were like some writers, but I like to cram my measure tight down, you see, and give you a great deal for your money, and in a word they had some bread and cheese and ale up stairs on the balcony of the inn. As they were drinking, drums and trumpets sounded nearer and nearer, the market-place was filled with soldiers, and his Royal Highness looking forth, recognised the Paflagonian banners, and the Paflagonian national air which the bands were playing.

The troops all made for the tavern at once, and as they came up Giglio exclaimed, on beholding their leader, "Whom do I see? Yes! No! It is, it is! Phoo! No, it can't be! Yes! It is my friend, my gallant faithful veteran, Captain Hedzoff! Ho! Hedzoff! Knowest thou not thy Prince, thy Giglio? Good Corporal, methinks we once were friends. Ha, Sergeant, an my memory serves me right, we have had many a bout at singlestick."

"I'faith, we have, a many, good my Lord," says the Sergeant.

"Tell me, what means this mighty armament," continued his Royal Highness from the balcony, "and whither march my Paflagonians?"

Hedzoff's head fell. "My Lord," he said, "we march as the allies of great Padella, Crim Tartary's monarch."

"Crim Tartary's usurper, gallant Hedzoff! Crim Tartary's grim tyrant, honest Hedzoff!" said the Prince, on the balcony, quite sarcastically.

"A soldier, Prince, must needs obey his orders: mine are to help his Majesty Padella. And also (though alack that I should say it!) to seize wherever I should light upon him—"

"First catch your hare! ha, Hedzoff!" exclaimed his Royal Highness.

"—On the body of *Giglio*, whilome Prince of Paflagonia," Hedzoff went on, with indescribable emotion. "My Prince, give up your sword without ado. Look! we are thirty thousand men to one!"

"Give up my sword! Giglio give up his sword!" cried the Prince; and stepping well forward on to the balcony, the royal youth, *without preparation*, delivered a speech so magnificent, that no report can do justice to it. It was all in blank verse, (in which, from this time, he invariably spoke, as more becoming his majestic station). It lasted for three days and three nights, during which not a single person who heard him was tired, or remarked the difference between daylight and dark. The soldiers only cheering tremendously, when occasionally, once in nine hours, the Prince paused to suck an orange, which Jones took out of the bag. He explained, in terms which we say we shall not attempt to convey, the whole history of the previous transaction, and his determination not only not to give up his sword, but to assume his rightful crown; and at the end of this extraordinary, this truly *gigantic* effort, Captain Hedzoff flung up his helmet, and cried, "Hurray! Hurray! Long live King Giglio!"

Such were the consequences of having employed his time well at College!

When the excitement had ceased, beer was ordered out for the army, and their Sovereign himself did not disdain a little! And now it was with some alarm that Captain Hedzoff told him his division was only the advance guard of the Paflagonian contingent,

hastening to King Padella's aid. The main force being a day's march in the rear under
his Royal Highness Prince Bulbo.

"We will wait here, good friend, to beat the Prince," his Majesty said, "and *then* will
make his royal Father wince."

X V

We Return to Rosalba.

K ING PADELLA made very similar proposals to Rosalba to those which she had received
from the various Princes who, as we have seen, had fallen in love with her. His Majesty
was a widower, and offered to marry his fair captive that instant, but she declined his
invitation in her usual polite gentle manner, stating that Prince Giglio was her love, and
that any other union was out of the question. Having tried tears and supplications in
vain, this violent-tempered monarch menaced her with threats and tortures; but she
declared she would rather suffer all these than accept the hand of her father's murderer,
who left her finally, uttering the most awful imprecations, and bidding her prepare for
death on the following morning.

All night long the King spent in advising how he should get rid of this obdurate
young creature. Cutting off her head was much too easy a death for her; hanging was so
common in his Majesty's dominions that it no longer afforded him any sport: finally, he
bethought himself of a pair of fierce lions which had lately been sent to him as presents,
and he determined, with these ferocious brutes, to hunt poor Rosalba down. Adjoining
his castle was an amphitheatre where the Prince indulged in bull-baiting, rat-hunting,
and other ferocious sports. The two lions were kept in a cage under this place; their
roaring might be heard over the whole city, the inhabitants of which, I am sorry to say,
thronged in numbers to see a poor young lady gobbled up by two wild beasts.

The King took his place in the royal box, having the officers of the Court around and
the Count Hogginarmo by his side, upon whom his Majesty was observed to look very
fiercely; the fact is, royal spies had told the monarch of Hogginarmo's behaviour, his
proposals to Rosalba, and his offer to fight for the crown. Black as thunder looked King
Padella at this proud noble, as they sat in the front seats of the theatre waiting to see the
tragedy whereof poor Rosalba was to be the heroine.

At length that Princess was brought out in her night-gown, with all her beautiful hair
falling down her back, and looking so pretty that even the beef-eaters and keepers of
the wild animals wept plentifully at seeing her. And she walked with her poor little feet
(only luckily the arena was covered with sawdust), and went and leaned up against a
great stone in the centre of the amphitheatre, round which the Court and the people
were seated in boxes with bars before them, for fear of the great, fierce, red-maned,
black-throated, long-tailed, roaring, bellowing, rushing lions. And now the gates were
opened, and with a wurrawarrurawarar two great lean, hungry, roaring lions rushed

out of their den, where they had been kept for three weeks on nothing but a little toast-and-water, and dashed straight up to the stone where poor Rosalba was waiting. Commend her to your patron saints, all you kind people, for she is in a dreadful state.

There was a hum and a buzz all through the circus, and the fierce King Padella even felt a little compassion. But Count Hogginarmo, seated by his Majesty, roared out, "Hurray! Now for it! Soo-soo-soo!" that nobleman being uncommonly angry still at Rosalba's refusal of him.

But O strange event! O remarkable circumstance! O extraordinary coincidence, which I am sure none of you could *by any possibility* have divined! When the lions came to Rosalba, instead of devouring her with their great teeth, it was with kisses they gobbled her up! They licked her pretty feet, they nuzzled their noses in her lap, they moo'd, they seemed to say, "Dear, dear sister, don't you recollect your brothers in the forest?" And she put her pretty white arms round their tawny necks, and kissed them.

King Padella was immensely astonished. The Count Hogginarmo was extremely disgusted. "Pooh!" the Count cried. "Gammon!" exclaimed his Lordship. "These lions are tame beasts come from Wombwell's or Astley's. It is a shame to put people off in this way. I believe they are little boys dressed up in door-mats. They are no lions at all."

"Ha!" said the King, "you dare to say 'gammon' to your Sovereign, do you? These lions are no lions at all, arn't they? Ho! my beef-eaters! Ho! my body-guard! Take this Count Hogginarmo and fling him into the circus! Give him a sword and buckler, let him keep his armour on, and his weather-eye out, and fight these lions."

The haughty Hogginarmo laid down his opera-glass, and looked scowling round at the King and his attendants. "Touch me not, dogs!" he said, "or by St. Nicholas the Elder, I will gore you! Your Majesty thinks Hogginarmo is afraid? No, not of a hundred thousand lions! Follow me down into the circus, King Padella, and match thyself against one of yon brutes. Thou darest not. Let them both come on, then!" And opening a grating of the box, he jumped lightly down into the circus.

Wurra wurra wurra wur-aw-aw-aw! ! !
In about two minutes
The Count Hogginarmo was
GOBBLED UP
by
those lions,
bones, boots, and all,
and
There was an
End of him.

At this, the King said, "Serve him right, the rebellious ruffian! And now, as those lions won't eat that young woman—"

"Let her off!—let her off!" cried the crowd.

"NO!" roared the King. "Let the beef-eaters go down and chop her into small pieces. If the lions defend her, let the archers shoot them to death. That hussey shall die in tortures!"

"A-a-ah!" cried the crowd. "Shame! shame!"

"Who dares cry out shame?" cried the furious potentate (so little can tyrants command their passions). "Fling any scoundrel who says a word down among the lions!" I warrant you there was a dead silence then, which was broken by a Pang arang pang pangkarangpang; and a Knight and a Herald rode in the farther end of the circus. The Knight, in full armour, with his vizor up, and bearing a letter on the point of his lance.

"Ha!" exclaimed the King, "by my fay, 'tis Elephant and Castle, pursuivant of my brother of Paflagonia; and the Knight, an my memory serves me, is the gallant Captain Hedzoff! What news from Paflagonia, gallant Hedzoff? Elephant and Castle, beshrew me, thy trumpeting must have made thee thirsty. What will my trusty herald like to drink?"

"Bespeaking first safe conduct from your Lordship," said Captain Hedzoff, "before we take a drink of anything, permit us to deliver our King's message."

"My Lordship, Ha!" said Crim Tartary, frowning terrifically. "That title soundeth strange in the anointed ears of a crowned King. Straightway speak out your message, Knight and Herald!"

Reining up his charger in a most elegant manner close under the King's balcony, Hedzoff turned to the herald, and bade him begin.

Elephant and Castle, dropping his trumpet over his shoulder, took a large sheet of paper out of his hat, and began to read:—

"O Yes! O Yes! O Yes! Know all men by these presents, that we, Giglio, King of Paflagonia, Grand Duke of Cappadocia, Sovereign Prince of Turkey and the Sausage Islands, having assumed our rightful throne and title, long time falsely borne by our usurping Uncle, styling himself King of Paflagonia,—"

"Ha!" growled Padella.

"Hereby summon the false traitor, Padella, calling himself King of Crim Tartary,"—

The King's curses were dreadful. "Go on, Elephant and Castle!" said the intrepid Hedzoff.

"—To release from cowardly imprisonment his liege lady and rightful Sovereign, Rosalba, Queen of Crim Tartary, and restore her to her royal throne: in default of which, I, Giglio, proclaim the said Padella sneak, traitor, humbug, usurper, and coward. I challenge him to meet me, with fists or with pistols, with battle-axe or sword, with blunderbuss or singlestick, alone or at the head of his army, on foot or on horseback; and will prove my words upon his wicked ugly body!"

"God save the King!" said Captain Hedzoff, executing a demivolte, two semilunes, and three caracols.

"Is that all?" said Padella, with the terrific calm of concentrated fury.

"That, sir, is all my royal master's message. Here is his Majesty's letter in autograph, and here is his glove, and if any gentleman of Crim Tartary chooses to find fault with his Majesty's expressions, I, Kutasoff Hedzoff, Captain of the Guard, am very much at his service," and he waved his lance, and looked at the assembly all round.

"And what says my good brother of Paflagonia, my dear son's father-in-law, to this rubbish?" asked the King.

"The King's uncle hath been deprived of the crown he unjustly wore," said Hedzoff gravely. "He and his ex-minister, Glumboso, are now in prison waiting the sentence of my royal master. After the battle of Bombardaro—"

"Of what?" asked the surprised Padella.

"Of Bombardaro, where my liege, his present Majesty, would have performed prodigies of valour, but that the whole of his uncle's army came over to our side, with the exception of Prince Bulbo."

"Ah! my boy, my boy, my Bulbo was no traitor!" cried Padella.

"Prince Bulbo, far from coming over to us, ran away, sir; but I caught him. The Prince is a prisoner in our army, and the most terrific tortures await him if a hair of the Princess Rosalba's head is injured."

"Do they?" exclaimed the furious Padella, who was now perfectly *livid* with rage. "Do they indeed? So much the worse for Bulbo. I've twenty sons as lovely each as Bulbo. Not one but is as fit to reign as Bulbo. Whip, whack, flog, starve, rack, punish, torture Bulbo—break all his bones—roast him or flay him alive—pull all his pretty teeth out one by one! But justly dear as Bulbo is to me,—Joy of my eyes, fond treasure of my soul!—Ha, ha, ha, ha! revenge is dearer still. Ho! torturers, rack-men, executioners—light up the fires and make the pincers hot! get lots of boiling lead!—Bring out Rosalba!"

XVI

How Hedzoff Rode Back Again to King Giglio.

CAPTAIN HEDZOFF rode away when King Padella uttered this cruel command, having done his duty in delivering the message with which his royal master had entrusted him. Of course he was very sorry for Rosalba, but what could he do?

So he returned to King Giglio's camp, and found the young monarch in a disturbed state of mind, smoking cigars in the royal tent. His Majesty's agitation was not appeased by the news that was brought by his ambassador. "The brutal ruthless ruffian royal wretch!" Giglio exclaimed. "As England's poesy has well remarked, 'The man that lays his hand upon a woman, save in the way of kindness, is a villain.' Ha, Hedzoff?"

"That he is, your Majesty," said the attendant.

"And didst thou see her flung into the oil? and didn't the soothing oil—the emollient oil, refuse to boil, good Hedzoff—and to spoil the fairest lady ever eyes did look on?"

"Faith, good my liege, I had no heart to look and see a beauteous lady boiling down; I took your royal message to Padella, and bore his back to you. I told him you would hold Prince Bulbo answerable. He only said that he had twenty sons as good as Bulbo, and forthwith he bade the ruthless executioners proceed."

"O cruel father—O unhappy son," cried the King. "Go, some of you, and bring Prince Bulbo hither."

Bulbo was brought in chains, looking very uncomfortable. Though a prisoner, he had been tolerably happy, perhaps because his mind was at rest, and all the fighting was over, and he was playing at marbles with his guards, when the King sent for him.

"O, my poor Bulbo," said his Majesty, with looks of infinite compassion, "hast thou heard the news (for you see Giglio wanted to break the thing gently to the Prince), thy brutal father has condemned Rosalba—p-p-p-ut her to death, P-p-p-prince Bulbo!"

"What, killed Betsinda, Boo-hoo-hoo," cried out Bulbo, "Betsinda! pretty Betsinda! dear Betsinda! She was the dearest little girl in the world. I love her better twenty thousand times even than Angelica," and he went on expressing his grief in so hearty and unaffected a manner, that the King was quite touched by it, and said, shaking Bulbo's hand, that he wished he had known Bulbo sooner.

Bulbo, quite unconsciously, and meaning for the best, offered to come and sit with his Majesty, and smoke a cigar with him, and console him. The *royal kindness* supplied Bulbo with a cigar; he had not had one, he said, since he was taken prisoner.

And now think what must have been the feelings of the most *merciful of monarchs*, when he informed his prisoner that, in consequence of King Padella's *cruel and dastardly behaviour* to Rosalba, Prince Bulbo must instantly be executed! The noble Giglio could not restrain his tears, nor could the Grenadiers, nor the officers, nor could Bulbo himself, when the matter was explained to him, and he was brought to understand that his Majesty's promise, of course, was *above every* thing, and Bulbo must submit. So poor Bulbo was led out. Hedzoff trying to console him, by pointing out that if he had won the battle of Bombardaro, he might have hanged Prince Giglio. "Yes! But that is no comfort to me now!" said poor Bulbo; nor indeed was it, poor fellow.

He was told the business would be done the next morning at eight, and was taken

back to his dungeon, where every attention was paid to him. The gaoler's wife sent him tea, and the turnkey's daughter begged him to write his name in her album, where a many gentlemen had wrote it on like occasions! "Bother your album!" says Bulbo. The Undertaker came and measured him for the handsomest coffin which money could buy—even this didn't console Bulbo. The Cook brought him dishes which he once used to like; but he wouldn't touch them: he sat down and began writing an adieu to Angelica, as the clock kept always ticking, and the hands drawing nearer to next morning. The Barber came in at night, and offered to shave him for the next day. Prince Bulbo kicked him away, and went on writing a few words to Princess Angelica, as the clock kept always ticking, and the hands hopping nearer and nearer to next morning. He got up on the top of a hat-box, on the top of a chair, on the top of his bed, on the top of his table, and looked out to see whether he might escape as the clock kept always ticking and the hands drawing nearer, and nearer, and nearer.

But looking out of the window was one thing, and jumping another: and the town clock struck seven. So he got into bed for a little sleep, but the gaoler came and woke him, and said, "Git up, your Royal Ighness, if you please, it's *ten minutes to eight.*"

So poor Bulbo got up: he had gone to bed in his clothes (the lazy boy), and he shook himself, and said he didn't mind about dressing, or having any breakfast, thank you; and he saw the soldiers who had come for him. "Lead on!" he said; and they led the way, deeply affected; and they came into the courtyard, and out into the square, and there was King Giglio come to take leave of him, and his Majesty most kindly shook hands with him, and the *gloomy procession* marched on:—when hark!

Haw—wurraw—wurraw—aworr!

A roar of wild beasts was heard. And who should come riding into the town, frightening away the boys, and even the beadle and policeman, but ROSALBA!

The fact is, that when Captain Hedzoff entered into the court of Snapdragon Castle, and was discoursing with King Padella, the Lions made a dash at the open gate, gobbled up the six beef-eaters in a jiffy, and away they went with Rosalba on the back of one of them, and they carried her, turn and turn about, till they came to the city where Prince Giglio's army was encamped.

When the KING heard of the QUEEN'S arrival, you may think how he rushed out of his breakfast-room to hand her Majesty off her Lion! The Lions were grown as fat as Pigs

now, having had Hogginarmo and all those beef-eaters, and were so tame, anybody might pat them.

While Giglio knelt (most gracefully) and helped the Princess, Bulbo, for his part, rushed up and kissed the Lion. He flung his arms round the forest monarch; he hugged him, and laughed and cried for joy. "O you darling old beast, O, how glad I am to see you, and the dear, dear Bets—that is, Rosalba."

"What, is it you? poor Bulbo," said the Queen. "O, how glad I am to see you;" and she gave him her hand to kiss. King Giglio slapped him most kindly on the back, and said, "Bulbo, my boy, I am delighted, for your sake, that her Majesty has arrived."

"So am I," said Bulbo; "and *you know why*." Captain Hedzoff here came up. "Sire, it is half-past eight: shall we proceed with the execution?"

"Execution, what for?" asked Bulbo.

"An officer only knows his orders," replied Captain Hedzoff, showing his warrant, on which his Majesty King Giglio smilingly said, "Prince Bulbo was reprieved this time," and most graciously invited him to breakfast.

X V I I

How a Tremendous Battle Took Place, and Who Won It.

As soon as King Padella heard, what we know already, that his victim, the lovely Rosalba, had escaped him, his Majesty's fury knew no bounds, and he pitched the Lord Chancellor, Lord Chamberlain, and every officer of the crown whom he could set eyes on, into the cauldron of boiling oil prepared for the Princess. Then he ordered out his whole army, horse, foot, and artillery; and set forth at the head of an innumerable host, and I should think twenty thousand drummers, trumpeters, and fifers.

King Giglio's advanced guard, you may be sure, kept that monarch acquainted with the enemy's dealings, and he was in no wise disconcerted. He was much too polite to alarm the Princess, his lovely guest, with any unnecessary rumours of battles impending; on the contrary, he did everything to amuse and divert her; gave her a most elegant breakfast, dinner, lunch, and got up a ball for her that evening, when he danced with her every single dance.

Poor Bulbo was taken into favour again, and allowed to go quite free now. He had new clothes given him, was called "My good cousin" by his Majesty, and was treated with the greatest distinction by everybody. But it was easy to see he was very melancholy. The fact is, the sight of Betsinda, who looked perfectly lovely in an elegant new dress, set poor Bulbo frantic in love with her again. And he never thought about Angelica, now Princess Bulbo, whom he had left at home, and who, as we know, did not care much about him.

The King, dancing the twenty-fifth polka with Rosalba, remarked with wonder the ring she wore; and then Rosalba told him how she had got it from Gruffanuff, who no doubt had picked it up when Angelica flung it away.

"Yes," says the Fairy Blackstick, who had come to see the young people, and who had very likely certain plans regarding them. "That ring I gave the Queen, Giglio's mother, who was not, saving your presence, a very wise woman; it is enchanted, and whoever wears it looks beautiful in the eyes of the world. I made poor Prince Bulbo, when he was christened, the present of a rose which made him look handsome while he had it; but he gave it to Angelica, who instantly looked beautiful again, whilst Bulbo relapsed into his natural plainness."

"Rosalba needs no ring, I am sure," says Giglio, with a low bow. "She is beautiful enough, in my eyes, without any enchanted aid."

"O, sir!" said Rosalba.

"Take off the ring and try," said the King, and resolutely drew the ring off her finger. In *his* eyes she looked just as handsome as before!

The King was thinking of throwing the ring away, as it was so dangerous and made all the people so mad about Rosalba; but being a Prince of great humour, and good-humour, too, he cast eyes upon a poor youth who happened to be looking on very disconsolately, and said—

"Bulbo, my poor lad! come and try on this ring. The Princess Rosalba makes it a present to you." The magic properties of this ring were uncommonly strong, for no sooner had Bulbo put it on, but lo and behold, he appeared a personable, agreeable young Prince enough—with a fine complexion, fair hair, rather stout, and with bandy legs; but these were encased in such a beautiful pair of yellow morocco boots that nobody remarked them. And Bulbo's spirits rose up almost immediately after he had looked in the glass, and he talked to their Majesties in the most lively, agreeable manner, and danced opposite the Queen with one of the prettiest maids of honour, and after looking at her Majesty, could not help saying—"How very odd; she is very pretty, but not so *extraordinarily* handsome." "Oh no, by no means!" says the Maid of Honour.

"But what care I, dear sir," says the Queen, who overheard them, "if *you* think I am good-looking enough?"

His Majesty's glance in reply to this affectionate speech was such that no painter could draw it. And the Fairy Blackstick said, "Bless you, my darling children! Now you are united and happy; and now you see what I said from the first, that a little misfortune has done you both good. *You*, Giglio, had you been bred in prosperity, would scarcely have learned to read or write—you would have been idle and extravagant, and could not have been a good King as you now will be. You, Rosalba, would have been so flattered, that your little head might have been turned like Angelica's, who thought herself too good for Giglio."

"As if anybody could be good enough for *him*," cried Rosalba.

"Oh, you, you darling!" says Giglio. And so she was; and he was just holding out his arms in order to give her a hug before the whole company, when a messenger came rushing in, and said, "My Lord, the enemy!"

"To arms!" cries Giglio.

"Oh, Mercy!" says Rosalba, and fainted of course. He snatched one kiss from her lips, and rushed *forth to the field* of battle!

The Fairy had provided King Giglio with a suit of armour, which was not only embroidered all over with jewels, and blinding to your eyes to look at, but was water-proof, gun-proof, and sword-proof; so that in the midst of the very hottest battles his Majesty rode about as calmly as if he had been a British Grenadier at Alma. Were I engaged in fighting for my country, *I* should like such a suit of armour as Prince Giglio wore; but, you know, he was a Prince of a fairy tale, and they always have these wonderful things.

Besides the fairy armour, the Prince had a fairy horse, which would gallop at any pace you please; and a fairy sword, which would lengthen, and run through a whole regiment of enemies at once. With such a weapon at command, I wonder, for my part, he thought of ordering his army out; but forth they all came, in magnificent new uniforms; Hedzoff and the Prince's two college friends each commanding a division, and his Majesty prancing in person at the head of them all.

Ah! if I had the pen of a Sir Archibald Alison, my dear friends, would I not now entertain you with the account of a most tremendous shindy? Should not fine blows be struck? dreadful wounds be delivered? arrows darken the air? cannon balls crash through the battalions? cavalry charge infantry? infantry pitch into cavalry? bugles blow; drums beat; horses neigh; fifes sing; soldiers roar, swear, hurray; officers shout out, "Forward, my men!" "This way, lads!" "Give it 'em, boys." "Fight for King Giglio, and the cause of right!" "King Padella for ever!" Would I not describe all this, I say, and in the very finest language, too? But this humble pen does not possess the skill necessary for the description of combats. In a word, the overthrow of King Padella's army was so

complete, that if they had been Russians you could not have wished them to be more utterly smashed and confounded.

As for that usurping monarch, having performed acts of valour much more considerable than could be expected of a royal ruffian and usurper, who had such a bad cause, and who was so cruel to women,—as for King Padella, I say, when his army ran away, the King ran away too, kicking his first general, Prince Punchikoff, from his saddle, and galloping away on the Prince's horse, having, indeed, had twenty-five or twenty-six of his own shot under him. Hedzoff coming up, and finding Punchikoff down, as you may imagine, very speedily disposed of *him*. Meanwhile King Padella was scampering off as hard as his horse could lay legs to ground. Fast as he scampered, I promise you somebody else galloped faster; and that individual, as no doubt you are aware, was the Royal Giglio, who kept bawling out, "Stay, traitor! Turn, miscreant, and defend thyself! Stand, tyrant, coward, ruffian, royal wretch, till I cut thy ugly head from thy usurping shoulders!" And, with his fairy sword, which elongated itself at will, his Majesty kept poking and prodding Padella in the back, until that wicked monarch roared with anguish.

When he was fairly brought to bay, Padella turned and dealt Prince Giglio a prodigious crack over the sconce with his battle-axe, a most enormous weapon, which had cut down I don't know how many regiments in the course of the afternoon. But, Law bless you! though the blow fell right down on his Majesty's helmet, it made no more impression than if Padella had struck him with a pat of butter: his battle-axe crumpled up in Padella's hand, and the Royal Giglio laughed for very scorn at the impotent efforts of that atrocious usurper.

At the ill success of his blow the Crim Tartar monarch was justly irritated. "If," says he to Giglio, "you ride a fairy horse, and wear fairy armour, what on earth is the use of my hitting you? I may as well give myself up a prisoner at once. Your Majesty won't, I suppose, be so mean as to strike a poor fellow who can't strike again?"

The justice of Padella's remark struck the magnanimous Giglio. "Do you yield yourself a prisoner, Padella?" says he.

"Of course, I do," says Padella.

"Do you acknowledge Rosalba as your rightful Queen, and give up the crown and all your treasures to your rightful mistress?"

"If I must I must," says Padella, who was naturally very sulky.

By this time King Giglio's aides-de-camp had come up, whom his Majesty ordered to bind the prisoner. And they tied his hands behind him, and bound his legs tight under his horse, having set him with his face to the tail; and in this fashion he was led back to King Giglio's quarters, and thrust into the very dungeon where young Bulbo had been confined.

Padella (who was a very different person in the depth of his distress, to Padella, the proud wearer of the Crim Tartar crown), now most affectionately and earnestly asked to see his son—his dear eldest boy—his darling Bulbo; and that good-natured young man never once reproached his haughty parent for his unkind conduct the day before, when he would have left Bulbo to be shot without any pity, but came to see his father, and spoke to him through the grating of the door, beyond which he was not allowed to go; and brought him some sandwiches from the grand supper which his Majesty was giving above stairs, in honour of the brilliant victory which had just been achieved.

"I cannot stay with you long, sir," says Bulbo, who was in his best ball dress, as he handed his father in the prog, "I am engaged to dance the next quadrille with her Majesty Queen Rosalba, and I hear the fiddles playing at this very moment."

So Bulbo went back to the ball-room, and the wretched Padella ate his solitary supper in silence and tears.

All was now joy in King Giglio's circle. Dancing, feasting, fun, illuminations, and jollifications of all sorts ensued. The people through whose villages they passed were ordered to illuminate their cottages at night, and scatter flowers on the roads during the day. They were requested, and I promise you they did not like to refuse, to serve the troops liberally with eatables and wine; besides, the army was enriched by the immense quantity of plunder which was found in King Padella's camp, and taken from his soldiers; who (after they had given up everything) were allowed to fraternise with the conquerors; and the united forces marched back by easy stages towards King Giglio's capital, his royal banner and that of Queen Rosalba being carried in front of the troops. Hedzoff was made a Duke and a Field Marshal. Smith and Jones were promoted to be Earls; the Crim Tartar Order of the Pumpkin and the Paflagonian decoration of the Cucumber were freely distributed by their Majesties to the army. Queen Rosalba wore the Paflagonian Ribbon of the Cucumber across her riding habit, whilst King Giglio never appeared without the grand Cordon of the Pumpkin. How the people cheered them as they rode along side by side! They were pronounced to be the handsomest couple ever seen: that was a matter of course; but they really *were* very handsome, and, had they been otherwise, would have looked so, they were so happy! Their Majesties were never separated during the whole day, but breakfasted, dined, and supped together always, and rode side by side, interchanging elegant compliments, and indulging in the most delightful conversation. At night, her Majesty's ladies of honour (who

had all rallied round her the day after King Padella's defeat,) came and conducted her to the apartments prepared for her; whilst King Giglio, surrounded by his gentlemen, withdrew to his own Royal quarters. It was agreed they should be married as soon as they reached the capital, and orders were dispatched to the Archbishop of Blombodinga, to hold himself in readiness to perform the interesting ceremony. Duke Hedzoff carried the message, and gave instructions to have the Royal Castle splendidly refurnished and painted afresh. The Duke seized Glumboso, the Ex-Prime Minister, and made him refund that considerable sum of money which the old scoundrel had secreted out of the late King's treasure. He also clapped Valoroso into prison, (who, by the way, had been dethroned for some considerable period past,) and when the Ex-Monarch weakly remonstrated, Hedzoff said, "A soldier, Sir, knows but his duty; my orders are to lock you up along with the Ex-King Padella, whom I have brought hither a prisoner under guard." So these two Ex-Royal personages were sent for a year to the House of Correction, and thereafter were obliged to become monks of the severest Order of Flagellants, in which state, by fasting, by vigils, by flogging, (which they administered to one another, humbly but resolutely,) no doubt they exhibited a repentance for their past misdeeds, usurpations, and private and public crimes.

As for Glumboso, that rogue was sent to the galleys, and never had an opportunity to steal any more.

XVIII

How They All Journeyed Back to the Capital.

THE FAIRY BLACKSTICK, by whose means this young King and Queen had certainly won their respective Crowns back, would come not unfrequently, to pay them a little visit—as they were riding in their triumphal progress towards Giglio's Capital—change her wand into a pony, and travel by their Majesties' side, giving them the very best advice. I am not sure that King Giglio did not think the Fairy and her advice rather a bore, fancying it was his own valour and merits which had put him on his throne, and conquered Padella: and, in fine, I fear he rather gave himself airs towards his best friend and patroness. She exhorted him to deal justly by his subjects, to draw mildly on the taxes, never to break his promise when he had once given it—and in all respects to be a good King.

"A good King, my dear Fairy!" cries Rosalba. "Of course he will. Break his promise! can you fancy my Giglio would ever do anything so improper, so unlike him? No! never!" And she looked fondly towards Giglio, whom she thought a pattern of perfection.

"Why is Fairy Blackstick always advising me, and telling me how to manage my government, and warning me to keep my word? Does she suppose that I am not a man of sense, and a man of honour?" asks Giglio, testily. "Methinks she rather presumes upon her position."

"Hush! dear Giglio," says Rosalba. "You know Blackstick has been very kind to us, and we must not offend her." But the Fairy was not listening to Giglio's testy observations, she had fallen back, and was trotting on her pony now, by Master Bulbo's side, who rode a donkey, and made himself generally beloved in the army by his cheerfulness, kindness, and good-humour to everybody. He was eager to see his darling Angelica. He thought there never was such a charming being. Blackstick did not tell him it was the possession of the Magic Rose that made Angelica so lovely in his eyes. She brought him the very best accounts of his little wife, whose misfortunes and humiliations had indeed very greatly improved her; and you see, she could whisk off on her wand a hundred miles in a minute, and be back in no time, and so carry polite messages from Bulbo to Angelica, and from Angelica to Bulbo, and comfort that young man upon his journey.

When the Royal party arrived at the last stage before you reach Blombodinga, who should be in waiting, in her carriage there with her lady of honour by her side, but the Princess Angelica. She rushed into her husband's arms, scarcely stopping to make a passing curtsey to the King and Queen. She had no eyes but for Bulbo, who appeared perfectly lovely to her on account of the fairy ring which he wore; whilst she herself, wearing the magic rose in her bonnet, seemed entirely beautiful to the enraptured Bulbo.

A splendid luncheon was served to the Royal party, of which the Archbishop, the Chancellor, the Duke Hedzoff, Countess Gruffanuff, and all our friends partook. The Fairy Blackstick being seated on the left of King Giglio, with Bulbo and Angelica beside. You could hear the joy-bells ringing in the capital, and the guns which the citizens were firing off in honour of their Majesties.

"What can have induced that hideous old Gruffanuff to dress herself up in such an absurd way? Did you ask her to be your bridesmaid, my dear?" says Giglio to Rosalba. "What a figure of fun Gruffy is!"

Gruffy was seated opposite their Majesties, between the Archbishop and the Lord Chancellor, and a figure of fun she certainly was, for she was dressed in a low white silk dress, with lace over, a wreath of white roses on her wig, a splendid lace veil, and her yellow old neck was covered with diamonds. She ogled the King in such a manner, that his Majesty burst out laughing.

"Eleven o'clock!" cries Giglio, as the great Cathedral bell of Blombodinga tolled that hour. "Gentlemen and ladies, we must be starting. Archbishop, you must be at church I think before twelve?"

"We must be at church before twelve," sighs out Gruffanuff in a languishing voice, hiding her old face behind her fan.

"And then I shall be the happiest man in my dominions," cries Giglio, with an elegant bow to the blushing Rosalba.

"O, my Giglio! O, my dear Majesty!" exclaims Gruffanuff; "and can it be that this happy moment at length has arrived"—

"Of course it has arrived," says the King.

"—And that I am about to become the enraptured bride of my adored Giglio!" continues Gruffanuff. "Lend me a smelling-bottle, somebody. I certainly shall faint with joy."

"*You* my bride?" roars out Giglio.

"*You* marry my Prince?" cries poor little Rosalba.

"Pooh! Nonsense! The woman's mad!" exclaims the King. And all the courtiers exhibited by their countenances and expressions, marks of surprise, or ridicule, or incredulity, or wonder.

"I should like to know who else is going to be married, if I am not?" shrieks out Gruffanuff. "I should like to know if King Giglio is a gentleman, and if there is such a thing as justice in Paflagonia? Lord Chancellor! my Lord Archbishop! will your Lordships sit by and see a poor, fond, confiding, tender creature put upon? Has not Prince Giglio promised to marry his Barbara? Is not this Giglio's signature? Does not this paper declare that he is mine, and only mine?" And she handed to his Grace the Archbishop the document which the Prince signed that evening, when she wore the magic ring, and Giglio drank so much champagne. And the old Archbishop, taking out his eye-glasses, read—" 'This is to give notice, that I, Giglio, only son of Savio, King of Paflagonia, hereby promise to marry the charming Barbara Griselda Countess Gruffanuff, and widow of the late Jenkins Gruffanuff, Esq.' "

"H'm," says the Archbishop, "the document is certainly a—a document."

"Phoo," says the Lord Chancellor, "the signature is not in his Majesty's hand-writing." Indeed, since his studies at Bosforo, Giglio had made an immense improvement in caligraphy.

"Is it your hand-writing, Giglio?" cries the Fairy Blackstick, with an awful severity of countenance.

"Y—y—y—es," poor Giglio gasps out, "I had quite forgotten the confounded paper: she can't mean to hold me by it. You old wretch, what will you take to let me off? Help the Queen, some one—her Majesty has fainted."

"Chop her head off!"   exclaim the impetuous Hedzoff,

"Smother the old witch!"   the ardent Smith, and the

"Pitch her into the river!"   faithful Jones.

But Gruffanuff flung her arms round the Archbishop's neck, and bellowed out, "Justice, justice, my Lord Chancellor!" so loudly, that her piercing shrieks caused everybody to pause. As for Rosalba, she was borne away lifeless by her ladies; and you may imagine the look of agony which Giglio cast towards that lovely being, as his hope, his joy, his darling, his all in all, was thus removed, and in her place the horrid old Gruffanuff rushed up to his side, and once more shrieked out, "Justice, justice!"

"Won't you take that sum of money which Glumboso hid?" says Giglio: "two hundred and eighteen thousand millions, or thereabouts. It's a handsome sum."

"I will have that and you too!" says Gruffanuff.

"Let us throw the crown jewels into the bargain," gasps out Giglio.

"I will wear them by my Giglio's side!" says Gruffanuff.

"Will half, three-quarters, five-sixths, nineteen-twentieths, of my kingdom do, Countess?" asks the trembling monarch.

"What were all Europe to me without *you*, my Giglio?" cries Gruff, kissing his hand.

"I won't, I can't, I shan't,—I'll resign the crown first," shouts Giglio, tearing away his hand; but Gruff clung to it.

"I have a competency, my love," she says, "and with thee and a cottage thy Barbara will be happy."

Giglio was half mad with rage by this time. "I will not marry her," says he. "Oh, Fairy, Fairy, give me counsel!" And as he spoke he looked wildly round at the severe face of the Fairy Blackstick.

" 'Why is Fairy Blackstick always advising me, and warning me to keep my word? Does she suppose that I am not a man of honour?' " said the Fairy, quoting Giglio's own haughty words. He quailed under the brightness of her eyes; he felt that there was no escape for him from that awful Inquisition.

"Well, Archbishop," said he, in a dreadful voice that made his Grace start, "since this Fairy has led me to the height of happiness but to dash me down into the depths of despair, since I am to lose Rosalba, let me at least keep my honour. Get up, Countess, and let us be married; I can keep my word, but I can die afterwards."

"O dear Giglio," cries Gruffanuff, skipping up, "I knew, I knew I could trust thee—I knew that my Prince was the soul of honour. Jump into your carriages, ladies and gentlemen, and let us go to church at once; and as for dying, dear Giglio, no, no:—thou wilt forget that insignificant little chambermaid of a queen—thou wilt live to be consoled by thy Barbara! She wishes to be a Queen, and not a Queen Dowager, my gracious Lord!" And hanging upon poor Giglio's arm, and leering and grinning in his face in the most disgusting manner, this old wretch tripped off in her white satin shoes, and jumped into the very carriage which had been got ready to convey Giglio and Rosalba to church. The cannons roared again, the bells peeled triple-bobmajors, the people came out flinging flowers upon the path of the royal bride and bridegroom, and Gruff looked out of the gilt coach window and bowed and grinned to them. Phoo! the horrid old wretch!

X I X

And Now We Come to the Last Scene in the Pantomime.

T HE MANY UPS AND DOWNS of her life had given the Princess Rosalba prodigious strength of mind, and that highly principled young woman presently recovered from her fainting-fit, out of which Fairy Blackstick, by a precious essence which the Fairy always carried in her pocket, awakened her. Instead of tearing her hair, crying, and bemoaning herself, and fainting again, as many young women would have done, Rosalba remembered that she owed an example of firmness to her subjects; and though she loved Giglio more than her life, was determined, as she told the Fairy, not to interfere between him and justice, or to cause him to break his royal word.

"I cannot marry him, but I shall love him always," says she to Blackstick; "I will go and be present at his marriage with the Countess, and sign the book, and wish them happy with all my heart. I will see, when I get home, whether I cannot make the new Queen some handsome presents. The Crim Tartary crown diamonds are uncommonly fine, and I shall never have any use for them. I will live and die unmarried like Queen Elizabeth, and, of course, I shall leave my crown to Giglio when I quit this world. Let us go and see them married, my dear Fairy, let me say one last farewell to him; and then, if you please, I will return to my own dominions."

So the Fairy kissed Rosalba with peculiar tenderness, and at once changed her wand into a very comfortable coach-and-four, with a steady coachman, and two respectable footmen behind, and the Fairy and Rosalba got into the coach, which Angelica and Bulbo entered after them. As for honest Bulbo, he was blubbering in the most pathetic manner, quite overcome by Rosalba's misfortune. She was touched by the honest fellow's sympathy, promised to restore to him the confiscated estates of Duke Padella his father, and created him, as he sat there in the coach, Prince, Highness, and First Grandee of the Crim Tartar Empire. The coach moved on, and, being a fairy coach, soon came up with the bridal procession.

Before the ceremony at church it was the custom in Paflagonia, as it is in other countries, for the bride and bridegroom to sign the Contract of Marriage, which was to be witnessed by the Chancellor, Minister, Lord Mayor, and principal officers of state. Now, as the royal palace was being painted and furnished anew, it was not ready for the reception of the King and his bride, who proposed at first to take up their residence at the Prince's palace, that one which Valoroso occupied when Angelica was born, and before he usurped the throne.

So the marriage party drove up to the palace: the dignitaries got out of their carriages and stood aside: poor Rosalba stepped out of her coach, supported by Bulbo, and stood almost fainting up against the railings so as to have a last look of her dear Giglio. As for Blackstick, she, according to her custom, had flown out of the coach window in some inscrutable manner, and was now standing at the palace door.

Giglio came up the steps with his horrible bride on his arm, looking as pale as if he was going to execution. He only frowned at the Fairy Blackstick—he was angry with her, and thought she came to insult his misery.

"Get out of the way, pray," says Gruffanuff, haughtily. "I wonder why you are always poking your nose into other people's affairs?"

"Are you determined to make this poor young man unhappy?" says Blackstick.

"To marry him, yes! What business is it of yours? Pray, madam, don't say 'you' to a Queen," cries Gruffanuff.

"You won't take the money he offered you?"

"No."

"You won't let him off his bargain, though you know you cheated him when you made him sign the paper."

"Impudence! Policemen, remove this woman!" cries Gruffanuff. And the policemen were rushing forward, but with a wave of her wand the Fairy struck them all like so many statues in their places.

"You won't take anything in exchange for your bond, Mrs. Gruffanuff," cries the Fairy, with awful severity. "I speak for the last time."

"No!" shrieks Gruffanuff, stamping with her foot. "I'll have my husband, my husband, my husband!"

"You SHALL HAVE YOUR HUSBAND!" the Fairy Blackstick cried; and advancing a step, laid her hand upon the nose of the KNOCKER.

As she touched it, the brass nose seemed to elongate, the open mouth opened still wider, and uttered a roar which made everybody start. The eyes rolled wildly; the arms and legs uncurled themselves, writhed about, and seemed to lengthen with each twist; the knocker expanded into a figure in yellow livery, six feet high; the screws by which it was fixed to the door unloosed themselves, and JENKINS GRUFFANUFF once more trod the threshold off which he had been lifted more than twenty years ago!

"Master's not at home," says Jenkins, just in his old voice; and Mrs. Jenkins, giving a dreadful *youp*, fell down in a fit, in which nobody minded her.

For everybody was shouting, "Huzzay! huzzay!" "Hip, hip, hurray!" "Long live the King and Queen!" "Were such things ever seen?" "No, never, never, never!" "The Fairy Blackstick for ever!"

The bells were ringing double peals, the guns roaring and banging most prodigiously. Bulbo was embracing everybody; the Lord Chancellor was flinging up his wig and shouting like a madman; Hedzoff had got the Archbishop round the waist, and they were dancing a jig for joy; and as for Giglio, I leave you to imagine what *he* was doing, and if he kissed Rosalba once, twice—twenty thousand times, I'm sure I don't think he was wrong.

So Gruffanuff opened the hall door with a low bow, just as he had been accustomed to do, and they all went in and signed the book, and then they went to church and were married, and the Fairy Blackstick sailed away on her cane, and was never more heard of in Paflagonia.

AND HERE ENDS THE FIRE-SIDE PANTOMIME.

Granny's Wonderful Chair

By FRANCES BROWNE

SELECTIONS

F RANCES BROWNE (1816–1879) was the seventh child of a village postmaster in County Donegal. She was born blind. As her brothers and sisters recited aloud each evening the lessons they were preparing for school next day, she listened and learned them by heart. She shouldered their chores in the household and told them stories in exchange for their reading aloud to her. Each night, after the other children had gone to sleep, she would repeat everything she had heard during the day. When she had learned geography and grammar in this way, she recited her lessons to the village teacher, who taught her French. While still in her teens she had listened to Scott's novels, to Byron's *Childe Harold*, and to Pope's translation of the *Iliad*. After listening for the first time to Homer, she burned a collection of poems she had written, and resolved to write no more poetry. But in her twenties she was inspired by hearing a volume of Irish songs and began to write verse for publication. With the first money she earned, she paid for the education of a younger sister, preparing her to read aloud and act as secretary. In 1847, with an annual income of twenty pounds from the Royal Bounty Fund, she and her sister moved to Edinburgh.

Ill health and poverty continued to plague her life. Somehow, on moving to London in 1852, she received a present of one hundred pounds from the Marquis of Lansdowne, which temporarily freed her from the most stringent pressures. In the fifties she wrote several books of stories for children, including *Granny's Wonderful Chair*, and began her first novels for adults. Little more is known of her life. Her book *My Share of the World: An Autobiography*, which appeared in three volumes in 1861, was actually not her own autobiography, but a novel, and whatever reminiscences it may contain are veiled and uncertain. Her reading and her interests ranged widely in time and space: she wrote about South African diamond mines, about the French Revolution, about Russia. Her books are hard to find; when found they prove to be original and surprising. But nothing that she wrote compared with *Granny's Wonderful Chair*.

Published at Christmas 1856 with the date 1857 on the title page, and with illustrations by the talented Kenny Meadows, *Granny's Wonderful Chair* was apparently well received but did not enjoy enough success to warrant reprinting. In the eighties, after Frances Browne was dead, however, it suddenly experienced a revival. A new edition appeared almost every year. In 1887 Frances Hodgson Burnett, whose *Little Lord Fauntleroy* (1886) had just made her famous, edited *Granny's Wonderful Chair* as *Stories from the Lost Fairy Book*, retold by the child who read them. It has since enjoyed great appreciation, was reprinted in full as late as 1963, and has even more recently been hailed as a "masterpiece of imaginative writing, all the more remarkable" because of Frances Browne's blindness.

For sheer beauty of imagery the story rivals Ruskin's *King of the Golden River*, while its language is far simpler. Frances Browne's vision of a fairy world has been described as a "place of rose-groves and nightingales, moss and moonlight, where men live on deer's milk and cakes of nut-flour, and shepherds on the hills pipe to their flocks at sunset." We would agree that the enchantment of the atmosphere is the "purest" in all of Victorian children's literature, but would firmly dispute the judgment that the tale is told "unmixed with any moral purpose" (G. Avery and A. Bull, *Nineteenth Century Children*, London: Hodder & Stoughton, 1965, p. 135).

When little Snowflower's magical chair takes her in search of grandmother, it is to the land of King Winwealth she goes. Winwealth has married Wantall, and their daughter is

139

Greedalind. Prince Wisewit has disappeared. At the court nobody cares for anything but money. As the chair tells the stories we are here omitting, the mean cobbler Scrub is discomfited and the generous cobbler Spare rewarded, but Greedalind wants their hut as a summerhouse, and the lesson is not learned. The wicked stewards, Reckoning Robin and Wary Will, dispossess their lords' children in favor of their own son and daughter, Hardhold and Drypenny, and are punished for it; but at the end the listening Greedalind only wants the great oak of the Lady Greensleeves for her own. The covetous brother Clutch and the warmhearted brother Kind learn the same lesson that was taught to Scrub and Spare, but Greedalind only demands the violet pasture as a playground. Even the delicate fable of the small-footed prince in the land of the big-footed people and the big-footed princess in the land of the small-footed people only arouses in Greedalind the yearning to possess the Fair Fountain, and in Queen Wantall the wish to be able to wash her money in the Growing Well.

Indeed, Frances Browne's stories teach the same lesson that Ruskin taught: the fatal wickedness of greed. In the materialistic world of Victorian England, it was a lesson that the authors of books for children—often men and women like Frances Browne who were themselves poor and undervalued—tried over and over again to teach. We shall find it in George MacDonald also. Its overshadowing presence in *Granny's Wonderful Chair* makes that delightful book not quite the work of timeless enchantment it has been called. Rather, it remains a children's book of distinguished quality that is also quintessentially Victorian.

The text of the selections from Granny's Wonderful Chair *is reprinted from an English edition (London: J.M. Dent and Sons, 1912).*

CHAPTER I

INTRODUCTORY

IN AN OLD TIME, long ago, when the fairies were in the world, there lived a little girl so uncommonly fair and pleasant of look, that they called her Snowflower. This girl was good as well as pretty. No one had ever seen her frown or heard her say a cross word, and young and old were glad when they saw her coming.

Snowflower had no relation in the world but a very old grandmother, called Dame Frostyface; people did not like her quite so well as her granddaughter, for she was cross enough at times, but always kind to Snowflower; and they lived together in a little cottage built of peat, and thatched with reeds, on the edge of a great forest; tall trees sheltered its back from the north wind; the mid-day sun made its front warm and cheerful; swallows built in the eaves; daisies grew thick at the door; but there were none in all that country poorer than Snowflower and her grandmother. A cat and two hens were all their live-stock: their bed was dry grass, and the only good piece of furniture in the cottage was a great arm-chair with wheels on its feet, a black velvet cushion, and many curious carvings of flowers and fawns on its dark oaken back.

On that chair Dame Frostyface sat spinning from morning till night to maintain herself and her granddaughter, while Snowflower gathered sticks for firing, looked after the hens and the cat, and did whatever else her grandmother bade her. There was nobody in the shire could spin such fine yarn as Dame Frostyface, but she spun very slowly. Her wheel was as old as herself, and far the more worn; indeed, the wonder was that it did not fall to pieces. So the dame's earnings were small, and their living meagre. Snowflower, however, felt no want of good dinners or fine clothes. Every evening, when the fire was heaped with the sticks she had gathered till it blazed and crackled up the cottage chimney, Dame Frostyface set aside her wheel, and told her a new story. Often did the little girl wonder where her grandmother had gathered so many stories, but she soon learned that. One sunny morning, at the time of the swallows coming, the dame rose up, put on the grey hood and mantle in which she carried her yarn to the fairs, and said, "My child, I am going a long journey to visit an aunt of mine, who lives far in the north country. I cannot take you with me, because my aunt is the crossest woman alive, and never liked young people: but the hens will lay eggs for you; there is barley-meal in the barrel; and, as you have been a good girl, I'll tell you what to do when you feel lonely. Lay your head gently down on the cushion of the arm-chair, and say, 'Chair of my grandmother, tell me a story.' It was made by a cunning fairy, who lived in the forest when I was young, and she gave it to me because she knew nobody could keep what they got hold of better. Remember, you must never ask a story more than once in the day; and if there be any occasion to travel, you have only to seat yourself in it, and say, 'Chair of my grandmother, take me such a way.' It will carry you wherever you wish; but mind to oil the wheels before you set out, for I have sat on it these forty years in that same corner."

Having said this, Dame Frostyface set forth to see her aunt in the north country. Snowflower gathered firing and looked after the hens and cat as usual. She baked herself a cake or two of the barley-meal; but when the evening fell the cottage looked lonely. Then Snowflower remembered her grandmother's words, and, laying her head gently down, she said, "Chair of my grandmother, tell me a story."

Scarce were the words spoken, when a clear voice from under the velvet cushion began to tell a new and most wonderful tale, which surprised Snowflower so much that she forgot to be frightened. After that the good girl was lonely no more. Every morning she baked a barley cake, and every evening the chair told her a new story; but she could never find out who owned the voice, though Snowflower showed her gratitude by polishing up the oaken back, and dusting the velvet cushion, till the chair looked as good as new. The swallows came and built in the eaves, the daisies grew thicker than ever at the door; but great misfortunes fell upon Snowflower. Notwithstanding all her care, she forgot to clip the hens' wings, and they flew away one morning to visit their friends, the pheasants, who lived far in the forest; the cat followed them to see its relations; the barley-meal was eaten up, except a couple of handfuls; and Snowflower had often strained her eyes in hopes of seeing the grey mantle, but there was no appearance of Dame Frostyface.

"My grandmother stays long," said Snowflower to herself; "and by and by there will be nothing to eat. If I could get to her, perhaps she would advise me what to do; and this is a good occasion for travelling."

Next day, at sunrise, Snowflower oiled the chair's wheels, baked a cake out of the last of the meal, took it in her lap by way of provision for the journey, seated herself, and said, "Chair of my grandmother, take me the way, she went."

Presently the chair gave a creak, and began to move out of the cottage, and into the forest the very way Dame Frostyface had taken, where it rolled along at the rate of a coach and six. Snowflower was amazed at this style of travelling, but the chair never stopped nor stayed the whole summer day, till as the sun was setting they came upon an open space, where a hundred men were hewing down the tall trees with their axes, a hundred more were cleaving them for firewood, and twenty waggoners, with horses and waggons, were carrying the wood away. "Oh! chair of my grandmother, stop!" said Snowflower, for she was tired, and also wished to know what this might mean. The chair immediately stood still, and Snowflower, seeing an old woodcutter, who looked civil, stepped up to him, and said, "Good father, tell me why you cut all this wood?"

"What ignorant country girl are you?" replied the man, "not to have heard of the great feast which our sovereign, King Winwealth, means to give on the birthday of his only daughter, the Princess Greedalind. It will last seven days. Everybody will be feasted, and this wood is to roast the oxen and the sheep, the geese and the turkeys, amongst whom there is a great lamentation throughout the land."

When Snowflower heard that she could not help wishing to see, and perhaps share in, such a noble feast, after living so long on barley cakes; so, seating herself, she said, "Chair of my grandmother, take me quickly to the palace of King Winwealth."

The words were hardly spoken, when off the chair started through the trees and out of the forest, to the great amazement of the woodcutters, who, never having seen such a sight before, threw down their axes, left their waggons, and followed Snowflower to the gates of a great and splendid city, fortified with strong walls and high towers, and standing in the midst of a wide plain covered with cornfields, orchards, and villages.

It was the richest city in all the land; merchants from every quarter came there to buy and sell, and there was a saying that people had only to live seven years in it to make their fortunes. Rich as they were, however, Snowflower thought she had never seen so many discontented, covetous faces as looked out from the great shops, grand houses, and fine coaches, when her chair rattled along the streets; indeed, the citizens did not stand high in repute for either good-nature or honesty; but it had not been so when King Winwealth was young, and he and his brother, Prince Wisewit, governed the land together—Wisewit was a wonderful prince for knowledge and prudence. He knew the whole art of government, the tempers of men, and the powers of the stars; moreover, he was a great magician, and it was said of him that he could never die or grow old. In his time there was neither discontent nor sickness in the city—strangers were hospitably entertained without price or questions. Lawsuits there were none, and no one locked his door at night. The fairies used to come there at May-day and Michaelmas, for they were Prince Wisewit's friends—all but one, called Fortunetta, a shortsighted but very cunning fairy, who hated everybody wiser than herself, and the prince especially, because she could never deceive him.

There was peace and pleasure for many a year in King Winwealth's city, till one day at midsummer Prince Wisewit went alone to the forest, in search of a strange herb for his garden, but he never came back; and though the king, with all his guards, searched far and near, no news was ever heard of him. When his brother was gone, King Winwealth grew lonely in his great palace, so he married a certain princess, called Wantall, and brought her home to be his queen. This princess was neither handsome nor agreeable. People thought she must have gained the king's love by enchantment, for her whole dowry was a desert island, with a huge pit in it that never could be filled, and her disposition was so covetous, that the more she got the greedier she grew. In process of time the king and queen had an only daughter, who was to be the heiress of all their dominions. Her name was the Princess Greedalind, and the whole city were making preparations to celebrate her birthday—not that they cared much for the princess, who was remarkably like her mother both in looks and temper, but being King Winwealth's only daughter, people came from far and near to the festival, and among them strangers and fairies who had not been there since the day of Prince Wisewit.

There was surprising bustle about the palace, a most noble building, so spacious that it had a room for every day in the year. All the floors were of ebony, and all the ceilings of silver, and there was such a supply of golden dishes used by the household, that five hundred armed men kept guard night and day lest any of them should be stolen. When these guards saw Snowflower and her chair, they ran one after the other to tell the king, for the like had never been seen nor heard of in his dominions, and the whole court crowded out to see the little maiden and her chair that came of itself.

When Snowflower saw the lords and ladies in their embroidered robes and splendid jewels, she began to feel ashamed of her own bare feet and linen gown; but at length taking courage, she answered all their questions, and told them everything about her wonderful chair. The queen and the princess cared for nothing that was not gilt. The courtiers had learned the same fashion, and all turned away in high disdain except the old king, who, thinking the chair might amuse him sometimes when he got out of spirits, allowed Snowflower to stay and feast with the scullion in his worst kitchen. The poor little girl was glad of any quarters, though nobody made her welcome—even the servants despised her bare feet and linen gown. They would give her chair no room but in a dusty corner behind the back door, where Snowflower was told she might sleep at night, and eat up the scraps the cook threw away.

That very day the feast began; it was fine to see the multitudes of coaches and people on foot and on horseback who crowded to the palace, and filled every room according to their rank. Never had Snowflower seen such roasting and boiling. There was wine for the lords and spiced ale for the common people, music and dancing of all kinds, and the best of gay dresses; but with all the good cheer there seemed little merriment, and a deal of ill-humour in the palace.

Some of the guests thought they should have been feasted in grander rooms; others were vexed to see many finer than themselves. All the servants were dissatisfied because they did not get presents. There was somebody caught every hour stealing the cups, and a multitude of people were always at the gates clamouring for goods and lands, which Queen Wantall had taken from them. The guards continually drove them away, but they came back again, and could be heard plainly in the highest banquet hall: so it was not wonderful that the old king's spirits got uncommonly low that evening after supper. His favourite page, who always stood behind him, perceiving this, reminded his majesty of the little girl and her chair.

"It is a good thought," said King Winwealth. "I have not heard a story this many a year. Bring the child and the chair instantly!"

The favourite page sent a messenger to the first kitchen, who told the master-cook, the master-cook told the kitchen-maid, the kitchen-maid told the chief-scullion, the chief-scullion told the dust-boy, and he told Snowflower to wash her face, rub up her chair, and go to the highest banquet hall, for the great king Winwealth wished to hear a story.

Nobody offered to help her, but when Snowflower had made herself as smart as she could with soap and water, and rubbed the chair till it looked as if dust had never fallen on it, she seated herself, and said:—"Chair of my grandmother, take me to the highest banquet hall."

Instantly the chair marched in a grave and courtly fashion out of the kitchen, up the grand staircase, and into the highest hall. The chief lords and ladies of the land were entertained there, besides many fairies and notable people from distant countries. There had never been such company in the palace since the time of Prince Wisewit; nobody wore less than embroidered satin. King Winwealth sat on his ivory throne in a robe of purple velvet, stiff with flowers of gold; the queen sat by his side in a robe of silver cloth, clasped with pearls; but the Princess Greedalind was finer still, the feast being in her honour. She wore a robe of cloth of gold clasped with diamonds; two waiting-ladies in white satin stood, one on either side, to hold her fan and handkerchief; and two pages, in gold-lace livery, stood behind her chair. With all that Princess Greedalind looked ugly and spiteful; she and her mother were angry to see a bare-footed girl and an old chair allowed to enter the banquet hall.

The supper-table was still covered with golden dishes, and the best of good things, but no one offered Snowflower a morsel: so, having made an humble courtesy to the king, the queen, the princess, and the good company most of whom scarcely noticed her, the poor little girl sat down upon the carpet, laid her head on the velvet cushion, as she used to do in the old cottage, and said:—"Chair of my grandmother, tell me a story."

Everybody was astonished, even to the angry queen and the spiteful princess, when a clear voice from under the cushion said:—"Listen to the story of the Christmas Cuckoo [here omitted]!"

CHAPTER VII

SOUR AND CIVIL

"ONCE UPON A TIME there stood upon the sea-coast of the west country a certain hamlet of low cottages, where no one lived but fishermen. All round it was a broad beach of snow-white sand, where nothing was to be seen but gulls and cormorants, and long tangled seaweeds cast up by the tide that came and went night and day, summer and winter. There was no harbour nor port on all that shore. Ships passed by at a distance, with their white sails set, and on the land-side there lay wide grassy downs, where peasants lived and shepherds fed their flocks. The fishermen thought themselves as well off as any people in that country. Their families never wanted for plenty of herrings and mackerel; and what they had to spare the landsmen bought from them at certain village markets on the downs, giving them in exchange butter, cheese, and corn.

"The two best fishermen in that village were the sons of two old widows, who had no other children, and happened to be near neighbours. Their family names were short, for they called the one Sour, and the other Civil. There was no relationship between them that ever I heard of; but they had only one boat, and always fished together, though their names expressed the difference of their humours—for Civil never used a hard word where a soft one would do, and when Sour was not snarling at somebody, he was sure to be grumbling at everything.

"Nevertheless they agreed wonderfully, and were lucky fishers. Both were strong, active, and of good courage. On winter's night or summer's morning they would steer out to sea far beyond the boats of their neighbours, and never came home without some fish to cook and some to spare. Their mothers were proud of them, each in her own fashion—for the saying held good, 'Like mother, like son.' Dame Civil thought the whole world didn't hold a better than her son; and her boy was the only creature at whom Dame Sour didn't scold and frown. The hamlet was divided in opinion concerning the young fishermen. Some thought Civil the best; some said, without Sour he would catch nothing. So things went on, till one day about the fall of winter, when mists were gathering darkly on sea and sky, and the air was chill and frosty, all the boatmen of the hamlet went out to fish, and so did Sour and Civil.

"That day they had not their usual luck. Cast their net where they would, not a single fish came in. Their neighbours caught boatsful, and went home, Sour said, laughing at them. But when the sea was growing crimson with the sunset their nets were empty, and they were tired. Civil himself did not like to go home without fish—it would damage the high repute they had gained in the village. Besides, the sea was calm and the evening fair, and, as a last attempt, they steered still further out, and cast their nets beside a rock which rose rough and grey above the water, and was called the Merman's Seat— from an old report that the fishermen's fathers had seen the mermen, or sea-people, sitting there on moonlight nights. Nobody believed that rumour now, but the villagers did not like to fish there. The water was said to be deep beyond measure, and sudden squalls were apt to trouble it; but Sour and Civil were right glad to see by the moving of their lines that there was something in their net, and gladder still when they found it so heavy that all their strength was required to draw it up. Scarcely had they landed it on the Merman's Seat, when their joy was changed to disappointment, for besides a few starved mackerel, the net contained nothing but a monstrous ugly fish as long as Civil (who was taller than Sour), with a huge snout, a long beard, and a skin covered with prickles.

" 'Such a horrid ugly creature!' said Sour, as they shook it out of the net on the rough rock, and gathered up the mackerel. 'We needn't fish here any more. How they will mock us in the village for staying out so late, and bringing home so little!'

" 'Let us try again,' said Civil, as he set his creel of mackerel in the boat.

" 'Not another cast will I make to-night;' and what more Sour would have said, was cut short by the great fish, for, looking round at them, it spoke out—

" 'I suppose you don't think me worth taking home in your dirty boat; but I can tell you that if you were down in my country, neither of you would be thought fit to keep me company.'

"Sour and Civil were terribly astonished to hear the fish speak. The first could not think of a cross word to say, but Civil made answer in his accustomed manner.

" 'Indeed, my lord, we beg your pardon, but our boat is too light to carry such a fish as you.'

" 'You do well to call me lord,' said the fish, 'for so I am, though it was hard to expect you could have known my quality in this dress. However, help me off the rock, for I must go home; and for your civility I will give you my daughter in marriage, if you will come and see me this day twelvemonth.'

"Civil helped the great fish off the rock as respectfully as his fear would allow him. Sour was so terrified at the whole transaction, that he said not a word till they got safe home; but from that day forward, when he wanted to put Civil down, it was his custom to tell him and his mother that he would get no wife but the ugly fish's daughter.

"Old Dame Sour heard this story from her son, and told it over the whole village. Some people wondered, but the most part laughed at it as a good joke; and Civil and his mother were never known to be angry but on that occasion. Dame Civil advised her son never to fish with Sour again; and as the boat happened to be his, Civil got an old skiff which one of the fishermen was going to break up for firewood, and cobbled it up for himself.

"In that skiff he went to sea alone all the winter, and all the summer; but though Civil was brave and skilful, he could catch little, because his boat was bad—and everybody but his mother began to think him of no value. Sour having the good boat got a new comrade, and had the praise of being the best fisherman.

"Poor Civil's heart was getting low as the summer wore away. The fish had grown scarce on that coast, and the fishermen had to steer further out to sea. One evening when he had toiled all day and caught nothing, Civil thought he would go further too, and try his fortune beside the Merman's rock. The sea was calm, and the evening fair; Civil did not remember that it was the very day on which his troubles began by the great fish talking to him twelve months before. As he neared the rock the sun was setting, and much astonished was the fisherman to see upon it three fair ladies, with sea-green gowns and strings of great pearls wound round their long fair hair; two of them were waving their hands to him. They were the tallest and stateliest ladies he had ever seen; but Civil could perceive as he came nearer that there was no colour in their cheeks, that their hair had a strange bluish shade, like that of deep sea-water, and there was a fiery light in their eyes that frightened him. The third, who was less of stature, did not notice him at all, but kept her eyes fixed on the setting sun. Though her look was mournful, Civil could see that there was a faint rosy bloom on her cheek—that her hair was a golden yellow, and her eyes were mild and clear like those of his mother.

" 'Welcome! welcome! noble fisherman!' cried the two ladies. 'Our father has sent us for you to visit him,' and with one bound they leaped into his boat, bringing with them the smaller lady, who said—

" 'Oh! bright sun and brave sky that I see so seldom!' But Civil heard no more, for his boat went down miles deep in the sea, and he thought himself drowning; but one lady had caught him by the right arm, and the other by the left, and pulled him into the mouth of a rocky cave, where there was no water. On they went, still down and down, as if on a steep hill-side. The cave was very long, but it grew wider as they came to the bottom. Then Civil saw a faint light, and walked out with his fair company into the country of the sea-people. In that land there grew neither grass nor flowers, bushes nor trees, but the ground was covered with bright-coloured shells and pebbles. There were hills of marble, and rocks of spar; and over all a cold blue sky with no sun, but a light clear and silvery as that of the harvest moon. The fisherman could see no smoking chimneys, but there were grottoes in the sparry rocks, and halls in the marble hills, where lived the sea-people—with whom, as old stories say, fishermen and mariners used to meet on lonely capes and headlands in the simple times of the world.

"Forth they came in all directions to see the stranger. Mermen with long white beards and mermaids such as walk with the fishermen, all clad in sea-green, and decorated with strings of pearls; but every one with the same colourless face, and the same wild light in their eyes. The mermaids led Civil up one of the marble hills to a great cavern with halls and chambers like a palace. Their floors were of alabaster, their walls of porphyry, and their ceilings inlaid with coral. Thousands of crystal lamps lit the palace. There were seats and tables hewn out of shining spar, and a great company sat feasting; but what most amazed Civil was the quantity of cups, flagons, and goblets, made of gold and silver, of such different shapes and patterns that they seemed to have been gathered from all the countries in the world. In the chief hall there sat a merman on a stately chair, with more jewels than all the rest about him. Before him the mermaids brought Civil, saying—

" 'Father, here is our guest.'

" 'Welcome, noble fisherman!' cried the merman, in a voice which Civil remembered with terror, for it was that of the great ugly fish; 'welcome to our halls! Sit down and feast with us, and then choose which of my daughters you will have for a bride.'

"Civil had never felt himself so thoroughly frightened in all his life. How was he to get home to his mother? and what would the old dame think when the dark night came without bringing him home? There was no use in talking—Civil had wisdom enough to see that: he therefore tried to take things quietly; and, having thanked the merman for his invitation, took the seat assigned him on his right hand. Civil was hungry with the long day at sea, but there was no want of fare on that table: meats and wines, such as he had never tasted, were set before him in the richest of golden dishes: but, hungry as he was, the fisherman perceived that everything there had the taste and smell of the sea.

"If the fisherman had been the lord of lands and castles he would not have been treated with more respect. The two mermaids sat by him—one filled his plate, another filled his goblet; but the third only looked at him in a stealthy, warning way when nobody perceived her. Civil soon finished his share of the feast, and then the merman showed him all the splendours of his cavern. The halls were full of company, some feasting, some dancing, and some playing all manner of games, and in every hall was the same abundance of gold and silver vessels; but Civil was most astonished when the merman brought him to a marble chamber full of heaps of precious stones. There were diamonds there whose value the fisherman knew not—pearls larger than ever a diver had gathered—emeralds, sapphires, and rubies, that would have made the jewellers of the world wonder; the merman then said—

" 'This is my eldest daughter's dowry.'

" 'Good luck attend her!' said Civil. 'It is the dowry of a queen.' But the merman led him on to another chamber: it was filled with heaps of gold coin, which seemed gathered from all times and nations. The images and inscriptions of all the kings that ever reigned were there; and the merman said:

" 'This is my second daughter's dowry.'

" 'Good luck attend her!' said Civil. 'It is a dowry for a princess.'

" 'So you may say,' replied the merman. 'But make up your mind which of the maidens you will marry, for the third has no portion at all, because she is not my daughter; but only, as you may see, a poor silly girl taken into my family for charity.'

" 'Truly, my lord,' said Civil, whose mind was already made up, 'both your daughters are too rich and far too noble for me; therefore I choose the third. Her poverty will best become my estate of a poor fisherman.'

" 'If you choose her,' said the merman, 'you must wait long for a wedding. I cannot allow an inferior girl to be married before my own daughters.' And he said a great deal more to persuade him; but Civil would not change his mind, and they returned to the hall.

"There was no more attention for the fisherman, but everybody watched him well. Turn where he would, master or guest had their eyes upon him, though he made them the best speeches he could remember, and praised all their splendours. One thing, however, was strange—there was no end to the fun and the feasting; nobody seemed tired, and nobody thought of sleep. When Civil's very eyes closed with weariness, and he slept on one of the marble benches—no matter how many hours—there were the company feasting and dancing away; there were the thousand lamps within, and the cold moonlight without. Civil wished himself back with his mother, his net, and his cobbled skiff. Fishing would have been easier than those everlasting feasts; but there was nothing else among the sea-people—no night for rest, no working day.

"Civil knew not how time went on, till, waking up from a long sleep, he saw, for the first time, that the feast was over, and the company gone. The lamps still burned, and the tables, with all their riches, stood in the empty halls; but there was no face to be seen, no sound to be heard, only a low voice singing beside the outer door; and there, sitting all alone, he found the mild-eyed maiden.

" 'Fair lady,' said Civil, 'tell me what means this quietness, and where are all the merry company?'

" 'You are a man of the land,' said the lady, 'and know not the sea-people. They never sleep but once a year, and that is at Christmas time. Then they go into the deep caverns, where there is always darkness, and sleep till the new year comes.'

" 'It is a strange fashion,' said Civil; 'but all folks have their way. Fair lady, as you and I are to be good friends, tell me, whence come all the wines and meats, and gold and silver vessels, seeing there are neither cornfields nor flocks here, workmen nor artificers?'

" 'The sea-people are heirs of the sea,' replied the maiden; 'to them come all the stores and riches that are lost in it. I know not the ways by which they come; but the lord of these halls keeps the keys of seven gates, where they go out and in; but one of the gates, which has not been open for thrice seven years, leads to a path under the sea, by which, I heard the merman say in his cups, one might reach the land. Good fisherman, if by chance you gain his favour, and ever open that gate, let me bear you company; for I was born where the sun shines and the grass grows, though my country and my parents are unknown to me. All I remember is sailing in a great ship, when a storm arose, and it was wrecked, and not one soul escaped drowning but me. I was then a little child, and a brave sailor had bound me to a floating plank before he was washed away. Here the sea-people came round me like great fishes, and I went down with them to this rich and weary country. Sometimes, as a great favour, they take me up with them to see the sun; but that is seldom, for they never like to part with one who has seen their country; and, fisherman, if you ever leave them, remember to take nothing with you that belongs to them, for if it were but a shell or a pebble, that will give them power over you and yours.'

" 'Thanks for your news, fair lady,' said Civil. 'A lord's daughter, doubtless, you must have been, while I am but a poor fisherman; yet, as we have fallen into the same misfortune, let us be friends, and it may be we shall find means to get back to the sunshine together.'

" 'You are a man of good manners,' said the lady, 'therefore, I accept your friendship; but my fear is that we shall never see the sunshine again.'

" 'Fair speeches brought me here,' said Civil, 'and fair speeches may help me back; but be sure I will not go without you.'

"This promise cheered the lady's heart, and she and Civil spent that Christmas time seeing the wonders of the sea country. They wandered through caves like that of the great merman. The unfinished feast was spread in every hall; the tables were covered with most costly vessels; and heaps of jewels lay on the floors of unlocked chambers. But for the lady's warning, Civil would fain have put away some of them for his mother.

"The poor woman was sad of heart by this time, believing her son to be drowned. On the first night when he did not come home, she had gone down to the sea and watched till morning. Then the fishermen steered out again, and Sour having found his skiff floating about, brought it home, saying, the foolish young man was doubtless lost; but what better could be expected when he had no discreet person to take care of him?

"This grieved Dame Civil sore. She never expected to see her son again; but, feeling lonely in her cottage at the evening hour when he used to come home, the good woman accustomed herself to go down at sunset and sit beside the sea. That winter happened to be mild on the coast of the west country, and one evening when the Christmas time was near, and the rest of the village preparing to make merry, Dame Civil sat, as usual, on the sands. The tide was ebbing and the sun going down, when from the eastward came a lady clad in black, mounted on a black palfrey, and followed by a squire in the same sad clothing; as the lady came near, she said—

" 'Woe is me for my daughter, and for all that have lost by the sea!'

" 'You say well, noble lady,' said Dame Civil. 'Woe is me also for my son, for I have none beside him.'

"When the lady heard that, she alighted from her palfrey, and sat down by the fisherman's mother, saying—

" 'Listen to my story. I was the widow of a great lord in the heart of the east country. He left me a fair castle, and an only daughter, who was the joy of my heart. Her name was Faith Feignless; but, while she was yet a child, a great fortune-teller told me that my daughter would marry a fisherman. I thought this would be a great disgrace to my noble family, and, therefore, sent my daughter with her nurse in a good ship, bound for a certain city where my relations live, intending to follow myself as soon as I could get my lands and castles sold. But the ship was wrecked, and my daughter drowned; and I have wandered over the world with my good Squire Trusty, mourning on every shore with those who have lost friends by the sea. Some with whom I have mourned grew to forget their sorrow, and would lament with me no more; others being sour and selfish, mocked me, saying, my grief was nothing to them: but you have good manners, and I will remain with you, however humble be your dwelling. My squire carries gold enough to pay all our charges.' So the mourning lady and her good Squire Trusty went home with Dame Civil, and she was no longer lonely in her sorrow, for when the dame said—

" 'Oh! if my son were alive, I should never let him go to sea in a cobbled skiff!' the lady answered—

" 'Oh! if my daughter were but living, I should never think it a disgrace though she married a fisherman!'

"The Christmas passed as it always does in the west country—shepherds made merry on the downs, and fishermen on the shore; but when the merrymakings and ringing of bells were over in all the land, the sea-people woke up to their continual feasts and dances. Like one that had forgotten all that was past, the merman again showed Civil the chamber of gold and the chamber of jewels, advising him to choose between his two daughters; but the fisherman still answered that the ladies were too noble, and far too rich for him. Yet as he looked at the glittering heap, Civil could not help recollecting the poverty of the west country, and the thought slipped out—

" 'How happy my old neighbours would be to find themselves here!'

" 'Say you so?' said the merman, who always wanted visitors.

" 'Yes,' said Civil, 'I have neighbours up yonder in the west country whom it would be hard to send home again if they got sight of half this wealth;' and the honest fisherman thought of Dame Sour and her son.

"The merman was greatly delighted with these speeches—he thought there was a probability of getting many land-people down, and by and by said to Civil—

" 'Suppose you took up a few jewels, and went up to tell your poor neighbours how welcome we might make them?'

"The prospect of getting back to his country rejoiced Civil's heart, but he had promised not to go without the lady, and therefore, answered prudently what was indeed true—

"Many thanks, my lord, for choosing such a humble man as I am to bear your message; but the people of the west country never believe anything without two witnesses at the least; yet if the poor maid whom I have chosen could be permitted to accompany me, I think they would believe us both.'

"The merman said nothing in reply, but his people, who had heard Civil's speech, talked it over among themselves till they grew sure that the whole west country would come down, if they only had news of the riches, and petitioned their lord to send up Civil and the poor maid by way of letting them know.

"As it seemed for the public good, the great merman consented; but, being determined to have them back, he gathered out of his treasure chamber some of the largest pearls and diamonds that lay convenient, and said—

" 'Take these as a present from me, to let the west country people see what I can do for my visitors.'

"Civil and the lady took the presents, saying—

" 'Oh, my lord, you are too generous. We want nothing but the pleasure of telling of your marvellous riches up yonder.'

" 'Tell everybody to come down, and they will get the like,' said the merman; 'and follow my eldest daughter, for she carries the key of the land gate.'

"Civil and the lady followed the mermaid through a winding gallery, which led from the chief banquet hall far into the marble hill. All was dark, and they had neither lamp nor torch, but at the end of the gallery they came to a great stone gate, which creaked like thunder on its hinges. Beyond that there was a narrow cave, sloping up and up like a steep hill-side. Civil and the lady thought they would never reach the top; but at last they saw a gleam of daylight, then a strip of blue sky, and the mermaid bade them stoop and creep through what seemed a crevice in the ground, and both stood up on the broad sea-beach as the day was breaking and the tide ebbing fast away.

" 'Good times to you among your west country people,' said the mermaid. 'Tell any of them that would like to come down to visit us, that they must come here midway between the high and low water-mark, when the tide is going out at morning or evening. Call thrice on the sea-people, and we will show them the way.'

"Before they could make answer, she had sunk down from their sight, and there was no track or passage there, but all was covered by the loose sand and sea-shells.

" 'Now,' said the lady to Civil, 'we have seen the heavens once more, and we will not go back. Cast in the merman's present quickly before the sun rises;' and taking the bag of pearls and diamonds, she flung it as far as she could into the sea.

"Civil never was so unwilling to part with anything as that bag, but he thought it better to follow a good example, and tossed his into the sea also. They thought they heard a long moan come up from the waters; but Civil saw his mother's chimney beginning to smoke, and with the fair lady in her sea-green gown he hastened to the good dame's cottage.

"The whole village were woke up that morning with cries of 'Welcome back, my son!' 'Welcome back, my daughter!' for the mournful lady knew it was her lost daughter, Faith Feignless, whom the fisherman had brought back, and all the neighbours assembled to hear their story. When it was told, everybody praised Civil for the prudence he had shown in his difficulties, except Sour and his mother: they did nothing but rail upon him for losing such great chances of making himself and the whole country rich. At last, when they heard over and over again of the merman's treasures, neither mother nor son would consent to stay any longer in the west country, and as nobody persuaded them, and they would not take Civil's direction, Sour got out his boat and steered away with his mother toward the Merman's Rock. From the voyage they never came back to the hamlet. Some say they went down and lived among the sea-people; others say—I know not how they learned it—that Sour and his mother grumbled and growled so much that even the sea-people grew weary of them, and turned them and their boat out on the open sea. What part of the world they chose to land on nobody is certain: by all accounts they have been seen everywhere, and I should not be surprised if they were in this good company. As for Civil, he married Faith Feignless, and became a great lord."

Here the voice ceased, and two that were clad in sea-green silk, with coronets of pearls, rose up, and said—

"That's our story."

"Oh, mamma, if we could get down to that country!" said Princess Greedalind.

"And bring all the treasures back with us!" answered Queen Wantall.

"Except the tale of yesterday, and the four that went before it, I have not heard such a story since my brother Wisewit went from me, and was lost in the forest," said King Winwealth. "Readyrein, the second of my pages, rise, and bring this maiden a purple velvet mantle."

The mantle was brought, and Snowflower having thanked the king, went down upon her grandmother's chair; but that night the little girl went no further than the lowest banquet hall, where she was bidden to stay and share the feast, and sleep hard by in a wainscot chamber. That she was well entertained there is no doubt, for King Winwealth had been heard to say that it was not clear to him how he could have got through the seven days' feast without her grandmother's chair and its stories; but next day being the last of the seven, things were gayer than ever in the palace. The music had never been so merry, the dishes so rich, or the wines so rare; neither had the clamours at the gate ever been so loud, nor the disputes and envies so many in the halls.

Perhaps it was these doings that brought the low spirits earlier than usual on King Winwealth, for after dinner his majesty fell into them so deeply that a message came down from the highest banquet hall, and the cupbearer told Snowflower to go up with her chair, for King Winwealth wished to hear another story.

Now the little girl put on all her finery, from the pink shoes to the purple mantle, and went up with her chair, looking so like a princess that the whole company rose to welcome her. But having made her courtesy, and laid down her head, saying, "Chair of my grandmother, tell me a story," the clear voice from under the cushion answered—

"Listen to the Story of Merrymind."

CHAPTER VIII

THE STORY OF MERRYMIND

"Once upon a time there lived in the north country a certain poor man and his wife, who had two corn-fields, three cows, five sheep, and thirteen children. Twelve of these children were called by names common in the north country—Hardhead, Stiffneck, Tightfingers, and the like; but when the thirteenth came to be named, either the poor man and his wife could remember no other name, or something in the child's look made them think it proper, for they called him Merrymind, which the neighbours thought a strange name, and very much above their station: however, as they showed no other signs of pride, the neighbours let that pass. Their thirteen children grew taller and stronger every year, and they had hard work to keep them in bread; but when the youngest was old enough to look after his father's sheep, there happened the great fair, to which everybody in the north country went, because it came only once in seven years, and was held on midsummer-day—not in any town or village, but on a green plain, lying between a broad river and a high hill, where it was said the fairies used to dance in old and merry times.

"Merchants and dealers of all sorts crowded to that fair from far and near. There was nothing known in the north country that could not be bought or sold in it, and neither old nor young were willing to go home without a fairing. The poor man who owned this large family could afford them little to spend in such ways; but as the fair happened only once in seven years, he would not show a poor spirit. Therefore, calling them about him, he opened the leathern bag in which his savings were stored, and gave every one of the thirteen a silver penny.

"The boys and girls had never before owned so much pocket-money; and, wondering what they should buy, they dressed themselves in their holiday clothes, and set out with their father and mother to the fair. When they came near the ground that midsummer morning, the stalls, heaped up with all manner of merchandise, from gingerbread upwards, the tents for fun and feasting, the puppet-shows, the rope-dancers, and the crowd of neighbours and strangers, all in their best attire, made those simple people think their north country fair the finest sight in the world. The day wore away in seeing wonders, and in chatting with old friends. It was surprising how far silver pennies went in those days; but before evening twelve of the thirteen had got fairly rid of their money. One bought a pair of brass buckles, another a crimson riband, a third green garters; the father bought a tobacco-pipe, the mother a horn snuffbox—in short, all had provided themselves with fairings except Merrymind.

"The cause of the silver penny remaining in his pocket was that he had set his heart upon a fiddle; and fiddles enough there were in the fair—small and large, plain and painted: he looked at and priced the most of them, but there was not one that came within the compass of a silver penny. His father and mother warned him to make haste with his purchase, for they must all go home at sunset, because the way was long.

"The sun was getting low and red upon the hill; the fair was growing thin, for many dealers had packed up their stalls and departed; but there was a mossy hollow in the great hill-side, to which the outskirts of the fair had reached, and Merrymind thought he would see what might be there. The first thing was a stall of fiddles, kept by a young merchant from a far country, who had many customers, his goods being fine and new; but hard by sat a little grey-haired man, at whom everybody had laughed that day, because he had nothing on his stall but one old dingy fiddle, and all its strings were broken. Nevertheless, the little man sat as stately, and cried, 'Fiddles to sell!' as if he had the best stall in the the fair.

" 'Buy a fiddle, my young master?' he said, as Merrymind came forward. 'You shall have it cheap: I ask but a silver penny for it; and if the strings were mended, its like would not be in the north country.'

"Merrymind thought this a great bargain. He was a handy boy, and could mend the strings while watching his father's sheep. So down went the silver penny on the little man's stall, and up went the fiddle under Merrymind's arm.

" 'Now, my young master,' said the little man, 'you see that we merchants have a deal to look after, and if you help me to bundle up my stall, I will tell you a wonderful piece of news about that fiddle.'

"Merrymind was good-natured and fond of news, so he helped him to tie up the loose boards and sticks that composed his stall with an old rope, and when they were hoisted on his back like a fagot, the little man said—

" 'About the fiddle, my young master: it is certain the strings can never be mended, nor made new, except by threads from the night-spinners, which, if you get, it will be a good pennyworth;' and up the hill he ran like a greyhound.

"Merrymind thought that was queer news, but being given to hope the best, he believed the little man was only jesting, and made haste to join the rest of the family, who were soon on their way home. When they got there every one showed his bargain, and Merrymind showed his fiddle; but his brothers and sisters laughed at him for buying such a thing when he had never learned to play. His sisters asked him what music he could bring out of broken strings; and his father said—

" 'Thou hast shown little prudence in laying out thy first penny, from which token I fear thou wilt never have many to lay out.'

"In short, everybody threw scorn on Merrymind's bargain except his mother. She, good woman, said if he laid out one penny ill, he might lay out the next better; and who knew but his fiddle would be of use some day? To make her words good, Merrymind fell to repairing the strings—he spent all his time, both night and day, upon them; but, true to the little man's parting words, no mending would stand, and no string would hold on that fiddle. Merrymind tried everything, and wearied himself to no purpose. At last he thought of inquiring after people who spun at night; and this seemed such a good joke to the north country people, that they wanted no other till the next fair.

"In the meantime Merrymind lost credit at home and abroad. Everybody believed in his father's prophecy; his brothers and sisters valued him no more than a herd-boy; the neighbours thought he must turn out a scapegrace. Still the boy would not part with his fiddle. It was his silver pennyworth, and he had a strong hope of mending the strings for all that had come and gone; but since nobody at home cared for him except his mother, and as she had twelve other children, he resolved to leave the scorn behind him, and go to seek his fortune.

"The family were not very sorry to hear of that intention, being in a manner ashamed of him; besides, they could spare one out of thirteen. His father gave him a barley cake, and his mother her blessing. All his brothers and sisters wished him well. Most of the neighbours hoped that no harm would happen to him; and Merrymind set out one summer morning with the broken-stringed fiddle under his arm.

"There were no highways then in the north country—people took whatever path pleased them best; so Merrymind went over the fair ground and up the hill, hoping to meet the little man, and learn something of the night-spinners. The hill was covered with heather to the top, and he went up without meeting any one. On the other side it was steep and rocky, and after a hard scramble down, he came to a narrow glen all overgrown with wild furze and brambles. Merrymind had never met with briars so sharp, but he was not the boy to turn back readily, and pressed on in spite of torn clothes and scratched hands, till he came to the end of the glen, where two paths met: one of them wound through a pine-wood, he knew not how far, but it seemed green and pleasant. The other was a rough, stony way leading to a wide valley surrounded by high hills, and overhung by a dull, thick mist, through it was yet early in the summer evening.

"Merrymind was weary with his long journey, and stood thinking of what path to choose, when, by the way of the valley, there came an old man as tall and large as any three men of the north country. His white hair and beard hung like tangled flax about him; his clothes were made of sackcloth; and on his back he carried a heavy burden of dust heaped high in a great pannier.

" 'Listen to me, you lazy vagabond!' he said, coming near to Merrymind: 'if you take the way through the wood I know not what will happen to you; but if you choose this path you must help me with my pannier, and I can tell you it's no trifle.'

" 'Well, father,' said Merrymind, 'you seem tired, and I am younger than you, though not quite so tall; so, if you please, I will choose this way, and help you along with the pannier.'

"Scarce had he spoken when the huge man caught hold of him, firmly bound one side of the pannier to his shoulders with the same strong rope that fastened it on his own back, and never ceased scolding and calling him names as they marched over the stony ground together. It was a rough way and a heavy burden, and Merrymind wished himself a thousand times out of the old man's company, but there was no getting off; and at length, in hopes of beguiling the way, and putting him in better humour, he began to sing an old rhyme which his mother had taught him. By this time they had entered the valley, and the night had fallen very dark and cold. The old man ceased scolding, and by a feeble glimmer of the moonlight, which now began to shine, Merrymind saw that they were close by a deserted cottage, for its door stood open to the night winds. Here the old man paused, and loosed the rope from his own and Merrymind's shoulders.

" 'For seven times seven years,' he said, 'have I carried this pannier, and no one ever sang while helping me before. Night releases all men, so I release you. Where will you sleep—by my kitchen fire, or in that cold cottage?'

"Merrymind thought he had got quite enough of the old man's society, and therefore answered—

" 'The cottage, good father, if you please.'

" 'A sound sleep to you, then!' said the old man, and he went off with his pannier.

"Merrymind stepped into the deserted cottage. The moon was shining through door and window, for the mist was gone, and the night looked clear as day; but in all the valley he could hear no sound, nor was there any trace of inhabitants in the cottage. The hearth looked as if there had not been a fire there for years. A single article of furniture was not to be seen; but Merrymind was sore weary, and, laying himself down in a corner, with his fiddle close by, he fell fast asleep.

"The floor was hard, and his clothes were thin, but all through his sleep there came a sweet sound of singing voices and spinning-wheels, and Merrymind thought he must have been dreaming when he opened his eyes next morning on the bare and solitary house. The beautiful night was gone, and the heavy mist had come back. There was no blue sky, no bright sun to be seen. The light was cold and grey, like that of mid-winter; but Merrymind ate the half of his barley cake, drank from a stream hard by, and went out to see the valley.

"It was full of inhabitants, and they were all busy in houses, in fields, in mills, and in forges. The men hammered and delved; the women scrubbed and scoured; the very children were hard at work: but Merrymind could hear neither talk nor laughter among them. Every face looked careworn and cheerless, and every word was something about work or gain.

"Merrymind thought this unreasonable, for everybody there appeared rich. The women scrubbed in silk, the men delved in scarlet. Crimson curtains, marble floors, and shelves of silver tankards were to be seen in every house; but their owners took neither ease nor pleasure in them, and every one laboured as it were for life.

"The birds of that valley did not sing—they were too busy pecking and building. The cats did not lie by the fire—they were all on the watch for mice. The dogs went out after hares on their own account. The cattle and sheep grazed as if they were never to get another mouthful; and the herdsmen were all splitting wood or making baskets.

"In the midst of the valley there stood a stately castle, but instead of park and gardens, brew-houses and washing-greens lay round it. The gates stood open, and Merrymind ventured in. The courtyard was full of coopers. They were churning in the banquet hall. They were making cheese on the dais, and spinning and weaving in all its principal chambers. In the highest tower of that busy castle, at a window from which she could see the whole valley, there sat a noble lady. Her dress was rich, but of a dingy drab colour. Her hair was iron-grey; her look was sour and gloomy. Round her sat twelve maidens of the same aspect, spinning on ancient distaffs, and the lady spun as hard as they, but all the yarn they made was jet black.

"No one in or out of the castle would reply to Merrymind's salutations, nor answer him any questions. The rich men pulled out their purses, saying, 'Come and work for wages!' The poor men said, 'We have no time to talk!' A cripple by the wayside wouldn't answer him, he was so busy begging; and a child by a cottage-door said it must go to work. All day Merrymind wandered about with his broken-stringed fiddle, and all day he saw the great old man marching round and round the valley with his heavy burden of dust.

" 'It is the dreariest valley that ever I beheld!' he said to himself. 'And no place to mend my fiddle in; but one would not like to go away without knowing what has come over the people, or if they have always worked so hard and heavily.'

"By this time the night again came on: he knew it by the clearing mist and the rising moon. The people began to hurry home in all directions. Silence came over house and field; and near the deserted cottage Merrymind met the old man.

" 'Good father,' he said, 'I pray you tell me what sport or pastime have the people of this valley?'

" 'Sport and pastime!' cried the old man, in great wrath. 'Where did you hear of the like? We work by day and sleep by night. There is no sport in Dame Dreary's land!' and, with a hearty scolding for his idleness and levity, he left Merrymind to sleep once more in the cottage.

"That night the boy did not sleep so sound: though too drowsy to open his eyes, he was sure there had been singing and spinning near him all night; and, resolving to find out what this meant before he left the valley, Merrymind ate the other half of his barley cake, drank again from the stream, and went out to see the country.

"The same heavy mist shut out sun and sky; the same hard work went forward wherever he turned his eyes; and the great old man with the dust-pannier strode on his accustomed round. Merrymind could find no one to answer a single question; rich and poor wanted him to work still more earnestly than the day before; and fearing that some of them might press him into service, he wandered away to the furthest end of the valley.

"There, there was no work, for the land lay bare and lonely, and was bounded by grey crags, as high and steep as any castle-wall. There was no passage or outlet, but through a great iron gate secured with a heavy padlock: close by it stood a white tent, and in the door a tall soldier, with one arm, stood smoking a long pipe. He was the first idle man Merrymind had seen in the valley, and his face looked to him like that of a friend; so coming up with his best bow, the boy said—

" 'Honourable master soldier, please to tell me what country is this, and why do the people work so hard?'

" 'Are you a stranger in this place, that you ask such questions?' answered the soldier.

" 'Yes,' said Merrymind; 'I came but the evening before yesterday.'

" 'Then I am sorry for you, for here you must remain. My orders are to let everybody in and nobody out; and the giant with the dust-pannier guards the other entrance night and day,' said the soldier.

" 'That is bad news,' said Merrymind; 'but since I am here, please to tell me why were such laws made, and what is the story of this valley?'

" 'Hold my pipe, and I will tell you,' said the soldier, 'for nobody else will take the time. This valley belongs to the lady of yonder castle, whom, for seven times seven years, men have called Dame Dreary. She had another name in her youth—they called her Lady Littlecare; and then the valley was the fairest spot in all the north country. The sun shone brightest there; the summers lingered longest. Fairies danced on the hill-tops; singing-birds sat on all the trees. Strongarm, the last of the giants, kept the pine-forest, and hewed yule logs out of it, when he was not sleeping in the sun. Two fair maidens, clothed in white, with silver wheels on their shoulders, came by night, and spun golden threads by the hearth of every cottage. The people wore homespun, and drank out of horn; but they had merry times. There were May-games, harvest-homes and Christmas cheer among them. Shepherds piped on the hill-sides, reapers sang in the fields, and laughter came with the red firelight out of every house in the evening. All that was changed, nobody knows how, for the old folks who remembered it are dead. Some say it was because of a magic ring which fell from the lady's finger; some because of a spring in the castle-court which went dry. However it was, the lady turned Dame Dreary. Hard work and hard times overspread the valley. The mist came down; the fairies departed; the giant Strongarm grew old, and took up a burden of dust; and the night-spinners were seen no more in any man's dwelling. They say it will be so till Dame Dreary lays down her distaff, and dances; but all the fiddlers of the north country have tried their merriest tunes to no purpose. The king is a wise prince and a great warrior. He has filled two treasure-houses, and conquered all his enemies; but he cannot change the order of Dame Dreary's land. I cannot tell you what great rewards he offered to any who could do it; but when no good came of his offers, the king feared that similar fashions might spread among his people, and therefore made a law that whomsoever entered should not leave it. His majesty took me captive in war, and placed me here to keep the gate, and save his subjects trouble. If I had not brought my pipe with me, I should have been working as hard as any of them by this time, with my one arm. Young master, if you take my advice you will learn to smoke.'

" 'If my fiddle were mended it would be better,' said Merrymind; and he sat talking with the soldier till the mist began to clear and the moon to rise, and then went home to sleep in the deserted cottage.

"It was late when he came near it, and the moonlight night looked lovely beside the misty day. Merrymind thought it was a good time for trying to get out of the valley. There was no foot abroad, and no appearance of the giant; but as Merrymind drew near to where the two paths met, there was he fast asleep beside a fire of pinecones, with his pannier at his head, and a heap of stones close by him. 'Is that your kitchen-fire?' thought the boy to himself, and he tried to steal past; but Strongarm started up, and pursued him with stones, and calling him bad names, half way back to the cottage.

"Merrymind was glad to run the whole way for fear of him. The door was still open, and the moon was shining in; but by the fireless hearth there sat two fair maidens, all in white, spinning on silver wheels, and singing together a blithe and pleasant tune like the larks of May-morning. Merrymind could have listened all night, but suddenly he bethought him that these must be the night-spinners, whose threads would mend his fiddle; so, stepping with reverence and good courage, he said—

" 'Honourable ladies, I pray you give a poor boy a thread to mend his fiddle-strings.'

" 'For seven times seven years,' said the fair maidens, 'have we spun by night in this deserted cottage, and no mortal has seen or spoken to us. Go and gather sticks through all the valley to make a fire for us on this cold hearth, and each of us will give you a thread for your pains'.

"Merrymind took his broken fiddle with him, and went through all the valley gathering sticks by the moonlight; but so careful were the people of Dame Dreary's land, that scarce a stick could be found, and the moon was gone, and the misty day had come before he was able to come back with a small fagot. The cottage-door was still open; the fair maidens and their silver wheels were gone; but on the floor where they sat lay two long threads of gold.

"Merrymind first heaped up his fagot on the hearth, to be ready against their coming at night, and next took up the golden threads to mend his fiddle. Then he learned the truth of the little man's saying at the fair, for no sooner were the strings fastened with those golden threads than they became firm. The old dingy fiddle too began to shine and glisten, and at length it was golden also. This sight made Merrymind so joyful, that, unlearned as he was in music, the boy tried to play. Scarce had his bow touched the strings when they began to play of themselves the same blithe and pleasant tune which the night-spinners sang together.

" 'Some of the workers will stop for the sake of this tune,' said Merrymind, and he went out along the valley with his fiddle. The music filled the air; the busy people heard it; and never was such a day seen in Dame Dreary's land. The men paused in their delving; the women stopped their scrubbing; the little children dropped their work; and every one stood still in their places while Merrymind and his fiddle passed on. When he came to the castle, the coopers cast down their tools in the court; the churning and cheesemaking ceased in the banquet hall; the looms and spinning-wheels stopped in the principal chambers; and Dame Dreary's distaff stood still in her hand.

"Merrymind played through the halls and up the tower-stairs. As he came near, the dame cast down her distaff, and danced with all her might. All her maidens did the like; and as they danced she grew young again—the sourness passed from her looks, and the greyness from her hair. They brought her the dress of white and cherry-colour she used to wear in her youth, and she was no longer Dame Dreary, but the Lady Littlecare, with golden hair, and laughing eyes, and cheeks like summer roses.

"Then a sound of merrymaking came up from the whole valley. The heavy mist rolled away over the hills; the sun shone out; the blue sky was seen; a clear spring gushed up in the castle-court; a white falcon came from the east with a golden ring, and put it on the lady's finger. After that Strongarm broke the rope, tossed the pannier of dust from his shoulder, and lay down to sleep in the sun. That night the fairies danced on the hill-tops; and the night-spinners, with their silver wheels, were seen by every hearth, and no more in the deserted cottage. Everybody praised Merrymind and his fiddle; and when news of his wonderful playing came to the king's ears, he commanded the iron gate to be taken away; he made the captive soldier a free man; and promoted Merrymind to be his first fiddler, which under that wise monarch was the highest post in his kingdom.

"As soon as Merrymind's family and neighbours heard of the high preferment his fiddle had gained for him, they thought music must be a good thing, and man, woman, and child took to fiddling. It is said that none of them ever learned to play a single tune except Merrymind's mother, on whom her son bestowed great presents."

Here the voice ceased, and one clothed in green and russet-coloured velvet rose up with a golden fiddle in his hand, and said—

"That's my story."

"Excepting yesterday's tale, and the five that went before it," said King Winwealth, "I have not heard such a story as that since my brother Wisewit went from me, and was lost in the forest. Fairfortune, the first of my pages, go and bring this maiden a golden girdle. And since her grandmother's chair can tell such stories, she shall go no more into low company, but feast with us in our chief banquet hall, and sleep in one of the best chambers of the palace!"

CHAPTER IX

PRINCE WISEWIT'S RETURN

Snowflower was delighted at the promise of feasting with those noble lords and ladies, whose wonderful stories she had heard from the chair. Her courtesy was twice as low as usual, and she thanked King Winwealth from the bottom of her heart. All the company were glad to make room for her, and when her golden girdle was put on, little Snowflower looked as fine as the best of them.

"Mamma," whispered the Princess Greedalind, while she looked ready to cry for spite, "only see that low little girl who came here in a coarse frock and barefooted, what finery and favour she has gained by her story-telling chair! All the court are praising her and overlooking me, though the feast was made in honour of my birthday. Mamma, I must have that chair from her. What business has a common little girl with anything so amusing?"

"So you shall, my daughter," said Queen Wantall—for by this time she saw that King Winwealth had, according to custom, fallen asleep on his throne. So calling two of her pages, Screw and Hardhands, she ordered them to bring the chair from the other end of the hall where Snowflower sat, and directly made it a present to Princess Greedalind.

Nobody in that court ever thought of disputing Queen Wantall's commands, and poor Snowflower sat down to cry in a corner; while Princess Greedalind, putting on what she thought a very grand air, laid down her head on the cushion, saying—

"Chair of my grandmother, tell me a story."

"Where did you get a grandmother?" cried the clear voice from under the cushion; and up went the chair with such force as to throw Princess Greedalind off on the floor, where she lay screaming, a good deal more angry than hurt.

All the courtiers tried in vain to comfort her. But Queen Wantall, whose temper was still worse, vowed that she would punish the impudent thing, and sent for Sturdy, her chief woodman, to chop it up with his axe.

At the first stroke the cushion was cut open, and, to the astonishment of everybody, a bird, whose snow-white feathers were tipped with purple, darted out and flew away through an open window.

"Catch it! catch it!" cried the queen and the princess; and all but King Winwealth, who still slept on his throne, rushed out after the bird. It flew over the palace garden and into a wild common, where houses had been before Queen Wantall pulled them down to search for a gold mine, which her majesty never found, though three deep pits were dug to come at it. To make the place look smart at the feast time these pits had been covered over with loose boughs and turf. All the rest of the company remembered this but Queen Wantall and Princess Greedalind. They were nearest to the bird, and poor Snowflower, by running hard, came close behind them, but Fairfortune, the king's first page, drew her back by the purple mantle, when, coming to the covered pit, boughs and turf gave way, and down went the queen and the princess.

Everybody looked for the bird, but it was nowhere to be seen; but on the common where they saw it alight there stood a fair and royal prince, clad in a robe of purple and a crown of changing colours, for sometimes it seemed of gold and sometimes of forest leaves.

Most of the courtiers stood not knowing what to think, but all the fairy people and all the lords and ladies of the chair's stories, knew him, and cried, "Welcome to Prince Wisewit!"

King Winwealth heard that sound where he slept, and came out glad of heart to welcome back his brother. When the lord high chamberlain and her own pages came out with ropes and lanthorns to search for Queen Wantall and Princess Greedalind, they found them safe and well at the bottom of the pit, having fallen on a heap of loose sand. The pit was of great depth, but some daylight shone down, and whatever were the yellow grains they saw glittering among the sand, the queen and the princess believed it was full of gold.

They called the miners false knaves, lazy rogues, and a score of bad names beside, for leaving so much wealth behind them, and utterly refused to come out of the pit; saying, that since Prince Wisewit was come, they could find no pleasure in the palace; but would stay there and dig for gold, and buy the world with it for themselves. King Winwealth thought the plan was a good one for keeping peace in his palace. He commanded shovels and picks to be lowered to the queen and the princess. The two pages, Screw and Hardhands, went down to help them, in hopes of halving the profits, and there they stayed, digging for gold. Some of the courtiers said they would find it; others believed they never could; and the gold was not found when this story was written.

As for Prince Wisewit, he went home, with the rest of the company, leading Snowflower by the hand, and telling them all how he had been turned into a bird by the cunning fairy Fortunetta, who found him off his guard in the forest; how she had shut him up under the cushion of that curious chair, and given it to old Dame Frostyface; and how all his comfort had been in little Snowflower, to whom he told so many stories.

King Winwealth was so rejoiced to find his brother again, that he commanded another feast to be held for seven days. All that time the gates of the palace stood open; all comers were welcome, all complaints heard. The houses and lands which Queen Wantall had taken away were restored to their rightful owners. Everybody got what they most wanted. There were no more clamours without, nor discontents within the palace; and on the seventh day of the feast who should arrive but Dame Frostyface, in her grey hood and mantle.

Snowflower was right glad to see her grandmother—so were the king and prince, for they had known the Dame in her youth. They kept the feast for seven days more; and when it was ended everything was right in the kingdom. King Winwealth and Prince Wisewit reigned once more together; and because Snowflower was the best girl in all that country, they chose her to be their heiress, instead of Princess Greedalind. From that day forward she wore white velvet and satin; she had seven pages, and lived in the grandest part of the palace. Dame Frostyface, too, was made a great lady. They put a new velvet cushion on her chair, and she sat in a gown of grey cloth, edged with gold, spinning on an ivory wheel in a fine painted parlour. Prince Wisewit built a great summer-house covered with vines and roses, on the spot where her old cottage stood. He also made a highway through the forest, that all good people might come and go there at their leisure; and the cunning fairy Fortunetta finding that her reign was over in those parts, set off on a journey round the world, and did not return in the time of this story. Good boys and girls, who may chance to read it, that time is long ago. Great wars, work, and learning, have passed over the world since then, and altered all its fashions. Kings make no seven-day feasts for all comers now. Queens and princesses, however greedy, do not mine for gold. Chairs tell no tales. Wells work no wonders; and there are no such doings on hills and forests, for the fairies dance no more. Some say it was the hum of schools—some think it was the din of factories that frightened them; but nobody has been known to have seen them for many a year, except, it is said, one Hans Christian Andersen, in Denmark, whose tales of the fairies are so good that they must have been heard from themselves.

It is certain that no living man knows the subsequent history of King Winwealth's country, nor what became of all the notable characters who lived and visited at his palace. Yet there are people who believe that the monarch still falls asleep on his throne, and into low spirits after supper; that Queen Wantall and Princess Greedalind have found the gold, and begun to buy; that Dame Frostyface yet spins—they cannot tell where; that Snowflower may still be seen at the new year's time in her dress of white velvet, looking out for the early spring; that Prince Wisewit has somehow fallen under a stronger spell and a thicker cushion, that he still tells stories to Snowflower and her friends, and when both cushion and spell are broken by another stroke of Sturdy's hatchet—which they expect will happen some time—the prince will make all things right again, and bring back the fairy times to the world

THE END

15

"Fairy Stories"

By JOHN RUSKIN

TWENTY-SEVEN YEARS after writing *The King of the Golden River* and seventeen after its publication, John Ruskin turned again briefly to the subject of fairy stories. In response to the request of a London publisher, John Camden Hotten, who was planning a reissue of Edgar Taylor's English translation of *German Popular Stories* (i.e., Grimm's *Fairy Tales*), originally published in 1823 and 1826 with Cruikshank's drawings, Ruskin in a few sonorous paragraphs delivered himself of his opinions about what a fairy tale should and should not be.

It should not overemphasize the glorious clothes worn by the fairies (perhaps a dig at Frances Browne's *Granny's Wonderful Chair*); it should not make fun of fairy subjects, even playfully (perhaps a dig at Thackeray's *Rose and the Ring*); it should not introduce a love story; it should emphatically not try to teach the children the moral lessons that their parents were properly responsible for teaching them (a dig at just about all *Kunstmärchen*, including Ruskin's own!); in fact, it should be a folk fairy story, and not retouched for moral purposes (here Ruskin echoes Dickens's blast of fifteen years earlier against Cruikshank's temperance Cinderella).

But the Cruikshank who had illustrated Grimm in the twenties was, as we know, not the fanatical temperance advocate who undertook to rewrite Cinderella and other favorites in the fifties. As the great authority on drawing, probably the greatest in nineteenth-century England, Ruskin was well within his own field in repeating here his praise of the earlier Cruikshank. He had compared Cruikshank to Rembrandt in his textbook *Elements of Drawing*, and now he eulogized him again.

Ruskin's mellifluous sentences with their rolling periods may seem to us to say rather little and to take a long time in saying it. He may seem to be pontificating. In fact he was pontificating; but in matters of taste he was the English pontiff, and it is a piece of good fortune to have preserved his considered opinion, as a man of almost fifty, about the literary genre we are examining. For the mature Ruskin, the nearer a fairy tale was to pure Grimm, the better a fairy tale it was.

The text of "Fairy Stories" is reprinted from E. T. Cook and A. Wedderburns, eds., The Works of John Ruskin, *Vol. XIX (1905), pp. 232–239.*

Long since, longer ago perhaps than the opening of some fairy tales, I was asked by the publisher who has been rash enough, at my request, to reprint these my favourite old stories in their earliest English form, to set down for him my reasons for preferring them to the more polished legends, moral and satiric, which are now, with rich adornment of every page by very admirable art, presented to the acceptance of the Nursery.

But it seemed to me to matter so little to the majestic independence of the child-public, who, beside themselves, liked, or who disliked, what they pronounced entertaining, that it is only on strict claims of a promise unwarily given that I venture on the impertinence of eulogy; and my reluctance is the greater, because there is in fact nothing very notable in these tales, unless it be their freedom from faults which for some time have been held to be quite the reverse of faults, by the majority of readers.

In the best stories recently written for the young, there is a taint which it is not easy to define, but which inevitably follows on the author's addressing himself to children bred in school-rooms and drawing-rooms, instead of fields and woods—children whose favourite amusements are premature imitations of the vanities of elder people, and whose conceptions of beauty are dependent partly on costliness of dress. The fairies who interfere in the fortunes of these little ones are apt to be resplendent chiefly in millinery and satin slippers, and appalling more by their airs than their enchantments.

The fine satire which, gleaming through every playful word, renders some of these recent stories as attractive to the old as to the young, seems to me no less to unfit them for their proper function. Children should laugh, but not mock; and when they laugh, it should not be at the weaknesses or faults of others. They should be taught, as far as they are permitted to concern themselves with the characters of those around them, to seek faithfully for good, not to lie in wait maliciously to make themselves merry with evil: they should be too painfully sensitive to wrong, to smile at it; and too modest to constitute themselves its judges.

With these minor errors a far graver one is involved. As the simplicity of the sense of beauty has been lost in recent tales for children, so also the simplicity of their conception of love. That word which, in the heart of a child, should represent the most constant and vital part of its being; which ought to be the sign of the most solemn thoughts that inform its awakening soul and, in one wide mystery of pure sunrise, should flood the zenith of its heaven, and gleam on the dew at its feet; this word, which should be consecrated on its lips, together with the Name which it may not take in vain, and whose meaning should soften and animate every emotion through which the inferior things and the feeble creatures, set beneath it in its narrow world, are revealed to its curiosity or companionship;—this word, in modern child-story, is too often restrained and darkened into the hieroglyph of an evil mystery, troubling the sweet peace of youth with premature gleams of uncomprehended passion, and flitting shadows of unrecognized sin.

These grave faults in the spirit of recent child-fiction are connected with a parallel folly of purpose. Parents who are too indolent and self-indulgent to form their children's characters by wholesome discipline, or in their own habits and principles of life are conscious of setting before them no faultless example, vainly endeavour to substitute the persuasive influence of moral precept, intruded in the guise of amusement, for the strength of moral habit compelled by righteous authority:—vainly think to inform the heart of infancy with deliberative wisdom, while they abdicate the guardianship of its unquestioning innocence; and warp into the agonies of an immature philosophy of conscience the once fearless strength of its unsullied and unhesitating virtue.

A child should not need to choose between right and wrong. It should not be capable of wrong; it should not conceive of wrong. Obedient, as bark to helm, not by sudden strain or effort, but in the freedom of its bright course of constant life; true, with an undistinguished, painless, unboastful truth, in a crystalline household world of truth; gentle, through daily entreatings of gentleness, and honourable trusts, and pretty prides of child-fellowship in offices of good; strong, not in bitter and doubtful contest with temptation, but in peace of heart, and armour of habitual right, from which temptation falls like thawing hail; self-commanding, not in sick restraint of mean appetites and covetous thoughts, but in vital joy of unluxurious life, and contentment in narrow possession, wisely esteemed.

Children so trained have no need of moral fairy tales; but they will find in the apparently vain and fitful courses of any tradition of old time, honestly delivered to them, a teaching for which no other can be substituted, and of which the power cannot be measured; animating for them the material world with inextinguishable life, fortifying them against the glacial cold of selfish science, and preparing them submissively, and with no bitterness of astonishment, to behold, in later years, the mystery—divinely appointed to remain such to all human thought—of the fates that happen alike to the evil and the good.

And the effect of the endeavour to make stories moral upon the literary merit of the work itself, is as harmful as the motive of the effort is false. For every fairy tale worth recording at all is the remnant of a tradition possessing true historical value;—historical, at least, in so far as it has naturally arisen out of the mind of a people under special circumstances, and risen not without meaning, nor removed altogether from their sphere of religious faith. It sustains afterwards natural changes from the sincere action of the fear or fancy of successive generations; it takes new colour from their manner of life, and new form from their changing moral tempers. As long as these changes are natural and effortless, accidental and inevitable, the story remains essentially true, altering its form, indeed, like a flying cloud, but remaining a sign of the sky; a shadowy image, as truly a part of the great firmament of the human mind as the light of reason which it seems to interrupt. But the fair deceit and innocent error of it cannot be interpreted nor restrained by a wilful purpose, and all additions to it by art do but defile, as the shepherd disturbs the flakes of morning mist with smoke from his fire of dead leaves.

There is also a deeper collateral mischief in this indulgence of licentious change and retouching of stories to suit particular tastes, or inculcate favourite doctrines. It directly destroys the child's power of rendering any such belief as it would otherwise have been in his nature to give to an imaginative vision. How far it is expedient to occupy his mind with ideal forms at all may be questionable to many, though not to me; but it is quite beyond question that if we do allow of the fictitous representation, that representation should be calm and complete, possessed to the full, and read down its utmost depth. The little reader's attention should never be confused or disturbed, whether he is possessing himself of fairy tale or history. Let him know his fairy tale accurately, and have perfect joy or awe in the conception of it as if it were real; thus he will always be exercising his power of grasping realities: but a confused, careless, and discrediting tenure of the fiction will lead to as confused and careless reading of fact. Let the circumstances of both be strictly perceived, and long dwelt upon, and let the child's own mind develop fruit of thought from both. It is of the greatest importance early to secure this habit of contemplation, and therefore it is a grave error, either to multiply unnecessarily, or to illustrate with extravagant richness, the incidents presented to the imagination. It should multiply and illustrate them for itself; and, if the intellect is of any real value, there will be a mystery and wonderfulness in its own dreams which would only be thwarted by external illustration. Yet I do not bring forward the text or the etchings in this volume as examples of what either ought to be in works of the kind: they are in many respects common, imperfect, vulgar; but their vulgarity is of a wholesome and harmless kind. It is not, for instance, graceful English, to say that a thought "popped into Catherine's head"; but it nevertheless is far better, as an initiation into literary style, that a child should be told this than that "a subject attracted Catherine's attention." And in genuine forms of minor tradition, a rude and more or less illiterate tone will always be discernible; for all the best fairy tales have owed their birth, and the greater part of their power, to narrowness of social circumstances; they belong properly to districts in which walled cities are surrounded by bright and unblemished country, and in which a healthy and bustling town life, not highly refined, is relieved by, and contrasted with, the calm enchantment of pastoral and woodland scenery, either under humble cultivation by peasant masters, or left in its natural solitude. Under conditions of this kind the imagination is enough excited to invent instinctively, (and rejoice in the invention of) spiritual forms of wildness and beauty, while yet it is restrained and made cheerful by the familiar accidents and relations of town life, mingling always in its fancy humorous and vulgar circumstances with pathetic ones, and never so much impressed with its supernatural phantasies as to be in danger of retaining them as any part of its religious faith. The good spirit descends gradually from an angel into a fairy, and the demon shrinks into a playful grotesque of diminutive malevolence, while yet both keep an accredited and vital influence upon the character and mind. But the language in which such ideas will be usually clothed must necessarily partake of their narrowness; and art is systematically incognizant of them, having only strength under the conditions which awake them to express itself in an irregular and gross grotesque, fit only for external architectural decoration.

The illustrations of this volume are almost the only exceptions I know to the general rule. They are of quite sterling and admirable art, in a class precisely parallel in elevation to the character of the tales which they illustrate; and the original etchings, as I have before said in the Appendix to my *Elements of Drawing*, were unrivalled in masterfulness of touch since Rembrandt; (in some qualities of delineation unrivalled even by him). These copies have been so carefully executed that at first I was deceived by them, and supposed them to be late impressions from the plates (and what is more, I believe the master himself was deceived by them, and supposed them to be his own); and although, on careful comparison with the first proofs, they will be found no exception to the terrible law that literal repetition of entirely fine work shall be, even to the hand that produced it,—much more to any other,—for ever impossible, they still represent, with sufficient fidelity to be in the highest degree instructive, the harmonious light and shade, the manly simplicity of execution, and the easy, unencumbered fancy, of designs which belonged to the best period of Cruikshank's genius. To make somewhat enlarged copies of them, looking at them through a magnifying-glass, and never putting two lines where Cruikshank has put only one, would be an exercise in decision and severe drawing which would leave afterwards little to be learnt in schools. I would gladly also say much in their praise as imaginative designs; but the power of genuine imaginative work, and its difference from that which is compounded and patched together from borrowed sources, is of all qualities of art the most difficult to explain; and I must be content with the simple assertion of it.

And so I trust the good old book, and the honest work that adorns it, to such favour as they may find with children of open hearts and lowly lives.

DENMARK HILL, *Easter*, 1868

At the Back
of the North Wind

By GEORGE MACDONALD

G EORGE MACDONALD (1824–1905) came of an ancient Highland family, reduced in his father's generation to the role of tenant farmers on the lands of a great landower, the Duke of Gordon. Although the family tradition was staunchly Calvinist, George Mac-Donald himself as a child rebelled against the harsh doctrine of the elect, and declared that he did not want God to love him if God did not love everybody. His mother died when he was eight years old, and although his father was kind and generous, the child felt deeply and permanently bereft. Tubercular like both his parents, he managed despite his illness and poverty to study for four years at King's College of the University of Aberdeen. Later he became a Congregational minister in England but was dismissed by his first congregation, narrow-minded and petty, who found him "tainted" with liberal theological opinion. For a Scot, there was something particularly humiliating about failure in the pulpit: MacDonald, in Scotch terms, was a "stickit" minister. In the "Broad Church" teachings of F. D. Maurice, MacDonald found comfort. He became a member of the Church of England but never took Anglican orders, preaching only through the pages of his fiction, which he regarded as sermons.

In his youth, tuberculosis killed not only his mother, and later his father, but many other members of his family. A morbidity often associated with the disease deeply affected MacDonald himself. In the life and writings of Friedrich von Hardenberg (1772–1801)—Novalis—who had died at twenty-nine of tuberculosis, MacDonald found a deep attraction. His first published work (1850) was a translation of Novalis's *Spiritual Songs*. All his life, he was influenced by Novalis, by E. T. A. Hoffmann (1776–1822) and other German romantics, by Wordsworth, and by a mystical tradition that went back to Jakob Boehme (1575–1624), Emanuel Swedenborg (1688–1772), and William Blake (1757–1827). Like the romantics and the mystics, MacDonald repudiated realism and reality, and espoused poesy, imagination, and dream. He adopted Novalis's view that mankind had evolved not only from animals but, before that, from plants and minerals; and added the invention that, as men behaved wickedly, they reverted to the shape of the animals they most resembled, while animals who had once been men might through repentance evolve upward toward humanity once more. MacDonald repudiated reason and the intellect in favor of the emotions. He preferred animals to people, children to adults, simple-minded or even idiotic human beings to normal ones.

These romantic currents blended in his writings with his distaste and resentment towards the rich of Victorian England and their false standards, and with his personal repudiation of Calvinism: in his novels, the stern paternal Calvinist God becomes softened and feminized into a figure more motherly than fatherly. He believed that death, paradoxically, should be eagerly sought, not as the antithesis to life, but as the real life. For MacDonald, as for Wordsworth, he who would save his life must lose it; when the caterpillar dies, he awakens as a butterfly: life without this "good" death, for MacDonald, was death itself; while the "good" death was truly life. Married to a devoted wife, affectionate father of eleven children, MacDonald struggled against illness, morbidity, and adversity. He wrote much verse, some forty-odd novels for adults, and two remarkable "fairy tales for adults," each a dream-romance: *Phantastes* (1858) at the beginning of his career, and *Lilith* (1895) near its very end. After an intermission of some years, tuberculosis raged among his children as it had among his immediate forebears and siblings. A second wave of deaths made it impossible for MacDonald to sustain his faith that evil in this world was only the best good that God could devise for us, however unpalatably disguised, and led him in his old age to the brink of despair and a passive resignation in silence.

Though George MacDonald's life was tragic, he knew long intervals of relative happiness, and he took justifiable pride in the achievements of those of his children who lived to grow up. He had many friends—Tennyson, Lewis Carroll, Kingsley, and Ruskin among them—and he enjoyed a wide popularity in England and America as a truly inspirational novelist. His major achievement is now seen in his writings for children: a series of short stories published mostly in the sixties, of which "The Golden Key" and "The Light Princess" are two of the best known; and three longer works, *At the Back of the North Wind* (1871), *The Princess and the Goblin* (1872), and its sequel, *The Princess and Curdie* (1877, book publication late in 1882). These have delighted and disturbed generation after generation of children, who, often with their elders, have read them without fully understanding their own reactions.

The Princess and the Goblin is probably MacDonald's best work of art: MacDonald himself called it "the most complete thing I have done." He beautifully realized the character of his Princess Irene, only eight years old, childlike but with true royal dignity and a conception of honor entirely befitting her station, and of her friend and rescuer, Curdie, the miner's son, who, though poor, is truly noble. The sinister goblins tunneling away beneath the castle, and their grotesque and horrible animal servants (all formerly people who have degenerated because of their wickedness), are balanced by the beautiful grandmother in her splendid tower room, with spinning wheel and lamp and white pigeons, who gives Irene a thread that will always bring her safe out of danger if she clings to it. To an adult reader the goblins may suggest the evil proclivities in our own human nature tunneling away in the subterranean chambers of our subconscious, and always threatening to take possession of the castle of our mind and soul unless we seek the help of our nobler self, which dwells, like grandmother, in the lofty towers of our personality. The thread we can envision as the thread of faith or love: the princess willingly believes that it will always bring her back to her grandmother, and it always does; but Curdie has to be convinced, and until he is convinced, he cannot see the thread. Children read the story with pleasure, without troubling themselves as to its interpretation. Yet despite its excellence it is too slight by itself to serve as an introduction to the original genius of MacDonald.

Those who prefer *The Princess and Curdie*—and it has its partisans—have somehow failed to see in it the despair of the author. Grandmother is now powerless. Although Irene and Curdie marry, they have no children, and after their death a king greedy for gold undermines the entire foundations of the capital city, which crashes into eternal destruction. Moreover, the selfish and wealthy inhabitants richly deserve their fate. In an apocalyptic mood, MacDonald filled this story with nastiness of all sorts—killings, filth, the transformation of people into beasts, and cruel and sadistic punishments: "they were smeared with rancid drippings; their faces were rubbed in maggots; I dare not tell all that was done to them." In his picture of the people of Irene's capital, and their self-satisified and fatal self-complacent prosperity, MacDonald was essaying political satire and striking out at what he felt to be the money-grubbing immorality of contemporary England. The rich are roundly denounced, and the poor praised; yet Curdie, in order to marry Irene, must be given royal blood. All this is revealing of MacDonald's own anger and frustration, and full of interest for students of his life and writing. But when read analytically, *The Princess and Curdie* hardly ranks as a children's book.

Flawed by occasional dull moments and oversentimental passages, and overlong for some modern tastes, *At the Back of the North Wind* is nonetheless one of the most strikingly original children's books of the ninteenth century, and unique for its combination of realism and fantasy. It takes place in two worlds, the real world of everyday Victorian London, and the dream world of little Diamond, the coachman's son, named after his father's beautiful horse. In moving back and forth between the real world and the dream world, MacDonald never changes his pace. The reader is not explicitly transferred—as in the *Alice* books or in MacDonald's own *Phantastes*—from the world of reality to the world of dreams. It is as if he had suddenly fallen asleep and passed from one world into the other, and at times the two worlds seem almost fused. Perhaps MacDonald was influenced here by E. T. A. Hoffmann's famous story *The Golden Pot*, which was a favorite of his.

The real world is a tough place in which Diamond's family suffers poverty, children as wretched as those in any of Hesba Stretton's "Street Arab" tales experience the brutality of drunken adults, toughs and bullies and foul-mouthed men abound, and the rich—with a few exceptions—are deeply to blame. Rich brewers build the pubs, like traps "to catch souls and bodies in." "Mr. Dyves"—mentioned only once with scorn—is *Dives*, the rich man, whose bed is like an ash-pit. Diamond's abused friend, Nanny, the little crossing-sweeper, is defiantly declared to be a lady, but when she dreams of visiting the moon, she finds herself even there accused of stealing and declared fit only for mud. When Diamond's father—having been reduced from coachman to cab driver—cannot drive his cab because of illness, Diamond himself drives it. It is probably the delightful matter-of-fact romance of the little boy sitting on the box of a hansom, and fearlessly driving his beloved horse through the streets of London, that has enthralled children for over a century.

But it is the dream world and the sudden transfers into it that make the book so mysterious and disturbing. MacDonald's own mythology is fully developed. The motherly or grandmotherly goddess figure (who appears in *Phantastes* and in the fairy tale called "The Carasoyn," in the Princess books and in *The Wise Woman*) here takes the form of North Wind, a woman with beautiful eyes, long fragrant hair, and a splendid bosom. She comes to Diamond in his dreams, she varies in size, and she takes him traveling with her. It is while flying over London in her arms that he first catches sight of Nanny and is set down to help her, as the two worlds momentarily fuse. North Wind sinks a ship at sea, as Diamond tries to understand why. There is a strange and beautiful country at the back of the north wind, to which Diamond wishes to go. When he is very ill, he actually does visit it: in the Arctic north, he finds her sitting on the doorstep of her house, as if dead on an icy ridge, and must pass directly through her to reach the country at her back. By reference to Dante and by quoting James Hogg's poem "Kilmeny," about a girl who had also visited the country, MacDonald makes it clear (to an adult) that the land at the back of the north wind is a kind of limbo, a way-station to paradise. Diamond returns; he has been at death's door; he has had a vision of paradise. And when, in MacDonald's book, Diamond does die, he goes to the back of the north wind.

North Wind loves and cherishes and embraces Diamond like the mighty loving grandmother-goddess of MacDonald's fantasy. But she sinks a ship; she turns herself into a wolf to frighten a drunken and incompetent nursemaid. Although people think her cruel, she is only doing what she must, and the people she drowns are carried to the land at her back. North Wind, then, is sometimes Death: but she is not precisely death, since she is also a divine motherly messenger, doing the work of a wind. The death she sometimes brings is the good, the welcome death that MacDonald celebrated and longed for; the death that is a reunion with the cosmos, with mother earth, with those who have gone before; the death that is not to be feared but sought.

As for Diamond, his mother's name is Martha and his father's Joseph; he sleeps in a manger; he is preternaturally good, loves everybody, and is always eager to help. The cabbies call him "God's baby," and it is widely believed that he is not right in the head. He is a Christlike child, we realize, a model of divine simplicity, a Wordsworthian simpleton or even almost an idiot, who lives only for others, and is too good for this world, which he must leave. Even North Wind does not know who gives her her assignments; but East Wind has told her that "it is all managed by a baby." So Diamond is the image on earth of the divine child who is in charge of the universe. George MacDonald was hinting here at his own mystic belief, and at his mighty efforts—eventually fruitless—to convince himself that apparent evil is only the best good. Together with the vision of Diamond's Christlike simplicity in a grubby, mean world so different from his dream life, it is MacDonald's personal faith that gives *At the Back of the North Wind* the quality of magic.

The text of At the Back of the North Wind, *with illustrations by Arthur Hughes, is reprinted from an American edition (New York: George Routledge and Sons, 1875).*

CHAPTER I

THE HAY-LOFT

I HAVE BEEN ASKED to tell you about the back of the North Wind. An old Greek writer mentions a people who lived there, and were so comfortable that they could not bear it any longer, and drowned themselves. My story is not the same as his. I do not think Herodotus had got the right account of the place. I am going to tell you how it fared with a boy who went there.

He lived in a low room over a coach-house; and that was not by any means at the back of the North Wind, as his mother very well knew. For one side of the room was built only of boards, and the boards were so old that you might run a pen-knife through into the north wind. And then let them settle between them which was the sharper! I know that when you pulled it out again the wind would be after it like a cat after a mouse, and you would know soon enough you were *not* at the back of the North Wind. Still, this room was not very cold, except when the north wind blew stronger than usual: the room I have to do with now was always cold, except in summer, when the sun took the matter into his own hands. Indeed, I am not sure whether I ought to call it a room at all; for it was just a loft where they kept hay and straw and oats for the horses. And when little Diamond—but stop: I must tell you that his father, who was a coachman, had named him after a favourite horse, and his mother had had no objection:—when little Diamond then lay there in bed, he could hear the horses under him munching away in the dark, or moving sleepily in their dreams. For Diamond's father had built him a bed in the loft with boards all around it, because they had so little room in their own end over the coach-house; and Diamond's father put old Diamond in the stall under the bed, because he was a quiet horse, and did not go to sleep standing, but lay down like a reasonable creature. But, although he was a surprisingly reasonable creature, yet, when young Diamond woke in the middle of the night, and felt the bed shaking in the blasts of the north wind, he could not help wondering whether, if the wind should blow the house down, and he were to fall through into the manger, old Diamond mightn't eat him up before he knew him in his nightgown. And although old Diamond was very quiet all night long, yet when he woke he got up like an earthquake, and then young Diamond knew what o'clock it was, or at least what was to be done next, which was—to go to sleep again as fast as he could.

There was hay at his feet and hay at his head, piled up in great trusses to the very roof. Indeed it was sometimes only through a little lane with several turnings, which looked as if it had been sawn out for him, that he could reach his bed at all. For the stock of hay was, of course, always in a state either of slow ebb or sudden flow. Sometimes the whole space of the loft, with the little panes in the roof for the stars to look in, would lie open before his open eyes as he lay in bed; sometimes a yellow wall of sweet-smelling fibres closed up his view at the distance of half a yard. Sometimes, when his mother had undressed him in her room, and told him to trot away to bed by himself, he would creep into the heart of the hay, and lie there thinking how cold it was outside in the wind, and how warm it was inside there in his bed, and how he could go to it

when he pleased, only he wouldn't just yet; he would get a little colder first. And ever as he grew colder, his bed would grow warmer, till at last he would scramble out of the hay, shoot like an arrow into his bed, cover himself up, and snuggle down, thinking what a happy boy he was. He had not the least idea that the wind got in at a chink in the wall, and blew about him all night. For the back of his bed was only of boards an inch thick, and on the other side of them was the north wind.

Now, as I have already said, these boards were soft and crumbly. To be sure, they were tarred on the outside, yet in many places they were more like tinder than timber. Hence it happened that the soft part having worn away from about it, little Diamond found one night, after he lay down, that a knot had come out of one of them, and that the wind was blowing in upon him in a cold and rather imperious fashion. Now he had no fancy for leaving things wrong that might be set right; so he jumped out of bed again, got a little strike of hay, twisted it up, folded it in the middle, and, having thus made it into a cork, stuck it into the hole in the wall. But the wind began to blow loud and angrily, and, as Diamond was falling asleep, out blew his cork and hit him on the nose, just hard enough to wake him up quite, and let him hear the wind whistling shrill in the hole. He searched for his hay-cork, found it, stuck it in harder, and was just dropping off once more, when, pop! with an angry whistle behind it, the cork struck him again, this time on the cheek. Up he rose once more, made a fresh stopple of hay, and corked the hole severely. But he was hardly down again before—pop! it came on his forehead. He gave it up, drew the clothes above his head, and was soon fast asleep.

Although the next day was very stormy, Diamond forgot all about the hole, for he was busy making a cave by the side of his mother's fire, with a broken chair, a three-legged stool, and a blanket, and then sitting in it. His mother, however, discovered it, and

pasted a bit of brown paper over it, so that, when Diamond had snuggled down the next night, he had no occasion to think of it.

Presently, however, he lifted his head and listened. Who could that be talking to him? The wind was rising again, and getting very loud, and full of rushes and whistles. He was sure some one was talking—and very near him too it was. But he was not frightened, for he had not yet learned how to be; so he sat up and hearkened. At last the voice, which, though quite gentle, sounded a little angry, appeared to come from the back of the bed. He crept nearer to it, and laid his ear against the wall. Then he heard nothing but the wind, which sounded very loud indeed. The moment, however, that he moved his head from the wall, he heard the voice again, close to his ear. He felt about with his hand, and came upon the piece of paper his mother had pasted over the hole. Against this he laid his ear, and then he heard the voice quite distinctly. There was, in fact, a little corner of the paper loose, and through that, as from a mouth in the wall, the voice came.

"What do you mean, little boy—closing up my window?"

"What window?" asked Diamond.

"You stuffed hay into it three times last night. I had to blow it out again three times."

"You can't mean this little hole! It isn't a window; it's a hole in my bed."

"I did not say it was *a* window: I said it was *my* window."

"But it can't be a window, because windows are holes to see out of."

"Well, that's just what I made this window for."

"But you are outside: you can't want a window."

"You are quite mistaken. Windows are to see out of, you say. Well, I'm in my house, and I want windows to see out of it."

"But you've made a window into my bed."

"Well, your mother has got three windows into my dancing-room, and you have three into my garret."

"But I heard father say, when my mother wanted him to make a window through the wall, that it was against the law, for it would look into Mr. Dyves's garden."

The voice laughed.

"The law would have some trouble to catch me!" it said.

"But if it's not right, you know," said Diamond, "that's no matter. You shouldn't do it."

"I am so tall I am above *that* law," said the voice.

"You must have a tall house, then," said Diamond.

"Yes; a tall house: the clouds are inside it."

"Dear me!" said Diamond, and thought a minute. "I think, then, you can hardly expect me to keep a window in my bed for you. Why don't you make a window into Mr. Dyves's bed?"

"Nobody makes a window into an ash-pit," said the voice, rather sadly. "I like to see nice things out of my windows."

"But he must have a nicer bed than I have, though mine is *very* nice—so nice that I couldn't wish a better."

"It's not the bed I care about: it's what is in it.—But you just open that window."

"Well, mother says I shouldn't be disobliging: but it's rather hard. You see the north wind will blow right in my face if I do."

"I am the North Wind."

"O-o-oh!" said Diamond, thoughtfully. "Then will you promise not to blow on my face if I open your window?"

"I can't promise that."

"But you'll give me the toothache. Mother's got it already."

"But what's to become of me without a window?"

"I'm sure I don't know. All I say is, it will be worse for me than for you."

"No; it will not. You shall not be the worse for it—I promise you that. You will be much the better for it. Just you believe what I say, and do as I tell you."

"Well, I *can* pull the clothes over my head," said Diamond, and feeling with his little sharp nails, he got hold of the open edge of the paper and tore it off at once.

In came a long whistling spear of cold, and struck his little naked chest. He scrambled and tumbled in under the bed-clothes, and covered himself up: there was no paper now between him and the voice, and he felt a little—not frightened exactly—I told you he had not learned that yet—but rather queer; for what a strange person this North Wind must be that lived in the great house—"called Out-of-Doors, I suppose," thought Diamond—and made windows into people's beds! But the voice began again; and he could hear it quite plainly, even with his head under the bed-clothes. It was a still more gentle voice now, although six times as large and loud as it had been, and he thought it sounded a little like his mother's.

"What is your name, little boy?" it asked.

"Diamond," answered Diamond, under the bed-clothes.

"What a funny name!"

"It's a very nice name," returned its owner.

"I don't know that," said the voice.

"Well, I do," retorted Diamond, a little rudely.

"Do you know to whom you are speaking?"

"No," said Diamond.

And indeed he did not. For to know a person's name is not always to know the person's self.

"Then I must not be angry with you.—You had better look and see, though."

"Diamond is a very pretty name," persisted the boy, vexed that it should not give satisfaction.

"Diamond is a useless thing rather," said the voice.

"That's not true. Diamond is very nice—as big as two—and so quiet all night! And doesn't he make a jolly row in the morning, getting up on his four great legs! It's like thunder."

"You don't seem to know what a diamond is."

"Oh, don't I just! Diamond is a great and good horse; and he sleeps right under me. He is Old Diamond, and I am Young Diamond; or, if you like it better, for you're very particular, Mr. North Wind, he's Big Diamond, and I'm Little Diamond; and I don't know which of us my father likes best."

A beautiful laugh, large but very soft and musical, sounded somewhere beside him, but Diamond kept his head under the clothes.

"I'm not Mr. North Wind," said the voice.

"You told me that you were the North Wind," insisted Diamond.

"I did not say *Mister* North Wind," said the voice.

"Well, then, I do; for mother tells me I ought to be polite."

"Then let me tell you I don't think it at all polite of you to say *Mister* to me."

"Well, I didn't know better. I'm very sorry."

"But you ought to know better."

"I don't know that."

"I do. You can't say it's polite to lie there talking—with your head under the bed-clothes, and never look up to see what kind of person you are talking to.—I want you to come out with me."

"I want to go to sleep," said Diamond, very nearly crying, for he did not like to be scolded, even when he deserved it.

"You shall sleep all the better to-morrow night."

"Besides," said Diamond, "you are out in Mr. Dyves's garden, and I can't get there. I can only get into our own yard."

"Will you take your head out of the bed-clothes?" said the voice, just a little angrily.

"No!" answered Diamond, half peevish, half frightened.

The instant he said the word, a tremendous blast of wind crashed in a board of the wall, and swept the clothes off Diamond. He started up in terror. Leaning over him was the large beautiful pale face of a woman. Her dark eyes looked a little angry, for they had just begun to flash; but a quivering in her sweet upper lip made her look as if she were going to cry. What was most strange was that away from her head streamed out her black hair in every direction, so that the darkness in the hayloft looked as if it were made of her hair; but as Diamond gazed at her in speechless amazement, mingled with confidence—for the boy was entranced with her mighty beauty—her hair began to gather itself out of the darkness, and fell down all about her again, till her face looked out of the midst of it like a moon out of a cloud. From her eyes came all the light by which Diamond saw her face and her hair; and that was all he did see of her yet. The wind was over and gone.

"Will you go with me now, you little Diamond? I am sorry I was forced to be so rough with you," said the lady.

"I will; yes, I will," answered Diamond, holding out both his arms. "But," he added, dropping them, "how shall I get my clothes? They are in mother's room, and the door is locked."

"Oh, never mind your clothes. You will not be cold. I shall take care of that. Nobody is cold with the North Wind."

"I thought everybody was," said Diamond.

"That is a great mistake. Most people make it, however. They are cold because they are not with the North Wind, but without it."

If Diamond had been a little older, and had supposed himself a good deal wiser, he would have thought the lady was joking. But he was not older, and did not fancy himself wiser, and therefore understood her well enough. Again he stretched out his arms. The lady's face drew back a little.

"Follow me, Diamond," she said.

"Yes," said Diamond, only a little ruefully.

"You're not afraid?" said the North Wind.

"No, ma'am; but mother never would let me go without shoes: she never said anything about clothes, so I dare say she wouldn't mind that."

"I know your mother very well," said the lady. "She is a good woman. I have visited her often. I was with her when you were born. I saw her laugh and cry both at once. I love your mother, Diamond."

"How was it you did not know my name, then, ma'am? Please am I to say *ma'am* to you, ma'am?"

"One question at a time, dear boy. I knew your name quite well, but I wanted to hear what you would say for it. Don't you remember that day when the man was finding fault with your name—how I blew the window in?"

"Yes, yes," answered Diamond, eagerly. "Our window opens like a door, right over the coach-house door. And the wind—you, ma'am—came in, and blew the bible out of the man's hands, and the leaves went all flutter flutter on the floor, and my mother picked it up and gave it back to him open, and there——"

"Was your name in the bible,—the sixth stone in the high-priest's breast-plate."

"Oh!—a stone, was it?" said Diamond. "I thought it had been a horse—I did."

"Never mind. A horse is better than a stone any day. Well, you see, I know all about you and your mother."

"Yes. I will go with you."

"Now for the next question: you're not to call me *ma'am*. You must call me just my own name—respectfully, you know—just North Wind."

"Well, please, North Wind, you are so beautiful, I am quite ready to go with you."

"You must not be ready to go with everything beautiful all at once, Diamond."

"But what's beautiful can't be bad. You're not bad, North Wind?"

"No; I'm not bad. But sometimes beautiful things grow bad by doing bad, and it takes some time for their badness to spoil their beauty. So little boys may be mistaken if they go after things because they are beautiful."

"Well, I will go with you because you are beautiful and good too."

"Ah, but there's another thing, Diamond:—What if I should look ugly without being bad—look ugly myself because I am making ugly things beautiful?—What then?"

"I don't quite understand you, North Wind. You tell me what then."

"Well, I will tell you. If you see me with my face all black, don't be frightened. If you see me flapping wings like a bat's, as big as the whole sky, don't be frightened. If you hear me raging ten times worse than Mrs. Bill, the blacksmith's wife—even if you see me looking in at people's windows like Mrs. Eve Dropper, the gardener's wife—you must believe that I am doing my work. Nay, Diamond, if I change into a serpent or a tiger, you must not let go your hold of me, for my hand will never change in yours if you keep a good hold. If you keep a hold, you will know who I am all the time, even when you look at me and can't see me the least like the North Wind. I may look something very awful. Do you understand?"

"Quite well," said little Diamond.

"Come along, then," said North Wind, and disappeared behind the mountain of hay.

Diamond crept out of bed and followed her.

CHAPTER II

THE LAWN

W HEN DIAMOND got round the corner of the hay, for a moment he hesitated. The stair by which he would naturally have gone down to the door was at the other side of the loft, and looked very black indeed; for it was full of North Wind's hair, as she descended before him. And just beside him was the ladder going straight down into the stable, up which his father always came to fetch the hay for Diamond's dinner. Through the opening in the floor the faint gleam of the stable lantern was enticing, and Diamond thought he would run down that way.

The stair went close past the loose-box in which Diamond the horse lived. When Diamond the boy was half-way down, he remembered that it was of no use to go this way, for the stable-door was locked. But at the same moment there was horse Diamond's great head poked out of his box on to the ladder, for he knew boy Diamond although he was in his night-gown, and wanted him to pull his ears for him. This Diamond did very gently for a minute or so, and patted and stroked his neck too, and kissed the big horse, and had begun to take the bits of straw and hay out of his mane, when all at once he recollected that the Lady North Wind was waiting for him in the yard.

"Good night, Diamond," he said, and darted up the ladder, across the loft, and down the stair to the door. But when he got out into the yard, there was no lady.

Now it is always a dreadful thing to think there is somebody and find nobody. Children in particular have not made up their minds to it; they generally cry at nobody, especially when they wake up at night. But it was an especial disappointment to Diamond, for his little heart had been beating with joy: the face of the North Wind was so grand! To have a lady like that for a friend—with such long hair, too! Why, it was longer than twenty Diamonds' tails! She was gone. And there he stood, with his bare feet on the stones of the paved yard.

It was a clear night overhead, and the stars were shining. Orion in particular was making the most of his bright belt and golden sword. But the moon was only a poor thin crescent. There was just one great, jagged, black and grey cloud in the sky, with a steep side to it like a precipice; and the moon was against this side, and looked as if she had tumbled off the top of the cloud-hill, and broken herself in rolling down the precipice. She did not seem comfortable, for she was looking down into the deep pit waiting for her. At least that was what Diamond thought as he stood for a moment staring at her. But he was quite wrong, for the moon was not afraid, and there was no pit she was going down into, for there were no sides to it, and a pit without sides to it is not a pit at all. Diamond, however, had not been out so late before in all his life, and things looked so strange about him!—just as if he had got into Fairyland, of which he knew quite as much as anybody; for his mother had no money to buy books to set him wrong on the subject. I have seen this world—only sometimes, just now and then, you know—look as strange as ever I saw Fairyland. But I confess that I have not yet seen Fairyland at its best. I am always *going* to see it so some time. But if you had been out in the face and not at the back of the North Wind, on a cold *rather* frosty night, and in your night-gown, you would have felt it all quite as strange as Diamond did. He cried a little, just a little, he was so disappointed to lose the lady: of course, you, little man, wouldn't have done that! But for my part, I don't mind people crying, so much as I mind what they cry about, and how they cry—whether they cry quietly like ladies and gentlemen, or go shrieking like vulgar emperors, or ill-natured cooks; for all emperors are not gentlemen, and all cooks are not ladies—nor all queens and princesses for that matter, either.

But it can't be denied that a little gentle crying does one good. It did Diamond good; for as soon as it was over he was a brave boy again.

"She shan't say it was my fault anyhow!" said Diamond. "I daresay she is hiding somewhere to see what I will do. I will look for her."

So he went round the end of the stable towards the kitchen-garden. But the moment he was clear of the shelter of the stable, sharp as a knife came the wind against his little chest and his bare legs. Still he would look in the kitchen-garden, and went on. But when he got round the weeping-ash that stood in the corner, the wind blew much stronger, and it grew stronger and stronger until he could hardly fight against it. And it was so cold! All the flashy spikes of the stars seemed to have got somehow into the wind. Then he thought of what the lady had said about people being cold because they were not *with* the North Wind. How it was that he should have guessed what she meant at that very moment I cannot tell, but I have observed that the most wonderful thing in the world is how people come to understand anything. He turned his back to the wind, and trotted again towards the yard; whereupon, strange to say, it blew so much more gently against his calves than it had blown against his shins, that he began to feel almost warm by contrast.

You must not think it was cowardly of Diamond to turn his back to the wind: he did so only because he thought Lady North Wind had said something like telling him to do so. If she had said to him that he must hold his face to it, Diamond would have held his face to it. But the most foolish thing is to fight for no good, and to please nobody.

Well, it was just as if the wind was pushing Diamond along. If he turned round, it grew very sharp on his legs especially, and so he thought the wind might really be Lady North Wind, though he could not see her, and he had better let her blow him wherever she pleased. So she blew and blew, and he went and went, until he found himself standing at a door in a wall, which door led from the yard into a little belt of shrubbery, flanking Mr. Coleman's house. Mr. Coleman was his father's master, and the owner of Diamond. He opened the door, and went through the shrubbery, and out into the middle of the lawn, still hoping to find North Wind. The soft grass was very pleasant to his bare feet, and felt warm after the stones of the yard; but the lady was nowhere to be seen. Then he began to think that after all he must have done wrong, and she was offended with him for not following close after her, but staying to talk to the horse, which certainly was neither wise nor polite.

There he stood in the middle of the lawn, the wind blowing his night-gown till it flapped like a loose sail. The stars were very shiny over his head; but they did not give light enough to show that the grass was green; and Diamond stood alone in the strange night, which looked half solid all about him. He began to wonder whether he was in a dream or not. It was important to determine this; "for," thought Diamond, "if I am in a dream, I am safe in my bed, and I needn't cry. But if I'm not in a dream, I'm out here, and perhaps I had better cry, or, at least, I'm not sure whether I can help it." He came

to the conclusion, however, that, whether he was in a dream or not, there could be no harm in not crying for a little while longer: he could begin whenever he liked.

The back of Mr. Coleman's house was to the lawn, and one of the drawing-room windows looked out upon it. The ladies had not gone to bed; for the light was still shining in that window. But they had no idea that a little boy was standing on the lawn in his night-gown, or they would have run out in a moment. And as long as he saw that light, Diamond could not feel quite lonely. He stood staring, not at the great warrior Orion in the sky, nor yet at the disconsolate, neglected moon going down in the west, but at the drawing-room window with the light shining through its green curtains. He had been in that room once or twice that he could remember at Christmas times; for the Colemans were kind people, though they did not care much about children.

All at once the light went nearly out: he could only see a glimmer of the shape of the window. Then, indeed, he felt that he was left alone. It was so dreadful to be out in the night after *everybody* was gone to bed! That was more than he *could* bear. He burst out crying in good earnest, beginning with a wail like that of the wind when it is waking up.

Perhaps you think this was very foolish; for could he not go home to his own bed again when he liked? Yes; but it looked dreadful to him to creep up that stair again and lie down in his bed again, and know that North Wind's window was open beside him, and she gone, and he might never see her again. He would be just as lonely there as here. Nay, it would be much worse if he had to think that the window was nothing but a hole in the wall.

At the very moment when he burst out crying, the old nurse, who had grown to be one of the family, for she had not gone away when Miss Coleman did not want any more nursing, came to the back-door, which was of glass, to close the shutters. She

thought she heard a cry, and, peering out with a hand on each side of her eyes like Diamond's blinkers, she saw something white on the lawn. Too old and too wise to be frightened, she opened the door, and went straight towards the white thing to see what it was. And when Diamond saw her coming he was not frightened either, though Mrs. Crump was a little cross sometimes; for there is a good kind of crossness that is only disagreeable, and there is a bad kind of crossness that is very nasty indeed. So she came up with her neck stretched out, and her head at the end of it, and her eyes foremost of all, like a snail's, peering into the night to see what it could be that went on glimmering white before her. When she did see, she made a great exclamation, and threw up her hands. Then without a word, for she thought Diamond was walking in his sleep, she caught hold of him, and led him towards the house. He made no objection, for he was just in the mood to be grateful for notice of any sort, and Mrs. Crump led him straight into the drawing-room.

Now, from the neglect of the new housemaid, the fire in Miss Coleman's bed-room had gone out, and her mother had told her to brush her hair by the drawing-room fire—a disorderly proceeding which a mother's wish could justify. The young lady was very lovely, though not nearly so beautiful as North Wind; and her hair was extremely long, for it came down to her knees—though that was nothing at all to North Wind's hair. Yet when she looked round, with her hair all about her, as Diamond entered, he thought for one moment that it was North Wind, and, pulling his hand from Mrs. Crump's, he stretched out his arms and ran towards Miss Coleman. She was so pleased that she threw down her brush, and almost knelt on the floor to receive him in her arms. He saw the next moment that she was not Lady North Wind, but she looked so like her he could not help running into her arms and bursting into tears afresh. Mrs.

Crump said the poor child had walked out in his sleep, and Diamond thought she ought to know, and did not contradict her: for anything he knew, it might be so indeed. He let them talk on about him, and said nothing; and when, after their astonishment was over, and Miss Coleman had given him a sponge-cake, it was decreed that Mrs. Crump should take him to his mother, he was quite satisfied.

His mother had to get out of bed to open the door when Mrs. Crump knocked. She was indeed surprised to see her boy; and having taken him in her arms and carried him to his bed, returned and had a long confabulation with Mrs. Crump, for they were still talking when Diamond fell fast asleep, and could hear them no longer.

CHAPTER III

OLD DIAMOND

Diamond woke very early in the morning, and thought what a curious dream he had had. But the memory grew brighter and brighter in his head, until it did not look altogether like a dream, and he began to doubt whether he had not really been abroad in the wind last night. He came to the conclusion that, if he had really been brought home to his mother by Mrs. Crump, she would say something to him about it, and that would settle the matter. Then he got up and dressed himself, but, finding that his father and mother were not yet stirring, he went down the ladder to the stable. There he found that even old Diamond was not awake yet, for he, as well as young Diamond, always got up the moment he woke, and now he was lying as flat as a horse could lie upon his nice trim bed of straw.

"I'll give old Diamond a surprise," thought the boy; and creeping up very softly, before the horse knew, he was astride of his back. Then it was young Diamond's turn to have more of a surprise than he had expected; for as with an earthquake, with a rumbling and a rocking hither and thither, a sprawling of legs and heaving as of many backs, young Diamond found himself hoisted up in the air, with both hands twisted in the horse's mane. The next instant old Diamond lashed out with both his hind legs, and giving one cry of terror young Diamond found himself lying on his neck, with his arms as far round it as they would go. But then the horse stood as still as a stone, except that he lifted his head gently up, to let the boy slip down to his back. For when he heard young Diamond's cry he knew that there was nothing to kick about; for young Diamond was a good boy, and old Diamond was a good horse, and the one was all right on the back of the other.

As soon as Diamond had got himself comfortable on the saddle place, the horse began pulling at the hay, and the boy began thinking. He had never mounted Diamond himself before, and he had never got off him without being lifted down. So he sat, while the horse ate, wondering how he was to reach the ground.

But while he meditated, his mother woke, and her first thought was to see her boy.

She had visited him twice during the night, and found him sleeping quietly. Now his bed was empty, and she was frightened.

"Diamond! Diamond! Where are you, Diamond?" she called out.

Diamond turned his head where he sat like a knight on his steed in enchanted stall, and cried aloud,—

"Here, mother!"

"Where, Diamond?" she returned.

"Here, mother, on Diamond's back."

She came running to the ladder, and peeping down, saw him aloft on the great horse.

"Come down, Diamond," she said.

"I can't," answered Diamond.

"How did you get up?" asked his mother.

"Quite easily," answered he; "but when I got up, Diamond would get up too, and so here I am."

His mother thought he had been walking in his sleep again, and hurried down the ladder. She did not much like going up to the horse, for she had not been used to horses; but she would have gone into a lion's den, not to say a horse's stall, to help her boy. So she went and lifted him off Diamond's back, and felt braver all her life after. She carried him in her arms up to her room; but afraid of frightening him at his own sleep-walking, as she supposed it, said nothing about last night. Before the next day was over, Diamond had almost concluded the whole adventure a dream.

For a week his mother watched him very carefully—going into the loft several times a night—as often, in fact, as she woke. Every time she found him fast asleep.

All that week it was hard weather. The grass showed white in the morning with the hoar-frost which clung like tiny comfits to every blade. And as Diamond's shoes were not good, and his mother had not quite saved up enough money to get him the new pair she so much wanted for him, she would not let him run out. He played all his games over and over indoors, especially that of driving two chairs harnessed to the baby's cradle; and if they did not go very fast, they went as fast as could be expected of the best chairs in the world, although one of them had only three legs, and the other only half a back.

At length his mother brought home his new shoes, and no sooner did she find they fitted him than she told him he might run out in the yard and amuse himself for an hour.

The sun was going down when he flew from the door like a bird from its cage. All the world was new to him. A great fire of sunset burned on the top of the gate that led from the stables to the house; above the fire in the sky lay a large lake of green light, above that a golden cloud, and over that the blue of the wintry heavens. And Diamond thought that, next to his own home, he had never seen any place he would like so much to live in as that sky. For it is not fine things that make home a nice place, but your mother and your father.

As he was yet looking at the lovely colours, the gates were thrown open, and there was old Diamond and his friend in the carriage, dancing with impatience to get at their stalls and their oats. And in they came. Diamond was not in the least afraid of his father driving over him, but, careful not to spoil the grand show he made with his fine horses and his multitudinous cape, with a red edge to every fold, he slipped out of the way and let him dash right on to the stables. To be quite safe he had to step into the recess of the door that led from the yard to the shrubbery.

As he stood there he remembered how the wind had driven him to this same spot on the night of his dream. And once more he was almost sure that it was no dream. At all events, he would go in and see whether things looked at all now as they did then. He opened the door, and passed through the little belt of shrubbery. Not a flower was to be seen in the beds on the lawn. Even the brave old chrysanthemums and Christmas roses had passed away before the frost. What? Yes! There was one! He ran and knelt down to look at it.

It was a primrose—a dwarfish thing, but perfect in shape—a baby-wonder. As he stooped his face to see it close, a little wind began to blow, and two or three long leaves that stood up behind the flower shook and waved and quivered, but the primrose lay still in the green hollow, looking up at the sky, and not seeming to know that the wind was blowing at all. It was just a one eye that the dull black wintry earth had opened to look at the sky with. All at once Diamond thought it was saying its prayers, and he ought not to be staring at it so. He ran to the stable to see his father make Diamond's bed. Then his father took him in his arms, carried him up the ladder, and set him down at the table where they were going to have their tea.

"Miss is very poorly," said Diamond's father; "Mis'ess has been to the doctor with her to-day, and she looked very glum when she came out again. I was a-watching of them to see what doctor had said."

"And didn't Miss look glum too?" asked his mother.

"Not half as glum as Mis'ess," returned the coachman. "You see——"

But he lowered his voice, and Diamond could not make out more than a word here and there. For Diamond's father was not only one of the finest of coachmen to look at, and one of the best of drivers, but one of the most discreet of servants as well. Therefore he did not talk about family affairs to any one but his wife, whom he had proved better than himself long ago, and was careful that even Diamond should hear nothing he could repeat again concerning master and his family.

It was bed-time soon, and Diamond went to bed and fell fast asleep.

He awoke all at once, in the dark.

"Open the window, Diamond," said a voice.

Now Diamond's mother had once more pasted up North Wind's window.

"Are you North Wind?" said Diamond: "I don't hear you blowing."

"No; but you hear me talking. Open the window, for I haven't overmuch time."

"Yes," returned Diamond. "But, please, North Wind, where's the use? You left me all alone last time."

He had got up on his knees, and was busy with his nails once more at the paper over the hole in the wall. For now that North Wind spoke again, he remembered all that had taken place before as distinctly as if it had happened only last night.

"Yes, but that was your fault," returned North Wind. "I had work to do; and, besides, a gentleman should never keep a lady waiting."

"But I'm not a gentleman," said Diamond, scratching away at the paper.

"I hope you won't say so ten years after this."

"I'm going to be a coachman, and a coachman is not a gentleman," persisted Diamond.

"We call your father a gentleman in our house," said North Wind.

"He doesn't call himself one," said Diamond.

"That's of no consequence: every man ought to be a gentleman, and your father is one."

Diamond was so pleased to hear this that he scratched at the paper like ten mice, and getting hold of the edge of it, tore it off. The next instant a young girl glided across the bed, and stood upon the floor.

"Oh dear!" said Diamond, quite dismayed; "I didn't know—who are you, please?"

"I'm North Wind."

"Are you really?"

"Yes. Make haste."

"But you're no bigger than me."

"Do you think I care about how big or how little I am? Didn't you see me this evening? I was less then."

"No. Where was you?"

"Behind the leaves of the primrose. Didn't you see them blowing?"

"Yes."

"Make haste, then, if you want to go with me."

"But you are not big enough to take care of me. I think you are only Miss North Wind."

"I am big enough to show you the way, anyhow. But if you won't come, why, you must stay."

"I must dress myself. I didn't mind with a grown lady, but I couldn't go with a little girl in my night-gown."

"Very well. I'm not in such a hurry as I was the other night. Dress as fast as you can, and I'll go and shake the primrose leaves till you come."

"Don't hurt it," said Diamond.

North Wind broke out in a little laugh like the breaking of silver bubbles, and was gone in a moment. Diamond saw—for it was a starlit night, and the mass of hay was at a low ebb now—the gleam of something vanishing down the stair, and, springing out of bed, dressed himself as fast as ever he could. Then he crept out into the yard, through the door in the wall, and away to the primrose. Behind it stood North Wind, leaning over it, and looking at the flower as if she had been its mother.

"Come along," she said, jumping up and holding out her hand.

Diamond took her hand. It was cold, but so pleasant and full of life, it was better than warm. She led him across the garden. With one bound she was on the top of the wall. Diamond was left at the foot.

"Stop, stop!" he cried. "Please, I can't jump like that."

"You don't try," said North Wind, who from the top looked down a foot taller than before.

"Give me your hand again, and I will try," said Diamond.

She reached down, Diamond laid hold of her hand, gave a great spring, and stood beside her.

"This *is* nice!" he said.

Another bound, and they stood in the road by the river. It was full tide, and the stars were shining clear in its depths, for it lay still, waiting for the turn to run down again to the sea. They walked along its side. But they had not walked far before its surface was covered with ripples, and the stars had vanished from its bosom.

And North Wind was now tall as a full-grown girl. Her hair was flying about her head, and the wind was blowing a breeze down the river. But she turned aside and went up a narrow lane, and as she went her hair fell down around her.

"I have some rather disagreeable work to do to-night," she said, "before I get out to sea, and I must set about it at once. The disagreeable work must be looked after first."

So saying, she laid hold of Diamond and began to run, gliding along faster and faster. Diamond kept up with her as well as he could. She made many turnings and windings, apparently because it was not quite easy to get him over walls and houses. Once they ran through a hall where they found back and front doors open. At the foot of the stair North Wind stood still, and Diamond, hearing a great growl, started in terror, and there, instead of North Wind, was a huge wolf by his side. He let go his hold in dismay, and the wolf bounded up the stair. The windows of the house rattled and shook as if guns were firing, and the sound of a great fall came from above. Diamond stood with white face staring up at the landing.

"Surely," he thought, "North Wind can't be eating one of the children!" Coming to himself all at once, he rushed after her with his little fist clenched. There were ladies in long trains going up and down the stairs, and gentlemen in white neckties attending on them, who stared at him, but none of them were of the people of the house, and they said nothing. Before he reached the head of the stair, however, North Wind met him, took him by the hand, and hurried down and out of the house.

"I hope you haven't eaten a baby, North Wind!" said Diamond, very solemnly.

North Wind laughed merrily, and went tripping on faster. Her grassy robe swept and swirled about her steps, and wherever it passed over withered leaves, they went fleeing and whirling in spirals, and running on their edges like wheels, all about her feet.

"No," she said at last, "I did not eat a baby. You would not have had to ask that foolish question if you had not let go your hold of me. You would have seen how I served a nurse that was calling a child bad names, and telling her she was wicked. She had been drinking. I saw an ugly gin bottle in a cupboard."

"And you frightened her?" said Diamond.

"I believe so!" answered North Wind, laughing merrily. "I flew at her throat, and she tumbled over on the floor with such a crash that they ran in. She'll be turned away to-morrow—and quite time, if they knew as much as I do."

"But didn't you frighten the little one?"

"She never saw me. The woman would not have seen me either if she had not been wicked."

"Oh!" said Diamond, dubiously.

"Why should you see things," returned North Wind, "that you wouldn't understand or know what to do with? Good people see good things; bad people, bad things."

"Then are you a bad thing?"

"No. For *you* see me, Diamond, dear," said the girl, and she looked down at him, and Diamond saw the loving eyes of the great lady beaming from the depths of her falling hair.

"I had to make myself look like a bad thing before she could see me. If I had put on any other shape than a wolf's she would not have seen me, for that is what is growing to be her own shape inside of her."

"I don't know what you mean," said Diamond, "but I suppose it's all right."

They were now climbing the slope of a grassy ascent. It was Primrose Hill, in fact, although Diamond had never heard of it. The moment they reached the top, North

Wind stood and turned her face towards London. The stars were still shining clear and cold overhead. There was not a cloud to be seen. The air was sharp, but Diamond did not find it cold.

"Now," said the lady, "whatever you do, do not let my hand go. I might have lost you the last time, only I was not in a hurry then: now I am in a hurry."

Yet she stood still for a moment.

CHAPTER IV

NORTH WIND

AND AS SHE STOOD looking towards London, Diamond saw that she was trembling.

"Are you cold, North Wind?" he asked.

"No, Diamond," she answered, looking down upon him with a smile; "I am only getting ready to sweep one of my rooms. Those careless, greedy, untidy children make it in such a mess."

As she spoke he could have told by her voice, if he had not seen with his eyes, that she was growing larger and larger. Her head went up and up towards the stars; and as she grew, still trembling through all her body, her hair also grew—longer and longer, and lifted itself from her head, and went out in black waves. The next moment, however, it fell back around her, and she grew less and less till she was only a tall woman. Then she put her hands behind her head, and gathered some of her hair, and began waving and knotting it together. When she had done, she bent down her beautiful face close to his, and said—

"Diamond, I am afraid you would not keep hold of me, and if I were to drop you, I don't know what might happen; so I have been making a place for you in my hair. Come."

Diamond held out his arms, for with that grand face looking at him, he believed like a baby. She took him in her hands, threw him over her shoulder, and said, "Get in, Diamond."

And Diamond parted her hair with his hands, crept between, and feeling about soon found the woven nest. It was just like a pocket, or like the shawl in which gipsy women carry their children. North Wind put her hands to her back, felt all about the nest, and finding it safe, said,—

"Are you comfortable, Diamond?"

"Yes, indeed," answered Diamond.

The next moment he was rising in the air. North Wind grew towering up to the place of the clouds. Her hair went streaming out from her, till it spread like a mist over the stars. She flung herself abroad in space.

Diamond held on by two of the twisted ropes which, parted and interwoven, formed his shelter, for he could not help being a little afraid. As soon as he had come to himself,

he peeped through the woven meshes, for he did not dare to look over the top of the nest. The earth was rushing past like a river or a sea below him. Trees, and water, and green grass hurried away beneath. A great roar of wild animals rose as they rushed over the Zoological Gardens, mixed with a chattering of monkeys and a screaming of birds; but it died away in a moment behind them. And now there was nothing but the roofs of houses, sweeping along like a great torrent of stones and rocks. Chimney-pots fell, and tiles flew from the roofs; but it looked to him as if they were left behind by the roofs and the chimneys as they scudded away. There was a great roaring, for the wind was dashing against London like a sea; but at North Wind's back Diamond, of course, felt nothing of it all. He was in a perfect calm. He could hear the sound of it, that was all.

By and by he raised himself and looked over the edge of his nest. There were the houses rushing up and shooting away below him, like a fierce torrent of rocks instead of water. Then he looked up to the sky, but could see no stars; they were hidden by the blinding masses of the lady's hair which swept between. He began to wonder whether she would hear him if he spoke. He would try.

"Please, North Wind," he said, "what is that noise?"

From high over his head came the voice of North Wind, answering him gently,—

"The noise of my besom. I am the old woman that sweeps the cobwebs from the sky; only I'm busy with the floor now."

"What makes the houses look as if they were running away?"

"I am sweeping so fast over them."

"But, please, North Wind, I knew London was very big, but I didn't know it was so big as this. It seems as if we should never get away from it."

"We are going round and round, else we should have left it long ago."

"Is this the way you sweep, North Wind?"

"Yes; I go round and round with my great besom."

"Please, would you mind going a little slower, for I want to see the streets?"

"You won't see much now."

"Why?"

"Because I have nearly swept all the people home."

"Oh! I forgot," said Diamond, and was quiet after that, for he did not want to be troublesome.

But she dropped a little towards the roofs of the houses, and Diamond could see down into the streets. There were very few people about, though. The lamps flickered and flared again, but nobody seemed to want them.

Suddenly Diamond espied a little girl coming along a street. She was dreadfully blown by the wind, and a broom she was trailing behind her was very troublesome. It seemed as if the wind had a spite at her—it kept worrying her like a wild beast, and tearing at her rags. She was so lonely there!

"Oh! please, North Wind," he cried, "won't you help that little girl?"

"No, Diamond; I mustn't leave my work."

"But why shouldn't you be kind to her?"

"I am kind to her: I am sweeping the wicked smells away."

"But you're kinder to me, dear North Wind. Why shouldn't you be as kind to her as you are to me?"

"There are reasons, Diamond. Everybody can't be done to all the same. Everybody is not ready for the same thing."

"But I don't see why I should be kinder used than she."

"Do you think nothing's to be done but what you can see, Diamond, you silly! It's all right. Of course you can help her if you like. You've got nothing particular to do at this moment; I have."

"Oh! do let me help her, then. But you won't be able to wait, perhaps?"

"No, I can't wait; you must do it yourself. And, mind, the wind will get a hold of you too."

"Don't you want me to help her, North Wind?"

"Not without having some idea what will happen. If you break down and cry, that won't be much of a help to her, and it will make a goose of little Diamond."

"I want to go," said Diamond. "Only there's just one thing—how am I to get home?"

"If you're anxious about that, perhaps you had better go with me. I am bound to take you home again, if you do."

"There!" cried Diamond, who was still looking after the little girl; "I'm sure the wind will blow her over, and perhaps kill her. Do let me go."

They had been sweeping more slowly along the line of the street. There was a lull in the roaring.

"Well, though I cannot promise to take you home," said North Wind, as she sank nearer and nearer to the tops of the houses, "I can promise you it will be all right in the end. You will get home somehow. Have you made up your mind what to do?"

"Yes; to help the little girl," said Diamond firmly.

The same moment North Wind dropt into the street and stood, only a tall lady, but with her hair flying up over the housetops. She put her hands to her back, took Diamond, and set him down in the street. The same moment he was caught in the fierce coils of the blast, and all but blown away. North Wind stepped back a pace, and at once towered in stature to the height of the houses. A chimney-pot clashed at Diamond's feet. He turned in terror, but it was to look for the little girl, and when he turned again the lady had vanished, and the wind was roaring along the street as if it had been the bed of an invisible torrent. The little girl was scudding before the blast, her hair flying too, and behind her she dragged her broom. Her little legs were going as fast as ever they could to keep her from falling. Diamond crept into the shelter of a doorway, thinking to stop her; but she passed him like a bird, crying gently and pitifully.

"Stop! stop! little girl," shouted Diamond, starting in pursuit.

"I can't," wailed the girl; "the wind won't leave go of me."

Diamond could run faster than she, and he had no broom. In a few moments he had caught her by the frock. But it tore in his hand, and away went the little girl. So he had to run again, and this time he ran so fast that he got before her, and turning round caught her in his arms, when down they went both together, which made the little girl laugh in the midst of her crying.

"Where are you going?" asked Diamond, rubbing the elbow that had stuck farthest out. The arm it belonged to was twined round a lamp-post as he stood between the little girl and the wind.

"Home," she said, gasping for breath.

"Then I will go with you," said Diamond.

And then they were silent for a while, for the wind blew worse than ever, and they had both to hold on to the lamp-post.

"Where is your crossing?" asked the girl at length.

"I don't sweep," answered Diamond.

"What *do* you do, then?" asked she. "You ain't big enough for most things."

"I don't know what I do do," answered he, feeling rather ashamed. "Nothing, I suppose. My father's Mr. Coleman's coachman."

"Have you a father?" she said, staring at him as if a boy with a father was a natural curiosity.

"Yes. Haven't *you?*" returned Diamond.

"No; nor mother neither. Old Sal's all I've got."

And she began to cry again.

"I wouldn't go to her if she wasn't good to me," said Diamond.

"But you must go somewheres."

"Move on," said the voice of a policeman behind them.

"I told you so," said the girl. "You must go somewheres. They're always at it."

"But old Sal doesn't beat you, does she?"

"I wish she would."

"What do you mean?" asked Diamond, quite bewildered.

"She would if she was my mother. But she wouldn't lie abed a-cuddlin' of her ugly old bones, and laugh to hear me crying at the door."

"You don't mean she won't let you in to-night?"

"It'll be a good chance if she does."

"Why are you out so late, then?" asked Diamond.

"My crossing's a long way off at the West End, and I had been indulgin' in door-steps and mewses."

"We'd better have a try anyhow," said Diamond. "Come along."

As he spoke Diamond thought he caught a glimpse of North Wind turning a corner in front of them; and when they turned the corner too, they found it quite quiet there, but he saw nothing of the lady.

"Now you lead me," he said, taking her hand, "and I'll take care of you."

The girl withdrew her hand, but only to dry her eyes with her frock, for the other had enough to do with her broom. She put it in his again, and led him, turning after turning, until they stopped at a cellar-door in a very dirty lane. There she knocked.

"I shouldn't like to live here," said Diamond.

"Oh yes, you would, if you had nowheres else to go to," answered the girl. "I only wish we may get in."

"I don't want to go in," said Diamond.

"Where do you mean to go, then?"

"Home to my home."

"Where's that?"

"I don't exactly know."

"Then you're worse off than I am."

"Oh no, for North Wind—" began Diamond, and stopped, he hardly knew why.

"What?" said the girl, as she held her ear to the door listening.

But Diamond did not reply. Neither did old Sal.

"I told you so," said the girl. "She is wide awake hearkening. But we don't get in."

"What will you do, then?" asked Diamond.

"Move on," she answered.

"Where?"

"Oh, anywheres. Bless you, I'm used to it."

"Hadn't you better come home with me, then?"

"That's a good joke, when you don't know where it is. Come on."

"But where?"

"Oh, nowheres in particular. Come on."

Diamond obeyed. The wind had now fallen considerably. They wandered on and on, turning in this direction and that, without any reason for one way more than another, until they had got out of the thick of the houses into a waste kind of place. By this time they were both very tired. Diamond felt a good deal inclined to cry, and thought he had been very silly to get down from the back of the North Wind; not that he would have minded it if he had done the girl any good; but he thought he had been of no use to her. He was mistaken there, for she was far happier for having Diamond with her than if she had been wandering about alone. She did not seem so tired as he was.

"Do let us rest a bit," said Diamond.

"Let's see," she answered. "There's something like a rail-way there. Perhaps there's an open arch."

They went towards it and found one, and, better still, there was an empty barrel lying under the arch.

"Hillo! here we are!" said the girl. "A barrel's the jolliest bed going—on the tramp, I mean. We'll have forty winks, and then go on again."

She crept in, and Diamond crept in beside her. They put their arms round each other, and when he began to grow warm, Diamond's courage began to come back.

"This *is* jolly!" he said. "I'm *so* glad!"

"I don't think so much of it," said the girl. "I'm used to it, I suppose. But I can't think how a kid like you comes to be out all alone this time o' the night."

She called him a *kid*, but she was not really a month older than he was; only she had had to work for her bread, and that so soon makes people older.

"But I shouldn't have been out so late if I hadn't got down to help you," said Diamond. "North Wind is gone home long ago."

"I think you must ha' got out o' one o' them Hidget Asylms," said the girl. "You said something about the north wind afore that I couldn't get the rights of."

So now, for the sake of his character, Diamond had to tell her the whole story.

She did not believe a word of it. She said she wasn't such a flat as to believe all that bosh. But as she spoke there came a great blast of wind through the arch, and set the barrel rolling. So they made haste to get out of it, for they had no notion of being rolled over and over as if they had been packed tight and wouldn't hurt, like a barrel of herrings.

"I thought we should have had a sleep," said Diamond; "but I can't say I'm very sleepy after all. Come, let's go on again."

They wandered on and on, sometimes sitting on a door-step, but always turning into lanes or fields when they had a chance.

They found themselves at last on a rising ground that sloped rather steeply on the other side. It was a waste kind of spot below, bounded by an irregular wall, with a few doors in it. Outside lay broken things in general, from garden rollers to flower-pots and wine-bottles. But the moment they reached the brow of the rising ground, a gust of wind seized them and blew them down hill as fast as they could run. Nor could Diamond stop before he went bang against one of the doors in the wall. To his dismay it burst open. When they came to themselves they peeped in. It was the back door of a garden.

"Ah, ah!" cried Diamond, after staring for a few moments, "I thought so! North Wind takes nobody in! Here I am in master's garden! I tell you what, little girl, you just bore a hole in old Sal's wall, and put your mouth to it, and say, 'Please, North Wind, mayn't I go out with you?' and then you'll see what'll come."

"I daresay I shall. But I'm out in the wind too often already to want more of it."

"I said *with* the North Wind, not *in* it."

"It's all one."

"It's *not* all one."

"It *is* all one."

"But I know best."

"And I know better. I'll box your ears," said the girl.

Diamond got very angry. But he remembered that even if she did box his ears, he mustn't box hers again, for she was a girl, and all that boys must do, if girls are rude, is to go away and leave them. So he went in at the door.

"Good-bye, mister," said the girl.

This brought Diamond to his senses.

"I'm sorry I was cross," he said. "Come in, and my mother will give you some breakfast."

"No, thank you. I must be off to my crossing. It's morning now."

"I'm very sorry for you," said Diamond.

"Well, it *is* a life to be tired of—what with old Sal, and so many holes in my shoes."

"I wonder you're so good. I should kill myself."

"Oh no, you wouldn't! When I think of it, I always want to see what's coming next, and so I always wait till next is over. Well! I suppose there's somebody happy somewheres. But it ain't in them carriages. Oh my! *how* they *do* look sometimes—fit to bite your head off! Good-bye!"

She ran up the hill and disappeared behind it. Then Diamond shut the door as he best could, and ran through the kitchen-garden to the stable. And wasn't he glad to get into his own blessed bed again!

CHAPTER V

THE SUMMER-HOUSE

DIAMOND SAID NOTHING to his mother about his adventures. He had half a notion that North Wind was a friend of his mother, and that, if she did not know *all* about it, at least she did not mind his going anywhere with the lady of the wind. At the same time he doubted whether he might not appear to be telling stories if he told all, especially as he could hardly believe it himself when he thought about it in the middle of the day, although when the twilight was once half-way on to night he had no doubt about it, at least for the first few days after he had been with her. The girl that swept the crossing had certainly refused to believe him. Besides, he felt sure that North Wind would tell him if he ought to speak.

It was some time before he saw the lady of the wind again. Indeed nothing remarkable took place in Diamond's history until the following week. This was what happened then. Diamond the horse wanted new shoes, and Diamond's father took him out of the stable, and was just getting on his back to ride him to the forge, when he saw his little boy standing by the pump, and looking at him wistfully. Then the coachman took his foot out of the stirrup, left his hold of the mane and bridle, came across to his boy, lifted him up, and setting him on the horse's back, told him to sit up like a man. He then led away both Diamonds together.

The boy atop felt not a little tremulous as the great muscles that lifted the legs of the horse knotted and relaxed against his legs, and he cowered towards the withers, grasping with his hands the bit of mane worn short by the collar; but when his father looked back at him, saying once more, "Sit up, Diamond," he let the mane go and sat up, notwithstanding that the horse, thinking, I suppose, that his master had said to him, *"Come* up, Diamond," stepped out faster. For both the Diamonds were just grandly obedient. And Diamond soon found that, as he was obedient to his father, so the horse was obedient to him. For he had not ridden far before he found courage to reach forward and catch hold of the bridle, and when his father, whose hand was upon it, felt the boy pull it towards him, he looked up and smiled, and, well pleased, let go his hold,

and left Diamond to guide Diamond; and the boy soon found that he could do so perfectly. It was a grand thing to be able to guide a great beast like that. And another discovery he made was that, in order to guide the horse, he had in a measure to obey the horse first. If he did not yield his body to the motions of the horse's body, he could not guide him; he must fall off.

The blacksmith lived at some distance, deeper into London. As they crossed the angle of a square, Diamond, who was now quite comfortable on his living throne, was glancing this way and that in a gentle pride, when he saw a girl sweeping a crossing scuddingly before a lady. The lady was his father's mistress, Mrs. Coleman, and the little girl was she for whose sake he had got off North Wind's back. He drew Diamond's bridle in eager anxiety to see whether her outstretched hand would gather a penny from Mrs. Coleman. But she had given one at the last crossing, and the hand returned only to grasp its broom. Diamond could not bear it. He had a penny in his pocket, the gift of the same lady the day before, and he tumbled off his horse to give it to the girl. He tumbled off, I say, for he did tumble when he reached the ground. But he got up in an instant, and ran, searching his pocket as he ran. She made him a pretty courtesy when he offered his treasure, but with a bewildered stare. She thought first: "Then he *was* on the back of the North Wind after all!" but, looking up at the sound of the horse's feet on the paved crossing, she changed her idea, saying to herself, "North Wind is his father's horse! That's the secret of it! Why couldn't he say so?" And she had a mind to refuse the penny. But his smile put it all right, and she not only took his penny but put it in her mouth with a "Thank you, mister. Did they wollop you then?"

"Oh no!" answered Diamond. "They never wollops me."

"Lor!" said the little girl, and was speechless.

Meantime his father, looking up, and seeing the horse's back bare, suffered a pang of awful dread, but the next moment catching sight of him, took him up and put him on, saying—

"Don't get off again, Diamond. The horse might have put his foot on you."

"No, father," answered the boy, and rode on in majestic safety.

The summer drew near, warm and splendid. Miss Coleman was a little better in health, and sat a good deal in the garden. One day she saw Diamond peeping through the shrubbery, and called him. He talked to her so frankly that she often sent for him after that, and by degrees it came about that he had leave to run in the garden as he pleased. He never touched any of the flowers or blossoms, for he was not like some boys who cannot enjoy a thing without pulling it to pieces, and so preventing every one from enjoying it after them.

A week even makes such a long time in a child's life, that Diamond had begun once more to feel as if North Wind were a dream of some far-off year.

One hot evening, he had been sitting with the young mistress, as they called her, in a little summer-house at the bottom of the lawn—a wonderful thing for beauty, the boy thought, for a little window in the side of it was made of coloured glass. It grew dusky, and the lady began to feel chill, and went in, leaving the boy in the summer-house. He sat there gazing out at a bed of tulips, which, although they had closed for the night, could not go quite asleep for the wind that kept waving them about. All at once he saw a great humble-bee fly out of one of the tulips.

"There! that is something done," said a voice—a gentle, merry, childish voice; but *so* tiny. "At last it was. I thought he would have had to stay there all night, poor fellow! I did."

Diamond could not tell whether the voice was near or far away, it was so small and yet so clear. He had never seen a fairy, but he had heard of such, and he began to look all about for one. And there was the tiniest creature sliding down the stem of the tulip!

"Are you the fairy that herds the bees?" he asked, going out of the summer-house, and down on his knees on the green shore of the tulip-bed.

"I'm not a fairy," answered the little creature.

"How do you know that?"

"It would become you better to ask how *you* are to know it."

"You've just told me."

"Yes. But what's the use of knowing a thing only because you're told it?"

"Well, how *am* I to know you are not a fairy? You do look very like one."

"In the first place, fairies are much bigger than you see me."

"Oh!" said Diamond reflectively; "I thought they were very little."

"But they might be tremendously bigger than I am, and yet not *very* big. Why, *I* could be six times the size I am, and not be very huge. Besides, a fairy can't grow big and little at will, though the nursery-tales do say so: they don't know better. You stupid Diamond! have you never seen me before?"

And, as she spoke, a moan of wind bent the tulips almost to the ground, and the creature laid her hand on Diamond's shoulder. In a moment he knew that it was North Wind.

"I *am* very stupid," he said; "but I never saw you so small before, not even when you were nursing the primrose."

"Must you see me every size that can be measured before you know me, Diamond?"

"But how could I think it was you taking care of a great stupid humble-bee?"

"The more stupid he was the more need he had to be taken care of. What with sucking honey and trying to open the door, he was nearly dazed; and when it opened in the morning to let the sun see the tulip's heart, what would the sun have thought to find such a stupid thing lying there—with wings too?"

"But how do you have time to look after bees?"

"I don't look after bees. I had this one to look after. It was hard work, though."

"Hard work! Why, you could blow a chimney down, or—or—a boy's cap off," said Diamond.

"Both are easier than blow a tulip open. But I scarcely know the difference between hard and easy. I am always able for what I have to do. When I see my work, I just rush at it—and it is done. But I mustn't chatter. I have got to sink a ship to-night."

"Sink a ship! What! with men in it!"

"Yes, and women too."

"How dreadful! I wish you wouldn't talk so."

"It is rather dreadful. But it is my work. I must do it."

"I hope you won't ask me to go with you."

"No, I won't ask you. But you must come for all that."

"I won't, then."

"Won't you?"

And North Wind grew a tall lady, and looked him in the eyes, and Diamond said—

"Please take me. You cannot be cruel."

"No; I could not be cruel if I would. I can do nothing cruel, although I often do what looks like cruel to those who do not know what I really am doing. The people they say I drown, I only carry away to—to—to—well, the back of the North Wind—that is what they used to call it long ago, only *I* never saw the place."

"How can you carry them there if you never saw it?"

"I know the way."

"But how is it you never saw it?"

"Because it is behind me."

"But you can look round."

"Not far enough to see my own back. No; I always look before me. In fact, I grow quite blind and deaf when I try to see my back. I only mind my work."

"But how does it be your work?"

"Ah, that I can't tell you. I only know it is, because when I do it I feel all right, and when I don't I feel all wrong. East Wind says—only one does not exactly know how much to believe of what she says, for she is very naughty sometimes—she says it is all managed by a baby; but whether she is good or naughty when she says that, I don't know. I just stick to my work. It is all one to me to let a bee out of a tulip, or to sweep the cobwebs from the sky. You would like to go with me to-night?"

"I don't want to see a ship sunk."

"But suppose I had to take you?"

"Why, then, of course I must go."

"There's a good Diamond—I think I had better be growing a bit. Only you must go to bed first. I can't take you till you're in bed. That's the law about children. So I had better go and do something else first."

"Very well, North Wind," said Diamond. "What are you going to do first, if you please?"

"I think I may tell you. Jump up on the top of the wall, there."

"I can't."

"Ah! and I can't help you—you haven't been to bed yet, you see. Come out to the road with me, just in front of the coach-house, and I will show you."

North Wind grew very small indeed, so small that she could not have blown the dust off a dusty miller, as the Scotch children call a yellow auricula. Diamond could not even see the blades of grass move as she flitted along by his foot. They left the lawn, went out by the wicket in the coach-house gates, and then crossed the road to the low wall that separated it from the river.

"You can get up on this wall, Diamond," said North Wind.

"Yes; but my mother has forbidden me."

"Then don't," said North Wind.

"But I can see over," said Diamond.

"Ah! to be sure. I can't."

So saying, North Wind gave a little bound, and stood on the top of the wall. She was just about the height a dragon-fly would be, if it stood on end.

"You darling!" said Diamond, seeing what a lovely little toy-woman she was.

"Don't be impertinent, Master Diamond," said North Wind. "If there's one thing makes me more angry than another, it is the way you humans judge things by their size. I am quite as respectable now as I shall be six hours after this, when I take an East

Indiaman by the royals, twist her round, and push her under. You have no right to address me in such a fashion."

But as she spoke, the tiny face wore the smile of a great grand woman. She was only having her own beautiful fun out of Diamond, and true woman's fun never hurts.

"But look there!" she resumed. "Do you see a boat with one man in it—a green and white boat?"

"Yes; quite well."

"That's a poet."

"I thought you said it was a bo-at."

"Stupid pet! Don't you know what a poet is?"

"Why, a thing to sail on the water in."

"Well, perhaps you're not so far wrong. Some poets do carry people over the sea. But I have no business to talk so much. The man is a poet."

"The boat is a boat," said Diamond.

"Can't you spell?" asked North Wind.

"Not very well."

"So I see. A poet is not a bo-at, as you call it. A poet is a man who is glad of something, and tries to make other people glad of it too."

"Ah! now I know. Like the man in the sweety-shop."

"Not very. But I see it is no use. I wasn't sent to tell you, and so I can't tell you. I must be off. Only first just look at the man."

"He's not much of a rower," said Diamond—"paddling first with one fin and then with the other."

"Now look here!" said North Wind.

And she flashed like a dragon-fly across the water, whose surface rippled and puckered as she passed. The next moment the man in the boat glanced about him, and bent to his oars. The boat flew over the rippling water. Man and boat and river were awake. The same instant almost, North Wind perched again upon the river wall.

"How did you do that?" asked Diamond.

"I blew in his face," answered North Wind.

"I don't see how that could do it," said Diamond.

"I daresay not. And therefore you will say you don't believe it could."

"No, no, dear North Wind. I know you too well not to believe you."

"Well, I blew in his face, and that woke him up."

"But what was the good of it?"

"Why! don't you see? Look at him—how he is pulling. I blew the mist out of him."

"How was that?"

"That is just what I cannot tell you."

"But you did it."

"Yes. I have to do ten thousand things without being able to tell how."

"I don't like that," said Diamond.

He was staring after the boat. Hearing no answer, he looked down to the wall.

North Wind was gone. Away across the river went a long ripple—what sailors call a cat's paw. The man in the boat was putting up a sail. The moon was coming to herself on the edge of a great cloud, and the sail began to shine white. Diamond rubbed his eyes, and wondered what it was all about. Things seemed going on around him, and all

to understand each other; but he could make nothing of it. So he put his hands in his pockets, and went in to have his tea. The night was very hot, for the wind had fallen again.

"You don't seem very well to-night, Diamond," said his mother.

"I am quite well, mother," returned Diamond, who was only puzzled.

"I think you had better go to bed," she added.

"Very well, mother," he answered.

He stopped for one moment to look out of the window. Above the moon the clouds were going different ways. Somehow or other this troubled him, but, notwithstanding, he was soon fast asleep.

He woke in the middle of the night and the darkness. A terrible noise was rumbling overhead, like the rolling beat of great drums echoing through a brazen vault. The roof of the loft in which he lay had no ceiling; only the tiles were between him and the sky. For a while he could not come quite awake, for the noise kept beating him down, so that his heart was troubled and fluttered painfully. A second peal of thunder burst over his head, and almost choked him with fear. Nor did he recover until the great blast that followed, having torn some tiles off the roof, sent a spout of wind down into his bed and over his face, which brought him wide awake, and gave him back his courage. The same moment he heard a mighty yet musical voice calling him.

"Come up, Diamond," it said. "It's all ready. I'm waiting for you."

He looked out of the bed, and saw a gigantic, powerful, but most lovely arm—with a hand whose fingers were nothing the less ladylike that they could have strangled a boa-constrictor, or choked a tigress off its prey—stretched down through a big hole in the roof. Without a moment's hesitation he reached out his tiny one, and laid it in the grand palm before him.

CHAPTER VI

OUT IN THE STORM

T HE HAND felt its way up his arm, and, grasping it gently and strongly above the elbow, lifted Diamond from the bed. The moment he was through the hole in the roof, all the winds of heaven seemed to lay hold upon him, and buffet him hither and thither. His hair blew one way, his night-gown another, his legs threatened to float from under him, and his head to grow dizzy with the swiftness of the invisible assailant. Cowering he clung with the other hand to the huge hand which held his arm, and fear invaded his heart.

"Oh, North Wind!" he murmured, but the words vanished from his lips as he had seen the soap-bubbles that burst too soon vanish from the mouth of his pipe. The wind caught them, and they were nowhere. They couldn't get out at all, but were torn away and strangled. And yet North Wind heard them, and in her answer it seemed to Diamond that just because she was so big and could not help it, and just because her ear and her mouth must seem to him so dreadfully far away, she spoke to him more tenderly and graciously than ever before. Her voice was like the bass of a deep organ, without the groan in it; like the most delicate of violin tones without the wail in it; like the most glorious of trumpet-ejaculations without the defiance in it; like the sound of falling water without the clatter and clash in it: it was like all of them and neither of them—all of them without their faults, each of them without its peculiarity: after all, it was more like his mother's voice than anything else in the world.

"Diamond, dear," she said, "be a man. What is fearful to you is not the least fearful to me."

"But it can't hurt you," murmured Diamond, "for you're *it*."

"Then if I'm *it*, and have you in my arms, how can it hurt you?"

"Oh yes! I see," whispered Diamond. "But it looks so dreadful, and it pushes me about so."

"Yes, it does, my dear. That is what it was sent for."

At the same moment, a peal of thunder which shook Diamond's heart against the sides of his bosom hurtled out of the heavens: I cannot say out of the sky, for there was no sky. Diamond had not seen the lightning, for he had been intent on finding the face of North Wind. Every moment the folds of her garment would sweep across his eyes and blind him, but between, he could just persuade himself that he saw great glories of woman's eyes looking down through rifts in the mountainous clouds over his head.

He trembled so at the thunder, that his knees failed him, and he sunk down at North Wind's feet, and clasped her round the column of her ankle. She instantly stooped and lifted him from the roof—up—up into her bosom, and held him there, saying, as if to an inconsolable child—

"Diamond, dear, this will never do."

"Oh yes, it will," answered Diamond. "I am all right now—quite comfortable, I assure you, dear North Wind. If you will only let me stay here, I shall be all right indeed."

"But you will feel the wind here, Diamond."

"I don't mind that a bit, so long as I feel your arms through it," answered Diamond, nestling closer to her grand bosom.

"Brave boy!" returned North Wind, pressing him closer.

"No," said Diamond, "I don't see that. It's not courage at all, so long as I feel you there."

"But hadn't you better get into my hair? Then you would not feel the wind; you will here."

"Ah, but, dear North Wind, you don't know how nice it is to feel your arms about me. It is a thousand times better to have them and the wind together, than to have only your hair and the back of your neck and no wind at all."

"But it is surely more comfortable there?"

"Well, perhaps; but I begin to think there are better things than being comfortable."

"Yes, indeed there are. Well, I will keep you in front of me. You will feel the wind, but not too much. I shall only want one arm to take care of you; the other will be quite enough to sink the ship."

"Oh, dear North Wind! how can you talk so?"

"My dear boy, I never talk; I always mean what I say."

"Then you do mean to sink the ship with the other hand?"

"Yes."

"It's not like you."

"How do you know that?"

"Quite easily. Here you are taking care of a poor little boy with one arm, and there you are sinking a ship with the other. It can't be like you."

"Ah! but which is me? I can't be two mes, you know."

"No. Nobody can be two mes."

"Well, which me is me?"

"Now I must think. There looks to be two."

"Yes. That's the very point—You can't be knowing the thing you don't know, can you?"

"No."

"Which me do you know?"

"The kindest, goodest, best me in the world," answered Diamond, clinging to North Wind.

"Why am I good to you?"

"I don't know."

"Have you ever done anything for me?"

"No."

"Then I must be good to you because I choose to be good to you."

"Yes."

"Why should I choose?"

"Because—because—because you like."

"Why should I like to be good to you?"

"I don't know, except it be because it's good to be good to me."

"That's just it; I am good to you because I like to be good."

"Then why shouldn't you be good to other people as well as to me?"

"That's just what I don't know. Why shouldn't I?"

"I don't know either. Then why shouldn't you?"

"Because I am."

"There it is again," said Diamond. "I don't see that you are. It looks quite the other thing."

"Well, but listen to me, Diamond. You know the one *me*, you say, and that is good."

"Yes."

"Do you know the other *me* as well?"

"No. I can't. I shouldn't like to."

"There it is. You don't know the other me. You are sure of one of them?"

"Yes."

"And you are sure there can't be two mes?"

"Yes."

"Then the me you don't know must be the same as the me you do know,—else there would be two mes?"

"Yes."

"Then the other me you don't know must be as kind as the me you do know?"

"Yes."

"Besides, *I* tell you that it is so, only it doesn't look like it. That I confess freely. Have you anything more to object?"

"No, no, dear North Wind; I am quite satisfied."

"Then I will tell you something you might object. You might say that the me you know is like the other me, and that I am cruel all through."

"I know that can't be, because you are so kind."

"But that kindness might be only a pretence for the sake of being more cruel afterwards."

Diamond clung to her tighter than ever, crying—

"No, no, dear North Wind; I can't believe that. I don't believe it. I won't believe it. That would kill me. I love you, and you must love me, else how did I come to love you? How could you know how to put on such a beautiful face if you did not love me and the rest? No. You may sink as many ships as you like, and I won't say another word. I can't say I shall like to see it, you know."

"That's quite another thing," said North Wind; and as she spoke she gave one spring from the roof of the hay-loft, and rushed up into the clouds, with Diamond on her left arm close to her heart. And as if the clouds knew she had come, they burst into a fresh jubilation of thunderous light. For a few moments, Diamond seemed to be borne up through the depths of an ocean of dazzling flame; the next, the winds were writhing around him like a storm of serpents. For they were in the midst of the clouds and mists, and they of course took the shapes of the wind, eddying and wreathing and whirling and shooting and dashing about like gray and black water, so that it was as if the wind itself had taken shape, and he saw the gray and black wind tossing and raving most madly all about him. Now it blinded him by smiting him upon the eyes; now it deafened him by bellowing in his ears; for even when the thunder came he knew now that it was the billows of the great ocean of the air dashing against each other in their haste to fill the hollow scooped out by the lightning; now it took his breath quite away by sucking it from his body with the speed of its rush. But he did not mind it. He only gasped first and then laughed, for the arm of North Wind was about him, and he was leaning against her bosom. It is quite impossible for me to describe what he saw. Did you ever watch a great wave shoot into a winding passage amongst rocks? If you ever did, you

would see that the water rushed every way at once, some of it even turning back and opposing the rest; greater confusion you might see nowhere except in a crowd of frightened people. Well, the wind was like that, except that it went much faster, and therefore was much wilder, and twisted and shot and curled and dodged and clashed and raved ten times more madly than anything else in creation except human passions. Diamond saw the threads of the lady's hair streaking it all. In parts indeed he could not tell which was hair and which was black storm and vapour. It seemed sometimes that all the great billows of mist-muddy wind were woven out of the crossing lines of North Wind's infinite hair, sweeping in endless intertwistings. And Diamond felt as the wind seized on his hair, which his mother kept rather long, as if he too was a part of the storm, and some of its life went out from him. But so sheltered was he by North Wind's arm and bosom that only at times, in the fiercer onslaught of some curl-billowed eddy, did he recognise for a moment how wild was the storm in which he was carried, nestling in its very core and formative centre.

It seemed to Diamond likewise that they were motionless in this centre, and that all the confusion and fighting went on around them. Flash after flash illuminated the fierce chaos, revealing in varied yellow and blue and gray and dusky red the vaporous contention; peal after peal of thunder tore the infinite waste; but it seemed to Diamond that North Wind and he were motionless, all but the hair. It was not so. They were sweeping with the speed of the wind itself towards the sea.

CHAPTER VII

THE CATHEDRAL

I MUST NOT GO ON describing what cannot be described, for nothing is more wearisome.

Before they reached the sea, Diamond felt North Wind's hair beginning to fall about him.

"Is the storm over, North Wind?" he called out.

"No, Diamond. I am only waiting a moment to set you down. You would not like to see the ship sunk, and I am going to give you a place to stop in till I come back for you."

"Oh! thank you," said Diamond. "I shall be sorry to leave you, North Wind, but I would rather not see the ship go down. And I'm afraid the poor people will cry, and I should hear them. Oh, dear!"

"There are a good many passengers on board; and to tell the truth, Diamond, I don't care about your hearing the cry you speak of. I am afraid you would not get it out of your little head again for a long time."

"But how can you bear it then, North Wind? For I am sure you are kind. I shall never doubt that again."

"I will tell you how I am able to bear it, Diamond: I am always hearing, through every noise, through all the noise I am making myself even, the sound of a far-off song. I do not exactly know where it is, or what it means; and I don't hear much of it, only the odour of its music, as it were, flitting across the great billows of the ocean outside this air in which I make such a storm; but what I do hear, is quite enough to make me able to bear the cry from the drowning ship. So it would you if you could hear it."

"No, it wouldn't," returned Diamond, stoutly. "For *they* wouldn't hear the music of the far-away song; and if they did, it wouldn't do them any good. You see you and I are not going to be drowned, and so *we* might enjoy it."

"But you have never heard the psalm, and you don't know what it is like. Somehow, I can't say how, it tells me that all is right; that it is coming to swallow up all cries."

"But that won't do them any good—the people, I mean," persisted Diamond.

"It must. It must," said North Wind, hurriedly. "It wouldn't be the song it seems to be if it did not swallow up all their fear and pain too, and set them singing it themselves with the rest. I am sure it will. And do you know, ever since I knew I had hair, that is, ever since it began to go out and away, that song has been coming nearer and nearer. Only I must say it was some thousand years before I heard it."

"But how can you say it was coming nearer when you did not hear it?" asked doubting little Diamond.

"Since I began to hear it, I know it is growing louder, therefore I judge it was coming nearer and nearer until I did hear it first. I'm not so very old, you know—a few thousand years only—and I was quite a baby when I heard the noise first, but I knew it must come from the voices of people ever so much older and wiser than I was. I can't sing at all, except now and then, and I can never tell what my song is going to be; I only know what it is after I have sung it.—But this will never do. Will you stop here?"

"I can't see anywhere to stop," said Diamond. "Your hair is all down like a darkness, and I can't see through it if I knock my eyes into it ever so much."

"Look then," said North Wind; and, with one sweep of her great white arm, she swept yards deep of darkness like a great curtain from before the face of the boy.

And lo! it was a blue night, lit up with stars. Where it did not shine with stars it shimmered with the milk of the stars, except where, just opposite to Diamond's face, the gray towers of a cathedral blotted out each its own shape of sky and stars.

"Oh! what's that?" cried Diamond, struck with a kind of terror, for he had never seen a cathedral, and it rose before him with an awful reality in the midst of the wide spaces, conquering emptiness with grandeur.

"A very good place for you to wait in," said North Wind. "But we shall go in, and you shall judge for yourself."

There was an open door in the middle of one of the towers, leading out upon the roof, and through it they passed. Then North Wind set Diamond on his feet, and he found himself at the top of a stone stair, which went twisting away down into the darkness. For only a little light came in at the door. It was enough, however, to allow Diamond to see that North Wind stood beside him. He looked up to find her face, and saw that she was no longer a beautiful giantess, but the tall gracious lady he liked best to see. She took his hand, and, giving him the broad part of the spiral stair to walk on, led him down a good way; then, opening another little door, led him out upon a narrow gallery that ran all round the central part of the church, on the ledges of the windows of the clerestory, and through openings in the parts of the wall that divided the windows from each other. It was very narrow, and except when they were passing through the wall, Diamond saw nothing to keep him from falling into the church. It lay below him like a great silent gulf hollowed in stone, and he held his breath for fear as he looked down.

"What are you trembling for, little Diamond?" said the lady, as she walked gently along, with her hand held out behind her leading him, for there was not breadth enough for them to walk side by side.

"I am afraid of falling down there," answered Diamond. "It is so deep down."

"Yes, rather," answered North Wind; "but you were a hundred times higher a few minutes ago."

"Ah, yes, but somebody's arm was about me then," said Diamond, putting his little mouth to the beautiful cold hand that had a hold of his.

"What a dear little warm mouth you've got!" said North Wind. "It is a pity you should talk nonsense with it. Don't you know I have a hold of you?"

"Yes; but I'm walking on my own legs, and they might slip. I can't trust myself so well as your arms."

"But I have a hold of you, I tell you, foolish child."

"Yes, but somehow I can't feel comfortable."

"If you were to fall, and my hold of you were to give way, I should be down after you in a less moment than a lady's watch can tick, and catch you long before you had reached the ground."

"I don't like it, though," said Diamond.

"*Oh! oh! oh!*" he screamed the next moment, bent double with terror, for North Wind had let go her hold of his hand, and had vanished, leaving him standing as if rooted to the gallery.

She left the words, "Come after me," sounding in his ears.

But move he dared not. In a moment more he would from very terror have fallen into the church, but suddenly there came a gentle breath of cool wind upon his face, and it kept blowing upon him in little puffs, and at every puff Diamond felt his faintness going away, and his fear with it. Courage was reviving in his little heart, and still the cool wafts of the soft wind breathed upon him, and the soft wind was so mighty and strong within its gentleness, that in a minute more Diamond was marching along the narrow ledge as fearless for the time as North Wind herself.

He walked on and on, with the windows all in a row on one side of him, and the great empty nave of the church echoing to every one of his brave strides on the other, until at last he came to a little open door, from which a broader stair led him down and down and down, till at last all at once he found himself in the arms of North Wind, who held him close to her, and kissed him on the forehead. Diamond nestled to her, and murmured into her bosom,—

"Why did you leave me, dear North Wind?"

"Because I wanted you to walk alone," she answered.

"But it is so much nicer here!" said Diamond.

"I daresay; but I couldn't hold a little coward to my heart. It would make me so cold!"

"But I wasn't brave of myself," said Diamond, whom my older readers will have already discovered to be a true child in this, that he was given to metaphysics. "It was the wind that blew in my face that made me brave. Wasn't it now, North Wind?"

"Yes: I know that. You had to be taught what courage was. And you couldn't know what it was without feeling it: therefore it was given you. But don't you feel as if you would try to be brave yourself next time?"

"Yes, I do. But trying is not much."

"Yes, it is—a very great deal, for it is a beginning. And a beginning is the greatest thing of all. To try to be brave is to be brave. The coward who tries to be brave is before the man who is brave because he is made so, and never had to try."

"How kind you are, North Wind!"

"I am only just. All kindness is but justice. We owe it."

"I don't quite understand that."

"Never mind; you will some day. There is no hurry about understanding it now."

"Who blew the wind on me that made me brave?"

"I did."

"I didn't see you."

"Therefore you can believe me."

"Yes, yes; of course. But how was it that such a little breath could be so strong?"

"That I don't know."

"But you made it strong?"

"No: I only blew it. I knew it would make you strong, just as it did the man in the boat, you remember. But how my breath has that power I cannot tell. It was put into it when I was made. That is all I know. But really I must be going about my work."

"Ah! the poor ship! I wish you would stop here, and let the poor ship go."

"That I dare not do. Will you stop here till I come back?"

"Yes. You won't be long?"

"Not longer than I can help. Trust me, you shall get home before the morning."

In a moment North Wind was gone, and the next Diamond heard a moaning about the church, which grew and grew to a roaring. The storm was up again, and he knew that North Wind's hair was flying.

The church was dark. Only a little light came through the windows, which were almost all of that precious old stained glass which is so much lovelier than the new. But Diamond could not see how beautiful they were, for there was not enough of light in the stars to show the colours of them. He could only just distinguish them from the walls. He looked up, but could not see the gallery along which he had passed. He could only tell where it was far up by the faint glimmer of the windows of the clerestory, whose sills made part of it. The church grew very lonely about him, and he began to feel like a child whose mother has forsaken it. Only he knew that to be left alone is not always to be forsaken.

He began to feel his way about the place, and for a while went wandering up and down. His little footsteps waked little answering echoes in the great house. It wasn't too big to mind him. It was as if the church knew he was there, and meant to make itself his house. So it went on giving back an answer to every step, until at length Diamond thought he should like to say something out loud, and see what the church would answer. But he found he was afraid to speak. He could not utter a word for fear of the loneliness. Perhaps it was as well that he did not, for the sound of a spoken word would have made him feel the place yet more deserted and empty. But he thought he could sing. He was fond of singing, and at home he used to sing, to tunes of his own, all the nursery rhymes he knew. So he began to try *Hey diddle diddle,* but it wouldn't do. Then he tried *Little Boy Blue,* but it was no better. Neither would *Sing a Song of Sixpence* sing itself at all. Then he tried *Poor old Cockytoo,* but he wouldn't do. They all sounded so silly! and he had never thought them silly before. So he was quiet, and listened to the echoes that came out of the dark corners in answer to his footsteps.

At last he gave a great sigh, and said, "I'm *so* tired." But he did not hear the gentle echo that answered from far away over his head, for at the same moment he came against the lowest of a few steps that stretched across the church, and fell down and hurt his arm. He cried a little first, and then crawled up the steps on his hands and knees. At the top he came to a little bit of carpet, on which he lay down; and there he lay staring at the dull window that rose nearly a hundred feet above his head.

Now this was the eastern window of the church, and the moon was at that moment just on the edge of the horizon. The next, she was peeping over it. And lo! with the moon, St. John and St. Paul, and the rest of them, began to dawn in the window in their lovely garments. Diamond did not know that the wonder-working moon was behind, and he thought all the light was coming out of the window itself, and that the good old men were appearing to help him, growing out of the night and the darkness, because he had hurt his arm, and was very tired and lonely, and North Wind was so long in coming. So he lay and looked at them backwards over his head, wondering when they would come down or what they would do next. They were very dim, for the moonlight was not strong enough for the colours, and he had enough to do with his eyes trying to make out their shapes. So his eyes grew tired, and more and more tired, and his eyelids grew so heavy that they would keep tumbling down over his eyes. He kept lifting them and lifting them, but every time they were heavier than the last. It was no use; they were too much for him. Sometimes before he had got them half up, down they were again; and at length he gave it up quite, and the moment he gave it up, he was fast asleep.

CHAPTER VIII

THE EAST WINDOW

THAT DIAMOND had fallen fast asleep is very evident from the strange things he now fancied as taking place. For he thought he heard a sound as of whispering up in the great window. He tried to open his eyes, but he could not. And the whispering went on and grew louder and louder, until he could hear every word that was said. He thought it was the Apostles talking about him. But he could not open his eyes.

"And how comes he to be lying there, St. Peter?" said one.

"I think I saw him a while ago up in the gallery, under the Nicodemus window. Perhaps he has fallen down. What do you think, St. Matthew?"

"I don't think he could have crept here after falling from such a height. He must have been killed."

"What are we to do with him? We can't leave him lying there. And we could not make him comfortable up here in the window; it's rather crowded already. What do you say, St. Thomas?"

"Let's go down and look at him."

There came a rustling, and a chinking, for some time, and then there was a silence, and Diamond felt somehow that all the Apostles were standing round him and looking down on him. And still he could not open his eyes.

"What is the matter with him, St. Luke?" asked one.

"There's nothing the matter with him," answered St. Luke, who must have joined the company of the Apostles from the next window, one would think. "He's in a sound sleep."

"I have it," cried another. "This is one of North Wind's tricks. She has caught him up and dropped him at our door, like a withered leaf or a foundling baby. I don't understand that woman's conduct, I must say. As if we hadn't enough to do with our money, without going taking care of other people's children! That's not what our forefathers built cathedrals for."

Now Diamond could not bear to hear such things against North Wind, who, he knew, never played anybody a trick. She was far too busy with her own work for that. He struggled hard to open his eyes, but without success.

"She should consider that a church is not a place for pranks, not to mention that *we* live in it," said another.

"It certainly is disrespectful of her. But she always is disrespectful. What right has she to bang at our windows as she has been doing the whole of this night? I dare say there is glass broken somewhere. I know my blue robe is in a dreadful mess with the rain first and the dust after. It will cost me shillings to clean it."

Then Diamond knew that they could not be Apostles, talking like this. They could only be the sextons and vergers, and such-like, who got up at night, and put on the robes of deans and bishops, and called each other grand names, as the foolish servants he had heard his father tell of call themselves lords and ladies, after their masters and mistresses. And he was so angry at their daring to abuse North Wind, that he jumped up, crying—

"North Wind knows best what she is about. She has a good right to blow the cobwebs from your windows, for she was sent to do it. She sweeps them away from grander places, I can tell you, for I've been with her at it."

This was what he began to say, but as he spoke his eyes came wide open, and behold, there were neither Apostles nor vergers there—not even a window with the effigies of holy men in it, but a dark heap of hay all about him, and the little panes in the roof of his loft glimmering blue in the light of the morning. Old Diamond was coming awake down below in the stable. In a moment more he was on his feet, and shaking himself so that young Diamond's bed trembled under him.

"He's grand at shaking himself," said Diamond. "I wish I could shake myself like that. But then I can wash myself, and he can't. What fun it would be to see Old Diamond washing his face with his hoofs and iron shoes! Wouldn't it be a picture?"

So saying, he got up and dressed himself. Then he went out into the garden. There must have been a tremendous wind in the night, for although all was quiet now, there lay the little summer-house crushed to the ground, and over it the great elm-tree, which the wind had broken across, being much decayed in the middle. Diamond almost cried to see the wilderness of green leaves, which used to be so far up in the blue air, tossing about in the breeze, and liking it best when the wind blew it most, now lying so near the ground, and without any hope of ever getting up into the deep air again.

"I wonder how old the tree is!" thought Diamond. "It must take a long time to get so near the sky as that poor tree was."

"Yes, indeed," said a voice beside him, for Diamond had spoken the last words aloud.

Diamond started, and looking round saw a clergyman, a brother of Mrs. Coleman, who happened to be visiting her. He was a great scholar, and was in the habit of rising early.

"Who are you, my man?" he added.

"Little Diamond," answered the boy.

"Oh! I have heard of you. How do you come to be up so early?"

"Because the sham Apostles talked such nonsense, they waked me up."

The clergyman stared. Diamond saw that he had better have held his tongue, for he could not explain things.

"You must have been dreaming, my little man," said he. "Dear! dear!" he went on, looking at the tree, "there has been terrible work here. This is the north wind's doing. What a pity! I wish we lived at the back door of it, I'm sure."

"Where is that, sir?" asked Diamond.

"Away in the Hyperborean regions," answered the clergyman, smiling.

"I never heard of the place," returned Diamond.

"I daresay not," answered the clergyman; "but if this tree had been there now, it would not have been blown down, for there is no wind there."

"But, please, sir, if it had been there," said Diamond, "we should not have had to be sorry for it."

"Certainly not."

"Then we shouldn't have had to be glad for it, either."

"You're quite right, my boy," said the clergyman, looking at him very kindly, as he turned away to the house, with his eyes bent towards the earth. But Diamond thought within himself, "I will ask North Wind next time I see her to take me to that country. I think she did speak about it once before."

CHAPTER IX

HOW DIAMOND GOT TO THE BACK OF THE NORTH WIND

W HEN DIAMOND went home to breakfast, he found his father and mother already seated at the table. They were both busy with their bread and butter, and Diamond sat himself down in his usual place. His mother looked up at him, and, after watching him for a moment, said:

"I don't think the boy is looking well, husband."

"Don't you? Well, I don't know. I think he looks pretty bobbish. How do you feel yourself, Diamond, my boy?"

"Quite well, thank you, father; at least, I think I've got a little headache."

"There! I told you," said his father and mother both at once.

"The child's very poorly," added his mother.

"The child's quite well," added his father.

And then they both laughed.

"You see," said his mother, "I've had a letter from my sister at Sandwich."

"Sleepy old hole!" said his father.

"Don't abuse the place; there's good people in it," said his mother.

"Right, old lady," returned his father; "only I don't believe there are more than two pair of carriage-horses in the whole blessed place."

"Well, people can get to heaven without carriages—or coachmen either, husband. Not that I should like to go without *my* coachman, you know. But about the boy?"

"What boy?"

"That boy, there, staring at you with his goggle-eyes."

"Have I got goggle-eyes, mother?" asked Diamond, a little dismayed.

"Not too goggle," said his mother, who was quite proud of her boy's eyes, only did not want to make him vain. "Not too goggle; only you need not stare so."

"Well, what about him?" said his father.

"I told you I had got a letter."

"Yes, from your sister; not from Diamond."

"La, husband! you've got out of bed the wrong leg first this morning, I do believe."

"I always get out with both at once," said his father, laughing.

"Well, listen then. His aunt wants the boy to go down and see her."

"And that's why you want to make out that he ain't looking well."

"No more he is. I think he had better go."

"Well, I don't care, if you can find the money," said his father.

"I'll manage that," said his mother; and so it was agreed that Diamond should go to Sandwich.

I will not describe the preparations Diamond made. You would have thought he had been going on a three months' voyage. Nor will I describe the journey, for our business is now at the place. He was met at the station by his aunt, a cheerful middle-aged woman, and conveyed in safety to the sleepy old town, as his father had called it. And no wonder that it was sleepy, for it was nearly dead of old age.

Diamond went about staring with his beautiful goggle-eyes, at the quaint old streets, and the shops, and the houses. Everything looked very strange, indeed; for here was a town abandoned by its nurse, the sea, like an old oyster left on the shore till it gaped for weariness. It used to be one of the five chief seaports in England, but it began to hold itself too high, and the consequence was the sea grew less and less intimate with it, gradually drew back, and kept more to itself, till at length it left it high and dry: Sandwich was a seaport no more; the sea went on with its own tide-business a long way off, and forgot it. Of course it went to sleep, and had no more to do with ships. That's what comes to cities and nations, and boys and girls, who say, "I can do without *your* help. I'm enough for myself."

Diamond soon made great friends with an old woman who kept a toyshop, for his mother had given him twopence for pocket-money before he left, and he had gone into her shop to spend it, and she got talking to him. She looked very funny, because she had not got any teeth, but Diamond liked her, and went often to her shop, although he had nothing to spend there after the twopence was gone.

One afternoon he had been wandering rather wearily about the streets for some time. It was a hot day, and he felt tired. As he passed the toyshop, he stepped in.

"Please may I sit down for a minute on this box?" he said, thinking the old woman was somewhere in the shop. But he got no answer, and sat down without one. Around him were a great many toys of all prices, from a penny up to shillings. All at once he heard a gentle whirring somewhere amongst them. It made him start and look behind him. There were the sails of a windmill going round and round almost close to his ear. He thought at first it must be one of those toys which are wound up and go with clockwork; but no, it was a common penny toy, with the windmill at the end of a whistle, and when the whistle blows the windmill goes. But the wonder was that there was no one at the whistle end blowing, and yet the sails were turning round and round—now faster, now slower, now faster again.

"What can it mean?" said Diamond, aloud.

"It means me," said the tiniest voice he had ever heard.

"Who are you, please?" asked Diamond.

"Well, really, I begin to be ashamed of you," said the voice. "I wonder how long it will be before you know me; or how often I might take you in before you got sharp enough to suspect me. You are as bad as a baby that doesn't know his mother in a new bonnet."

"Not quite so bad as that, dear North Wind," said Diamond, "for I didn't see you at all, and indeed I don't see you yet, although I recognise your voice. Do grow a little, please."

"Not a hair's-breadth," said the voice, and it was the smallest voice that ever spoke. "What are you doing here?"

"I am come to see my aunt. But, please, North Wind, why didn't you come back for me in the church that night?"

"I did. I carried you safe home. All the time you were dreaming about the glass apostles, you were lying in my arms."

"I'm so glad," said Diamond. "I thought that must be it, only I wanted to hear you say so. Did you sink the ship, then?"

"Yes."

"And drown everybody?"

"Not quite. One boat got away with six or seven men in it."

"How could the boat swim when the ship couldn't?"

"Of course I had some trouble with it. I had to contrive a bit, and manage the waves a little. When they're once thoroughly waked up, I have a good deal of trouble with them sometimes. They're apt to get stupid with tumbling over each other's heads. That's when they're fairly at it. However, the boat got to a desert island before noon next day."

"And what good will come of that?"

"I don't know. I obeyed orders. Good bye."

"Oh! stay, North Wind, *do* stay!" cried Diamond, dismayed to see the windmill get slower and slower.

"What is it, my dear child?" said North Wind, and the windmill began turning again so swiftly that Diamond could scarcely see it. "What a big voice you've got! and what a noise you do make with it! What is it you want? I have little to do, but that little must be done."

"I want you to take me to the country at the back of the north wind."

"That's not so easy," said North Wind, and was silent for so long that Diamond thought she was gone indeed. But after he had quite given her up, the voice began again.

"I almost wish old Herodotus had held his tongue about it. Much he knew of it!"

"Why do you wish that, North Wind?"

"Because then that clergyman would never have heard of it, and set you wanting to go. But we shall see. We shall see. You must go home now, my dear, for you don't seem very well, and I'll see what can be done for you. Don't wait for me. I've got to break a few of old Goody's toys: she's thinking too much of her new stock. Two or three will do. There! go now."

Diamond rose, quite sorry, and without a word left the shop, and went home.

It soon appeared that his mother had been right about him, for that same afternoon his head began to ache very much, and he had to go to bed.

He awoke in the middle of the night. The lattice window of his room had blown open, and the curtains of his little bed were swinging about in the wind.

"If that should be North Wind now!" thought Diamond.

But the next moment he heard some one closing the window, and his aunt came to the bedside. She put her hand on his face, and said—

"How's your head, dear?"

"Better, auntie, I think."

"Would you like something to drink?"

"Oh, yes! I should, please."

So his aunt gave him some lemonade, for she had been used to nursing sick people, and Diamond felt very much refreshed, and laid his head down again to go very fast asleep, as he thought. And so he did, but only to come awake again, as a fresh burst of wind blew the lattice open a second time. The same moment he found himself in a cloud of North Wind's hair, with her beautiful face, set in it like a moon, bending over him.

"Quick, Diamond!" she said. "I have found such a chance!"

"But I'm not well," said Diamond.

"I know that, but you will be better for a little fresh air. You shall have plenty of that."

"You want me to go, then?"

"Yes, I do. It won't hurt you."

"Very well," said Diamond; and getting out of the bed-clothes, he jumped into North Wind's arms.

"We must make haste before your aunt comes," said she, as she glided out of the open lattice and left it swinging.

The moment Diamond felt her arms fold around him he began to feel better. It was a moonless night, and very dark, with glimpses of stars when the clouds parted.

"I used to dash the waves about here," said North Wind, "where cows and sheep are feeding now; but we shall soon get to them. There they are."

And Diamond, looking down, saw the white glimmer of breaking water far below him.

"You see, Diamond," said North Wind, "it is very difficult for me to get you to the back of the north wind, for that country lies in the very north itself, and of course I can't blow northwards."

"Why not?" asked Diamond.

"You little silly!" said North Wind. "Don't you see that if I were to blow northwards I should be South Wind, and that is as much as to say that one person could be two persons?"

"But how can you ever get home at all, then?"

"You are quite right—that is my home, though I never get farther than the outer door. I sit on the doorstep, and hear the voices inside. I am nobody there, Diamond."

"I'm very sorry."

"Why?"

"That you should be nobody."

"Oh, I don't mind it. Dear little man! you will be very glad some day to be nobody yourself. But you can't understand that now, and you had better not try; for if you do, you will be certain to go fancying some egregious nonsense, and making yourself miserable about it."

"Then I won't," said Diamond.

"There's a good boy. It will all come in good time."

"But you haven't told me how you get to the doorstep, you know."

"It is easy enough for me. I have only to consent to be nobody, and there I am. I draw into myself, and there I am on the doorstep. But you can easily see, or you have less sense than I think, that to drag you, you heavy thing, along with me, would take centuries, and I could not give the time to it."

"Oh, I'm so sorry!" said Diamond.

"What for now, pet?"

"That I'm so heavy for you. I would be lighter if I could, but I don't know how."

"You silly darling! Why, I could toss you a hundred miles from me if I liked. It is only when I am going home that I shall find you heavy."

"Then you are going home with me?"

"Of course. Did I not come to fetch you just for that?"

"But all this time you must be going southwards."

"Yes. Of course I am."

"How can you be taking me northwards, then?"

"A very sensible question. But you shall see. I will get rid of a few of these clouds—only they do come up so fast! It's like trying to blow a brook dry. There! What do you see now?"

"I think I see a little boat, away there, down below."

"A little boat, indeed! Well! She's a yacht of two hundred tons; and the captain of it is a friend of mine; for he is a man of good sense, and can sail his craft well. I've helped him many a time when he little thought it. I've heard his grumbling at me, when I was doing the very best I could for him. Why, I've carried him eighty miles a day, again and again, right north."

"He must have dodged for that," said Diamond, who had been watching the vessels, and had seen that they went other ways than the wind blew.

"Of course he must. But don't you see, it was the best I could do? I couldn't be South Wind. And besides it gave him a share in the business. It is not good at all—mind that, Diamond—to do everything for those you love, and not give them a share in the doing.

It's not kind. It's making too much of yourself, my child. If I had been South Wind, he would only have smoked his pipe all day, and made himself stupid."

"But how could he be a man of sense and grumble at you when you were doing your best for him?"

"Oh! you must make allowances," said North Wind, "or you will never do justice to anybody.—You do understand, then, that a captain may sail north—"

"In spite of a north wind—yes," supplemented Diamond.

"Now, I do think you must be stupid, my dear," said North Wind. "Suppose the north wind did not blow, where would he be then?"

"Why then the south wind would carry him."

"So you think that when the north wind stops the south wind blows. Nonsense. If I didn't blow, the captain couldn't sail his eighty miles a day. No doubt South Wind would carry him faster, but South Wind is sitting on her doorstep then, and if I stopped there would be a dead calm. So you are all wrong to say he can sail north in spite of me; he sails north by my help, and my help alone. You see that, Diamond?"

"Yes, I do, North Wind. I am stupid, but I don't want to be stupid."

"Good boy! I am going to blow you north in that little craft, one of the finest that ever sailed the sea. Here we are, right over it. I shall be blowing against you; you will be sailing against me; and all will be just as we want it. The captain won't get on so fast as he would like, but he will get on, and so shall we. I'm just going to put you on board. Do you see in front of the tiller—that thing the man is working, now to one side, now to the other—a round thing like the top of a drum?"

"Yes," said Diamond.

"Below that is where they keep their spare sails, and some stores of that sort. I am going to blow that cover off. The same moment I will drop you on deck, and you must tumble in. Don't be afraid, it is of no depth, and you will fall on a roll of sail-cloth. You will find it nice and warm and dry—only dark; and you will know I am near you by every roll and pitch of the vessel. Coil yourself up and go to sleep. The yacht shall be my cradle, and you shall be my baby."

"Thank you, dear North Wind. I am not a bit afraid," said Diamond.

In a moment they were on a level with the bulwarks, and North Wind sent the hatch of the after-store rattling away over the deck to leeward. The next, Diamond found himself in the dark, for he had tumbled through the hole as North Wind had told him, and the cover was replaced over his head. Away he went rolling to leeward, for the wind began all at once to blow hard. He heard the call of the captain, and the loud trampling of the men over his head, as they hauled at the main sheet to get the boom on board that they might take in a reef in the mainsail. Diamond felt about until he had found what seemed the most comfortable place, and there he snuggled down and lay.

Hours after hours, a great many of them, went by; and still Diamond lay there. He never felt in the least tired or impatient, for a strange pleasure filled his heart. The straining of the masts, the creaking of the boom, the singing of the ropes, the banging of the blocks as they put the vessel about, all fell in with the roaring of the wind above, the surge of the waves past her sides, and the thud with which every now and then one would strike her; while through it all Diamond could hear the gurgling, rippling, talking flow of the water against her planks, as she slipped through it, lying now on this side, now on that—like a subdued air running through the grand music his North Wind was making about him to keep him from tiring as they sped on towards the country at the back of her doorstep.

How long this lasted Diamond had no idea. He seemed to fall asleep sometimes, only through the sleep he heard the sounds going on. At length the weather seemed to get worse. The confusion and trampling of feet grew more frequent over his head; the vessel lay over more and more on her side, and went roaring through the waves, which banged and thumped at her as if in anger. All at once arose a terrible uproar. The hatch was blown off; a cold fierce wind swept in upon him; and a long arm came with it which laid hold of him and lifted him out. The same moment he saw the little vessel far below him righting herself. She had taken in all her sails and lay now tossing on the waves like a sea-bird with folded wings. A short distance to the south lay a much larger vessel, with two or three sails set, and towards it North Wind was carrying Diamond. It was a German ship, on its way to the North Pole.

"That vessel down there will give us a lift now," said North Wind; "and after that I must do the best I can."

She managed to hide him amongst the flags of the big ship, which were all snugly stowed away, and on and on they sped towards the north. At length one night she whispered in his ear, "Come on deck, Diamond;" and he got up at once and crept on deck. Everything looked very strange. Here and there on all sides were huge masses of floating ice, looking like cathedrals, and castles, and crags, while away beyond was a blue sea.

"Is the sun rising or setting?" asked Diamond.

"Neither or both, which you please. I can hardly tell which myself. If he is setting now, he will be rising the next moment."

"What a strange light it is!" said Diamond. "I have heard that the sun doesn't go to bed all the summer in these parts. Miss Coleman told me that. I suppose he feels very sleepy, and that is why the light he sends out looks so like a dream."

"That will account for it well enough for all practical purposes," said North Wind.

Some of the icebergs were drifting northward: one was passing very near the ship. North Wind seized Diamond, and with a single bound lighted on one of them—a huge thing, with sharp pinnacles and great clefts. The same instant a wind began to blow from the south. North Wind hurried Diamond down the north side of the iceberg, stepping by its jags and splintering; for this berg had never got far enough south to be melted and smoothed by the summer sun. She brought him to a cave near the water, where she entered, and, letting Diamond go, sat down as if weary on a ledge of ice.

Diamond seated himself on the other side, and for a while was enraptured with the colour of the air inside the cave. It was a deep, dazzling, lovely blue, deeper than the deepest blue of the sky. The blue seemed to be in constant motion, like the blackness when you press your eyeballs with your fingers, boiling and sparkling. But when he looked across to North Wind he was frightened; her face was worn and livid.

"What is the matter with you, dear North Wind?" he said.

"Nothing much. I feel very faint. But you mustn't mind it, for I can bear it quite well. South Wind always blows me faint. If it were not for the cool of the thick ice between me and her, I should faint altogether. Indeed, as it is, I fear I must vanish."

Diamond stared at her in terror, for he saw that her form and face were growing, not small, but transparent, like something dissolving, not in water, but in light. He could see the side of the blue cave through her very heart. And she melted away till all that was left was a pale face, like the moon in the morning, with two great lucid eyes in it.

"I am going, Diamond," she said.

"Does it hurt you?" asked Diamond.

"It's very uncomfortable," she answered; "but I don't mind it, for I shall come all right again before long. I thought I should be able to go with you all the way, but I cannot. You must not be frightened though. Just go straight on, and you will come all right. You'll find me on the doorstep."

As she spoke, her face too faded quite away, only Diamond thought he could still see her eyes shining through the blue. When he went closer, however, he found that what he thought her eyes were only two hollows in the ice. North Wind was quite gone; and Diamond would have cried, if he had not trusted her so thoroughly. So he sat still in the blue air of the cavern listening to the wash and ripple of the water all about the base of the iceberg, as it sped on and on into the open sea northwards. It was an excellent craft to go with a current, for there was twice as much of it below water as above. But a light south wind was blowing too, so it went fast.

After a little while Diamond went out and sat on the edge of his floating island, and looked down into the ocean beneath him. The white sides of the berg reflected so much light below the water, that he could see far down into the green abyss. Sometimes he fancied he saw the eyes of North Wind looking up at him from below, but the fancy never lasted beyond the moment of its birth. And the time passed he did not know how, for he felt as if he were in a dream. When he got tired of the green water, he went into the blue cave; and when he got tired of the blue cave he went out and gazed all about him on the blue sea, ever sparkling in the sun, which kept wheeling about the sky, never going below the horizon. But he chiefly gazed northwards, to see whether any land were appearing. All this time he never wanted to eat. He broke off little bits of the berg now and then and sucked them, and he thought them very nice.

At length, one time he came out of his cave, he spied, far off upon the horizon, a shining peak that rose into the sky like the top of some tremendous iceberg; and his vessel was bearing him straight towards it. As it went on the peak rose and rose higher and higher above the horizon; and other peaks rose after it, with sharp edges and jagged ridges connecting them. Diamond thought this must be the place he was going to; and he was right; for the mountains rose and rose, till he saw the line of the coast at their feet, and at length the iceberg drove into a little bay, all round which were lofty precipices with snow on their tops, and streaks of ice down their sides. The berg floated slowly up to a projecting rock. Diamond stepped on shore, and without looking behind him began to follow a natural path which led windingly towards the top of the precipice.

When he reached it, he found himself on a broad table of ice, along which he could walk without much difficulty. Before him, at a considerable distance, rose a lofty ridge of ice, which shot up into fantastic pinnacles and towers and battlements. The air was very cold, and seemed somehow dead, for there was not the slightest breath of wind.

In the centre of the ridge before him appeared a gap like the opening of a valley. But as he walked towards it, gazing, and wondering whether that could be the way he had to take, he saw that what had appeared a gap was the form of a woman seated against the ice front of the ridge, leaning forward with her hands in her lap, and her hair hanging down to the ground.

"It is North Wind on her doorstep," said Diamond joyfully, and hurried on.

He soon came up to the place, and there the form sat, like one of the great figures at the door of an Egyptian temple, motionless, with drooping arms and head. Then Diamond grew frightened, because she did not move nor speak. He was sure it was North Wind, but he thought she must be dead at last. Her face was white as the snow, her eyes were blue as the air in the ice-cave, and her hair hung down straight, like icicles. She had on a greenish robe, like the colour in the hollows of a glacier seen from far off.

He stood up before her, and gazed fearfully into her face for a few minutes before he ventured to speak. At length, with a great effort and a trembling voice, he faltered out—

"North Wind!"

"Well, child?" said the form, without lifting its head.

"Are you ill, dear North Wind?"

"No. I am waiting."

"What for?"

"Till I'm wanted."

"You don't care for me any more," said Diamond, almost crying now.

"Yes, I do. Only I can't show it. All my love is down at the bottom of my heart. But I feel it bubbling there."

"What do you want me to do next, dear North Wind?" said Diamond, wishing to show his love by being obedient.

"What do you want to do yourself?"

"I want to go into the country at your back."

"Then you must go through me."

"I don't know what you mean."

"I mean just what I say. You must walk on as if I were an open door, and go right through me."

"But that will hurt you."

"Not in the least. It will hurt you, though."

"I don't mind that, if you tell me to do it."

"Do it," said North Wind.

Diamond walked towards her instantly. When he reached her knees, he put out his hand to lay it on her, but nothing was there save an intense cold. He walked on. Then all grew white about him; and the cold stung him like fire. He walked on still, groping through the whiteness. It thickened about him. At last, it got into his heart, and he lost all sense. I would say that he fainted—only whereas in common faints all grows black about you, he felt swallowed up in whiteness. It was when he reached North Wind's heart that he fainted and fell. But as he fell, he rolled over the threshold, and it was thus that Diamond got to the back of the north wind.

CHAPTER X

AT THE BACK OF THE NORTH WIND

I HAVE NOW come to the most difficult part of my story.

And why? Because I do not know enough about it. And why should I not know as much about this part as about any other part? for of course I could know nothing about the story except Diamond had told it; and why should not Diamond tell about the country at the back of the north wind, as well as about his adventures in getting there? Because, when he came back, he had forgotten a great deal, and what he did remember was very hard to tell. Things there are so different from things here! The people there do not speak the same language for one thing. Indeed, Diamond insisted that there they do not speak at all. I do not think he was right, but it may well have appeared so to Diamond. The fact is, we have different reports of the place from the most trustworthy people. Therefore we are bound to believe that it appears somewhat different to different people. All, however, agree in a general way about it.

I will tell you something of what two very different people have reported, both of whom knew more about it, I believe, than Herodotus. One of them speaks from his own experience, for he visited the country; the other from the testimony of a young peasant girl who came back from it for a month's visit to her friends. The former was a great Italian of noble family, who died more than five hundred years ago; the latter a Scotch shepherd who died not forty years ago.

The Italian, then, informs us that he had to enter that country through a fire so hot that he would have thrown himself into boiling glass to cool himself. This was not

Diamond's experience, but then Durante—that was the name of the Italian, and it means Lasting, for his books will last as long as there are enough men in the world worthy of having them—Durante was an elderly man, and Diamond was a little boy, and so their experience must be a little different. The peasant girl, on the other hand, fell fast asleep in the wood, and woke in the same country.

In describing it, Durante says that the ground everywhere smelt sweetly, and that a gentle, even-tempered wind, which never blew faster or slower, breathed in his face as he went, making all the leaves point one way, not so as to disturb the birds in the tops of the trees, but, on the contrary, sounding a bass to their song. He describes also a little river which was so full that its little waves, as it hurried along, bent the grass, full of red and yellow flowers, through which it flowed. He says that the purest stream in the world beside this one would look as if it were mixed with something that did not belong to it, even although it was flowing ever in the brown shadow of the trees, and neither sun nor moon could shine upon it. He seems to imply that it is always the month of May in that country. It would be out of place to describe here the wonderful sights he saw, for the music of them is in another key from that of this story, and I shall therefore only add from the account of this traveller, that the people there are so free and so just and so healthy, that every one of them has a crown like a king and a mitre like a priest.

The peasant girl—Kilmeny was her name—could not report such grand things as Durante, for, as the shepherd says, telling her story as I tell Diamond's—

> "Kilmeny had been she knew not where,
> And Kilmeny had seen what she could not declare;
> Kilmeny had been where the cock never crew,
> Where the rain never fell, and the wind never blew;
> But it seemed as the harp of the sky had rung,
> And the airs of heaven played round her tongue,
> When she spoke of the lovely forms she had seen,
> And a land where sin had never been;
> A land of love and a land of light,
> Withouten sun, or moon, or night;
> Where the river swayed a living stream,
> And the light a pure and cloudless beam:
> The land of vision it would seem,
> And still an everlasting dream."

The last two lines are the shepherd's own remark, and a matter of opinion. But it is clear, I think, that Kilmeny must have described the same country as Durante saw, though, not having his experience, she could neither understand nor describe it so well.

Now I must give you such fragments of recollection as Diamond was able to bring back with him.

When he came to himself after he fell, he found himself at the back of the north wind. North Wind herself was nowhere to be seen. Neither was there a vestige of snow or of ice within sight. The sun too had vanished; but that was no matter, for there was plenty of a certain still rayless light. Where it came from he never found out; but he thought it belonged to the country itself. Sometimes he thought it came out of the flowers, which were very bright, but had no strong colour. He said the river—for all agree that there is a river there—flowed not only through, but over grass: its channel, instead of being rock, stones, pebbles, sand, or anything else, was of pure meadow grass, not over long. He insisted that if it did not sing tunes in people's ears, it sung tunes in their heads, in proof of which I may mention, that, in the troubles which followed, Diamond was often heard singing; and when asked what he was singing, would answer, "One of the tunes the river at the back of the north wind sung." And I may as well say at once that Diamond never told these things to any one but—no, I had better not say who it was; but whoever it was told me, and I thought it would be well to write them for my child-readers.

He could not say he was very happy there, for he had neither his father nor mother with him, but he felt so still and quiet and patient and contented, that, as far as the mere feeling went, it was something better than mere happiness. Nothing went wrong at the back of the north wind. Neither was anything quite right, he thought. Only everything was going to be right some day. His account disagreed with that of Durante, and agreed with that of Kilmeny, in this, that he protested there was no wind there at all. I fancy he missed it. At all events *we* could not do without wind. It all depends on how big our lungs are whether the wind is too strong for us or not.

When the person he told about it asked him whether he saw anybody he knew there, he answered, "Only a little girl belonging to the gardener, who thought he had lost her, but was quite mistaken, for there she was safe enough, and was to come back some day, as I came back, if they would only wait."

"Did you talk to her, Diamond?"

"No. Nobody talks there. They only look at each other, and understand everything."

"Is it cold there?"

"No."

"Is it hot?"

"No."

"What is it then?"

"You never think about such things there."

"What a queer place it must be!"

"It's a very good place."

"Do you want to go back again?"

"No: I don't think I have ever left it; I feel it here, somewhere."

"Did the people there look pleased?"

"Yes—quite pleased, only a little sad."

"Then they didn't look glad?"

"They looked as if they were waiting to be gladder some day."

This was how Diamond used to answer questions about that country. And now I will take up the story again, and tell you how he got back to this country.

CHAPTER XI

HOW DIAMOND GOT HOME AGAIN

W HEN ONE at the back of the north wind wanted to know how things were going with any one he loved, he had to go to a certain tree, climb the stem, and sit down in the branches. In a few minutes, if he kept very still, he would see something at least of what was going on with the people he loved.

One day when Diamond was sitting in this tree, he began to long very much to get home again, and no wonder, for he saw his mother crying. Durante says that the people there may always follow their wishes, because they never wish but what is good. Diamond's wish was to get home, and he would fain follow his wish.

But how was he to set about it? If he could only see North Wind! But the moment he had got to her back, she was gone altogether from his sight. He had never seen her back. She might be sitting on her doorstep still, looking southwards, and waiting, white and thin and blue-eyed, until she was wanted. Or she might have again become a mighty creature, with power to do that which was demanded of her, and gone far away upon many missions. She must be somewhere, however. He could not go home without her, and therefore he must find her. She could never have intended to leave him always away from his mother. If there had been any danger of that, she would have told him, and given him his choice about going. For North Wind was right honest. How to find North Wind, therefore, occupied all his thoughts.

In his anxiety about his mother, he used to climb the tree every day, and sit in its branches. However many of the dwellers there did so, they never incommoded one another; for the moment one got into the tree, he became invisible to every one else; and it was such a wide-spreading tree that there was room for every one of the people of the country in it, without the least interference with each other. Sometimes, on getting down, two of them would meet at the root, and then they would smile to each other more sweetly than at any other time, as much as to say, "Ah, you've been up there too!"

One day he was sitting on one of the outer branches of the tree, looking southwards after his home. Far away was a blue shining sea, dotted with gleaming and sparkling specks of white. Those were the icebergs. Nearer he saw a great range of snow-capped mountains, and down below him the lovely meadow-grass of the country, with the stream flowing and flowing through it, away towards the sea. As he looked he began to wonder, for the whole country lay beneath him like a map, and that which was near him looked just as small as that which he knew to be miles away. The ridge of ice which encircled it appeared but a few yards off, and no larger than the row of pebbles with which a child will mark out the boundaries of the kingdom he has appropriated on the sea-shore. He thought he could distinguish the vapoury form of North Wind, seated as he had left her, on the other side. Hastily he descended the tree, and to his amazement found that the map or model of the country still lay at his feet. He stood in it. With one stride he had crossed the river; with another he had reached the ridge of ice; with the third he stepped over its peaks, and sank wearily down at North Wind's knees. For there

she sat on her doorstep. The peaks of the great ridge of ice were as lofty as ever behind her, and the country at her back had vanished from Diamond's view.

North Wind was as still as Diamond had left her. Her pale face was white as the snow, and her motionless eyes were as blue as the caverns in the ice. But the instant Diamond touched her, her face began to change like that of one waking from sleep. Light began to glimmer from the blue of her eyes. A moment more, and she laid her hand on Diamond's head, and began playing with his hair. Diamond took hold of her hand, and laid his face to it. She gave a little start.

"How very alive you are, child!" she murmured. "Come nearer to me."

By the help of the stones all around he clambered up beside her, and laid himself against her bosom. She gave a great sigh, slowly lifted her arms, and slowly folded them about him, until she clasped him close. Yet a moment, and she roused herself, and came quite awake; and the cold of her bosom, which had pierced Diamond's bones, vanished.

"Have you been sitting here ever since I went through you, dear North Wind?" asked Diamond, stroking her hand.

"Yes," she answered, looking at him with her old kindness.

"Ain't you very tired?"

"No; I've often had to sit longer. Do you know how long you have been?"

"Oh! years and years," answered Diamond.

"You have just been seven days," returned North Wind.

"I thought I had been a hundred years!" exclaimed Diamond.

"Yes, I dare say," replied North Wind. "You've been away from here seven days; but how long you may have been in there is quite another thing. Behind my back and before my face things are so different! They don't go at all by the same rule."

"I'm very glad," said Diamond, after thinking a while.

"Why?" asked North Wind.

"Because I've been such a long time there, and such a little while away from mother. Why, she won't be expecting me home from Sandwich yet!"

"No. But we mustn't talk any longer. I've got my orders now, and we must be off in a few minutes."

Next moment Diamond found himself sitting alone on the rock. North Wind had vanished. A creature like a great humble-bee or cockchafer flew past his face; but it could be neither, for there were no insects amongst the ice. It passed him again and again, flying in circles around him, and he concluded that it must be North Wind herself, no bigger than Tom Thumb when his mother put him in the nutshell lined with flannel. But she was no longer vapoury and thin. She was solid, although tiny. A moment more, and she perched on his shoulder.

"Come along, Diamond," she said in his ear, in the smallest and highest of treble voices; "it is time we were setting out for Sandwich."

Diamond could just see her, by turning his head towards his shoulder as far as he could, but only with one eye, for his nose came between her and the other.

"Won't you take me in your arms and carry me?" he said in a whisper, for he knew she did not like a loud voice when she was small.

"Ah! you ungrateful boy," returned North Wind, smiling, "how dare you make game of me? Yes, I will carry you, but you shall walk a bit for your impertinence first. Come along."

She jumped from his shoulder, but when Diamond looked for her upon the ground, he could see nothing but a little spider with long legs that made its way over the ice towards the south. It ran very fast indeed for a spider, but Diamond ran a long way before it, and then waited for it. It was up with him sooner than he had expected, however, and it had grown a good deal. And the spider grew and grew and went faster and faster, till all at once Diamond discovered that it was not a spider, but a weasel; and away glided the weasel, and away went Diamond after it, and it took all the run there was in him to keep up with the weasel. And the weasel grew, and grew, and grew, till all at once Diamond saw that the weasel was not a weasel but a cat. And away went the cat, and Diamond after it. And when he had run half a mile, he found the cat waiting for him, sitting up and washing her face not to lose time. And away went the cat again, and Diamond after it. But the next time he came up with the cat, the cat was not a cat, but a hunting-leopard. And the hunting-leopard grew to a jaguar, all covered with spots like eyes. And the jaguar grew to a Bengal tiger. And at none of them was Diamond afraid, for he had been at North Wind's back, and he could be afraid of her no longer whatever she did or grew. And the tiger flew over the snow in a straight line for the south, growing less and less to Diamond's eyes till it was only a black speck upon the whiteness; and then it vanished altogether. And now Diamond felt that he would rather not run any farther, and that the ice had got very rough. Besides, he was near the precipices that bounded the sea, so he slackened his pace to a walk, saying aloud to himself:

"When North Wind has punished me enough for making game of her, she will come back to me; I know she will, for I can't go much farther without her."

"You dear boy! It was only in fun. Here I am!" said North Wind's voice behind him.

Diamond turned, and saw her as he liked best to see her, standing beside him, a tall lady.

"Where's the tiger?" he asked, for he knew all the creatures from a picture book that Miss Coleman had given him. "But, of course," he added, "you were the tiger. I was puzzled and forgot. I saw it such a long way off before me, and there you were behind me. It's so odd, you know."

"It must look very odd to you, Diamond: I see that. But it is no more odd to me than to break an old pine in two."

"Well, that's odd enough," remarked Diamond.

"So it is! I forgot. Well, none of these things are odder to me than it is to you to eat bread and butter."

"Well, that's odd too, when I think of it," persisted Diamond. "I should just like a slice of bread and butter! I'm afraid to say how long it is—how long it seems to me, that is—since I had anything to eat."

"Come then," said North Wind, stooping and holding out her arms. "You shall have some bread and butter very soon. I am glad to find you want some."

Diamond held up his arms to meet hers, and was safe upon her bosom. North Wind bounded into the air. Her tresses began to lift and rise and spread and stream and flow and flutter; and with a roar from her hair and an answering roar from one of the great glaciers beside them, whose slow torrent tumbled two or three icebergs at once into the waves at their feet, North Wind and Diamond went flying southwards.

CHAPTER XII

WHO MET DIAMOND AT SANDWICH

As THEY FLEW, so fast they went that the sea slid away from under them like a great web of shot silk, blue shot with grey, and green shot with purple. They went so fast that the stars themselves appeared to sail away past them overhead, "like golden boats," on a blue sea turned upside down. And they went so fast that Diamond himself went the other way as fast—I mean he went fast asleep in North Wind's arms.

When he woke, a face was bending over him; but it was not North Wind's; it was his mother's. He put out his arms to her, and she clasped him to her bosom and burst out crying. Diamond kissed her again and again to make her stop. Perhaps kissing is the best thing for crying, but it will not always stop it.

"What is the matter, mother?" he said.

"Oh, Diamond, my darling! you have been so ill!" she sobbed.

"No, mother dear. I've only been at the back of the north wind," returned Diamond.

"I thought you were dead," said his mother.

But that moment the doctor came in.

"Oh! there!" said the doctor with gentle cheerfulness; "we're better to-day, I see."

Then he drew the mother aside, and told her not to talk to Diamond, or to mind what he might say; for he must be kept as quiet as possible. And indeed Diamond was not much inclined to talk, for he felt very strange and weak, which was little wonder, seeing that all the time he had been away he had only sucked a few lumps of ice, and there could not be much nourishment in them.

Now while he is lying there, getting strong again with chicken broth and other nice things, I will tell my readers what had been taking place at his home, for they ought to be told it.

They may have forgotten that Miss Coleman was in a very poor state of health. Now there were three reasons for this. In the first place, her lungs were not strong. In the second place, there was a gentleman somewhere who had not behaved very well to her. In the third place, she had not anything particular to do. These three *nots* together are enough to make a lady very ill indeed. Of course she could not help the first cause; but if the other two causes had not existed, that would have been of little consequence; she would only have had to be a little careful. The second she could not help quite; but if she had had anything to do, and had done it well, it would have been very difficult for any man to behave badly to her. And for this third cause of her illness, if she had had anything to do that was worth doing, she might have borne his bad behaviour so that even that would not have made her ill. It is not always easy, I confess, to find something to do that is worth doing, but the most difficult things are constantly being done, and she might have found something if she had tried. Her fault lay in this, that she had not tried. But, to be sure, her father and mother were to blame that they had never set her going. Only then again, nobody had told her father and mother that they ought to set her going in that direction. So as none of them would find it out of themselves, North Wind had to teach them.

We know that North Wind was very busy that night on which she left Diamond in the cathedral. She had in a sense been blowing through and through the Colemans' house the whole of the night. First, Miss Coleman's maid had left a chink of her mistress's window open, thinking she had shut it, and North Wind had wound a few of her hairs round the lady's throat. She was considerably worse the next morning. Again, the ship which North Wind had sunk that very night belonged to Mr. Coleman. Nor will my readers understand what a heavy loss this was to him until I have informed them that he had been getting poorer and poorer for some time. He was not so successful in his speculations as he had been, for he speculated a great deal more than was right, and it was time he should be pulled up. It is a hard thing for a rich man to grow poor; but it is an awful thing for him to grow dishonest, and some kinds of speculation lead a man deep into dishonesty before he thinks what he is about. Poverty will not make a man worthless—he may be worth a great deal more when he is poor than he was when he was rich; but dishonesty goes very far indeed to make a man of no value—a thing to be thrown out in the dust-hole of the creation, like a bit of a broken basin, or a dirty rag. So North Wind had to look after Mr. Coleman, and try to make an honest man of him. So she sank the ship which was his last venture, and he was what himself and his wife and the world called ruined.

Nor was this all yet. For on board that vessel Miss Coleman's lover was a passenger; and when the news came that the vessel had gone down, and that all on board had perished, we may be sure she did not think the loss of their fine house and garden and furniture the greatest misfortune in the world.

Of course, the trouble did not end with Mr. Coleman and his family. Nobody can suffer alone. When the cause of suffering is most deeply hidden in the heart, and

nobody knows anything about it but the man himself, he must be a great and a good man indeed, such as few of us have known, if the pain inside him does not make him behave so as to cause all about him to be more or less uncomfortable. But when a man brings money-troubles on himself by making haste to be rich, then most of the people he has to do with must suffer in the same way with himself. The elm-tree which North Wind blew down that very night, as if small and great trials were to be gathered in one heap, crushed Miss Coleman's pretty summer-house: just so the fall of Mr. Coleman crushed the little family that lived over his coach-house and stable. Before Diamond was well enough to be taken home, there was no home for him to go to. Mr. Coleman—or his creditors, for I do not know the particulars—had sold house, carriage, horses, furniture, and everything. He and his wife and daughter and Mrs. Crump had gone to live in a small house in Hoxton, where he would be unknown, and whence he could walk to his place of business in the City. For he was not an old man, and hoped yet to retrieve his fortunes. Let us hope that he lived to retrieve his honesty, the tail of which had slipped through his fingers to the very last joint, if not beyond it.

Of course, Diamond's father had nothing to do for a time, but it was not so hard for him to have nothing to do as it was for Miss Coleman. He wrote to his wife that, if her sister would keep her there till he got a place, it would be better for them, and he would be greatly obliged to her. Meantime, the gentleman who had bought the house had allowed his furniture to remain where it was for a little while.

Diamond's aunt was quite willing to keep them as long as she could. And indeed Diamond was not yet well enough to be moved with safety.

When he had recovered so far as to be able to go out, one day his mother got her sister's husband, who had a little pony-cart, to carry them down to the sea-shore, and leave them there for a few hours. He had some business to do further on at Ramsgate, and would pick them up as he returned. A whiff of the sea-air would do them both good, she said, and she thought besides she could best tell Diamond what had happened if she had him quite to herself.

CHAPTER XIII

THE SEASIDE

DIAMOND AND HIS MOTHER sat down upon the edge of the rough grass that bordered the sand. The sun was just far enough past its highest not to shine in their eyes when they looked eastward. A sweet little wind blew on their left side, and comforted the mother without letting her know what it was that comforted her. Away before them stretched the sparkling waters of the ocean, every wave of which flashed out its own delight back in the face of the great sun, which looked down from the stillness of its blue house with gloriously silent face upon its flashing children. On each hand the shore rounded outwards, forming a little bay. There were no white cliffs here, as further north and south, and the place was rather dreary, but the sky got at them so much the better. Not a house, not a creature was within sight. Dry sand was about their feet, and under them tiny wiry grass, that just managed to grow out of the poverty-stricken shore.

"Oh dear!" said Diamond's mother, with a deep sigh, "it's a sad world!"

"Is it?" said Diamond; "I didn't know."

"How should you know, child? You've been too well taken care of, I trust."

"Oh yes, I have," returned Diamond. "I'm so sorry! I thought you were taken care of too. I thought my father took care of you. I will ask him about it. I think he must have forgotten."

"Dear boy!" said his mother; "your father's the best man in the world."

"So I thought!" returned Diamond with triumph. "I was sure of it!—Well, doesn't he take very good care of you?"

"Yes, yes, he does," answered his mother, bursting into tears. "But who's to take care of him? And how is he to take care of us if he's got nothing to eat himself?"

"Oh dear!" said Diamond with a gasp; "hasn't he got anything to eat? Oh! I must go home to him."

"No, no, child. He's not come to that yet. But what's to become of us, I don't know."

"Are you very hungry, mother? There's the basket. I thought you put something to eat in it."

"O you darling stupid! I didn't say I was hungry," returned his mother, smiling through her tears.

"Then I don't understand you at all," said Diamond. "Do tell me what's the matter."

"There *are* people in the world who have nothing to eat, Diamond."

"Then I suppose they don't stop in it any longer. They—they—what you call—die—don't they?"

"Yes, they do. How would you like that?"

"I don't know. I never tried. But I suppose they go where they get something to eat."

"Like enough they don't want it," said his mother, petulantly.

"That's all right then," said Diamond, thinking I dare say more than he chose to put in words.

"Is it though? Poor boy! how little *you* know about things! Mr. Coleman's lost all his money, and your father has nothing to do, and we shall have nothing to eat by and by."

"Are you sure, mother?"

"Sure of what?"

"Sure that we shall have nothing to eat."

"No, thank Heaven! I'm not sure of it. I hope not."

"Then I *can't* understand it, mother. There's a piece of gingerbread in the basket, I know."

"O you little bird! You have no more sense than a sparrow that picks what it wants, and never thinks of the winter and the frost and the snow."

"Ah—yes—I see. But the birds get through the winter, don't they?"

"Some of them fall dead on the ground."

"They must die some time. They wouldn't like to be birds always. Would you, mother?"

"What a child it is!" thought his mother, but she said nothing.

"Oh! now I remember," Diamond went on. "Father told me that day I went to Epping Forest with him, that the rose-bushes, and the may-bushes, and the holly-bushes were the birds' barns, for there were the hips, and the haws, and the holly-berries, all ready for the winter."

"Yes; that's all very true. So you see the birds are provided for. But there are no such barns for you and me, Diamond."

"Ain't there?"

"No. We've got to work for our bread."

"Then let's go and work," said Diamond, getting up.

"It's no use. We've not got anything to do."

"Then let's wait."

"Then we shall starve."

"No. There's the basket. Do you know, mother, I think I shall call that basket the barn."

"It's not a very big one. And when it's empty—where are we then?"

"At auntie's cupboard," returned Diamond promptly.

"But we can't eat auntie's things all up and leave her to starve."

"No, no. We'll go back to father before that. He'll have found a cupboard somewhere by that time."

"How do you know that?"

"I don't know it. But *I* haven't got even a cupboard, and I've always had plenty to eat. I've heard you say I had too much, sometimes."

"But I tell you that's because I've had a cupboard for you, child."

"And when yours was empty, auntie opened hers."

"But that can't go on."

"How do you know? I think there must be a big cupboard somewhere, out of which the little cupboards are filled, you know, mother."

"Well, I wish I could find the door of that cupboard," said his mother. But the same moment she stopped, and was silent for a good while. I cannot tell whether Diamond knew what she was thinking, but I think I know. She had heard something at church the day before, which came back upon her—something like this, that she hadn't to eat for to-morrow as well as for to-day; and that what was not wanted couldn't be missed. So, instead of saying anything more, she stretched out her hand for the basket, and she and Diamond had their dinner.

And Diamond did enjoy it. For the drive and the fresh air had made him quite hungry; and he did not, like his mother, trouble himself about what they should dine off that day week. The fact was he had lived so long without any food at all at the back of the north wind, that he knew quite well that food was not essential to existence; that in fact, under certain circumstances, people could live without it well enough.

His mother did not speak much during their dinner. After it was over she helped him to walk about a little, but he was not able for much and soon got tired. He did not get fretful, though. He was too glad of having the sun and the wind again, to fret because he could not run about. He lay down on the dry sand, and his mother covered him with a shawl. She then sat by his side, and took a bit of work from her pocket. But Diamond felt rather sleepy, and turned on his side and gazed sleepily over the sand. A few yards off he saw something fluttering.

"What is that, mother?" he said.

"Only a bit of paper," she answered.

"It flutters more than a bit of paper would, I think," said Diamond.

"I'll go and see if you like," said his mother. "My eyes are none of the best."

So she rose and went and found that they were both right, for it was a little book, partly buried in the sand. But several of its leaves were clear of the sand, and these the wind kept blowing about in a very flutterful manner. She took it up and brought it to Diamond.

"What is it, mother?" he asked.

"Some nursery rhymes, I think," she answered.

"I'm too sleepy," said Diamond. "Do read some of them to me."

"Yes, I will," she said, and began one—"But this is such nonsense!" she said again. "I will try to find a better one."

She turned the leaves searching, but three times, with sudden puffs, the wind blew the leaves rustling back to the same verses.

"Do read that one," said Diamond, who seemed to be of the same mind as the wind. "It sounded very nice. I am sure it is a good one."

So his mother thought it might amuse him, though she couldn't find any sense in it. She never thought he might understand it, although she could not.

Now I do not exactly know what the mother read, but this is what Diamond heard, or thought afterwards that he had heard. He was, however, as I have said, very sleepy, and when he thought he understood the verses he may have been only dreaming better ones. This is how they went—

> I know a river
> whose waters run asleep
> run run ever
> singing in the shallows
> dumb in the hollows
> sleeping so deep
> and all the swallows
> that dip their feathers
> in the hollows
> or in the shallows
> are the merriest swallows of all
> for the nests they bake
> with the clay they cake
> with the water they shake
> from their wings that rake
> the water out of the shallows
> or the hollows
> will hold together
> in any weather
> and so the swallows
> are the merriest fellows
> and have the merriest children
> and are built so narrow
> like the head of an arrow

to cut the air
and go just where
the nicest water is flowing
and the nicest dust is blowing
for each so narrow
like head of an arrow
is only a barrow
to carry the mud he makes
from the nicest water flowing
and the nicest dust that is blowing
to build his nest
for her he loves best
with the nicest cakes
which the sunshine bakes
all for their merry children
all so callow
with beaks that follow
gaping and hollow
wider and wider
after their father
or after their mother
the food-provider
who brings them a spider
or a worm the poor hider
down in the earth
so there's no dearth
for their beaks as yellow
as the buttercups growing
beside the flowing
of the singing river
always and ever
growing and blowing
for fast as the sheep
awake or asleep
crop them and crop them
they cannot stop them
but up they creep
and on they go blowing
and so with the daisies
the little white praises
they grow and they blow
and they spread out their crown
and they praise the sun
and when he goes down
their praising is done
and they fold up their crown

and they sleep every one
till over the plain
he's shining amain
and they're at it again
praising and praising
such low songs raising
that no one hears them
but the sun who rears them
and the sheep that bite them
are the quietest sheep
awake or asleep
with the merriest bleat
and the little lambs
are the merriest lambs
they forget to eat
for the frolic in their feet
and the lambs and their dams
are the whitest sheep
with the woolliest wool
and the longest wool
and the trailingest tails
and they shine like snow
in the grasses that grow
by the singing river
that sings for ever
and the sheep and the lambs
are merry for ever
because the river
sings and they drink it
and the lambs and their dams
are quiet
and white
because of their diet
for what they bite
is buttercups yellow
and daisies white
and grass as green
as the river can make it
with wind as mellow
to kiss it and shake it
as never was seen
but here in the hollows
beside the river
where all the swallows
are merriest of fellows
for the nests they make

with the clay they cake
in the sunshine bake
till they are like bone
as dry in the wind
as a marble stone
so firm they bind
the grass in the clay
that dries in the wind
the sweetest wind
that blows by the river
flowing for ever
but never you find
whence comes the wind
that blows on the hollows
and over the shallows
where dip the swallows
alive it blows
the life as it goes
awake or asleep
into the river
that sings as it flows
and the life it blows
into the sheep
awake or asleep
with the woolliest wool
and the trailingest tails
and it never fails
gentle and cool
to wave the wool
and to toss the grass
as the lambs and the sheep
over it pass
and tug and bite
with their teeth so white
and then with the sweep
of their trailing tails
smooth it again
and it grows amain
and amain it grows
and the wind as it blows
tosses the swallows
over the hollows
and down on the shallows
till every feather
doth shake and quiver
and all their feathers

go all together
blowing the life
and the joy so rife
into the swallows
that skim the shallows
and have the yellowest children
for the wind that blows
is the life of the river
flowing for ever
that washes the grasses
still as it passes
and feeds the daisies
the little white praises
and buttercups bonny
so golden and sunny
with butter and honey
that whiten the sheep
awake or asleep
that nibble and bite
and grow whiter than white
and merry and quiet
on the sweet diet
fed by the river
and tossed for ever
by the wind that tosses
the swallow that crosses
over the shallows
dipping his wings
to gather the water
and bake the cake
that the wind shall make
as hard as a bone
as dry as a stone
it's all in the wind
that blows from behind
and all in the river
that flows for ever
and all in the grasses
and the white daisies
and the merry sheep
awake or asleep
and the happy swallows
skimming the shallows
and it's all in the wind
that blows from behind.

Here Diamond became aware that his mother had stopped reading.

"Why don't you go on, mother dear?" he asked.

"It's such nonsense!" said his mother. "I believe it would go on for ever."

"That's just what it did," said Diamond.

"What did?" she asked.

"Why, the river. That's almost the very tune it used to sing."

His mother was frightened, for she thought the fever was coming on again. So she did not contradict him.

"Who made that poem?" asked Diamond.

"I don't know," she answered. "Some silly woman for her children, I suppose—and then thought it good enough to print."

"She must have been at the back of the north wind some time or other, anyhow," said Diamond. "She couldn't have got a hold of it anywhere else. That's just how it went." And he began to chant bits of it here and there; but his mother said nothing for fear of making him worse; and she was very glad indeed when she saw her brother-in-law jogging along in his little cart. They lifted Diamond in, and got up themselves, and away they went, "home again, home again, home again," as Diamond sang. But he soon grew quiet, and before they reached Sandwich he was fast asleep and dreaming of the country at the back of the north wind.

CHAPTER XIV

OLD DIAMOND

AFTER THIS DIAMOND RECOVERED so fast, that in a few days he was quite able to go home as soon as his father had a place for them to go. Now his father having saved a little money, and finding that no situation offered itself, had been thinking over a new plan. A strange occurrence it was which turned his thoughts in that direction. He had a friend in the Bloomsbury region, who lived by letting out cabs and horses to the cabmen. This man, happening to meet him one day as he was returning from an unsuccessful application, said to him:

"Why don't you set up for yourself now—in the cab line, I mean?"

"I haven't enough for that," answered Diamond's father.

"You must have saved a goodish bit, I should think. Just come home with me now and look at a horse I can let you have cheap. I bought him only a few weeks ago, thinking he'd do for a Hansom, but I was wrong. He's got bone enough for a waggon, but a waggon ain't a Hansom. He ain't got go enough for a Hansom. You see parties as takes Hansoms wants to go like the wind, and he ain't got wind enough, for he ain't so young as he once was. But for a four-wheeler as takes families and their luggages, he's the very horse. He'd carry a small house any day. I bought him cheap, and I'll sell him cheap."

"Oh, I don't want him," said Diamond's father. "A body must have time to think

over an affair of so much importance. And there's the cab too. That would come to a deal of money."

"I could fit you there, I dare say," said his friend. "But come and look at the animal, anyhow."

"Since I lost my own old pair, as was Mr. Coleman's," said Diamond's father, turning to accompany the cab-master, "I ain't almost got the heart to look a horse in the face. It's a thousand pities to part man and horse."

"So it is," returned his friend sympathetically.

But what was the ex-coachman's delight, when, on going into the stable where his friend led him, he found the horse he wanted him to buy was no other than his own old Diamond, grown very thin and bony and long-legged, as if they had been doing what they could to fit him for Hansom work!

"*He* ain't a Hansom horse," said Diamond's father indignantly.

"Well, you're right. He ain't handsome, but he's a good un," said his owner.

"Who says he ain't handsome? He's one of the handsomest horses a gentleman's coachman ever druv," said Diamond's father; remarking to himself under his breath—"though I says it as shouldn't"—for he did not feel inclined all at once to confess that his own old horse could have sunk so low.

"Well," said his friend, "all I say is—There's a animal for you, as strong as a church; an' 'll go like a train, leastways a parly," he added, correcting himself.

But the coachman had a lump in his throat and tears in his eyes. For the old horse, hearing his voice, had turned his long neck, and when his old friend went up to him and laid his hand on his side, he whinnied for joy, and laid his big head on his master's breast. This settled the matter. The coachman's arms were round the horse's neck in a moment, and he fairly broke down and cried. The cab-master had never been so fond of a horse himself as to hug him like that, but he saw in a moment how it was. And he must have been a good-hearted fellow, for I never heard of such an idea coming into the head of any other man with a horse to sell: instead of putting something on to the price because he was now pretty sure of selling him, he actually took a pound off what he had meant to ask for him, saying to himself it was a shame to part old friends.

Diamond's father, as soon as he came to himself, turned and asked how much he wanted for the horse.

"I see you're old friends," said the owner.

"It's my own old Diamond. I liked him far the best of the pair, though the other was good. You ain't got him too, have you?"

"No; nothing in the stable to match *him* there."

"I believe you," said the coachman. "But you'll be wanting a long price for *him, I* know."

"No, not so much. I bought him cheap, and as I say, he ain't for my work."

The end of it was that Diamond's father bought old Diamond again, along with a four-wheeled cab. And as there were some rooms to be had over the stable, he took them, wrote to his wife to come home, and set up as a cabman.

CHAPTER XV

THE MEWS

IT WAS LATE in the afternoon when Diamond and his mother and the baby reached London. I was so full of Diamond that I forgot to tell you a baby had arrived in the meantime. His father was waiting for them with his own cab, but they had not told Diamond who the horse was; for his father wanted to enjoy the pleasure of his surprise when he found it out. He got in with his mother without looking at the horse, and his father having put up Diamond's carpet-bag and his mother's little trunk, got upon the box himself and drove off; and Diamond was quite proud of riding home in his father's own carriage. But when he got to the mews, he could not help being a little dismayed at first; and if he had never been to the back of the north wind, I am afraid he would have cried a little. But instead of that, he said to himself it was a fine thing all the old furniture was there. And instead of helping his mother to be miserable at the change, he began to find out all the advantages of the place; for every place has some advantages, and they are always better worth knowing than the disadvantages. Certainly the weather was depressing, for a thick dull persistent rain was falling by the time they reached home. But happily the weather is very changeable; and besides, there was a good fire burning in the room, which their neighbour with the drunken husband had attended to for them; and the tea-things were put out, and the kettle was boiling on the fire. And with a good fire, and tea and bread and butter, things cannot be said to be miserable.

Diamond's father and mother were, notwithstanding, *rather* miserable, and Diamond began to feel a kind of darkness beginning to spread over his own mind. But the same moment he said to himself, "This will never do. I can't give in to this. I've been to the back of the north wind. Things go right there, and so I must try to get things to go right here. I've got to fight the miserable things. They shan't make me miserable if I can help it." I do not mean that he thought these very words. They are perhaps too grown-up for him to have thought, but they represent the kind of thing that was in his heart and his head. And when heart and head go together, nothing can stand before them.

"What nice bread and butter this is!" said Diamond.

"I'm glad you like it, my dear," said his father. "I bought the butter myself at the little shop round the corner."

"It's very nice, thank you, father. Oh, there's baby waking! I'll take him."

"Sit still, Diamond," said his mother. "Go on with your bread and butter. You're not strong enough to lift him yet."

So she took the baby herself, and set him on her knee. Then Diamond began to amuse him, and went on till the little fellow was shrieking with laughter. For the baby's world was his mother's arms; and the drizzling rain, and the dreary mews, and even his father's troubled face could not touch him. What cared baby for the loss of a hundred situations? Yet neither father nor mother thought him hard-hearted because he crowed and laughed in the middle of their troubles. On the contrary, his crowing and laughing were infectious. His little heart was so full of merriment that it could not hold it all, and it ran over into theirs. Father and mother began to laugh too, and Diamond laughed till he had a fit of coughing which frightened his mother, and made them all stop. His father took the baby, and his mother put him to bed.

But it was indeed a change to them all, not only from Sandwich, but from their old place. Instead of the great river where the huge barges with their mighty brown and yellow sails went tacking from side to side like little pleasure-skiffs, and where the long thin boats shot past with eight and sometimes twelve rowers, their windows now looked out upon a dirty paved yard. And there was no garden more for Diamond to run into when he pleased, with gay flowers about his feet, and solemn sun-filled trees over his head. Neither was there a wooden wall at the back of his bed with a hole in it for North Wind to come in at when she liked. Indeed, there was such a high wall, and there were so many houses about the mews, that North Wind seldom got into the place at all, except when something *must* be done, and she had a grand cleaning out like other housewives; while the partition at the head of Diamond's new bed only divided it from the room occupied by a cabman who drank too much beer, and came home chiefly to quarrel with his wife and pinch his children. It was dreadful to Diamond to hear the scolding and the crying. But it could not make him miserable, because he had been at the back of the north wind.

If my reader find it hard to believe that Diamond should be so good, he must remember that he had been to the back of the north wind. If he never knew a boy so good, did he ever know a boy that had been to the back of the north wind? It was not in the least strange of Diamond to behave as he did; on the contrary, it was thoroughly sensible of him.

We shall see how he got on.

CHAPTER XVI

DIAMOND MAKES A BEGINNING

THE WIND blew loud, but Diamond slept a deep sleep, and never heard it. My own impression is that every time when Diamond slept well and remembered nothing about it in the morning, he had been all that night at the back of the north wind. I am almost sure that was how he woke so refreshed, and felt so quiet and hopeful all the day. Indeed he said this much, though not to me,—that always when he woke from such a sleep there was a something in his mind, he could not tell what—could not tell whether it was the last far-off sounds of the river dying away in the distance, or some of the words of the endless song his mother had read to him on the seashore. Sometimes he thought it must have been the twittering of the swallows—over the shallows, you know; but it *may* have been the chirping of the dingy sparrows picking up their breakfast in the yard—how can I tell? I don't know what I know, I only know what I think; and to tell the truth, I am more for the swallows than the sparrows. When he knew he was coming awake, he would sometimes try hard to keep hold of the words of what seemed a new song, one he had not heard before—a song in which the words and the music somehow appeared to be all one; but even when he thought he had got them well fixed in his mind, ever as he came *awaker*—as he would say—one line faded away out of it, and then another, and then another, till at last there was nothing left but some lovely picture of water or grass or daisies, or something else very common, but with all the commonness polished off it, and the lovely soul of it, which people so seldom see, and, alas! yet seldomer believe in, shining out. But after that he would sing the oddest, loveliest little songs to the baby—of his own making, his mother said; but Diamond said he did not make them; they were made somewhere inside him, and he knew nothing about them till they were coming out.

When he woke that first morning he got up at once, saying to himself, "I've been ill long enough, and have given a great deal of trouble; I must try and be of use now, and help my mother." When he went into her room he found her lighting the fire, and his father just getting out of bed. They had only the one room, besides the little one, not much more than a closet, in which Diamond slept. He began at once to set things to rights, but the baby waking up, he took him, and nursed him till his mother had got the breakfast ready. She was looking gloomy, and his father was silent; and indeed except Diamond had done all he possibly could to keep out the misery that was trying to get in at doors and windows, he too would have grown miserable, and then they would have been all miserable together. But to try to make others comfortable is the only way to get right comfortable ourselves, and that comes partly of not being able to think so much about ourselves when we are helping other people. For our Selves will always do pretty well if we don't pay them too much attention. Our Selves are like some little children who will be happy enough so long as they are left to their own games, but when we begin to interfere with them, and make them presents of too nice playthings, or too many sweet things, they begin at once to fret and spoil.

"Why, Diamond, child!" said his mother at last, "you're as good to your mother as if you were a girl—nursing the baby, and toasting the bread, and sweeping up the hearth! I declare a body would think you had been among the fairies."

Could Diamond have had greater praise or greater pleasure? You see when he forgot his Self his mother took care of his Self, and loved and praised his Self. Our own praises poison our Selves, and puff and swell them up, till they lose all shape and beauty, and become like great toadstools. But the praises of father or mother do our Selves good, and comfort them and make them beautiful. *They* never do them any harm. If they do any harm, it comes of our mixing some of our own praises with them, and that turns them nasty and slimy and poisonous.

When his father had finished his breakfast, which he did rather in a hurry, he got up and went down into the yard to get out his horse and put him to the cab.

"Won't you come and see the cab, Diamond?" he said.

"Yes, *please*, father—if mother can spare me a minute," answered Diamond.

"Bless the child! I don't want him," said his mother cheerfully.

But as he was following his father out of the door, she called him back.

"Diamond, just hold the baby one minute. I have something to say to your father."

So Diamond sat down again, took the baby in his lap, and began poking his face into its little body, laughing and singing all the while, so that the baby crowed like a little bantam. And what he sang was something like this—such nonsense to those that couldn't understand it! but not to the baby, who got all the good in the world out of it:—

baby's a-sleeping
wake up baby
for all the swallows
are the merriest fellows
and have the yellowest children
who would go sleeping
and snore like a gaby
disturbing his mother
and father and brother
and all a-boring
their ears with his snoring
snoring snoring
for himself and no other
for himself in particular
wake up baby
sit up perpendicular
hark to the gushing
hark to the rushing
where the sheep are the woolliest
and the lambs the unruliest
and their tails the whitest
and their eyes the brightest
and baby's the bonniest
and baby's the funniest

and baby's the shiniest
and baby's the tiniest
and baby's the merriest
and baby's the worriest
of all the lambs
that plague their dams
and mother's the whitest
of all the dams
that feed the lambs
that go crop-cropping
without stop-stopping
and father's the best
of all the swallows
that build their nest
out of the shining shallows
and he has the merriest children
that's baby and Diamond
and Diamond and baby
and baby and Diamond
and Diamond and baby

Here Diamond's knees went off in a wild dance which tossed the baby about and shook the laughter out of him in immoderate peals. His mother had been listening at the door to the last few lines of his song, and came in with the tears in her eyes. She took the baby from him, gave him a kiss, and told him to run to his father.

By the time Diamond got into the yard, the horse was between the shafts, and his father was looping the traces on. Diamond went round to look at the horse. The sight of him made him feel very queer. He did not know much about different horses, and all other horses than their own were very much the same to him. But he could not make it out. This was Diamond and it wasn't Diamond. Diamond didn't hang his head like that; yet the head that was hanging was very like the one that Diamond used to hold so high. Diamond's bones didn't show through his skin like that; but the skin they pushed out of shape so was very like Diamond's skin; and the bones might be Diamond's bones, for he had never seen the shape of *them*. But when he came round in front of the old horse, and he put out his long neck, and began sniffing at him and rubbing his upper lip and his nose on him, then Diamond saw it *could* be no other than old Diamond, and he did just as his father had done before—put his arms round his neck and cried—but not much.

"Ain't it jolly, father?" he said. "Was there ever anybody so lucky as me? Dear old Diamond."

And he hugged the horse again, and kissed both his big hairy cheeks. He could only manage one at a time however—the other cheek was so far off on the other side of his big head.

His father mounted the box with just the same air, as Diamond thought, with which he had used to get upon the coachbox, and Diamond said to himself, "Father's as grand as ever anyhow." He had kept his brown livery-coat, only his wife had taken the silver buttons off and put brass ones instead, because they did not think it polite to Mr. Coleman in his fallen fortunes to let his crest be seen upon the box of a cab. Old Diamond had kept just his collar; and that had the silver crest upon it still, for his master thought nobody would notice that, and so let it remain for a memorial of the better days of which it reminded him—not unpleasantly, seeing it had been by no fault either of his or of the old horse's that they had come down in the world together.

"Oh, father, do let me drive a bit," said Diamond, jumping up on the box beside him.

His father changed places with him at once, putting the reins into his hands. Diamond gathered them up eagerly.

"Don't pull at his mouth," said his father; "just feel at it gently to let him know you're there and attending to him. That's what I call talking to him through the reins."

"Yes, father, I understand," said Diamond. Then to the horse he said, "Go on, Diamond." And old Diamond's ponderous bulk began at once to move to the voice of the little boy.

But before they had reached the entrance of the mews, another voice called after young Diamond, which, in his turn, he had to obey, for it was that of his mother. "Diamond! Diamond!" it cried; and Diamond pulled the reins, and the horse stood still as a stone.

"Husband," said his mother, coming up, "you're never going to trust *him* with the reins—a baby like that?"

"He must learn some day, and he can't begin too soon. I see already he's a born coachman," said his father proudly. "And I don't see well how he could escape it, for my father and my grandfather, that's his great-grandfather, was all coachmen, I'm told; so it must come natural to him, any one would think. Besides, you see, old Diamond's as proud of him as we are our own selves, wife. Don't you see how he's turning round his ears, with the mouths of them open, for the first word he speaks to tumble in? He's too well bred to turn his head, you know."

"Well, but, husband, I can't do without him to-day. Everything's got to be done, you know. It's my first day here. And there's that baby!"

"Bless you, wife! I never meant to take him away—only to the bottom of Endell Street. He can watch his way back."

"No, thank you, father; not to-day," said Diamond. "Mother wants me. Perhaps she'll let me go another day."

"Very well, my man," said his father, and took the reins which Diamond was holding out to him.

Diamond got down, a little disappointed of course, and went in with his mother, who was too pleased to speak. She only took hold of his hand as tight as if she had been afraid of his running away instead of glad that he would not leave her.

Now, although they did not know it, the owner of the stables, the same man who had sold the horse to his father, had been standing just inside one of the stable-doors, with his hands in his pockets, and had heard and seen all that passed; and from that day John Stonecrop took a great fancy to the little boy. And this was the beginning of what came of it.

That same evening, just as Diamond was feeling tired of the day's work, and wishing

his father would come home, Mr. Stonecrop knocked at the door. His mother went and
opened it.

"Good evening, ma'am," said he. "Is little master in?"

"Yes, to be sure he is—at your service, I'm sure, Mr. Stonecrop," said his mother.

"No, no, ma'am; it's I'm at his service. I'm just a-going out with my own cab, and if he
likes to come with me, he shall drive my old horse till he's tired."

"It's getting rather late for him," said his mother thoughtfully. "You see he's been an
invalid."

Diamond thought, what a funny thing! How could he have been an invalid when he
did not even know what the word meant? But, of course, his mother was right.

"Oh well," said Mr. Stonecrop, "I can just let him drive through Bloomsbury Square,
and then he shall run home again."

"Very good, sir. And I'm much obliged to you," said his mother. And Diamond,
dancing with delight, got his cap, put his hand in Mr. Stonecrop's, and went with him to
the yard where the cab was waiting. He did not think the horse looked nearly so nice as
Diamond, nor Mr. Stonecrop nearly so grand as his father; but he was none the less
pleased. He got up on the box, and his new friend got up beside him.

"What's the horse's name?" whispered Diamond, as he took the reins from the man.

"It's not a nice name," said Mr. Stonecrop. "You needn't call him by it. I didn't give it
him. He'll go well enough without it. Give the boy a whip, Jack. I never carries one
when I drives old—"

He didn't finish the sentence. Jack handed Diamond a whip, with which, by holding it
half down the stick, he managed just to flack the haunches of the horse; and away he
went.

"Mind the gate," said Mr. Stonecrop; and Diamond did mind the gate, and guided the
nameless horse through it in safety, pulling him this way and that according as was
necessary. Diamond learned to drive all the sooner that he had been accustomed to do
what he was told, and could obey the smallest hint in a moment. Nothing helps one to
get on like that. Some people don't know how to do what they are told: they have not
been used to it, and they neither understand quickly nor are able to turn what they do
understand into action quickly. With an obedient mind one learns the rights of things
fast enough; for it is the law of the universe, and to obey is to understand.

"Look out!" cried Mr. Stonecrop, as they were turning the corner into Bloomsbury
Square.

It was getting dusky now. A cab was approaching rather rapidly from the opposite
direction, and Diamond pulling aside, and the other driver pulling up, they only just
escaped a collision. Then they knew each other.

"Why, Diamond, it's a bad beginning to run into your own father," cried the driver.

"But, father, wouldn't it have been a bad ending to run into your own son?" said
Diamond in return; and the two men laughed heartily.

"This is very kind of you, I'm sure, Stonecrop," said his father.

"Not a bit. He's a brave fellow, and'll be fit to drive on his own hook in a week or two.
But I think you'd better let him drive you home now, for his mother don't like his
having over much of the night air, and I promised not to take him farther than the
square."

"Come along then, Diamond," said his father, as he brought his cab up to the other, and moved off the box to the seat beside it. Diamond jumped across, caught at the reins, said "Good night, and thank you, Mr. Stonecrop," and drove away home, feeling more of a man than he had ever yet had a chance of feeling in all his life. Nor did his father find it necessary to give him a single hint as to his driving. Only I suspect the fact that it was old Diamond, and old Diamond on his way to his stable, may have had something to do with young Diamond's success.

"Well, child," said his mother, when he entered the room, "you've not been long gone."

"No, mother; here I am. Give me the baby."

"The baby's asleep," said his mother.

"Then give him to me, and I'll lay him down."

But as Diamond took him, he woke up and began to laugh. For he was indeed one of the merriest children. And no wonder, for he was as plump as a plum-pudding, and had never had an ache or pain that lasted more than five minutes at a time. Diamond sat down with him and began to sing to him.

> baby baby babbing
> your father's gone a-cabbing
> to catch a shilling for its pence
> to make the baby babbing dance
> for old Diamond's a duck
> they say he can swim
> but the duck of diamonds
> is baby that's him
> and of all the swallows
> the merriest fellows
> that bake their cake
> with the water they shake
> out of the river
> flowing for ever
> and make dust into clay
> on the shiniest day
> to build their nest
> father's the best
> and mother's the whitest
> and her eyes are the brightest
> of all the dams
> that watch their lambs
> cropping the grass
> where the waters pass
> singing for ever
> and of all the lambs
> with the shakingest tails
> and the jumpingest feet
> baby's the funniest
> baby's the bonniest

and he never wails
and he's always sweet
and Diamond's his nurse
and Diamond's his nurse
and Diamond's his nurse

When Diamond's rhymes grew scarce, he always began dancing the baby. Some people wondered that such a child could rhyme as he did, but his rhymes were not very good, for he was only trying to remember what he had heard the river sing at the back of the north wind.

CHAPTER XVII

DIAMOND GOES ON

DIAMOND BECAME a great favourite with all the men about the mews. Some may think it was not the best place in the world for him to be brought up in; but it must have been, for there he was. At first, he heard a good many rough and bad words; but he did not like them, and so they did him little harm. He did not know in the least what they meant, but there was something in the very sound of them, and in the tone of voice in which they were said, which Diamond felt to be ugly. So they did not even stick to him, not to say get inside him. He never took any notice of them, and his face shone pure and good in the middle of them, like a primrose in a hailstorm. At first, because his face was so quiet and sweet, with a smile always either awake or asleep in his eyes, and because he never heeded their ugly words and rough jokes, they said he wasn't all there, meaning that he was half an idiot, whereas he was a great deal more there than they had the sense to see. And before long the bad words found themselves ashamed to come out of the men's mouths when Diamond was near. The one would nudge the other to remind him that the boy was within hearing, and the words choked themselves before they got any farther. When they talked to him nicely he had always a good answer, sometimes a smart one, ready, and that helped much to make them change their minds about him.

One day Jack gave him a curry-comb and a brush to try his hand upon old Diamond's coat. He used them so deftly, so gently, and yet so thoroughly, as far as he could reach, that the man could not help admiring him.

"You must make haste and grow," he said. "It won't do to have a horse's belly clean and his back dirty, you know."

"Give me a leg," said Diamond, and in a moment he was on the old horse's back with the comb and brush. He sat on his withers, and reaching forward as he ate his hay, he curried and he brushed, first at one side of his neck, and then at the other. When that was done he asked for a dressing-comb, and combed his mane thoroughly. Then he pushed himself on to his back, and did his shoulders as far down as he could reach.

Then he sat on his croup, and did his back and sides; then he turned round like a monkey, and attacked his hind-quarters, and combed his tail. This last was not so easy to manage, for he had to lift it up, and every now and then old Diamond would whisk it out of his hands, and once he sent the comb flying out of the stable door, to the great amusement of the men. But Jack fetched it again, and Diamond began once more, and did not leave off till he had done the whole business fairly well, if not in a first-rate, experienced fashion. All the time the old horse went on eating his hay, and, but with an occasional whisk of his tail when Diamond tickled or scratched him, took no notice of the proceeding. But that was all a pretence, for he knew very well who it was that was perched on his back, and rubbing away at him with the comb and the brush. So he was quite pleased and proud, and perhaps said to himself something like this—

"I'm a stupid old horse, who can't brush his own coat; but there's my young godson on my back, cleaning me like an angel."

I won't vouch for what the old horse was thinking, for it is very difficult to find out what any old horse is thinking.

"Oh dear!" said Diamond when he had done, "I'm so tired!"

And he laid himself down at full length on old Diamond's back.

By this time all the men in the stable were gathered about the two Diamonds, and all much amused. One of them lifted him down, and from that time he was a greater favourite than before. And if ever there was a boy who had a chance of being a prodigy at cab-driving, Diamond was that boy, for the strife came to be who should have him out with him on the box.

His mother, however, was a little shy of the company for him, and besides she could not always spare him. Also his father liked to have him himself when he could; so that he was more desired than enjoyed among the cabmen.

But one way and another he did learn to drive all sorts of horses, and to drive them well, and that through the most crowded streets in London city. Of course there was the man always on the box-seat beside him, but before long there was seldom the least occasion to take the reins out of his hands. For one thing he never got frightened, and consequently was never in too great a hurry. Yet when the moment came for doing something sharp, he was always ready for it. I must once more remind my readers that he had been to the back of the north wind.

One day, which was neither washing-day nor cleaning-day, nor marketing-day, nor Saturday, nor Monday—upon which consequently Diamond could be spared from the baby—his father took him on his own cab. After a stray job or two by the way, they drew up in the row upon the stand between Cockspur Street and Pall Mall. They waited a long time, but nobody seemed to want to be carried anywhere. By and by ladies would be going home from the Academy exhibition, and then there would be a chance of a job.

"Though, to be sure," said Diamond's father—with what truth I cannot say, but he believed what he said—"some ladies is very hard, and keeps you to the bare sixpence a mile, when every one knows that ain't enough to keep a family *and* a cab upon. To be sure it's the law; but mayhap they may get more law than they like some day themselves."

As it was very hot, Diamond's father got down to have a glass of beer himself, and give another to the old waterman.

He left Diamond on the box.

A sudden noise got up and Diamond looked round to see what was the matter.

There was a crossing near the cab-stand, where a girl was sweeping. Some rough young imps had picked a quarrel with her, and were now hauling at her broom to get it away from her. But as they did not pull all together, she was holding it against them, scolding and entreating alternately.

Diamond was off his box in a moment, and running to the help of the girl. He got hold of the broom at her end and pulled along with her. But the boys proceeded to rougher measures, and one of them hit Diamond on the nose, and made it bleed; and as he could not let go the broom to mind his nose, he was soon a dreadful figure. But presently his father came back, and missing Diamond, looked about. He had to look twice, however, before he could be sure that that was his boy in the middle of the tumult. He rushed in, and sent the assailants flying in all directions. The girl thanked Diamond, and began sweeping as if nothing had happened, while his father led him away. With the help of old Tom, the waterman, he was soon washed into decency, and his father set him on the box again, perfectly satisfied with the account he gave of the cause of his being in a fray.

"I couldn't let them behave so to a poor girl—could I, father?" he said.

"Certainly not, Diamond," said his father, quite pleased, for Diamond's father was a gentleman.

A moment after, up came the girl, running, with her broom over her shoulder, and called, "Cab, there! cab!"

Diamond's father turned instantly, for he was the foremost in the rank, and followed the girl. One or two other passing cabs heard the cry, and made for the place, but the girl had taken care not to call till she was near enough to give her friends the first chance. When they reached the curbstone—who should it be waiting for the cab but Mrs. and Miss Coleman! They did not look at the cabman, however. The girl opened the door for them; they gave her the address, and a penny; she told the cabman, and away they drove.

When they reached the house, Diamond's father got down and rang the bell. As he opened the door of the cab, he touched his hat as he had been wont to do. The ladies both stared for a moment, and then exclaimed together:

"Why, Joseph! can it be you?"

"Yes, ma'am; yes, miss;" answered he, again touching his hat, with all the respect he could possibly put into the action. "It's a lucky day which I see you once more upon it."

"Who would have thought it?" said Mrs. Coleman. "It's changed times for both of us, Joseph, and it's not very often we can have a cab even; but you see my daughter is still very poorly, and she can't bear the motion of the omnibuses. Indeed we meant to walk a bit first before we took a cab, but just at the corner, for as hot as the sun was, a cold wind came down the street, and I saw that Miss Coleman must not face it. But to think we should have fallen upon you, of all the cabmen in London! I didn't know you had got a cab."

"Well, you see, ma'am, I had a chance of buying the old horse, and I couldn't resist *him*. There he is, looking at you, ma'am. Nobody knows the sense in that head of his."

The two ladies went near to pat the horse, and then they noticed Diamond on the box.

"Why, you've got both Diamonds with you," said Miss Coleman. "How do you do, Diamond?"

Diamond lifted his cap, and answered politely.

"He'll be fit to drive himself before long," said his father, proudly. "The old horse is a-teaching of him."

"Well, he must come and see us, now you've found us out. Where do you live?"

Diamond's father gave the ladies a ticket with his name and address printed on it; and then Mrs. Coleman took out her purse, saying:

"And what's your fare, Joseph?"

"No, thank you, ma'am," said Joseph. "It was your own old horse as took you; and me you paid long ago."

He jumped on his box before she could say another word, and with a parting salute drove off, leaving them on the pavement, with the maid holding the door for them.

It was a long time now since Diamond had seen North Wind, or even thought much about her. And as his father drove along, he was thinking not about her, but about the crossing-sweeper, and was wondering what made him feel as if he knew her quite well, when he could not remember anything of her. But a picture arose in his mind of a little girl running before the wind and dragging her broom after her; and from that, by degrees, he recalled the whole adventure of the night when he got down from North Wind's back in a London street. But he could not quite satisfy himself whether the whole affair was not a dream which he had dreamed when he was a very little boy. Only he had been to the back of the north wind since—there could be no doubt of that; for when he woke every morning, he always knew that he had been there again. And as he thought and thought, he recalled another thing that had happened that morning, which, although it seemed a mere accident, might have something to do with what had happened since. His father had intended going on the stand at King's Cross that morning, and had turned into Gray's Inn Lane to drive there, when they found the way blocked up, and upon inquiry were informed that a stack of chimneys had been blown down in the night, and had fallen across the road. They were just clearing the rubbish away. Diamond's father turned, and made for Charing Cross.

That night the father and mother had a great deal to talk about.

"Poor things!" said the mother; "it's worse for them than it is for us. You see they've been used to such grand things, and for them to come down to a little poky house like that—it breaks my heart to think of it."

"I don't know," said Diamond thoughtfully, "whether Mrs. Coleman had bells on her toes."

"What do you mean, child?" said his mother.

"She had rings on her fingers anyhow," returned Diamond.

"Of course she had, as any lady would. What has that to do with it?"

"When we were down at Sandwich," said Diamond, "you said you would have to part with your mother's ring, now we were poor."

"Bless the child! he forgets nothing," said his mother. "Really, Diamond, a body would need to mind what they say to you."

"Why?" said Diamond. "I only think about it."

"That's just why," said the mother.

"Why is that why?" persisted Diamond, for he had not yet learned that grown-up people are not often so much grown up that they never talk like children—and spoilt ones too.

"Mrs. Coleman is none so poor as all that yet. No, thank Heaven! she's not come to that."

"Is it a *great* disgrace to be poor?" asked Diamond, because of the tone in which his mother had spoken.

But his mother, whether conscience-stricken I do not know, hurried him away to bed, where after various attempts to understand her, resumed and resumed again in spite of invading sleep, he was conquered at last, and gave in, murmuring over and over to himself, "Why is why?" but getting no answer to the question.

CHAPTER XVIII

THE DRUNKEN CABMAN

A FEW NIGHTS after this, Diamond woke up suddenly, believing he heard the North Wind thundering along. But it was something quite different. South Wind was moaning round the chimneys, to be sure, for she was not very happy that night, but it was not her voice that had wakened Diamond. Her voice would only have lulled him the deeper asleep. It was a loud, angry voice, now growling like that of a beast, now raving like that of a madman; and when Diamond came a little wider awake, he knew that it was the voice of the drunken cabman, the wall of whose room was at the head of his bed. It was anything but pleasant to hear, but he could not help hearing it. At length there came a cry from the woman, and then a scream from the baby. Thereupon Diamond thought it time that somebody did something, and as himself was the only somebody at hand, he must go and see whether he could not do the something. So he got up and put on part of his clothes, and went down the stairs, for the cabman's room did not open upon their stair, and he had to go out into the yard, and in at the next door. This, fortunately, the cabman, being drunk, had left open. By the time he reached their stair, all was still except the voice of the crying baby, which guided him to the right door. He opened it softly, and peeped in. There, leaning back in a chair, with his arms hanging down by his sides, and his legs stretched out before him and supported on his heels, sat the drunken cabman. His wife lay in her clothes upon the bed, sobbing, and the baby was wailing in the cradle. It was very miserable altogether.

Now the way most people do when they see anything very miserable is to turn away from the sight, and try to forget it. But Diamond began as usual to try to destroy the misery. The little boy was just as much one of God's messengers as if he had been an angel with a flaming sword, going out to fight the devil. The devil he had to fight just then was Misery. And the way he fought him was the very best. Like a wise soldier, he attacked him first in his weakest point—that was the baby; for Misery can never get such a hold of a baby as of a grown person. Diamond was knowing in babies, and he knew he could do something to make the baby happy; for although he had only known one baby as yet, and although not one baby is the same as another, yet they are so very much alike in some things, and he knew that one baby so thoroughly, that he had good reason to believe he could do something for any other. I have known people who would have begun to fight the devil in a very different and a very stupid way. They would have begun by scolding the idiotic cabman; and next they would make his wife angry by saying it must be her fault as well as his, and by leaving ill-bred though well-meant shabby little books for them to read, which they were sure to hate the sight of; while all the time they would not have put out a finger to touch the wailing baby. But Diamond had him out of the cradle in a moment, set him up on his knee, and told him to look at the light. Now all the light there was came only from a lamp in the yard, and it was a very dingy and yellow light, for the glass of the lamp was dirty, and the gas was bad; but the light that came from it was, notwithstanding, as certainly light as if it had come from the sun itself, and the baby knew that, and smiled to it; and although it was indeed a

wretched room which that lamp lighted—so dreary, and dirty, and empty, and hopeless!
—there in the middle of it sat Diamond on a stool, smiling to the baby, and the baby on
his knees smiling to the lamp. The father of him sat staring at nothing, neither asleep
nor awake, not quite lost in stupidity either, for through it all he was dimly angry with
himself, he did not know why. It was that he had struck his wife. He had forgotten it,
but was miserable about it, notwithstanding. And this misery was the voice of the great
Love that had made him and his wife and the baby and Diamond, speaking in his heart,
and telling him to be good. For that great Love speaks in the most wretched and dirty
hearts; only the tone of its voice depends on the echoes of the place in which it sounds.
On Mount Sinai, it was thunder; in the cabman's heart it was *misery;* in the soul of St.
John it was perfect blessedness.

By and by he became aware that there was a voice of singing in the room. This, of
course, was the voice of Diamond singing to the baby—song after song, every one as
foolish as another to the cabman, for he was too tipsy to part one word from another: all
the words mixed up in his ear in a gurgle without division or stop; for such was the way
he spoke himself, when he was in this horrid condition. But the baby was more than
content with Diamond's songs, and Diamond himself was so contented with what the
songs were all about, that he did not care a bit about the songs themselves, if only baby
liked them. But they did the cabman good as well as the baby and Diamond, for they
put him to sleep, and the sleep was busy all the time it lasted, smoothing the wrinkles
out of his temper.

At length Diamond grew tired of singing, and began to talk to the baby instead. And
as soon as he stopped singing, the cabman began to wake up. His brain was a little
clearer now, his temper a little smoother, and his heart not quite so dirty. He began to

listen and he went on listening, and heard Diamond saying to the baby something like this, for he thought the cabman was asleep:

"Poor daddy! Baby's daddy takes too much beer and gin, and that makes him somebody else, and not his own self at all. Baby's daddy would never hit baby's mammy if he didn't take too much beer. He's very fond of baby's mammy, and works from morning to night to get her breakfast and dinner and supper, only at night he forgets, and pays the money away for beer. And they put nasty stuff in the beer, I've heard my daddy say, that drives all the good out, and lets all the bad in. Daddy says when a man takes to drink, there's a thirsty devil creeps into his inside, because he knows he will always get enough there. And the devil is always crying out for more drink, and that makes the man thirsty, and so he drinks more and more, till he kills himself with it. And then the ugly devil creeps out of him, and crawls about on his belly, looking for some other cabman to get into, that he may drink, drink, drink. That's what *my* daddy says, baby. And he says, too, the only way to make the devil come out, is to give him plenty of cold water and tea and coffee, and nothing at all that comes from the public-house; for the devil can't abide that kind of stuff, and creeps out pretty soon, for fear of being drowned in it. But your daddy *will* drink the nasty stuff, poor man! I wish he wouldn't, for it makes mammy cross with him, and no wonder! and then when mammy's cross, he's crosser, and there's nobody in the house to take care of them but baby; and you *do* take care of them, baby—don't you, baby? I know you do. Babies always take care of their fathers and mothers—don't they, baby? That's what they come for—isn't it, baby? And when daddy stops drinking beer and nasty gin with turpentine in it, father says, then mammy *will* be so happy, and look so pretty! and daddy will be so good to baby! and baby will be as happy as a swallow, which is the merriest fellow! And Diamond will be so happy too! And when Diamond's a man, he'll take baby out with him on the box, and teach him to drive a cab."

He went on with chatter like this till baby was asleep, by which time he was tired, and father and mother were both wide awake,—only rather confused—the one from the beer, the other from the blow—and staring, the one from his chair, the other from her bed, at Diamond. But he was quite unaware of their notice, for he sat half-asleep, with his eyes wide open, staring in his turn, though without knowing it, at the cabman, while the cabman could not withdraw his gaze from Diamond's white face and big eyes. For Diamond's face was always rather pale, and now it was paler than usual with sleeplessness, and the light of the street-lamp upon it. At length he found himself nodding, and he knew then it was time to put the baby down, lest he should let him fall. So he rose from the little three-legged stool, and laid the baby in the cradle, and covered him up—it was well it was a warm night, and he did not want much covering—and then he all but staggered out of the door, he was so tipsy himself with sleep.

"Wife," said the cabman, turning towards the bed, "I do somehow believe that wur a angel just gone. Did you see him, wife? He warn't wery big, and he hadn't got none o' them wingses, you know. It wur one o' them baby-angels you sees on the gravestones, you know."

"Nonsense, hubby!" said his wife; "but it's just as good. I might say better, for you can ketch hold of *him* when you like. That's little Diamond as everybody knows, and a duck o' diamonds he is! No woman could wish for a better child than he be."

"I ha' heerd on him in the stable, but I never see the brat afore. Come, old girl, let bygones be bygones, and gie us a kiss, and we'll go to bed."

The cabman kept his cab in another yard, although he had his room in this. He was often late in coming home, and was not one to take notice of children, especially when he was tipsy, which was oftener than not. Hence, if he had ever seen Diamond, he did not know him. But his wife knew him well enough, as did every one else who lived all day in the yard. She was a good-natured woman. It was she who had got the fire lighted and the tea ready for them when Diamond and his mother came home from Sandwich. And her husband was not an ill-natured man either, and when in the morning he recalled not only Diamond's visit, but how he himself had behaved to his wife, he was very vexed with himself, and gladdened his poor wife's heart by telling her how sorry he was. And for a whole week after, he did not go near the public-house, hard as it was to avoid it, seeing a certain rich brewer had built one, like a trap to catch souls and bodies in, at almost every corner he had to pass on his way home. Indeed, he was never quite so bad after that, though it was some time before he began really to reform.

CHAPTER XIX

DIAMOND'S FRIENDS

ONE DAY when old Diamond was standing with his nose in his bag between Pall Mall and Cockspur Street, and his master was reading the newspaper on the box of his cab, which was the last of a good many in the row, little Diamond got down for a run, for his legs were getting cramped with sitting. And first of all he strolled with his hands in his pockets up to the crossing, where the girl and her broom were to be found in all weathers. Just as he was going to speak to her, a tall gentleman stepped upon the crossing. He was pleased to find it so clean, for the streets were muddy, and he had nice boots on: so he put his hand in his pocket, and gave the girl a penny. But when she gave him a sweet smile in return, and made him a pretty courtesy, he looked at her again, and said:

"Where do you live, my child?"

"Paradise Row," she answered; "next door to the Adam and Eve—down the area."

"Whom do you live with?" he asked.

"My wicked old grannie," she replied.

"You shouldn't call your grannie wicked," said the gentleman.

"But she is," said the girl, looking up confidently in his face. "If you don't believe me, you can come and take a look at her."

The words sounded rude, but the girl's face looked so simple that the gentleman saw she did not mean to be rude, and became still more interested in her.

"Still you shouldn't say so," he insisted.

"Shouldn't I? Everybody calls her wicked old grannie—even them that's as wicked as her. You should hear her swear. There's nothing like it in the Row. Indeed, I assure you, sir, there's ne'er a one of them can shut my grannie up once she begins and gets right a-going. You must put her in a passion first, you know. It's no good till you do that—she's so old now. How she *do* make them laugh, to be sure!"

Although she called her wicked, the child spoke so as plainly to indicate pride in her grannie's pre-eminence in swearing.

The gentleman looked very grave to hear her, for he was sorry that such a nice little girl should be in such bad keeping. But he did not know what to say next, and stood for a moment with his eyes on the ground. When he lifted them, he saw the face of Diamond looking up in his.

"Please, sir," said Diamond, "her grannie's very cruel to her sometimes, and shuts her out in the streets at night, if she happens to be late."

"Is this your brother?" asked the gentleman of the girl.

"No, sir."

"How does he know your grandmother, then? He does not look like one of her sort."

"Oh no, sir! He's a good boy—quite."

Here she tapped her forehead with her finger in a significant manner.

"What do you mean by that?" asked the gentleman, while Diamond looked on smiling.

"The cabbies call him God's baby," she whispered. "He's not right in the head, you know. A tile loose."

Still Diamond, though he heard every word, and understood it too, kept on smiling. What could it matter what people called him, so long as he did nothing he ought not to do? And, besides, *God's baby* was surely the best of names!

"Well, my little man, and what can you do?" asked the gentleman, turning towards him—just for the sake of saying something.

"Drive a cab," said Diamond.

"Good; and what else?" he continued; for, accepting what the girl had said, he regarded the still sweetness of Diamond's face as a sign of silliness, and wished to be kind to the poor little fellow.

"Nurse a baby," said Diamond.

"Well—and what else?"

"Clean father's boots, and make him a bit of toast for his tea."

"You're a useful little man," said the gentleman. "What else can you do?"

"Not much that I know of," said Diamond. "I can't curry a horse, except somebody puts me on his back. So I don't count that."

"Can you read?"

"No; but mother can and father can, and they're going to teach me some day soon."

"Well, here's a penny for you."

"Thank you, sir."

"And when you have learned to read, come to me, and I'll give you sixpence and a book with fine pictures in it."

"Please, sir, where am I to come?" asked Diamond, who was too much a man of the world not to know that he must have the gentleman's address before he could go and see him.

"You're no such silly!" thought he, as he put his hand in his pocket, and brought out a card. "There," he said, "your father will be able to read that, and tell you where to go."

"Yes, sir. Thank you, sir," said Diamond, and put the card in his pocket.

The gentleman walked away, but turning round a few paces off, saw Diamond give his penny to the girl, and, walking slower, heard him say:

"I've got a father, and mother, and little brother, and you've got nothing but a wicked old grannie. You may have my penny."

The girl put it beside the other in her pocket, the only trust-worthy article of dress she wore. Her grandmother always took care that she had a stout pocket.

"Is she as cruel as ever?" asked Diamond.

"Much the same. But I gets more coppers now than I used to, and I can get summats to eat, and take browns enough home besides to keep her from grumbling. It's a good thing she's so blind, though."

"Why?" asked Diamond.

" 'Cause if she was as sharp in the eyes as she used to be, she would find out I never eats her broken wittles, and then she'd know as I must get something somewheres."

"Doesn't she watch you, then?"

"O' course she do. Don't she just! But I make believe and drop it in my lap, and then hitch it into my pocket."

"What would she do if she found you out?"

"She'd never give me no more."

"But you don't want it!"

"Yes, I do want it."

"What do you do with it, then?"

"Give it to cripple Jim."

"Who's cripple Jim?"

"A boy in the Row. His mother broke his leg when he wur a kid, so he's never come to much; but he's a good boy, is Jim, and I love Jim dearly. I always keeps off a penny for Jim—leastways as often as I can.—But there, I must sweep again, for them busses makes no end o' dirt."

"Diamond! Diamond!" cried his father, who was afraid he might get no good by talking to the girl; and Diamond obeyed, and got up again upon the box. He told his father about the gentleman, and what he had promised him if he would learn to read, and showed him the gentleman's card.

"Why, it's not many doors from the Mews!" said his father, giving him back the card. "Take care of it, my boy, for it may lead to something. God knows, in these hard times a man wants as many friends as he's ever likely to get."

"Haven't you got friends enough, father?" asked Diamond.

"Well, I have no right to complain; but the more the better, you know."

"Just let me count," said Diamond.

And he took his hands from his pockets, and spreading out the fingers of his left hand, began to count, beginning at the thumb.

"There's mother first; and then baby, and then me. Next there's old Diamond—and the cab—no, I won't count the cab, for it never looks at you, and when Diamond's out of the shafts, it's nobody. Then there's the man that drinks next door, and his wife, and his baby."

"They're no friends of mine," said his father.

"Well, they're friends of mine," said Diamond.

His father laughed.

"Much good they'll do you!" he said.

"How do you know they won't?" returned Diamond.

"Well, go on," said his father.

"Then there's Jack and Mr. Stonecrop, and, deary me! not to have mentioned Mr. Coleman and Mrs. Coleman, and Miss Coleman, and Mrs. Crump. And then there's the clergyman that spoke to me in the garden that day the tree was blown down."

"What's his name?"

"I don't know his name."

"Where does he live?"

"I don't know."

"How can you count him, then?"

"He did talk to me, and very kindlike too."

His father laughed again.

"Why, child, you're just counting everybody you know. That don't make 'em friends."

"Don't it? I thought it did. Well, but they shall be my friends. I shall make 'em."

"How will you do that?"

"They can't help themselves then, if they would. If I choose to be their friend, you know, they can't prevent me. Then there's that girl at the crossing."

"A fine set of friends you do have, to be sure, Diamond!"

"Surely *she*'s a friend anyhow, father. If it hadn't been for her, you would never have got Mrs. Coleman and Miss Coleman to carry home."

His father was silent, for he saw that Diamond was right, and was ashamed to find himself more ungrateful than he had thought.

"Then there's the new gentleman," Diamond went on.

"If he do as he say," interposed his father.

"And why shouldn't he? I daresay sixpence ain't too much for him to spare. But I don't quite understand, father: is nobody your friend but the one that does something for you?"

"No, I won't say that, my boy. You would have to leave out baby then."

"Oh no, I shouldn't. Baby can laugh in your face, and crow in your ears, and make you feel so happy. Call you that nothing, father?"

The father's heart was fairly touched now. He made no answer to this last appeal, and Diamond ended off with saying:

"And there's the best of mine to come yet—and that's you, daddy—except it be mother, you know. You're my friend, daddy, ain't you? And I'm your friend, ain't I?"

"And God for us all," said his father, and then they were both silent, for that was very solemn.

CHAPTER XX

DIAMOND LEARNS TO READ

THE QUESTION of the tall gentleman as to whether Diamond could read or not, set his father thinking it was high time he could; and as soon as old Diamond was suppered and bedded, he began the task that very night. But it was not much of a task to Diamond, for his father took for his lesson-book those very rhymes his mother had picked up on the sea-shore; and as Diamond was not beginning too soon, he learned very fast indeed. Within a month he was able to spell out most of the verses for himself.

But he had never come upon the poem he thought he had heard his mother read from it that day. He had looked through and through the book several times after he knew the letters and a few words, fancying he could tell the look of it, but had always failed to find one more like it than another. So he wisely gave up the search till he could really read. Then he resolved to begin at the beginning, and read them all straight through. This took him nearly a fortnight. When he had almost reached the end, he came upon the following verses, which took his fancy much, although they were certainly not very like those he was in search of.

LITTLE BOY BLUE

Little Boy Blue lost his way in a wood.
Sing apples and cherries, roses and honey:

He said, "I would not go back if I could,
It's all so jolly and funny."

He sang, "This wood is all my own,
Apples and cherries, roses and honey;
So here I'll sit, like a king on my throne,
All so jolly and funny."

A little snake crept out of the tree,
Apples and cherries, roses and honey;
"Lie down at my feet, little snake," said he,
All so jolly and funny.

A little bird sang in the tree overhead,
Apples and cherries, roses and honey,
"Come and sing your song on my finger instead,
All so jolly and funny."

The snake coiled up; and the bird flew down,
And sang him the song of Birdie Brown.

Little Boy Blue found it tiresome to sit,
And he thought he had better walk on a bit.

So up he got, his way to take,
And he said, "Come along, little bird and snake."

And waves of snake o'er the damp leaves passed,
And the snake went first and Birdie Brown last;

By Boy Blue's head, with flutter and dart,
Flew Birdie Brown with its song in its heart.

He came where the apples grew red and sweet:
"Tree, drop me an apple down at my feet."

He came where the cherries hung plump and red:
"Come to my mouth, sweet kisses," he said.

And the boughs bow down, and the apples they dapple
The grass, too many for him to grapple.

And the cheeriest cherries, with never a miss,
Fall to his mouth, each a full-grown kiss.

He met a little brook singing a song.
He said, "Little brook, you are going wrong.

"You must follow me, follow me, follow, I say,
Do as I tell you, and come this way."

And the song-singing, sing-songing forest brook
Leaped from its bed and after him took,

Followed him, followed. And pale and wan,
The dead leaves rustled as the water ran.

And every bird high up on the bough,
And every creature low down below,

He called, and the creatures obeyed the call,
Took their legs and their wings and followed him all;

Squirrels that carried their tails like a sack,
Each on his own little humpy brown back;

Householder snails, and slugs all tails,
And butterflies, flutterbies, ships all sails;

And weasels, and ousels, and mice, and larks,
And owls, and rere-mice, and harkydarks;

All went running, and creeping, and flowing,
After the merry boy fluttering and going;

The dappled fawns fawning, the fallow-dear following,
The swallows and flies, flying and swallowing;

Cockchafers, henchafers, cockioli-birds,
Cockroaches, henroaches, cuckoos in herds.

The spider forgot and followed him spinning,
And lost all his thread from end to beginning.

The gay wasp forgot his rings and his waist,
He never had made such undignified haste.

The dragon-flies melted to mist with their hurrying.
The mole in his moleskins left his barrowing burrowing.

The bees went buzzing, so busy and beesy,
And the midges in columns so upright and easy.

But Little Boy Blue was not content,
Calling for followers still as he went,

Blowing his horn, and beating his drum,
And crying aloud, "Come all of you, come!"

He said to the shadows, "Come after me;"
And the shadows began to flicker and flee,

And they flew through the wood all flattering and fluttering,
Over the dead leaves flickering and muttering.

And he said to the wind, "Come, follow; come, follow,
With whistle and pipe, and rustle and hollo."

And the wind wound round at his desire,
As if he had been the gold cock on the spire.

And the cock itself flew down from the church,
And left the farmers all in the lurch.

They run and they fly, they creep and they come,
Everything, everything, all and some.

The very trees they tugged at their roots,
Only their feet were too fast in their boots,

After him leaning and straining and bending,
As on through their boles he kept walking and wending,

Till out of the wood he burst on a lea,
Shouting and calling, "Come after me!"

And then they rose up with a leafy hiss,
And stood as if nothing had been amiss.

Little Boy Blue sat down on a stone,
And the creatures came round him every one.

And he said to the clouds, "I want you there;"
And down they sank through the thin blue air.

And he said to the sunset far in the west,
"Come here; I want you; I know best."

And the sunset came and stood up on the wold,
And burned and glowed in purple and gold.

Then Little Boy Blue began to ponder:
"What's to be done with them all, I wonder."

Then Little Boy Blue, he said, quite low,
"What to do with you all I am sure I don't know."

Then the clouds clodded down till dismal it grew;
The snake sneaked close; round Birdie Brown flew;

The brook sat up like a snake on its tail;
And the wind came up with a *what-will-you* wail;

And all the creatures sat and stared;
The mole opened his very eyes and glared;

And for rats and bats and the world and his wife,
Little Boy Blue was afraid of his life.

Then Birdie Brown began to sing,
And what he sang was the very thing:

"You have brought us all hither, Little Boy Blue,
Pray what do you want us all to do?"

"Go away! go away!" said Little Boy Blue;
"I'm sure I don't want you—get away—do."

"No, no; no, no; no, yes, and no, no,"
Sang Birdie Brown, "it mustn't be so.

"We cannot for nothing come here, and away.
Give us some work, or else we stay."

"Oh dear! and oh dear!" with sob and with sigh,
Said Little Boy Blue, and began to cry.

But before he got far, he thought of a thing;
And up he stood, and spoke like a king.

"Why do you hustle and jostle and bother?
Off with you all! Take me back to my mother."

The sunset stood at the gates of the west.
"Follow *me*, follow *me*," came from Birdie Brown's breast.

"I am going that way as fast as I can,"
Said the brook, as it sank and turned and ran.

Back to the woods fled the shadows like ghosts:
"If we stay, we shall all be missed from our posts."

Said the wind with a voice that had changed its cheer,
"I was just going there, when you brought me here."

"That's where I live," said the sack-backed squirrel,
And he turned his sack with a swing and a swirl.

Said the cock of the spire, "His father's churchwarden."
Said the brook running faster, "I run through his garden."

Said the mole, "Two hundred worms—there I caught 'em
Last year, and I'm going again next autumn."

Said they all, "If that's where you want us to steer for,
What in earth or in water did you bring us here for?"

"Never you mind," said Little Boy Blue;
"That's what I tell you. If that you won't do,

"I'll get up at once, and go home without you.
I think I will; I begin to doubt you."

He rose; and up rose the snake on its tail,
And hissed three times, half a hiss, half a wail.

Little Boy Blue he tried to go past him;
But wherever he turned, sat the snake and faced him.

"If you don't get out of my way," he said,
"I tell you, snake, I will break your head."

The snake he neither would go nor come;
So he hit him hard with the stick of his drum.

The snake fell down as if he were dead,
And Little Boy Blue set his foot on his head.

And all the creatures they marched before him,
And marshalled him home with a high cockolorum.

And Birdie Brown sang Twirrrr twitter twirrrr twee
  Apples and cherries, roses and honey;
Little Boy Blue has listened to me—
  All so jolly and funny.

CHAPTER XXI

SAL'S NANNY

Diamond managed with many blunders to read this rhyme to his mother.
"Isn't it nice, mother?" he said.
"Yes, it's pretty," she answered.
"I think it means something," returned Diamond.
"I'm sure I don't know what," she said.
"I wonder if it's the same boy—yes, it must be the same—Little Boy Blue, you know. Let me see—how does that rhyme go?

Little Boy Blue, come blow me your horn—

Yes, of course it is—for this one went 'blowing his horn and beating his drum.' He had a drum too.

Little Boy Blue, come blow me your horn;
The sheep's in the meadow, the cow's in the corn.

He had to keep them out, you know. But he wasn't minding his work. It goes—

Where's the little boy that looks after the sheep?
He's under the haystack, fast asleep.

There, you see, mother! And then, let me see—

Who'll go and wake him? No, not I;
For if I do, he'll be sure to cry.

So I suppose nobody did wake him. He was a rather cross little boy, I dare say, when woke up. And when he did wake of himself, and saw the mischief the cow had done to the corn, instead of running home to his mother, he ran away into the wood and lost himself. Don't you think that's very likely, mother?"

"I shouldn't wonder," she answered.

"So you see he was naughty; for even when he lost himself he did not want to go home. Any of the creatures would have shown him the way if he had asked it—all but the snake. He followed the snake, you know, and he took him farther away. I suppose it was a young one of the same serpent that tempted Adam and Eve. Father was telling us about it last Sunday, you remember."

"Bless the child!" said his mother to herself; and then added aloud, finding that Diamond did not go on, "Well, what next?"

"I don't know, mother. I'm sure there's a great deal more, but what it is I can't say. I only know that he killed the snake. I suppose that's what he had a drumstick for. He couldn't do it with his horn."

"But surely you're not such a silly as to take it all for true, Diamond?"

"I think it must be. It looks true. That killing of the snake looks true. It's what *I*'ve got to do so often."

His mother looked uneasy. Diamond smiled full in her face, and added—

"When baby cries and won't be happy, and when father and you talk about your troubles, I mean."

This did little to reassure his mother; and lest my reader should have his qualms about it too, I venture to remind him once more that Diamond had been to the back of the north wind.

Finding she made no reply, Diamond went on—

"In a week or so, I shall be able to go to the tall gentleman and tell him I can read. And I'll ask him if he can help me to understand the rhyme."

But before the week was out, he had another reason for going to Mr. Raymond.

For three days, on each of which, at one time or other, Diamond's father was on the same stand near the National Gallery, the girl was not at her crossing, and Diamond got quite anxious about her, fearing she must be ill. On the fourth day, not seeing her yet, he said to his father, who had that moment shut the door of his cab upon a fare—

"Father, I want to go and look after the girl. She can't be well."

"All right," said his father. "Only take care of yourself, Diamond."

So saying he climbed on his box and drove off.

He had great confidence in his boy, you see, and would trust him anywhere. But if he had known the kind of place in which the girl lived, he would perhaps have thought twice before he allowed him to go alone. Diamond, who did know something of it, had not, however, any fear. From talking to the girl he had a good notion of where about it was, and he remembered the address well enough; so by asking his way some twenty times, mostly of policemen, he came at length pretty near the place. The last policeman he questioned looked down upon him from the summit of six feet two inches, and replied with another question, but kindly:

"What do you want there, my small kid? It ain't where you was bred, I guess."

"No, sir," answered Diamond. "I live in Bloomsbury."

"That's a long way off," said the policeman.

"Yes, it's a good distance," answered Diamond; "but I find my way about pretty well. Policemen are always kind to me."

"But what on earth do you want here?"

Diamond told him plainly what he was about, and of course the man believed him, for nobody ever disbelieved Diamond. People might think he was mistaken, but they never thought he was telling a story.

"It's an ugly place," said the policeman.

"Is it far off?" asked Diamond.

"No. It's next door almost. But it's not safe."

"Nobody hurts me," said Diamond.

"I must go with you, I suppose."

"Oh, no! please not," said Diamond. "They might think I was going to meddle with them, and I ain't, you know."

"Well, do as you please," said the man, and gave him full directions.

Diamond set off, never suspecting that the policeman, who was a kind-hearted man, with children of his own, was following him close, and watching him round every corner. As he went on, all at once he thought he remembered the place, and whether it really was so, or only that he had laid up the policeman's instructions well in his mind, he went straight for the cellar of old Sal.

"He's a sharp little kid, anyhow, for as simple as he looks," said the man to himself. "Not a wrong turn does he take! But old Sal's a rum un for such a child to pay a morning visit to. She's worse when she's sober than when she's half drunk. I've seen her when she'd have torn him in pieces."

Happily then for Diamond, old Sal had gone out to get some gin. When he came to her door at the bottom of the area-stair and knocked, he received no answer. He laid his ear to the door, and thought he heard a moaning within. So he tried the door, and found it was not locked. It was a dreary place indeed,—and very dark, for the window was below the level of the street, and covered with mud, while over the grating which kept people from falling into the area, stood a chest of drawers, placed there by a dealer in second-hand furniture, which shut out almost all the light. And the smell in the place was dreadful. Diamond stood still for a while, for he could see next to nothing, but he heard the moaning plainly enough now. When he got used to the darkness, he discovered his friend lying with closed eyes and a white suffering face on a heap of little better than rags in a corner of the den. He went up to her and spoke; but she made him no answer. Indeed, she was not in the least aware of his presence, and Diamond saw that he could do nothing for her without help. So taking a lump of barley-sugar from his pocket, which he had bought for her as he came along, and laying it beside her, he left the place, having already made up his mind to go and see the tall gentleman, Mr. Raymond, and ask him to do something for Sal's Nanny, as the girl was called.

By the time he got up the area-steps, three or four women who had seen him go down were standing together at the top waiting for him. They wanted his clothes for their children; but they did not follow him down lest Sal should find them there. The moment he appeared, they laid their hands on him, and all began talking at once, for each wanted to get some advantage over her neighbours. He told them quite quietly, for he was not frightened, that he had come to see what was the matter with Nanny.

"What do you know about Nanny?" said one of them fiercely. "Wait till old Sal comes home, and you'll catch it, for going prying into her house when she's out. If you don't give me your jacket directly, I'll go and fetch her."

"I can't give you my jacket," said Diamond. "It belongs to my father and mother, you know. It's not mine to give. Is it now? You would not think it right to give away what wasn't yours—would you now?"

"Give it away! No, that I wouldn't; I'd keep it," she said, with a rough laugh. "But if the jacket ain't yours, what right have you to keep it? Here, Cherry, make haste. It'll be one go apiece."

They all began to tug at the jacket, while Diamond stooped and kept his arms bent to resist them. Before they had done him or the jacket any harm, however, suddenly they all scampered away; and Diamond, looking in the opposite direction, saw the tall policeman coming towards him.

"You had better have let me come with you, little man," he said, looking down in Diamond's face, which was flushed with his resistance.

"You came just in the right time, thank you," returned Diamond. "They've done me no harm."

"They would have if I hadn't been at hand, though."

"Yes; but you were at hand, you know, so they couldn't."

Perhaps the answer was deeper in purport than either Diamond or the policeman knew. They walked away together, Diamond telling his new friend how ill poor Nanny was, and that he was going to let the tall gentleman know. The policeman put him in the nearest way for Bloomsbury, and stepping out in good earnest, Diamond reached Mr. Raymond's door in less than an hour. When he asked if he was at home, the servant, in return, asked what he wanted.

"I want to tell him something."

"But I can't go and trouble him with such a message as that."

"He told me to come to him—that is, when I could read—and I can."

"How am I to know that?"

Diamond stared with astonishment for one moment, then answered:

"Why, I've just told you. That's how you know it."

But this man was made of coarser grain than the policeman, and instead of seeing that Diamond could not tell a lie, he put his answer down as impudence, and saying, "Do you think I'm going to take your word for it?" shut the door in his face.

Diamond turned and sat down on the doorstep, thinking with himself that the tall gentleman must either come in or come out, and he was therefore in the best possible position for finding him. He had not waited long before the door opened again; but when he looked round, it was only the servant once more.

"Get away," he said. "What are you doing on the doorstep?"

"Waiting for Mr. Raymond," answered Diamond, getting up.

"He's not at home."

"Then I'll wait till he comes," returned Diamond, sitting down again with a smile.

What the man would have done next I do not know, but a step sounded from the hall, and when Diamond looked round yet again, there was the tall gentleman.

"Who's this, John?" he asked.

"I don't know, sir. An imperent little boy as will sit on the doorstep."

"Please, sir," said Diamond, "he told me you weren't at home, and I sat down to wait for you."

"Eh, what!" said Mr. Raymond. "John! John! This won't do. Is it a habit of yours to turn away my visitors? There'll be some one else to turn away, I'm afraid, if I find any more of this kind of thing. Come in, my little man. I suppose you've come to claim your sixpence?"

"No, sir, not that."

"What! can't you read yet?"

"Yes, I can now, a little. But I'll come for that next time. I came to tell you about Sal's Nanny."

"Who's Sal's Nanny?"

"The girl at the crossing you talked to the same day."

"Oh, yes; I remember. What's the matter? Has she got run over?"

Then Diamond told him all.

Now Mr. Raymond was one of the kindest men in London. He sent at once to have the horse put to the brougham, took Diamond with him, and drove to the Children's Hospital. There he was well known to everybody, for he was not only a large subscriber, but he used to go and tell the children stories of an afternoon. One of the doctors promised to go and find Nanny, and do what could be done—have her brought to the hospital, if possible.

That same night they sent a litter for her, and as she could be of no use to old Sal until she was better, she did not object to having her removed. So she was soon lying in the fever ward—for the first time in her life in a nice clean bed. But she knew nothing of the whole affair. She was too ill to know anything.

CHAPTER XXII

MR. RAYMOND'S RIDDLE

MR. RAYMOND took Diamond home with him, stopping at the Mews to tell his mother that he would send him back soon. Diamond ran in with the message himself, and when he reappeared he had in his hand the torn and crumpled book which North Wind had given him.

"Ah! I see," said Mr. Raymond; "you are going to claim your sixpence now."

"I wasn't thinking of that so much as of another thing," said Diamond. "There's a rhyme in this book I can't quite understand. I want you to tell me what it means, if you please."

"I will if I can," answered Mr. Raymond. "You shall read it to me when we get home, and then I shall see."

Still with a good many blunders, Diamond did read it after a fashion. Mr. Raymond took the little book and read it over again.

Now Mr. Raymond was a poet himself, and so, although he had never been at the back of the north wind, he was able to understand the poem pretty well. But before saying anything about it, he read it over aloud, and Diamond thought he understood it much better already.

"I'll tell you what I think it means," he then said. "It means that people may have their way for a while, if they like, but it will get them into such troubles they'll wish they hadn't had it."

"I know, I know!" said Diamond. "Like the poor cabman next door. He drinks too much."

"Just so," returned Mr. Raymond. "But when people want to do right, things about them will try to help them. Only they must kill the snake, you know."

"I was sure the snake had something to do with it," cried Diamond triumphantly.

A good deal more talk followed, and Mr. Raymond gave Diamond his sixpence.

"What will you do with it?" he asked.

"Take it home to my mother," he answered. "She has a teapot—such a black one! —with a broken spout, and she keeps all her money in it. It ain't much; but she saves it up to buy shoes for me. And there's baby coming on famously, and he'll want shoes soon. And every sixpence is something—ain't it, sir?"

"To be sure, my man. I hope you'll always make as good a use of your money."

"I hope so, sir," said Diamond.

"And here's a book for you, full of pictures and stories and poems. I wrote it myself, chiefly for the children of the hospital where I hope Nanny is going. I don't mean I printed it, you know. I made it," added Mr. Raymond, wishing Diamond to understand that he was the author of the book.

"I know what you mean. I make songs myself. They're awfully silly, but they please baby, and that's all they're meant for."

"Couldn't you let me hear one of them now?" said Mr. Raymond.

"No, sir, I couldn't. I forget them as soon as I've done with them. Besides, I couldn't make a line without baby on my knee. We make them together, you know. They're just as much baby's as mine. It's he that pulls them out of me."

"I suspect the child's a genius," said the poet to himself, "and that's what makes people think him silly."

Now if any of my child readers want to know what a genius is—shall I try to tell them, or shall I not? I will give them one very short answer: it means one who understands things without any other body telling him what they mean. God makes a few such now and then to teach the rest of us.

"Do you like riddles?" asked Mr. Raymond, turning over the leaves of his own book.

"I don't know what a riddle is," said Diamond.

"It's something that means something else, and you've got to find out what the something else is."

Mr. Raymond liked the old-fashioned riddle best, and had written a few—one of which he now read.

> I have only one foot, but thousands of toes;
> My one foot stands, but never goes.
> I have many arms, and they're mighty all;
> And hundreds of fingers, large and small.
> From the ends of my fingers my beauty grows.
> I breathe with my hair, and I drink with my toes,
> I grow bigger and bigger about the waist,
> And yet I am always very tight laced.
> None e'er saw me eat—I've no mouth to bite;
> Yet I eat all day in the full sunlight.
> In the summer with song I shake and quiver,
> But in winter I fast and groan and shiver.

"Do you know what that means, Diamond?" he asked, when he had finished.

"No, indeed, I don't," answered Diamond.

"Then you can read it for yourself, and think over it, and see if you can find it out," said Mr. Raymond, giving him the book. "And now you had better go home to your mother. When you've found the riddle, you can come again."

If Diamond had had to find out the riddle in order to see Mr. Raymond again, I doubt if he would ever have seen him.

"Oh then," I think I hear some little reader say, "he could not have been a genius, for a genius finds out things without being told."

I answer, "Genius finds out truths, not tricks." And if you do not understand that, I am afraid you must be content to wait till you grow older and know more.

CHAPTER XXIII

THE EARLY BIRD

WHEN DIAMOND got home he found his father at home already, sitting by the fire and looking rather miserable, for his head ached and he felt sick. He had been doing night work of late, and it had not agreed with him, so he had given it up, but not in time, for he had taken some kind of fever. The next day he was forced to keep his bed, and his wife nursed him, and Diamond attended to the baby. If he had not been ill, it would have been delightful to have him at home; and the first day Diamond sang more songs than ever to the baby, and his father listened with some pleasure. But the next he could not bear even Diamond's sweet voice, and was very ill indeed; so Diamond took the baby into his own room, and had no end of quiet games with him there. If he did pull all his bedding on the floor, it did not matter, for he kept baby very quiet, and made the bed himself again, and slept in it with baby all the next night, and many nights after.

But long before his father got well, his mother's savings were all but gone. She did not say a word about it in the hearing of her husband, lest she should distress him; and one night, when she could not help crying, she came into Diamond's room that his father might not hear her. She thought Diamond was asleep, but he was not. When he heard her sobbing, he was frightened, and said—

"Is father worse, mother?"

"No, Diamond," she answered, as well as she could; "he's a good bit better."

"Then what are you crying for, mother?"

"Because my money is almost all gone," she replied.

"O mammy, you make me think of a little poem baby and I learned out of North Wind's book to-day. Don't you remember how I bothered you about some of the words?"

"Yes, child," said his mother heedlessly, thinking only of what she should do after to-morrow.

Diamond began and repeated the poem, for he had a wonderful memory.

> A little bird sat on the edge of her nest;
>   Her yellow-beaks slept as sound as tops;
> That day she had done her very best,
>   And had filled every one of their little crops.
> She had filled her own just over-full,
> And hence she was feeling a little dull.
>
> 'Oh dear!' she sighed, as she sat with her head
>   Sunk in her chest, and no neck at all,
> While her crop stuck out like a feather bed
>   Turned inside out, and rather small;
> 'What shall I do if things don't reform?
> I don't know where there's a single worm.
>
> 'I've had twenty to-day, and the children five each,
>   Besides a few flies, and some very fat spiders:
> No one will say I don't do as I preach—
>   I'm one of the best of bird-providers;
> But where's the use? We want a storm—
> I don't know where there's a single worm.'
>
> 'There's five in my crop,' said a wee, wee bird,
>   Which woke at the voice of his mother's pain;
> 'I know where there's five.' And with the word
>   He tucked in his head, and went off again.
> 'The folly of childhood,' sighed his mother,
> 'Has always been my especial bother.'
>
> The yellow-beaks they slept on and on—
>   They never had heard of the bogy To-morrow;
> But the mother sat outside, making her moan—

> She'll soon have to beg, or steal, or borrow;
> For she never can tell the night before
> Where she shall find one red worm more.
>
> The fact, as I say, was, she'd had too many;
>   She couldn't sleep, and she called it virtue,
> Motherly foresight, affection, any
>   Name you may call it that will not hurt you;
> So it was late ere she tucked her head in,
> And she slept so late it was almost a sin.
>
> But the little fellow who knew of five,
>   Nor troubled his head about any more,
> Woke very early, felt quite alive,
>   And wanted a sixth to add to his store:
> He pushed his mother, the greedy elf,
> Then thought he had better try for himself.
>
> When his mother awoke and had rubbed her eyes,
>   Feeling less like a bird, and more like a mole,
> She saw him—fancy with what surprise—
>   Dragging a huge worm out of a hole!
> 'Twas of this same hero the proverb took form:
> *'Tis the early bird that catches the worm.*

"There, mother!" said Diamond, as he finished; "ain't it funny?"

"I wish you were like that little bird, Diamond, and could catch worms for yourself," said his mother, as she rose to go and look after her husband.

Diamond lay awake for a few minutes, thinking what he could do to catch worms. It was very little trouble to make up his mind, however, and still less to go to sleep after it.

CHAPTER XXIV

ANOTHER EARLY BIRD

HE GOT UP in the morning as soon as he heard the men moving in the yard. He tucked in his little brother so that he could not tumble out of bed, and then went out, leaving the door open, so that if he should cry his mother might hear him at once. When he got into the yard he found the stable-door just opened.

"I'm the early bird, I think," he said to himself. "I hope I shall catch the worm."

He would not ask any one to help him, fearing his project might meet with disapproval and opposition. With great difficulty, but with the help of a broken chair he brought down from his bedroom, he managed to put the harness on Diamond. If the

old horse had had the least objection to the proceeding, of course he could not have done it; but even when it came to the bridle, he opened his mouth for the bit, just as if he had been taking the apple which Diamond sometimes gave him. He fastened the cheek-strap very carefully, just in the usual hole, for fear of choking his friend, or else letting the bit get amongst his teeth. It was a job to get the saddle on; but with the chair he managed it. If old Diamond had had an education in physics to equal that of the camel, he would have knelt down to let him put it on his back, but that was more than could be expected of him, and then Diamond had to creep quite under him to get hold of the girth. The collar was almost the worst part of the business; but there Diamond could help Diamond. He held his head very low till his little master had got it over and turned it round, and then he lifted his head, and shook it on to his shoulders. The yoke was rather difficult; but when he had laid the traces over the horse's neck, the weight was not too much for him. He got him right at last, and led him out of the stable.

By this time there were several of the men watching him, but they would not interfere, they were so anxious to see how he would get over the various difficulties. They followed him as far as the stable-door, and there stood watching him again as he put the horse between the shafts, got them up one after the other into the loops, fastened the traces, the belly-band, the breeching, and the reins.

Then he got his whip. The moment he mounted the box, ten men broke into a hearty cheer of delight at his success. But they would not let him go without a general inspection of the harness; and although they found it right, for not a buckle had to be shifted, they never allowed him to do it for himself again all the time his father was ill.

The cheer brought his mother to the window, and there she saw her little boy setting out alone with the cab in the gray of the morning. She tugged at the window, but it was stiff; and before she could open it, Diamond, who was in a great hurry, was out of the mews, and almost out of the street. She called "Diamond! Diamond!" but there was no answer except from Jack.

"Never fear for him, ma'am," said Jack. "It 'ud be only a devil as would hurt him, and there ain't so many o' them as some folk 'ud have you believe. A boy o' Diamond's size as can 'arness a 'oss o' t'other Diamond's size, and put him to, right as a trivet—if he do upset the keb—'ll fall on *his* feet, ma'am."

"But he won't upset the cab, will he, Jack?"

"Not he, ma'am. Leastways he won't go for to do it."

"I know as much as that myself. What do you mean?"

"I mean he's as little likely to do it as the oldest man in the stable. How's the gov'nor to-day, ma'am?"

"A good deal better, thank you," she answered, closing the window in some fear lest her husband should have been made anxious by the news of Diamond's expedition. He knew pretty well, however, what his boy was capable of, and although not quite easy was less anxious than his mother. But as the evening drew on, the anxiety of both of them increased, and every sound of wheels made his father raise himself in his bed, and his mother peep out of the window.

Diamond had resolved to go straight to the cabstand where he was best known, and never to crawl for fear of getting annoyed by idlers. Before he got across Oxford Street, however, he was hailed by a man who wanted to catch a train, and was in too great a hurry to think about the driver. Having carried him to King's Cross in good time, and got a good fare in return, he set off again in great spirits, and reached the stand in safety. He was the first there after all.

As the men arrived they all greeted him kindly, and inquired after his father.

"Ain't you afraid of the old 'oss running away with you?" asked one.

"No, he wouldn't run away with *me*," answered Diamond. "He knows I'm getting the shillings for father. Or if he did he would only run home."

"Well, you're a plucky one, for all your girl's looks!" said the man; "and I wish ye luck."

"Thank you, sir," said Diamond. "I'll do what I can. I came to the old place, you see, because I knew you would let me have my turn here."

In the course of the day one man did try to cut him out, but he was a stranger; and the shout the rest of them raised let him see it would not do, and made him so far ashamed besides, that he went away crawling.

Once, in a block, a policeman came up to him, and asked him for his number. Diamond showed him his father's badge, saying with a smile:

"Father's ill at home, and so I came out with the cab. There's no fear of me. I can drive. Besides, the old horse could go alone."

"Just as well, I dare say. You're a pair of 'em. But you *are* a rum 'un for a cabby—ain't you now?" said the policeman. "I don't know as I ought to let you go."

"I ain't done nothing," said Diamond. "It's not my fault I'm no bigger. I'm big enough for my age."

"That's where it is," said the man. "You ain't fit."

"How do you know that?" asked Diamond, with his usual smile, and turning his head like a little bird.

"Why, how are you to get out of this ruck now, when it begins to move?"

"Just you get up on the box," said Diamond, "and I'll show you. There, that van's a-moving now. Jump up."

The policeman did as Diamond told him, and was soon satisfied that the little fellow could drive.

"Well," he said, as he got down again, "I don't know as I should be right to interfere. Good luck to you, my little man!"

"Thank you, sir," said Diamond, and drove away.

In a few minutes a gentleman hailed him.

"Are you the driver of this cab?" he asked.

"Yes, sir," said Diamond, showing his badge, of which he was proud.

"You're the youngest cabman I ever saw. How am I to know you won't break all my bones?"

"I would rather break all my own," said Diamond. "But if you're afraid, never mind me; I shall soon get another fare."

"I'll risk it," said the gentleman; and, opening the door himself, he jumped in.

He was going a good distance, and soon found that Diamond got him over the ground well. Now when Diamond had only to go straight ahead, and had not to mind so much what he was about, his thoughts always turned to the riddle Mr. Raymond had set him; and this gentleman looked so clever that he fancied he must be able to read it for him. He had given up all hope of finding it out for himself, and he could not plague his father about it when he was ill. He had thought of the answer himself, but fancied it could not be the right one, for to see how it all fitted required some knowledge of physiology. So, when he reached the end of his journey, he got down very quickly, and with his head just looking in at the window, said, as the gentleman gathered his gloves and newspapers:

"Please, sir, can you tell me the meaning of a riddle?"

"You must tell me the riddle first," answered the gentleman, amused.

Diamond repeated the riddle.

"Oh! that's easy enough," he returned. "It's a tree."

"Well, it ain't got no mouth, sure enough; but how then does it eat all day long?"

"It sucks in its food through the tiniest holes in its leaves," he answered. "Its breath is its food. And it can't do it except in the daylight."

"Thank you, sir, thank you," returned Diamond. "I'm sorry I couldn't find it out myself; Mr. Raymond would have been better pleased with me."

"But you needn't tell him any one told you."

Diamond gave him a stare which came from the very back of the north wind, where that kind of thing is unknown.

"That would be cheating," he said at last.

"Ain't you a cabby, then?"

"Cabbies don't cheat."

"Don't they? I am of a different opinion."

"I'm sure my father don't."

"What's your fare, young innocent?"

"Well, I think the distance is a good deal over three miles—that's two shillings. Only father says sixpence a mile is too little, though we can't ask for more."

"You're a deep one. But I think you're wrong. It's over four miles—not much, but it is."

"Then that's half-a-crown," said Diamond.

"Well, here's three shillings. Will that do?"

"Thank you kindly, sir. I'll tell my father how good you were to me—first to tell me my riddle, then to put me right about the distance, and then to give me sixpence over. It'll help father to get well again, it will."

"I hope it may, my man. I shouldn't wonder if you're as good as you look, after all."

As Diamond returned, he drew up at a stand he had never been on before: it was time to give Diamond his bag of chopped beans and oats. The men got about him, and began to chaff him. He took it all good-humouredly, until one of them, who was an ill-conditioned fellow, began to tease old Diamond by poking him roughly in the ribs, and making general game of him. That he could not bear, and the tears came in his eyes. He undid the nose-bag, put it in the boot, and was just going to mount and drive away, when the fellow interfered, and would not let him get up. Diamond endeavoured to persuade him, and was very civil, but he would have his fun out of him, as he said. In a few minutes a group of idle boys had assembled, and Diamond found himself in a very uncomfortable position. Another cab drew up at the stand, and the driver got off and approached the assemblage.

"What's up here?" he asked, and Diamond knew the voice. It was that of the drunken cabman.

"Do you see this young oyster? He pretends to drive a cab," said his enemy.

"Yes, I do see him. And I sees you too. You'd better leave him alone. He ain't no oyster. He's a angel come down on his own business. You be off, or I'll be nearer you than quite agreeable."

The drunken cabman was a tall, stout man, who did not look one to take liberties with.

"Oh! if he's a friend of yours," said the other, drawing back.

Diamond got out the nose-bag again. Old Diamond should have his feed out now.

"Yes, he is a friend o' mine. One o' the best I ever had. It's a pity he ain't a friend o' yourn. You'd be the better for it, but it ain't no fault of hisn."

When Diamond went home at night, he carried with him one pound one shilling and sixpence, besides a few coppers extra, which had followed some of the fares.

His mother had got very anxious indeed—so much so that she was almost afraid, when she did hear the sound of his cab, to go and look, lest she should be yet again disappointed, and should break down before her husband. But there was the old horse, and there was the cab all right, and there was Diamond on the box, his pale face looking triumphant as a full moon in the twilight.

When he drew up at the stable-door, Jack came out, and after a good many friendly questions and congratulations, said:

"You go in to your mother, Diamond. I'll put up the old 'oss. I'll take care on him. He do deserve some small attention, he do."

"Thank you, Jack," said Diamond, and bounded into the house, and into the arms of his mother, who was waiting him at the top of the stair.

The poor, anxious woman led him into his own room, sat down on his bed, took him on her lap as if he had been a baby, and cried.

"How's father?" asked Diamond, almost afraid to ask.

"Better, my child," she answered, "but uneasy about you, my dear."

"Didn't you tell him I was the early bird gone out to catch the worm?"

"*That* was what put it in your head, was it, you monkey?" said his mother, beginning to get better.

"That or something else," answered Diamond, so very quietly that his mother held his head back and stared in his face.

"Well! of all the children!" she said, and said no more.

"And here's my worm," resumed Diamond.

But to see her face as he poured the shillings and sixpences and pence into her lap! She burst out crying a second time, and ran with the money to her husband.

And how pleased he was! It did him no end of good. But while he was counting the coins, Diamond turned to baby, who was lying awake in his cradle, sucking his precious thumb, and took him up, saying:

"Baby, baby! I haven't seen you for a whole year."

And then he began to sing to him as usual. And what he sang was this, for he was too happy either to make a song of his own or to sing sense. It was one out of Mr. Raymond's book.

THE TRUE HISTORY OF THE CAT AND THE FIDDLE

Hey, diddle, diddle!
The cat and the fiddle!
He played such a merry tune,
   That the cow went mad
   With the pleasure she had,
And jumped right over the moon.
   But then, don't you see?
   Before that could be,
The moon had come down and listened.
   The little dog hearkened,
   So loud that he barkened,
   "There's nothing like it, there isn't."

Hey, diddle, diddle!
Went the cat and the fiddle,
Hey diddle, diddle, dee, dee!
   The dog laughed at the sport
   Till his cough cut him short,
It was hey diddle, diddle, oh me!
   And back came the cow
   With a merry, merry low,
For she'd humbled the man in the moon.
   The dish got excited,
   The spoon was delighted,
And the dish waltzed away with the spoon.

   But the man in the moon,
   Coming back too soon
From the famous town of Norwich,
   Caught up the dish,
   Said, "It's just what I wish
To hold my cold plum-porridge!"
   Gave the cow a rat-tat,
   Flung water on the cat,
And sent him away like a rocket.
   Said, "O Moon, there you are!"
   Got into her car,
And went off with the spoon in his pocket.

   Hey ho! diddle, diddle!
   The wet cat and wet fiddle,
They made such a caterwauling,
   That the cow in a fright,
   Stood bolt upright
Bellowing now, and bawling;
   And the dog on his tail,

Stretched his neck with a wail.
But "Ho! ho!" said the man in the moon—
"No more in the South
Shall I burn my mouth,
For I've found a dish and a spoon."

CHAPTER XXV

DIAMOND'S DREAM

"THERE, BABY!" said Diamond; "I'm so happy that I can only sing nonsense. Oh, father, think if you had been a poor man, and hadn't had a cab and old Diamond! What should I have done?"

"I don't know indeed what you could have done," said his father from the bed.

"We should have all starved, my precious Diamond," said his mother, whose pride in her boy was even greater than her joy in the shillings. Both of them together made her heart ache, for pleasure can do that as well as pain.

"Oh no! we shouldn't," said Diamond. "I could have taken Nanny's crossing till she came back; and then the money, instead of going for Old Sal's gin, would have gone for father's beef-tea. I wonder what Nanny will do when she gets well again. Somebody else will be sure to have taken the crossing by that time. I wonder if she will fight for it, and whether I shall have to help her. I won't bother my head about that. Time enough yet! Hey diddle! hey diddle! hey diddle diddle! I wonder whether Mr. Raymond would take me to see Nanny. Hey diddle! hey diddle! hey diddle diddle! The baby and fiddle! O, mother, I'm such a silly! But I can't help it. I wish I could think of something else, but there's nothing will come into my head but *hey diddle diddle! the cat and the fiddle!* I wonder what the angels do—when they're extra happy, you know—when they've been driving cabs all day and taking home the money to their mothers. Do you think they ever sing nonsense, mother?"

"I dare say they've got their own sort of it," answered his mother, "else they wouldn't be like other people."

She was thinking more of her twenty-one shillings and sixpence, and of the nice dinner she would get for her sick husband next day, than of the angels and their nonsense, when she said it. But Diamond found her answer all right.

"Yes, to be sure," he replied. "They wouldn't be like other people if they hadn't their nonsense sometimes. But it must be very pretty nonsense, and not like that silly hey diddle diddle! the cat and the fiddle! I wish I could get it out of my head. I wonder what the angels' nonsense is like. Nonsense is a very good thing, ain't it, mother?—a little of it now and then; more of it for baby, and not so much for grown people like cabmen and their mothers? It's like the pepper and salt that goes in the soup—that's

it—isn't it, mother? There's baby fast asleep! Oh, what a nonsense baby it is—to sleep so much! Shall I put him down, mother?"

Diamond chattered away. What rose in his happy little heart ran out of his mouth, and did his father and mother good. When he went to bed, which he did early, being more tired, as you may suppose, than usual, he was still thinking what the nonsense could be like which the angels sang when they were too happy to sing sense. But before coming to any conclusion he fell fast asleep. And no wonder, for it must be acknowledged a difficult question.

That night he had a very curious dream which I think my readers would like to have told them. They would, at least, if they are as fond of nice dreams as I am, and don't have enough of them of their own.

He dreamed that he was running about in the twilight in the old garden. He thought he was waiting for North Wind, but she did not come. So he would run down to the back gate, and see if she were there. He ran and ran. It was a good long garden out of his dream, but in his dream it had grown so long and spread out so wide that the gate he wanted was nowhere. He ran and ran, but instead of coming to the gate found himself in a beautiful country, not like any country he had ever been in before. There were no trees of any size; nothing bigger in fact than hawthorns, which were full of may-blossom. The place in which they grew was wild and dry, mostly covered with grass, but having patches of heath. It extended on every side as far as he could see. But although it was so wild, yet wherever in an ordinary heath you might have expected furze bushes, or holly, or broom, there grew roses—wild and rare—all kinds. On every side, far and near, roses were glowing. There too was the gum-cistus, whose flowers fall every night and come again the next morning, lilacs and syringas and laburnums, and many shrubs besides, of which he did not know the names; but the roses were everywhere. He wandered on and on, wondering when it would come to an end. It was of no use going back, for there was no house to be seen anywhere. But he was not frightened, for you know Diamond was used to things that were rather out of the way. He threw himself down under a rose-bush, and fell asleep.

He woke, not out of his dream, but into it, thinking he heard a child's voice, calling "Diamond, Diamond!" He jumped up, but all was still about him. The rose-bushes were pouring out their odours in clouds. He could see the scent like mists of the same colour as the rose, issuing like a slow fountain and spreading in the air till it joined the tiny rosy vapour which hung over all the wilderness. But again came the voice calling him, and it seemed to come from over his head. He looked up, but saw only the deep blue sky full of stars—more brilliant, however, than he had seen them before; and both sky and stars looked nearer to the earth.

While he gazed up, again he heard the cry. At the same moment he saw one of the biggest stars over his head give a kind of twinkle and jump, as if it went out and came in again. He threw himself on his back, and fixed his eyes upon it. Nor had he gazed long before it went out, leaving something like a scar in the blue. But as he went on gazing he saw a face where the star had been—a merry face, with bright eyes. The eyes appeared not only to see Diamond, but to know that Diamond had caught sight of them, for the face withdrew the same moment. Again came the voice, calling "Diamond, Diamond;" and in jumped the star to its place.

Diamond called as loud as he could, right up into the sky:

"Here's Diamond, down below you. What do you want him to do?"

The next instant many of the stars round about that one went out, and many voices shouted from the sky,—

"Come up; come up. We're so jolly! Diamond! Diamond!"

This was followed by a peal of the merriest, kindliest laughter, and all the stars jumped into their places again.

"How am I to come up?" shouted Diamond.

"Go round the rose-bush. It's got its foot in it," said the first voice.

Diamond got up at once, and walked to the other side of the rose-bush.

There he found what seemed the very opposite of what he wanted—a stair down into the earth. It was of turf and moss. It did not seem to promise well for getting into the sky, but Diamond had learned to look through the look of things. The voice must have meant that he was to go down this stair; and down this stair Diamond went, without waiting to think more about it.

It was such a nice stair, so cool and soft—all the sides as well as the steps grown with moss and grass and ferns! Down and down Diamond went—a long way, until at last he heard the gurgling and plashing of a little stream; nor had he gone much farther before he met it—yes, met it coming up the stairs to meet him, running up just as naturally as if it had been doing the other thing. Neither was Diamond in the least surprised to see it pitching itself from one step to another as it climbed towards him: he never thought it was odd—and no more it was, there. It would have been odd here. It made a merry tune as it came, and its voice was like the laughter he had heard from the sky. This appeared

promising; and he went on, down and down the stair, and up and up the stream, till at last he came where it hurried out from under a stone, and the stair stopped altogether. And as the stream bubbled up, the stone shook and swayed with its force; and Diamond thought he would try to lift it. Lightly it rose to his hand, forced up by the stream from below; and, by what would have seemed an unaccountable perversion of things had he been awake, threatened to come tumbling upon his head. But he avoided it, and when it fell, got upon it. He now saw that the opening through which the water came pouring in was over his head, and with the help of the stone he scrambled out by it, and found himself on the side of a grassy hill which rounded away from him in every direction, and down which came the brook which vanished in the hole. But scarcely had he noticed so much as this before a merry shouting and laughter burst upon him, and a number of naked little boys came running, every one eager to get to him first. At the shoulders of each fluttered two little wings, which were of no use for flying, as they were mere buds; only being made for it they could not help fluttering as if they were flying. Just as the foremost of the troop reached him, one or two of them fell, and the rest with shouts of laughter came tumbling over them till they heaped up a mound of struggling merriment. One after another they extricated themselves, and each as he got free threw his arms round Diamond and kissed him. Diamond's heart was ready to melt within him from clear delight. When they had all embraced him,—

"Now let us have some fun," cried one, and with a shout they all scampered hither and thither, and played the wildest gambols on the grassy slopes. They kept constantly coming back to Diamond, however, as the centre of their enjoyment, rejoicing over him as if they had found a lost playmate.

There was a wind on the hillside which blew like the very embodiment of living gladness. It blew into Diamond's heart, and made him so happy that he was forced to sit down and cry.

"Now let's go and dig for stars," said one who seemed to be the captain of the troop.

They all scurried away, but soon returned, one after another, each with a pickaxe on his shoulder and a spade in his hand. As soon as they were gathered, the captain led them in a straight line to another part of the hill. Diamond rose and followed.

"Here is where we begin our lesson for to-night," he said. "Scatter and dig."

There was no more fun. Each went by himself, walking slowly with bent shoulders and his eyes fixed on the ground. Every now and then one would stop, kneel down, and look intently, feeling with his hands and parting the grass. One would get up and walk on again, another spring to his feet, catch eagerly at his pickaxe and strike it into the ground once and again, then throw it aside, snatch up his spade, and commence digging at the loosened earth. Now one would sorrowfully shovel the earth into the hole again, trample it down with his little bare white feet, and walk on. But another would give a joyful shout, and after much tugging and loosening would draw from the hole a lump as big as his head, or no bigger than his fist; when the under side of it would pour such a blaze of golden or bluish light into Diamond's eyes that he was quite dazzled. Gold and blue were the commoner colours: the jubilation was greater over red or green or purple. And every time a star was dug up all the little angels dropped their tools and crowded about it, shouting and dancing and fluttering their wing-buds.

When they had examined it well, they would kneel down one after the other and peep through the hole; but they always stood back to give Diamond the first look. All that Diamond could report, however, was, that through the star-holes he saw a great many things and places and people he knew quite well, only somehow they were different—there was something marvellous about them—he could not tell what. Every time he rose from looking through a star-hole, he felt as if his heart would break for joy; and he said that if he had not cried, he did not know what would have become of him.

As soon as all had looked, the star was carefully fitted in again, a little mould was strewn over it, and the rest of the heap left as a sign that that star had been discovered.

At length one dug up a small star of a most lovely colour—a colour Diamond had never seen before. The moment the angel saw what it was, instead of showing it about, he handed it to one of his neighbours, and seated himself on the edge of the hole, saying:

"This will do for me. Good-bye. I'm off."

They crowded about him, hugging and kissing him; then stood back with a solemn stillness, their wings lying close to their shoulders. The little fellow looked round on them once with a smile, and then shot himself headlong through the star-hole. Diamond, as privileged, threw himself on the ground to peep after him, but he saw nothing.

"It's no use," said the captain. "I never saw anything more of one that went that way."

"His wings can't be much use," said Diamond, concerned and fearful, yet comforted by the calm looks of the rest.

"That's true," said the captain. "He's lost them by this time. They all do that go that way. You haven't got any, you see."

"No," said Diamond. "I never did have any."

"Oh! didn't you?" said the captain.

"Some people say," he added, after a pause, "that they come again. I don't know. I've never found the colour I care about myself. I suppose I shall some day."

Then they looked again at the star, put it carefully into its hole, danced round it and over it—but solemnly, and called it by the name of the finder.

"Will you know it again?" asked Diamond.

"Oh yes. We never forget a star that's been made a door of."

Then they went on with their searching and digging.

Diamond having neither pickaxe nor spade, had the more time to think.

"I don't see any little girls," he said at last.

The captain stopped his shovelling, leaned on his spade, rubbed his forehead thoughtfully with his left hand—the little angels were all left-handed—repeated the words "little girls," and then, as if a thought had struck him, resumed his work, saying—

"I think I know what you mean. I've never seen any of them, of course; but I suppose that's the sort you mean. I'm told—but mind I don't say it is so, for I don't know—that when we fall asleep, a troop of angels very like ourselves, only quite different, goes round to all the stars we have discovered, and discovers them after us. I suppose with our shovelling and handling we spoil them a bit; and I dare say the clouds that come up from below make them smoky and dull sometimes. They say—mind, I say *they say*—these other angels take them out one by one, and pass each round as we do, and breathe over it, and rub it with their white hands, which are softer than ours, because they don't do any pick-and-spade work, and smile at it, and put it in again; and that is what keeps them from growing dark."

"How jolly!" thought Diamond. "I should like to see *them* at their work too.—When do you go to sleep?" he asked the captain.

"When we grow sleepy," answered the captain. "They do say—but mind I say *they say*—that it is when those others—what do you call them? I don't know if that is their name; I am only guessing that may be the sort you mean—when they are on their rounds and come near any troop of us we fall asleep. They live on the west side of the hill. None of *us* have ever been to the top of it yet."

Even as he spoke, he dropped his spade. He tumbled down beside it, and lay fast asleep. One after the other each of the troop dropped his pickaxe or shovel from his listless hands, and lay fast asleep by his work.

"Ah!" thought Diamond to himself, with delight, "now the girl-angels are coming, and I, not being an angel, shall not fall asleep like the rest, and I shall see the girl-angels."

But the same moment he felt himself growing sleepy. He struggled hard with the invading power. He put up his fingers to his eyelids and pulled them open. But it was of no use. He thought he saw a glimmer of pale rosy light far up the green hill, and ceased to know.

When he awoke, all the angels were starting up wide awake too. He expected to see them lift their tools, but no, the time for play had come. They looked happier than ever, and each began to sing where he stood. He had not heard them sing before.

"Now," he thought, "I shall know what kind of nonsense the angels sing when they are merry. They don't drive cabs, I see, but they dig for stars, and they work hard enough to be merry after it."

And he did hear some of the angels' nonsense; for if it was all sense to them, it had only just as much sense to Diamond as made good nonsense of it. He tried hard to set it down in his mind, listening as closely as he could, now to one, now to another, and now to all together. But while they were yet singing he began, to his dismay, to find that he was coming awake—faster and faster. And as he came awake, he found that, for all the goodness of his memory, verse after verse of the angels' nonsense vanished from it. He always thought he could keep the last, but as the next began he lost the one before it, and at length awoke, struggling to keep hold of the last verse of all. He felt as if the effort to keep from forgetting that one verse of the vanishing song nearly killed him. And yet by the time he was wide awake he could not be sure of that even. It was something like this:

> White hands of whiteness
>   Wash the stars' faces,
> Till glitter, glitter, glit, goes their brightness
>   Down to poor places.

This, however, was so near sense that he thought it could not be really what they did sing.

CHAPTER XXVI

DIAMOND TAKES A FARE
THE WRONG WAY RIGHT

THE NEXT MORNING Diamond was up almost as early as before. He had nothing to fear from his mother now, and made no secret of what he was about. By the time he reached the stable, several of the men were there. They asked him a good many questions as to his luck the day before, and he told them all they wanted to know. But when he proceeded to harness the old horse, they pushed him aside with rough kindness, called him a baby, and began to do it all for him. So Diamond ran in and had another mouthful of tea and bread and butter; and although he had never been so tired as he was the night before, he started quite fresh this morning. It was a cloudy day, and the wind blew hard from the north—so hard sometimes that, perched on the box with just his toes touching the ground, Diamond wished that he had some kind of strap to fasten himself down with lest he should be blown away. But he did not really mind it.

His head was full of the dream he had dreamed; but it did not make him neglect his work, for his work was not to dig stars but to drive old Diamond and pick up fares. There are not many people who can think about beautiful things and do common work at the same time. But then there are not many people who have been to the back of the north wind.

There was not much business doing. And Diamond felt rather cold, notwithstanding

his mother had herself put on his comforter and helped him with his greatcoat. But he was too well aware of his dignity to get inside his cab as some do. A cabman ought to be above minding the weather—at least so Diamond thought. At length he was called to a neighbouring house, where a young woman with a heavy box had to be taken to Wapping for a coast-steamer.

He did not find it at all pleasant, so far east and so near the river; for the roughs were in great force. However, there being no block, not even in Nightingale Lane, he reached the entrance of the wharf, and set down his passenger without annoyance. But as he turned to go back, some idlers, not content with chaffing him, showed a mind to the fare the young woman had given him. They were just pulling him off the box, and Diamond was shouting for the police, when a pale-faced man, in very shabby clothes, but with the look of a gentleman somewhere about him, came up, and making good use of his stick, drove them off.

"Now, my little man," he said, "get on while you can. Don't lose any time. This is not a place for you."

But Diamond was not in the habit of thinking only of himself. He saw that his new friend looked weary, if not ill, and very poor.

"Won't you jump in, sir?" he said. "I'll will take you wherever you like."

"Thank you, my man; but I have no money; so I can't."

"Oh! I don't want any money. I shall be much happier if you will get in. You have saved me all I had. I owe you a lift, sir."

"Which way are you going?"

"To Charing Cross; but I don't mind where I go."

"Well, I am very tired. If you will take me to Charing Cross, I shall be greatly obliged to you. I have walked from Gravesend, and had hardly a penny left to get through the tunnel."

So saying, he opened the door and got in, and Diamond drove away.

But as he drove, he could not help fancying he had seen the gentleman—for Diamond knew he was a gentleman—before. Do all he could, however, he could not recall where or when. Meantime his fare, if we may call him such, seeing he was to pay nothing, whom the relief of being carried had made less and less inclined to carry himself, had been turning over things in his mind, and, as they passed the Mint, called to Diamond, who stopped his horse, got down, and went to the window.

"If you didn't mind taking me to Chiswick, I should be able to pay you when we got there. It's a long way, but you shall have the whole fare from the Docks—and something over."

"Very well, sir," said Diamond. "I shall be most happy."

He was just clambering up again, when the gentleman put his head out of the window and said—

"It's The Wilderness—Mr. Coleman's place; but I'll direct you when we come into the neighbourhood."

It flashed upon Diamond who he was. But he got upon his box to arrange his thoughts before making any reply.

The gentleman was Mr. Evans, to whom Miss Coleman was to have been married, and Diamond had seen him several times with her in the garden. I have said that he had not behaved very well to Miss Coleman. He had put off their marriage more than once in a cowardly fashion, merely because he was ashamed to marry upon a small income, and live in a humble way. When a man thinks of what people will say in such a case, he may love, but his love is but a poor affair. Mr. Coleman took him into the firm as a junior partner, and it was in a measure through his influence that he entered upon those speculations which ruined him. So his love had not been a blessing. The ship which North Wind had sunk was their last venture, and Mr. Evans had gone out with it in the hope of turning its cargo to the best advantage. He was one of the single boat-load which managed to reach a desert island, and he had gone through a great many hardships and sufferings since then. But he was not past being taught, and his troubles had done him no end of good, for they had made him doubt himself, and begin to think, so that he had come to see that he had been foolish as well as wicked. For, if he had had Miss Coleman with him in the desert island, to build her a hut, and hunt for her food, and make clothes for her, he would have thought himself the most fortunate of men; and when he was at home, he would not marry till he could afford a man-servant. Before he got home again, he had even begun to understand that no man can make haste to be rich without going against the will of God, in which case it is the one frightful thing to be successful. So he had come back a more humble man, and longing to ask Miss Coleman to forgive him. But he had no idea what ruin had fallen upon them, for he had never made himself thoroughly acquainted with the firm's affairs. Few speculative people do know their own affairs. Hence he never doubted he should find matters much as he left them, and expected to see them all at The Wilderness as before. But if he had not fallen in with Diamond, he would not have thought of going there first.

What was Diamond to do? He had heard his father and mother drop some remarks concerning Mr. Evans which made him doubtful of him. He understood that he had not been so considerate as he might have been. So he went rather slowly till he should make up his mind. It was, of course, of no use to drive Mr. Evans to Chiswick. But if he should tell him what had befallen them, and where they lived now, he might put off going to see them, and he was certain that Miss Coleman, at least, must want very much to see Mr. Evans. He was pretty sure also that the best thing in any case was to bring them together, and let them set matters right for themselves.

The moment he came to this conclusion, he changed his course from westward to northward, and went straight for Mr. Coleman's poor little house in Hoxton. Mr. Evans was too tired and too much occupied with his thoughts to take the least notice of the streets they passed through, and had no suspicion, therefore, of the change of direction.

By this time the wind had increased almost to a hurricane, and as they had often to head it, it was no joke for either of the Diamonds. The distance, however, was not great. Before they reached the street where Mr. Coleman lived it blew so tremendously, that when Miss Coleman, who was going out a little way, opened the door, it dashed against the wall with such a bang, that she was afraid to venture, and went in again. In five minutes after, Diamond drew up at the door. As soon as he had entered the street, however, the wind blew right behind them, and when he pulled up, old Diamond had so much ado to stop the cab against it, that the breeching broke. Young Diamond jumped off his box, knocked loudly at the door, then turned to the cab and said—before Mr. Evans had quite begun to think something must be amiss:

"Please, sir, my harness has given way. Would you mind stepping in here for a few minutes? They're friends of mine. I'll take you where you like after I've got it mended. I shan't be many minutes, but you can't stand in this wind."

Half stupid with fatigue and want of food, Mr. Evans yielded to the boy's suggestion, and walked in at the door which the maid held with difficulty against the wind. She took Mr. Evans for a visitor, as indeed he was, and showed him into the room on the ground-floor. Diamond, who had followed into the hall, whispered to her as she closed the door—

"Tell Miss Coleman. It's Miss Coleman he wants to see."

"I don't know," said the maid.—"He don't look much like a gentleman."

"He is, though; and I know him, and so does Miss Coleman."

The maid could not but remember Diamond, having seen him when he and his father brought the ladies home. So she believed him, and went to do what he told her.

What passed in the little parlour when Miss Coleman came down does not belong to my story, which is all about Diamond. If he had known that Miss Coleman thought Mr. Evans was dead, perhaps he would have managed it differently. There was a cry and a running to and fro in the house, and then all was quiet again.

Almost as soon as Mr. Evans went in, the wind began to cease, and was now still. Diamond found that by making the breeching just a little tighter than was quite comfortable for the old horse he could do very well for the present; and, thinking it better to let him have his bag in this quiet place, he sat on the box till the old horse should have eaten his dinner. In a little while Mr. Evans came out, and asked him to come in. Diamond obeyed, and to his delight Miss Coleman put her arms round him and kissed him, and there was payment for him! not to mention the five precious shillings she gave him, which he could not refuse because his mother wanted them so

much at home for his father. He left them nearly as happy as they were themselves.

The rest of the day he did better, and, although he had not so much to take home as the day before, yet on the whole the result was satisfactory. And what a story he had to tell his father and mother about his adventures, and how he had done, and what was the result! They asked him such a multitude of questions! some of which he could answer, and some of which he could not answer; and his father seemed ever so much better from finding that his boy was already not only useful to his family but useful to other people, and quite taking his place as a man who judged what was wise, and did work worth doing.

For a fortnight Diamond went on driving his cab, and keeping his family. He had begun to be known about some parts of London, and people would prefer taking his cab because they liked what they heard of him. One gentleman who lived near the mews, engaged him to carry him to the City every morning at a certain hour; and Diamond was punctual as clockwork—though to effect that, required a good deal of care, for his father's watch was not much to be depended on, and had to be watched itself by the clock of St. George's church. Between the two, however, he did make a success of it.

After that fortnight, his father was able to go out again. Then Diamond went to make inquiries about Nanny: and this led to something else.

CHAPTER XXVII

THE CHILDREN'S HOSPITAL

T HE FIRST DAY his father resumed his work, Diamond went with him as usual. In the afternoon, however, his father, having taken a fare to the neighbourhood, went home, and Diamond drove the cab the rest of the day. It was hard for old Diamond to do all the work, but they could not afford to have another horse. They contrived to save him as much as possible, and fed him well, and he did bravely.

The next morning his father was so much stronger that Diamond thought he might go and ask Mr. Raymond to take him to see Nanny. He found him at home. His servant had grown friendly by this time, and showed him in without any cross-questioning. Mr. Raymond received him with his usual kindness, consented at once, and walked him to the Hospital, which was close at hand. It was a comfortable old-fashioned house, built in the reign of Queen Anne, and in her day, no doubt, inhabited by rich and fashionable people: now it was a home for poor sick children, who were carefully tended for love's sake. There are regions in London where a hospital in every other street might be full of such children, whose fathers and mothers are dead, or unable to take care of them.

When Diamond followed Mr. Raymond into the room where those children who had got over the worst of their illness and were growing better lay, he saw a number of little iron bedsteads, with their heads to the walls, and in every one of them a child, whose face was a story in itself. In some, health had begun to appear in a tinge upon the cheeks, and a doubtful brightness in the eyes, just as out of the cold dreary winter the spring comes in blushing buds and bright crocuses. In others there were more of the signs of winter left. Their faces reminded you of snow and keen cutting winds, more than of sunshine and soft breezes and butterflies; but even in them the signs of suffering told that the suffering was less, and that if the spring-time had but arrived, it had yet arrived.

Diamond looked all round, but could see no Nanny. He turned to Mr. Raymond with a question in his eyes.

"Well?" said Mr. Raymond.

"Nanny's not here," said Diamond.

"Oh, yes, she is."

"I don't see her."

"I do, though. There she is."

He pointed to a bed right in front of where Diamond was standing.

"That's not Nanny," he said.

"It *is* Nanny. I have seen her many times since you have. Illness makes a great difference."

"Why, that girl must have been to the back of the north wind!" thought Diamond, but he said nothing, only stared; and as he stared, something of the old Nanny began to dawn through the face of the new Nanny. The old Nanny, though a good girl, and a friendly girl, had been rough, blunt in her speech, and dirty in her person. Her face would always have reminded one who had already been to the back of the north wind of something he had seen in the best of company, but it had been coarse notwithstanding, partly from the weather, partly from her living amongst low people, and partly from having to defend herself: now it was so sweet, and gentle, and refined, that she might have had a lady and gentleman for a father and mother. And Diamond could not help thinking of words which he had heard in the church the day before: "Surely it is good to be afflicted;" or something like that. North Wind, somehow or other, must have had to do with her! She had grown from a rough girl into a gentle maiden.

Mr. Raymond, however, was not surprised, for he was used to see such lovely changes—something like the change which passes upon the crawling, many-footed creature, when it turns sick and ill, and revives a butterfly, with two wings instead of many feet. Instead of her having to take care of herself, kind hands ministered to her, making her comfortable and sweet and clean, soothing her aching head, and giving her cooling drink when she was thirsty; and kind eyes, the stars of the kingdom of heaven, had shone upon her; so that, what with the fire of the fever and the dew of tenderness, that which was coarse in her had melted away, and her whole face had grown so refined and sweet that Diamond did not know her. But as he gazed, the best of the old face, all the true and good part of it, that which was Nanny herself, dawned upon him, like the moon coming out of a cloud, until at length, instead of only believing Mr. Raymond that this was she, he saw for himself that it was Nanny indeed—very worn, but grown beautiful.

He went up to her. She smiled. He had heard her laugh, but had never seen her smile before.

"Nanny, do you know me?" said Diamond.

She only smiled again, as if the question was amusing.

She was not likely to forget him; for although she did not yet know it was he who had got her there, she had dreamed of him often, and had talked much about him when delirious. Nor was it much wonder, for he was the only boy except Joe who had ever shown her kindness.

Meantime Mr. Raymond was going from bed to bed, talking to the little people. Every one knew him, and every one was eager to have a look, and a smile, and a kind word from him. Diamond sat down on a stool at the head of Nanny's bed. She laid her hand in his. No one else of her old acquaintance had been near her.

Suddenly a little voice called aloud—

"Won't Mr. Raymond tell us a story?"

"Oh, yes, please do! please do!" cried several little voices which also were stronger than the rest. For Mr. Raymond was in the habit of telling them a story when he went to see them, and they enjoyed it far more than the other nice things which the doctor permitted him to give them.

"Very well," said Mr. Raymond, "I will. What sort of a story shall it be?"

"A true story," said one little girl.

"A fairy tale," said a little boy.

"Well," said Mr. Raymond, "I suppose, as there is a difference, I may choose. I can't think of any true story just at this moment, so I will tell you a sort of a fairy one."

"Oh, jolly!" exclaimed the little boy who had called out for a fairy tale.

"It came into my head this morning as I got out of bed," continued Mr. Raymond; "and if it turns out pretty well, I will write it down, and get somebody to print it for me, and then you shall read it when you like."

"Then nobody ever heard it before?" asked one older child.

"No, nobody."

"Oh!" exclaimed several, thinking it very grand to have the first telling; and I dare say there might be a peculiar freshness about it, because everything would be nearly as new to the story-teller himself as to the listeners.

Some were only sitting up and some were lying down, so there could not be the same busy gathering, and bustling, and shifting to and fro with which children generally prepare themselves to hear a story; but their faces, and the turning of their heads, and many feeble exclamations of expected pleasure, showed that all such preparations were making within them.

Mr. Raymond stood in the middle of the room, that he might turn from side to side, and give each a share of seeing him. Diamond kept his place by Nanny's side, with her hand in his. I do not know how much of Mr. Raymond's story the smaller children understood; indeed, I don't quite know how much there was in it to be understood, for in such a story every one has just to take what he can get. But they all listened with apparent satisfaction, and certainly with great attention. Mr. Raymond wrote it down afterwards, and here it is—somewhat altered no doubt, for a good story-teller tries to make his stories better every time he tells them. I cannot myself help thinking that he was somewhat indebted for this one to the old story of The Sleeping Beauty.

CHAPTER XXVIII

LITTLE DAYLIGHT

No house of any pretension to be called a palace is in the least worthy of the name, except it has a wood near it—very near it—and the nearer the better. Not all round it—I don't mean that, for a palace ought to be open to the sun and wind, and stand high and brave, with weathercocks glittering and flags flying; but on one side of every palace there must be a wood. And there was a very grand wood indeed beside the palace of the king who was going to be Daylight's father; such a grand wood, that nobody yet had ever got to the other end of it. Near the house it was kept very trim and nice, and it was free of brushwood for a long way in; but by degrees it got wild, and it grew wilder, and wilder, and wilder, until some said wild beasts at last did what they liked in it. The king and his courtiers often hunted, however, and this kept the wild beasts far away from the palace.

One glorious summer morning, when the wind and sun were out together, when the vanes were flashing and the flags frolicking against the blue sky, little Daylight made her appearance from somewhere—nobody could tell where—a beautiful baby, with such bright eyes that she might have come from the sun, only by and by she showed such lively ways that she might equally well have come out of the wind. There was great jubilation in the palace, for this was the first baby the queen had had, and there is as much happiness over a new baby in a palace as in a cottage.

But there is one disadvantage of living near a wood; you do not know quite who your neighbours may be. Everybody knew there were in it several fairies, living within a few miles of the palace, who always had had something to do with each new baby that came; for fairies live so much longer than we, that they can have business with a good many generations of human mortals. The curious houses they lived in were well known also,—one, a hollow oak; another, a birch-tree, though nobody could ever find how that fairy made a house of it; another, a hut of growing trees intertwined, and patched up with turf and moss. But there was another fairy who had lately come to the place, and nobody even knew she was a fairy except the other fairies. A wicked old thing she was, always concealing her power, and being as disagreeable as she could, in order to tempt people to give her offence, that she might have the pleasure of taking vengeance upon them. The people about thought she was a witch, and those who knew her by sight were careful to avoid offending her. She lived in a mud house, in a swampy part of the forest.

In all history we find that fairies give their remarkable gifts to prince and princess, or any child of sufficient importance in their eyes, always at the christening. Now this we can understand, because it is an ancient custom amongst human beings as well; and it is not hard to explain why wicked fairies should choose the same time to do unkind things; but it is difficult to understand how they should be able to do them, for you would fancy all wicked creatures would be powerless on such an occasion. But I never knew of any interference on the part of a wicked fairy that did not turn out a good thing in the end. What a good thing, for instance, it was that one princess should sleep for a hundred years! Was she not saved from all the plague of young men who were not worthy of her? And did she not come awake exactly at the right moment when the right

prince kissed her? For my part, I cannot help wishing a good many girls would sleep till just the same fate overtook them. It would be happier for them, and more agreeable to their friends.

Of course all the known fairies were invited to the christening. But the king and queen never thought of inviting an old witch. For the power of the fairies they have by nature; whereas a witch gets her power by wickedness. The other fairies, however, knowing the danger thus run, provided as well as they could against accidents from her quarter. But they could neither render her powerless, nor could they arrange their gifts in reference to hers beforehand, for they could not tell what those might be.

Of course the old hag was there without being asked. Not to be asked was just what she wanted, that she might have a sort of a reason for doing what she wished to do. For somehow even the wickedest of creatures likes a pretext for doing the wrong thing.

Five fairies had one after the other given the child such gifts as each counted best, and the fifth had just stepped back to her place in the surrounding splendour of ladies and gentlemen, when, mumbling a laugh between her toothless gums, the wicked fairy hobbled out into the middle of the circle, and at the moment when the archbishop was handing the baby to the lady at the head of the nursery department of state affairs, addressed him thus, giving a bite or two to every word before she could part with it:

"Please your Grace, I'm very deaf; would your Grace mind repeating the princess's name?"

"With pleasure, my good woman," said the archbishop, stooping to shout in her ear: "the infant's name is little Daylight."

"And little daylight it shall be," cried the fairy, in the tone of a dry axle, "and little

good shall any of her gifts do her. For I bestow upon her the gift of sleeping all day long, whether she will or not. Ha, ha! He, he! Hi, hi!"

Then out started the sixth fairy, who, of course; the others had arranged should come after the wicked one, in order to undo as much as she might.

"If she sleep all day," she said, mournfully, "she shall, at least, wake all night."

"A nice prospect for her mother and me!" thought the poor king; for they loved her far too much to give her up to nurses, especially at night, as most kings and queens do—and are sorry for it afterwards.

"You spoke before I had done," said the wicked fairy. "That's against the law. It gives me another chance."

"I beg your pardon," said the other fairies, all together.

"She did. I hadn't done laughing," said the crone. "I had only got to Hi, hi! and I had to go through Ho, ho! and Hu, hu! So I decree that if she wakes all night she shall wax and wane with its mistress the moon. And what that may mean I hope her royal parents will live to see. Ho, ho! Hu, hu!"

But out stepped another fairy, for they had been wise enough to keep two in reserve, because every fairy knew the trick of one.

"Until," said the seventh fairy, "a prince comes who shall kiss her without knowing it."

The wicked fairy made a horrid noise like an angry cat, and hobbled away. She could not pretend that she had not finished her speech this time, for she had laughed Ho, ho! and Hu, hu!

"I don't know what that means," said the poor king to the seventh fairy.

"Don't be afraid. The meaning will come with the thing itself," said she.

The assembly broke up, miserable enough—the queen, at least, prepared for a good

many sleepless nights, and the lady at the head of the nursery department anything but
comfortable in the prospect before her, for of course the queen could not do it all. As
for the king, he made up his mind, with what courage he could summon, to meet the
demands of the case, but wondered whether he could with any propriety require the
First Lord of the Treasury to take a share in the burden laid upon him.

I will not attempt to describe what they had to go through for some time. But at last
the household settled into a regular system—a very irregular one in some respects. For
at certain seasons the palace rang all night with bursts of laughter from little Daylight,
whose heart the old fairy's curse could not reach; she was Daylight still, only a little in
the wrong place, for she always dropped asleep at the first hint of dawn in the east. But
her merriment was of short duration. When the moon was at the full, she was in
glorious spirits, and as beautiful as it was possible for a child of her age to be. But as the
moon waned, she faded, until at last she was wan and withered like the poorest, sickliest
child you might come upon in the streets of a great city in the arms of a homeless
mother. Then the night was quiet as the day, for the little creature lay in her gorgeous
cradle night and day with hardly a motion, and indeed at last without even a moan, like
one dead. At first they often thought she was dead, but at last they got used to it, and
only consulted the almanac to find the moment when she would begin to revive, which,
of course, was with the first appearance of the silver thread of the crescent moon. Then
she would move her lips, and they would give her a little nourishment; and she would
grow better and better and better, until for a few days she was splendidly well. When
well, she was always merriest out in the moonlight; but even when near her worst, she
seemed better when, in warm summer nights, they carried her cradle out into the light
of the waning moon. Then in her sleep she would smile the faintest, most pitiful smile.

For a long time few people ever saw her awake. As she grew older she became such a
favourite, however, that about the palace there were always some who would contrive to
keep awake at night, in order to be near her. But she soon began to take every chance of
getting away from her nurses and enjoying her moonlight alone. And thus things went
on until she was nearly seventeen years of age. Her father and mother had by that time
got so used to the odd state of things that they had ceased to wonder at them. All their
arrangements had reference to the state of the Princess Daylight, and it is amazing how
things contrive to accommodate themselves. But how any prince was ever to find and
deliver her, appeared inconceivable.

As she grew older she had grown more and more beautiful, with the sunniest hair
and the loveliest eyes of heavenly blue, brilliant and profound as the sky of a June day.
But so much more painful and sad was the change as her bad time came on. The more
beautiful she was in the full moon, the more withered and worn did she become as the
moon waned. At the time at which my story has now arrived, she looked, when the
moon was small or gone, like an old woman exhausted with suffering. This was the
more painful that her appearance was unnatural; for her hair and eyes did not change.
Her wan face was both drawn and wrinkled, and had an eager hungry look. Her skinny
hands moved as if wishing, but unable, to lay hold of something. Her shoulders were
bent forward, her chest went in, and she stooped as if she were eighty years old. At last
she had to be put to bed, and there await the flow of the tide of life. But she grew to
dislike being seen, still more being touched by any hands, during this season. One lovely
summer evening, when the moon lay all but gone upon the verge of the horizon, she

vanished from her attendants, and it was only after searching for her a long time in great terror, that they found her fast asleep in the forest, at the foot of a silver birch, and carried her home.

A little way from the palace there was a great open glade, covered with the greenest and softest grass. This was her favourite haunt; for here the full moon shone free and glorious, while through a vista in the trees she could generally see more or less of the dying moon as it crossed the opening. Here she had a little rustic house built for her, and here she mostly resided. None of the court might go there without leave, and her own attendants had learned by this time not to be officious in waiting upon her, so that she was very much at liberty. Whether the good fairies had anything to do with it or not I cannot tell, but at last she got into the way of retreating further into the wood every night as the moon waned, so that sometimes they had great trouble in finding her; but as she was always very angry if she discovered they were watching her, they scarcely dared to do so. At length one night they thought they had lost her altogether. It was morning before they found her. Feeble as she was, she had wandered into a thicket a long way from the glade, and there she lay—fast asleep, of course.

Although the fame of her beauty and sweetness had gone abroad, yet as everybody knew she was under a bad spell, no king in the neighbourhood had any desire to have her for a daughter-in-law. There were serious objections to such a relation.

About this time in a neighbouring kingdom, in consequence of the wickedness of the nobles, an insurrection took place upon the death of the old king, the greater part of the nobility was massacred, and the young prince was compelled to flee for his life, disguised like a peasant. For some time, until he got out of the country, he suffered much from hunger and fatigue; but when he got into that ruled by the princess's father, and had no longer any fear of being recognized, he fared better, for the people were kind. He did not abandon his disguise, however. One tolerable reason was that he had no other clothes to put on, and another that he had very little money, and did not know where to get any more. There was no good in telling everybody he met that he was a prince, for he felt that a prince ought to be able to get on like other people, else his rank only made a fool of him. He had read of princes setting out upon adventure; and here he was out in similar case, only without having had a choice in the matter. He would go on, and see what would come of it.

For a day or two he had been walking through the palace-wood, and had had next to nothing to eat, when he came upon the strangest little house, inhabited by a very nice tidy motherly old woman. This was one of the good fairies. The moment she saw him she knew quite well who he was and what was going to come of it; but she was not at liberty to interfere with the orderly march of events. She received him with the kindness she would have shown to any other traveller, and gave him bread and milk, which he thought the most delicious food he had ever tasted, wondering that they did not have it for dinner at the palace sometimes. The old woman pressed him to stay all night. When he woke he was amazed to find how well and strong he felt. She would not take any of the money he offered, but begged him, if he found occasion of continuing in the neighbourhood, to return and occupy the same quarters.

"Thank you much, good mother," answered the prince; "but there is little chance of that. The sooner I get out of this wood the better."

"I don't know that," said the prince.

"What do you mean?" asked the prince.

"Why how *should* I know?" returned she.

"I can't tell," said the prince.

"Very well," said the fairy.

"How strangely you talk!" said the prince.

"Do I?" said the fairy.

"Yes, you do," said the prince.

"Very well," said the fairy.

The prince was not used to be spoken to in this fashion, so he felt a little angry, and turned and walked away. But this did not offend the fairy. She stood at the door of her little house looking after him till the trees hid him quite. Then she said "At last!" and went in.

The prince wandered and wandered, and got nowhere. The sun sank and sank and went out of sight, and he seemed no nearer the end of the wood than ever. He sat down on a fallen tree, ate a bit of bread the old woman had given him, and waited for the moon; for, although he was not much of an astronomer, he knew the moon would rise some time, because she had risen the night before. Up she came, slow and slow, but of a good size, pretty nearly round indeed; whereupon, greatly refreshed with his piece of bread, he got up and went—he knew not whither.

After walking a considerable distance, he thought he was coming to the outside of the forest; but when he reached what he thought the last of it, he found himself only upon the edge of a great open space in it, covered with grass. The moon shone very bright, and he thought he had never seen a more lovely spot. Still it looked dreary because of its loneliness, for he could not see the house at the other side. He sat down weary again, and gazed into the glade. He had not seen so much room for several days.

All at once he spied something in the middle of the grass. What could it be? It moved; it came nearer. Was it a human creature, gliding across—a girl dressed in white, gleaming in the moonshine? She came nearer and nearer. He crept behind a tree and watched, wondering. It must be some strange being of the wood—a nymph whom the moonlight and the warm dusky air had enticed from her tree. But when she came close to where he stood, he no longer doubted she was human—for he had caught sight of her sunny hair, and her clear blue eyes, and the loveliest face and form that he had ever seen. All at once she began singing like a nightingale, and dancing to her own music, with her eyes ever turned towards the moon. She passed close to where he stood, dancing on by the edge of the trees and away in a great circle towards the other side, until he could see but a spot of white in the yellowish green of the moonlit grass. But when he feared it would vanish quite, the spot grew, and became a figure once more. She approached him again, singing and dancing and waving her arms over her head, until she had completed the circle. Just opposite his tree she stood, ceased her song, dropped her arms, and broke out into a long clear laugh, musical as a brook. Then, as if tired, she threw herself on the grass, and lay gazing at the moon. The prince was almost afraid to breathe lest he should startle her, and she should vanish from his sight. As to venturing near her, that never came into his head.

She had lain for a long hour or longer, when the prince began again to doubt concerning her. Perhaps she was but a vision of his own fancy. Or was she a spirit of the wood, after all? If so, he too would haunt the wood, glad to have lost kingdom and

everything for the hope of being near her. He would build him a hut in the forest, and there he would live for the pure chance of seeing her again. Upon nights like this at least she would come out and bask in the moonlight, and make his soul blessed. But while he thus dreamed she sprang to her feet, turned her face full to the moon, and began singing as if she would draw her down from the sky by the power of her entrancing voice. She looked more beautiful than ever. Again she began dancing to her own music, and danced away into the distance. Once more she returned in a similar manner; but although he was watching as eagerly as before, what with fatigue and what with gazing, he fell fast asleep before she came near him. When he awoke it was broad daylight, and the princess was nowhere.

He could not leave the place. What if she should come the next night! He would gladly endure a day's hunger to see her yet again: he would buckle his belt quite tight. He walked round the glade to see if he could discover any prints of her feet. But the grass was so short, and her steps had been so light, that she had not left a single trace behind her.

He walked half-way round the wood without seeing anything to account for her presence. Then he spied a lovely little house, with thatched roof and low eaves, surrounded by an exquisite garden, with doves and peacocks walking in it. Of course this must be where the gracious lady who loved the moonlight lived. Forgetting his appearance, he walked towards the door, determined to make inquiries, but as he passed a little pond full of gold and silver fishes, he caught sight of himself and turned to find the door to the kitchen. There he knocked, and asked for a piece of bread. The good-natured cook brought him in, and gave him an excellent breakfast, which the prince found nothing the worse for being served in the kitchen. While he ate, he talked with his entertainer, and learned that this was the favourite retreat of the Princess Daylight. But he learned nothing more, both because he was afraid of seeming inquisitive, and because the cook did not choose to be heard talking about her mistress to a peasant lad who had begged for his breakfast.

As he rose to take his leave, it occurred to him that he might not be so far from the old woman's cottage as he had thought, and he asked the cook whether she knew anything of such a place, describing it as well as he could. She said she knew it well enough, adding with a smile—

"It's there you're going, is it?"

"Yes, if it's not far off."

"It's not more than three miles. But mind what you are about, you know."

"Why do you say that?"

"If you're after any mischief, she'll make you repent it."

"The best thing that could happen under the circumstances," remarked the prince.

"What do you mean by that?" asked the cook.

"Why, it stands to reason," answered the prince, "that if you wish to do anything wrong, the best thing for you is to be made to repent of it."

"I see," said the cook. "Well, I think you may venture. She's a good old soul."

"Which way does it lie from here?" asked the prince.

She gave him full instructions; and he left her with many thanks.

Being now refreshed, however, the prince did not go back to the cottage that day: he remained in the forest, amusing himself as best he could, but waiting anxiously for the night, in the hope that the princess would again appear. Nor was he disappointed, for, directly the moon rose, he spied a glimmering shape far across the glade. As it drew nearer, he saw it was she indeed—not dressed in white as before: in a pale blue like the sky, she looked lovelier still. He thought it was that the blue suited her yet better than the white; he did not know that she was really more beautiful because the moon was nearer the full. In fact the next night was full moon, and the princess would then be at the zenith of her loveliness.

The prince feared for some time that she was not coming near his hiding-place that night; but the circles in her dance ever widened as the moon rose, until at last they embraced the whole glade, and she came still closer to the trees where he was hiding than she had come the night before. He was entranced with her loveliness, for it was indeed a marvellous thing. All night long he watched her, but dared not go near her. He would have been ashamed of watching her too, had he not become almost incapable of thinking of anything but how beautiful she was. He watched the whole night long, and saw that as the moon went down she retreated in smaller and smaller circles, until at last he could see her no more.

Weary as he was, he set out for the old woman's cottage, where he arrived just in time for her breakfast, which she shared with him. He then went to bed, and slept for many hours. When he awoke, the sun was down, and he departed in great anxiety lest he should lose a glimpse of the lovely vision. But, whether it was by the machinations of the swamp-fairy, or merely that it is one thing to go and another to return by the same road, he lost his way. I shall not attempt to describe his misery when the moon rose, and he saw nothing but trees, trees, trees. She was high in the heavens before he reached the glade. Then indeed his troubles vanished, for there was the princess coming dancing towards him, in a dress that shone like gold, and with shoes that glimmered through the grass like fire-flies. She was of course still more beautiful than before. Like an embodied sunbeam she passed him, and danced away into the distance.

Before she returned in her circle, clouds had begun to gather about the moon. The wind rose, the trees moaned, and their lighter branches leaned all one way before it. The prince feared that the princess would go in, and he should see her no more that night. But she came dancing on more jubilant than ever, her golden dress and her sunny hair streaming out upon the blast, waving her arms towards the moon, and in the exuberance of her delight ordering the clouds away from off her face. The prince could hardly believe she was not a creature of the elements, after all.

By the time she had completed another circle, the clouds had gathered deep, and there were growlings of distant thunder. Just as she passed the tree where he stood, a flash of lightning blinded him for a moment; and when he saw again, to his horror, the princess lay on the ground. He darted to her, thinking she had been struck; but when she heard him coming, she was on her feet in a moment.

"What do you want?" she asked.

"I beg your pardon. I thought—the lightning—" said the prince, hesitating.

"There is nothing the matter," said the princess, waving him off rather haughtily.

The poor prince turned and walked towards the wood.

"Come back," said Daylight: "I like you. You do what you are told. Are you good?"

"Not so good as I should like to be," said the prince.

"Then go and grow better," said the princess.

Again the disappointed prince turned and went.

"Come back," said the princess.

He obeyed, and stood before her waiting.

"Can you tell me what the sun is like?" she asked.

"No," he answered. "But where's the good of asking what you know?"

"But I don't know," she rejoined.

"Why, everybody knows."

"That's the very thing: I'm not everybody. I've never seen the sun."

"Then you can't know what it's like till you do see it."

"I think you must be a prince," said the princess.

"Do I look like one?" said the prince.

"I can't quite say that."

"Then why do you think so?"

"Because you both do what you are told and speak the truth.—Is the sun so very bright?"

"As bright as the lightning."

"But it doesn't go out like that, does it?"

"Oh no. It shines like the moon, rises and sets like the moon, is much the same shape as the moon, only so bright that you can't look at it for a moment."

"But I *would* look at it," said the princess.

"But you couldn't," said the prince.

"But I could," said the princess.

"Why don't you, then?"

"Because I can't."

"Why can't you?"

"Because I can't wake. And I never shall wake until——"

Here she hid her face in her hands, turned away, and walked in the slowest, stateliest manner towards the house. The prince ventured to follow her at a little distance, but she turned and made a repellent gesture, which, like a true gentleman-prince, he obeyed at once. He waited a long time, but as she did not come near him again, and as the night had now cleared, he set off at last for the old woman's cottage.

It was long past midnight when he reached it, but, to his surprise, the old woman was paring potatoes at the door. Fairies are fond of doing odd things. Indeed, however they may dissemble, the night is always their day. And so it is with all who have fairy blood in them.

"Why, what are you doing there, this time of the night, mother?" said the prince; for that was the kind way in which any young man in his country would address a woman who was much older than himself.

"Getting your supper ready, my son," she answered.

"Oh! I don't want any supper," said the prince.

"Ah! you've seen Daylight," said she.

"I've seen a princess who never saw it," said the prince.

"Do you like her?" asked the fairy.

"Oh! don't I?" said the prince. "More than you would believe, mother."

"A fairy can believe anything that ever was or ever could be," said the old woman.

"Then are you a fairy?" asked the prince.

"Yes," said she.

"Then what do you do for things not to believe?" asked the prince.

"There's plenty of them—everything that never was nor ever could be."

"Plenty, I grant you," said the prince. "But do you believe there could be a princess who never saw the daylight? Do you believe that, now?"

This the prince said, not that he doubted the princess, but that he wanted the fairy to tell him more. She was too old a fairy, however, to be caught so easily.

"Of all people, fairies must not tell secrets. Besides, she's a princess."

"Well, I'll tell *you* a secret. I'm a prince."

"I know that."

"How do you know it?"

"By the curl of the third eyelash on your left eyelid."

"Which corner do you count from?"

"That's a secret."

"Another secret? Well, at least, if I am a prince, there can be no harm in telling me about a princess."

"It's just princes I can't tell."

"There ain't any more of them—are there?" said the prince.

"What! you don't think you're the only prince in the world, do you?"

"Oh, dear, no! not at all. But I know there's one too many just at present, except the princess——"

"Yes, yes, that's it," said the fairy.

"What's *it?*" asked the prince.

But he could get nothing more out of the fairy, and had to go to bed unanswered, which was something of a trial.

Now wicked fairies will not be bound by the laws which the good fairies obey, and this always seems to give the bad the advantage over the good, for they use means to gain their ends which the others will not. But it is all of no consequence, for what they do never succeeds; nay, in the end it brings about the very thing they are trying to prevent. So you see that somehow, for all their cleverness, wicked fairies are dreadfully stupid, for, although from the beginning of the world they have really helped instead of thwarting the good fairies, not one of them is a bit the wiser for it. She will try the bad thing just as they all did before her; and succeeds no better of course.

The prince had so far stolen a march upon the swamp-fairy that she did not know he was in the neighbourhood until after he had seen the princess those three times. When she knew it, she consoled herself by thinking that the princess must be far too proud and too modest for any young man to venture even to speak to her before he had seen her six times at least. But there was even less danger than the wicked fairy thought; for, however much the princess might desire to be set free, she was dreadfully afraid of the wrong prince. Now, however, the fairy was going to do all she could.

She so contrived it by her deceitful spells, that the next night the prince could not by any endeavour find his way to the glade. It would take me too long to tell her tricks. They would be amusing to us, who know that they could not do any harm, but they were something other than amusing to the poor prince. He wandered about the forest till daylight, and then fell fast asleep. The same thing occurred for seven following days, during which neither could he find the good fairy's cottage. After the third quarter of the moon, however, the bad fairy thought she might be at ease about the affair for a fortnight at least, for there was no chance of the prince wishing to kiss the princess during that period. So the first day of the fourth quarter he did find the cottage, and the next day he found the glade. For nearly another week he haunted it. But the princess never came. I have little doubt she was on the farther edge of it some part of every night, but at this period she always wore black, and, there being little or no light, the prince never saw her. Nor would he have known her if he had seen her. How could he have taken the worn decrepit creature she was now, for the glorious Princess Daylight?

At last, one night when there was no moon at all, he ventured near the house. There he heard voices talking, although it was past midnight; for her women were in considerable uneasiness, because the one whose turn it was to watch her had fallen asleep, and had not seen which way she went, and this was a night when she would probably wander very far, describing a circle which did not touch the open glade at all, but stretched away from the back of the house, deep into that side of the forest—a part of which the prince knew nothing. When he understood from what they said that she had disappeared, and that she must have gone somewhere in the said direction, he plunged at once into the wood to see if he could find her. For hours he roamed with nothing to guide him but the vague notion of a circle which on one side bordered on the house, for so much had he picked up from the talk he had overheard.

It was getting towards the dawn, but as yet there was no streak of light in the sky, when he came to a great birch-tree, and sat down weary at the foot of it. While he sat—very miserable, you may be sure—full of fear for the princess, and wondering how her attendants could take it so quietly, he bethought himself that it would not be a bad plan to light a fire, which, if she were anywhere near, would attract her. This he managed with a tinder-box, which the good fairy had given him. It was just beginning to blaze up, when he heard a moan, which seemed to come from the other side of the tree. He sprung to his feet, but his heart throbbed so that he had to lean for a moment against the tree before he could move. When he got round, there lay a human form in a little dark heap on the earth. There was light enough from his fire to show that it was not the princess. He lifted it in his arms, hardly heavier than a child, and carried it to the flame. The countenance was that of an old woman, but it had a fearfully strange look. A black hood concealed her hair, and her eyes were closed. He laid her down as comfortably as he could, chafed her hands, put a little cordial from a bottle, also the gift of the fairy, into her mouth; took off his coat and wrapped it about her, and in short did the best he could. In a little while she opened her eyes and looked at him—so pitifully! The tears rose and flowed down her gray wrinkled cheeks, but she said never a word. She closed her eyes again, but the tears kept on flowing, and her whole appearance was so utterly pitiful that the prince was very near crying too. He begged her to tell him what was the matter, promising to do all he could to help her; but still she did not speak. He thought she was dying, and took her in his arms again to carry her to the princess's house, where he thought the good-natured cook might be able to do something for her. When he lifted her, the tears flowed yet faster, and she gave such a sad moan that it went to his very heart.

"Mother, mother!" he said——"Poor mother!" and kissed her on the withered lips.

She started; and what eyes they were that opened upon him! But he did not see them, for it was still very dark, and he had enough to do to make his way through the trees towards the house.

Just as he approached the door, feeling more tired than he could have imagined possible—she was such a little thin old thing—she began to move, and became so restless that, unable to carry her a moment longer, he thought to lay her on the grass. But she stood upright on her feet. Her hood had dropped, and her hair fell about her. The first gleam of the morning was caught on her face: that face was bright as the never-aging Dawn, and her eyes were lovely as the sky of darkest blue. The prince recoiled in over-mastering wonder. It was Daylight herself whom he had brought from the forest! He fell at her feet, nor dared look up until she laid her hand upon his head. He rose then.

"You kissed me when I was an old woman: there! I kiss you when I am a young princess," murmured Daylight—"Is that the sun coming?"

CHAPTER XXIX

RUBY

T HE CHILDREN were delighted with the story, and made many amusing remarks upon it. Mr. Raymond promised to search his brain for another, and when he had found one to bring it to them. Diamond having taken leave of Nanny, and promised to go and see her again soon, went away with him.

Now Mr. Raymond had been turning over in his mind what he could do both for Diamond and for Nanny. He had therefore made some acquaintance with Diamond's father, and had been greatly pleased with him. But he had come to the resolution, before he did anything so good as he would like to do for them, to put them all to a certain test. So as they walked away together, he began to talk with Diamond as follows:—

"Nanny must leave the hospital soon, Diamond."

"I'm glad of that, sir."

"Why? Don't you think it's a nice place?"

"Yes, very. But it's better to be well and doing something, you know, even if it's not quite so comfortable."

"But they can't keep Nanny so long as they would like. They can't keep her till she's *quite* strong. There are always so many sick children they want to take in and make better. And the question is, What will she do when they send her out again?"

"That's just what I can't tell, though I've been thinking of it over and over, sir. Her crossing was taken long ago, and I couldn't bear to see Nanny fighting for it, especially with such a poor fellow as has taken it. He's quite lame, sir."

"She doesn't look much like fighting, now, does she, Diamond?"

"No, sir. She looks too like an angel. Angels don't fight—do they, sir?"

"Not to get things for themselves, at least," said Mr. Raymond.

"Besides," added Diamond, "I don't quite see that she would have any better right to the crossing than the boy who has got it. Nobody gave it to her; she only took it. And now he has taken it."

"If she were to sweep a crossing—soon at least—after the illness she has had, she would be laid up again the very first wet day," said Mr. Raymond.

"And there's hardly any money to be got except on the wet days," remarked Diamond reflectively. "Is there nothing else she could do, sir?"

"Not without being taught, I'm afraid."

"Well, couldn't somebody teach her something?"

"Couldn't you teach her, Diamond?"

"I don't know anything myself, sir. I *could* teach her to dress the baby; but nobody would give her anything for doing things like that: they are so easy. There wouldn't be much good in teaching her to drive a cab, for where would she get the cab to drive? There ain't fathers and old Diamonds everywhere. At least poor Nanny can't find any of them, I doubt."

"Perhaps if she were taught to be nice and clean, and only speak gentle words——"

"Mother could teach her that," interrupted Diamond.

"And to dress babies, and feed them, and take care of them," Mr. Raymond proceeded, "she might get a place as a nurse somewhere, you know. People do give money for that."

"Then I'll ask mother," said Diamond.

"But you'll have to give her her food then; and your father, not being strong, has enough to do already without that."

"But here's me," said Diamond: "I help him out with it. When he's tired of driving, up I get. It don't make any difference to old Diamond. I don't mean he likes me as well as my father—of course he can't, you know—nobody could; but he does his duty all the same. It's got to be done, you know, sir; and Diamond's a good horse—isn't he, sir?"

"From your description I should say certainly; but I have not the pleasure of his acquaintance myself."

"Don't you think he will go to heaven, sir?"

"That I don't know anything about," said Mr. Raymond. "I confess I should be glad to think so," he added, smiling thoughtfully.

"I'm sure he'll get to the back of the north wind, anyhow," said Diamond to himself; but he had learned to be very careful of saying such things aloud.

"Isn't it rather too much for him to go in the cab all day and every day?" resumed Mr. Raymond.

"So father says, when he feels his ribs of a morning. But then he says the old horse *do* eat well, and the moment he's had his supper, down he goes, and never gets up till he's called; and, for the legs of him, father says that makes no end of a differ. Some horses, sir! they won't lie down all night long, but go to sleep on their four pins, like a haystack, father says. *I* think it's very stupid of them, and so does old Diamond. But then I suppose they don't know better, and so they can't help it. We mustn't be too hard upon them, father says."

"Your father must be a good man, Diamond."

Diamond looked up in Mr. Raymond's face, wondering what he could mean.

"I said your father must be a good man, Diamond."

"Of course," said Diamond. "How could he drive a cab if he wasn't?"

"There are some men drive cabs who are not very good," objected Mr. Raymond.

Diamond remembered the drunken cabman, and saw that his friend was right.

"Ah! but," he returned, "he *must* be, you know, with such a horse as old Diamond."

"That does make a difference," said Mr. Raymond. "But it is quite enough that he *is* a good man, without our trying to account for it. Now, if you like, I will give you a proof that *I* think him a good man. I am going away on the Continent for a while—for three months, I believe—and I am going to let my house to a gentleman who does not want the use of my brougham. My horse is nearly as old, I fancy, as your Diamond, but I don't want to part with him, and I don't want him to be idle; for nobody, as you say, ought to be idle; but neither do I want him to be worked very hard. Now, it has come into my head that perhaps your father would take charge of him, and work him under certain conditions."

"My father will do what's right," said Diamond. "I'm sure of that."

"Well, so I think. Will you ask him when he comes home to call and have a little chat with me—to-day, some time?"

"He must have his dinner first," said Diamond. "No, he's got his dinner with him to-day. It must be after he's had his tea."

"Of course, of course. Any time will do. I shall be at home all day."

"Very well, sir. I will tell him. You may be sure he will come. My father thinks you a very kind gentleman, and I know he is right, for I know your very own self, sir."

Mr. Raymond smiled, and as they had now reached his door, they parted, and Diamond went home. As soon as his father entered the house, Diamond gave him Mr. Raymond's message, and recounted the conversation that had preceded it. His father said little, but took thought-sauce to his bread and butter, and as soon as he had finished his meal, rose, saying:

"I will go to your friend directly, Diamond. It would be a grand thing to get a little more money. We do want it."

Diamond accompanied his father to Mr. Raymond's door, and there left him.

He was shown at once into Mr. Raymond's study, where he gazed with some wonder at the multitude of books on the walls, and thought what a learned man Mr. Raymond must be.

Presently Mr. Raymond entered, and after saying much the same about his old horse, made the following distinct proposal—one not over-advantageous to Diamond's father, but for which he had reasons—namely, that Joseph should have the use of Mr. Raymond's horse while he was away, on condition that he never worked him more than six hours a day, and fed him well, and that, besides, he should take Nanny home as soon as she was able to leave the hospital, and provide for her as for one of his own children, neither better nor worse—so long, that is, as he had the horse.

Diamond's father could not help thinking it a pretty close bargain. He should have both the girl and the horse to feed, and only six hours' work out of the horse.

"It will save your own horse," said Mr. Raymond.

"That is true," answered Joseph; "but all I can get by my own horse is only enough to keep us, and if I save him and feed your horse and the girl—don't you see, sir?"

"Well, you can go home and think about it, and let me know by the end of the week. I am in no hurry before then."

So Joseph went home and recounted the proposal to his wife, adding that he did not think there was much advantage to be got out of it.

"Not much that way, husband," said Diamond's mother; "but there would be an advantage, and what matter who gets it!"

"I don't see it," answered her husband. "Mr. Raymond is a gentleman of property, and I don't discover any much good in helping him to save a little more. He won't easily get one to make such a bargain, and I don't mean he shall get me. It would be a loss rather than a gain—I do think—at least, if I took less work out of our own horse."

"One hour would make a difference to old Diamond. But that's not the main point. You must think what an advantage it would be to the poor girl that hasn't a home to go to!"

"She *is* one of Diamond's friends," thought his father.

"I could be kind to her, you know," the mother went on, "and teach her housework, and how to handle a baby; and, besides, she would help me, and I should be the stronger for it, and able to do an odd bit of charing now and then, when I got the chance."

"I won't hear of that," said her husband. "Have the girl by all means. I'm ashamed I did not think of both sides of the thing at once. I wonder if the horse is a great eater. To be sure, if I gave Diamond two hours' additional rest, it would be all the better for the old bones of him, and there would be four hours extra out of the other horse. That would give Diamond something to do every day. He could drive old Diamond after dinner, and I could take the other horse out for six hours after tea, or in the morning, as I found best. It might pay for the keep of both of them,—that is, if I had good luck. I should like to oblige Mr. Raymond, though he be rather hard, for he has been very kind to our Diamond, wife. Hasn't he now?"

"He has indeed, Joseph," said his wife, and there the conversation ended.

Diamond's father went the very next day to Mr. Raymond, and accepted his proposal; so that the week after, having got another stall in the same stable, he had two horses instead of one. Oddly enough, the name of the new horse was Ruby, for he was a very red chestnut. Diamond's name came from a white lozenge on his forehead. Young Diamond said they *were* rich now, with such a big diamond and such a big ruby.

CHAPTER XXX

NANNY'S DREAM

NANNY WAS NOT FIT to be moved for some time yet, and Diamond went to see her as often as he could. But being more regularly engaged now, seeing he went out every day for a few hours with old Diamond, and had his baby to mind, and one of the horses to attend to, he could not go so often as he would have liked.

One evening, as he sat by her bedside, she said to him:

"I've had such a beautiful dream, Diamond! I should like to tell it you."

"Oh! do," said Diamond; "I am so fond of dreams!"

"She must have been to the back of the north wind," he said to himself.

"It was a very foolish dream, you know. But somehow it was so pleasant! What a good thing it is that you believe the dream all the time you are in it!"

My readers must not suppose that poor Nanny was able to say what she meant so well as I put it down here. She had never been to school, and had heard very little else than vulgar speech until she came to the hospital. But I have been to school, and although that could never make me able to dream so well as Nanny, it has made me able to tell her dream better than she could herself. And I am the more desirous of doing this for her that I have already done the best I could for Diamond's dream, and it would be a shame to give the boy all the advantage.

"I will tell you all I know about it," said Nanny. "The day before yesterday, a lady came to see us—a very beautiful lady, and very beautifully dressed. I heard the matron say to her that it was very kind of her to come in blue and gold; and she answered that she knew we didn't like dull colours. She had such a lovely shawl on, just like redness dipped in milk, and all worked over with flowers of the same colour. It didn't shine much; it *was* silk, but it kept in the shine. When she came to my bedside, she sat down, just where you are sitting, Diamond, and laid her hand on the counterpane. I was sitting up, with my table before me, ready for my tea. Her hand looked so pretty in its blue

glove, that I was tempted to stroke it. I thought she wouldn't be angry, for everybody that comes to the hospital is kind. It's only in the streets they ain't kind. But she drew her hand away, and I almost cried, for I thought I had been rude. Instead of that, however, it was only that she didn't like giving me her glove to stroke, for she drew it off, and then laid her hand where it was before. I wasn't sure, but I ventured to put out my ugly hand."

"Your hand ain't ugly, Nanny," said Diamond; but Nanny went on—

"And I stroked it again, and then she stroked mine,—think of that! And there was a ring on her finger, and I looked down to see what it was like. And she drew it off, and put it upon one of my fingers. It was a red stone, and she told me they called it a ruby."

"Oh, that is funny!" said Diamond. "Our new horse is called Ruby. We've got another horse—a red one—such a beauty!"

But Nanny went on with her story.

"I looked at the ruby all the time the lady was talking to me,—it was so beautiful! And as she talked I kept seeing deeper and deeper into the stone. At last she rose to go away, and I began to pull the ring off my finger; and what do you think she said?—'Wear it all night, if you like. Only you must take care of it. I can't give it you, for some one gave it to me; but you may keep it till to-morrow.' Wasn't it kind of her? I could hardly take my tea, I was so delighted to hear it; and I do think it was the ring that set me dreaming; for, after I had taken my tea, I leaned back, half lying and half sitting, and looked at the ring on my finger. By degrees I began to dream. The ring grew larger and larger, until at last I found that I was not looking at a red stone, but at a red sunset, which shone in at the end of a long street near where Grannie lives. I was dressed in rags as I used to be, and I had great holes in my shoes, at which the nasty mud came through to my feet. I didn't use to mind it before, but now I thought it horrid. And there was the great red sunset, with streaks of green and gold between, standing looking at me. Why couldn't I live in the sunset instead of in that dirt? Why was it so far away always? Why did it never come into our wretched street? It faded away, as the sunsets always do, and at last went out altogether. Then a cold wind began to blow, and flutter all my rags about——"

"That was North Wind herself," said Diamond.

"Eh?" said Nanny, and went on with her story.

"I turned my back to it, and wandered away. I did not know where I was going, only it was warmer to go that way. I don't think it was a north wind, for I found myself somewhere in the west end at last. But it doesn't matter in a dream which wind it was."

"I don't know that," said Diamond. "I believe North Wind can get into our dreams—yes, and blow in them. Sometimes she has blown me out of a dream altogether."

"I don't know what you mean, Diamond," said Nanny.

"Never mind," answered Diamond. "Two people can't always understand each other. They'd both be at the back of the north wind directly, and what would become of the other places without them?"

"You do talk so oddly!" said Nanny. "I sometimes think they must have been right about you."

"What did they say about me?" asked Diamond.

"They called you God's baby."

"How kind of them! But I knew that."

"Did you know what it meant, though? It meant that you were not right in the head."

"I feel all right," said Diamond, putting both hands to his head, as if it had been a globe he could take off and set on again.

"Well, as long as you are pleased I am pleased," said Nanny.

"Thank you, Nanny. Do go on with your story. I think I like dreams even better than fairy tales. But they must be nice ones, like yours, you know."

"Well, I went on, keeping my back to the wind, until I came to a fine street on the top of a hill. How it happened I don't know, but the front door of one of the houses was open, and not only the front door, but the back door as well, so that I could see right through the house—and what do you think I saw? A garden place with green grass, and the moon shining upon it! Think of that! There was no moon in the street, but through the house there was the moon. I looked and there was nobody near: I would not do any harm, and the grass was so much nicer than the mud! But I couldn't think of going on the grass with such dirty shoes: I kicked them off in the gutter, and ran in on my bare feet, up the steps, and through the house, and on to the grass; and the moment I came into the moonlight, I began to feel better."

"That's why North Wind blew you there," said Diamond.

"It came of Mr. Raymond's story about the Princess Daylight," returned Nanny. "Well, I lay down upon the grass in the moonlight without thinking how I was to get out again. Somehow the moon suited me exactly. There was not a breath of the north wind you talk about; it was quite gone."

"You didn't want her any more, just then. She never goes where she's not wanted," said Diamond. "But she blew you into the moonlight, anyhow."

"Well, we won't dispute about it," said Nanny: "you've got a tile loose, you know."

"Suppose I have," returned Diamond, "don't you see it may let in the moonlight, or the sunlight for that matter?"

"Perhaps yes, perhaps no," said Nanny.

"And you've got your dreams, too, Nanny."

"Yes, but I know they're dreams."

"So do I. But I know besides they are something more as well."

"Oh! do you?" rejoined Nanny. "I don't."

"All right," said Diamond. "Perhaps you will some day."

"Perhaps I won't," said Nanny.

Diamond held his peace, and Nanny resumed her story.

"I lay a long time, and the moonlight got in at every tear in my clothes, and made me feel so happy——"

"There, I tell you!" said Diamond.

"What do you tell me?" returned Nanny.

"North Wind——"

"It was the moonlight, I tell you," persisted Nanny, and again Diamond held his peace.

"All at once I felt that the moon was not shining so strong. I looked up, and there was a cloud, all crapey and fluffy, trying to drown the beautiful creature. But the moon was so round, just like a whole plate, that the cloud couldn't stick to her; she shook it off, and said *there*, and shone out clearer and brighter than ever. But up came a thicker cloud,—and 'You shan't' said the moon; and 'I will' said the cloud,—but it couldn't: out shone the moon, quite laughing at its impudence. I knew her ways, for I've always been used to watch her. She's the only thing worth looking at in our street at night."

"Don't call it *your* street," said Diamond. "You're not going back to it. You're coming to us, you know."

"That's too good to be true," said Nanny.

"There are very few things good enough to be true," said Diamond; "but I hope this is. Too good to be true it can't be. Isn't *true* good? and isn't *good* good? And how, then, can anything be too good to be true? That's like old Sal—to say that."

"Don't abuse Grannie, Diamond. She's a horrid old thing, she and her gin bottle; but she'll repent some day, and then you'll be glad not to have said anything against her."

"Why?" said Diamond.

"Because you'll be sorry for her."

"I am sorry for her now."

"Very well. That's right. She'll be sorry too. And there'll be an end of it."

"All right. You come to us," said Diamond.

"Where was I?" said Nanny.

"Telling me how the moon served the clouds."

"Yes. But it wouldn't do, all of it. Up came the clouds and the clouds, and they came faster and faster, until the moon was covered up. You couldn't expect her to throw off a hundred of them at once—could you?"

"Certainly not," said Diamond.

"So it grew very dark; and a dog began to yelp in the house. I looked and saw that the door to the garden was shut. Presently it was opened—not to let me out, but to let the dog in—yelping and bounding. I thought if he caught sight of me, I was in for a biting first, and the police after. So I jumped up, and ran for a little summer-house in the

corner of the garden. The dog came after me, but I shut the door in his face. It was well it had a door—wasn't it?"

"You dreamed of the door because you wanted it," said Diamond.

"No, I didn't; it came of itself. It was there, in the true dream."

"There—I've caught you!" said Diamond. "I knew you believed in the dream as much as I do."

"Oh, well, if you will lay traps for a body!" said Nanny. "Anyhow, I was safe inside the summer-house. And what do you think?—There was the moon beginning to shine again—but only through one of the panes—and that one was just the colour of the ruby. Wasn't it funny?"

"No, not a bit funny," said Diamond.

"If you will be contrary!" said Nanny.

"No, no," said Diamond; "I only meant that was the very pane I should have expected her to shine through."

"Oh, very well!" returned Nanny.

What Diamond meant, I do not pretend to say. He had curious notions about things.

"And now," said Nanny, "I didn't know what to do, for the dog kept barking at the door, and I couldn't get out. But the moon was so beautiful that I couldn't keep from looking at it through the red pane. And as I looked it got larger and larger till it filled the whole pane and outgrew it, so that I could see it through the other panes; and it grew till it filled them too and the whole window, so that the summer-house was nearly as bright as day.

"The dog stopped barking, and I heard a gentle tapping at the door, like the wind blowing a little branch against it."

"Just like her," said Diamond, who thought everything strange and beautiful must be done by North Wind.

"So I turned from the window and opened the door; and what do you think I saw?"

"A beautiful lady," said Diamond.

"No—the moon itself, as big as a little house, and as round as a ball, shining like yellow silver. It stood on the grass—down on the very grass: I could see nothing else for the brightness of it. And as I stared and wondered, a door opened in the side of it, near the ground, and a curious little old man, with a crooked thing over his shoulder, looked out, and said: 'Come along, Nanny; my lady wants you. We're come to fetch you.' I wasn't a bit frightened. I went up to the beautiful bright thing, and the old man held down his hand, and I took hold of it, and gave a jump, and he gave me a lift, and I was inside the moon. And what do you think it was like? It was such a pretty little house, with blue windows and white curtains! At one of the windows sat a beautiful lady, with her head leaning on her hand, looking out. She seemed rather sad, and I was sorry for her, and stood staring at her.

" 'You didn't think I had such a beautiful mistress as that!' said the queer little man. 'No, indeed!' I answered: 'who would have thought it?' 'Ah! who indeed? But you see you don't know everything.' The little man closed the door, and began to pull at a rope which hung behind it with a weight at the end. After he had pulled a while, he said—'There, that will do; we're all right now.' Then he took me by the hand and opened a little trap in the floor, and led me down two or three steps, and I saw like a great hole below me. 'Don't be frightened,' said the little man. 'It's not a hole. It's only a window. Put your face down and look through.' I did as he told me, and there was the garden and the summer-house, far away, lying at the bottom of the moonlight. 'There!' said the little man; 'we've brought you off! Do you see the little dog barking at us down there in the garden?' I told him I couldn't see anything so far. 'Can *you* see anything so small and so far off?' I said. 'Bless you, child!' said the little man; 'I could pick up a needle out of the grass if I had only a long enough arm. There's one lying by the door of the summer-house now.' I looked at his eyes. They were very small, but so bright that I think he saw by the light that went out of them. Then he took me up, and up again by a little stair in a corner of the room, and through another trap-door, and there was one great round window above us, and I saw the blue sky and the clouds, and such lots of stars, all so big, and shining as hard as ever they could!"

"The little girl-angels had been polishing them," said Diamond.

"What nonsense you do talk!" said Nanny.

"But my nonsense is just as good as yours, Nanny. When you have done, I'll tell you my dream. The stars are in it—not the moon, though. She was away somewhere. Perhaps she was gone to fetch you then. I don't think that, though, for my dream was longer ago than yours. She might have been to fetch some one else, though; for we can't fancy it's only us that get such fine things done for them. But do tell me what came next."

Perhaps one of my child-readers may remember whether the moon came down to fetch him or her the same night that Diamond had his dream. I cannot tell, of course. I know she did not come to fetch me, though I did think I could make her follow me when I was a boy—not a very tiny one either.

"The little man took me all round the house, and made me look out of every window.

Oh, it was beautiful! There we were, all up in the air, in such a nice clean little house! 'Your work will be to keep the windows bright,' said the little man. 'You won't find it very difficult, for there ain't much dust up here. Only, the frost settles on them sometimes, and the drops of rain leave marks on them.' 'I can easily clean them inside,' I said; 'but how am I to get the frost and the rain off the outside of them?' 'Oh!' he said, 'it's quite easy. There are ladders all about. You've only got to go out at the door, and climb about. There are a great many windows you haven't seen yet, and some of them look into places you don't know anything about. I used to clean them myself, but I'm getting rather old, you see. Ain't I now?' 'I can't tell,' I answered. 'You see I never saw you when you were younger.' 'Never saw the man in the moon?' said he. 'Not very near,' I answered—'not to tell how young or how old he looked. I have seen the bundle of sticks on his back.' For Jim had pointed that out to me. Jim was very fond of looking at the man in the moon. Poor Jim! I wonder he hasn't been to see me. I'm afraid he's ill too."

"I'll try to find out," said Diamond, "and let you know."

"Thank you," said Nanny. "You and Jim ought to be friends."

"But what did the man in the moon say, when you told him you had seen him with the bundle of sticks on his back?"

"He laughed. But I thought he looked offended too. His little nose turned up sharper, and he drew the corners of his mouth down from the tips of his ears into his neck. But he didn't look cross, you know."

"Didn't he say anything?"

"Oh, yes! He said: 'That's all nonsense. What you saw was my bundle of dusters. I was going to clean the windows. It takes a good many, you know. Really, what they do say of their superiors down there!' 'It's only because they don't know better,' I ventured to say. 'Of course, of course,' said the little man. 'Nobody ever does know better. Well, I forgive them, and *that* sets it all right, I hope.' 'It's very good of you,' I said. 'No!' said he, 'it's not in the least good of me. I couldn't be comfortable otherwise.' After this he said nothing for a while, and I laid myself on the floor of his garret, and stared up and around at the great blue beautifulness. I had forgotten him almost, when at last he said: 'Ain't you done yet?' 'Done what?' I asked. 'Done saying your prayers,' says he. 'I wasn't saying my prayers,' I answered. 'Oh yes, you were,' said he, 'though you didn't know it! And now I must show you something else.'

"He took my hand and led me down the stair again, and through a narrow passage, and through another, and another, and another. I don't know how there could be room for so many passages in such a little house. The heart of it must be ever so much farther from the sides than they are from each other. How could it have an inside that was so independent of its outside? There's the point. It was funny—wasn't it, Diamond?"

"No," said Diamond. He was going to say that that was very much the sort of thing at the back of the north wind; but he checked himself and only added, "All right. I don't see it. I don't see why the inside should depend on the outside. It ain't so with the crabs. They creep out of their outsides and make new ones. Mr. Raymond told me so."

"I don't see what that has got to do with it," said Nanny.

"Then go on with your story, please," said Diamond. "What did you come to, after going through all those winding passages into the heart of the moon?"

"I didn't say they were winding passages. I said they were long and narrow. They didn't wind. They went by corners."

"That's worth knowing," remarked Diamond. "For who knows how soon he may have to go there? But the main thing is, what did you come to at last?"

"We came to a small box against the wall of a tiny room. The little man told me to put my ear against it. I did so, and heard a noise something like the purring of a cat, only not so loud, and much sweeter. 'What is it?' I asked. 'Don't you know the sound?' returned the little man. 'No,' I answered. 'Don't you know the sound of bees?' he said. I had never heard bees, and could not know the sound of them. 'Those are my lady's bees,' he went on. I had heard that bees gather honey from the flowers. 'But where are the flowers for them?' I asked. 'My lady's bees gather their honey from the sun and the stars,' said the little man. 'Do let me see them,' I said. 'No. I daren't do that,' he answered. 'I have no business with them. I don't understand them. Besides, they are so bright that if one were to fly into your eye, it would blind you altogether.' 'Then you have seen them?' 'Oh, yes! Once or twice, I think. But I don't quite know: they are so very bright—like buttons of lightning. Now I've showed you all I can to-night, and we'll go back to the room.' I followed him, and he made me sit down under a lamp that hung from the roof, and gave me some bread and honey.

"The lady had never moved. She sat with her forehead leaning on her hand, gazing out of the little window, hung like the rest with white cloudy curtains. From where I was sitting I looked out of it too, but I could see nothing. Her face was very beautiful, and very white, and very still, and her hand was as white as the forehead that leaned on it. I did not see her whole face—only the side of it, for she never moved to turn it full upon me, or even to look at me.

"How long I sat after I had eaten my bread and honey, I don't know. The little man was busy about the room, pulling a string here, and a string there, but chiefly the string at the back of the door. I was thinking with some uneasiness that he would soon be wanting me to go out and clean the windows, and I didn't fancy the job. At last he came up to me with a great armful of dusters. 'It's time you set about the windows,' he said; 'for there's rain coming, and if they're quite clean before, then the rain can't spoil them.' I got up at once. 'You needn't be afraid,' he said. 'You won't tumble off. Only you must be careful. Always hold on with one hand while you rub with the other.' As he spoke, he opened the door. I started back in a terrible fright, for there was nothing but blue air to be seen under me, like a great water without a bottom at all. But what must be must, and to live up here was so much nicer than down in the mud with holes in my shoes, that I never thought of not doing as I was told. The little man showed me how and where to lay hold while I put my foot round the edge of the door on to the first round of a ladder. 'Once you're up,' he said, 'you'll see how you have to go well enough.' I did as he told me, and crept out very carefully. Then the little man handed me the bundle of dusters, saying, 'I always carry them on my reaping hook, but I don't think you could manage it properly. You shall have it if you like.' I wouldn't take it, however, for it looked dangerous.

"I did the best I could with the dusters, and crawled up to the top of the moon. But what a grand sight it was! The stars were all over my head, so bright and so near that I could almost have laid hold of them. The round ball to which I clung went bobbing and floating away through the dark blue above and below and on every side. It was so beautiful that all fear left me, and I set to work diligently. I cleaned window after window. At length I came to a very little one, in at which I peeped. There was the room with the box of bees in it! I laid my ear to the window, and heard the musical hum quite distinctly. A great longing to see them came upon me, and I opened the window and crept in. The little box had a door like a closet. I opened it—the tiniest crack—when out came the light with such a sting that I closed it again in terror—not, however, before three bees had shot out into the room, where they darted about like flashes of lightning. Terribly frightened, I tried to get out of the window again, but I could not: there was no way to the outside of the moon but through the door; and that was in the room where the lady sat. No sooner had I reached the room, than the three bees, which had followed me, flew at once to the lady, and settled upon her hair. Then first I saw her move. She started, put up her hand, and caught them; then rose and, having held them into the flame of the lamp one after the other, turned to me. Her face was not so sad now as stern. It frightened me much. 'Nanny, you have got me into trouble,' she said. 'You have been letting out my bees, which it is all I can do to manage. You have forced me to burn them. It is a great loss, and there will be a storm.' As she spoke, the clouds had gathered all about us. I could see them come crowding up white about the windows. 'I am sorry to find,' said the lady, 'that you are not to be trusted. You must go home again—you won't do for us.' Then came a great clap of thunder, and the moon rocked and swayed. All grew dark about me, and I fell on the floor, and lay half-stunned. I could hear everything but could see nothing. 'Shall I throw her out of the door, my lady?' said the little man. 'No,' she answered; 'she's not quite bad enough for that. I don't think there's much harm in her; only she'll never do for us. She would make dreadful mischief up here. She's only fit for the mud. It's a great pity. I am sorry for her. Just take that ring off her finger. I am sadly afraid she has stolen it.' The little man caught hold of my hand, and I felt him tugging at the ring. I tried to speak what was true about it, but, after a terrible effort, only gave a groan. Other things began to come into my head. Somebody else had a hold of me. The little man wasn't there. I opened my eyes at last, and saw the nurse. I had cried out in my sleep, and she had come and waked me. But, Diamond, for all it was only a dream, I cannot help being ashamed of myself yet for opening the lady's box of bees."

"You wouldn't do it again—would you—if she were to take you back?" said Diamond.

"No. I don't think anything would ever make me do it again. But where's the good? I shall never have the chance."

"I don't know that," said Diamond.

"You silly baby! It was only a dream," said Nanny.

"I know that, Nanny, dear. But how can you tell you mayn't dream it again?"

"That's not a bit likely."

"I don't know that," said Diamond.

"You're always saying that," said Nanny. "I don't like it."

"Then I won't say it again—if I don't forget," said Diamond. "But it was such a beautiful dream!—wasn't it, Nanny? What a pity you opened that door and let the bees out! You might have had such a long dream, and such nice talks with the moon-lady! Do try to go again, Nanny. I do so want to hear more."

But now the nurse came and told him it was time to go; and Diamond went, saying to himself, "I can't help thinking that North Wind had something to do with that dream. It would be tiresome to lie there all day and all night too—without dreaming. Perhaps if she hadn't done that, the moon might have carried her to the back of the north wind—who knows?"

CHAPTER XXXI

THE NORTH WIND DOTH BLOW

Iᴛ ᴡᴀs ᴀ ɢʀᴇᴀᴛ ᴅᴇʟɪɢʜᴛ to Diamond when at length Nanny was well enough to leave the hospital and go home to their house. She was not very strong yet, but Diamond's mother was very considerate of her, and took care that she should have nothing to do she was not quite fit for. If Nanny had been taken straight from the street, it is very probable she would not have been so pleasant in a decent household, or so easy to teach; but after the refining influences of her illness and the kind treatment she had had in the hospital, she moved about the house just like some rather sad pleasure haunting the mind. As she got better, and the colour came back to her cheeks, her step grew lighter and quicker, her smile shone out more readily, and it became certain that she would soon be a treasure of help. It was great fun to see Diamond teaching her how to hold the baby, and wash and dress him, and often they laughed together over her awkwardness. But she had not many such lessons before she was able to perform those duties quite as well as Diamond himself.

Things however did not go well with Joseph from the very arrival of Ruby. It almost seemed as if the red beast had brought ill luck with him. The fares were fewer, and the pay less. Ruby's services did indeed make the week's income at first a little beyond what it used to be, but then there were two more to feed. After the first month he fell lame, and for the whole of the next Joseph dared not attempt to work him. I cannot say that he never grumbled, for his own health was far from what it had been; but I can say that he tried to do his best. During all that month, they lived on very short commons indeed, seldom tasting meat except on Sundays, and poor old Diamond, who worked hardest of all, not even then—so that at the end of it he was as thin as a clothes-horse, while Ruby was as plump and sleek as a bishop's cob.

Nor was it much better after Ruby was able to work again, for it was a season of great depression in business, and that is very soon felt amongst the cabmen. City men look more after their shillings, and their wives and daughters have less to spend. It was besides a wet autumn, and bread rose greatly in price. When I add to this that Diamond's mother was but poorly, for a new baby was coming, you will see that these were not very jolly times for our friends in the Mews.

Notwithstanding the depressing influences around him, however, Joseph was able to keep a little hope alive in his heart; and when he came home at night, would get Diamond to read to him, and would also make Nanny produce her book that he might

see how she was getting on. For Diamond had taken her education in hand, and as she was a clever child, she was very soon able to put letters and words together.

Thus the three months passed away, but Mr. Raymond did not return. Joseph had been looking anxiously for him, chiefly with the desire of getting rid of Ruby—not that he was absolutely of no use to him, but that he was a constant weight upon his mind. Indeed, as far as provision went, he was rather worse off with Ruby and Nanny than he had been before, but on the other hand, Nanny was a great help in the house, and it was a comfort to him to think that when the new baby did come, Nanny would be with his wife.

Of God's gifts a baby is of the greatest; therefore it is no wonder that when this one came, she was as heartily welcomed by the little household as if she had brought plenty with her. Of course she made a great difference in the work to be done—far more difference than her size warranted, but Nanny was no end of help, and Diamond was as much of a sunbeam as ever, and began to sing to the new baby the first moment he got her in his arms. But he did not sing the same songs to her that he had sung to his brother; for, he said, she was a new baby and must have new songs; and besides, she was a sister-baby and not a brother-baby, and of course would not like the same kind of songs. Where the difference in his songs lay, however, I do not pretend to be able to point out. One thing I am sure of, that they not only had no small share in the education of the little girl, but helped the whole family a great deal more than they were aware.

How they managed to get through the long dreary expensive winter, I can hardly say. Sometimes things were better, sometimes worse. But at last the spring came, and the winter was over and gone, and that was much. Still Mr. Raymond did not return, and

although the mother would have been able to manage without Nanny now, they could not look for a place for her so long as they had Ruby; and they were not altogether sorry for this.

One week at last was worse than they had yet had. They were almost without bread before it was over. But the sadder he saw his father and mother looking, the more Diamond set himself to sing to the two babies.

One thing which had increased their expenses was, that they had been forced to hire another little room for Nanny. When the second baby came, Diamond gave up his room that Nanny might be at hand to help his mother, and went to hers, which, although a fine place to what she had been accustomed to, was not very nice in his eyes. He did not mind the change though, for was not his mother the more comfortable for it? And was not Nanny more comfortable too? And indeed was not Diamond himself more comfortable that other people were more comfortable? And if there was more comfort every way, the change was a happy one.

CHAPTER XXXII

DIAMOND AND RUBY

IT WAS FRIDAY NIGHT, and Diamond, like the rest of the household, had had very little to eat that day. The mother would always pay the week's rent before she laid out anything even on food. His father had been very gloomy—so gloomy that he had actually been cross to his wife. It is a strange thing how the pain of seeing the suffering of those we love will sometimes make us add to their suffering by being cross with them. This comes of not having faith enough in God, and shows how necessary this faith is, for when we lose it, we lose even the kindness which alone can soothe the suffering. Diamond in consequence had gone to bed very quiet and thoughtful—a little troubled indeed.

It had been a very stormy winter; and even now that the spring had come, the north wind often blew. When Diamond went to his bed, which was in a tiny room in the roof, he heard it like the sea moaning; and when he fell asleep he still heard the moaning. All at once he said to himself, "Am I awake, or am I asleep?" But he had no time to answer the question, for there was North Wind calling him. His heart beat very fast, it was such a long time since he had heard that voice. He jumped out of bed, and looked everywhere, but could not see her. "Diamond, come here," she said again and again; but where the *here* was he could not tell. To be sure the room was all but quite dark, and she might be close beside him.

"Dear North Wind," said Diamond, "I want so much to go to you, but I can't tell where."

"Come here, Diamond," was all her answer.

Diamond opened the door, and went out of the room, and down the stair and into the yard. His little heart was in a flutter, for he had long given up all thought of seeing her again. Neither now was he to see her. When he got out, a great puff of wind came against him, and in obedience to it he turned his back, and went as it blew. It blew him right up to the stable-door, and went on blowing.

"She wants me to go into the stable," said Diamond to himself; "but the door is locked."

He knew where the key was, in a certain hole in the wall—far too high for him to get at. He ran to the place, however: just as he reached it there came a wild blast, and down fell the key clanging on the stones at his feet. He picked it up, and ran back and opened the stable-door, and went in. And what do you think he saw?

A little light came through the dusty window from a gas-lamp, sufficient to show him Diamond and Ruby with their two heads up, looking at each other across the partition of their stalls. The light showed the white mark on Diamond's forehead, but Ruby's eye shone so bright, that he thought more light came out of it than went in. This is what he saw.

But what do you think he heard?

He heard the two horses talking to each other—in a strange language, which yet, somehow or other, he could understand, and turn over in his mind in English. The first words he heard were from Diamond, who apparently had been already quarrelling with Ruby.

"Look how fat you are, Ruby!" said old Diamond. "You are so plump and your skin shines so, you ought to be ashamed of yourself."

"There's no harm in being fat," said Ruby in a deprecating tone. "No, nor in being sleek. I may as well shine as not."

"No harm?" retorted Diamond. "Is it no harm to go eating up all poor master's oats, and taking up so much of his time grooming you, when you only work six hours—no, not six hours a day, and, as I hear, get along no faster than a big dray-horse with two tons behind him?—So they tell me."

"Your master's not mine," said Ruby. "I must attend to my own master's interests, and eat all that is given me, and be as sleek and fat as I can, and go no faster than I need."

"Now really if the rest of the horses weren't all asleep, poor things—*they* work till they're tired—I do believe they would get up and kick you out of the stable. You make me ashamed of being a horse. You dare to say my master ain't your master! That's your gratitude for the way he feeds you and spares you! Pray where would your carcass be if it weren't for him?"

"He doesn't do it for my sake. If I were his own horse, he would work me as hard as he does you."

"And I'm proud to be so worked. I wouldn't be as fat as you—not for all you're worth. You're a disgrace to the stable. Look at the horse next you. *He's* something like a horse—all skin and bone. And his master ain't over kind to him either. He put a stinging lash on his whip last week. But that old horse knows he's got the wife and children to keep—as well as his drunken master—and he works *like* a horse. I dare say he grudges his master the beer he drinks, but I don't believe he grudges anything else."

"Well, I don't grudge yours what he gets by me," said Ruby.

"Gets!" retorted Diamond. "What he gets isn't worth grudging. It comes to next to nothing—what with your fat and your shine."

"Well, at least you ought to be thankful you're the better for it. You get a two hours' rest a day out of it."

"I thank my master for that—not you, you lazy fellow! You go along like a buttock of beef upon castors—you do."

"Ain't you afraid I'll kick, if you go on like that, Diamond?"

"Kick! You couldn't kick if you tried. You might heave your rump up half a foot, but for lashing out—oho! If you did, you'd be down on your belly before you could get your legs under you again. It's my belief, once out, they'd stick out for ever. Talk of kicking! Why don't you put one foot before the other now and then when you're in the cab? The abuse master gets for your sake is quite shameful. No decent horse would bring it on him. Depend upon it, Ruby, no cabman likes to be abused any more than his fare. But *his* fares, at least when you are between the shafts, are very much to be excused. Indeed they are."

"Well, you see, Diamond, I don't want to go lame again."

"I don't believe you were so very lame after all—there!"

"Oh, but I was."

"Then I believe it was all your own fault. I'm not lame. I never was lame in all my life. You don't take care of your legs. You never lay them down at night. There you are with your huge carcass crushing down your poor legs all night long. You don't even care for your own legs—so long as you can eat, eat, and sleep, sleep. You a horse indeed!"

"But I tell you I *was* lame."

"I'm not denying there was a puffy look about your off-pastern. But my belief is, it wasn't even grease—it was fat."

"I tell you I put my foot on one of those horrid stones they make the roads with, and it gave my ankle such a twist."

"Ankle indeed! Why should you ape your betters? Horses ain't got any ankles: they're only pasterns. And so long as you don't lift your feet better, but fall asleep between every step, you'll run a good chance of laming all your *ankles* as you call them, one after another. It's not your lively horse that comes to grief in that way. I tell you I believe it wasn't much, and if it was, it was your own fault. There! I've done. I'm going to sleep. I'll try to think as well of you as I can. If you would but step out a bit and run off a little of your fat!"

Here Diamond began to double up his knees; but Ruby spoke again, and, as young Diamond thought, in a rather different tone.

"I say, Diamond, I can't bear to have an honest old horse like you, think of me like that. I will tell you the truth: it was my own fault that I fell lame."

"I told you so," returned the other, tumbling against the partition as he rolled over on his side to give his legs every possible privilege in their narrow circumstances.

"I meant to do it, Diamond."

At the words, the old horse arose with a scramble like thunder, shot his angry head and glaring eye over into Ruby's stall, and said—

"Keep out of my way, you unworthy wretch, or I'll bite you. You a horse! Why did you do that?"

"Because I wanted to grow fat."

"You grease-tub! Oh! my teeth and tail! I thought you were a humbug! Why did you want to get fat? There's no truth to be got out of you but by cross-questioning. You ain't fit to be a horse."

"Because once I *am* fat, my nature is to keep fat for a long time; and I didn't know when master might come home and want to see me."

"You conceited, good-for-nothing brute! You're only fit for the knacker's yard. You wanted to look handsome, did you? Hold your tongue, or I'll break my halter and be at you—with your handsome fat!"

"Never mind, Diamond. You're a good horse. You can't hurt me."

"Can't hurt you! Just let me once try."

"No, you can't."

"Why then?"

"Because I'm an angel."

"What's that?"

"Of course you don't know."

"Indeed I don't."

"I know you don't. An ignorant, rude old human horse, like you, couldn't know it. But there's young Diamond listening to all we're saying; and he knows well enough there are horses in heaven for angels to ride upon, as well as other animals, lions and eagles and bulls, in more important situations. The horses the angels ride, must be angel-horses, else the angels couldn't ride upon them. Well, I'm one of them."

"You ain't."

"Did you ever know a horse tell a lie?"

"Never before. But you've confessed to shamming lame."

"Nothing of the sort. It was necessary I should grow fat, and necessary that good Joseph, your master, should grow lean. I could have pretended to be lame, but that no horse, least of all an angel-horse, would do. So I must *be* lame, and so I sprained my ankle—for the angel-horses *have* ankles—they don't talk horse-slang up there—and it hurt me very much, I assure you, Diamond, though you mayn't be good enough to be able to believe it."

Old Diamond made no reply. He had lain down again, and a sleepy snort, very like a snore, revealed that, if he was not already asleep, he was past understanding a word that Ruby was saying. When young Diamond found this, he thought he might venture to take up the dropt shuttlecock of the conversation.

"I'm good enough to believe it, Ruby," he said.

But Ruby never turned his head, or took any notice of him. I suppose he did not understand more of English than just what the coachmen and stablemen were in the habit of addressing him with. Finding, however, that his companion made no reply, he shot his head over the partition and looking down at him said—

"You just wait till to-morrow, and you'll see whether I'm speaking the truth or not.—I declare the old horse is fast asleep!—Diamond!—No I won't."

Ruby turned away, and began pulling at his hay-rack in silence.

Diamond gave a shiver, and looking round saw that the door of the stable was open. He began to feel as if he had been dreaming, and after a glance about the stable to see if North Wind was anywhere visible, he thought he had better go back to bed.

CHAPTER XXXIII

THE PROSPECT BRIGHTENS

T HE NEXT MORNING, Diamond's mother said to his father, "I'm not quite comfortable about that child again."

"Which child, Martha?" asked Joseph. "You've got a choice now."

"Well, Diamond I mean. I'm afraid he's getting into his queer ways again. He's been at his old trick of walking in his sleep. I saw him run up the stair in the middle of the night."

"Didn't you go after him, wife?"

"Of course I did—and found him fast asleep in his bed. It's because he's had so little meat for the last six weeks, I'm afraid."

"It may be that. I'm very sorry. But if it don't please God to send us enough, what *am* I to do, wife?"

"You can't help it, I know, my dear good man," returned Martha. "And after all I don't know. I don't see why he shouldn't get on as well as the rest of us. There I'm nursing baby all this time, and I get along pretty well. I'm sure, to hear the little man singing, you wouldn't think there was much amiss with him."

For at that moment Diamond was singing like a lark in the clouds. He had the new baby in his arms, while his mother was dressing herself. Joseph was sitting at his breakfast—a little weak tea, dry bread, and very dubious butter—which Nanny had set for him, and which he was enjoying because he was hungry. He had groomed both horses, and had got old Diamond harnessed ready to put to.

"Think of a fat angel, Dulcimer!" said Diamond.

The baby had not been christened yet, but Diamond, in reading his bible, had come upon the word *dulcimer*, and thought it so pretty that ever after he called his sister Dulcimer.

"Think of a red fat angel, Dulcimer!" he repeated; "for Ruby's an angel of a horse, Dulcimer. He sprained his ankle and got fat on purpose."

"What purpose, Diamond?" asked his father.

"Ah! that I can't tell. I suppose to look handsome when his master comes," answered Diamond—"What do *you* think, Dulcimer? It must be for some good, for Ruby's an angel."

"I wish I were rid of him, anyhow," said his father; "for he weighs heavy on my mind."

"No wonder, father: he's so fat," said Diamond. "But you needn't be afraid, for everybody says he's in better condition than when you had him."

"Yes, but he may be as thin as a tin horse before his owner comes. It was too bad to leave him on my hands this way."

"Perhaps he couldn't help it," suggested Diamond. "I dare say he has some good reason for it."

"So I should have said," returned his father, "if he had not driven such a hard bargain with me at first."

"But we don't know what may come of it yet, husband," said his wife. "Mr. Raymond may give a little to boot, seeing you've had more of the bargain than you wanted or reckoned upon."

"I'm afraid not: he's a hard man," said Joseph, as he rose and went to get his cab out.

Diamond resumed his singing. For some time he carolled snatches of everything or anything; but at last it settled down into something like what follows. I cannot tell where or how he got it.

> Where did you come from, baby dear?
> Out of the everywhere into here.
>
> Where did you get your eyes so blue?
> Out of the sky as I came through.
>
> What makes the light in them sparkle and spin?
> Some of the starry spikes left in.
>
> Where did you get that little tear?
> I found it waiting when I got here.
>
> What makes your forehead so smooth and high?
> A soft hand stroked it as I went by.
>
> What makes your cheek like a warm white rose?
> I saw something better than any one knows.
>
> Whence that three-cornered smile of bliss?
> Three angels gave me at once a kiss.
>
> Where did you get this pearly ear?
> God spoke, and it came out to hear.
>
> Where did you get those arms and hands?
> Love made itself into hooks and bands.
>
> Feet, whence did you come, you darling things?
> From the same box as the cherubs' wings.
>
> How did they all just come to be you?
> God thought about me, and so I grew.
>
> But how did you come to us, you dear?
> God thought about you, and so I am here.

"*You* never made that song, Diamond," said his mother.

"No, mother. I wish I had. No, I don't. That would be to take it from somebody else. But it's mine for all that."

"What makes it yours?"

"I love it so."

"Does loving a thing make it yours?"

"I think so, mother—at least more than anything else can. If I didn't love baby (which couldn't be, you know), she wouldn't be mine a bit. But I do love baby, and baby is my very own Dulcimer."

"The baby's mine, Diamond."

"That makes her the more mine, mother."

"How do you make that out?"

"Because you're mine, mother."

"Is that because you love me?"

"Yes, just because. Love makes the only myness," said Diamond.

When his father came home to have his dinner, and change Diamond for Ruby, they saw him look very sad, and he told them he had not had a fare worth mentioning the whole morning.

"We shall all have to go to the workhouse, wife," he said.

"It would be better to go to the back of the north wind," said Diamond, dreamily, not intending to say it aloud.

"So it would," answered his father. "But how are we to get there, Diamond?"

"We must wait till we're taken," returned Diamond.

Before his father could speak again, a knock came to the door, and in walked Mr. Raymond with a smile on his face. Joseph got up and received him respectfully, but not very cordially. Martha set a chair for him, but he would not sit down.

"You are not very glad to see me," he said to Joseph. "You don't want to part with the old horse."

"Indeed, sir, you *are* mistaken there. What with anxiety about him, and bad luck, I've wished I were rid of him a thousand times. It was only to be for three months, and here it's eight or nine."

"I'm sorry to hear such a statement," said Mr. Raymond. "Hasn't he been of service to you?"

"Not much, not with his lameness——"

"Ah!" said Mr. Raymond, hastily—"you've been laming him—have you? That accounts for it. I see, I see."

"It wasn't my fault, and he's all right now. I don't know how it happened, but——"

"He did it on purpose," said Diamond. "He put his foot on a stone just to twist his ankle."

"How do you know that, Diamond?" said his father, turning to him. "I never said so, for I could not think how it came."

"I heard it—in the stable," answered Diamond.

"Let's have a look at him," said Mr. Raymond.

"If you'll step into the yard," said Joseph, "I'll bring him out."

They went, and Joseph, having first taken off his harness, walked Ruby into the middle of the yard.

"Why," said Mr. Raymond, "you've not been using him well."

"I don't know what you mean by that, sir. I didn't expect to hear that from you. He's sound in wind and limb—as sound as a barrel."

"And as big, you might add. Why, he's as fat as a pig! You don't call that good usage!"

Joseph was too angry to make any answer.

"You've not worked him enough, I say. That's not making a good use of him. That's not doing as you'd be done by."

"I shouldn't be sorry if I was served the same, sir."

"He's too fat, I say."

"There was a whole month I couldn't work him at all, and he did nothing but eat his head off. He's an awful eater. I've taken the best part of six hours a day out of him since, but I'm always afraid of his coming to grief again, and so I couldn't make the most even of that. I declare to you, sir, when he's between the shafts, I sit on the box as miserable as if I'd stolen him. He looks all the time as if he was a bottling up of complaints to make of me the minute he set eyes on you again. There! look at him now, squinting round at me with one eye! I declare to you, on my word, I haven't laid the whip on him more than three times."

"I'm glad to hear it. He never did want the whip."

"I didn't say that, sir. If ever a horse wanted the whip, he do. He's brought me to beggary almost with his snail's pace. I'm very glad you've come to rid me of him."

"I don't know that," said Mr. Raymond. "Suppose I were to ask you to buy him of me—cheap."

"I wouldn't have him in a present, sir. I don't like him. And I wouldn't drive a horse that I didn't like—no, not for gold. It can't come to good where there's no love between 'em."

"Just bring out your own horse, and let me see what sort of a pair they'd make."

Joseph laughed rather bitterly as he went to fetch Diamond.

When the two were placed side by side, Mr. Raymond could hardly keep his countenance, but from a mingling of feelings. Beside the great red round barrel Ruby, all body and no legs, Diamond looked like a clothes-horse with a skin thrown over it. There was hardly a spot of him where you could not descry some sign of a bone underneath. Gaunt and grim and weary he stood, kissing his master, and heeding no one else.

"You haven't been using him well," said Mr. Raymond.

"I must say," returned Joseph, throwing an arm round his horse's neck, "that the remark had better have been spared, sir. The horse is worth three of the other now."

"I don't think so. I think they make a very nice pair. If the one's too fat, the other's too lean—so that's all right. And if you won't buy my Ruby, I must buy your Diamond."

"Thank you, sir," said Joseph, in a tone implying anything but thanks.

"You don't seem to like the proposal," said Mr. Raymond.

"I don't," returned Joseph. "I wouldn't part with my old Diamond for his skin as full of nuggets as it is of bones."

"Who said anything about parting with him?"

"You did now, sir."

"No; I didn't. I only spoke of buying him to make a pair with Ruby. We could pare Ruby and patch Diamond a bit. And for height, they are as near a match as I care about. Of course you would be the coachman—if only you would consent to be reconciled to Ruby."

Joseph stood bewildered, unable to answer.

"I've bought a small place in Kent," continued Mr. Raymond, "and I must have a pair to my carriage, for the roads are hilly thereabouts. I don't want to make a show with a pair of high-steppers. I think these will just do. Suppose for a week or two, you set yourself to take Ruby down and bring Diamond up. If we could only lay a pipe from Ruby's sides into Diamond's, it would be the work of a moment. But I fear that wouldn't answer."

A strong inclination to laugh intruded upon Joseph's inclination to cry, and made speech still harder than before.

"I beg your pardon, sir," he said at length. "I've been so miserable, and for so long, that I never thought you was only a chaffing of me when you said I hadn't used the horses well. I did grumble at you, sir, many's the time in my trouble; but whenever I said anything, my little Diamond would look at me with a smile, as much as to say: 'I know him better than you, father;' and upon my word, I always thought the boy must be right."

"Will you sell me Diamond then?"

"I will, sir, on one condition—that if ever you want to part with him or me, you give me the option of buying him. I could *not* part with him, sir. As to who calls him his, that's nothing; for, as Diamond says, it's only loving a thing that can make it yours—and I do love old Diamond, sir, dearly."

"Well, there's a cheque for twenty pounds, which I wrote to offer you for him, in case I should find you had done the handsome thing by Ruby. Will that be enough?"

"It's too much, sir. His body ain't worth it—shoes and all. It's only his heart, sir—that's worth millions—but his heart'll be mine all the same—so it's too much, sir."

"I don't think so. It won't be, at least, by the time we've got him fed up again. You take it and welcome. Just go on with your cabbing for another month, only take it out of Ruby and let Diamond rest; and by that time I shall be ready for you to go down into the country."

"Thank you, sir; thank you. Diamond set you down for a friend, sir, the moment he saw you. I do believe that child of mine knows more than other people."

"I think so too," said Mr. Raymond as he walked away.

He had meant to test Joseph when he made the bargain about Ruby, but had no intention of so greatly prolonging the trial. He had been taken ill in Switzerland, and had been quite unable to return sooner. He went away now highly gratified at finding that he had stood the test, and was a true man.

Joseph rushed in to his wife who had been standing at the window anxiously waiting the result of the long colloquy. When she heard that the horses were to go together in double harness, she burst forth into an immoderate fit of laughter. Diamond came up with the baby in his arms and made big anxious eyes at her, saying,

"What is the matter with you, mother dear? Do cry a little. It will do you good. When father takes ever so small a drop of spirits, he puts water to it."

"You silly darling!" said his mother; "how could I but laugh at the notion of that great fat Ruby going side by side with our poor old Diamond?"

"But why not, mother? With a month's oats, and nothing to do, Diamond'll be nearer Ruby's size than you will father's. I think it's very good for different sorts to go together. Now Ruby will have a chance of teaching Diamond better manners."

"How dare you say such a thing, Diamond?" said his father, angrily. "To compare the two for manners, there's no comparison possible. Our Diamond's a gentleman."

"I don't mean to say he isn't, father; for I dare say some gentlemen judge their neighbours unjustly. That's all I mean. Diamond shouldn't have thought such bad things of Ruby. He didn't try to make the best of him."

"How do you know that, pray?"

"I heard them talking about it one night."

"Who?"

"Why, Diamond and Ruby. Ruby's an angel."

Joseph stared and said no more. For all his new gladness, he was very gloomy as he re-harnessed the angel, for he thought his darling Diamond was going out of his mind.

He could not help thinking rather differently, however, when he found the change that had come over Ruby. Considering his fat, he exerted himself amazingly, and got over the ground with incredible speed. So willing, even anxious, was he to go now, that Joseph had to hold him quite tight.

Then, as he laughed at his own fancies, a new fear came upon him lest the horse should break his wind, and Mr. Raymond have good cause to think he had not been using him well. He might even suppose that he had taken advantage of his new instructions, to let out upon the horse some of his pent-up dislike; whereas in truth, it had so utterly vanished that he felt as if Ruby too had been his friend all the time.

CHAPTER XXXIV

IN THE COUNTRY

Before the end of the month, Ruby had got respectably thin, and Diamond respectably stout. They really began to look fit for double harness.

Joseph and his wife had got their affairs in order, and every thing ready for migrating at the shortest notice; and they felt so peaceful and happy that they judged all the trouble they had gone through well worth enduring. As for Nanny, she had been so happy ever since she left the hospital, that she expected nothing better, and saw nothing attractive in the notion of the country. At the same time, she had not the least idea of what the word *country* meant, for she had never seen anything about her but streets and gas-lamps. Besides, she was more attached to Jim than to Diamond: Jim was a reasonable being, Diamond in her eyes at best only an amiable, over-grown baby, whom no amount of expostulation would ever bring to talk sense, not to say think it. Now that she could manage the baby as well as he, she judged herself altogether his superior. Towards his father and mother, she was all they could wish.

Diamond had taken a great deal of pains and trouble to find Jim, and had at last succeeded through the help of the tall policeman, who was glad to renew his acquaintance with the strange child. Jim had moved his quarters, and had not heard of Nanny's illness till some time after she was taken to the hospital, where he was too shy to go and inquire about her. But when at length she went to live with Diamond's family, Jim was willing enough to go and see her. It was after one of his visits, during which they had been talking of her new prospects, that Nanny expressed to Diamond her opinion of the country.

"There ain't nothing in it but the sun and moon, Diamond."

"There's trees and flowers," said Diamond.

"Well, they ain't no count," returned Nanny.

"Ain't they? They're so beautiful, they make you happy to look at them."

"That's because you're such a silly."

Diamond smiled with a far-away look, as if he were gazing through clouds of green leaves and the vision contented him. But he was thinking with himself what more he could do for Nanny; and that same evening he went to find Mr. Raymond, for he had heard that he had returned to town.

"Ah! how do you do, Diamond?" said Mr. Raymond; "I am glad to see you."

And he was indeed, for he had grown very fond of him. His opinion of him was very different from Nanny's.

"What do you want now, my child?" he asked.

"I'm always wanting something, sir," answered Diamond.

"Well, that's quite right, so long as what you want is right. Everybody is always wanting something; only we don't mention it in the right place often enough. What is it now?"

"There's a friend of Nanny's, a lame boy, called Jim."

"I've heard of him," said Mr. Raymond. "Well?"

"Nanny doesn't care much about going to the country, sir."

"Well, what has that to do with Jim?"

"You couldn't find a corner for Jim to work in—could you, sir?"

"I don't know that I couldn't. That is, if you can show good reason for it."

"He's a good boy, sir."

"Well, so much the better for him."

"I know he can shine boots, sir."

"So much the better for us."

"You want your boots shined in the country—don't you, sir?"

"Yes, to be sure."

"It wouldn't be nice to walk over the flowers with dirty boots—would it, sir?"

"No, indeed."

"They wouldn't like it—would they?"

"No, they wouldn't."

"Then Nanny would be better pleased to go, sir."

"If the flowers didn't like dirty boots to walk over them, Nanny wouldn't mind going to the country? Is that it? I don't quite see it."

"No, sir; I didn't mean that. I meant, if you would take Jim with you to clean your boots, and do odd jobs, you know, sir, then Nanny would like it better. She's so fond of Jim!"

"Now you come to the point, Diamond. I see what you mean, exactly. I will turn it over in my mind. Could you bring Jim to see me?"

"I'll try, sir. But they don't mind me much.—They think I'm silly," added Diamond, with one of his sweetest smiles.

What Mr. Raymond thought, I dare hardly attempt to put down here. But one part of it was, that the highest wisdom must ever appear folly to those who do not possess it.

"I think he would come though—after dark, you know," Diamond continued. "He does well at shining boots. People's kind to lame boys, you know, sir. But after dark, there ain't so much doing."

Diamond succeeded in bringing Jim to Mr. Raymond, and the consequence was that he resolved to give the boy a chance. He provided new clothes for both him and Nanny; and upon a certain day, Joseph took his wife and three children, and Nanny and Jim, by train to a certain station in the county of Kent, where they found a cart waiting to carry them and their luggage to The Mound, which was the name of Mr. Raymond's new residence. I will not describe the varied feelings of the party as they went, or when they arrived. All I will say is, that Diamond, who is my only care, was full of quiet delight—a gladness too deep to talk about.

Joseph returned to town the same night, and the next morning drove Ruby and Diamond down, with the carriage behind them, and Mr. Raymond and a lady in the carriage. For Mr. Raymond was an old bachelor no longer: he was bringing his wife with him to live at The Mound. The moment Nanny saw her, she recognized her as the lady who had lent her the ruby-ring. That ring had been given her by Mr. Raymond.

The weather was very hot, and the woods very shadowy. There were not a great many wild flowers, for it was getting well towards autumn, and the most of the wild flowers rise early to be before the leaves, because if they did not, they would never get a glimpse of the sun for them. So they have their fun over, and are ready to go to bed again by the time the trees are dressed. But there was plenty of the loveliest grass and daisies about

the house, and Diamond's chief pleasure seemed to be to lie amongst them, and breathe the pure air. But all the time, he was dreaming of the country at the back of the north wind, and trying to recall the songs the river used to sing. For this was more like being at the back of the north wind than anything he had known since he left it. Sometimes he would have his little brother, sometimes his little sister, and sometimes both of them in the grass with him, and then he felt just like a cat with her first kittens, he said, only he couldn't purr—all he could do was to sing.

These were very different times from those when he used to drive the cab, but you must not suppose that Diamond was idle. He did not do so much for his mother now, because Nanny occupied his former place; but he helped his father still, both in the stable and the harness-room, and generally went with him on the box that he might learn to drive a pair, and be ready to open the carriage-door. Mr. Raymond advised his father to give him plenty of liberty.

"A boy like that," he said, "ought not to be pushed."

Joseph assented heartily, smiling to himself at the idea of pushing Diamond. After doing everything that fell to his share, the boy had a wealth of time at his disposal. And a happy, sometimes a merry time it was. Only for two months or so, he neither saw nor heard anything of North Wind.

CHAPTER XXXV

I MAKE DIAMOND'S ACQUAINTANCE

M R. RAYMOND'S HOUSE was called The Mound, because it stood upon a little steep knoll, so smooth and symmetrical that it showed itself at once to be artificial. It had, beyond doubt, been built for Queen Elizabeth as a hunting-tower—a place, namely, from the top of which you could see the country for miles on all sides, and so be able to follow with your eyes the flying deer and the pursuing hounds and horsemen. The mound had been cast up to give a good basement-advantage over the neighbouring heights and woods. There was a great quarry-hole not far off, brimful of water, from which, as the current legend stated, the materials forming the heart of the mound—a kind of stone unfit for building—had been dug. The house itself was of brick, and they said the foundations were first laid in the natural level, and then the stones and earth of the mound were heaped about and between them, so that its great height should be well buttressed.

Joseph and his wife lived in a little cottage a short way from the house. It was a real cottage, with a roof of thick thatch, which, in June and July, the wind sprinkled with the red and white petals it shook from the loose topmost sprays of the rose-trees climbing the walls. At first Diamond had a nest under this thatch—a pretty little room with white muslin curtains; but afterwards Mr. and Mrs. Raymond wanted to have him for a page in the house, and his father and mother were quite pleased to have him employed without his leaving them. So he was dressed in a suit of blue, from which his pale face and fair hair came out like the loveliest blossom, and took up his abode in the house.

"Would you be afraid to sleep alone, Diamond?" asked his mistress.

"I don't know what you mean, ma'am," said Diamond. "I never was afraid of anything that I can recollect—not much, at least."

"There's a little room at the top of the house—all alone," she returned: "perhaps you would not mind sleeping there?"

"I can sleep anywhere, and I like best to be high up. Should I be able to see out?"

"I will show you the place," she answered; and taking him by the hand, she led him up and up the oval-winding stair in one of the two towers.

Near the top they entered a tiny little room, with two windows from which you could see over the whole country. Diamond clapped his hands with delight.

"You would like this room, then, Diamond?" said his mistress.

"It's the grandest room in the house," he answered. "I shall be near the stars, and yet not far from the tops of the trees. That's just what I like."

I daresay he thought also, that it would be a nice place for North Wind to call at in passing; but he said nothing of that sort. Below him spread a lake of green leaves, with glimpses of grass here and there at the bottom of it. As he looked down, he saw a squirrel appear suddenly, and as suddenly vanish amongst the topmost branches.

"Aha! little squirrel," he cried, "my nest is built higher than yours."

"You can be up here with your books as much as you like," said his mistress. "I will have a little bell hung at the door, which I can ring when I want you. Half-way down the stair is the drawing-room."

So Diamond was installed as page, and his new room got ready for him.

It was very soon after this that I came to know Diamond. I was then a tutor in a family whose estate adjoined the little property belonging to The Mound. I had made the acquaintance of Mr. Raymond in London some time before, and was walking up the drive towards the house to call upon him one fine warm evening, when I saw Diamond for the first time. He was sitting at the foot of a great beech-tree, a few yards from the road, with a book on his knees. He did not see me. I walked up behind the tree, and peeping over his shoulder, saw that he was reading a fairy-book.

"What are you reading?" I said, and spoke suddenly, with the hope of seeing a startled little face look round at me. Diamond turned his head as quietly as if he were only obeying his mother's voice, and the calmness of his face rebuked my unkind desire and made me ashamed of it.

"I am reading the story of the Little Lady and the Goblin Prince," said Diamond.

"I am sorry I don't know the story," I returned. "Who is it by?"

"Mr. Raymond made it."

"Is he your uncle?" I asked at a guess.

"No. He's my master."

"What do you do for him?" I asked respectfully.

"Anything he wishes me to do," he answered. "I am busy for him now. He gave me this story to read. He wants my opinion upon it."

"Don't you find it rather hard to make up your mind?"

"Oh dear no! Any story always tells me itself what I'm to think about it. Mr. Raymond doesn't want me to say whether it is a clever story or not, but whether I like it, and why I like it. I never can tell what they call clever from what they call silly, but I always know whether I like a story or not."

"And can you always tell why you like it or not?"

"No. Very often I can't at all. Sometimes I can. I always know, but I can't always tell why. Mr. Raymond writes the stories, and then tries them on me. Mother does the same when she makes jam. She's made such a lot of jam since we came here! And she always makes me taste it to see if it'll do. Mother knows by the face I make whether it will or not."

At this moment I caught sight of two more children approaching. One was a handsome girl, the other a pale-faced, awkward-looking boy, who limped much on one leg. I withdrew a little, to see what would follow, for they seemed in some consternation. After a few hurried words, they went off together, and I pursued my way to the house, where I was as kindly received by Mr. and Mrs. Raymond as I could have desired. From them I learned something of Diamond, and was in consequence the more glad to find him, when I returned, seated in the same place as before.

"What did the boy and girl want with you, Diamond?" I asked.

"They had seen a creature that frightened them."

"And they came to tell you about it?"

"They couldn't get water out of the well for it. So they wanted me to go with them."

"They're both bigger than you."

"Yes, but they were frightened at it."

"And weren't you frightened at it?"

"No."

"Why?"

"Because I'm silly. I'm never frightened at things."

I could not help thinking of the old meaning of the word *silly*.

"And what was it?" I asked.

"I think it was a kind of an angel—a very little one. It had a long body and great wings, which it drove about it so fast that they grew a thin cloud all round it. It flew backwards and forwards over the well, or hung right in the middle, making a mist of its wings, as if its business was to take care of the water."

"And what did you do to drive it away?"

"I didn't drive it away. I knew, whatever the creature was, the well was to get water out of. So I took the jug, dipped it in, and drew the water."

"And what did the creature do?"

"Flew about."

"And it didn't hurt you?"

"No. Why should it? I wasn't doing anything wrong."

"What did your companions say then?"

"They said—'Thank you, Diamond. What a dear silly you are!' "

"And weren't you angry with them?"

"No! Why should I? I should like if they would play with me a little; but they always like better to go away together when their work is over. They never heed me. I don't mind it much, though. The other creatures are friendly. They don't run away from me. Only they're all so busy with their own work, they don't mind me much."

"Do you feel lonely, then?"

"Oh, no! When nobody minds me, I get into my nest, and look up. And then the sky does mind me, and thinks about me."

"Where is your nest?"

He rose, saying, "I will show you," and led me to the other side of the tree.

There hung a little rope-ladder from one of the lower boughs. The boy climbed up the ladder and got upon the bough. Then he climbed further into the leafy branches, and went out of sight.

After a little while, I heard his voice coming down out of the tree.

"I am in my nest now," said the voice.

"I can't see you," I returned.

"I can't see you either, but I can see the first star peeping out of the sky. I should like to get up into the sky. Don't you think I shall, some day?"

"Yes, I do. Tell me what more you see up there."

"I don't see anything more, except a few leaves, and the big sky over me. It goes swinging about. The earth is all behind my back. There comes another star! The wind is like kisses from a big lady. When I get up here I feel as if I were in North Wind's arms."

This was the first I heard of North Wind.

The whole ways and look of the child, so full of quiet wisdom, yet so ready to accept the judgment of others in his own dispraise, took hold of my heart, and I felt myself wonderfully drawn towards him. It seemed to me, somehow, as if little Diamond possessed the secret of life, and was himself what he was so ready to think the lowest living thing—an angel of God with something special to say or do. A gush of reverence came over me, and with a single *good night*, I turned and left him in his nest.

I saw him often after this, and gained so much of his confidence that he told me all I have told you. I cannot pretend to account for it. I leave that for each philosophical reader to do after his own fashion. The easiest way is that of Nanny and Jim, who said often to each other that Diamond had a tile loose. But Mr. Raymond was much of my opinion concerning the boy; while Mrs. Raymond confessed that she often rang her bell just to have once more the pleasure of seeing the lovely stillness of the boy's face, with those blue eyes which seemed rather made for other people to look into than for himself to look out of.

It was plainer to others than to himself that he felt the desertion of Nanny and Jim. They appeared to regard him as a mere toy, except when they found he could minister to the increase of their privileges or indulgences, when they made no scruple of using him—generally with success. They were however well-behaved to a wonderful degree; while I have little doubt that much of their good behaviour was owing to the unconscious influence of the boy they called God's baby.

One very strange thing is, that I could never find out where he got some of his many songs. At times they would be but bubbles blown out of a nursery rhyme, as was the following, which I heard him sing one evening to his little Dulcimer. There were about a score of sheep feeding in a paddock near him, their white wool dyed a pale rose in the light of the setting sun. Those in the long shadows from the trees were dead white; those in the sunlight were half glorified with pale rose.

> Little Bo Peep, she lost her sheep,
>   And didn't know where to find them;
> They were over the height and out of sight,

Trailing their tails behind them.

Little Bo Peep woke out of her sleep,
 Jump'd up and set out to find them:
"The silly things, they've got no wings,
 And they've left their trails behind them:

"They've taken their tails, but they've left their trails,
 "And so I shall follow and find them;"
For wherever a tail had dragged a trail,
 The long grass grew behind them.

And day's eyes and butter-cups, cow's lips and crow's feet
 Were glittering in the sun.
She threw down her book, and caught up her crook,
 And after her sheep did run.

She ran, and she ran, and ever as she ran,
 The grass grew higher and higher;
Till over the hill the sun began
 To set in a flame of fire.

She ran on still—up the grassy hill,
 And the grass grew higher and higher;
When she reached its crown, the sun was down,
 And had left a trail of fire.

The sheep and their tails were gone, all gone—
 And no more trail behind them;
Yes, yes! they were there—long-tailed and fair,
 But, alas! she could not find them.

Purple and gold, and rosy and blue,
 With their tails all white behind them,
Her sheep they did run in the trail of the sun;
 She saw them, but could not find them.

After the sun, like clouds they did run,
 But she knew they were her sheep:
She sat down to cry, and look up at the sky,
 But she cried herself asleep.

And as she slept the dew fell fast,
 And the wind blew from the sky;
And strange things took place that shun the day's face.
 Because they are sweet and shy.

Nibble, nibble, crop! she heard as she woke:
 A hundred little lambs
Did pluck and eat the grass so sweet
 That grew in the trails of their dams.

Little Bo Peep caught up her crook,
  And wiped the tears that did blind her;
And nibble nibble crop! without a stop,
  The lambs came eating behind her.

Home, home she came, both tired and lame,
  With three times as many sheep.
In a month or more, they'll be as big as before,
  And then she'll laugh in her sleep.

But what would you say, if one fine day,
  When they've got their bushiest tails,
Their grown up game should be just the same,
  And she have to follow their trails?

Never weep, Bo Peep, though you lose your sheep,
  And do not know where to find them;
'Tis after the sun the mothers have run,
  And there are their lambs behind them.

I confess again to having touched up a little, but it loses far more in Diamond's sweet voice singing it than it gains by a rhyme here and there.

Some of them were out of books Mr. Raymond had given him. These he always knew, but about the others he could seldom tell. Sometimes he would say, "I made that one;" but generally he would say, "I don't know; I found it somewhere;" or "I got it at the back of the north wind."

One evening I found him sitting on the grassy slope under the house, with his Dulcimer in his arms and his little brother rolling on the grass beside them. He was chanting in his usual way, more like the sound of a brook than anything else I can think of. When I went up to them he ceased his chant.

"Do go on, Diamond. Don't mind me," I said.

He began again at once. While he sang, Nanny and Jim sat a little way off, one hemming a pocket-handkerchief, and the other reading a story to her, but they never heeded Diamond. This is as near what he sang as I can recollect, or reproduce rather.

What would you see if I took you up
  To my little nest in the air?
You would see the sky like a clear blue cup
  Turned upside downwards there.

What would you do if I took you there
  To my little nest in the tree?
My child with cries would trouble the air,
  To get what she could but see.

What would you get in the top of the tree
  For all your crying and grief?
Not a star would you clutch of all you see—
  You could only gather a leaf.

But when you had lost your greedy grief,
    Content to see from afar,
You would find in your hand a withering leaf,
    In your heart a shining star.

As Diamond went on singing, it grew very dark, and just as he ceased there came a great flash of lightning, that blinded us all for a moment. Dulcimer crowed with pleasure; but when the roar of thunder came after it, the little brother gave a loud cry of terror. Nanny and Jim came running up to us, pale with fear. Diamond's face too was paler than usual, but with delight. Some of the glory seemed to have clung to it, and remained shining.

"You're not frightened—are you, Diamond?" I said.

"No. Why should I be?" he answered with his usual question, looking up in my face with calm shining eyes.

"He ain't got sense to be frightened," said Nanny, going up to him and giving him a pitying hug.

"Perhaps there's more sense in not being frightened, Nanny," I returned. "Do you think the lightning can do as it likes?"

"It might kill you," said Jim.

"Oh no, it mightn't!" said Diamond.

As he spoke there came another great flash, and a tearing crack.

"There's a tree struck!" I said; and when we looked round, after the blinding of the flash had left our eyes, we saw a huge bough of the beech-tree in which was Diamond's nest, hanging to the ground like the broken wing of a bird.

"There!" cried Nanny; "I told you so. If you had been up there you see what would have happened, you little silly!"

"No, I don't," said Diamond, and began to sing to Dulcimer. All I could hear of the song, for the other children were going on with their chatter, was—

> The clock struck one,
> And the mouse came down,
> Dickery, dickery, dock!

Then there came a blast of wind, and the rain followed in straight-pouring lines, as if out of a watering-pot. Diamond jumped up with his little Dulcimer in his arms, and Nanny caught up the little boy; and they ran for the cottage. Jim vanished with a double shuffle, and I went into the house.

When I came out again to return home, the clouds were gone, and the evening sky glimmered through the trees, blue, and pale-green towards the west, I turned my steps a little aside to look at the stricken beech. I saw the bough torn from the stem, and that was all the twilight would allow me to see. While I stood gazing, down from the sky came a sound of singing, but the voice was neither of lark nor of nightingale: it was sweeter than either: it was the voice of Diamond, up in his airy nest:

> The lightning and thunder,
>   They go and they come;
> But the stars and the stillness
>   Are always at home.

And then the voice ceased:

"Good night, Diamond," I said.

"Good night, sir," answered Diamond.

As I walked away pondering, I saw the great black top of the beech swaying about against the sky in an upper wind, and heard the murmur as of many dim half-articulate voices filling the solitude around Diamond's nest.

CHAPTER XXXVI

DIAMOND QUESTIONS NORTH WIND

MY READERS will not wonder that, after this, I did my very best to gain the friendship of Diamond. Nor did I find this at all difficult, the child was so ready to trust. Upon one subject alone was he reticent—the story of his relations with North Wind. I fancy he could not quite make up his mind what to think of them. At all events it was some little time before he trusted me with this, only then he told me everything. If I could not regard it all in exactly the same light as he did, I was, while guiltless of the least pretence, fully sympathetic, and he was satisfied without demanding of me any theory of difficult points involved. I let him see plainly enough, that whatever might be the explanation of the marvellous experience, I would have given much for a similar one myself.

On an evening soon after the thunderstorm, in a late twilight, with a half-moon high in the heavens, I came upon Diamond in the act of climbing by his little ladder into the beech-tree.

"What are you always going up there for, Diamond?" I heard Nanny ask, rather rudely, I thought.

"Sometimes for one thing, sometimes for another, Nanny," answered Diamond, looking skywards as he climbed.

"You'll break your neck some day," she said.

"I'm going up to look at the moon to-night," he added, without heeding her remark.

"You'll see the moon just as well down here," she returned.

"I don't think so."

"You'll be no nearer to her up there."

"Oh, yes! I shall. I must be nearer her, you know. I wish I could dream as pretty dreams about her as you can, Nanny."

"You silly! you never have done about that dream. I never dreamed but that one, and it was nonsense enough, I'm sure."

"It wasn't nonsense. It was a beautiful dream—and a funny one too, both in one."

"But what's the good of talking about it that way, when you know it was only a dream? Dreams ain't true."

"That one was true, Nanny. You know it was. Didn't you come to grief for doing what you were told not to do? And isn't that true?'

"I can't get any sense into him," exclaimed Nanny, with an expression of mild despair. "Do you really believe, Diamond, that there's a house in the moon, with a beautiful lady, and a crooked old man and dusters in it?"

"If there isn't, there's something better," he answered, and vanished in the leaves over our heads.

I went into the house, where I visited often in the evenings. When I came out, there was a little wind blowing, very pleasant after the heat of the day, for although it was late summer now it was still hot. The tree-tops were swinging about in it. I took my way past the beech, and called up to see if Diamond were still in his nest in its rocking head.

"Are you there, Diamond?" I said.

"Yes, sir," came his clear voice in reply.

"Isn't it growing too dark for you to get down safely?"

"Oh, no, sir—if I take time to it. I know my way so well, and never let go with one hand till I've a good hold with the other."

"Do be careful," I insisted—foolishly, seeing the boy was as careful as he could be already.

"I'm coming," he returned. "I've got all the moon I want to-night."

I heard a rustling and a rustling drawing nearer and nearer. Three or four minutes elapsed, and he appeared at length creeping down his little ladder. I took him in my arms, and set him on the ground.

"Thank you, sir," he said. "That's the north wind blowing, isn't it, sir?"

"I can't tell," I answered. "It feels cool and kind, and I think it may be. But I couldn't be sure except it were stronger; for a gentle wind might turn any way amongst the trunks of the trees."

"I shall know when I get up to my own room," said Diamond. "I think I hear my mistress's bell. Good night, sir."

He ran to the house, and I went home.

His mistress had rung for him only to send him to bed, for she was very careful over him, and I daresay thought he was not looking well. When he reached his own room, he opened both his windows, one of which looked to the north and the other to the east, to find how the wind blew. It blew right in at the northern window. Diamond was very glad, for he thought perhaps North Wind herself would come now: a real north wind had never blown all the time since he left London. But, as she always came of herself, and never when he was looking for her, and indeed almost never when he was thinking of her, he shut the east window, and went to bed. Perhaps some of my readers may wonder that he could go to sleep with such an expectation; and, indeed, if I had not known him, I should have wondered at it myself; but it was one of his peculiarities, and seemed nothing strange in him. He was so full of quietness that he could go to sleep almost any time, if he only composed himself and let the sleep come. This time he went fast asleep as usual.

But he woke in the dim blue night. The moon had vanished. He thought he heard a knocking at his door.

"Somebody wants me," he said to himself, and jumping out of bed, ran to open it.

But there was no one there. He closed it again, and, the noise still continuing, found that another door in the room was rattling. It belonged to a closet, he thought, but he had never been able to open it. The wind blowing in at the window must be shaking it. He would go and see if it was so.

The door now opened quite easily, but to his surprise, instead of a closet he found a long narrow room. The moon, which was sinking in the west, shone in at an open window at the further end. The room was low with a coved ceiling, and occupied the whole top of the house, immediately under the roof. It was quite empty. The yellow light of the half-moon streamed over the dark floor. He was so delighted at the discovery of the strange desolate moonlit place close to his own snug little room, that he began to dance and skip about the floor. The wind came in through the door he had left open, and blew about him as he danced, and he kept running towards it that it might blow in his face. He kept picturing to himself the many places, lovely and desolate, the hill-sides and farm-yards and tree-tops and meadows, over which it had blown on its way to the Mound. And as he danced, he grew more and more delighted with the motion and the wind; his feet grew stronger, and his body lighter, until at length it seemed as if he were borne up on the air, and could almost fly. So strong did his feeling become, that at last he began to doubt whether he was not in one of those precious dreams he had so often had, in which he floated about on the air at will. But something made him look up, and to his unspeakable delight, he found his uplifted hands lying in those of North Wind, who was dancing with him, round and round the long bare room, her hair now falling to the floor, now filling the arched ceiling, her eyes shining on him like thinking stars, and the sweetest of grand smiles playing breezily about her beautiful mouth. She was, as so often before, of the height of a rather tall lady. She did not stoop in order to dance with him, but held his hands high in hers. When he saw her, he gave one spring, and his arms were about her neck, and her arms holding him to her bosom. The same moment she swept with him through the open window in at which the moon was shining, made a circuit like a bird about to alight, and settled with him in his nest on the top of the great beech-tree. There she placed him on her lap and began to hush him as if he were her own baby, and Diamond was so entirely happy that he did not care to speak a word. At length, however, he found that he was going to sleep, and that would be to lose so much, that, pleasant as it was, he could not consent.

"Please, dear North Wind," he said, "I am so happy that I'm afraid it's a dream. How am I to know that it's not a dream?"

"What does it matter?" returned North Wind.

"I should cry," said Diamond.

"But why should you cry? The dream, if it is a dream, is a pleasant one—is it not?"

"That's just why I want it to be true."

"Have you forgotten what you said to Nanny about her dream?"

"It's not for the dream itself—I mean, it's not for the pleasure of it," answered Diamond, "for I have that, whether it be a dream or not; it's for you, North Wind: I can't bear to find it a dream, because then I should lose you. You would be nobody then, and I could not bear that. You ain't a dream, are you, dear North Wind? Do say *No*, else I shall cry, and come awake, and you'll be gone for ever. I daren't dream about you once again if you ain't anybody."

"I'm either not a dream, or there's something better that's not a dream, Diamond," said North Wind, in a rather sorrowful tone, he thought.

"But it's not something better—it's you I want, North Wind," he persisted, already beginning to cry a little.

She made no answer, but rose with him in her arms and sailed away over the tree-tops till they came to a meadow, where a flock of sheep was feeding.

"Do you remember what the song you were singing a week ago says about Bo-Peep—how she lost her sheep, but got twice as many lambs?" asked North Wind, sitting down on the grass, and placing him in her lap as before.

"Oh yes, I do, well enough," answered Diamond; "but I never just quite liked that rhyme."

"Why not, child?"

"Because it seems to say one's as good as another, or two new ones are better than one that's lost. I've been thinking about it a great deal, and it seems to me that although any one sixpence is as good as any other sixpence, not twenty lambs would do instead of one sheep whose face you knew. Somehow, when once you've looked into anybody's eyes, right deep down into them, I mean, nobody will do for that one any more. Nobody, ever so beautiful or so good, will make up for that one going out of sight. So you see, North Wind, I can't help being frightened to think that perhaps I am only dreaming, and you are nowhere at all. Do tell me that you are my own real beautiful North Wind."

Again she rose, and shot herself into the air, as if uneasy because she could not answer him; and Diamond lay quiet in her arms, waiting for what she would say. He tried to see up into her face, for he was dreadfully afraid she was not answering him because she could not say that she was not a dream; but she had let her hair fall over her face so that he could not see it. This frightened him still more.

"Do speak, North Wind," he said at last.

"I never speak when I have nothing to say," she replied.

"Then I do think you must be a real North Wind, and no dream," said Diamond.

"But I'm looking for something to say all the time."

"But I don't want you to say what's hard to find. If you were to say one word to comfort me that wasn't true, then I should know you must be a dream, for a great beautiful lady like you could never tell a lie."

"But she mightn't know how to say what she had to say, so that a little boy like you would understand it," said North Wind. "Here, let us get down again, and I will try to tell you what I think. You mustn't suppose I am able to answer all your questions, though. There are a great many things I don't understand more than you do."

She descended on a grassy hillock, in the midst of a wild furzy common. There was a rabbit-warren underneath, and some of the rabbits came out of their holes, in the moonlight, looking very sober and wise, just like patriarchs standing in their tent-doors, and looking about them before going to bed. When they saw North Wind, instead of turning round and vanishing again with a thump of their heels, they cantered slowly up to her and snuffed all about her with their long upper lips, which moved every way at once. That was their way of kissing her; and, as she talked to Diamond, she would every now and then stroke down their furry backs, or lift and play with their long ears. They would, Diamond thought, have leaped upon her lap, but that he was there already.

"I think," said she, after they had been sitting silent for a while, "that if I were only a dream, you would not have been able to love me so. You love me when you are not with me, don't you?"

"Indeed I do," answered Diamond, stroking her hand. "I see! I see! How could I be able to love you as I do if you weren't there at all, you know? Besides, I couldn't be able to dream anything half so beautiful all out of my own head; or if I did, I couldn't love a fancy of my own like that, could I?"

"I think not. You might have loved me in a dream, dreamily, and forgotten me when you woke, I daresay, but not loved me like a real being as you love me. Even then, I don't think you could dream anything that hadn't something real like it somewhere. But you've seen me in many shapes, Diamond: you remember I was a wolf once—don't you?"

"Oh yes—a good wolf that frightened a naughty drunken nurse."

"Well, suppose I were to turn ugly, would you rather I weren't a dream then?"

"Yes; for I should know that you were beautiful inside all the same. You would love me, and I should love you all the same. I shouldn't like you to look ugly, you know. But I shouldn't believe it a bit."

"Not if you saw it?"

"No, not if I saw it ever so plain."

"There's my Diamond! I will tell you all I know about it then. I don't think I am just what you fancy me to be. I have to shape myself various ways to various people. But the heart of me is true. People call me by dreadful names, and think they know all about me. But they don't. Sometimes they call me Bad Fortune, sometimes Evil Chance, sometimes Ruin; and they have another name for me which they think the most dreadful of all."

"What is that?" asked Diamond, smiling up in her face.

"I won't tell you that name. Do you remember having to go through me to get into the country at my back?"

"Oh yes, I do. How cold you were, North Wind! and so white, all but your lovely eyes! My heart grew like a lump of ice, and then I forgot for a while."

"You were very near knowing what they call me then. Would you be afraid of me if you had to go through me again?"

"No. Why should I? Indeed I should be glad enough, if it was only to get another peep of the country at your back."

"You've never seen it yet."

"Haven't I, North Wind? Oh! I'm so sorry! I thought I had. What did I see then?"

"Only a picture of it. The real country at my real back is ever so much more beautiful than that. You shall see it one day—perhaps before very long."

"Do they sing songs there?"

"Don't you remember the dream you had about the little boys that dug for the stars?"

"Yes, that I do. I thought you must have had something to do with that dream, it was so beautiful."

"Yes; I gave you that dream."

"Oh! thank you. Did you give Nanny her dream too—about the moon and the bees?"

"Yes. I was the lady that sat at the window of the moon."

"Oh, thank you. I was almost sure you had something to do with that too. And did you tell Mr. Raymond the story about the Princess Daylight?"

"I believe I had something to do with it. At all events he thought about it one night when he couldn't sleep. But I want to ask you whether you remember the song the boy-angels sang in that dream of yours."

"No. I couldn't keep it, do what I would, and I did try."

"That was my fault."

"How could that be, North Wind?"

"Because I didn't know it properly myself, and so I couldn't teach it to you. I could only make a rough guess at something like what it would be, and so I wasn't able to make you dream it hard enough to remember it. Nor would I have done so if I could, for it was not correct. I made you dream pictures of it, though. But you will hear the very song itself when you do get to the back of——"

"My own dear North Wind," said Diamond, finishing the sentence for her, and kissing the arm that held him leaning against her.

"And now we've settled all this—for the time, at least," said North Wind.

"But I can't feel quite sure yet," said Diamond.

"You must wait a while for that. Meantime you may be hopeful, and content not to be quite sure. Come now, I will take you home again, for it won't do to tire you too much."

"Oh! no, no. I'm not the least tired," pleaded Diamond.

"It is better, though."

"Very well; if you wish it," yielded Diamond with a sigh.

"You are a dear good boy," said North Wind. "I will come for you again to-morrow night and take you out for a longer time. We shall make a little journey together, in fact. We shall start earlier; and as the moon will be later, we shall have a little moonlight all the way."

She rose, and swept over the meadow and the trees. In a few moments the Mound appeared below them. She sank a little, and floated in at the window of Diamond's room. There she laid him on his bed, covered him over, and in a moment he was lapt in a dreamless sleep.

CHAPTER XXXVII

ONCE MORE

THE NEXT NIGHT Diamond was seated by his open window, with his head on his hand, rather tired, but so eagerly waiting for the promised visit that he was afraid he could not sleep. But he started suddenly, and found that he had been already asleep. He rose, and looking out of the window saw something white against his beech-tree. It was North Wind. She was holding by one hand to a top branch. Her hair and her garments went floating away behind her over the tree, whose top was swaying about while the others were still.

"Are you ready, Diamond?" she asked.

"Yes," answered Diamond, "quite ready."

In a moment she was at the window, and her arms came in and took him. She sailed away so swiftly that he could at first mark nothing but the speed with which the clouds above and the dim earth below went rushing past. But soon he began to see that the sky

was very lovely, with mottled clouds all about the moon, on which she threw faint colours like those of mother-of-pearl, or an opal. The night was warm, and in the lady's arms he did not feel the wind which down below was making waves in the ripe corn, and ripples on the rivers and lakes. At length they descended on the side of an open earthy hill, just where, from beneath a stone, a spring came bubbling out.

"I am going to take you along this little brook," said North Wind. "I am not wanted for anything else to-night, so I can give you a treat."

She stooped over the stream, and holding Diamond down close to the surface of it, glided along level with its flow as it ran down the hill. And the song of the brook came up into Diamond's ears, and grew and grew and changed with every turn. It seemed to Diamond to be singing the story of its life to him. And so it was. It began with a musical tinkle which changed to a babble and then to a gentle rushing. Sometimes its song would almost cease, and then break out again, tinkle, babble, and rush, all at once. At the bottom of the hill they came to a small river, into which the brook flowed with a muffled but merry sound. Along the surface of the river, darkly clear below them in the moonlight, they floated; now, where it widened out into a little lake, they would hover for a moment over a bed of water-lilies, and watch them swing about, folded in sleep, as the water on which they leaned swayed in the presence of North Wind; and now they would watch the fishes asleep among their roots below. Sometimes she would hold Diamond over a deep hollow curving into the bank, that he might look far into the cool stillness. Sometimes she would leave the river and sweep across a clover-field. The bees were all at home, and the clover was asleep. Then she would return and follow the river. It grew wider and wider as it went. Now the armies of wheat and of oats would hang over its rush from the opposite banks; now the willows would dip low branches in its still waters; and now it would lead them through stately trees and grassy banks into a lovely garden, where the roses and lilies were asleep, the tender flowers quite folded up, and only a few wide-awake and sending out their life in sweet strong odours. Wider and wider grew the stream, until they came upon boats lying along its banks, which rocked a little in the flutter of North Wind's garments. Then came houses on the banks, each standing in a lovely lawn, with grand trees; and in parts the river was so high that some of the grass and the roots of some of the trees were under water, and Diamond, as they glided through between the stems, could see the grass at the bottom of the water. Then they would leave the river and float about and over the houses, one after another— beautiful rich houses, which, like fine trees, had taken centuries to grow. There was scarcely a light to be seen, and not a movement to be heard: all the people in them lay fast asleep.

"What a lot of dreams they must be dreaming!" said Diamond.

"Yes," returned North Wind. "They can't surely be all lies—can they?"

"I should think it depends a little on who dreams them," suggested Diamond.

"Yes," said North Wind. "The people who think lies, and do lies, are very likely to dream lies. But the people who love what is true will surely now and then dream true things. But then something depends on whether the dreams are home-grown, or whether the seed of them is blown over somebody else's garden-wall. Ah! there's some one awake in this house!"

They were floating past a window in which a light was burning. Diamond heard a moan, and looked up anxiously in North Wind's face.

"It's a lady," said North Wind. "She can't sleep for pain."

"Couldn't you do something for her?" said Diamond.

"No, I can't. But you could."

"What could I do?"

"Sing a little song to her."

"She wouldn't hear me."

"I will take you in, and then she will hear you."

"But that would be rude, wouldn't it? You can go where you please, of course, but I should have no business in her room."

"You may trust me, Diamond. I shall take as good care of the lady as of you. The window is open. Come."

By a shaded lamp, a lady was seated in a white wrapper, trying to read, but moaning every minute. North Wind floated behind her chair, set Diamond down, and told him to sing something. He was a little frightened, but he thought a while, and then sang:—

> The sun is gone down,
>   And the moon's in the sky;
> But the sun will come up,
>   And the moon be laid by
>
> The flower is asleep,
>   But it is not dead;
> When the morning shines,
>   It will lift its head.

> When winter comes,
> It will die—no, no;
> It will only hide
> From the frost and the snow.

> Sure is the summer,
> Sure is the sun;
> The night and the winter
> Are shadows that run.

The lady never lifted her eyes from her book, or her head from her hand.

As soon as Diamond had finished, North Wind lifted him and carried him away.

"Didn't the lady hear me?" asked Diamond, when they were once more floating down with the river.

"Oh, yes, she heard you," answered North Wind.

"Was she frightened then?"

"Oh, no."

"Why didn't she look to see who it was?"

"She didn't know you were there."

"How could she hear me then?"

"She didn't hear you with her ears."

"What did she hear me with?"

"With her heart."

"Where did she think the words came from?"

"She thought they came out of the book she was reading. She will search all through it to-morrow to find them, and won't be able to understand it at all."

"Oh, what fun!" said Diamond. "What *will* she do?"

"I can tell you what she won't do: she'll never forget the meaning of them; and she'll never be able to remember the words of them."

"If she sees them in Mr. Raymond's book, it will puzzle her, won't it?"

"Yes, that it will. She will never be able to understand it."

"Until she gets to the back of the north wind," suggested Diamond.

"Until she gets to the back of the north wind," assented the lady.

"Oh!" cried Diamond, "I know now where we are. Oh! do let me go into the old garden, and into mother's room, and Diamond's stall. I wonder if the hole is at the back of my bed still. I should like to stay there all the rest of the night. It won't take you long to get home from here, will it, North Wind?"

"No," she answered; "you shall stay as long as you like."

"Oh, how jolly!" cried Diamond, as North Wind sailed over the house with him, and set him down on the lawn at the back.

Diamond ran about the lawn for a little while in the moonlight. He found part of it cut up into flower-beds, and the little summer-house with the coloured glass and the great elm-tree gone. He did not like this, and ran into the stable. There were no horses there at all. He ran upstairs. The rooms were empty. The only thing left that he cared about was the hole in the wall where his little bed had stood; and that was not enough to make him wish to stop. He ran down the stair again, and out upon the lawn. There he threw himself down and began to cry. It was all so dreary and lost!

"I thought I liked the place so much," said Diamond to himself, "but I find I don't care about it. I suppose it's only the people in it that make you like a place, and when they're gone, it's dead, and you don't care a bit about it. North Wind told me I might stop as long as I liked, and I've stopped longer already—North Wind!" he cried aloud, turning his face towards the sky.

The moon was under a cloud, and all was looking dull and dismal. A star shot from the sky, and fell in the grass beside him. The moment it lighted, there stood North Wind.

"Oh!" cried Diamond, joyfully, "were you the shooting star?"

"Yes, my child."

"Did you hear me call you then?"

"Yes."

"So high up as that?"

"Yes; I heard you quite well."

"Do take me home."

"Have you had enough of your old home already?"

"Yes, more than enough. It isn't a home at all now."

"I thought that would be it," said North Wind. "Everything, dreaming and all, has got a soul in it, or else it's worth nothing, and we don't care a bit about it. Some of our thoughts are worth nothing, because they've got no soul in them. The brain puts them into the mind, not the mind into the brain."

"But how can you know about that, North Wind? You haven't got a body."

"If I hadn't, you wouldn't know anything about me. No creature can know another without the help of a body. But I don't care to talk about that. It is time for you to go home."

So saying, North Wind lifted Diamond and bore him away.

CHAPTER XXXVIII

AT THE BACK OF THE NORTH WIND

I DID NOT SEE DIAMOND for a week or so after this, and then he told me what I have now told you. I should have been astonished at his being able even to report such conversations as he said he had had with North Wind, had I not known already that some children are profound in metaphysics. But a fear crosses me, lest, by telling so much about my friend, I should lead people to mistake him for one of those consequential, priggish little monsters, who are always trying to say clever things, and looking to see whether people appreciate them. When a child like that dies, instead of having a silly book written about him, he should be stuffed like one of those awful big-headed fishes you see in museums. But Diamond never troubled his head about what people thought of him. He never set up for knowing better than others. The wisest things he said came

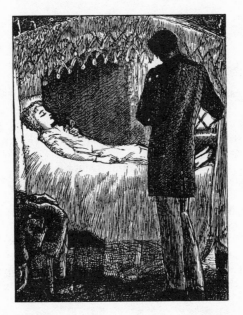

out when he wanted one to help him with some difficulty he was in. He was not even offended with Nanny and Jim for calling him a silly. He supposed there was something in it, though he could not quite understand what. I suspect however that the other name they gave him, *God's Baby*, had some share in reconciling him to it.

Happily for me, I was as much interested in metaphysics as Diamond himself, and therefore, while he recounted his conversations with North Wind, I did not find myself at all in a strange sea, although certainly I could not always feel the bottom, being indeed convinced that the bottom was miles away.

"*Could* it be all dreaming, do you think, sir?" he asked anxiously.

"I daren't say, Diamond," I answered. "But at least there is one thing you may be sure of, that there is a still better love than that of the wonderful being you call North Wind. Even if she be a dream, the dream of such a beautiful creature could not come to you by chance."

"Yes, I know," returned Diamond; "I know."

Then he was silent, but, I confess, appeared more thoughtful than satisfied.

The next time I saw him, he looked paler than usual.

"Have you seen your friend again?" I asked him.

"Yes," he answered, solemnly.

"Did she take you out with her?"

"No. She did not speak to me. I woke all at once, as I generally do when I am going to see her, and there she was against the door into the big room, sitting just as I saw her sit on her own door-step, as white as snow, and her eyes as blue as the heart of an iceberg. She looked at me, but never moved or spoke."

"Weren't you afraid?" I asked.

"No. Why should I?" he answered. "I only felt a little cold."

"Did she stay long?"

"I don't know. I fell asleep again. I think I have been rather cold ever since though," he added with a smile.

I did not quite like this, but I said nothing.

Four days after, I called again at the Mound. The maid who opened the door looked grave, but I suspected nothing. When I reached the drawing-room, I saw Mrs. Raymond had been crying.

"Haven't you heard?" she said, seeing my questioning looks.

"I've heard nothing," I answered.

"This morning we found our dear little Diamond lying on the floor of the big attic-room, just outside his own door—fast asleep, as we thought. But when we took him up, we did not think he was asleep. We saw that——"

Here the kind-hearted lady broke out crying afresh.

"May I go and see him?" I asked.

"Yes," she sobbed. "You know your way to the top of the tower."

I walked up the winding stair, and entered his room. A lovely figure, as white and almost as clear as alabaster, was lying on the bed. I saw at once how it was. They thought he was dead. I knew that he had gone to the back of the north wind.

The Boy in Grey

By HENRY KINGSLEY

THE BOY IN GREY

AND

OTHER STORIES AND SKETCHES

BY

HENRY KINGSLEY

New Edition

WITH A FRONTISPIECE BY A. FORESTIER

NONE OF THE STANDARD STUDIES of Victorian children's literature mentions Henry Kingsley (1830–1876), scapegrace younger brother of the famous Charles, the Broad Church parson and novelist so often referred to in these headnotes. Most readers of an anthology of this kind would expect to find here Charles's *Water-Babies* (1863)—which all the books *do* mention with respect and some admiration. *Water-Babies* is not only well known, however, but boring to the modern reader; those who wish to read it will find it readily available elsewhere. Henry Kingsley, himself a novelist whose admirers prefer his *Ravenshoe* (1861) to Charles's *Westward Ho!* (1855), and his *Recollections of Geoffrey Hamlyn* (1859), with its remarkable scenes of Australian life, to any fiction that Charles ever wrote, also produced a now wholly forgotten children's story that serves our purposes here far better than *Water-Babies*. *The Boy in Grey* is not resuscitated here in order to perpetuate the rather silly fraternal rivalry that plagued Henry Kingsley so severely in his lifetime, or because it can be defended as a memorable or brilliant children's story in itself. Most readers will find it irritating, opaque, jaunty where it should be serious, flawed in taste, even irreverent in its effort to be reverent. It is, however, a remarkable Victorian period piece, and it illustrates neatly certain interesting aspects of Victorian society in general and of the children's literature industry in particular.

It is impossible to imagine *The Boy in Grey* without the *Alice* books. Everyone knows how many writers dashed off their own imitations of Lewis Carroll's splendid nonsense, and vainly strove to follow him in shedding the inevitable moral that had clung so tightly to every fairy tale previously written, even to those by Catherine Sinclair or Frances Browne, for example, in whom modern scholars sometimes have failed to find the moral that is obviously there. Victorian morality clung also to the imitators of Carroll, and his genius eluded them all, even the most popular, like George Edward Farrow, whose *Wallypug of Why* (1895) is often regarded as the best imitation. Henry Kingsley's *Boy in Grey* is an early effort to imitate the *Alice* books: animals and birds appear unexpectedly and converse with the child hero, advising him, helping him on his journey, commenting indirectly about many subjects. But of course, like all the other imitations, this one fails.

There was much pathos in the author's life. Disgraced, it is supposed, for heavy drinking and for a homosexual episode at Oxford, he went off to Australia to find gold. He drove cattle, hunted bandits for a time as a mounted policeman, and wandered about as a "sundowner," or tramp on horseback. At twenty-eight, he returned to England and published *Geoffrey Hamlyn*, reflecting his Australian adventures. He seemed launched on a promising career as a successful novelist. But a disastrous marriage to a nagging spendthrift wife brought continued financial anxiety. He continued to drink too much. He smoked incessantly and contracted cancer of the tongue. He died at forty-six. He loved children and never had any. He was simple, direct, bluff, humorous, and a little disreputable, cultivating an Australian accent in part to annoy his proper relatives, notably his sister-in-law, Charles's wife. At his best he was capable of superb English prose descriptions. He wrote twenty-two books in the years between 1859 and his death in 1876, several of which were undeservedly neglected, and almost all of which have some literary merit.

The Boy in Grey is a potpourri. It is partly an allegory, like so many of the fairy tales of the time. But instead of giving his characters obvious English names like Winwealth or

Wisewit, Henry Kingsley put the names into Greek or otherwise concealed their meaning. A modern reader—let alone a Victorian schoolboy—needs a key. The hero, Prince Philarete, is a "lover of virtue." His three friends—Arturio, Polemos, and Athanasio— stand respectively for nobility, the military, and the church. The fairy Anangke is "necessity," and Cacodemos is "evil populace." The Boy in Grey is Christ, whom Philarete must seek on a journey which, he thinks, takes only three days, but which in fact occupies eleven years; so that he is twenty-one when it is over—a time-distortion like that in George MacDonald's "Golden Key," in which years go by while the characters think them days. Philarete's search for Christ takes his whole boyhood; when he returns to face Revolution, he is a man, and prepared to deal with it, for Christ is his friend now, and comes to his side to save him from the mob, spurred on by the wicked premier, Cacodemos.

The story is, then, highly political. Aristocracy (the priggish Arturio, so named surely because of the Arthurian Round Table legends), the soldiery (Polemos, the Greek word for war), and even the church (Athanasio, who has had an ancient feud with the military about the righteousness of war) are all slain. But Christ in his humility (bare-legged and bare-footed) saves the state. And the state, unfortunately for the literary merit of *The Boy in Grey*, is not merely a fairy kingdom: it is Great Britain. In its confused way, the book seems to teach that proper Christian piety will be Britain's salvation. Philarete's journey to find the Boy in Grey takes him to India, Canada, and Australia, where he encounters local animals, birds, and personages of fiction, and is called upon to hear opinions on local issues, cryptically expressed. There is an allegorical vision of the British Navy (as a ship called *Ancient Mariner*) and of the American Navy (as a ship called *Flying Dutchman*), complete with a description of the American melting pot, and an affirmation of the two nations' permanent friendship (both seek the Boy in Grey) despite their ancient rivalry and many past battles. In the Canadian wilderness, Philarete encounters whole groups of favorite characters from fiction, some—like the boys from *Tom Brown's School Days*—already enshrined in these pages; others—like Meg Merrilies from Scott's *Guy Mannering* or Elsie Venner from Oliver Wendell Holmes's popular but now forgotten novel—needing identification; others—like the Queen of Hearts "looking more cross than ever Tenniel made her look"—still familiar to us all. Philarete intervenes intelligently in a dispute over prices and wages; he encounters Apollo's serpent, who represents science as well as the Evil One. Into the jumbled pages of *The Boy in Grey*, Henry Kingsley even put an overt plea to squabbling sects—Dissenters, Romanists, Tractarians—to seek the Boy in Grey. There are even barely concealed references to Turkey as the sick man of Europe and to the problems of Indian colonial officials.

The constant intrusion into a fairy romance of the world of every day, and not only the children's world of every day with mathematics to learn and geography to ponder— which also (but how differently!) intrudes even into the *Alice* books—but the adult world of economics, politics, and religious and territorial strife, ruins the story as a work of art. What is left is suffocatingly sentimental for our tastes, and even uncomfortable. The kiss on the mouth that Philarete gives the Boy in Grey, and their lying "warm together" as the Prince calls the Boy "My darling," makes the modern reader queasy. "We are too old to kiss," says the boy later, when he realizes that both are now young men, but the modern Freudian does not believe it, seeing in the story more than a suspicion of the homosexual leanings that had once been its author's downfall.

As Christ, the Boy in Grey has no particular characteristics, a great contrast to George MacDonald's Diamond. *The Boy in Grey*, then, is a failure. But as an example of an *Alice* imitation, written in haste by a novelist of great talent, distraught by debt, too busy to do more than stuff a literary rag-bag in the vain hope of financial success, it retains considerable interest. What redeems it still further is the occasional haunting beauty of the original lyrics that Henry Kingsley scattered through his story. The reader who is impatient with the text of *The Boy in Grey* will find himself rewarded by the verses about the blackbird and Mary Magdalen. Frederick Yorke Powell, a folklorist and astute critic of letters, once urged Jack Yeats to illustrate this poem. It was Henry Kingsley's "best thing," he said, adding, "It used to make me cry when I was a boy, and it makes me feel uncommon creepy even now."

The text of The Boy in Grey *is reprinted from an English edition (London: Ward, Lock and Bowden, 1895).*

CHAPTER I

IT WAS PRINCE PHILARETE'S tenth birthday, and if you will find the "Court Circular" for that date, you will read what beautiful presents he had.

First, a great brass top, or, as Mr. Jenkins called it, a gyrotrope, which spun for two hours and forty-six minutes, making all the time a noise like the loudest railway whistle, only louder; which was a charming toy.

Next, a Noah's Ark, in which the elephant was as big as a Newfoundland dog, and would serve for a rantoone; and Noah was as big as your sister's largest doll. All the animals had cloth hides, coloured exactly like nature. If you wound up the brown bear with a watch-key, he would run about for five minutes (that was done by little wheels on his toes), and growl (that was done by a bellows in his inside). And the rarer and more recently discovered ones, such as the Wandoodle and Teezyweezy, and the Rumtifoozle, had only just been made, under the joint superintendence of Mr. Frank Buckland and Mr. Tegetmeier.

There was another great fact about this Noah's Ark of his. Professor Huxley had superintended the models of all the extinct animals, even to that of the Xylopodotherium, the gigantic armadillo, with a wooden leg, recently discovered in the drift of the Appalachian mountains, near Millidgeville. The Professor would not have taken that trouble for every one. But he knew that this Prince could dree out the weird of the Boy in Grey, and so he did it for *him*. For the Professor talks much to the Boy in Grey, and the Boy in Grey loves him.

"That was a fine Noah's Ark," you say; "he must have been glad."

We will see about that presently.

Next he had a box of French soldiers, each three inches high, exactly like life. There were I don't know how many of these beautiful wooden soldiers, and the band of the little army was mounted on a musical box like a triumphal arch, inside of which was a barrel with two tunes—"Partant pour la Syrie," and the "Marseillaise;" and when you wound it up, you never knew which it was going to play next, which was great fun—to folks at a distance.

Well, with all these lovely presents, Prince Philarete was not enjoying his birthday at all. As his uncle, Prince Thalasses, Lord High Admiral of Liberia, remarked, "The boy was not making good weather of it." Prince Thalasses had brought to his nephew, the future Emperor of Liberia, one of the most beautiful presents you ever saw. It was a little war-steamer, wound up by clockwork, which would run for a quarter of an hour, and fire its guns three times. After this it was no good whatever unless the works were greased with the *best* butter, like the March Hare's watch.

Prince Philarete cared for none of these things. The weird of the Boy in Grey was on him, as it was, speaking with deep reverence, on some twelve men more than eighteen hundred years ago. The child wished to be alone, he knew not why, but he wanted utter solitude. Men have lived in the desert, and have come down into towns, and said the very words which, after a thousand years, we are acting on now—words which make some men mad with pure joy, now they see them being acted on, and which make old men sing "Nunc Dimittis" with a new emphasis. He wanted to be alone.

Prince Philarete had loved all his friends as a good boy should. And indeed they were good friends enough, for they could die for him, and one lad can do no more than that for another, unless he can live for him. Arturio was the one who came to him first, finding that he was alone. Arturio was one of his pages, a boy of a great house, who was with him day and night; the boy who knew his ways and his thoughts beyond all boys.

Arturio found him sitting at the window alone. Arturio was a very solemn boy. He was dressed in snow-white trousers, fitting close to his leg, a black velvet tunic, a black velvet bonnet, and he had on his breast, clasping his velvet tunic, a blazing diamond. The Prince had often asked him to exchange this splendid cold pure diamond for the flaming ruby which the Prince wore on the same place. Arturio had always refused the offer, saying, "The latter branch of our house has always worn the diamond. You are mixed in blood with the Lancelots. I cannot exchange. I will not have my heart burnt out, even to serve my Lord and Prince."

Arturio, with his black velvet and diamond, bowed himself on this occasion, and told his Prince that their supper was ready. Prince Philarete said that he was tired of his toys, and that he was not coming to supper at all.

Arturio agreed that the toys were all nonsense, and that his Highness was right in refusing supper: but the company of his equals would surely please him.

"I have no equals," said Prince Philarete; "I shall have a thousand years hence, and then I shall be dead. But I have no equals now."

"Your family traditions, Prince, make it necessary for me to say that my family, had things been different, would have been as good as yours;" whereupon he kicked the Xylopodotherium.

"Don't be cross, Arturio," said the Prince; "I can't come."

Arturio was not in the least cross: he never was, according to his own account; but he kicked the Xylopodotherium up into the air, so that it fell on the nose of young Duke Polemos, who was coming also to summon the Prince to supper.

"Oh, hang it," said Duke Polemos, "you have broken my nose. You have shied a rocking-horse at me now: last time it was one of your wooden generals."

"It was only a carefully-executed model of a Xylopodotherium," said Duke Arturio.

"Who's he?" said Duke Polemos. "Some of *your* lot, I doubt. I'm of the Tenth Heavy Dragoons, and I don't care a hang who knows it. What do you make of that, for instance?"

"Nothing," said Duke Arturio, coldly.

"Well then, Prince, my dear, come to supper, for I am hungry. There is jam, woodcock, ice-cream, and barley-sugar. Come to supper."

"I want no supper," said the Prince; "but come near to me, Polemos."

Polemos came at once. He was a bold, thoughtless, possibly cruel boy, but he loved the Prince. He was dressed like Arturio, his legs in close-fitting white, but his tunic was green, and it was clasped at the breast by a great emerald. Arturio went, and left the Prince alone with the stupid boy, the boy of the emerald. And the boy of the emerald knelt beside his Prince, and said—

"What is it, my dear one?"

"Change thine emerald for my ruby, Polemos: my ruby burns my heart. I have asked Arturio for his cold clear diamond, and he will not give it to me. Give me thine emerald."

"Never, my Prince, will I give thee my emerald. Wear thy bonny ruby—that is the jewel of a good prince. See, look at my emerald: does it shine?"

"It is quite dull."

"Then there is peace in the land," said the stupid Polemos. "See, my beloved, how your ruby is blazing."

"It is bright indeed," said the Prince.

"Do you know," said Polemos, "that when your ruby blazes brightest, and when it burns your heart most, my old enemy, the Boy in Grey, who wears the great sapphire upon his breast, engraven with characters which no man can read, is nearest to you. He is near now."

"The Boy in Grey! I have not heard of him."

"No; and that is just the bother," said Duke Polemos. "Your family has always put up mine to fight him, and so *we* know something of him. *We* in our rude way love him. His brothers are dear to us, and die for us. You will not come to supper, then? Here is Athanasio. I will begin without you."

"Athanasio," said the Prince, when they were alone, "bid me not to supper. Tell me, my Athanasio, dost thou know aught of a Boy in Grey?"

Athanasio was clothed like the other pages; but his tunic, which was black, was a little longer, and on his breast he wore a great opal, which changed in colour as he moved. He crossed his hands on his breast and began bowing towards the door.

"Athanasio, come back and tell me of this Boy in Grey!"

Athanasio declined. "My lord," he said, "my family has been in such perpetual debate with yours about this Boy for eighteen centuries, that I would prefer to leave you two to a personal interview."

"Give me thine opal, and I will give thee my ruby," cried the Prince.

"The Boy in Grey would tear your heart out, my lord, if he saw my opal there. Better wear your ruby. It is burning bright to-night. The Boy is near."

And so Athanasio left him all alone, as the others had done, in the window-seat in the shadow of the curtain.

And the ruby on his brave maroon tunic burnt bright and steady, and warmed his heart. It flashed out great rays of light, which lit up the limited landscape outside the window: only a mass of rapidly falling snow. After a time the Prince slept, and was only awakened by voices in the room.

The King in his royal robes; the Queen also dressed up for a great occasion; and some one else, more important and greater than king or kaiser ever could be: a fairy—the Fairy Anangke. A very dear old friend of mine, whom I have known almost as long as any one.

Will you please to remark that when you know Fairy Anangke you know the best lady whom you can know. But if you can't know Fairy Anangke intimately, you should try to make her acquaintance in some sort even at second-hand through the poor. For unless you do, you are simply naught.

She was standing and talking to the King and Queen. She was a pale woman with large eyes; of very solemn aspect. She was dressed in a long sweeping robe of black velvet, which covered her feet, so that the wisest of our men never knew exactly which way she would walk. I am only telling you the simple truth when I say that she carried on her breast, one below the other, the jewels which I have told you the boys whom I have described wore upon their bosoms, all save the sapphire—the wine-dark sapphire, in whose cold dark depths lay utter infinity, and the character, on which were read nearly two thousand years ago, and have been forgotten, that she had given to the Boy in Grey.

The King and the Queen and she were talking earnestly together, and the Queen was crying bitterly, but the Prince could not hear what they said.

"My dear old friend," said the Queen, kneeling down, "is it not possible that he could be spared? Did I not give my Henri, and you know how that ended: did I not give my Louis, and where is he? Spare me this one."

"I have nothing to do with it. The weird of the Boy in Grey is upon him, and he must dree it."

"And be killed by the Boy! Ah, cruel, cruel Necessity!"

"I am not cruel, Queen, indeed," said Fairy Anangke. "I am a person of very little power, too. I am only cruel, after all, to fools. Men can fight me, and beat me. I came only to tell you that the weird is on him, and he *must* go."

"Will he die?" said the Queen, at her feet. "Will my bonny child be killed like the others? You know. You can say."

"I do *not* know," said the Fairy. "But this I do know: the others met the Boy and kissed him, Henri on the brow, Louis on the cheek; the Boy should be kissed fully and fairly on the lips. If Philarete does so, all will go well."

"Let me tell him," said the Queen, eagerly.

"Impossible," said the Fairy. "He must find it out for himself."

"I *will* tell my darling."

"If you offer to do so, I will make you and your husband dumb: you know I can do that. I did so once or twice before. I have the appointment of your Ministers nowadays, and I will strike you both dumb once more by appointing Cacodemos if you dare to say a word to the child."

So the King and Queen, terrified into submission, departed slowly and sorrowfully upstairs, to receive their guests for the grand dinner and ball which was to be given that night.

Would you like to go with me? Well, we will just look in: we must not stay long lest we should miss the Prince, who is lying in the window-seat looking out upon the falling snow, with his ruby blazing brightly. We will keep near him, and yet see some of the company. For myself, I am very fond of fine company, and, what is more, I believe that every one else is too.

CHAPTER II

Now the guests began to come; rattery-tattery-tattery-tat-tat-tat went the knocker; and the footmen had the door open in half a minute, and shut it instantly for fear two people should get in at once without each of them making that horrible noise all over again. This is the very highest breeding known; All The World's footmen do it.

They were all Ambassadors who came to dinner. After dinner, to the ball, there were invited All The World and his wife; Mr. Nobody with all his relations, including his aunt's baby, whose portrait was painted by the late Charles Bennett in "Nursery Fun;" and Everybody Else. We have only to do with the Ambassadors.

The Turcomanian Ambassador came first. He was very cold, and took off his goloshes in the hall, and was making himself tidy, shivering over the fire, when the Muscovite Ambassador arrived, and coming up to him, said—

"Grumph, it is hot here! Are you any better?"

"I am as well as ever I was in my life," said the Turcoman Ambassador; "you are always saying I am sick. You said it too often once, you know."

"Your constitution is ruined," said the Muscovite.

"You never had one any more than I," retorted the Turk.

"Hein! hein!" said the Gallic Ambassador; "but, Messieurs, consider!"

And the English Ambassador said, "Come, gentlemen! gentlemen! Pray!"

And the Hellenic Ambassador said, "That for his part he thought his Excellency of Muscovy was quite correct"; whereupon all the other Ambassadors, Muscovy included, told him to hold his tongue. Which he did.

The next arrival was the Ambassador from Columbia, who said to the footman, "Young man, there is my best hat: treat it as if my head was inside it, and as soon as the exchange drops I'll give you a quarter dollar currency.—Why, if here ain't the Etruscan Ambassador and the Latin Nuncio! Well, I do admire! How air you, neighbours? Folks have been telling me that there have been words between you two about the busting down of some rails between your two lots. Anything I can do in the way of kind offices, I am sure—always happy. Here is the young man come to say that the King and Queen are fixed up tight and spry, and ready to receive. Won't you go first, Gaul? Well, if you won't, I will. Come along."

This was uncommonly cool of the Columbian Ambassador, and he seemed to think so himself, for he half turned round as he walked upstairs to give them some of his conversation, and the Prince heard him say—

"You didn't notice the Boy in Grey outside, did you, Muscovy?"

"No," said the Muscovite Ambassador, "I did not. He never comes after me. I go after him. I have just been after him lately."

"Well done," said the Columbian Ambassador, "so you have. Nor you, Gaul?"

"He is dead," said the Gallic Ambassador.

"He is outside among the carriages now," said the Columbian Minister.

And the Prince peered more and more eagerly into the darkness and the snow.

At last he saw him. He came and stood straight in front of the window, and looked the Prince straight in the eyes.

Save for a grey seamless tunic, which reached half-way down his thigh and half-way down his arm, the Boy was perfectly naked, and stood with his bare feet in the snow, and his bare head in the wind. His head was erect, majestic, and beautiful, and his hair was wild. At his throat, as a clasp, like all the boys we have seen, he wore a large jewel. His was a sapphire, bright as the moon in a frost, blue as the sea on a summer's day, with varying light flashing from it on the Prince's face, and seeming to show letters which he had never seen before.

The Boy neither spoke nor beckoned. For a few seconds only the light from the Boy's sapphire mingled with the light from the Prince's ruby, and made the falling snow purple. Then the Boy turned and went away, and the Prince, bareheaded and thinly clad as he was, rose and followed him swiftly.

The guests were coming in to the ball as the Prince passed through them quickly. They most of them knew—courtiers generally can see—what had happened to him. They fell away right and left, and spoke in terrified whispers. "He is going after the Boy in Grey as his brother did," was what they said, and grew pale and horror-stricken. And the funds went down four and three-quarters on the night, as the City intelligence said; at least the earliest men on the Exchange found it so the first thing next morning.

"He is off," said the old seneschal, drawing back from the door to let him pass, with a solemn and tender awe on his old face; "off, bareheaded, just as my two boys went."

"Did they come back, Master Clerk of Owsenford?" said a young footman in a whisper.

"Oh, yes, they came back again," said he; "the cruel Mayor of Paris thought he had got them safe, but they came back again. Why, you know—

'It fell about the Martinmas,
    When nights were long and mirk,
The clerk's two sons came home again;
    Their hats were of the birk.

'It grew not by the bonny hill-side,
    Nor yet by holt and sheugh;
But by the gates of Paradise,
    That birk grew fair eneugh.'

Yes; they came back safe enough to Usher's Well; but they went away again.

'The cock doth craw, the day doth daw,
    The chaunering worm doth chide;
Gin we be missed out of our place,
    A sair pain we must bide.' "

But the Prince was gone, and we must go after him. How far? As near about thirty-five thousand miles as need be. I fancy a little more, but certainly not less. He ran down the steps, and diving in among the fretting horses and blazing carriage-lamps, disappeared into the darkness and the drifting snow.

CHAPTER III

T HE LIGHTS of the blazing windows of the palace guided him a little at first; but as the sound of the music died upon his ear the light died away also, and he found himself alone in the dark in the lower and poorer quarter of the town, with no light but his ruby. There was no doubt about his way, for the ruby was very bright now, and before him, pressed firmly into the snow, were the naked footprints of the Boy in Grey. The Prince walked very fast, and peered before him into the darkness for a glimpse of the sapphire, but there was nothing to be seen. The cowering poverty around him was asleep and silent, and he soon cleared the City Augusta, and got into the great forest which lies beyond it. And which forest is Fairyland:

> "Oh! see you not that bonny road
>   That winds along the fernie brae?
> Oh! yon's the road to Fairyland,
>   Where thou and I this e'en must gae."

In that forest there is no snow or frost at any time of the year: nobody ever feels pain in Fairyland, and nobody ever cries there. There is no hunger or thirst in Fairyland. Every one is happy in Fairyland; but God's mercy on the boy or man who goes to sleep there and thinks that it is heaven! As our noble old Bunyan teaches us, there is a "bye-way to hell out of it." And so the Prince found himself at once in a warm beautiful summer's night with a bright moon, which would have rejoiced him extremely, only it got so very difficult to follow the tread of the Boy in Grey through the grass and the flowers. It is always easy enough in the snow; any one can do it then, but only a few can follow his footsteps in the summer-time.

In a narrow pleasant path among hazel trees, down by a bright stream, he met a beautiful lady all in black, with jewels on her breast, and he said to her—

"If you please, ma'am, how am I to follow the Boy in Grey?"

And she said, "Ask every one you meet," and looked kindly at him. After which she said, "You could not do this?" and, whiff! she vanished away; and the Prince laughed till the wood rang, for it was really fine sport if you had seen it. I need not tell you that this was the Fairy Anangke.

CHAPTER IV

THERE WAS SOMETHING scuttling along in front of him, and when he came up to it, he found it was a hedgehog.

"Have you seen the Boy in Grey?" said the Prince.

"Eh!" replied the hedgehog. "Speak louder—I am hard of hearing."

"Have you seen the Boy in Grey?" he said, louder.

"No!" shouted the hedgehog. "Have you seen my wife?"

"No, I have not," said the Prince.

"Then there is a pair of us," said the hedgehog. "I thought one fool was enough at a time. She has been out ever since the morning after some partridge eggs, and I don't know what is become of her."

"I am sorry for that," said the Prince.

"It is not much business of yours, that I know of," said the hedgehog. "If you see her, tell her she will catch it when she comes home."

"Then, perhaps she won't come home at all," said the Prince.

"She'll come fast enough," said the hedgehog; "because she knows, if she don't come, that I shall come and fetch her. And she wouldn't like that. She knows *me*."

At this point the hedgehog tucked his toes in, rolled himself up in a ball, and lay for dead, with all his prickles up. But, from the centre of the ball, like a person speaking from under bedclothes, came a thin wiry voice, which said—

"It is no use trying it on. You have tried it on too often, and you never made anything of it. Come on! Come on!"

The Prince thought that the hedgehog was alluding to him, and was getting indignant: when he became aware of a pair of bright eyes, and looking down, he saw that a beautiful fox was cowering at his feet.

"Ho! then it is *you* that the hedgehog is afraid of?"

"Without reason, dear Royal Highness," said the fox; "I assure you without reason. Our friend is too suspicious: if he would only uncoil himself for a moment, I would——"

"No doubt you would," said the hedgehog, from under the bed-clothes. "But he knows a trick worth two of that. Come on! Why don't you come on?"

The fox shrugged his shoulders at the Prince.

"Our friend's temper gets the better of him sometimes. But he is amiable. Oh yes, without doubt he is amiable. Can I serve your Royal Highness?"

"Have you seen the Boy in Grey go by? I want to follow him: he must be somewhere close by."

Whereupon the fox, exclaiming, "Traps and shot guns, and no fair law allowed!" took to his heels and sped away.

And the hedgehog, uncoiling himself, said, "I am going to fetch my wife back with a flea in her ear;" and off *he* went, but not the same way as the fox. And the Prince went on, following the footsteps, until he should meet some one else.

But before he met any one else, the moon had got low and pale, the east had brightened from white to green, from green to gold, and morning pierced the beautiful wood with millions of beams of light. This was glorious for the Prince, for he knew that a long summer's day was before him, and there are few boys who do not know that that is the most glorious happiness which this earth can bring.

The wood was filled with infinite birds, singing in rivalry: the nightingale, who had slept an hour or so, found that he was in the wood, and began again, "Tereu, Tereu, by-and-bye," till the Prince stood and hollowed his hand against his ear, to catch such sweet cadence. The thrush said, "Lirripo, Lirripo!" and the bold glorious blackbird said, "Love! Love! Love! Love lies a-bleeding. Pick him up! Pick him up! Pretty sweet! Pretty sweet! Pick him up! Pretty sweet! Pretty sweet! Pick him up! Pick him up!"

"How beautifully you sing!" said the Prince, "and what a fine golden bill you have!"

"My ancestor, sir, got that golden bill at Glastonbury, hundreds and hundreds of years ago. Were you ever there?"

"No. Tell me the story."

"At Glastonbury is the thorn planted by Joseph of Arithmathæa down in the valley, and at the top of the hill called 'Weary All' was the church of St. Michael. And somebody toiled up that hill one wild early spring evening; and my ancestor (who afterwards took the title of Earl of Chysorinchus, not now continued in the family, in consequence of our great lawsuit with the ring-ouzels about their assuming the white collar of the order of St. Agnes, which we have discarded) was on the bush; and we sing the story like this:

> Magdalen at Michael's gate
>   Tirled at the pin;
> On Joseph's thorn sang the blackbird,
> "Let her in! Let her in!"
>
> "Hast thou seen the wounds?" said Michael,
>   "Know'st thou thy sin?"
> "It is evening, evening," sang the blackbird,
>   "Let her in! Let her in!"
>
> "Yes, I have seen the wounds,
>   And I know my sin."
> "She knows it well, well, well," sang the blackbird,
>   "Let her in! Let her in!"
>
> "Thou bringest no offerings," said Michael,
>   "Nought save sin."
> And the blackbird sang, "She is sorry, sorry, sorry.
>   Let her in! Let her in!"
>
> When he had sung himself to sleep,
>   And night did begin,
> One came and opened Michael's gate,
>   And Magdalen went in.

"I am *very* glad of that," said the Prince. "I can't *tell* you how glad I am of that; and she must have been so very glad too. And that's why you have a golden bill, yet. I am very glad they let her in. Why did you quarrel with the ring-ouzels, did you say?"

"*We* are of the order of St. Cecilia," said the blackbird, proudly.

But the jay said, "Yar! Crar! here's somebody coming, and we shall all be murdered in our beds." And the rook said, "Caw daw! I wish I was in bed again." And the starling sat on a tree, and chattered very fast, "My wife ought to have got up and boiled the kettle." And the magpie said nothing at all, for he had his eye on the Prince's ruby. But his wife told him that it wouldn't do, and he agreed with regret that it wouldn't.

Here and there he could see the naked footstep which had preceded his, sometimes on dewy turf, sometimes on the sand by some clear stream, where the sleepy trout floated like the peacocks of the water. Once in an open glade he missed the trail, and looked about. Instantly there dashed down before him a beautiful butterfly, a butterfly so beautiful that it fills one's mind with humble awe and wonder to look at it. Its flight was like the eagle's, and it hovered up and down before him.

"Oh, you glorious creature! who are you?" said the Prince.

"I am the Purple Emperor," said the butterfly. "I inhabit the tops of the highest oak trees in the New Forest, and I am the most artistically coloured of all European butterflies. I have come down to show you the way."

And it flew before him to the next stream, and then it flew up towards the sun, for the boy's feet were plain again now. And the Prince, as he stepped across the brook, sang out, loud, clear, and joyfully:

> "Wilt thou stay, or must I follow
> O'er the brae and through the hollow?
>   Stay, stay, Boy in Grey.
> Rest thee, rest, at evening's gloaming:
> Wilful one, wilt thou be roaming
>   Till the breaking of the day?
> All night long I'll walk till morning;
> Let me find thee at the dawning;
>   Stay, stay, Boy in Grey."

And the most remarkable thing was that the very next morn——But I must not tell you too much at once. It would spoil the story if I told it all to you at once. At least, so they say.

What with one pleasure and another, with flowers and insects to look at, with health, youth, and vitality, the Prince was rather dawdling, when he was aware of a pair of eyes, and looking up, he saw a very large greyish bird, with its back towards him, but which had turned its head right round, and was looking down the back of its neck.

"You mustn't do that," said the Prince; "you will make yourself ill."

"Not a bit of it," said the great snowy owl; "we often do it for hours together."

"Why?"

"Because none of the English owls can, except us."

"That is not much of a reason," said the Prince.

"Good enough for us," said the owl. "I am going to fly to Greenland directly; this is too hot for me. Did you ever see me fly?"

"Never," said the Prince; "but if you fly with your head turned that way, you will fly up against something and hurt yourself. You can't possibly see which way you are going like that."

"Well, here goes, anyhow," said the owl, "before I am roasted." And away he skipped over the tops of the trees like a woodcock.

"If you please, sir," said a gentle voice, like a sigh, near him, "I am the stag."

"So I should have gathered from your personal appearance," said the Prince, who was not behind in the *royal art* of making a shrewd guess who people were he had never seen before. "I have seen your portrait at the Royal Academy, by Sir Edwin Landseer: it was very like. What are you crying about, for there are tears coursing themselves down your innocent nose?"

"Mere habit," said the stag. "It is my lachrymathingamy gland. Mere habit."

"Get over it," said the Prince. "We hate whimpering at our place."

And so he went on, singing, from old echoes:

> "Stay, stay, Boy in Grey,
> The brave birds sing on every spray;
> Stay, stay, stay for me,
> And see the things I will give thee.

I follow swift, but thou art fleeter:
Sure the present time is sweeter.
Bonny, bonny Boy, this merry, merry wood
Laughs around with all things good.
For the morrow means but sorrow;
Of the future let us borrow:
If the morrow means but pain,
Days like these come not again.
Stay for me one summer's day,
Boy in Grey, Boy in Grey."

How long the Prince would have continued singing like this I don't know, but he was stopped by a voice from the top of a tree, saying that the Prince was singing mere Crambo, and that he could make that sort of stuff by the yard. Looking up to see who had uttered the impertinence, he saw that it was the magpie, who had followed him in the hopes of his dropping his ruby. And, indeed, the rest of this poem is lost to European literature. For at this moment, crossing the small brook which divides his European from his Asiatic dominions, he came on a spectacle so *absurd* and *ridiculous,* and at the same time so *humiliating* to every well-regulated mind, that I must take another chapter even to speak of it.

CHAPTER V

"BAROORA! BAROORA! BAROO!" said somebody, so loud and so near that the Prince drew up short, and the whole wood echoed, "Baroo! Baroo!" and turning to the right, the Prince saw a ridiculous black bear, with very long hair, and an absurd black-and-tan nose; which sat on its haunches, rocked itself to and fro, and scratched its stomach with its fore paws.

"You must not make that noise here," said the Prince; "I cannot permit it for an instant."

"I am the Isabella bear! Doodle-doodle-do!" said the bear, weeping bitterly.

"That makes not the least difference," said the Prince; "I cannot allow such a noise from you or any other bear. You really must not do it. What is the matter with you?"

"I am the Isabella bear," said the poor thing, dissolving into tears. "Doodle-doodle! Baroo! baroo!"

"You are a very ridiculous person," said the Prince. "Have *you* seen the Boy in Grey?"

The bear rubbed her nose with her fore paws, but did not seem inclined to answer.

"I believe that you are a thorough-going humbug, and that there is nothing the matter with you at all," said the Prince, looking back; and immediately after he fell headlong over something flat on his face. It was only a lion, so it did not much matter. "You stupid old ass!" said the Prince, "why do you lie across the road like that?"

"Gnorr hrump!" said the lion. "I was watching here to show your Highness the way; and, gnorr hum garr! I went to sleep. He is on ahead. The tiger will show you the way to my brother now."

"But what are you doing *here?*" said the Prince.

"I am occasionally found on the north-west of India," said the lion, sitting down and scratching his head with his hind paw, just like a cat.

"But that is not giving a good account of yourself," said the Prince. "Get up!"

And the lion got up.

"I want to stroke your nose," said the Prince; "it is a very nice nose."

"Gar! garoar! your Royal Highness is welcome. Put your head into my mouth and look at my teeth. Do you know the use of them?"

"No."

"They are for your Royal Highness's enemies—that is to say, if it be true that you are following the Boy."

"They are fine teeth," said the Prince.

"The hyæna has better," said the lion; "he can crunch up bones which I can't."

"Where shall I meet the hyæna?" said the Prince.

"When you come into Africa, you will meet him at the Cape," said the lion. "Look out, sir; here is a messenger. Give me a good report, sir. Gnarr, snorr, churruk!"

And as the lion stood rubbing his beard against the Prince's legs, there descended from the sky a bird so amazingly wonderful, that I would have hesitated even to mention it lest I should be accused of invention. I can only say that there is such a bird, because somebody killed one once, and got it skinned, and a lady I know wears its skin in her hat at social gatherings. And whenever I look at the bird I am less and less puzzled; for I know more and more strongly that there is a great beneficent Will.

As for describing this bird, I cannot do it. Shakespeare and Raphael could not have done it either. It is a bird so amazing in its real artistic beauty, and in the thoughts which it brings on those who choose to think, that I decline to say anything about it. It lit down on the Prince's shoulder, and covered the Prince's ruby with its tail; and the lion said, "Humph, snurr! this will do!" And the bird twittered in the Prince's ear, very low:

"Stop not, stay not, pretty pretty master;
  Follow, follow on to the very very last.
Stay not, fear not, follow, follow faster;
  Hold the Boy, kiss the Boy, hold him fast.
Hold him, kiss him mouth to mouth,
All the world, from north to south,
From east to west, from night to day,
Shall laugh when thou kissest the Boy in Grey."

And the lion purred like a great cat, and said—

"That is something like talk. I thought he would have a messenger." And the Prince said to the bird, "Let us sit down and talk a few minutes." And the bird said, "Yes, my lord, we will sit on the lion for a few minutes; I have a few more words to say."

And the lion lay down, with his nose between his fore paws, and the Prince sat on him, and played with his mane, and the bird sat on the Prince's shoulder, with its tail falling all down the maroon velvet of the Prince's tunic, and whispered in his ear, and

> The lion heard every word,
> But not a word said he:
> "When princes talk to the Paradise bird,
> There is no word for me."

"Grumph! Will he go through with it!"

What the bird said to the Prince you must find out for yourself. *I* know; and I know where I learnt it, too. But this is a fairy tale, and my reverence for the Bible is so deep that I dislike to do more than just hint at it in a fantastic story like this.

CHAPTER VI

THE END of the conversation with the bird I may give.

"Bird," said the Prince, "you have not told me your name."

"I am the Bird of Paradise. I have come down to bring you this message."

"Ha! I thought I knew you;" said the Prince; "and that was done for him eighteen hundred years ago. Well, birdie, I will do *that* for him. Just what Arturio and Athanasio are always telling me. I say, pretty bird, cannot you come with me?"

And the Bird of Paradise twittered—

> "All alone, all alone, pretty dear,
> Through the moss-hags and marshes drear;
> By the stream, through the wood, through the glen;
> By the crag, by the hollow, by the den:
> By the ocean shore vacant and wide,
> Left bare in the sleep of the tide;
> Till the dawning of the day
> You must hunt the Boy in Grey.
> All you want is resolution—"

If you can find a decent rhyme for the last line, you will be able to finish the verse. You do not know what rhymes with that last word. But if you don't go after the Boy in Grey, you will find it out when you least think it.

The Bird of Paradise said, "I must go now."

"Won't you come with me, pretty bird?" said the Prince.

"No," said the bird, "I am going up there, and you must meet him all alone. Not one solitary creature must be with you when you two meet. Mind what I told you, and don't dawdle."

"Shall I ever see you again, sweet bird?" said the Prince.

The Bird of Paradise was poising itself on its wings, and preparing to fly upwards; but when it heard these words, it came and fluttered in front of the Prince's breast.

And it said, "If you do as I have told you, and if all goes well, you *will* see me again. In the darkest midnight of the darkest night, in the darkest day of all thy life, when resolution has grown to obstinacy, courage to fury, love to despair—when thy friends are dead, thy fair name blackened, thy faith wavering, then I will be with thee, if all goes well by to-morrow morning."

"Shall I call for thee, bird?"

"The Bird of Paradise needs no calling from him who drees the weird of the Boy in Grey. I will be with you, if you do what I tell you. I can say no more. I want to fly up and warm my wings."

And up he went towards the sky.

For a time the Prince could see him curling round and round, bright as a star, but at last he was lost in the light of the sun.

"You'll mind what he told you," said the lion. "I knew they'd send a messenger here; and I'll tell you another thing: there will be another messenger."

"What is her name?" asked the Prince.

"White's thrush," said the lion; "and he is first cousin to the Bird of Paradise, and also to the lyre-bird of Australia, and he also will have something to tell you. Kiss me, Prince, and let me go, for here is the royal Bengal tiger coming, and I don't want to have a turn up before your Royal Highness. Kiss me, dear. Garr garr, garoo!"

In another instant the tiger had bounded out of the jungle and close to the Prince's legs, and with lifted lips and gleaming fangs was face to face with the lion. The lion, silent as the grave, inexorable as death, cold as fate, crouched also, belly to the earth, and waited for his spring. Every gigantic muscle was tense and sharp, and his fore paws clawed the ground in the delicious anticipation of onset. The tiger, standing erect, snarled and scowled. Between the two stood the Prince, with his hands in the pockets of his tight-fitting white trousers, who said—

"Now, you two, steady. You are losing your tempers" (which was perfectly obvious); "you are in reality the best friends in the world. Lion, old man!"

"Yes, my lord," said the lion.

"Go away, that's a dear."

And the lion went.

"Now, tiger, old boy! tell us the way to the elephant!"

Was there anything that the tiger would not do for the beautiful young Sahib? Nothing. He salaamed until his head was right down between his paws. Beautiful Sahib! It was his humble and deferential duty to inform his Royal Highness that the elephant was a large animal with a long trunk, and that his food was entirely vegetable.

"Well, I suppose I know that, stupid," said the Prince.

"Oh, doubtless!" with another salaam. "Of course his Highness knew. Doubtless his Highness was also aware that he (the tiger) fed very much on the reindeer in certain parts?"

"No, I didn't know that," said the Prince. "That *can't* be true."

"We cross one another in the north of Asia, your Highness," said the tiger with a humble smile. "My father and the lion's father have had many a battle over the carcase of a reindeer."

And, indeed, it was perfectly true, as the Prince found out when he got more familiar with Humboldt's "Aspects" and Keith Johnstone's "Physical Atlas," strange as it seems the first time you read it.

"Well, can you show me the way to the King Elephant?" said the Prince.

"He is to be found close to the very summit of Adam's Peak, in your island of Ceylon," said the tiger; "your Royal Highness knows that, of course."

"It is impossible that it could be so," said the Prince. "The Peak is as sharp as the Matterhorn, and eight thousand feet high."

"Sweet Sahib, Sir Emerson Tennent saw his footsteps there: you will believe *him*."

The tiger was getting rather the best of it; but arguing with an Asiatic is rather difficult. The Prince said, "Hm! well, *he* must know. I think I will go on and find a common elephant." So he turned away, and all of a sudden the tiger set up such a "Garr, buck buck, buck goor," that the whole wood rang, and 2,469 monkeys, who had been sitting in rows on the boughs of trees, unobserved, and listening to every word, went up one bough higher in columns of battalions in echelon from the left. And the oldest monkey said that $x^2 + 17 + \sqrt[2]{y+9}$ = the square described on the hypothenuse of the triangle of the First Life-Guards' band. He thought he had better say something, and so he said that—which did not happen to mean anything at all.

"What are you making that noise about?" said the Prince, turning on the tiger.

"I could not help it, Sahib," said the tiger, crouching.

"You had *better*," said the Prince; "you made that noise once before, and you remember what came of it." And on he went, until he was arrested by a very beautiful sight.

On a great straight bough, which stretched over his path, there sat twenty-nine peacocks in a row, with their backs towards him and their tails drooping down. He was immensely delighted at the beautiful sight, and was standing with his hands behind his back, when the bird on the extreme left—who was, in reality, the drill-sergeant—said—

" 'Tention! Open order from the left." And all the birds shifted along the bough until there were five feet between each.

"Right about face!" said the sergeant; and at once all the peacocks shifted their tails over the bough, and confronted the Prince.

"Prepare spread TAILS!" shouted the drill-sergeant; and the Prince heard him say, in a lower voice, very rapidly, "Now, at the second word of command, I want to see all them tails go up together, same as in presenting of arms. I want 'em all up together, and no fumbling with 'em—like a swell with a new umbrella in a hailstorm. Spread TAILS!"

And up they all went. All except 23's, which wouldn't go up at all. He explained to the sergeant afterwards that it was congenital weakness in his dorsal muscles, and that the doctor never should have passed him; but the sergeant reported him all the same, and the elder Duke Polemos was absolutely *furious*. However, in spite of 23's mishap, the spectacle was extremely fine. The Prince, from his *royal education*, knew enough of drill to keep their tails up till they were tired, and then tell them to put them down again. So, after a few minutes, he sang out, "Drop *tails*. Stand at EASE!" which they did.

After such a splendid pageant, of course there was nothing to do but to make a speech. He knew enough to know *that*. He had never done it before, but as the Columbian Ambassador might say, "waded in." He put his left hand inside the right breast of his tunic, advanced his left leg, and began.

"Gentlemen, I can assure you that I am profoundly moved by the generous manner in which you have drunk your tails—I should say, spread my health. In the whole world, gentlemen, I can conceive of no whatsaname which is more gratifying to one's feelings than a spectacle like this. The safety of this great empire, gentlemen, upon which the sun never sets, is in my mind twenty-five hours out of the twenty-four. And when I come to a remote part of it, such, for instance, as Canada or New Zealand, and find twenty-nine such peacocks as I have seen to-day, presenting tails in such a manner as the peacocks before me, I lay my head on my pillow in peace, knowing that the safety of our empire is secured. Gentlemen, once more I beg to thank you in my own name and the name of my father for the way in which you have thingamied your whatsanames."

The sergeant called for three cheers, but the birds were all shoving and pecking, because some had too much Orange on their necks, and some too much Green. So they never cheered at all.

The Prince beckoned the sergeant down, and he floated down, and alighted at his feet.

"Why," said the Prince, "are there twenty-nine of you?"

"The Fairy Anangke said that there were to be three peacocks for every year of your Royal Highness's life, just to make .333, which is the nearest we can get to 1,000 by decimals, which is the length of your Royal Highness's life, and which is doubled in the number of the beast; and three times 10 is 29."

"But three times 10 is 30," said the Prince.

"Not in the colonies, your Royal Highness," said the sergeant. "No! no! Look at the seven per cent. *ad valorem* duty which Canada puts upon British imports. No, no! Peacock as I am, I know that in the colonies two and two make five."

A low voice, like a vast gigantic sigh behind the Prince, said—

$$x = 20$$
$$y = 20$$

But

$$x^{2569} + y^{2569} = 50."$$

"That is the most absolute and perfect nonsense which ever was talked. How dare you say that of numbers? How dare you say that two and two could make five in any possible combination of any conceivable powers of numbers?"

And, turning round, the Prince found himself face to face with a great grey elephant, who was kneeling down with a log of wood, six feet long, tight held in his trunk.

"Why, goodness me!" said the Prince, "it is *you*. I was coming after you. Why did you say that two and two made five?"

"To call your attention from the peacock," said the elephant, "who was saying just the same. Anangke says that you may ride on me for a little way. Are you afraid of me, my pretty master?"

"Afraid of *you*, dear? I was coming for you."

"Then," said the elephant, "stand still"; and he put down the log of wood, and he curled the trunk round the Prince's waist, and hoisted him up on his shoulder.

"That *is* nice," said the Prince; "but why are you taking up that log of wood again? We don't want *that*."

"It is a railway sleeper," said the elephant.

"*I see*," said the Prince. "Arturio and Athanasio say that the railways have done no good. Polemoi, father and son, say they will extinguish war! and the Polemoi say that war is bad, and though it is their trade they are sick of it. What do *you* think, my old?"

And the elephant said "Hough!" and he didn't say anything else just then, but he trotted on with the Prince on his shoulders and the railway sleeper in his trunk, until they came to the Elephantpoor Junction of the Bombay, Madras, and Calcutta Railway, at which place were assembled 500 elephants, 500 mahouts, 9,400 grass-cutters, 7,220 native troops, and 120 men of the Royal Artillery to keep them in order, and knock their heads together when they misbehaved: which they did most effectually.

"Has the Boy in Grey come here, for I have lost his footsteps?" said the Prince.

And the elephant put down the railway sleeper in its proper place, and then pointed steadily to the great stone railway station with his trunk, saying, "That is one of his footsteps. Did Lord Arturio and Lord Athanasio say that railways were no good?"

"Yes."

"Stuff and nonsense, and rubbish and humbug!" said the elephant with a grunt. "Rapid interchange of commodities brings about rapid interchange of ideas, and the earth not belonging to the devil, the majority of ideas are good, and will get acted on the more rapidly by increased means of communication. Believe an old Indian elephant. I say, Prince, my dear, speak to this gentleman; you are under great obligations to him."

The Prince gave a *royal bow* to a camel who was gawking and maundering by the road-side, and the camel bowed low in return. When they were out of earshot, the Prince said—

"Elephant, please tell me why I am under obligations to him."

"My Prince, it was he who brought mathematics and chemistry from the East to the shore of the Mediterranean, and rendered the railway and the telegraph possible."

"Law!" said the Prince.

"Yes, that is true," said the elephant. "Did you ever hear of the great city he founded?"

"No."

"They call it Palmyra now; formerly it was called Tadmor-in-the-Desert."

"I have heard of it. It was a beautiful city. Did he found it?"

"It was his *stable*," said the elephant. "Damascus was his home. But what between the Chorasmians, the Moguls, and the Crusaders, and the Saracens all getting together by the ears at one and the same time, Palmyra got ruined, and is what you see it now."

"That *is* wonderful," said the Prince. "I wish I had been more polite to him."

"You will meet him again," said the elephant.

"And where will that be?"

"In the centre of Australia," said the elephant; "opening out new lands of inestimable wealth for the brothers and sisters of the Boy in Grey, your subjects. One M'Kinlay is leading him there now."

The Prince sat forward on the elephant's back, with his hand over his forehead, thinking deeply.

"O elephant," he said, "wisest of beasts, tell me some more."

And they had arrived at the bank of the Ganges. And the elephant turned his trunk over his shoulder, and, taking the Prince round the waist, set him down on the sand, with his face to the left, opposite a little heap of black ashes. The Prince backed between the elephant's legs, and said—

"Elephant, I am frightened; there has been a suttee."

And then the elephant took him round the waist once more, and turned him to the right. And the Prince saw a bone sticking up through the sand. And the Prince began to cry.

"O elephant, do not make me look on death. I am too young to look on death. I know that this is the place where the old people were left to die; but do not let me look on death."

But the elephant held him fast for a minute, and then turned him sharp round towards the jungle through which they had come.

And lo! a British officer of artillery, clothed all in white, with a white puggery down his back, and a cloud of natives round him making representations.

And R. A. said, "What is the good of lying like that? The girl is only fourteen, and she don't want it, and the old man is not seventy, and he don't want it—he will live for ten years. And I'll tell you another thing: if I catch any of you at either of these two abominations, *I'll hang you up to the next tree.* It is indecent and abominable, superstitious savagery. *I won't have it!* I have been hard at work killing the tigers which you have not pluck to kill for yourselves, and I have missed the train listening to your lies. There!"

And in fact at that moment the train went roaring over the viaduct across the Ganges. And R. A. lost his temper to that extent that there and then, summing up matters according to the Rabelaisian manner, he boxed, cuffed, and banged his eighteen syces, his punkah wallah, his moonshee, his clean linen wallah, his dirty linen wallah, his powder wallah, his shot wallah, his wads wallah, his caps wallah.

Then he had another turn at the moonshee, who, he said, was the most thundering humbug of the lot. Then he made an onslaught on his bath wallah, his sponge wallah, his toothbrush wallah, his nailbrush wallah, his soap wallah, his hookabadar, his fixature—the best thing for curling the moustaches—wallah.

And then he had a pipe, and left the other two hundred and fifty wallahs in peace.

"What makes him so angry with them?" said the Prince.

"They lie so to him," said the elephant. "And your people hate it, and never forgive it. But high caste people like me know what we owe to R. A."

"Was he the man who put a stop to suttees and exposure?" said the Prince.

"He has put a stop to many things," said the elephant. "I wish he would put a stop to Calcutta. Dalhousie, Canning, Elgin, all dead in that abominable swamp. But, pretty master, we have missed the train, and you must get right on the top of my head and cross your legs to keep your feet dry. For we must swim."

"I don't mind wetting my feet," said the Prince.

"Yes, but you must," said the elephant; "you will be in a cold country this very evening."

"What country?" asked the Prince.

"Canada," said the elephant. "We have dawdled here too long, and the Boy is at the Cape now, if he travels at his usual speed; and you will have to take ship straight from Cape Cormorin to Vancouver's Island. You must miss the Cape."

"Then I shall not see the hyæna," said the Prince.

"But it is your only chance of catching the Boy," said the elephant. "Sit tight, Prince."

And so the elephant swam over the river, and trotted southward through India with the Prince on his head. And the Prince liked it, for in point of conversation there is no one like the elephant. He never *says* anything to you or me, but that renders his conversation the more delightful, because, don't you see? there is no one to contradict you. *To princes,* however, the elephant will talk, and he talked gently to Prince Philarete as he trotted through India.

"If the Boy is gone from the shore," said the Prince, "shall I find a ship to carry me after him?"

Said the elephant, jogging on faster and faster, "There will be two ships waiting for selection by your Royal Highness. I, who know nearly everything, know that. Shall I tell you about them?"

"Please, dear."

"They are the ships of the Ancient Mariner and the Flying Dutchman, and they have been racing home from China, to get the first cargo of tea into London. And they have come to illimitable grief. You have heard of the great annual race home from China?"

The Prince had heard of it.

"Well, these two ships were first favourites for the race (I hope you don't know what *that* means, because if you do you were better dead), and they both sailed together from Hong Kong, loaded with tea. And when they were in the China Sea it came on to blow a cyclone, and all their masts went overboard. Whereupon the Ancient Mariner rigged up a jury fore-topmast on the stump of her foremast, put a rag of a sail on her, put his ship to the wind, lashed the helm, and passed the word for all hands to turn in till further orders. Which his crew did. And when the skipper heard them all snoring, he went below and turned in himself.

"But the Flying Dutchman, my dear Prince," said the elephant, "did nothing of the kind. When his masts were carried overboard, he was determined to assert himself; and he ordered both watches on deck, and pointed out to them that he was the original Flying Dutchman, and that his mother kept the sign of the 'Crooked Billet' at the Five Points, New York. And that didn't do any good in any way, because the starboard watch were mostly negroes and Irish, and the larboard watch was composed of those people who have generally given your Royal Highness a jolly good licking whenever you have meddled with them.

"Then the Flying Dutchman started all his tea overboard, like the Boston folks; but the crew said that was only cutting off his nose to spite his face. 'Let *them* try what they could do,' they said; 'there was the Ancient Mariner not three miles to windward making tolerable weather, and every hand asleep, with the helm lashed.'

"And the skipper said they might try if they'd a mind, but he wanted to try something else first. So he had both watches up to the capstan, and read the Declaration of Independence in his Fire Brigade uniform; but *that* didn't do, and so the crew began to see what *they* could do.

"First of all they tried an ovation; but they all got chucked into the lee-scuppers together by a sudden pitch to larboard, which, of course, pitched the starboard watch, composed of Irish and negroes, on the larboard watch, composed of the Bunker's Hillites; and all the whitewash came off the Irish, and all the black came off the negroes, and there was a nice mess.

"Then they gave the captain a serenade, and as soon as he had got them to leave off he came to the fore part of the quarter-deck, and, in a speech of four hours and twenty-six minutes, again pointed out to them that he was the original Flying Dutchman, and that his mother kept the sign of the 'Crooked Billet' at the Five Points, New York, and that any man who said she did not was a low horse thief. But that did no good.

"But it all came to the same in the end, my dear," said the elephant; "the Ancient Mariner and the Flying Dutchman mean the same thing, for they love the Boy in Grey. When the storm was over, they both made to the same port. We shall see them directly; either of them will take you after the Boy, if he is gone. See, here is the shore of the sea."

"And there is the print of his foot on the sand," said the Prince. "He is gone. O my elephant, where shall I find him?"

"Well, I will tell you," said the elephant. "When the emu wren lights on your shoulder as the Bird of Paradise did, and when White's thrush sings its tor-r-r-oo, tor-r-r-oo, you are not far from him. You have much to go through, and only an afternoon and a night. Good-bye, love! Come again! come again!"

And the elephant trotted away through the forest, and there came to him the Ancient Mariner and the Flying Dutchman.

At first he thought that the Ancient Mariner was a boy, for his gait was so elastic, and his eye and his complexion were clear; but looking at his head, he saw that his short cropped hair was whitened with the snows of eleven centuries. He was dressed only in the man-of-war's shirt and trousers, with bare feet and bare bosom, like a man-of-war's boy, and his bare breast was tattooed over with names innumerable, which the Prince tried to read; and as he tried to read them, he felt that the ruby was not only burning his breast, but was illuminating certain letters on the old young man's left breast over *his* heart. And the Prince read, all crowded together without order:—"Sluys, 1340." "Sally, the Girl of my Heart." "Aboukir." "Franklin." "Magpie schooner." "Rattlesnake." "Fox yacht." "Trafalgar." "Lifeboat." "Warwick and Parliament, 1642." "Atlantic Cable." "Drake for Acapulco." "Fitzroy." And there were many more; but the Prince read no more, but said instantly to the Ancient Mariner, "I will sail with you, please."

The Flying Dutchman spoke at once, and the Prince looked at him. He was a glorious creature, nine hundred years younger in years than the Ancient Mariner, yet not much younger in work. He also had some names tattooed on his bare bosom, but they were names which the Prince hated to look at:—"Chesapeake." "Macedonian."

"It was a foolish quarrel, that of my fathers," he said.

"I shall have other names scored on my heart soon," said the Flying Dutchman. Indeed he had, poor boy; for soon after this he fell to loggerheads with his brother about the relative height of two stools, and Prince Philarete, trying to sit on both at once, to show that there was no difference in the height of them, came down by the run, and has to pay his own doctor's bill. At least, so they say; and all this is true; that is the point of the joke, if there be any joke at having such words as "Antietam" or "Chancellorsville" written on your heart.

"Sorry you can't sail with me, Prince," said the Flying Dutchman; "however, we are both bound for the same port in the end. *He* will show you to the Boy in Grey as well as I."

And the Prince went on board the Ancient Mariner's ship, which had come to grief in the China race, just like the Flying Dutchman's. It was a remarkable ship, very much tinkered up, but an uncommon good ship for sailing.

When they got the anchor up, and had put some sail on her, and she was moving through the water, the Ancient Mariner gave his orders: "Lash the helm to windward!" and they did that. "All hands turn in!" and they did that too, like winking. And when the Ancient Mariner heard them all snoring in their bunks, he went below and turned in himself, leaving the Prince on the quarter-deck singing out, "Hi! here! hallo! This won't do, you know! Get up, some of you!" but they didn't mind him a bit in the world.

"The ship will go to the bottom," said the Prince.

But she didn't, but got to British Columbia that very afternoon, after a slow passage of one hour and twenty-two minutes.

This may appear incredible to certain captious and incredulous readers; but I can only say that I who write, and live thirty-five miles from London, walked to my neighbour's door the other day at half-past eleven. And I said to him, "Congress vetoed that bill of the President's last night. I thought they would." I forget what the matter was now: something which interested us for a time. It is a standing joke with us now. The *Times*, from which I got my information, must have had it by half-past six in the morning. To amuse one, as the French say, let us recall the great telegraphic banquet given, I think, at the Langham Hotel; when after dinner they telegraphed healths to New York and to Calcutta, and received complimentary replies while still over their wine, with an account of the weather. The worst danger of all this is, that if we mislay our tempers we shall be at war before we have time to find them again; at least, that is the elephant's opinion.

The Prince met the Russian Bear and the American Bear out a-walking the other day in Alaska, and asked their opinion on this subject; but they were diplomatic. The Russian Bear said, "Grumph!" and the American Bear spoke for two hours and forty-five minutes, using the most beautiful tropes and figures you ever heard; and ended by saying that after this short expression of his sentiments he would conclude.

CHAPTER VII

IT WAS A LONG BROAD OCEAN SHORE on which the Prince landed, but the naked footsteps were there before him, and he held his way steadily across the broad sands towards the melancholy forest capes which fringed them, and so plunged boldly and at once into the great pine-forests of British Columbia, where he saw nothing at all; but coming on to the tracks of Lord Milton and Doctor Cheadle, and finding that the Boy in Grey's trail was the same as theirs, he stepped out and got over the Rocky Mountains into Canada in about half an hour, singing—

> "Earth moves on with accumulative forces:
> Where should we be but for those who've gone before?
> Shanks's mare, the iron foal, steamships, camels, horses,
> Toiling onward night and day by desert, stream, and shore.
>   But Shanks his mare is always first,
>   Spite of hunger, danger, thirst;
>   So here's a health, and three good cheers,

> For all glorious pioneers.
> There are none on the earth who can compare
> With those who ride on Shanks his mare."

"The sentiment's very pretty," said a voice on a tree close to him, "but it don't seem to me to scan out clean. Our people are insisting on good scanning now, except in the case of Walt Whitman, who don't go in for that line of art. I can't offer more than eighteen dollars, and I wouldn't offer more than fourteen if you weren't a Prince. I would make it more if I could, but I have a large family, and I really can't. I'll guarantee you a circulation in our bi-weekly of two hundred and fifty thousand. Write it down, and I'll hand over the cash."

And the Prince said, "I'll see you blowed first—as my father's herald said to his new trumpet before he bought it." By which piece of *courtly dexterity* the Prince only just saved himself from making a most *low* and *vulgar* remark.

"Well, I don't blame you for holding out," said the American mocking-bird. "Say twenty dollars. Come, I will sing you a song."

And he sung him one, a real American.

"Hah!" said the Prince; "I heard that you could sing if you chose."

And he tried to sing himself as he passed on into the forest. But after that he did not make much hand of it, and after a time let it alone. He began again, seeking for the *divine afflatus.*

> "Here's good health, and three good cheers,
> To our glorious pioneers."

And the two pioneers in question were as near as possible finding their names wedded to immortal verse, but for the life of him the Prince could not find any rhyme for "Milton" except "Stilton," or for "Cheadle" except "Beadle." And they neither of them suited, for no *gentleman*, leave alone a *prince*, would take a liberty with another gentleman's name. So he sang a song which had been taught him by a young lady-in-waiting when he was very young. And he remembered with sadness that she died soon, before his brother Henri, and how sorry his mother had been. This was the song:

> " 'Who will be my love,
>   Now while the cowslip blows,
> Bending as I pass,
>   Watching the wild hedge-rose?'

> " 'I will be thy love,'
>   Rang the bluebell loud and deep;
> 'I am blue as thine own eyes, darling,
>   And the rose is asleep.'

> " 'I will be thine,' said the oak-leaf.
>   'Cowslip and bluebell fade,
> They faint and die in summer
>   Under my shade.'

"The wild rose woke at last,
    Sung out loud and free,
'I am thy love, thine own love,
    Come to me.

" 'I am the flower of delight,
    Of memory, music, and song;
I sleep through the winter night,—
    I have slept long.

" 'At the sound of thy feet in the dew,
    At the sound of thy voice in the mead.
I awakened and budded and blew,
    Thy love indeed.'

"With a kiss for the bluebell and rose,
    And a smile for the oak overhead,
He bore back his heart to the cowslip,
    But the cowslip was dead."

And then he turned to whistling, and he whistled "Acis and Galatea" all through until he was near the very end. But when he was nearly done, some one, sitting on a pine bough, who turned out to be the carrion crow, said—

"Hawk. Crawk. That is only falsetto. The pitch is much too high. Don't you know that we are all going to have new pitch forks, I mean tuning forks, the vibrations of which will be just $30,000^{\text{nth}}$—$20^4\sqrt{x+48,000}^2$ lower than the old ones? You are not up to the time."

"My time was very good," said the Prince; "and your formula is nonsensical and impossible."

"That is what they say about here, anyhow," said the Crow. "The old pitch murders my larynx. Hawk. Shaw. Gah.

That is the way to sing."

"You are rather hoarse, sir," said the Prince.

"Like Falstaff, with Hallelujahing and singing of anthems," said the crow. "Crawk. Here is the humming-bird. Now he is going to take my character away. I fell into trouble when I was younger, I allow that; but I have been a respectable character for these three days, and am likely to be so for another week if they don't leave their things lying about."

The humming bird sang,

And then he passed into prose, and said in Canadian French, very jerky, with all the short syllables huddled together, and all the long syllables lengthened into a drawl—

"Sir-r-r, I proceed to precise my accusation against the gentleman in black on the bough there, who has just abandoned speech. At one time parson, at one time priest; at one time politician, at one time philanthropist; at one time burglar, at one time pickpocket. Now a stealer of pence out of the trays of blind men's dogs; at another the robber of the slippers of the faithful at the door of a mosque during prayer time. He is *roleur, coquin, brigand*. I precise my accusation by accusing him of stealing my wife's eggs."

"Why did she leave them about, then?" bawled the carrion crow. "I am one of the criminal classes, I am; and what I want is to be kep' out of temptation. And I don't want my moral tone lowered by corporal punishment. That don't suit me, that don't."

The Prince briefly explained to the carrion crow that he was after the Boy in Grey, and that he should be returning with him to-morrow. And he told the carrion crow what he and the Boy in Grey would do with him if they found him there on their return.

And the carrion crow said, "Oh, blow that!" and he flew away through the wood, right against Colonel Henderson, who having studied the works and ways, and also the hopes and chances, of the criminal class, as Governor of West Australia, wisely and well, happened to be walking homewards through this very wood to see what he could do for the Prince, when the crow flew against him.

And he knew his bird in an instant, did Colonel Henderson. And the Colonel boxed his ears and put him in his coat pocket, and there he is now. Only the Colonel takes him out once a year, boxes his ears, and puts him in again. Since which course of proceeding the Registrar-General noticed that eggs, as an article of human food, have increased .228 beyond the average of the last ten years. This is at all events a result; and as it comes out of a State paper from Fetter Lane, you cannot for a moment suppose that there is anything *ex parte* about it.

The next person the Prince met was an ermine in his summer clothes. And the ermine said, "Bother *you*. Why can't your mother wear Russian, and leave her own ermines alone?" And he cut and ran for his life.

And the next person the Prince met was a noble young Highlander, in deer-skin leggings, but with a plaid over his shoulders, who was sitting in a canoe reading, and who bowed to him and said—

"Ye're late, sir, and he is on before. But I would leave no Indian to have the guiding of you. Get in, Prince, and talk to me. There is no portage now between us and the great Atlantic. Dare you go over Saute Sainte Marie with me?"

"Has *he* gone?"

"Yes, he has gone," said the Highlander.

So the Prince got into the canoe, and nestled against the Highlander. And the

Highlander's name was Gil Macdonald. And once this Highlander wrote a book, about how he got from Hudson's Bay to the Red River in a canoe. The book is out of print and I have forgotten even the title; but it remains one of the best books of travel which I have read.

CHAPTER VIII

Aₛ ₛₒₒₙ ₐₛ the Prince was comfortably packed into the birch-bark canoe beside the young Highlander, it occurred to the Prince to ask the Highlander what he was.

"Clerk in the Hudson's Bay Company. Detailed by the Fairy Anangke and the Boy in Grey to help you on."

"We must go very fast."

"One thousand miles the hour. Ye'll be in time. You are to go in shore at a hail. Mind the bough, dear."

And so they began their quaint voyage through Canada.

"What is the name of this river, please?" asked the Prince.

"This is the Minneseewahaha, or River of Happy Recollections," answered Gil Macdonald. "You will see some bodies ye ken weel enow."

"It is very solemn and beautiful," said the Prince.

Indeed it was. It was a broad limestone river, ever growing wider, crystal clear, with swift streams and eddies, and it swept on walled by gigantic hemlock firs, sometimes by feathering oaks and beeches; very solemn, still, and silent indeed. The canoe scarcely wanted the aid of Gil's paddle, and the Prince, with his cheek on the deer-skin knee of Gil, looking dreamily into the tree-tops as they sped swiftly along.

"Look over the side," said Gil.

And looking down, the Prince said, "Why, there are peacocks in this water."

"They are the *Salmo fontalis*, the burn trout of Canada" (he *said* Salma fontaaleese, which King James I. of England and some *more recent authorities* tell us is the *proper* way of pronouncing Latin); "they are brighter in colour than our *Salma fleuveeaateleese*, and are not to be confounded with them."

At this moment they rounded a turn in the river, and the Prince made a jump to one side of the canoe, and with a loud glad cry held out his arms.

"Ha' a care, Prince! Ha' a care!" cried Gil. "Ye'll wholme us keel uppermost. These are unco kittle craft of ours, ye must ken. I'll put ye ashore to the daft rintherout callant e'en now."

On the point of the rock stretching into the stream stood a boy in light belted flannel trousers and a blue flannel shirt, who executed a small short dance when he saw them. It was Scud East.

"Scud! Scud!" said the Prince, "who would have thought of seeing *you* here?" and as he jumped ashore up ran Tom Brown and Arthur, and there was such a cackling of happy recollections that you could hardly hear yourself speak.

"But where is Martin?" said the Prince at last.

Scud put his hands to his mouth, and sent a shout through the forest. "Madman! Madman! here is Philarete."

The answer came from one hundred and fifty feet in the air, and it was, "Don't kick up that beastly row, Scud. I have got the eggs, and I have got a live raccoon round the neck. He has bit me to the bone three times, but I have got him, and I am coming down."

There was a slithering noise, and a terrible cracking of broken boughs, and down came the Madman by the run; sticking, however, tight to his raccoon.

"Here," said the raccoon, "you keep your hands off me. What were you doing up *my* tree? I wasn't up to nothink. I'll have you took to the Doctor as sure as you're born. Let me go, I tell you."

Martin offered him to the Prince, who let him go, and he ran away. And he ran up into a tree, and began preaching a sermon about Naboth's vineyard, or, as he put it, the invasion of other chaps' little places. He began his sermon then, which was many years ago, and he hasn't finished it yet. The last time I saw him he was hammering away at it as hard as ever.

"We must cut, Philarete," said Tom Brown, "or we shall be late for locking-up. The Boy in Grey was with us to-day. Remember what the Bird of Paradise said."

" 'Ware louts!" cried Scud East.

And they turned towards the forest, and saw two dim figures stalking through it; both dressed like Indians.

"It is only Pathfinder and Chingachgook," said Tom Brown, "going to set their beaver-traps. I say, Philarete, old boy, look on the beavers when they hail you. Good-bye."

And so the Prince was in the canoe again speeding down the river. He looked back at the next bend, and he saw Tom, Scud, Arthur, and Martin standing in a row, watching him, with their arms twined as closely round one another's necks as they have twined them round our hearts.

The next turn in the river brought them a new adventure. Gil with dexterity ran the canoe up a little sandy cove, right at the feet of an aged gentleman in the costume of the early part of the eighteenth century, who sat in a chair, with one leg crossed over the other, thinking. Behind him was a black gentleman, with a sky-blue tail coat down to his heels, and his collar up to his eyes, and a large eye-glass, who also appeared lost in thought.

"How do you do, sir," said the Prince.

"I am perfectly well, sir," said Robinson Crusoe.

"Do you always sit like that?" said the Prince, for he thought he *might* have risen even if he had sat down directly afterwards.

"No, sir," said Robinson Crusoe, changing his legs; "I sometimes sit like that."

"What do you do to pass away your time, sir?"

"Think," said Robinson Crusoe.

"What do you think about?" asked the Prince.

"The permission of evil."

"And what do *you* think about, for instance?" asked the Prince, turning round to the gentleman in the sky-blue tail coat.

"Brack jebblem, sar," replied Friday, "him likewise think about permissions of evil."

"Could you not give me a tune on your banjo?" asked the Prince.

"He has quitted such vanities," said Robinson Crusoe.

And the Prince got into the canoe again.

But he most solemnly avers that he saw the end of Mr. Friday's banjo sticking out from under Robinson Crusoe's chair at the time he was talking to him. He says he is *sure* of it. And Gil declares that before they turned the next bend Friday had taken it out and was hard at it, thrumpty thrumpty, with—

"Guinea-corn, I love to hyam you."

"Two of the best fellows who ever lived," remarked Gil. "But they have talked themselves to a deadlock, and there they are. They dare not even get their banjoes out if any one's looking."

So they sailed on past another bend, and on a point were two gentlemen arm in arm, standing waiting for them, and beside them was a little young lady dressed for a ball *with only one shoe on*. The Prince landed, walked up to them, and said—

"Dear Colonel Dobbin, I hope you are quite well. Colonel Crawley, you are not looking well: I fear Coventry Island does not agree with you. Give my love to Rawdy. Miss Cinderella, I was delighted to hear that you got home from the Mansion House ball quite safe; I believe that I have to *congratulate* you. Give my love to Toto, and ask him to come and play with me. I have such fine toys; I have a beautiful new Xylopodo——"

Here the Prince broke off quite short, and retreated hurriedly to the canoe. For he saw, coming swiftly through the forest, a tall old lady in a dressing gown and nightcap, with a bundle of tracts in one hand and a black dose in the other. And he knew her, for it was Lady Southdown come to convert the Indians; so he fled, and left Dobbin, Crawley, and Cinderella standing together on the dim shore of the Minneseewahaha.

When he was afloat again he began to cry, which was not much in his line. And when Gil asked him "what gar'd him greet," he said, "I am so sorry for poor Colonel Crawley."

And Gil said, "There is more joy in heaven over the sinner that repenteth, than over ninety and nine just men who need no repentance. See to her, for instance, now. Do you mind what the blackbird sang at Glastonbury?"

The group which confronted the Prince at this landing was the strangest and quaintest he had met yet. The woman to whom Gil had pointed with his paddle was dressed in grey, with a scarlet letter on her bosom. What the original letter was is no matter now, for it was gone, and turned into a great red flaming R. And his ruby burnt so hot upon his heart that he held it off his breast. Beside her stood a tall gentleman about fifty, with a folded paper in his hand, in clothes which apparently were not made for him, but towards whom the Prince instantly conceived a deep devotion. Beside him stood a dead young lady of great beauty, awful, beautiful, but apparently silent for ever, under whose feet lay two rattlesnakes, crushed, thank Heaven! to death at last.

Colonel Sprowle began the conversation.

"I bid you welcome, sir. You are after the Boy in Grey. Yes, sir. I have induced my two friends, Mrs. Hester Prynne and Miss Elsie Venner, to assist with me in giving you an ovation, and, if agreeable, a serenade. I was killed, sir, as you no doubt remember, in a piece of forest-land beyond the Chickahominy. I have a neat oration wrote out, ready to deliver, sir, by old Waxworks Ward, of Baldwinsville, Indiana, who came to a heap of trouble down South himself. Instead of speaking it, sir, I will just hand it over for you to read as you go down stream in your dug-out. Our time is very short, sir; we must be back immediately."

Elsie Venner said, without a hiss in her voice now, but in round sound English—

> "The cock is crowing a merry midnight;
> I wot the wild fowls are boding day;
> The Psalms of Heaven will soon be sung,
> And we'll be missed away."

And so *they* were gone, and the canoe went onwards, but the Prince was crying again. He was crying about Colonel Sprowle now; thinking how Colonel Sprowle, when the Southerners had the best of it, had defended that narrow place in the woodlands with a shrewdness and valour beyond all praise, knowing that he was defending the retreat of the Northern army; and how at night, when Colonel Bernard came in with a flag of truce to sort the dead, he found Colonel Sprowle nearest of all of them to the enemy save two—two young men, the sons of the wild gipsy woman who lived up the mountain and brought Bernard the rattlesnakes, and were content to die with the Colonel, having seen his works and his ways, and having made up their minds that he was a good man. You say, young one, that this is all Greek to you. Read "Elsie Venner," and it will be Greek no longer.

"Dinna greet ower 'em," said Gil; "they died the death of men, fighting for their ain cause: would ye have better death than *that*? I wished them ill at one time, but they will doubtless respect the claims both of the Hudson's Bay and the North-west Company. Wipe your een, man; wipe your een. Here's a whole lot more of them."

And indeed there were. In a pretty savannah, hemmed in by the great forest, with one point of it running out into the stream, there was such a crowd of faces that the Prince was quite confused.

CHAPTER IX

THERE WAS NO DOUBT about one thing. The fat old lady in the black bonnet, who was at the very point of the meadow, and was hailing them by wildly waving a green umbrella, was Mrs. Gamp; and it was also perfectly evident that Mrs. Gamp was tipsy, for she fell into the water sideways, and was pulled out by Tim Linkinwater and Mr. Tapley. She *said* that she slipped, but Captain Cuttle and Mrs. Nickleby agreed that she had had too much to drink, and had overbalanced herself. So they left her to be watched, and, as far as possible, dried, by Joe Gargery and Mr. Snodgrass.

The proceedings were also disagreeably enlivened on the landing of the Prince, by a terrible squabble between Aunt Clegg, Aunt Pullet, Mr. Pecksniff, and the Queen of Hearts. Aunt Clegg's thesis was that Mr. Pecksniff was not sober, and had lost one of his shoes, a most undeniable major. But Aunt Pullet, taking up the argument, made such a wild wandering affair of it, that the Queen of Hearts, looking more cross than ever Tenniel made her look, declared that in future all syllogisms were to be kept in celarunt, under penalty of decapitation. And Mr. Pecksniff, a man who never spoke the truth, applauded her highly.

Said Alice to Silas Marner, "How they squabble and fight! Come away with me, and show me your loom, my dear; and show me the place where you hid your money."

And so those two trotted off, and Tom Pinch ran after them, and said, "Hi! here! Silas Marner, wait for me. Show me your loom, and I will show you my organ."

So in consequence the Prince saw nothing of Silas Marner, Tom Pinch, or Alice: those three went to Wonderland together. But he had an interview with Aunt Clegg, for all that.

I am not in a position to state what passed. She succeeded in exasperating him beyond mortal endurance, and he lost his temper. Arthur Pendennis, Don Quixote, and Sir Joshua Reynolds, three men always willing to make peace, interfered; but it was no good. She only said that three fools added to one made four. So they sent, by the Hon. Elijah Pogram's advice, for Doctor Johnson, who said to Arthur Pendennis, "That which is nearest to us affects us most: the passions rise higher at domestic than at imperial tragedies." But Aunt Clegg had nailed her colours to the mast, and said that you could always tell the biggest fools in a company by the length of their words. There was nothing to be done with her at all, until Père Goriot, Mr. Jaggers, Falstaff, and Madame Bonbeck got her in conversation and led her away.

The elder Mr. Chuzzlewit said, "Really, that lady seems to have mislaid her temper. We wanted to give the Prince a welcome among us. Now I warn you, that if any *gentleman* mislays his temper, I shall send for John Halifax;" and then this party were among the past.

In a shady place by the river-side they saw Mr. Punch walking up and down arm in arm with a Bishop. Mr. Punch was faultlessly dressed in a blue frock coat with velvet collar, white waist-coat, and large watch chain, a beautiful new hat, and straw-coloured kid gloves: the respectable millionaire all over. The Prince hardly knew him; but he could not help wondering what the Bishop would say, if he knew that only the week before, Mr. Punch, *in far other costume,* had beaten the Beadle's brains out, and that he and his friends had stood by laughing and encouraging him, and that Athanasio had given him a three-penny-piece to do it again.

He rather thought that he had best not land under the circumstances; particularly as there was a bagpipe and fiddle plainly audible in the next reach. They were soon round the bend, and there was a crowd there with a vengeance.

CHAPTER X

THIS CROWD WAS more motley than the last, but Philarete knew them better than those he had last seen.

Foremost among them, close to the water's edge, were two great Scotch stag-hounds, which he knew to be Bran and Buscar, and between them stood a little withered man in the dress of the last century, whom he recognised in an instant as Peter Peebles.

"And what are ye saying till it a', Prince?" he began as soon as the canoe touched the shore. "Ye look brawly. But I hae nae doubt ye are ganging a gait which will guide ye to sorrow. Ye are in ill company, for a breekit Hielandman is a Hielandman still. When the deil gangs to kirk, he pits his tail down his trouser-leg. A skeeley tod can make the same stink as a puir brock when the dogs are at the cairn's mouth. Aweel. I hae to apply to your Highness for letters of law-burrow against——"

"Haud your whist, mun!" said Gil, furious at his insolence against the Highlanders; "the Prince does not understand Scottish law."

"And haud *your* whist, ye ill-looking, land-louping vagabond!" replied Peter. "It is little that you or your forbears ever kenned of Scottish law, save the big gallows at Crieff. Ye are just as Hieland as the muckle deil himself. I apply to his gracious Highness for letters of law-burrow against Alexander Sanders, or Alick Glengoldnie of that ilk, vulgarly known as Alick Dhu, for that he, having conceived a great and deadly malice against the said complainer, he himself, his wife, bairns, men tenants, servants, and others, in his name, does continually cause, send, hound out, and command resett, assistance, and rehabilitation to ane Meg Merrilies——"

Here the Prince began to laugh, for he saw what was coming.

"——who casts down his dikes, destroys his henings, wins peats without license, liberty, or tolerance; the whilk Meg Merrilies is a daft randy quean, a spaewife and gipsy——"

Here he got a box on the ear which sent him staggering, and Philarete found himself standing face to face with a woman whom he had never dreaded at her worst, but had always loved; and he saw that, scarred and smitten as the face was with eighty years of sorrow, it was more beautiful than ever. She raised him, and sat him on her strong arm, and he kissed her on the cheek, just as the Baron of Bradwardine came up and demanded to take off his boots after his battle with Peter Peebles; a ceremony which the Prince graciously pretermitted.

And then came a glorious hour, an hour the like of which can come twice to no boy; an hour with the people whom Scott created.

He thought he had been but a few minutes when he heard Gil crying for him, and Meg Merrilies hurried him down to the canoe. Peter Peebles had disappeared for no good, thought Meg; and now once more they were afloat on the Minneseewahaha.

CHAPTER XI

"WHO ARE THOSE TWO," asked the Prince in a whisper, "who are lying there asleep together under the yew? See, she has her hand on his breast, and he has his hand in her hair."

"Whist!" said Gil; "they are no asleep, they are dead. It is Romeo and Juliet. Sair misguided in this world by dynastic tradition, but no divided in their death."

"Here are some others," said Philarete. "Who are those two pretty ones sitting fishing and sucking oranges, and who are those two beside them cracking nuts with their teeth?"

"The twa with the oranges," said Gil, "are Paul and Virginia; the twa cracking nuts are Benedick and Beatrix."

"Are Benedick and Beatrix cross to one another now?"

"No," said Gil, "they studied one another's tempers, and they have but one soul between them till the crack of doom."

"Please, Gil," said Philarete, "what became of Maggie and Tom Tulliver?"

"They live in the block house called Expiation, which is in the centre of Lake Manitou, where we shall be directly. Lake Manitou, ye doubtless ken, means the Lake of God; the place where He has prepared peace on earth for those that He thinks need it. The brother and sister live there all alone, and no canoe goes by their house. The Boy in Grey was with them for an hour yestreen, but he is gone forward."

"Does any one else live on Lake Manitou?"

"Only Hamlet, with Jacques to see after him and mind his house. We shall see the lake directly, but we must go ashore here. Did you hear that hail?"

"I heard some one grunting," said Philarete.

"It is the beavers," said Gil. "Mind what Tom Brown asked of you."

They now landed in a very swampy place, and the Prince got over one of his shoes in mud at once, and dirtied his white silk stockings. "I shall have both my shoes off here directly," he said. So Gil hoisted him on his back, and the Prince went in that fashion to the interview with the beavers.

And a nice mess they were making of it. There were two streams which met inland, one called Capital and the other Labour. Now, the older beavers had, from time immemorial, possessed the stream called Capital, and had dammed it, and had got on very well for many years, because their progeny were always killed off by the Hudson Bay trappers to make beaver hats.

But a time came when Lincoln and Bennett invented silk hats, and then there was much less demand for beaver-skins. Then their progeny, not being killed off in war, began to grow on them, and it was necessary to come to some arrangement.

So the young beavers said that they must marry and live, and that they would go to the brook Labour, and dam that. And the elder beavers said, "All right; our brook is the biggest."

But the younger beavers made such an enormously big dam that they sent half the water over into the elder beavers' dam, and flooded their lodges. Whereupon the elder beavers, after scratching their heads with their tails, set to work and raised their dam one foot, whereby they certainly succeeded in flooding the lodges of the junior beavers, but were put to the expense of putting an extra storey on their own, which the junior beavers could not afford.

Consequently at the Prince's arrival, the whole place was in a state of crock and mud. Gil, carrying the Prince, lost both his moccasins, and drew his stockinged feet out of the dirt like drawing corks. At last he perched the Prince on the master beaver's lodge, and the beavers from both rivers rallied round him. The master beaver had rheumatism in the fishy part of his tail, and could not appear; but the Prince heard him as he sat on the roof of his lodge, underneath him, grunting.

The Prince sat cross-legged on the roof of the master beaver's lodge, while matters were explained to him by both the Capital and Labour beavers. When he had read all they had to say, he answered—

"Lower away both your dams, so as not to annoy one another," which, for a boy of ten years old, was not so bad. The beavers set to work doing it at once.

But the skunk was furious. He had climbed out on to the dam to listen, and when he heard the decision of the Prince he made such a smell that the beavers chivied him and pulled him into the clean water—a thing he hated.

But the beavers were greatly pleased with the Prince's decision. The youngest and most hot-headed of the junior beavers said that really after this the question between an hereditary and an elective presidency was open to discussion. In fact, the Prince was a success. The junior beavers at once held a mass meeting, and unanimously resolved to leave off gnawing through a tall tree called Commerce, which, had they continued, would have fallen right across the senior beavers' lodges.

And then the Great Master Beaver of all Beavers (G.M.B.O.A.B. *he* called himself), in spite of his rheumatism, came out of his lodge under water, and said with a grunt—

"Come into the Great Lodge and be made a Beaver. Come and be initiated."

Philarete said that he must hurry along after the Boy in Grey, and that he could not go under water in his best clothes.

"We will make you $\pi \beta \phi \pi \tau$."

"I don't think I should like it," said Philarete.

"We will make you duplex $\sigma \sigma$ duplex $\tau \tau$."

"I really have not time," said Philarete.

"Will you be $\kappa \lambda \chi \delta \Theta$?" said the G.M.B.O.A.B.

"I have not got so far in my Buttmann's Greek grammar as that. I remember $\lambda \mu \nu \rho$, but I don't like it."

"Well," said the Master Beaver, "you will be with us in time. Take," he continued, "these two gentlemen to the river, wash the Prince's silk stockings clean, and find Mr. Macdonald's moccasins. Are you going to take him over the Saute Sainte Marie?" he added to Gil Macdonald, in a whisper.

"Yes."

"You will try his metal there."

"It wants no trying," said Gil. "I have tried it, and it rings true."

"Ah!" said the Master Beaver, "what Princes could do if they chose!"

"Ye may weel say that," replied Gil. "Alternate plagues and blessings; but Presidents and Emperors are but little better. By the by, our people are not troubling yours just now. Beaver-skins are no worth a bawbee."

"Well, that is a good thing," said the Master Beaver.

"I suppose ye've heard that the Hudson's Bay Company are about selling their territory to the Dominion, and that you will be at the tender mercy of the settlers?"

The Master Beaver instantly dived into his lodge without saying good-bye, and made his will, leaving the whole of his property to the Hudson's Bay Company. But as he had not got any it did not much matter, and they never took the trouble to prove his will, as you will see if you examine the papers at this moment before Parliament.

The junior beavers cleaned the Prince's stockings, and found Gil's moccasins. After which they had another mass meeting, and unanimously voted that it was Whit Monday (it was nothing of the sort, it was the Saturday before the Tenth Sunday after Trinity, but *public opinion* prevailed), and that consequently they must all go to Greenwich fair in steamboats. Which they did.

"Where next, Gil?" said Philarete.

"Lake Manitou," replied Gil, and added, "Mind, ye are no to say one word to any one, save me, all the time ye cross it."

"May I not say one word to Hamlet, just to tell him how sorry I was about the accident with Polonius?"

"Not one word."

"May I not kiss Maggie Tulliver? Oh, please!"

"Ye maun do nothing of the kind. Both she and Hamlet are dreeing their weird, whilk the Papists have erected into the superstition of purgatory, an idle and foolish thing, but for which they say they find Scripture in John xx. verse 17, and elsewhere. It is a thrawn thing to believe, but mind ye dinna speak to Hamlet or Maggie Tulliver."

The river widened among majestic islands until it expanded into the lake, a calm sheet of water among towering woodlands. Gil had scarcely begun paddling across it, when he bent down his head, and whispered in Philarete's ear, "Yon's Maggie."

She was bare headed, and was pushing her canoe up a narrow creek which ran into the forest, reading a book the while. The dark night of her hair was towards them, and the Prince said—

"Will she turn her head?"

"No fear," said Gil. "She reads nought but her Thomas à Kempis now. Be quiet, man! ye are among the deid folk."

"Does Tom love her now?" asked Philarete, in spite of the caution.

"Who could help it? But she is not as she was. Her face is always turned now towards that great God who inspired a woman with the genius that created her." Which was Greek to Philarete, beyond Buttmann.

"Is that Hamlet?" he asked.

"The gentleman fishing with a cork float off the little block house? No, that is Jacques. He is sitting there and thinking about God's permission of evil and cruelty anent wounded staigs and such cattle, just as Robinson Crusoe did, you remember, and impinging live worms on his hook the while, to catch fish for Lord Hamlet's dinner. He represents one kind of sentimentality. Prince Hamlet (a bonny chiel, but misguided) sits up near the roof, looking for his father's ghaist, and thinking that he had cut one man's throat too few. The O'Donoghue's ghaist came from the Lake of Killarney to plague him, but he would have none of it, and threepit to the American Government anent the nuisance. But the American Government made reply, that although the O'Donoghue of that time had without doubt committed murder, spulsie, deforcement, raid, violent incoming, and arson, yet it was committed on patriotic grounds; and that therefore they could not move in the matter. So Prince Hamlet retired north of the Eider."

"I don't understand that last," said Philarete.

"No fear you would. It only means this. England was stalemated by America, and Prince Hamlet went to the wall, about the Denmark business."

They had crossed the lake now, and were in the great river again. Into the reservoir which they had crossed so quickly innumerable rivers had poured their floods, and when Gil and the Prince got into the new river they saw that it was four times the size of the old one—broader, more majestic, more powerful. There is no resisting these great American rivers; you must swim with the tide. Sometimes, however, old formations, like that of the old sandstone at Niagara, rise and torture these rivers, which is a great trouble.

"Sit again with your head on my knees, Prince," said Gil. "Are you frightened?"

"No," said Philarete. "I am afraid of nothing with you."

"We are going over the Saute Sainte Marie," said Gil. "Do ye ken the mystery of it?" Said Philarete, "No."

"The boy who dares to stand up in the canoe when she dips over the lip of the Saute Sainte Marie—whilk, ye ken, is the Fall of the Virgin—will live long, and see the Boy in Grey. The boy who dares not stand up will see him never, in this world or in the next."

As Gil spoke, the terrible roar of the great cataract was in their ears. The river, gathered from innumerable sources, was overwhelmingly powerful, but glassy, smooth, and swift, walled by tall pine trees. Passing rapidly round a bend in the river, Philarete saw what was before him. He said, suddenly, "Must we go?"

"After the Boy in Grey? Yes," said Gil.

Philarete rose and stood in the bow of the canoe, with outspread arms to balance himself. Water and earth alike fell away from them utterly, and before he had time to say more than "O God, who stillest the raging of the waters," he was alone with Gil in a frail canoe among the hissing eddies of the most famous of American rapids.

When the canoe gave the first sickening dip into the tortured raging waters, he gave himself up for lost, the whole matter seemed so helpless and horrible. For three-quarters of a mile before him he saw nothing but a seething hill of water, dipping one foot in thirty-seven, the roar of which was heard for thirty miles. Where were his father and mother now? Where were Polemos, Arturio, and Athanasio now? What were they doing or thinking about? But the Boy in Grey was on before, and the weird was on him, and so he stood with his arms out in the bow of the canoe and balanced himself.

Peter Peebles was the last man they saw in this terrible part of their journey. He had discovered a statute against the deforcement and wilful misguidement of princes ("and sic cattle," *he* said), "passed by the Scottish Parliament after the assault on the pious body of the amiable and excellent Jamie Sixth of Scotland, First of England, by the daft rintherout callant Ruthven at Perth. Whilk Act provided that any one, leave alone a Hieland cattle-lifter, who should commit deforcement, or in any way bring into danger, or have suspicion of doing constructive spulsie on the Lord's anointed, should thereby and then——"

They lost a lot of his argument here, for he was flying from one rock to another, as if he were Mr. Bright, and they were a salmon. And his wig was off, and his old coat-tails were flying about his ears. The last they heard of him was—

"And so the aforesaid Peter Peebles deponeth and maketh oath, that the aforesaid Gil or Gilbert Macdonald of Glen Strae, in opposition of the law above mentioned, has violently possessed himself of the person of an anointed prince, with a pair of silken hose worth one hundred pounds Scots, and a ruby worth two hundred millions Scots, whilk——"

They saw no more of him after this. The Prince once looked back on to the leaping wall of water which they had passed, and wondered that they had lived. Yet they were alive.

"No more law now, Gil," he said.

"Only a newer and a better one," said Gil, "and a stricter."

And that was the end of the Saute Sainte Marie. They were out on a lake three hundred miles in length, and on the first island they came to was the Fairy Anangke, sitting and netting nets for the catching of crawfish.

"Well, and what do *you* think of the Saute Sainte Marie?" she asked.

"I like it now it is over," said the Prince.

"Why did you fear it at first, then?" said the Fairy. "Take it all in all, they are as good as you."

"I don't understand you," said the Prince.

"I never supposed you would, my dear; but there, hurry away after the Boy in Grey. Dree out this weird, child, and you are safe. Causes produce effects, child. As you behave now, your actions will react. In the dark horror which you will have to pass through, you will find the results of your own actions. Has he been good, Gil?"

"He'll do, madam."

"Well, your report is a good one; though you are not to be trusted about princes. Why did you Scotch Highlanders harbour the Pretender at Benbecula and South Uist?"

"Now *I* am going to catch it," Gil whispered to the Prince. "Sentimental grounds, Madam Anangke."

"Sentimental grounds!" said Fairy Anangke, scornfully. "It was on sentimental grounds that the blessed Restoration was accomplished by your Duke of Albemarle, for the benefit of Lady Castlemaine mainly. And the poor sailors lying dying in Pepys' yard of starvation for their money, while the Dutch were burning Chatham. Pish! Take him to Australia."

"She is very cross," said the Prince when they were alone.

"She *is*," said Gil.

"How far are you to go with me, Gil?"

"All the way to Australia. *She* says, and none can resist her."

"Do you mean that you and I are to go all round Cape Horn, or through Magellan's Straits, in this canoe?"

"Ye may go by the Cape if ye will."

"Shall I be frightened?" said the Prince.

"Ye'll never be frightened any more," said Gil. "You have come down the Great Rapid, and you will never know fear now; not even when you give up your soul to God. You have trusted in God and in man, and have seen that neither would betray you."

CHAPTER XII

GIL MACDONALD and Prince Philarete went safely round Cape Horn in about fifteen hours, and this was, for one reason at least, the most remarkable part of their voyage.

Not because it was done in a birch-bark canoe, against the great booming west wind which plagued Magellan and nearly ruined Anson. Pigafetta felt it, and Byron will tell you of that wind. The reason why this part of their journey was the most remarkable was this. When they came through Canada they saw plenty of things; round the Horn they saw *nothing at all.*

You say that there is nothing remarkable about that. I beg your pardon. Did *you* ever see nothing at all? *I* never did, and should very much like to make the acquaintance of a man who had.

Because, don't you see, you *cannot see* nothing at all. And yet that was all they saw, and therefore they must have seen that.

Let us be cool and logical. Let us not heat ourselves unnecessarily over this question. Let us get at the crux of it. There is no greater mistake in this world than unnecessary heat over deep matters of thought like this. It involves the great question of Iamity.

They did not see anything at all, and therefore they saw nothing. But you cannot see nothing. But they did. Therefore they couldn't have.

Nonsense? Yes. But you will have worse and more pernicious nonsense than this to sort out for yourself before you have worn out three pair of trousers—that is, if you mean to be a man.

Well, they saw something when they approached the Australian shore. All the male adult colonists were down on the shore; and every man had brought his grandmother, and every man had brought an egg, and was showing his grandmother how to suck it.

"Come here," they cried, as Gil and the Prince coasted along; "come here, you two, and learn to suck eggs. We will teach you to suck all kinds of eggs, not merely those of the emu and talegalla, but those of the blue-throated warbler. And we will teach you to suck eggs which we have never seen. Come ashore, come ashore."

But they never came ashore for all that, but coasted on till the high wooded capes, no longer jutting in the sea, trended inland, and at last were lost to the eye. Then began a long continuous beach of sand, backed with low rolling sandhills. Then even these were gone, and the coast got so low that it was only distinguished from the grey wild sea by the line of mad bursting surf which broke up. The sea which the Greeks called barren was swarming with life, beauty, and vitality; the land was barren, hideous, and seemed accursed.

A long black cloud lay along their southern horizon towards the Pole, and from it came a blast from the Antarctic ice, cold as the hand of death upon the heart, yet as mad in its rage as the Mistral. A pelting, pitiless shower deluged them, and hid sea and sky and land as Gil hurried their frail bark towards the leaping breakers, and whispered—

"Ye must land here. Good-bye."

That was all. How it happened he does not know; how long it took he does not know. There was wild confusion for a little time, and then he found himself standing high and dry on the awful desolate shore alone—with God.

The blinding shower had cleared away, but the deadly cold wind remained. He looked towards the sea—a mad wild stretch of tumbled waters gnawing at the land. No signs of Gil or the canoe. Gil had disappeared by glamour of his nation; his mother had been a noted spaewife, so that was not surprising. He turned towards the land; it was nothing but a level sea of sand and salt, stretching away indefinitely northward, hideous, barren, but only marked by the track of two resolute naked little feet, not yet obliterated by the driving dust.

He was on the track now, and the ruby blazed and flamed out finely, warming his heart. And he broke into song, even in that hideous place, which God seemed to have forgotten.

> All alone, thou and I in the desert,
>   In the land all forgotten of God,
> In the land the last raised from the ocean,
>   In the land which no footsteps have trod,
> In the land where the lost pioneer
>   Falls stricken in heart as in head,
> In the land where his bones lie sand-buried,
>   In the land of the dead.
>
> Hear me, darling, the hope of the nation,
>   Stay thy feet as thou crossest the sand:
> Thou art far on before me to landward;
>   I look seaward—no help is at hand.
> Stay thy feet in thy swiftness, I pray thee,
>   Through this region of drouth and of light:
> Boy in Grey, I beseech thee to stay thee;
>   Let me meet thee at night.
>
> One said, who was never in error,
>   That the poor we had with us alway,
> And in all times of sadness and terror,
>   When night is more bright than the day,
> We can then lay our heads on thy bosom,
>   And, forgetful of false friends and old,
> Find there all we wanted in this world,
>   Warm when others were cold.

CHAPTER XIII

He was so very much pleased with his little song that he thought the best thing he could do would be to sing it over again. A theatrical friend of mine tells me that encores are very seldom successful: this one was a failure.

He began—

> All alone, thou and I in the desert,
> In the land all forgotten of God—

and there he broke down. *Was* it forgotten of God?

It seemed like it. A plain of level baking sand and salt as far as the eye could reach, with a sky of brass overhead: not one blade of grass or one drop of fresh water. Surely forgotten of God if ever land was. He tried the song once more, but the words stuck in his throat.

"Peem! Peem!" Who is this alone with us in this hideous blazing desert? A little golden fly; in some ways more beautifully organised than ourselves: a beautiful little golden fly, in comparison to whose flight that of the eagle is a clumsy flapping, and that of the woodcock a clumsy dash. That little fly makes nine thousand strokes a minute with his pretty little wings. What does he say as he hovers before Philarete, passes him, goes behind him, round his head, and at last lights on his shoulder? He is a very little fly, like a small stingless wasp, and he says this—

"We are rather out of bounds, you and I. This is the desert, where God is at work to found in future ages a new place for the Boy in Grey's plough. This weary land is, chemically speaking, already richer than the Polders which the Dutch reclaimed. It is being gradually upheaved so that it can carry watercourses in hollow places where there is but little evaporation. And the armies of God are advancing on it, to shield it from the sun. A few hundred miles northward you will meet their advance guard: first skirmishers of bent grass, the little whorls of Banksia; then a forest of full-grown trees; then Casuarinæ, at which point man can live. Walk swiftly, and you will be among the towering box forests of the gold land before you know where you are."

And so the fly flew away, and the Prince sped on several hundred miles, until out of the salt desert he saw a small shattered mountain, and under that mountain was a pool of fresh water, with an old gum tree by the side of it. And the pool of fresh water said to him—

"I am Jackson's Creek, and I am the finish and the end of it. I can't get any further at present, but I will be down to the sea some day."

And the old blue gum said, "You and I have been a long time about it."

"I am not going to be much longer," said the water-hole: "there has been a great storm up northward."

And as he spoke the Prince saw a hill of water coming down the gully, carrying with it broken boughs, and sticks, and straw, and dead kangaroos. And it burst into the pool and went seaward, making a largeish lake in the desert, but scooping out a fresh-water hole below the other.

"He is off," said the old gum-tree; "we will soon have the place in order at this rate.—Hi! here! don't go yet."

This last exclamation was not addressed to Prince Philarete, but to a small tortoise, who had emerged from the old water-hole, and was steadily bent down the side of the new stream to the desert.

"I'm off too," said the tortoise. "I'm sick of seeing your old boughs blown about. And you have been struck with lightning three times—a thing you can't deny. I'm off to see the fun." And away he pegged, twenty yards an hour.

"They are all leaving me," said the gum tree, weeping resinous tears like the Prince's ruby. "The opossums will come soon and live in my inside, and keep me awake all night; the centipedes will come and give me the tic-douloureux; and the cockatoos will come and pull and peck. And then the blackfellows will come and make shields out of my bark, and will cut steps in me to get at the opossums, and very likely set me on fire to burn them out. I wish I was dead! There is no place left in the world for a gentleman of fixed opinions."

"You take this matter too much to heart, sir," said the Prince.

"Heart!" said the gum tree. "If you could only see my inside, you would see that it has been gone for years. I shall flare up like a foul chimney when they do set me on fire."

So he did; but the oddest thing is that, although set on fire three times, he is as well as ever. I have a personal acquaintance with him, and on one occasion took the liberty of lighting a fire in front of him, and sleeping inside him.

About a hundred miles on, the Prince came into a very pretty country of acacias, with grass and everlasting flowers, where he met a running brook, and he asked the brook where it was going; for, do you see, he had come that way himself, and wondered.

And the brook said, "As far as I can at present. Not farther than the larger Banksias. This evaporation is telling on my constitution already."

"You will not get to the sea, then?"

"Not for a thousand years. In about that time I shall get there."

"Hawk! crawk! chawk! Wee! wah! chawk!" said somebody, to whom the Prince turned and wished "Good morning."

"Say that again."

"Good morning, sir."

"Ho! I am the Black Cockatoo with the yellow tail. I am the worst tempered among the Scansores. I am the biggest blackguard under the sun: that is about what I am." And he hung on upside down, and pecked, and bit, and clawed, using *the most awful language* all the time, until the Prince walked away and left him, never stopping until he was brought up by a pair of eyes in the grass.

"How do you do?" said the Prince. But the eyes were there still, though the mouth belonging to them said not one word.

This was not very comfortable. So the Prince advanced towards the eyes, and found that they belonged to an insignificant looking grey lizard, not nine inches long. . "Get up," he said.

Whereupon the lizard said, "Piperry wip!" emphatically, and bolted out of the grass down the sandy path, full gallop, as if he was going in for the Derby: he made such caracoles and demivoltes as you never saw in your life; and when he had gone down the path for about fifty yards, he dashed into the heather again, and was gone, leaving a cloud of dust behind him. I do not know this gentleman's name. Philarete calls him the galloping lizard.

Now in this sandy path there was a strange thing. The naked footsteps of the Boy in Grey were plain enough, but in the sandy path Philarete began to be aware that they were accompanied by a fresh trail, and wherever he saw the Boy's footsteps in the sand after this, even to nearly the last (as you will hear), he saw this strange trail beside the Boy in Grey's naked footprints.

It puzzled him. The trail was so singular that I, who have seen it often, can scarcely describe it. It was as though you put your hand into the surface of the sand, and at intervals pushed it from right to left; that was all. What could it be?

In a turn of the road, in a pleasant, happy, quiet little gully, such as are to be seen in Australia and nowhere else—in a gully of shadow, and trickling waters, and flowers, and the murmur of birds, in the earthly Paradise of the Australian spring—Philarete met a quaint pretty little fellow, something like a small raccoon, with white bands all over him, and a brush like a fox; and, seeing something intelligent in his eye, determined to converse with him on the subject of this strange trail, now parallel to that of the Boy in Grey.

"What is your name, if you please?" asked Philarete.

"They call me Myrmecobius now," he said; "but I have not got any real name. I was born before man and before speech, and I have thirty-three molars. I am the oldest beast alive, and the she-oak is the oldest tree. The she-oak has no real name either, it is only a consolidated Equisetum."

"That is a very fine name, though," said Philarete. "But look here, I want you to tell me something. What is the name of that—person—who seems to be leaving his trail beside my friend the Boy in Grey?"

"Why," said the Myrmecobius, "the settlers call him the Carpet Snake."

"Is that his real name?"

"Well, it is hard to say what his real name is," said the Myrmecobius.

"Is he, like you, too old to *have* a name?"

"Oh no, he comes into historical times. You can read of him in the third chapter of Genesis. He has kept his name, too, very well. Cuvier gives him exactly the same name as the old Greeks did."

"And what is that?"

"Python."

"The snake of Apollo?"

"The very same. Some call him 'Science' now; and he still lives in the tree of knowledge of good and evil, which, as you are doubtless aware, grows between the devil and the deep sea."

The frightened Prince said, "Why does he go with the Boy in Grey?"

"To catch you and speak to you."

"Will he follow the Boy in Grey to the end?"

"No; your turn first, his afterwards. The time for the meeting of the Python and the Boy in Grey alone is not yet. If the two meet without you, there will be evil such as no man has seen. Is Athanasio with you?"

"No."

"I wish he was. There is a great deal more to be got out of *him* yet; however, if you must get on without him, get on. Don't hurry, and don't dawdle. There is plenty of time, but remember that the night cometh in which no man can work." After saying which the Myrmecobius quietly skulked away into the heather.

The next person he met was an American professor of natural history, in green spectacles, who was, as he said, "Kinder looking round and sorting things." He never said one single word, but he took off the Prince's cap and felt his head, after which he went straight off, and wrote his great paper on the solitary occurrence of a Doleco-cephalous Pithecoid in the interior of Australia. Such is democratic respect for princes!

The moment he was out of sight there was such a noise as you never heard. If all the beasts in the Regent's Park were to have nothing to eat for a fortnight, there would be a fine noise, I doubt not; but it would be nothing to the noise which arose the instant the naturalist's back was turned. The Prince stopped his ears, but all the beasts and the birds in the bush resolved themselves into an indignation meeting, and carried him into the chair by acclamation.

White's thrush (who had been in America) always declared to the day of his death that all the pow-wows he'd ever seen were fizzle to this.

Philarete, finding himself actually in the chair, bethought himself of his *princely duties*, and called for "Order!" to which the spur-winged plover began yelling "Hear! hear!" and found himself unable to leave off for above a quarter of an hour, notwithstanding that all the other birds kept yelling and howling "Silence!" at him.

At last there was a dead silence, which was broken by the kangaroo, who moved the first resolution by saying "Poof."

"I deny it," said the scorpion, running round and round in the sand; "I deny it."

Whereupon the laughing jackass came down off his tree, ate up the scorpion, and flew up into his tree again; whereupon the duck-billed porcupine, bristling up his quills, moved that the "laughing jackass was out of order."

The laughing jackass replied only "Ho! ho! ho! Hah! hah! he!"

The porcupine was not going to be laughed out of his motion to order. He called for a seconder.

The brush-turkey said "that two courses only were open to the meeting, either to condemn the laughing jackass for his proceedings with regard to the scorpion, or not to do so. For his part he recommended the meeting to do neither."

The crow said that that was a recurrent negation.

The brush-turkey said he had left his dictionary on the piano, and so he could not reply to his honourable friend's long words.

Meanwhile there had come about a free fight between the opossum and the native cat, who had got their teeth into one another, and were making the dust fly, I can tell you. The meeting were highly delighted and excited, making a disorderly ring round the combatants.

"Go it!" yelled the eagle; "three to two on the native cat! Go it, Dasyurus! get your teeth in his nose and hold on. Go it!" And the old rascal, who had no more fight in him than your grandmother, went on bobbing up and down in the most ridiculous manner, drooping his wings and yelling, until the Prince caught him a good box on the ears, and sent him sprawling.

"What are they fighting about?" asked the Prince of the kangaroo, who seemed the most sensible person present.

"Nothing at all," said the kangaroo; "that is the point of the joke. It's a prize fight."

"It is one of our national sports," said the porcupine.

"Oh! it is one of your national sports, is it? And what is the object of this meeting?"

"To protest against the naturalist, who has been killing us for specimens," said the kangaroo. "We have not been able to call our souls our own. He says he wants to observe our habits, and immediately kills us indiscriminately. I don't call that natural history. Blow that. Poof."

"He wants to examine your internal construction," said the Prince, who, like all true princes, was a patron of science.

"Internal construction!" said the porcupine, with all his quills up. "What odds is my inside to *him*? I don't want to bother with *his* inside. If I had the examination of his internal construction, I'd do it in a way *he* wouldn't like: yes, indeed."

The Prince argued that some of our highest poets and novel-writers were in the habit of turning themselves inside out for the inspection of the public, and that when the public got tired of that, they generally took an historical or other character and tried to turn *him* inside out; but the porcupine could not be brought to see matters in this light.

"Let him leave my inside alone, and I'll go bail I leave *his* alone," was all that he would say, and that very sulkily.

The Prince finding that the rest of the meeting were all mad over the prize fight between the opossum and the native cat, and that to argue about the first principles of art with an ignorance as crass as that of the porcupine, was useless, quietly vacated the chair and slipped away into the wood.

CHAPTER XIV

Now HE CAME into the solemn towering box forest. All around him were great trees, as large as his father's largest oaks, beneath which the level turf stretched away for miles in long flats, with brave flowers, orchises and everlasting flowers; and sometimes these forest flats would be broken by little abrupt rocky ridges, with red clay and white quartz showing amidst the scant grass and thick flowers; and here the gold lay about so thick that you could see it as you walked; and on one hillside there were sapphires like blue stars, and they told him of the Boy in Grey, and how he had gone by with a sapphire on his bosom bigger than any of them.* Here also were snakes in plenty, harmless and venomous; but they never troubled him, poor things, any more than they will trouble you, if you leave them alone. These rocky rises, with glimpses of the distant blue mountains between the tree-stems, were the most peaceful and beautiful places which he had seen; and here he met the king of the kangaroos. And the king of the kangaroos asked him what o'clock it was.

"Greenwich time?" asked Philarete.

"Did you say Greenwich fair?" said the kangaroo, who stood seven feet high and looked rather stupid.

"No, Greenwich time. Eight hours difference, you know."

"Ho!" said the kangaroo; "just scratch my head, will you have the goodness?"

And the Prince did so.

---

* Black Hill, Buninyong. The writer there found a great number of sapphires, but, not thinking what they were, ultimately lost them all.

"I have got a message for you," said the kangaroo.

"From the Boy in Grey?"

"Yes."

"And what is it?"

"I have forgotten all about it. Or at least I have forgotten whether I remember it or not; or, to be more correct, I can't remember whether I have forgotten it."

"Can't you think of it?" said Philarete.

"Oh, yes, I can think of it, but I can't remember one word of it."

"What was it about?"

"It was about as long as my tail," said the kangaroo.

"How did it begin?"

"At the beginning," returned the kangaroo, promptly. "At least, I am not sure that it did not begin in the middle."

"Do you think it began at the end?"

"Very likely, for aught I know," said the kangaroo.

It was no use talking to the silly thing, and so he walked on. But he had not gone a hundred yards before the kangaroo called out, "Hi! hullo! come back!" And the Prince went.

"Just scratch my head, will you?" said the kangaroo. And Philarete walked away quite angry.

There were parrots enough here of all colours to have stocked Jamrach's for a twelvemonth, whistling and jabbering and contradicting. A solemn emu whom he met, and of whom he asked the way, told him that this place was called Jaw Fair, corresponding to Bunyan's Prating Row, and that this was the great day of the year with the Parrots' Benefit Societies, on which they spent annually twenty-five per cent. of their savings. Pretty as the parrots were, Philarete was glad enough to get out of the noise, and thankfully accepted a seat on the emu's back: who nevertheless stood still after the Prince was comfortably between his shoulders, and bent his beautiful neck and head in all directions.

"I am waiting for the white cockatoo," he explained. "He has to come with us. He is attending Jaw Fair."

"Does *he* spend his money?" asked Philarete.

The emu made a noise in his stomach like the rattling of pebbles. It was his way of laughing.

"Not *he*," he said. "He is too wide-awake for that. But he likes society, and has great powers of conversation; so he goes. There is the eagle ready for us there on that bough. Oh, here is the cockatoo. So off we go."

He bent his breast nearly to the ground, and away they went twenty miles an hour. The eagle dipped off his bough, rushed upwards like a rocket into the sky until he seemed a speck, wheeled round, and came rushing close past the Prince's ear like a whirlwind; after which he took up the position which he held all through their wonderful journey, just a hundred yards in front of the emu, ten feet from the ground.

The swift elastic motion of the emu at first engaged Philarete's attention, and then he began looking at the eagle as they sped headlong forward. With wings fifteen feet across, this bird held his magnificent course before them. Through the deep forest, where the green and yellow lights fell flickering on his chocolate and orange back, he held on like a meteor before them, until the forest grew thinner and thinner, and they came on the wild wide open plain, with a dim blue mountain here and there upon the wide sea-like horizon—still before them always the steadfast eagle, with his flying shadow upon the golden grass.

Northward ever, beyond the bounds of human knowledge, past solitary lakes covered with black swans, ducks, and pelicans; now racing across the lower spurs of some lonely extinct volcano, now crossing some deep ravine scooped out of the table-land by some fretting creek, growing silent before the coming summer. But as day waned, the day of all days in the Prince's life, they came to a pleasant peaceful granite country, where there were trees and ferns, as if in a European park, and a silent creek, with lilies, and reeds, and rushes, which whispered and rustled in the melancholy evening wind.

The eagle sat upon a tree, and the emu drank at the creek, holding up his head after each draught, like the Interpreter's fowl, to give thanks to Heaven. Now for the first time the Prince saw that the cockatoo was with them, and thought that he would like a little conversation; but the cockatoo only said in a whisper, "We cannot talk here."

"What place is this," said Philarete, "so solemn, so sad, and yet so beautiful?"

"This is the Creek Mestibethiwong, the Creek of the Lost Footsteps: follow me."

So he flew a little way and lighted on a tree, under which there lay a human figure on its side, withered long since by rain and sun, with the cheek pressed in the sand. So lies Leichardt, so lay Wills.

While Philarete was looking on him, not with terror but with deep pity, the cockatoo lit upon his shoulder, and said—

"He set his feet before the feet of his fellows, and here his feet failed him, and he lay down and died."

"All alone?" said Philarete. "Alas! to die so, away from all! All alone?"

"Not alone," whispered the pretty bird. "See there, go and look. You are not afraid."

Philarete went up undismayed to look. By the dead man's hand was a Bible, and Philarete read—

"When thou passest through the waters, I will be with thee; and through the rivers, they shall not overflow thee."

"Not alone," said Philarete; "I see."

At this moment there burst on his astonished ear such a ravishing flood of melody that his breath came thick and short with pleasure. Beginning with a few short sharp notes of perfect quality, it rolled up into a trumpet-like peal, and then died off in a few bars like the booming of minster-bells on a still evening in a deep wooded valley, in the land which had become a dim memory.

"In all my father's land are no such bells as those. Who is it that rings them over the dead man?"

"That is the Australian magpie," said his companion. "Now lie down a little."

The setting sun was smiting the highest boughs as he laid his head on the sand. For a little time he looked across to where the dead man lay, and in a little time he slept. When he awoke it was dark night, and his clothes were wet with dew. The emu, the eagle, and the cockatoo were gone, and he was alone by the silent creek with the dead man.

Philarete rose, and in the daze which followed his sleep called to the dead pioneer to arise also. But the dead pioneer was past calling by all princes: he lay quite quiet by the side of the Creek of the Lost Footsteps. Philarete was now absolutely alone, with a horror upon him. Now he knew that the dead man was dead; now he knew that he was 14,000 miles from home, alone and without help, in the company of a dead man who had lain down and died here. Who could help him in this terrible strait and in this black midnight, under the strange Southern Cross, and Magellan's clouds?

There was but One who could help the poor child, God Himself; and the poor little man knelt down in the sand and prayed that God would tell him how to follow the Boy in Grey, as Christ did, and that he would be good to Arturio, Polemos, and Athanasio. The boy was very humble. He was alone with death, and he did not wish to die until he had seen the Boy in Grey. Sometimes he wished he was back with his toys, sometimes he wished he was with rioting Polemos, sometimes he wished that he was with Arturio, in spite of Arturio's priggishness; but when he said his poor little prayer he thought more of Athanasio than any one; for Athanasio had loved the Boy in Grey, and his family had quarrelled with the family of Athanasio on the subject. But the poor little Prince said his prayer, as he looked on the dead man by the silent creek, and his prayer was answered in a most singular and remarkable way. From this moment he had no fear whatever. He knew now that he could dree out his weird to the end, without any fear of failure. He had been doing his very best, and his work had been accepted; the Great Cause was sending to him inferior beasts to teach him the great lesson, that the higher animals are far before us men in what is now called virtue. The poor little man had been taught to pray, and he prayed; and his poor little prayer, arriving from his heart, was answered.

There was a tiny wind on his cheek, and a tiny voice in his ear: a little bird lit on his shoulder, I doubt a democratic bird, and said, "Don't be afraid of it now, Prince; go through with it. He is not far;" and then the Prince saw that the emu wren had lit on his left shoulder; then he remembered what the elephant had told him in India. He had no fear now, for the Elephant's words were coming true, word for word. No fear or halting now: the emu wren was on his shoulder, and the Boy in Grey was not far.

"Will you come on to my finger?" said the Prince.

The emu wren did so. When he saw it the Prince gave a great sigh. It was only a little bird, one of the smallest birds in existence; it was only a little grey bird, without any "tropical" colour at all; but yet the most astoundingly beautiful bird in creation. Conceive a little tiny wren, which has a grey tail more delicate than that of the Bird of Paradise. How did it get that tail? I, believing in a good God, cannot tell you. Competition and selection I do believe in, but I have seen things which tell me that there is a great *Will*, and the emu wren is one.

Such a very little bird, with such a very long tail. It lit on the Prince's forefinger in the dark, and it said, "Look at my tail."

"I can't see," said the Prince; "and he is dead."

"I am sorry you can't see my tail," said the emu wren, "because I am a very humble little bird, and I like to be admired sometimes. However, I had to come to you in the dark, and I have come. Do you think that my tail came by competition or selection?"

"I don't suppose it matters much," said the Prince.

"He don't think it matters much," said the emu wren. "Pipe up."

"Who are you talking to?" said the Prince, with that disregard of grammar which is not confined to princes, but which has actually been attributed to deans.

(If you want a piece of fun, young man, just examine the "grammar" of the last sentence—"a disregard of grammar which is not confined to princes." It means absolutely nothing at all, but you never would have seen it if I hadn't told you).

"Who are you talking to?" he repeated.

"It's White's thrush," said the emu wren; and White's thrush flew up on a tree, and said, "Toroo! toroo! the night is dark, but he must meet him before the morning, or the world will lapse back into its old folly. Hurry him on. I live in all lands, and I tell you he must go."

"Take me on your shoulder," said the emu wren.

"Bonny sweet, of course I will," said the Prince. "But why?"

"Because of the carpet snake."

"Must I meet him?" said Philarete.

"Yes, he is slower than the Boy in Grey. You must be quiet, and let him have his will of you. You must be very quiet and submissive, or you will never see the Boy in Grey, and then the whole world will be ruined."

They sped on, these three, through the night, leaving the dead man, the lost pioneer, lying where he was by the creek; it seemed nearly morning, when White's thrush said, "Toroo! here he is."

"The Boy in Grey?" whispered Philarete.

"No, the python," said White's thrush.

They were rising on to the mountains now, and Philarete put his friend the emu wren off his shoulder on to a bush, for the python, or carpet snake, had ceased following the Boy in Grey, and was lying a dark mass on the sandy path before him. You see that the emu wren had a suspicion or fancy, and the Prince, being a real prince, was afraid that the snake of Apollo would charm her, and then gobble her up and swallow her. The Prince, being *au fait* with affairs, knew that the thing had happened several times before, and his *statesmanlike intellect* told him that it was very likely to happen again (as it has). So he put the emu-wren on a bush before he had his interview with the python, or carpet snake.

Yet the ruby on his breast was blazing out now with a vengeance. The Boy in Grey is not far off when the python is near. The carpet snake raised his head from the ground, and lashing his tail round the Prince's heel, passed his head between his legs, and raised his head so that it nearly touched the Prince's face. Its eyes were for one instant like beryl, and the Prince said, "I understand, and I will go first:" then the python, or carpet snake, uncoiled himself from the boy's body and let him go. The Prince was alone with the emu wren and White's thrush, and it was very dark, but he knew that if he could dree out the weird a light would break on the world such as the world had never seen yet. He had looked into the python's eyes, and he had learnt something, for you learn quick in that school. He had learned something from the King and Queen, his father and mother; now the only thing was to catch the Boy in Grey before it was too late.

Some people older than children will read this story; to them we should say, "Help to catch the Boy in Grey. Whether you are Dissenters, Romanists, Tractarians—whatsoever you are, catch the Boy in Grey, even if you walk as far as Philarete after him." Speaking now to my equals or superiors, I do appeal in favour of the Boy in Grey. It would seem that they are going to keep the very Bible from him. *"Aux armes, Citoyens!"*

The Python dropped from Philarete's body into the sand, and he was free to go on through the darkness of the Australian night, through the rustling Australian forest.

The Prince went very quickly; the emu wren and White's thrush said each of them that they had something to say to him, but the Prince only said, "I have seen the python." The boy said that it was merely a matter of time; the python had not spoken to him, but he had seen two things in the eyes of the python—Love and Hate. Young man, you had better listen to this: Love, played with and abused, is very apt to become furious Hate. I heard of a country called Ireland once; but that is no matter. Prince Philarete saw that he must hurry after the Boy in Grey.

Whither? There were no footsteps in the sand now. White's thrush had left him, and would guide him no more; only the little emu wren was on his finger, and he asked her, "How shall we find the Boy in Grey?" and she said, "I don't exactly know."

"I would give you anything," said Philarete, "if you could guide me to him."

"My dear," said the emu wren, "we have neither of us got anything, that would come to the same thing in the end, and it is not the least use asking the black cockatoo, he is so terribly *emporté*."

"Hah! hah! you two," said a voice over their heads. "Wee, wah! you're a pretty couple of fools. I saw Eyre through the great Australian bight. I *am* the black cockatoo, and I have heard every word you have said. I was Eyre's pilot. Do you think I could not manage two such twopenny fools as you? The Boy in Grey is just over the mountain. Look sharp!"

"I am afraid you are a very sad blackguard, sir," said the Prince.

"Well, if ye have not found out *that* before you *must* be a fool," said the black cockatoo. "You keep my counsel, and hang Henderson, that's all we convicts want of you. We black cockatoos don't like Henderson—he knows too much. We don't mind Bruce so much, but we don't like Henderson."

But we are leaving our Prince alone, utterly alone in the desert. The black cockatoo flew away *before* the Prince in the direction of the Boy in Grey, and the emu wren stepped away and saw she could go no farther.

The night was very dark and the wood was very wild, the hill was very steep, too, now, and he was utterly and entirely alone. There was a great thicket of *Eucalypus Dumosa* in her way, but the naked feet of the Boy in Grey had crushed it down right and left so that the Prince could follow.

But as he rose into the dim breezy solitude of the upper and more open forest, he saw that he was getting into such a presence as he had never seen before. The night was very dark and dim, and night winds were making lonely whispers like the voices of dead men among the boughs of the mountain forest trees. Yet there was a light growing in his eye, and before he could tell what light that was, he was out of the dark wood on to a breezy down, where the night wind sighed old memories in the grass. Before him was a profound valley, dark as the pit, and beyond that a vast alp leaping up into the black sky with sheets of snow. That was the light.

It was such a wild, bare, bald down, and it was so far from home, and such a hopeless place, that the Prince would have been frightened had not Cowardice and he parted company. So unutterably solitary so terribly magnificent. Around him, hundreds of miles in every direction, was an ocean of rolling woodlands, untrodden by human foot. The solitude of the plains is terrible, but the solitude of the mountain forest is overwhelming.

The wind whistled through the grass and moved it. There seemed to be nothing here save himself, and the stars, and the alp; but there was something else too. There was the Boy in Grey. A cry rose in that solitary desert which seemed to bring fresh flashes from the Southern Cross, for the Boy in Grey, with naked feet, was lying in the grass before him, and the Prince cried out, "My darling, I have got you at last! let us lie warm together, for I am so very very cold."

So prince and peasant lay together in the long grass on the windy solitary down. And as the Prince kissed the Boy in Grey, with one kiss for Henri, one for Louis, and one for Philarete, morning came down on the summit of the alp and made it blaze again.

CHAPTER XV

WHEN THEY AWOKE and rose to turn back together, the alp was all one sheet of glory and light, and they laughed, those two together, with their arms round one another's necks.

"I thought I should never catch you," said the Prince.

"And I thought you were never coming," said the Boy in Grey.

"Where were you going?" said the Prince.

"Down there," said the Boy in Grey.

"Into that dark and horrible valley?" said the Prince. "What is the name of it?"

"Revolution," said the Boy in Grey.

"But you are coming back with me now?" said Philarete.

"Yes."

"What is the name of the alp, boy?"

"Duty," said the Boy in Grey.

"*I* see," said Philarete. "You were going to scale it through the Valley of Revolution. Could we have gone up it together?"

"I don't know. I cannot tell in any way. It is a dark matter. But if you had not come I should have tried it by myself. But you were true to the time which old Anangke settled, and so we will go happily home together."

"You will live with me now, you will live with Polemos, Arturio, and Athanasio?" said the Prince.

"I think not," said the Boy in Grey. "If Polemos would give up his fury, if Arturio would give up being a prig, and Athanasio being a bore, I could get on much better with your lot; at present I don't exactly like them. But with regard to yourself, I am with you, my own love, to the world's end."

And so they walked back, and everybody saw that a coalition had been made between the Prince and the Boy in Grey. The Black Cockatoo was perfectly furious. He screeched and yelled to that extent that the feathers went flying off the top of his head, and he had to borrow an old wig from the Duck-billed Echidna, before he could go to the International Exhibition at Melbourne. And a nice figure he looked with his head all over porcupine-quills. The Carrion Crow hated this arrangement, and being out on ticket-of-leave, called a meeting on Clerkenwell Green; but Colonel Henderson, having been round by Field Lane with Lord Shaftesbury, happened to attend that meeting in an accidental way, and very soon settled the Carrion Crow. There was a good deal said about the coalition between the Prince and the Boy in Grey. The very *Ornithorhyncus paradoxus* having come into it, a gentleman I know well, but not free of speech; the Whale makes no objection, the Emu is perfectly charmed. The Parrot don't care, because it is only something more to talk about; but the Echidna or Porcupine says there is a dereliction of principle. But what are you to do with a porcupine? Blackfellows brought us two one afternoon, and we desired to tame them, and let them go. They at once buried themselves in the earth with a nimbleness and dexterity which the Right Hon. Robert Lowe, a countryman of theirs, has never equalled at his best. Porcupines are not dangerous. The Boy in Grey went quietly home with Prince Philarete, caring nothing about what was said of them.

Swiftly as they went back to their home, the enemy was swifter. The Prince and the Boy in Grey had been separated too long, and fearful mischief had occurred. The Prince and the Boy in Grey thought that only three nights had passed since one had been away after the other into the snow on the night of the great ball at the palace. The Cockatoo soon set them right on that point.

They were hurrying into town towards the palace as fast as they could go, when some one sung out "Hi! you two!" and they stopped. And the Prince looked round to see who spoke, and it was the White Cockatoo in a cage, hung out of window, holding on upside down by his perch, and screaming at intervals.

"Hullo, you sir!" they said. "What are you doing here?"

"I have been caught by a blackfellow, and sold to a nigger, and the nigger taught me American, and then he sold me to a sailor who taught me to swear (which he could), and the sailor sold me to a Jew, who sold me to a first mate, and I learnt a deal more bad language on the voyage, and the mate sold me to Jamrach, and Jamrach sold me to my present proprietor. *She* is an old lady of religious proclivities, and she don't approve of me because I sometimes swear in conversation. I am trying to get over it, and perhaps I may. I say, you two, you have made a nice mess of it between you. Where the dickens have you been so long, you two?"

"So long!" said Philarete; "we have only been away three days."

"You fool!" said the Cockatoo (for he is a very impudent person), "you and the Boy in Grey have been away for eleven years, and everything has gone to mops and brooms" (it was his vulgar way of speaking). "We thought you were dead. The Carrion Crow has been here and kicked up no end of a row about you two."

They hurried on. "Come to the palace, darling," said the Prince to the Boy in Grey.

"No," said the Boy. "Is it true that we have been eleven years away? Let us look at one another."

And they turned: they had been in Fairyland, where all things are possible, and the idiotic old Cockatoo was right.

When they looked at one another now in the light of the summer's evening, each saw in the other a magnificent young man, full of power, grace, and potential fury.

"I will not go to the palace," said the Boy in Grey. "I must hurry to my brothers: we have been too long away, and I must see to matters. We are too old to kiss, and I must be off. In the darkest hour of the night which is coming I will be with you. But you must call, or our people will not hear. Good-night, until the dawn smites the cathedral spire as it did the alp."

And then he was gone, and his sapphire blazed no longer.

Philarete went on to the palace gate, and at the palace gate he met a gallant young gentleman, of gigantic stature, on whose breast was an emerald, burning brightly. "Who goes there?" said the grand young man, clashing his hand on his sword. He did not know Philarete, but Philarete knew him: he said very quietly, "Polemos," and the noble old lad knew him at once, and said, not with effusion, because a true soldier never effuses—well, we will not repeat what Polemos said: it wouldn't do to repeat what Polemos said; we always said that we could not report in detail the language of Polemos, and we have not done so. There cannot be the least harm, however, in saying that Polemos took the *outrageous liberty* of smacking the Prince on the back, and saying, "None too soon, boy, none too soon."

Polemos *bellowed*—I can use no other expression—and forth came Athanasio, a fine young man, but at this time a little weak in the back (his family are troubled with chronic rickets, and have given the State a deal of trouble one way or another, though they have done much service). Athanasio came out and blessed the arrangement generally, which made Polemos take the *diametrically opposite line.* But the more Polemos went on, the more Athanasio went on the opposite track—to use the words of Boileau, *"Il bênit subitement le guerrier consterné"*—so dexterously every time he opened his mouth, that Polemos got utterly sulky and dumb, and let the quarrel stand over until the year 2666, in which year it is wildly possible this squabble between soldier and priest may be ended.

Athanasio then informed Philarete that his father and mother were both dead, that Cacodemus was Prime Minister, and that it was all Philarete's fault for going away for eleven years and six months, when——

Arturio, with his diamond blazing brightly, dashed out of the door, and said, "You fools! where is my boy?" and the splendid young giant put his arm over Philarete's shoulder, and led him in. Of all his friends, Philarete had loved Arturio least; but now—but now his heart beat only one solitary measure with his.

"Are they really dead?" said Philarete.

"They are dead," said Arturio, "and you will see them no more, for ever. You do not fear *death?*"

"I am not come to that yet," said Philarete, quickly; "I should be glad to have time to weep for them."

"Work first, weeping after," said Arturio. "To-night is the night of all time. You have kissed the Boy in Grey, and the Carrion Crow has babbled out the fact. My Prince, my beloved, have I ever been hard with you?"

"It is all forgiven now, Arturio. You have never been so well beloved as you are now."

"I shall die to-night," said Arturio, "I know it. It was not given to me to kiss the Boy in Grey. But, Prince, I wish you to see and to act. Cacodemus, weary of your long delay, is in revolution, and we must fight this night. Our only hope is in you, and in the Boy in Grey."

No time for sorrow over his lost parent; no time for anything save action. It was his dawdling which had ruined everything, as he thought. It was his dawdling after the Boy in Grey which saved the kingdom, I say.

It is no use talking politics here. Any child nowadays can understand me when I say that Cacodemus had gone to the bad altogether. He had not only deserted the monarchy, a thing we do not like, but he had been talking excited bosh among people who could not argue with him, and who, in consequence, believed in him. We have seen the same thing a hundred times over.

"We must fight to-night or never," said Arturio, and the Cockatoo quite agreed; for the Cockatoo had, it seemed, been at the Ballarat riots, and had thought it necessary to open its cage and get out, for the purpose of advising the Prince. For a similar reason the Myrmecobius came in and said that he had thirty-two molars, which was not to the point in any way; but he was a deputation, and was dismissed with politeness. The American Bear and Tom Brown also got up a deputation; but the American Bear fell downstairs (as plantigrades will) and broke a gas lamp, and said that Tom Brown must pay it, or he'd hire a judge and make him. In fact, there were endless deputations, in the middle of which the Carrion Crow escaped and carried off all the plate and a good deal of the jewellery. In fact, there was a terrible fight on hand, and Arturio, no bad politician with all his faults, could not for a moment say which way it was going.

Arturio hoped that Philarete would live through it. As for himself, he knew he must die in the quarrel, and he was content. But would Athanasio be killed? that was the question. What I am telling you is perfectly true, that Arturio would die for Athanasio. The real aristocrat will die for the Churchman. It is an old bargain. I am not sure that it is any business of mine, I only speak of matters as I find them. On that night of storm and war Arturio was more anxious about Athanasio than he was about Philarete or the Boy in Grey.

Cacodemus had played his cards very well. He had said two lies: he had said that the Boy in Grey and the Prince were dead. The dog knew better—he knew that they had met, had kissed, and were coming. The Fly of the desert had told him that the Cockatoo had told all the other cockatoos about it, and cockatoos spread intelligence very fast, as every one knows. But he lied on, and said that they were dead. The Tiger and the Elephant had an interview with him, and begged him to mind what he was at, for they did not want the old story over again. He kicked the Tiger (Cacodemus has pluck), and ordered the Elephant out of the room. The Elephant at once departed to Jamrach's, and on his way he met the Boy in Grey and told him *his* opinion, and the Boy in Grey, now grown to a noble young giant, told him *his* opinion. The Elephant offered his services, combined with those of his friend the Tiger, but the Boy in Grey thought he had better not avail himself of them save in case of emergency. I want you to pay particular attention to this. If you have our Boy in Grey with you, you can do without either the Tiger or the Elephant. You don't see it? Wait till you are forty.

But the night was a night of storm and fury. At seven o'clock that night the attack on the palace began, and poor young Prince Philarete, who had been eleven years in Fairyland, like his elder brother Louis XVI., found himself face to face with an infuriated mob directed by Cacodemus.

Louis XVI., Philarete's elder brother, never kissed the Boy fairly. Our Prince had— that makes the difference between the two princes. The supreme and awful hour was nearly the same with both, but "you may wear your rue with a difference." There was a seething howling hell of the wrath and rage of a neglected population outside Philarete's palace. Then shattering file-firing from his soldiers, under the direction of Polemos. Then the terrible bursting of doors by the mob; then the doors burst open and the mob in; then his gallant guards fighting from stair to stair; then his gallant men and brave gentlemen lying dead around him. Polemos dead, with his sword clutched tightly in his hand; Arturio dead and perfectly quiet, having worked till death; Athanasio dead with his arms crossed (he had not fought, but was shot down). All his friends dead, and he, poor Prince, standing at the top of the great marble staircase, with the ruby blazing like fire, praying to the mad neglected mob to hold their hands.

They would not hold their hands. Their wrongs were very deep, and that grand young prince had been away eleven years in Fairyland. They would have his life as they had had those of Polemos, Arturio, and Athanasio; they came rushing up the staircase towards the Prince, when the struggling crowd flickered and waved like a flame suddenly blown by the wind.

For the Boy in Grey had his arm round the Prince's neck, and had his cheek against his. The gallant young men stood there together, and the mob fell back. The bare legs and the naked feet of the Boy in Grey saved that State. I am under the impression myself (I may be mistaken), that those bare legs and naked feet are a little wanted, not only in England, but in America.

And I have come to a most singular conclusion also, to which I beg to draw your particular attention; and my conclusion is that I have told my story, and the time is come when I have no more to say. I wish other writers of stories would leave off when they come to an end and finish. In point of fact, I wish I could myself. I really won't be long. It is not me, it is the Cockatoo.

The Cockatoo declares in the *most emphatic manner* that the Boy in Grey *never* made any speech at the Prince's wedding. Now, the Elephant, the Emu, the Myrmecobius, the Tiger, and the Xylopodotherium, or the extinct animal with a wooden leg, are perfectly unanimous in telling me that the Cockatoo is an old fool. I don't know whether the Cockatoo is right or I am right. I disagree with the Cockatoo on many points. I think that he sits too late at his club, and is apt to say (like the late Mr. Richard Swiveller) the first thing which comes into his head. These are habits of which I cannot approve; yet your Cockatoo is a gentleman. It seems to me that you never know when you are right. But the Prince Philarete did his best. You go do your best, and you won't come far wrong.

Do as the Wombat does. The other day I had an interview with the Wombat. He wanted to be scratched on his back, and *he told me so*. I refused to do it, but there was no bad blood between us. We are as good friends as ever.

Therefore we most earnestly hope that the Cockatoo is wrong.

THE END

18

"The Good Little Girl"

By "F. ANSTEY"

The Good Little Girl

T HIS DELIGHTFUL SHORT STORY, originally published in 1890, is peculiarly fitted to close our series of reprinted texts from Victorian children's literature. It is a satirical story of real life, making effective sport of the good good children of the sort we found in Hesba Stretton; but it simultaneously satirizes the fairy tale. So it pokes genial fun at the two genres that have occupied us in these volumes, and by that very token signalizes that a new age may be beginning. And in the 1890s the strength in fact departed from both the old tried and true forms. Although moral tales of domestic life and fanciful or nonsensical fairy tales continued to pour from the presses, they showed little originality. The authorities on children's literature generally point to Kenneth Grahame's *Golden Age* (1895)—in which the children show not merely rebellion against the adult world, as in *Castle Blair*, but total contempt for it, and in which the author sides with the children—as heralding the premature opening of our own twentieth century. They are probably right in singling out *The Golden Age* as the first monument of a new era, lying beyond our Victorian period spiritually, even if still inside it chronologically by six years. But to make the transition into the new era seem rational, it is useful, as well as amusing, to have before us Anstey's cheerfully ridiculous farewell to the old.

"F. Anstey" was the pseudonym of Thomas Anstey Guthrie (1856–1934), a barrister. *Vice-Versa; or, A Lesson to Fathers* (1882), his first book, launched him resoundingly. It tells of a pompous businessman, Mr. Bultitude, who is always wishing aloud that he could change places with Dick, his schoolboy son, of the magical transformation by which the exchange is actually effected, and of Mr. Bultitude's comic distress. Adults as well as children loved the book, and Anstey forgot about his legal practice. One of his other novels, *The Tinted Venus* (1885), became a successful musical comedy in the United States some six or seven decades after its first appearance. "The Good Little Girl" is a fine example of his gentle wit.

The text of "The Good Little Girl" is reprinted from Paleface and Redskin and Other Stories for Boys and Girls *(New York and London: D. Appleton and Sons, 1924).*

Her name was Priscilla Prodgers, and she was a very good little girl indeed. So good was she, in fact, that she could not help being aware of it herself, and that is a stage to which very many quite excellent persons never succeed in attaining. She was only just a child, it is true, but she had read a great many beautiful story-books, and so she knew what a powerful reforming influence a childish and innocent remark, or a youthful example, or a happy combination of both, can exert over grown-up people. And early in life—she was but eleven at the date of this history—early in life she had seen clearly that her mission was to reform her family and relatives generally. This was a heavy task for one so young, particularly in Priscilla's case, for, besides a father, mother, brother, and sister, in whom she could not but discern many and serious failings, she possessed an aunt who was addicted to insincerity, two female cousins whose selfishness and unamiability were painful to witness, and a male cousin who talked slang and was so worldly that he habitually went about in yellow boots! Nevertheless Priscilla did not flinch, although, for some reason, her earnest and unremitting efforts had hitherto failed to produce any deep impression. At times she thought this was owing to the fact that she tried to reform all her family together, and that her best plan would be to take each one separately, and devote her whole energies to improving that person alone. But then she never could make up her mind which member of the family to begin with. It is small wonder that she often felt a little disheartened, but even that was a cheering symptom, for in the books it is generally just when the little heroine becomes most discouraged that the seemingly impenitent relative exhibits the first sign of softening.

So Priscilla persevered: sometimes with merely a shocked glance of disapproval, which she had practised before the looking-glass until she could do it perfectly; sometimes with some tender, tactful little hint. "Don't you think, dear papa," she would say softly, on a Sunday morning, "don't you *think* you could write your newspaper article on some *other* day—is it a work of *real* necessity?" Or she would ask her mother, who was certainly fond of wearing pretty things, "How much bread for poor starving people would the price of your new bonnet buy, mother? I should *so* like to work it out on my little slate!"

Then she would remind her brother Alick that it would be so much better if, instead of wasting his time in playing with silly little tin soldiers, he would try to learn as much as he could before he was sent to school; while she was never tired of quoting to her sister Betty the line, "Be good, sweet maid, and let who will be clever!" which Betty, quite unjustly, interpreted to mean that Priscilla thought but poorly of her sister's intellectual capacity. Once when, as a great treat, the children were allowed to read "Ivanhoe" aloud, Priscilla declined to participate until she had conscientiously read up the whole Norman period in her English history; and on another occasion she cried bitterly on hearing that her mother had arranged for them to learn dancing, and even endured bread and water for an entire day rather than consent to acquire an accomplishment which she feared, from what she had read, would prove a snare. On the second day—well, there was roast beef and Yorkshire pudding for dinner, and Priscilla yielded; but she made the resolution—and kept it too—that, if she went to the dancing class, she would firmly refuse to take the slightest pains to learn a single step.

I only mention all these traits to show that Priscilla really was an unusually good child, which makes it the more sad and strange that her family should have profited so little by her example. She was neither loved nor respected as she ought to have been, I am

grieved to say. Her papa, when he was not angry, made the cruellest fun of her mild reproofs; her mother continued to spend money on dresses and bonnets, and even allowed the maid to say that her mistress was "not at home," when she was merely unwilling to receive visitors. Alick and Betty, too, only grew more exasperated when Priscilla urged them to keep their tempers, and altogether she could not help feeling how wasted and thrown away she was in such a circle.

But she never quite lost heart; her papa was a literary man and wrote tales, some of which she feared were not as true as they affected to be, while he invariably neglected to insert a moral in any of them; frequently she dropped little remarks before him with apparent carelessness, in the hope that he might put them in print—but he never did; she never could recognise herself as a character in any of his stories, and so at last she gave up reading them at all!

But one morning she came more near to giving up in utter despair than ever before. Only the previous day she had been so hopeful! her father had really seemed to be beginning to appreciate his little daughter, and had presented her with sixpence in the new coinage to put in her money-box. This had emboldened her to such a degree that, happening on the following morning to hear him ejaculate "Confound it!" she had, pressing one hand to her beating heart and laying the other hand softly upon his shoulder (which is the proper attitude on these occasions), reminded him that such an expression was scarcely less reprehensible than actual bad language. Upon which her hard-hearted papa had told her, almost sharply, *"not to be a little prig!"*

Priscilla forgave him, of course, and freely, because he was her father and it was her duty to bear with him; but she felt the injustice deeply, for all that. Then, when she went up into the nursery, Alick and Betty made a frantic uproar, merely because she insisted on teaching them the moves in chess, when they perversely wanted to play Halma! So, feeling baffled and sick at heart, she had put on her hat and run out all alone to a quiet lane near her home, where she could soothe her troubled mind by thinking over the ingratitude and lack of appreciation with which her efforts were met.

She had not gone very far up the lane when she saw, seated on a bench, a bent old woman in a poke-bonnet with a crutch-handled stick in her hands, and this old woman Priscilla (who was very quick of observation) instantly guessed to be a fairy—in which, as it fell out, she was perfectly right.

"Good-day, my pretty child!" croaked the old dame.

"Good-day to you, ma'am!" answered Priscilla politely (for she knew that it was not only right but prudent to be civil to fairies, particularly when they take the form of old women). "But, if you please, you mustn't call me pretty—because I am not. At least," she added, for she prided herself upon her truthfulness, "not *exactly* pretty. And I should hate to be always thinking about my looks, like poor Milly—she's our housemaid, you know—and I so often have to tell her that she did not make her *own* face."

"I don't alarm you, I see," said the old crone; "but possibly you are not aware that you're talking to a fairy?"

"Oh, yes, I am—but I'm not a bit afraid, because, you see, fairies can only hurt *bad* children."

"Ah, and you're a good little child—that's not difficult to see!"

"They don't see it at home!" said Priscilla, with a sad little sigh, "or they would listen more when I tell them of things they oughtn't to do."

"And what things do they do that they oughtn't to, my child—if you don't mind telling me?"

"Oh, I don't mind in the *least!*" Priscilla hastened to assure her; and then she told the old woman all her family's faults, and the trial it was to bear with them and go on trying to induce them to mend their ways. "And papa is getting worse than ever," she concluded dolefully; "only fancy, this very morning, he called me a little prig!"

"Tut, tut!" said the fairy sympathetically, "deary, deary me! So he called you *that*, did he?—'a little prig!' And *you*, too! Ah, the world's coming to a pretty pass! I suppose, now, your papa and the rest of them have got it into their heads that you are too young and too inexperienced to set up as their adviser—is that it?"

"I'm afraid so," admitted Priscilla; "but we mustn't blame them," she added gently, "we must remember that they don't know any better—mustn't we, ma'am?"

"You sweet child!" said the old lady with enthusiasm; "I must see if I can't do something to help you, though I'm not the fairy I used to be—still, there are tricks I can manage still, if I'm put to it. What you want is something that will prove to them that they ought to pay more attention to you, eh?—something there can be no possible mistake about?"

"Yes!" cried Priscilla eagerly, "and—and—how would it be if you changed them into something else, just to *show* them, and then I could ask for them to be transformed back again, you know?"

"What an ingenious little thing you are!" exclaimed the fairy; "but, let us see—if you came home and found your cruel papa doing duty as the family hatstand, or strutting about as a Cochin China fowl—"

"Oh, *yes;* and I'd feed him every day, till he was sorry?" interrupted the warm-hearted little girl impulsively.

"Ah, but you're so hasty, my dear. Who would write all the clever articles and tales to earn bread and meat for you all?—fowls can't use a pen. No, we must find a prettier trick than that—there *was* one I seem to remember, long, long ago, performing for a good little ill-used girl, just like you, my dearie, just like you! Now what was it? some gift I gave her whenever she opened her lips——"

"Why, *I* remember—how funny that you should have forgotten! Whenever she opened her lips, roses, and diamonds, and rubies fell out. That would be the very thing! Then they'd *have* to attend to me! Oh, do be a kind old fairy and give me a gift like that—do, *do!*"

"Now, don't be so impetuous! You forget that this is not the time of year for roses, and, as for jewels, well, I don't think I can be very far wrong in supposing that you open your lips pretty frequently in the course of the day?"

"Alick does call me a 'mag,'" said Priscilla; "but that's wrong, because I never speak without having something to say. I don't think people ought to—it may do so *much* harm; mayn't it?"

"Undoubtedly. But, anyhow, if we made it *every* time you opened your lips, you would soon ruin me in precious stones, that's plain! No, I think we had better say that the jewels shall only drop when you are saying something you wish to be particularly improving—how will that do?"

"Very nicely indeed, ma'am, thank you," said Priscilla, "because, you see, it comes to just the same thing."

"Ah, well, try to be as economical of your good things as you can—remember that in these hard times a poor old fairy's riches are not as inexhaustible as they used to be."

"And jewels really will drop out?"

"Whenever they are wanted to 'point a moral and adorn a tale,'" said the old woman (who, for a fairy, was particularly well-read). "There, run along home, do, and scatter your pearls before your relations."

It need scarcely be said that Priscilla was only too willing to obey; she ran all the way home with a light heart, eager to exhibit her wonderful gift. "How surprised they will be!" she was thinking. "If it had been Betty, instead of me, I suppose she would have come back talking toads! It would have been a good lesson for her—but still, toads are nasty things, and it would have been rather unpleasant for the rest of us. I think I won't tell Betty *where* I met the fairy."

She came in and took her place demurely at the family luncheon, which was the children's dinner; they were all seated already, including her father, who had got through most of his writing in the course of the morning.

"Now make haste and eat your dinner, Priscilla," said her mother, "or it will be quite cold."

"I always let it get a little cold, mother," replied the good little girl, "so that I mayn't come to think too much about eating, you know."

As she uttered this remark, she felt a jewel producing itself in some mysterious way from the tip of her tongue, and saw it fall with a clatter into her plate. "I'll pretend not to notice anything," she thought.

"Hullo!" exclaimed Alick, pausing in the act of mastication, "I say—*Prissie!*"

"If you ask mother, I'm sure she will tell you that it is most ill-mannered to speak with your mouth full," said Priscilla, her speech greatly impeded by an immense emerald.

"I like that!" exclaimed her rude brother; "who's speaking with their mouth full *now?*"

" '*Their*' is not grammar, dear," was Priscilla's only reply to this taunt, as she delicately ejected a pearl, "you should say *her* mouth full." For Priscilla's grammar was as good as her principles.

"But really, Priscilla, dear," said her mother, who felt some embarrassment at so novel an experience as being obliged to find fault with her little daughter, "you should not eat sweets just before dinner, and—and couldn't you get rid of them in some other manner?"

"Sweets!" cried Priscilla, considerably annoyed at being so misunderstood, "they are not *sweets,* mother. Look!" And she offered to submit one for inspection.

"If I may venture to express an opinion," observed her father, "I would rather that a child of mine should suck sweets than coloured beads, and in either case I object to having them prominently forced upon my notice at meal-times. But I daresay I'm wrong. I generally am."

"Papa is quite right, dear," said her mother, "it *is* such a dangerous habit—suppose you were to swallow one, you know! Put them in the fire, like a good girl, and go on with your dinner."

Priscilla rose without a word, her cheeks crimsoning, and dropped the pearl, ruby, and emerald, with great accuracy, into the very centre of the fire. This done, she returned to her seat, and went on with her dinner in silence, though her feelings prevented her from eating very much.

"If they choose to think my pearls are only beads, or jujubes, or acidulated drops," she said to herself, bitterly, "I won't waste any more on them, that's all! I won't open my lips again, except to say quite ordinary things—so *there!*"

If Priscilla had not been such a very good little girl, you might almost have thought she was in a temper; but she was not,—her feelings were wounded, that was all, which is quite a different thing.

That afternoon, her aunt Margarine, Mrs. Hoyle, came to call. She was the aunt whom we have already mentioned as being given to insincerity; she was not well off, and had a tendency to flatter people; but Priscilla was fond of her notwithstanding, and she had never detected her in any insincerity towards herself. She was sent into the drawing-room to entertain her aunt until her mother was ready to come down, and her aunt, as usual, overwhelmed her with affectionate admiration. "How pretty and well you are looking, my pet!" she began, "and oh, what a beautiful frock you have on!"

"The little silkworms wore it before I did, aunt," said Priscilla, modestly.

"How sweet of you to say so! But they never looked half so well in it, I'll be bou——

Why, my child, you've dropped a stone out of a brooch or something. Look—on the carpet there!"

"Oh," said Priscilla carelessly, "it was out of my mouth—not out of a brooch, I never wear jewellery. I think jewellery makes people grow so conceited; don't you, Aunt Margarine?"

"Yes, indeed, dearest—indeed you are *so* right!" said her aunt (who wore a cameo-brooch as large as a tart upon her cloak), "and—and surely that can't be a *diamond* in your lap?"

"Oh, yes, it is. I met a fairy this morning in the lane and so——" and here Priscilla proceeded to narrate her wonderful experience. "I thought it might perhaps make papa and mamma value me a little more than they do," she said wistfully, as she finished her story, "but they don't take the least notice; they made me put the jewels on the fire—they did, really!"

"What blindness!" cried her aunt; "how *can* people shut their eyes to such a treasure? And—and may I just have *one* look? What, you really don't want them?—I may keep them for my very own? You precious love! Ah, I know a humble home where you would be appreciated at your proper worth. What would I not give for my poor naughty Belle and Cathie to have the advantage of seeing more of such a cousin!"

"I don't know whether I could do them much good," said Priscilla, "but I would try my best."

"I am sure you would!" said Aunt Margarine, "and now, dearest sweet, I am going to ask your dear mamma to spare you to us for just a little while; we must both beg very hard."

"I'll go and tell nurse to pack my things now, and then I can go away with you," said the little girl.

When her mother heard of the invitation, she consented quite willingly. "To tell you the truth, Margarine," she said, "I shall be very glad for the child to have a change. She seems a little unhappy at home with us, and she behaved most unlike her usual self at lunch; it *can't* be natural for a child of her age to chew large glass beads. Did your Cathie and Belle ever do such a thing?"

"Never," said Aunt Margarine, coughing. "It is a habit that certainly ought to be checked, and I promise you, my dear Lucy, that if you will only trust Priscilla to me, I will take away anything of that kind the very moment I find it. And I do think, poor as we are, we shall manage to make her feel at home. We are all so fond of your sweet Priscilla!"

So the end of it was that Priscilla went to stay with her aunt that very afternoon, and her family bore the parting with the greatest composure.

"I can't give you nice food, or a pretty bedroom to sleep in such as you have at home," said her kind aunt. "We are very plain people, my pet; but at least we can promise you a warm welcome."

"Oh, auntie," protested Priscilla, "you mustn't think I mind a little hardship! Why, if beds weren't hard and food not nicely cooked now and then, we should soon grow too luxurious to do our duty, and that would be so very bad for us!"

"Oh, what *beauties!*" cried her aunt involuntarily, as she stooped to recover several sparkling gems from the floor of the cab. "I mean—it's better to pick them up, dear, don't you think? they might get in people's *way*, you know. What a blessing you will be in

our simple home! I want you to do all you can to instruct your cousins; don't be afraid of telling them of any faults you may happen to see. Poor Cathie and Belle, I fear they are very far from being all they should be!" and Aunt Margarine heaved a sigh.

"Never mind, auntie; they will be better in time, I am sure. *I* wasn't *always* a good girl."

Priscilla thoroughly enjoyed the first few days of her visit; even her aunt was only too grateful for instruction, and begged that Priscilla would tell her, quite candidly, of any shortcomings she might notice. And Priscilla, very kindly and considerately, always *did* tell her. Belle and Catherine were less docile, and she saw that it would take her some time to win their esteem and affection; but this was just what Priscilla liked: it was the usual experience of the heroines in the books, and much more interesting, too, than conquering her cousins' hearts at once.

Still, both Catherine and Belle persistently hardened their hearts against their gentle little cousin in the unkindest way; they would scarcely speak to her, and chose to make a grievance out of the fact that one or other of them was obliged, by their mother's strict orders, to be constantly in attendance upon her, in order to pick up and bring Mrs. Hoyle all the jewels that Priscilla scattered in profusion wherever she went.

"If you would only carry a plate about with you, Priscilla," complained Belle one day, "you could catch the jewels in that."

"But I don't *want* to catch the jewels, dear Belle," said Priscilla, with a playful but very sweet smile; "if other people prize such things, that is not my fault, is it? *Jewels* do not make people any happier, Belle!"

"I should think not!" exclaimed Belle. "I'm sure my back perfectly aches with stooping, and so does Cathie's. There! that big topaz has just gone and rolled under the sideboard, and mother will be *so* angry if I don't get it out! It is too bad of you, Priscilla! *I* believe you do it on purpose!"

"Ah, you will know me better some day, dear," was the gentle response.

"Well, at all events, I think you might be naughty just now and then, Prissie, and give Cathie and me a half-holiday."

"I would do anything else to please you, dear, but not that; you must not ask me to do what is impossible."

Alas! not even this angelic behaviour, not even the loving admonitions, the tender

rebukes, the shocked reproaches that fell, accompanied by perfect cascades of jewels, from the lips of our pattern little Priscilla, succeeded in removing the utterly unfounded prejudices of her cousins, though it was some consolation to feel that she was gradually acquiring a most beneficial influence over her aunt, who called Priscilla "her little conscience." For, you see, Priscilla's conscience had so little to do on her own account that it was always at the service of other people, and indeed quite enjoyed being useful, as was only natural to a conscientious conscience which felt that it could never have been created to be idle.

Very soon another responsibility was added to little Priscilla's burdens. Her cousin Dick, the worldly one with the yellow boots, came home after his annual holiday, which, as he was the junior clerk in a large bank, he was obliged to take rather late in the year. She had looked forward to his return with some excitement. Dick, she knew, was frivolous and reckless in his habits—he went to the theatre occasionally and frequently spent an evening in playing billiards and smoking cigars at a friend's house. There would be real credit in reforming poor cousin Dick.

He was not long, of course, in hearing of Priscilla's marvellous endowment, and upon the first occasion they were alone together treated her with a respect and admiration which he had very certainly never shown her before.

"You're wonderful, Prissie!" he said; "I'd no idea you had it in you!"

"Nor had I, Dick; but it shows that even a little girl can do something."

"I should rather think so! and—and the way you look—as grave as a judge all the time! Prissie, I wish you'd tell me how you manage it, I wouldn't tell a soul."

"But I don't know, Dick. I only talk and the jewels come—that is all."

"You artful little girl! you can keep a secret, I see, but so can I. And you might tell me how you do the trick. What put you up to the dodge? I'm to be trusted, I assure you."

"Dick, you can't—you mustn't—think there is any trickery about it! How can you believe I could be such a wicked little girl as to play tricks? It was an old fairy that gave me the gift. I'm sure I don't know why—unless she thought that I was a good child and deserved to be encouraged."

"By Jove!" cried Dick, "I never knew you were half such fun!"

"I am not fun, Dick. I think fun is generally so very vulgar, and oh, I wish you wouldn't say 'by Jove!' Surely you know he was a heathen god!"

"I seem to have heard of him in some such capacity," said Dick. "I say, Prissie, what a ripping big ruby!"

"Ah, Dick, Dick, you are like the others! I'm afraid you think more of the jewels than any words I may say—and yet *jewels* are common enough!"

"They seem to be with you. Pearls, too, and such fine ones! Here, Priscilla, take them; they're your property."

Priscilla put her hands behind her: "No, indeed, Dick, they are of no use to me. Keep them, please; they may help to remind you of what I have said."

"It's awfully kind of you," said Dick, looking really touched. "Then—since you put it in that way—thanks, I will, Priscilla. I'll have them made into a horse-shoe pin."

"You mustn't let it make you too fond of dress, then," said Priscilla; "but I'm afraid you're that already, Dick."

"A diamond!" he cried; "go on, Priscilla, I'm listening—pitch into me, it will do me a *lot* of good!

But Priscilla thought it wisest to say no more just then.

That night, after Priscilla and Cathie and Belle had gone to bed, Dick and his mother sat up talking until a late hour.

"Is dear little cousin Priscilla to be a permanency in this establishment?" began her cousin, stifling a yawn, for there had been a rather copious flow of precious stones during the evening.

"Well, I shall keep her with us as long as I can," said Mrs. Hoyle, "she's such a darling, and they don't seem to want her at home. I'm sure, limited as my means are, I'm most happy to have such a visitor."

"She seems to pay her way—only her way is a trifle trying at times, isn't it? She lectured me for half an hour on end without a single check!"

"Are you sure you picked them all up, dear boy?"

"Got a few of the best in my waistcoat-pocket now. I'm afraid I scrunched a pearl or two, though: they were all over the place, you know. I suppose you've been collecting too, mater?"

"I picked up one or two," said his mother; "I should think I must have nearly enough now to fill a bandbox. And that brings me to what I wanted to consult you about, Richard. How are we to dispose of them? She has given them all to me."

"You haven't done anything with them yet, then?"

"How could I? I have been obliged to stay at home: I've been so afraid of letting that precious child go out of my sight for a single hour, for fear some unscrupulous persons might get hold of her. I thought that perhaps, when you came home, you would dispose of the jewels for me."

"But, mater," protested Dick, "I can't go about asking who'll buy a whole bandbox full of jewels!"

"Oh, very well, then; I suppose we must go on living this hugger-mugger life when we have the means of being as rich as princes, just because you are too lazy and selfish to take a little trouble!"

"I know something about these things," said Dick. "I know a fellow who's a diamond merchant, and it's not so easy to sell a lot of valuable stones as you seem to imagine, mother. And then Priscilla really overdoes it, you know—why, if she goes on like this, she'll make diamonds as cheap as currants!"

"*I* should have thought that was a reason for selling them as soon as possible; but I'm only a woman, and of course *my* opinion is worth nothing! Still you might take some of the biggest to your friend, and accept whatever he'll give you for them—there are plenty more, you needn't haggle over the price."

"He'd want to know all about them, and what should I say? I can't tell him a cousin of mine produces them whenever she feels disposed."

"You could say they have been in the family for some time, and you are obliged to part with them; I don't ask you to tell a falsehood, Richard."

"Well, to tell you the honest truth," said Dick, "i'd rather have nothing to do with it. I'm not proud, but I shouldn't like it to get about among our fellows at the bank that I went about hawking diamonds."

"But you stupid, undutiful boy, don't you see that you could leave the bank—you need never do anything any more—we should all live rich and happy somewhere in the country, if we could only sell those jewels! And you won't do that one little thing!"

"Well," said Dick, "I'll think over it. I'll see what I can do."

And his mother knew that it was perfectly useless to urge him any further; for, in some things, Dick was as obstinate as a mule, and, in others far too easy-going and careless ever to succeed in life. He had promised to think over it, however, and she had to be contented with that.

On the evening following this conversation cousin Dick entered the sitting-room the moment after his return from the city, and found his mother to all appearances alone.

"What a dear sweet little guileless angel cousin Priscilla is, to be sure!" was his first remark.

"Then you *have* sold some of the stones!" cried Aunt Margarine. "Sit down, like a good boy, and tell me all about it."

"Well," said Dick, "I took the finest diamonds and rubies and pearls that escaped from that saintlike child last night in the course of some extremely disparaging comments on my character and pursuits—I took those jewels to Faycett and Rosewater's in New Bond Street—you know the shop, on the right-hand side as you go up——"

"Oh, go on, Dick; go on—never mind *where* it is—how much did you get for them?"

"I'm coming to that; keep cool, dear mamma. Well, I went in, and I saw the manager, and I said: 'I want you to make these up into a horse-shoe scarf-pin for me.'"

"You said that! You never tried to sell one? Oh, Dick, you are too provoking!"

"Hold on, mater; I haven't done yet. So the manager—a very gentlemanly person, rather thin on the top of the head—not that that affects his business capacities; for, after all——"

"Dick, do you want to drive me frantic?"

"I can't conceive any domestic occurrence which would be more distressing or generally inconvenient, mother dear. You do interrupt a fellow so! I forget where I was now—oh, the manager, ah, yes! Well, the manager said, 'We shall be very happy to have the stones made in any design you may select'—jewellery, by the way, seems to exercise a most refining influence upon the manners: this man had the deportment of a duke—'you may select,' he said; 'but of course I need not tell you that none of these stones are genuine.'"

"Not genuine!" cried Aunt Margarine, excitedly. "They must be—he was lying!"

"West-end jewellers never lie," said Dick; "but naturally, when he said that, I told him

I should like to have some proof of his assertion. 'Will you take the risk of testing?' said he. 'Test away, my dear man!' said I. So he brought a little wheel near the emerald—'whizz!' and away went the emerald! Then he let a drop of something fall on the ruby—and it fizzled up for all the world like pink champagne. 'Go on, don't mind *me!*' I told him, so he touched the diamond with an electric wire—'phit!' and there was only something that looked like the ash of a shocking bad cigar. Then the pearls—and they popped like so many air-balloons. 'Are you satisfied?' he asked.

" 'Oh, perfectly,' said I, 'you needn't trouble about the horse-shoe pin now. Good evening,' and so I came away, after thanking him for his very amusing scientific experiments."

"And do you believe that the jewels are all shams, Dick?—do you really?"

"I think it so probable that nothing on earth will induce me to offer a single one for sale. I should never hear the last of it at the bank. No, mater, dear little Priscilla's sparkling conversation may be unspeakably precious from a moral point of view, but it has no commercial value. Those jewels are bogus—shams every stone of them!"

Now, all this time our heroine had been sitting unperceived in a corner behind a window-curtain, reading the "Wide, Wide World," a work which she was never weary of perusing. Some children would have come forward earlier, but Priscilla was never a forward child, and she remained as quiet as a little mouse up to the moment when she could control her feelings no longer.

"It isn't true!" she cried passionately, bursting out of her retreat and confronting her cousin; "its cruel and unkind to say my jewels are shams! They are real—they are, they *are!*"

"Hullo, Prissie!" said her abandoned cousin; "so you combine jewel-dropping with eavesdropping, eh?"

"How dare you!" cried Aunt Margarine, almost beside herself, "you odious little prying minx, setting up to teach your elders and your betters with your cut and dried priggish maxims! When I think how I have petted and indulged you all this time, and borne with the abominable litter you left in every room you entered—and now to find you are only a little, conceited, hypocritical impostor—oh, *why* haven't I words to express my contempt for such conduct—why am I dumb at such a moment as this?"

"Come, mother," said her son soothingly, "that's not such a bad beginning; I should call it fairly fluent and expressive, myself."

"Be quiet, Dick! I'm speaking to this wicked child, who has obtained our love and sympathy and attention on false pretences, for which she ought to be put in prison—yes, in *prison*, for such a heartless trick on relatives who can ill afford to be so cruelly disappointed!"

"But, aunt!" expostulated poor Priscilla, "you always said you only kept the jewels as souvenirs, and that it did you so much good to hear me talk!"

"Don't argue with *me*, miss! If I had known the stones were wretched tawdry imitations, do you imagine for an instant——?"

"Now, mother," said Dick, "be fair—they were uncommonly good imitations, you must admit that!"

"Indeed, indeed, I thought they were real, the fairy never told me!"

"After all," said Dick, "it's not Priscilla's fault. She can't help it if the stones aren't real, and she made up for quality by quantity anyhow; didn't you, Prissie?"

"Hold your tongue, Richard; she *could* help it, she knew it all the time, and she's a hateful, sanctimonious little stuck-up viper, and so I tell her to her face!"

Priscilla could scarcely believe that kind, indulgent, smooth-spoken Aunt Margarine could be addressing such words to her; it frightened her so much that she did not dare to answer, and just then Cathie and Belle came into the room.

"Oh, mother," they began penitently, "we're *so* sorry, but we couldn't find dear Prissie anywhere, so we haven't picked up anything the whole afternoon!"

"Ah, my poor darlings, you shall never be your cousin's slaves any more. Don't go near her, she's a naughty, deceitful wretch; her jewels are false, my sweet loves, false! She has imposed upon us all, she does not deserve to associate with you!"

"I always said Prissie's jewels looked like the things you get on crackers!" said Belle, tossing her head.

"Now we shall have a little rest, I hope," chimed in Cathie.

"I shall send her home to her parents this very night," declared Aunt Margarine; "she shall not stay here to pervert our happy household with her miserable *gewgaws!*"

Here Priscilla found her tongue. "Do you think I *want* to stay?" she said proudly; "I see now that you only wanted to have me here because—because of the horrid jewels, and I never knew they were false, and I let you have them all, every one, you know I did; and I wanted you to mind what I said and not trouble about picking them up, but you *would* do it! And now you all turn round upon me like this! What have I done to be treated so? What have I done?"

"Bravo, Prissie!" cried Dick. "Mother, if you ask me, I think it serves us all jolly well right, and it's a downright shame to bullyrag poor Prissie in this way!"

"I *don't* ask you," retorted his mother, sharply; "so you will kindly keep your opinions to yourself."

"Tra-la-la!" sang rude Dick, "we are a united family—we are, we are, we *are!*"—a vulgar refrain he had picked up at one of the burlesque theatres he was only too fond of frequenting.

But Priscilla came to him and held out her hand quite gratefully and humbly. "Thank you, Dick," she said; "*you* are kind, at all events. And I am sorry you couldn't have your horse-shoe pin!"

"Oh, *hang* the horse-shoe pin!" exclaimed Dick, and poor Priscilla was so thoroughly cast down that she quite forgot to reprove him.

She was not sent home that night after all, for Dick protested against it in such strong terms that even Aunt Margarine saw that she must give way; but early on the following morning Priscilla quitted her aunt's house, leaving her belongings to be sent on after her.

She had not far to walk, and it so happened that her way led through the identical lane in which she had met the fairy. Wonderful to relate, there, on the very same stone and in precisely the same attitude, sat the old lady, peering out from under her poke-bonnet, and resting her knotty old hands on her crutch-handled stick!

Priscilla walked past with her head in the air pretending not to notice her, for she considered that the fairy had played her a most malicious and ill-natured trick.

"Heyday!" said the old lady (it is only fairies who can permit themselves such old-fashioned expressions nowadays). "Heyday, why, here's my good little girl again! Isn't she going to speak to me?"

"No, she's not," said Priscilla—but she found herself compelled to stop, notwithstanding.

"Why, what's all this about? You're not going to sulk with me, my dear, are you?"

"I think you're a very cruel, bad, unkind old woman for deceiving me like this!"

"Goodness me! Why, didn't the jewels come, after all?"

"Yes—they came, only they were all horrid artificial ones—and it is a shame, it *is!*" cried poor Priscilla from her bursting heart.

"Artificial, were they? that really is very odd! Can you account for that at all, now?"

"Of course I can't! You told me that they would drop out whenever I said anything to improve people—and I was *always* saying *something* improving! Aunt had a bandbox in her room quite full of them."

"Ah, you've been very industrious, evidently; it's unfortunate your jewels should all have been artificial—most unfortunate. I don't know how to explain it, unless"—(and here the old lady looked up queerly from under her white eyelashes), "unless your goodness was artificial too?"

"How do you mean?" asked Priscilla, feeling strangely uncomfortable. "I'm sure I've never done anything the least bit naughty—how can my goodness possibly be artificial?"

"Ah, that I can't explain; but I think (I only say I *think,* mind) that a little girl so young as you must have some faults hidden about her somewhere, and that perhaps on the whole she would be better employed in trying to find them out and cure them before she attempted to correct those of other people. And I'm sure it can't be good for any child to be always seeing herself in a little picture, just as she likes to fancy other people see her. But of course, my dear, you never made such a mistake as that!"

Priscilla turned very red, and began to scrape one of her feet against the other; she was thinking, and her thoughts were not at all pleasant ones.

"Oh, fairy," she said at last, "I'm afraid that's just what I *did* do. I was always thinking how good I was and putting everybody—papa, mamma, Alick, Betty, Aunt Margarine,

Cathie, Belle, and even poor cousin Dick—right! I have been a horrid little hateful prig, and that's why all the jewels were rubbish. But, oh, shall I have to go on talking sham diamonds and things all the rest of my life?"

"That," said the fairy, "depends entirely on yourself. You have the remedy in your own hands—or lips."

"Ah, you mean I needn't talk at all? But I must—sometimes. I couldn't bear to be dumb as long as I lived—and it would look so odd, too!"

"I never said you were not to open your lips at all. But can't you try to talk simply and naturally—not like little girls or boys in any story-books whatever—not to 'show off' or improve people; only as a girl would talk who remembers that, after all, her elders are quite as likely as she is to know what they ought or ought not to do and say?"

"I shall forget sometimes, I know I shall!" said Priscilla disconsolately.

"If you do, there will be something to remind you, you know. And by-and-by, perhaps, as you grow up you may, quite by accident, say something sincere and noble and true—and then a jewel will fall which will really be of value!"

"No!" cried Priscilla, "no, *please!* Oh, fairy, let me off that! If I *must* drop them, let them be false ones to punish me—not real. I don't want to be rewarded any more for being good—if I ever am really good!"

"Come," said the fairy, with a much pleasanter smile, "you are not a hopeless case, at all events. It shall be as you wish, then, and perhaps it will be the wisest arrangement for all parties. Now run away home, and see how little use you can make of your fairy gift."

Priscilla found her family still at breakfast.

"Why," observed her father, raising his eyebrows as she entered the door, "here's our little monitor—(or is it *monitress*, eh, Priscilla?)—back again. Children, we shall all have to mind our p's and q's—and, indeed, our entire alphabet, now!"

"I'm sure," said her mother, kissing her fondly, "Priscilla knows we're all delighted to have her home!"

"*I'm* not," said Alick, with all a boy's engaging candour.

"Nor am I," added Betty, "it's been ever so much nicer at home while she's been away!"

Priscilla burst into tears as she hid her face upon her mother's protecting shoulder. "It's true!" she sobbed, "I don't deserve that you should be glad to see me—I've been hateful and horrid, I know—but, oh, if you'll only forgive me and love me and put up with me a little, I'll try not to preach and be a prig any more—I will truly!"

And at this her father called her to his side and embraced her with a fervour he had not shown for a very long time.

* * * * *

I should not like to go so far as to assert that no imitation diamond, ruby, pearl, or emerald ever proceeded from Priscilla's lips again. Habits are not cured in a day, and fairies—however old they may be—are still fairies; so it *did* occasionally happen that a mock jewel made an unwelcome appearance after one of Priscilla's more unguarded utterances. But she was always frightfully ashamed and abashed by such an accident, and buried the imitation stones immediately in a corner of the garden. And as time went on the jewels grew smaller and smaller, and frequently dissolved upon her tongue, leaving a faintly bitter taste, until at last they ceased altogether, and Priscilla became as pleasant and unaffected a girl as she who may now be finishing this history.

Aunt Margarine never sent back the contents of that bandbox; she kept the biggest stones and had a brooch made of them, while, as she never mentioned that they were false, no one out of the family ever so much as suspected it.

But, for all that, she always declared that her niece Priscilla had bitterly disappointed her expectations—which was perhaps the truest thing that Aunt Margarine ever said.

A Select Bibliography
of Primary Works

HANS CHRISTIAN ANDERSEN

Danish Fairy-legends and Tales. Translated by Caroline Peachey. Glasgow: Pickering, 1846.
A Danish Story Book. Translated by Charles Boner. London: Cundall, 1846.
The Nightingale and Other Stories. Translated by Charles Boner. London: Cundall, 1846.
Wonderful Stories for Children. Translated by Mary Howitt. London: Chapman & Hall, 1846.
Fairy Tales from Hans Christian Andersen. Translated by E. V. Lucas. London: Dent, 1899.
    Reprint. New York: Grossett, 1945.
Hans Andersen: Forty-two Stories. Translated by Montague Rhodes James. London: Faber &
    Faber, 1930.
It's Perfectly True and Other Stories. Translated by Paul Leyssac. New York: Harcourt, 1938.
The Complete Andersen. Translated by Jean Hersholt. New York: Heritage, 1942.
Hans Christian Andersen's Fairy Tales. Translated by R. P. Keigwin, edited by Svend Larsen.
    Odense, Denmark: World Editions, 1950.
Hans Christian Andersen's Fairy Tales. Translated by Reginald Spink. New York: Dutton, 1953.
Seven Tales. Translated by Eva Le Gallienne, illustrated by Maurice Sendak. New York:
    Harper, 1959.
Hans Andersen's Fairy Tales. Translated by L. W. Kingsland, illustrated by Ernest Shepard.
    London: Oxford, 1961.
The Complete Fairy Tales and Stories. Translated by Erik Haugaard. New York: Doubleday,
    1974.

FRANCES BROWNE

Granny's Wonderful Chair and the Tales It Told. Illustrated by Kenny Meadows. London:
    Griffith & Farrow, 1856. Reprinted as *The Story of the Lost Fairy Book.* Edited by Frances
    Hodgson Burnett. London, 1887.
Pictures and Songs from Home. London: Nelson, 1856.
Our Uncle the Traveler. London: Kent, 1859.
The Young Foresters. London, 1860.
Granny's Wonderful Chair. London: J. M. Dent & Sons, 1912.

CHARLES DICKENS

A Christmas Carol, in Prose, Being a Ghost Story of Christmas. Illustrated by John Leech. London:
    Chapman & Hall, 1843.

Christmas Books. 5 vols. London: Chapman & Hall, 1843–48.

The Chimes: A Goblin Story of Some Bells That Rang an Old Year Out and a New Year In. London: Chapman & Hall, 1845.

The Cricket on the Hearth: A Fairy Tale of Home. Illustrated by D. Maclise, R. A., R. Doyle, S. Stanfield, J. Leech, and E. Landseer. London: Bradbury & Evans, 1846.

A Child's History of England. 3 vols. London: Bradbury & Evans, 1852–54. Reprint. New York: Dutton, 1970.

Charles Dickens' Stories from the Christmas Numbers of "Household Words" and "All Year Round," 1852–1867. Edited and introduced by Charles Dickens the younger. New York and London: Macmillan, 1886.

Christmas Stories, and Sketches by Boz Illustrative of Every-day People. Illustrated by S. Eytinge, Jr. Boston: Ticknor & Fields, 1867.

A Holiday Romance. Boston: Ticknor & Fields, 1868. Reprint. London: Cecil Palmer, 1920.

A Child's Dream of a Star. Boston: Osgood, 1871.

The Chimes. Illustrated by C. E. Brock. London: Dent; New York: Dutton, 1905.

The Cricket on the Hearth. Illustrated by C. E. Brock. London: Dent; New York: Dutton, 1905.

The Magic Fishbone: A Holiday Romance from the Pen of Miss Alice Rainbird, Aged 7. London: James Nisbet, 1911.

The Trial of William Tinkling, Written by Himself at the Age of 8. Orange Tree Series of Children's Books, no. 3. London: Constable, 1912.

Captain Boldheart and the Latin-grammar Master: A Holiday Romance from the Pen of Lieut-Col. Robin Redforth, Aged 9. Orange Tree Series of Children's Books, no. 4. London: Constable, 1912.

A Christmas Carol. Illustrated by Arthur Rackham. London: Heinemann, 1915.

The Magic Fishbone. Illustrated by F. D. Bedford. London: Warne, 1921.

A Christmas Carol. Illustrated by F. D. Bedford. London: Macmillan, 1923.

The Chimes. Illustrated by Arthur Rackham, introduction by Edward Wagenknecht. London: G. W. Jones for the Limited Editions Club, 1931.

The Cricket on the Hearth. Illustrated by Hugh Thomson. Waltham St. Lawrence, England: Golden Cockerel Press for the Limited Editions Club, 1933.

A Christmas Carol. Illustrated by Gordon Ross, introduction by Stephen Leacock. Boston: Merrymount Press for the Limited Editions Club, 1934.

A Christmas Carol. Illustrated by Philip Reed. Chicago: Holiday, 1940. Reprint. New York: Atheneum, 1960.

Mrs. Orange. Illustrated by Robert Stewart Sherriffs. London: Herbert Jenkins, 1948.

The Magic Fishbone. Illustrated by Louis Slobodkin. New York: Vanguard, 1953.

The Chimes. Illustrated by Landseer, Maclise, Tenniel, and Stanfield, introduction by Eleanor Farjeon. London: Oxford, 1954.

A Christmas Carol. Facsimile of the first edition. Introduction and bibliography by Edgar Johnson. New York: Columbia University Press, 1956.

A Christmas Carol. Facsimile of the manuscript in the Pierpont Morgan Library. Illustrated by John Leech. London: Heinemann, 1967. Reprint. New York: Dover, 1971.

The Chimes. 2 vols. Harmondsworth, England: Penguin, 1971.

The Annotated Christmas Carol. Introduction and bibliography by Michael Hearn. New York: Potter, 1976.

A Charles Dickens Christmas: "A Christmas Carol," "The Chimes," "The Cricket on the Hearth." Illustrated by Warren Chappell. New York: Oxford, 1976.

A Holiday Romance. Reprinted in *The King of the Golden River [Ruskin], A Holiday Romance, and Petsetilla's Posy [Hood].* Introduction by Diane Johnson. Classics of Children's Literature, 1621–1932. New York: Garland, 1976.

JULIANA HORATIA EWING

Mrs. Overtheway's Remembrances. London: Bell & Daldy, 1869. Reprint. Classics of Children's Literature, 1621–1932. New York: Garland, 1977.

The Brownies and Other Tales. Illustrated by G. Cruikshank. London: Bell & Daldy, 1870.

A Flat-Iron for a Farthing; or, Some Passages in the Life of an Only Son. London: Bell & Daldy, 1873.

Lob Lie-by-the-fire. London: Bell & Daldy, 1874. Reprint. Classics of Children's Literature, 1621–1932. New York: Garland, 1977.

Jan of the Windmill: A Story of the Plains. London: Bell & Daldy, 1876.

Six to Sixteen: A Story for Girls. London: G. Bell, 1876. Reprint. Classics of Children's Literature, 1621–1932. New York: Garland, 1976.

A Great Emergency, and Other Tales. London: G. Bell, 1877.

We and the World: A Book for Boys. London: G. Bell, 1881.

Brothers of Pity, and Other Tales of Beasts and Men. London: Society for Promoting Christian Knowledge, 1882.

Old-fashioned Fairy Tales. London: Society for Promoting Christian Knowledge, 1882.

Daddy Darwin's Dovecot. London: Society for Promoting Christian Knowledge, 1884. Reprint. Classics of Children's Literature, 1621–1932. New York: Garland, 1977.

Jackanapes. Illustrated by Randolph Caldecott. London: Society for Promoting Christian Knowledge, 1884. Reprint. Preface by Alison Lurie. Classics of Children's Literature, 1621–1932. New York: Garland, 1977.

Mother's Birthday Review, and Seven Other Tales in Verse. Illustrated by R. Andre. London: Society for Promoting Christian Knowledge, 1885.

The Story of a Short Life. London: Society for Promoting Christian Knowledge, 1885.

Daddy Darwin's Dovecot, Melchior's Dream, and Other Tales. Illustrated by Randolph Caldecott, Gordon Browne, et al. Boston: Little, 1909.

Mary's Meadow, and Other Tales of Fields and Flowers. Edited by Horatia K. F. Eden. London: Bell & Daldy, 1915.

A Great Emergency and a Very Ill-tempered Family. New York: Schocken, 1969.

FREDERIC W. FARRAR

Eric; or, Little by Little. A Tale of Roslyn School. Edinburgh: Adam & Charles Black, 1858. Reprint. Introduction by John Rowe Townsend. London: Hamish Hamilton, 1971.

Julian Home: A Tale of College Life. Edinburgh: Adam & Charles Black, 1859.

St. Winifred's; or, The World of School. Edinburgh: Adam & Charles Black, 1862.

["F. T. L. Hope."] *The Three Homes: A Tale for Fathers and Sons.* London: Cassell, Bates & Co., 1872.

Darkness and Dawn; or, Scenes in the Days of Nero. London: Longmans, 1891.

Eric; or, Little by Little. Edinburgh: Adam & Charles Black, 1892. Reprint. Introduction by Gillian Avery. Classics of Children's Literature, 1621–1932. New York: Garland, 1977.

Gathering Clouds. London: Longmans, 1895.

Eric; or, Little by Little. Illustrated by Gordon Browne. London: Adam & Charles Black, 1898.

Christmas Carols. New York: Thomas Whittaker, n.d.

T. ANSTEY GUTHRIE ("F. ANSTEY")

Vice-Versa; or, A Lesson to Fathers. London: Smith, Elder & Co., 1882.
The Talking Horse. London: Smith, Elder & Co., 1892.
Paleface and Redskin and Other Stories for Boys and Girls. London: Richards, 1898.
The Brass Bottle. London: Smith, Elder & Co., 1900.
Only Toys! London: Richards, 1903.
Paleface and Redskin and Other Stories for Boys and Girls. New York and London: D. Appleton & Sons, 1924.

MARY HOWITT

Peter Parley's Fable of the Spider and the Fly. London: Carter, 1830.
Sketches of Natural History. London: Darton, 1834. Reprint. New York: Johnson, 1970.
Tales in Prose for the Young. London: Darton, 1836.
Tales in Verse. London: Darton, 1836.
Birds and Flowers and Other Country Things. London: Darton, 1838.
Other Country Things. London: Darton, 1838.
The Christmas Library . . . Hymns and Fireside Verses. London: Darton, 1839.
Hope On! Hope Ever! or, The Boyhood of Felix Law. London: Munroe, 1840.
Sowing and Reaping; or, What Will Come of It. London: Munroe, 1840. Reprint. New York: Johnson, 1970.
Strive and Thrive: A Tale. London: Tegg, 1840.
Who Shall Be Greatest? London: Munroe, 1841.
Little Coin, Much Care; or, How Poor Men Live. New York: Appleton, 1842.
Which Is the Wiser? or, People Abroad: A Tale for Youth. London: Tegg, 1842.
Alice Franklin: A Tale. New York: Appleton, 1843.
Love and Money: An Every-day Tale. London: Tegg, 1843.
No Sense Like Common Sense. New York: Appleton, 1843.
Work and Wages; or, Life in Service. New York: Appleton, 1843.
My Own Story; or, The Autobiography of a Child. New York: Appleton, 1844.
Speckter, Otto. *The Child's Picture and Verse Book, Commonly Called Otto Speckter's Fable Book.* Translated from the German by Mary Howitt. London: Tegg, 1844.
Stober, Karl. *The Curate's Favorite Pupil.* Translated from the German by Mary Howitt, illustrated by John Absolon. London: Orr, 1844.
Andersen, Hans Christian. *Wonderful Stories for Children.* Translated from the Danish by Mary Howitt. London: Chapman & Hall, 1846.
Ballads, and Other Poems. London: Longman, Brown, 1847.
The Children's Year. Illustrated by John Absolon. London: Longman, Brown, 1847.
The Childhood of Mary Leeson. Boston: Crosby, Nichols, 1848.
Our Cousins in Ohio. London: Darton, 1849.
My Juvenile Days, and Other Tales. New York: Appleton, 1850.
Midsummer Flowers, for the Young. Philadelphia: Lindsay & Blakiston, 1854.
Stories in Rhyme. Boston: Brown, Bazin & Co., 1855.
Lillieslea; or, Lost and Found: A Story for the Young. Illustrated by John Absolon. London: Routledge, 1861.
Tales of English Life, including Middleton and the Middletons. London: Warne, 1881.

THOMAS HUGHES

Tom Brown's School Days, by an Old Boy. Cambridge: Macmillan, 1857.
The Scouring of the White Horse. London: Macmillan, 1859.
Tom Brown at Oxford. 3 vols. Cambridge: Macmillan, 1861.
Brown and Arthur: An Episode from "Tom Brown's School Days." Richmond, Va.: West & Johnston, 1861.
Tom Brown's School Days. Boston: Houghton, 1895.
Tom Brown's School Days. Illustrated by Arthur Hughes and Sydney Prior Hall. London: Macmillan, 1900.
Tom Brown's School Days. Introduction by W. D. Howells, illustrated by Louis Rhead. New York: Harper, 1911.
Tom Brown's School Days. Edited by F. Sidgwick, illustrated by W. F. Loveday, preface by Lord Kilbracken. London: Sidgwick & Jackson, 1913.

ANNIE KEARY

[With Eliza Keary.] *The Heroes of Asgard and the Giants of Jotunheim; or, The Week and Its Story.* London: W. Kent & Co., 1857.
The Rival Kings. London: W. Kent & Co., 1857.
Father Phim. London: W. Kent & Co., 1879.

HENRY KINGSLEY

The Boy in Grey. London: Ward, Lock, & Bowden, 1895.

MARK LEMON

The Enchanted Doll. Illustrated by Richard Doyle. London: Bradbury & Evans, 1849.
Fairy Tales. London: Stark, 1865.
Tinikin's Transformations: A Child's Story. Illustrated by C. Green. London: Stark, 1869.

GEORGE MACDONALD

Adela Cathcart. London, 1864.
Dealings with the Fairies. Illustrated by Arthur Hughes. London: Strahan, 1867.
At the Back of the North Wind. Illustrated by Arthur Hughes. London: Strahan, 1871.
"Poems for Children." In *Works of George MacDonald,* vol. 3. London: Strahan, 1871.
Ronald Bannerman's Boyhood. London, 1871.
Gutta Percha Willie. London, 1873.
At the Back of the North Wind. New York: George Routledge & Sons, 1875.
The Gifts of the Child Christ, and Other Tales. 2 vols. London: Sampson, Low, 1882.
The Princess and Curdie. Illustrated by James Allen. London: Chatto & Windus, 1883.
The Princess and the Goblin. Illustrated by Arthur Hughes. London: Chatto & Windus, 1883.
A Rough Shaking. London: Blackie, 1890.
The Light Princess, and Other Fairy Tales. London: Blackie, 1890.
The Light Princess. Illustrated by Dorothy Lathrop. New York: Macmillan, 1926.
The Golden Key. Illustrated by Maurice Sendak, afterword by W. H. Auden. New York: Farrar, 1967.
The Light Princess. Illustrated by Maurice Sendak. New York: Farrar, 1969.

At the Back of the North Wind. Preface by Glenn E. Sadler. Classics of Children's Literature, 1621–1932. New York: Garland, 1976.
The Wise Woman: A Parable. Preface by Mark Zaitchick. Classics of Children's Literature, 1621–1932. New York: Garland, 1977.

HARRIET MOZLEY

The Fairy Bower; or, The History of a Month. 1841.
The Lost Brooch. 2 vols. 1841.
The Fairy Bower. New York and Philadelphia: D. Appleton & Co., 1847.

JOHN RUSKIN

The King of the Golden River; or, The Black Brothers: A Legend of Stiria. Illustrated by Richard Doyle. London: Smith & Elder, 1851.
The Ethics of the Dust. N.p., 1866.
The King of the Golden River. Illustrated by Richard Doyle. Kent: George Allen, 1882.
Dame Wiggins of Lee and Her Seven Wonderful Cats. Illustrated by Kate Greenaway. London: Allen, 1885.
The King of the Golden River. East Aurora, N.Y.: Roycrofters, 1900.
The King of the Golden River. Illustrated by Arthur Rackham. Philadelphia: Lippincott, 1932.
The King of the Golden River. Illustrated by Fritz Kredel, introduction by May Lamberton Becker. Rainbow Classics. Cleveland: World, 1946.
The King of the Golden River. Illustrated by Josef Vyetal. London: Hamlyn, 1973.
The King of the Golden River. Reprinted in *The King of the Golden River, A Holiday Romance [Dickens], and Petsetilla's Posy [Hood].* Introduction by Diane Johnson. Classics of Children's Literature, 1621–1932. New York: Garland, 1976.

FLORA SHAW

Castle Blair. Boston: Roberts, 1878.
Phyllis Browne. Boston: Roberts, 1882.
Hector. London: Bell, 1883.

CATHERINE SINCLAIR

Charlie Seymour; or, The Good Aunt and the Bad Aunt. London: Carter, 1832.
Holiday House: A Book for the Young. Edinburgh: W. Whyte, 1839. Reprint. Preface by Alison Lurie. Classics of Children's Literature, 1621–1932. New York: Garland, 1976.
Frank Vansittart; or, The Model Schoolboys. London, 1853.
The Picture Letter by Catherine Sinclair. N.p., 1861.
Another Letter from Catherine Sinclair. N.p., 1862.
A Crossman's Letter by Catherine Sinclair. N.p., 1862.
A Sunday Letter by Catherine Sinclair. N.p., 1862.
The First of April Picture Letter by Catherine Sinclair. Edinburgh: W. Whyte, 1864.
Holiday House. New York: Robert Carter & Brothers, 1864.
"Uncle David's Nonsensical Story about Giants and Fairies." Reprinted in *Old Fashioned Tales,* compiled by Edward Verrall Lucas. London: Wells Gardner, 1905.
A Bible Picture Letter. N.p., n.d.

SARAH SMITH ("HESBA STRETTON")

Jessica's First Prayer. London: Religious Tract Society, 1867.
Little Meg's Children. London: Religious Tract Society, 1868.
Alone in London. London: Religious Tract Society, 1869.
Lost Gip. London: Religious Tract Society, 1873.

WILLIAM MAKEPEACE THACKERAY ("M. A. TITMARSH")

Dr. Birch and His Young Friends, by M. A. Titmarsh. Illustrated by W. Thackeray. London: Chapman & Hall, 1849.
The Rose and the Ring; or, The History of Prince Giglio and Prince Bulbo: A Fire-side Pantomime for Great and Small Children, by Mr. M. A. Titmarsh. Illustrated by W. Thackeray. London: Smith & Elder, 1855.
The Christmas Books of Mr. M. A. Titmarsh. Illustrated by W. Thackeray. London: Chapman & Hall, 1857.
The Rose and the Ring. Illustrated by W. Thackeray. London: Smith, Elder, & Co., 1909.
The Rose and the Ring. Illustrated by Gordon Browne. London: Stokes, 1909.
The Thackeray Alphabet. Illustrated by W. Thackeray. London: Murray, 1929.
The Rose and the Ring. Facsimile of the original illustrated manuscript. Introduction by Gordon N. Ray. New York: Pierpont Morgan Library, 1929.

CHARLOTTE M. YONGE

The Heir of Redclyffe. 2 vols. London: J. W. Parker, 1853.
The Little Duke; or, Richard the Fearless. London: J. W. Parker, 1854.
The Lances of Lynwood. London: Macmillan, 1855.
The Daisy Chain; or, Aspirations: A Family Chronicle. 2 vols. London: J. W. Parker, 1856.
The Daisy Chain. London: Macmillan, 1860. Reprint. Introduction by Susan M. Kenney. Classics of Children's Literature, 1621–1932. New York: Garland, 1977.
Countess Kate. London: Mozley, 1862.
A Book of Golden Deeds of All Times and All Lands, Gathered and Narrated by the Author of the "Heir of Redclyffe." London: Macmillan, 1864.
The Trial: More Links of the Daisy Chain. 2 vols. London: Macmillan, 1864.
The Dove in the Eagle's Nest. 2 vols. London: Macmillan, 1866.
Countess Kate. Boston: Loring, 1866.
The Chaplet of Pearls; or, The White and Black Ribaumont. London: Macmillan, 1868.
Unknown to History: A Story of the Captivity of Mary of Scotland. London: Macmillan, 1882.
The Heir of Redclyffe. Illustrated by Kate Greenaway. London: Macmillan, 1914.
The Dove in the Eagle's Nest. Illustrated by Marguerite de Angeli. Children's Classics. New York: Macmillan, 1926.
The Heir of Redclyffe. London: Duckworth, 1964.